NEWSPAPER EXTRACTS FROM

THE MARIN JOURNAL
MARIN COUNTY TOCSIN

SAN RAFAEL
MARIN COUNTY, CALIFORNIA

JANUARY 5, 1893 TO DECEMBER 27, 1894

Abstracted by
Carolyn Schwab

Marin County Genealogical Society
P.O. Box 1511
Novato, California 94948

HERITAGE BOOKS
2006

HERITAGE BOOKS
AN IMPRINT OF HERITAGE BOOKS, INC.

Books, CDs, and more—Worldwide

For our listing of thousands of titles see our website
at
www.HeritageBooks.com

Published 2006 by
HERITAGE BOOKS, INC.
Publishing Division
65 East Main Street
Westminster, Maryland 21157-5026

Copyright © 2006 Carolyn Schwab
Marin County Genealogical Society

Other Heritage Books by Carolyn Schwab and the Marin County Genealogical Society:

*Newspaper Extracts from The Marin Journal, Marin County Tocsin
San Rafael, Marin County, California, January 3, 1889 to December 27, 1890.*

*Newspaper Extracts from The Marin Journal, Marin County Tocsin
San Rafael, Marin County, California, January 1, 1891 to December 31, 1892*

*Newspaper Extracts from The Marin Journal, San Rafael, Marin County,
California, January 6, 1881 to December 25, 1884*

*Newspaper Extracts from The Marin Journal, San Rafael, Marin County,
California, January 1, 1885 to December 27, 1888*

Other Heritage Books by Carolyn Schwab:

Newspaper Abstracts from "The Hoosier State", Newport, Vermillion County, Indiana, January 2, 1868 to December 25, 1873
Newspaper Abstracts from "The Hoosier State", Newport, Vermillion County, Indiana, January 1, 1874 to December 30, 1875
Newspaper Abstracts from "The Hoosier State", Newport, Vermillion County, Indiana, January 6, 1876 to December 27, 1877
Newspaper Abstracts from "The Hoosier State", Newport, Vermillion County, Indiana, January 3, 1878 to December 31, 1879
Newspaper Extracts from Sausalito News, Sausalito, Marin County, California, February 12, 1885 to December 26, 1890
The Hoosier State Newspapers, 1880-1881

All rights reserved. No part of this book may be reproduced or transmitted in any form
or by any means, electronic or mechanical, including photocopying, recording or by any
information storage and retrieval system without written permission from the author,
except for the inclusion of brief quotations in a review.

International Standard Book Number: 978-0-7884-3849-2

I have copied more information from the newpapers than just the vital statistics in this book. Since the 1890 Census was lost, many births, marriages, and deaths were never known about because there is a twenty year gap. I have copied voter lists, orphans records, lists of letters, and notes of when people living out of state visit their relatives. When people move to another place, we often lose them. I hope this book helps you find those lost people.

                    Carolyn Schwab
            Marin County Genealogical Society

Table of Contents

1893 1
1894 139
Index 271

MARIN COUNTY NEWSPAPERS 1893

Marin Journal
Thursday, January 5, 1893

In Memoriam
On Thursday, December 15, 1892, the funeral of GEORGE CLEMENT SNOOK, an unusually gifted young man took place. He was well known for his musical and artistic ability; also his intellectual attainments. He was the son of GEORGE A. SNOOK, one of our early pioneer merchants, and had it not been for his delicate health, would surely have made a name for himself. The deceased was a native of San Francisco, a student of the State University and of the Art Association; also a member of the Loring Club. His sweet tenor voice has been listened to with pleasure for many years in the churches of this city, Oakland, and San Rafael, and every call for charity was cheerfully responded to. Well educated and brilliant, modest unassuming, and earnest, he was endeared to hosts of friends, who sympathize with his afflicted family.
S.F.Chronicle

A Serious Accident
On Tuesday, while playing about the Wilkins' building, now in course of erection, opposite the Post Office, RAFAEL DUFFICY, the youngest son of Judge DUFFICY, fell from a plank to the basement, a distance of nearly 8 feet, and broke the bone of the left arm, the bone coming through the flesh and lacerating it in a fearful manner. There is danger that the wound will compel the amputation of the arm, although the attending physicians are doing all that is possible to prevent this. Judge and Mrs. DUFFICY have the sympathy of the entire community.

Mere Mention
Mrs. SHIELDS, who has been suffering from a severe attack of pneumonia, is now on the way to recovery.

Miss ANNIE GOSS of Petaluma is in San Rafael on a visit. She is the guest of Mr. GEORGE F. FANNING.

Real Estate Transfers
    J.E. BETTENCOURT to FRANCES BETTENCOURT
    1. NW Tamalpais Ave. and 4th Street, San Rafael
    2. N. 4th Street and Tamalpais Ave.
    3. SW 5th and Tamalpais Ave.
    Gift

    Estate of JANE LA PAGE to CHARLES A. ZINKAND
    NW 4th and B Street, San Rafael - $19,500

    Sausalito Bay & Land Co. to ROBINSON NUGENT
    1. Lots 17 & 18, Blk 8, Map 3, Sausalito Bay & Land Co.
    2. Alleyway between Lots 7 & 8, 17 & 18, Blk 8
    $10

    Belvedere Land Co. to HUGO D. KEIL
    Lot 1, Blk 7, Belvedere - $10

    JOHN W. MACKAY etal to MARY A. BUSTIN
    Lot 4th & Irwin Streets - $650

    THOMAS MENZIES etal to JANE STIMPSON
    Lot in Forbes Reserve - $10

    ANTONIO FIORI to MATTHEW TOMASINI etal
    Land in Nicasio - $10

    ELLA F. PARK to ARTHUR CROSBY
    Lot in San Rafael - $5

    JESUS M. SAIS vs. VINCENTA PACHECO etal
    Partition of portion of Sais Rancho – Decree

JOHN E. SHOOBERT to ELIZABETH J. SHOOBERT
Lot 2, Blk 31, & NE ptn Lot 1, Blk 31, Sausalito Land and Ferry Co.
Gift

Sausalito Bay & Land Co. to JOSEPHINE WOLFERT
Lot 3, Blk 14, Map 6, Sausalito Bay Land Co. - $10

Letter List

ADAMS, RUBY	CREDON, H.
CATTYMENOS, --	GIBSON, A.
GREEN, A.	JOHNSON, C.F.
LAFRANCHI, P.	MORGAN, E.J.
MAHONEY, M.J.	McALLISTER, J.L.
NEAL, J.	REYNOLDS, E.W.
SINCLAIR, A.M.	SMITH, J.
SMITH, R.	WOODWARD, J.
TROUETTE, A.	WATSON, J.H.
WARNER, ---	

Foreign

GITTI, G.	ROSSI, L.
MAGUS, M.S.	MARCHATS, D.
TIMONY, F.	

Superior Court

E. WORMOUTH vs. GARDNER etal
Cause stand committed

J.B. CAUZZA vs. GEORGE W. BURBANK
Judgment in favor of contestee for costs

People vs. W.A. ALEXANDER
Arraignment set for January 16

Estate of L. MACHADO
Over one week

JULIA LEONARDA vs. F.S. AZEVEDO
Dem. Withdrawn, 10 days

Estate of PAT HAYES
Final account settled and estate distributed as prayed

G.A. FERGUSON vs. His Creditors
Bond of receiver fixed in sum of $1,000

CHARLES HARLAN etux vs. Their Creditors
Continued for two weeks

R.K. PATTRIDGE vs. F.E. SUTCLIFFE
Case dismissed as to H. WYATT, Attorney fees $60

Died
CABRALL – In Santa Margarita Valley, January 2, 1893, ROSIE CABRALL, aged 3 months.

Marin Journal
Thursday, January 12, 1893

Letter List

ALBANO, J.	ALEXANDER, CHARLES
ALLEN, L.H.	BYRNE, M.
CRISP, --	LORD, J.
GARCIA, --	GREEN, --

HAMMEL, R.
MILLER, CLARA
McLEAN, J.N.
MOUETTE, P.
O'BRIEN, EVA
WELLS, M.M.

Marriage Licenses
- FRANZ FREY, 27, San Francisco, to Miss ANNA LARICHE, 25, San Francisco
- CHARLES L. WILLIAMS, 47, Alameda, to HELOISE R.C. VELAN, 40, Alameda
- ANDREW DENNISON, 22, Boulder Creek, to Miss MAUD FITZROY, 21, San Rafael
- JAMES CRAIG, 32, Ross Station, to Miss ROSENA L. DuBOIS, 37, St. Helena
- JAMES A. CAREY, 39, San Francisco, to Miss MAY A. FOSTER, 23, San Francisco
- LEOPOLD STRASSER, 29, San Francisco, to Miss REBECCA MORRIS, 23, San Francisco
- WILLIAM S. THAXTER, 44, Oakland, to Mrs. GEORGIA MARTINA HUMPHREY, 34, Oakland

Superior Court

People vs. ROBERT WILSON
Application of District Attorney not sufficient to convict
Ordered the information dismissed and defendant discharged

M. GREENWOOD vs. A.W. FOSTER
Plaintiff takes nothing by his action, defendant taking nothing by counter claim
Defendant to recover costs, plaintiff attorneys to prepare findings within 10 days

A.C. DIGGINS vs. TIMOTHY MAHON etal
Demurrer overruled, 10 days to answer

Estate of M. DeS. DE BOTTA
Held over one week

A PIXLEY vs. N.P.C.R.R.
Motion of plaintiff over the term

People vs. J.A.C. ROEDER
Motion of district attorney over one week

Notice to Creditors
Estate of PETER MORRISSEY, deceased
EDWARD EDEN, Admr.
E.B. MAHON, Attorney for Admr.
October 13, 1892

Estate of WELMAN LOSEE
The widow of WELMAN LOSEE of Novato, whose sad and untimely death was heretofore mentioned in the Journal, has filed her petition for letters of administration on his estate. The estate under probate is small, not exceeding $1,000. Acquaintances of the deceased who are informed of the facts will be surprised at the smallness of the estate, believing that he was a man of considerable means. He had considerable money, but he invested in real estate situated in Sonoma County, and a good while before his death conveyed it all to his wife. The deeds are recorded in Sonoma County, where the land is situated. This relieves the probate court here of a good deal of labor and saves the widow considerable expense.

Town Talk
Mr. COBDEN of San Rafael has gone to Denver.

ROY BARNEY is attending Heald's Business College in the city.

Mrs. MARY DAVIES from Santa Barbara is staying at Cypress Villa.

HIRAM TOWNE, from Kansas, is visiting his brother, A.N. TOWNE, of San Rafael. When he left home the mercury was 10 degrees below zero.

Mere Mention
Mrs. WYNANS is dangerously ill with pneumonia.

Miss M.S. HOTCHKISS desires to inform the ladies of San Rafael and vicinity that she is prepared to give massage and galvanism (electricity) at the residences of patrons, or at her home, B and Bay Streets, San Rafael.

Conductor MURRAY, of North Pacific Coast railroad, has perfected a water motor for the running of light machinery which he will place on exhibition this year at the Mechanic's fair.

County Surveyor ELLISON is now installed in his office in the courthouse, and with his assistants, is very busy surveying new roads.

Much favorable comment has been excited by the crayon portrait of Wells Fargo Agent ARMSTRONG, which can be seen in the window of WOLFE's drug store. The portrait is the work of Miss R. ARMSTRONG, and certainly proves that the fair artist has attained great skill in this department of art. Miss ARMSTRONG has had the best instruction and shows she has profited thereby.

The Companions of the Forest held a meeting last Friday at the Chosen Friends' Hall. Mrs. SCOTT was awarded a handsome badge for having secured the most new members during the year.

Constable FOSTER received a very handsome bulldog for Christmas.

Miss NELLIE BUNN has accepted a fine position with the Sterling Furniture Co. of San Francisco.

Marin Journal
Thursday, January 19, 1893

List of Grand Jurors 1893

ATCHLEY, G.W.	San Rafael
BULLIS, R.	San Rafael
BOYD, JOHN F.	San Rafael
BONETTI, LUCA	Tomales
BUTLER, M.	Pt. Reyes
CAESAR, WILLIAM	San Rafael
CHRISTIESON, J.P.	San Rafael
CONDONI, G.	Pt. Reyes
COBBALL, A.	Sausalito
DODGE, GEORGE M.	San Rafael
DILLON, GEORGE	Tomales
EASKOOT, A.D.	Bolinas
FRASIER, DANIEL	Nicasio
GRANDI, SALVATORE	Nicasio
HANSEN, THOMAS	San Rafael
HAYDEN, D.L.	Novato
HUBBELL, O.	Tomales
LEE, ALLAN	San Rafael
MAGNES, R.	San Rafael
MAHON, T.J.	San Rafael
MAACK, C.A.	San Antonio
MAGEE, RICHARD	Nicasio
MARTINELLI, LOUIS	Nicasio
MYERS, DAVID	Pt. Reyes
MAGEE, R.D.	Sausalito
MILLS, W.G.	Sausalito
McCARTHY, E.W.	San Rafael
PETER, LOUIS	San Rafael
PAGE, ARTHUR	Sausalito
PETERSON, JOHANNES	San Rafael
ROY, THOMAS B.	Nicasio
SALE, WILLIAM T.	San Rafael
SWEETSER, JOHN R.	Novato
SHAFTER, P.J.	Pt. Reyes
SCHNELL, JOHN	Sausalito
SHOOBERT, JOHN E.	Sausalito

STRAIN, HENRY — Bolinas
WARDEN, DAVID — San Rafael
WALSH, F.S. — San Rafael
WOODWORTH, A. — Tomales

Letter List

- EARL, --
- GREENFIELD, S.E.
- MATTLIES, H.
- McGEE, CHARLES
- OSWALL, L.
- SHIELDS, MARCIA
- STATTER, --
- WALLS, A.W.
- EREASE, A.
- KELLEY, K.
- MILTON, --
- OHAE, D.C.
- PONJCAN, A.M.
- SRIVERS, H.
- WELLS, O.T.

Foreign

- OLIVEIRA, J.V.
- FIGUERA, N.
- MESA, M.R.

Superior Court

J.F. HILLS as admr. Etal vs. F.W. RUSSELL etal
Judgment ordered entered, plaintiff
$1383, interest, attorney fees, and costs
Deft. Judgment $3,000, interest, attorney fees, and costs

Estate of JAMES M. DONAHUE
Motion for counsel fees, over until February 24

J.A. ROY vs. N.P.C.R.R.
Set for trial February 8

P.W. RIORDAN vs. F. SMITH
Jury waived, set for trial February 15

People vs. J.A. ROEDER
Over one week

People vs. W.A. ALEXANDER
Motion of District Attorney to dismiss for insufficient evidence
Taken under advisement

Estate of W. LOSEE
Letters of administration to LYDIA T. LOSEE

C.A. BOLAND vs. County of Marin
Set for February 8

Estate of JOHN F. WELCH
Homestead set apart to widow

Estate of JAMES M. DONAHUE
McCLASHAN vs. administrator
Compromise ratified to $2,000 to be paid during due course of administration

Estate of JANE LA PAGE
No order

Estate of LUCAS MACHADO
Final account settled and allowed and estate distributed

Estate of MARY DE SILVA BOTTA
Letters of administration ordered to HENRY SMITH

Real Estate transfers

JOHN W. MACKEY etal to P.W. JONES
Lot on Irwin Street, San Rafael, 325 acres - $1200

A.P. HOTALING and wife to HEPBURN WILKINS
Lot 4th and E Streets, San Rafael - $10

MILLARD F. HUDSON and wife to GUSTAV MARCUS
Subs 1 & 2, Lot 163, and sub 2, lot 166, Tam Land & Water Co. - $10

GUSTAV MARENS to LEO ELOESSER
Ptn Lot 163, Tam Land & Water Co. - $10

Home and Farm Co. to WILLIAM J. WHITNEY
Lots 14 & 15, Block G, Novato - $10

OLIVIA A. GORDON etal to CHARLES C. STRATTON
Lot 4, Blk 12, Short's addition to San Rafael - $10

MARY HAYES to MARTIN B. MAGNESEN
Hayes Ranch of 150 acres

Sausalito Bay Land Co. to EDWARD D. SPARROW
Lot 13, Blk 14, Lots 9 & 10, blk 13, old Sausalito - $10

REGINALD B. BIRCH to LAURA S. WHITE
Lots 47, 50, 76, 77, and part lot 75, Tam Land & Water Co. - $10

HAMILTON PAGE and wife to JOHN T. COCHRANE
Lot Bayview and E Street, San Rafael - $10

ANNIE A. MAILLIARD to THOMAS B. ROY etal
112.52 acres on Olema Road across from San Geronimo Creek

Estate JANE LA PAGE to CHARLES A. ZINKAND
Lot 4th and B Streets, San Rafael

Estate SARAH C. PIERCE to WILLIAM S. PIERCE
2259 Acres Ptn Rancho Punta de los Reyes at Tomales Point, Distn.

Estate PATRICK HAYES to MARY HAYES
Lot 1, Blk 14, San Rafael
Hayes Ranch 110 acres by Jessup – Distn.

REGINALD W. BIRCH to LAURA J. WHITE
All interest in estate of WILLIAM A. BIRCH, decd.

Home & Farm Co. to JOHANNES KEANER
Lot 11, Reservoir Hill, Rancho de Novato - $10

WENDELL EASTON etal to JOHN MORRIS
Lots 9, 10, 11, 12, 13, 14, 15, and 16, Blk 17, Sunnyside Tract - $10

LOUISA BROZ etal to WILHELM HUG
Lot 25, blk 2, Sunnyside Tract - $10

FRANK BROZ and wife to WILHELM HUG
Lot 24, blk 2, Sunnyside Tract - $10

American Land & Trust Co. to CHARLES MEYER
Lot 9, blk 11, Larkspur

JOHN M. SANTANA to JACOB ROSENBERG
Lot 9, blk 18, Sausalito Land & Ferry Co.

Born
NOWELL – In San Francisco, January 9, 1893, to the wife of GEORGE NOWELL, a girl.

Marin Journal
Thursday, January 26, 1893

Real Estate Transfers
CHARLES H. BENSON and wife to HENRY KNITTEL
Lot on Grand Ave., San Rafael - $10

O.C. MILLER etal to LAURA E. WHITAKER
Agreement to convey Villa Lot 19, subdn Campbell Tract, Sausalito - $3500

CHARLES S. DRAKE to IGNAZIO SARTORI
Lot 6th and Forbes Ave., San Rafael - $6200

ROSA FAGGIANO to J.B. FAGGIANO
Ptn. Rancho San Jose - $10

J.W. TAYLOR to S.F. & N.P. Co.
Right of way Olompali Ranch, 5.6 acres - $224

Sausalito Bay Land Co. to ALVIRA JANE RIDEOUT
Lots 1, 2, 11, and 12, blk 12, Sausalito Bay Land Co., Map 8 - $10

PETER WILLIAMS and wife to JOHN SHINE
Lot E Street and Clayton, San Rafael - $10

Marriage Licenses
ELMER E. COTTLE, 27, San Jose, to Miss AIMEE A. BRONSON, 21, San Jose
JOHN WATTS, 34, Tomales, to Miss LILLA BEAN, 32, Tomales
HENRY G. HAYS, 27, San Francisco, to Miss ANNIE CROWLEY, 24, San Francisco
MANUEL F. MADRUGA, 40, Sausalito, to MARIA F. PIMENTEL, 28, Sausalito
JOAO DE AZEVEDO CABRAL, 28, Novato, to Miss CLARA PEIRERA CARDOZA, 17, Novato

Superior Court
VALENTINE vs. SLOSS etal
Motion for new trial argued, five days to answer

JOHN A. ROY etal vs. N.P.C.R.R. Co.
Continued to February 20 for jury trial

MICHAEL MURRAY vs. CHARLES BYRNE
J.D. BYRNE, admr. substituted for CHARLES BYRNE as deft.

C.A. BOLAND vs. Marin County
Set for trial February 8

OHM vs. OHM
Motion for alimony denied

People vs. J.A. ROEDER
Order affirming judgment of the Justice's court

Letter list
AUSTIN, FRANK	BROWN, FRED
BALEARINI, L.	BURKE, J.T.
CROSBIE, W.	ENGEL, J.G.
GRANT, --	HOVER, A.

JONES, MARY	KELLEY, A.C.
KAHN, A.	MORRIS, K.M.
WATSON, J.W.	POWELL, M.

Foreign

MACHADO, F.	FERNANDEZ, M.S.
SOARES, F.	ORLOVERE, L.
SOARES, A.J.	THOMAY, A.

Born

MAGGETTI – In San Anselmo, January 9, 1893, to the wife of J. MAGGETTI, a daughter.

AZEVEDO – In San Rafael, January 13, 1893, to the wife of MANUEL AZEVEDO, a daughter.

SHEEHY – In San Rafael, January 13, 1893, to the wife of JOHN SHEEHY, a daughter.

FULLER – In San Rafael, January 22, 1893, to the wife of HENRY FULLER, a daughter.

Mere Mention

Mrs. A. CROSBY is receiving a visit from her brother, Mr. BURKE, of New Jersey, who will pass the winter here.

Marin County Tocsin
Saturday, January 28, 1893

JAMES H. WILKINS
    Editor of Marin County Tocsin

HENRY I. KOWALSKY
    Attorney and Counselor-at-Law
    San Francisco

CHARLES S. BARNEY
    Real Estate, Insurance Agent, Notary Public
    San Rafael

HEPBURN WILKINS
    Attorney at Law
    San Rafael

Official Directory

Judge of Superior Court	F.M. ANGELLOTTI
Member of Assembly	THOMAS G. ESTEY
Sheriff and Tax Collector	FRANK HEALY
County Clerk	T.S. BONNEAU
Treasurer	R.T. COTTINGHAM
District Attorney	JAMES W. COCHRANE
Auditor and Recorder	CHARLES H. BENSON
Assessor	WILLIAM VANDERBILT
Surveyor	G.M. DODGE
Superintendent, Public Instruction	R. FURLONG
Coroner and Public Admin.	E. EDEN
Supervisors	
District No. 1	J.A. HARDING
District No. 2	R. KINSELLA
District No. 3	W.H. HANNON
District No. 4	GEORGE W. BURBANK
District No. 5	A.C. MATHESON
Justices of the Peace	
San Rafael	M.C. DUFFICY, R.P. TROY
Sausalito	J.S. BELLRUDE, G.W. SIMPTON
Nicasio	M.B. MILLER

        Tomales   A.L. FISHER
        Bolinas   W.A. ANDREWS, H. BETTEN
        Olema   JERRY ADAMS
                                          W.O.L. CRANDALL

J.G. McREA
    Proprietor, Sheppard Hotel
    San Quentin

E.B. MAHON
    Attorney-at-Law
    San Rafael

KINSELLA & JOHNSON
    Plumbing, Gasfitting, Stoves
    San Rafael

WALTER ADAMS
    Proprietor, Ocean House
    Bolinas

A SOLDAVINI & A. ARBINI
    Hay Pressed
    San Anselmo

T.J. MAHON
    Mahon House
    San Rafael

JOHANNES PETERSON
    Builder and Contractor
    San Rafael

J.P. CHRISTIESON
    Pioneer Mill and Lumber Co.
    San Rafael

M. MURRAY
    Bayview Livery and Sale Stable
    San Rafael

GANNON & HAWKINS
    Royal Billiard Hall
    San Rafael

M. BLUMENTHAL
    New California Market
    San Rafael

JACOB OBITZ
    Proprietor, Linden House
    San Rafael

A.B. THOMSON
    Dry Goods Merchant
    San Rafael

Superior Court
    People vs. W.A. ALEXANDER
    Action dismissed and bail exonerated

Estate of PETER WEBER, deceased
Continued to January 30

FINNERTY vs. LAGAN, Admr.
Trial set for February 8

Local News
Justice RODDEN imposed a fine of $25 each on Mr. and Mrs. JERRY SHINE, convicted of assault and battery on Mrs. B. BRENNFLECK.

Father McKINNON has terminated his connection with St. Vincent's Orphanage and will be assigned to other duty. During his administration, a marked improvement in the institution has been visible in all departments.

Manager BRENNAN was in San Rafael Sunday, looking over the Hotel Rafael. He says he has been engaged to take charge during the coming season, but the exact date of the opening has not been fixed.

Capt. H.A. GORLEY has accepted an invitation to deliver an address before the California Commandery of the Military Order of the Loyal Legion of the United States, at the Occidental Hotel, on the evening of January 31st. The Loyal Legion is justly considered one of the highest organizations of ex-soldiers in the land, and an invitation to address it is considered a high compliment.

Absconds with a Music Teacher
A few of the aborigines of San Rafael, like JACK GANNON, remember the D'HEIRRY family. Old Dr. PAUL D'HIERRY was one of the early settlers of the town. He and his wife came here in the first part of the fifties, and were notable people in their day and generation. The Dr. was a French gentleman of the old school, courteous as become his race, but dignified no end. He fought a duel down on the marsh with some mooseback for treading on his toe, or something of the sort, and tried to induce old JOHN SIMS to go on the field of honor with him, but failed. D'HIERRY was once Chairman of the Board of Supervisors and at his instance, he and his associates resigned from office simultaneously, after discharging a fiery proclamation at the county officials, who are accused of all manner of crime and turpitude. The document, still on file, is probably one of the most remarkable public papers in existence.
More than a quarter of a century ago, the family pulled up stakes and left for other parts. The old people died soon after, leaving two young boys, just about able to take care of themselves. They struck out and were soon lost in the shuffle. A glimpse into the later history of one of them, PAUL D'HIERRY, has recently been afforded by the enterprise of the Associated Press and has been followed with deep interest by old residents of San Rafael. It seems that the young man went to Seattle many years ago, when it was a small village. With its unexampled growth, he prospered and became a leading lawyer, a newspaper proprietor, and a man of means. These facts came to light through the recent unfortunate notoriety of his domestic affairs. His wife absconded a few months ago with a music teacher, thoughtfully taking $10,000 of her husband's money with her, a circumstance indicating that he must be pretty well fixed. D'HIERRY pursued the fugitives to New York and recovered his wife and child, but not the money, which the amorous music teacher was probably most solicitous about retaining. We wish our ex-townsman better luck next time.

Sudden Death
Last Wednesday afternoon an elderly man stepped hastily into Schneider's store on Fourth Street and sat down on the edge of a large box standing near the doorway. Almost immediately thereafter, he fell to the floor and after a few gasps, expired. A crowd gathered immediately, but no one recognized the deceased, who appeared to be an entire stranger. His large traveling bag, however, bore the name of H. TOWNE, and it was surmised that he might be some relation of A.P. TOWNE, Esq., of Point San Pedro. This proved to be the case. The deceased was a brother of Mr. A.P. TOWNE, and had recently come to California from Kansas in search of health. His full name was HIRAM TOWNE. On his arrival in this State, he had come direct to his brother's home and left there about 2 weeks ago for a trip to Southern California, from which he had just returned. Coroner EDEN took charge of the remains and an autopsy proved that death resulted from paralysis of the heart and a jury returned a verdict in accordance. Mr. A.P. TOWNE, who was deeply moved at his brother's sudden end, had the body embalmed and shipped to relatives in the East.

Real Estate
A.B. CASTIGAN to A. ROULLIER
Lot 43, Mill Valley - $1300

Home and Farm Co. to THOMAS BOREMAN
Lots 1 & 2, blk I; Lots 3 & 22, blk J, and Lot 11, blk H, Novato

J.O.B. SHORT and wife to WALTER SHORT
Lots 21 & 22, blk A, Short's Addition, San Rafael - $10

J.O.B. SHORT and wife to F.G. WRIGHT
Lots 29 & 30, blk A, Short's Addition, San Rafael - $10

GEORGE W. HOPKINS to GILES H. GRAY
Lots 51 & 52, and parts of 84 & 85, Marinita Park Tract, San Rafael - $5

Notice to Creditors
    Estate of MARY DE SILVA BOTTA, deceased
    HENRY SCHMIDT, Admr.
    JAMES W. COCHRANE, Attorney for Admr.
    January 16, 1893

Notice to Creditors
    Estate of ALEXIS PERILLAT, deceased
    MARIE PERILLAT, executrix of will
    HEPBURN WILKINS, Attorney for Exec.
    December 19, 1892

Notice to Creditors
    Estate of WILLIAM E. HOLLOWAY, deceased
    JOHN H. ROSSETER, Admr. With the will annexed
    San Francisco, October 12, 1892

Bonita Circle, No. 133, C. of F.
Estrella Circle, No. 120, Companions of the Forest, of San Rafael, went to Sausalito Wednesday evening by special train, to institute a new Circle at that place. Following are the names of the grand officers who officiated:

    Miss N.A. RODMAN, S.C.C.   Mrs. KATE FLYNN, S.S.C.C.
    Mrs. HARDENBURG, D.G.C.C.   Mr. J.S. FALCONAR, S.C.C.

Bonita, No. 133, is the name and number of the new Circle. The following officers were installed:

    Miss P. COLLINS, P.C.C.   Miss J. WASSER, C.C.
    Mrs. L. WALTERS, S.C.C.   Mrs. JOHNSON, Treasurer
    Miss E. MEYER, F.S.   Miss D. ADAMS, R.S.
    Mrs. L. FROST, R.G.   Miss N. WHALEY, L.G.
    Mrs. STRITTMATTER, I.G.   Mr. J.S. AMARAL, O.G.

Among those present from San Rafael were:
Mrs. H. SCOTT, C.C.; Miss B. McDONALD, S.C.; Mrs. A. KAPPENMAN, Treasurer; Miss S. SHOBERG, F.S.; Miss ARMSTRONG, L.G.; Miss E. McKEON, P.C.; Mrs. ARMSTRONG, Mrs. DONAHUE, Mrs. JOHNSON, Mrs. JORDAN, Mrs. RICHARDSON, Mrs. GILLERAN, Mrs. KELLY, Mrs. MACKIN, Mrs. SHIPPLER, Mrs. LAKIN, Mrs. McDONALD, Mrs. FOSTER, Mrs. SCHWEISAU, Misses H. and M. CLARK, Misses M. and A. CURTIS, Miss MASTRUP, Miss HAYES, Messrs. FOSTER, KAPPENMAN, RUSSELL, FORTIO, URSCHMAN, CLARK and JONES.

C. PINOT & P. KROUGLAIR
    Proprietors, Hotel de Paris
    San Rafael

M. HERZOG
    The New San Rafael Market
    San Rafael

JAMES I. TAYLOR
    Proprietor, Camp Taylor
    Marin County

Town Talk
Mr. and Mrs. BODEN were agreeably surprised on Tuesday evening last by a sudden visitation upon them of a score of their friends, the occasion being their first wedding anniversary.

Marin Journal
Thursday, February 2, 1893

Marriage Licenses
LEON E. PRATT, 27, San Francisco, to SOPHIE W. PEARL, 27, San Jose
JOSE JOAQUIN, 50, San Rafael, to ANNA RAMOS, 40, San Rafael
MAURICE A. CHOYNSKI, 26, San Francisco, to MAUD LACY, 19, Chico

Superior Court
CHARLES & MARIE HARLAN vs. Their Creditors
Certain property ordered set apart to insolvents as exempt from execution

EDNEY S. LIBBEY, insolvent
Order of adjudication in insolvency made

T.B. VALENTINE vs. SLOSS etal
Motion for new trial denied

E. WORMOUTH vs. J. and P. GARDNER
Judgment for defendant's attorney to preface findings within 10 days

Estate of G. BELGERI, deceased
Continued to February 6th

Estate of M.C. COBB, deceased
Will admitted to probate, H.A. COBB appointed executor

El Paso National Bank vs. W. LICHTENBERG
Motion to vacate judgment

G.W. FOX vs. SUSAN FOX
Motion dismissed without prejudice

F.W. SPENCER vs. VINCENT NEALE
Over one week

P.A. DE FRIEZE vs. L. QUINT
Plaintiff allowed to amend complaint

Estate of PETER WEBER, deceased
Will admitted to probate and letters issued

G.A. FERGUSON, insolvent
M.F. COCHRANE appointed assignee in bond of $2500

Letter List

AITKEN, MAY	BURNETT, H.D.
DUARTE, A.	FITZSIMMONS, J.
JOHNSON, C.S.	SANCIVEN, M.
SCHMIDT, A.	SMITH, A.
TAYLOR, T.W.	TARR, C.B.

Foreign

IGNACIO, M.	MORRIS, M.
REGENDES, A.T.	JONJOR, A.L.
PEREIRA, J.	AZEVEDO, F.S.

Marin County Tocsin
Saturday, February 4, 1893

Born
MANNY – In San Rafael, January 28, 1893, to the wife of JAMES MANNY, a daughter

Married
CHOYNSKI-LACY – In San Rafael, January 31, 1893, by Justice of Peace E. ARDNER, MAURICE A. CHOYNSKI of San Francisco to Miss MAUD LACY of Chico.

Estray Notice
Came to my place in Ross Valley, about 6 months ago, one small roan Mare, blind in the left eye.
    EDWARD McNAMARA

M.F. GROVE, MD
  Physician and Surgeon
  San Rafael

CHARLES LEZZINI
  Wood for sale, also pasturage and cattle
  Fairfax

Five Dollars Reward
Will be paid by the undersigned for information that will lead to the arrest and conviction of any person hunting or digging claims on my premises, without my permission.
    A.P. TOWNE

Notice to Creditors
  Estate of MELVINA C. COBB, deceased
    HENRY ALFRED COBB, Exec. Of Will
    JAMES W. COCHRANE, Attorney for Executor
  February 3, 1893

Local News
Col. SLINKEY, of the News, is meditating starting a newspaper at Sausalito.

A.B. MORETTI has bought half interest in H. DALESSI's Austin Ranch dairy business.

P. HENRY PETERSON, son of Contractor PETERSON, has gone abroad for a rest. He will be absent six months.

Mr. WILLIAM LAWRENCE has purchased a one half interest in the grocery business of F. SILVEIRA on Fourth Street, San Rafael.

Mr. LOUIS TOMASINI, Manager of the Dairyman's Union, spent last Monday in San Rafael on legal business.

Dr. M.F. GROVE, late of Healdsburg, has succeeded Dr. P.B. MORGAN, as a medical practitioner. His residence and office are in the building formerly occupied by Dr. MORGAN, southeast corner of Fourth and E Streets.

Coroner EDEN brought the remains of a man to the Morgue yesterday morning, who was found floating in Raccoon Straights, at Tiburon. Deceased must have been in the water about 3 weeks. There was nothing on the body whereby it could be identified.

Real Estate Transfers
  KATE L. BROOKS etal to WILL BROOKS
  Trust deed to property of estate of B.S. BROOKS, deceased, nominal

  JACOB NAGEL to C.H.W. KOERNER
  Part of block 12, Short's addition, San Rafael - $10

T.B. JOHNSON and HAPPY ISABEL JOHNSON to AUGUST BODIN
Lot on South 4th Street, near Marin Street, San Rafael - $10

Estate of B.S. BROOKS, deceased
Decree of distribution to WILL BROOKS, trustee

Sausalito Land & Ferry Co. to DOMINGO G. DE ROSAS
Lot 5, blk 59, Sausalito - $10

A.F.L. BELL to S.A. McADAMS
Lots 3, 4, 14, & 15, blk 9, and lots 30 & 31, blk 2, and lot 20, blk 4, Sunnyside Tract - $10

S.C. BIGELOW and wife to BARRY BARROS
Part of lot K of Richardson Bay tide lots - Reconveyance

W. BROOKS and W. LEVISTON to E. SCHWIESAU
Lot on D Street, near Taylor - $5

Estate of WILLIAM FEENEY to JOHN STUMPF
1 ¼ acres at Bolinas - $1500

Marin Journal
Thursday, February 9, 1893

W.B. WINN
Editor and Publisher, Marin Journal
San Rafael

Superior Court
County of Marin vs. L. TOMASINI
Demurrer of KOWALSKY withdrawn, 10 days to answer
Demurrer of TOMASINI etal over one week

Estate of JANE LA PAGE, deceased
Comp. Of claim of ELLEN FINNERTY ordered in sum of $250

El Paso National Bank vs. W. LICHTENBERG
Motion to vacate judgment on the pleadings denied

Estate of G. BELGERI, deceased
Letters of admr. ordered issued to L. TOMASINI, bond of $2,000

GEORGE PENMAN vs. His Creditors
No creditors appearing, the sheriff was appointed assignee

F.W. SPENCER vs. V. NEALE etal
Demurrers argued and submitted

A Wedding Celebration
On Saturday evening, the Mulberry restaurant on B Street was the scene of lively festivities, the occasion being the celebration of the wedding of Mr. JOE KING to Miss ANNA D. RAMOS, both of whom are well known and highly respected and esteemed by the people of this county, and especially by the Portuguese portion of the community. The wedding occurred in Sausalito, after the principals came to San Rafael, accompanied by nearly 100 friends, and repaired to the Mulberry restaurant, where elaborate preparations had been made for their reception. One of the large dining rooms had been cleared for dancing, and in the other room the tables fairly groaned with an abundant supply of eatables and drinkables. Good music had been provided, and there was dancing and merry making till broad daylight. The utmost good cheer and hospitality prevailed, and everyone appreciated the endeavors of Messrs. PERRY and RAMOS, the proprietors of the restaurant, to make the affair one to be remembered with pleasure by all who had the good fortune to participate in the enjoyment of the evening.

A Card from Dr. MORGAN
Having left San Rafael to enter the practice of medicine in San Francisco, I wish to commend to all my past patrons and to the public generally, Dr. M.F. GROVE, who has just located in the house I formerly occupied in San Rafael. I believe Dr. GROVE to be a gentleman of integrity, a well read and skillful physician, and cheerfully endorse him as a worthy representative of homeopathic medicine.
P. BRETT MORGAN

Went Crazy
A week ago last Saturday, Mrs. KATHERINE BRAZIL, a Portuguese woman, came to the house of JOHN BETTENCOURT to stay for a few days until arrangements could be made to secure a divorce between herself and her husband, ANTONE BRAZIL, who is employed at the Patent Brickyard. On Friday night she began to act queer, and by Sunday she went violently insane, so that the sheriff had to be called to take her to the jail, to which place she was taken with difficulty by the sheriff with plenty of assistance. On Monday, she was pronounced insane by the examining physicians, and taken to the insane asylum. She left 2 children, one a cripple and the other an infant of 7 weeks. These children were sent to the Poor Farm on Tuesday by Supervisor HARDING, but the superintendent refused to receive them on the ground that he was not prepared to take care of them. The children were then brought back and are now being cared for by a nurse at the expense of the county.

Letter List
- AUSTIN, H.S.
- DOUGLAS, JAMES
- DICKMANN, --
- FITZSIMMONS, J.
- McGEE, THOMAS
- POTTER, H.W.
- WATSON, M.
- COLLINS, E.M.
- BEVIER, H.N.
- DAYTON, E.
- MURPHY, A.B.
- REINFELT, M.
- SMITH, K.

Foreign
- BOSSANI, J.
- DU REIS, S.
- DA COSTA, A.
- ROSFARINI, V.

Married
DEAS-LEWIS – In Alameda, January 25, 1893, by the Rev. A.T. PERKINS, Dr. W.B. DEAS, formerly of Olema, to Miss RUTH LEWIS, of Pt. Reyes Station, Marin County

KING-RAMOS – At Sausalito, February 5, 1893, by Rev. Father VALENTINI, JOE KING, of San Rafael, to Miss ANNA D. RAMOS, of Sausalito

Marriage Licenses
ARTHUR W. BRYANT, 33, San Francisco, to Mrs. FRANCES M. LOPLAND, 17, San Francisco
THOMAS F. BUTLER, 28, Oakland, to Miss MARY HOWARD, 26, Oakland

Real Estate Transfers
A.B. COSTIGAN to A. ROULLIER
Lot 43, Tamalpais Land & Water Co. - $1300

Home and Farm Co. to THOMAS BOREMAN
Lot 1 & 2, Blk 1, Lots 3 & 22, Blk J, Lot 11, Blk H, Novato - $10

J.O. B. SHORT and wife to WALTER E. SHORT
Lot C Street and Bayview, San Rafael - $10

J.O.B. SHORT and wife to JOHN P. STALFORD
Lot Bayview and C Street, San Rafael

J.O.B. SHORT and wife to FREDERICK G. WRIGHT
Lot San Rafael Ave., San Rafael

Home and Farm Co. to HENRY B. WOOD
Lots 16, 17, & 28, Reservoir Hill Place, Novato - $10

GEORGE W. HOPKINS to GILES H. GRAY
Lots 61 & 62, and portions of lots 84 & 85, Marinita Park - $5

JAMES L. HYDES etal to E.J. McCUTCHEON
1 ½ acres, portion 1st Q, San Anselmo Valley

JACOB NAGEL and wife to H.W. KOERNER
Lot Taylor and E, San Rafael - $10

Belvedere Land Co. to HUGH D. KELF
Lot 1, Blk 7, Belvedere - $10

Belvedere Land Co. to KARL KELLOGG
Lot 27, Blk 1, Belvedere - $10

THADDEUS B. JOHNSON etal to AUGUST BODIN
Lot 4th Street and Marin Street, San Rafael - $10

Estate of B.S. BROOKS to WILL BROOKS
All deed interest in estate - Distribution

Sausalito Land & Ferry Co. to DOMINGO G. DE ROSAS
Lot 5, Blk 59, Sausalito Land & Ferry Co. - $10

ARTHUR F.L. BELL to S.A. McADAMS
Lots 3,4,14, 7 15, Blk 9; lots 30 & 31, Blk 2; lot 20, Blk 4, Sunnyside tract - $10

WILL BROOKS to E. SCHWIESAU
Lot D Street and Taylor, San Rafael - $5

Estate ANN FEENEY to JOHN STUMPF
1 ½ acres near Bolinas Point - $1500

KATE L. BROOKS to WILL BROOKS
All interest in estate of B.S. BROOKS - Deed of trust

County School Items
The County School Superintendent has recently appointed the following:
New School district of San Anselmo
Dr. WILLIAM ALEXANDER, of Ross Valley
W.P. TAYLOR, of Ross Valley
JAMES COFFIN, of Ross Valley
Tocaloma – G.A. CODINI
Olema – MARK CARR
Pt. Reyes – H.P. CLAUSSEN, and J.R. REEVES
Pierce – CHARLES MALTZEN
Nicasio – CHARLES CASAROTTE
San Jose – G. PACHECO
Franklin – FRANK CLARK
Tomales – E.R. COX, and Mrs. L.E. REYNOLDS
Richardson – JAMES B. DAVIDSON, Miss C.L. FIEDLER, Miss JENNIE FARRELL, and Miss ANNIE FARRELL
San Quentin – Miss GEORGIE SCOTT
Dixie – Miss McDONNELL
Black – Miss K.A. CHANDLER (succeeds Miss DOWLING)

Mr. J. NEWCOMER, who for 10 successive years taught the Aurora School near Tomales, has accepted a position of principal of the Pescadero Schools in San Mateo County. Mr. S. CORNELL, lately of Bay District, has found a new field of labor in teaching Tehama County youth. Two teachers graduated from the State Normal at San Jose last month; Miss EDNA M. NELSON of Olema, and Miss MYRETA W. MORE of San Quentin.

Born
PAULINO – At San Geronimo, February 5, 1893, to the wife of JOE PAULINO, a daughter.

Marin Journal
Thursday, February 16, 1893

A Narrow Escape
On Sunday last, Dr. GEORGE RODDEN, the dentist, had a narrow escape from serious injury while shooting with some companions near Bolinas. The doctor and FRED ELLIOTT were about 100 feet apart with ELLIOTT on the hill. A quail started up, and in bringing up his gun to shoot, ELLIOTT caught the trigger on the lapel of his coat causing the gun to go off. It happened to be pointed straight at the doctor, and most of the charge landed in the right side of his face, neck, and chest. A local surgeon soon had nearly all the shot picked out of the doctor's epidermis.

Superior Court
JULIA SHAFTER HAMILTON, admr. Vs. JOHN SHIELD
Judgment for plaintiff in accord with prayer of complaint

Estate of WILLIAM GARZOLI
Final account settled and estate distributed
ROSA GARZOLI appointed guardian in bond of $500 to each minor

Application of WEISTENSTEIN on habeas corpus
Writ dismissed and applicant remanded to San Quentin

GEORGE W. FOX vs. SUSAN FOX
Motion to open default of defendant denied

G.A. FERGUSON vs. His Creditors
Account of receiver set for February 17

Born
COSTELLO – In San Rafael, February 12, 1893, to the wife of JOHN COSTELLO, a daughter.

Marriage Licenses
EDWARD F. WOSSER, 24, Sausalito to WILHEMINE L. MARDER, 19, San Francisco
W.R. HARWOOD, 31, San Francisco to IVY SWANWELL, 19, Oakland
MANUEL RESENDES, 23, Tomales to EMMA SEPES, 16, Marshall

List of Letters

BURKE, H.	CARROLL, THOMAS
DALY, H.	FRANCE, W.M.
GRIFFITH, ---	HARWOOD, W.R.
LARSSEN, ---	JOSEPHINE, E.
POMEROY, W.	POTTER, H.W.

Marin County Tocsin
Saturday, February 18, 1893

Born
RASMUSSEN – In San Rafael, February 16, 1893, to the wife of PETER RASMUSSEN, a son

Local News
Mr. POOLE STEMPLE, late of Tomales, is said to have gathered in $15,000 from the Louisiana lottery.

Coroner EDEN received a telephone message from Tiburon last evening, stating that a BODY had been found dead in the brush in Belvedere. The Coroner will go down today and bring the remains to San Rafael.

A case of smallpox developed at Taylor's paper mill, this week, the sufferer being Engineer GEDDING. He had just returned from a visit to San Francisco, where he undoubtedly contracted it. The patient was at once removed to an isolated building, which was strictly quarantined.

Superior Court
- M.W. KAIN vs. LOUIS VESARIA
  Judgment for plaintiff for $834.80

- Marin County vs. LOUIS TOMASINI etal
  Executrix of Will of S.A. MARSHALL substituted as defendant
  Allowed to withdraw demurrer and answer in 15 days

- Estate of WELMAN LOSEE, deceased
  Continued to Monday, February 20

- Simpson Lumber Co. vs. A.S. SPENCE
  Order dismissing action, without prejudice

Marin Journal
Thursday, February 23, 1893

Letter List

COLLINS, C.D.	CARROLL, C.
CAREY, K.	CHADWICK, G.
CHRISTENSEN, C.	DUTRAN, M.
FREESE, M.	GLYNN, E.
GALRACHAER, B.	HAGERTY, N.
MORRIS, MARY	MURPHY, P.
McGEE, THOMAS	McKENNA, B.
REESE, C.	STOW, S.H.
SMITH, JEAN	WELLMORE, I.R.

Real Estate transfers
- Sausalito Bay Land Co. to G.P. RIXFORD
  Villa lot 2, Blk 23; Villa lots 35, 36, 37, 38, 54, 55, Blk 19; Villa lots 6, 7, 8, 9, 10, 15, 16, 17, 18, 19, 20, Blk 4, Sausalito Bay Land Co., Map 3 - $10

- Mt. Tamalpais Cemetery to EMILY F. GLOVER etal
  Lot 106, Section J, Tamalpais Cemetery - $52.50

- Belvedere Land Co. to WILLIAM BACHR Jr.
  Lot 19, Blk 7, Belvedere - $10

- Belvedere Land Co. to ALBERT GERBERDING
  Lot 20, Blk 7, Belvedere - $10

- Home & Farm Co. to HUGH McCORNICK
  Lot 2, Mahlstedt Park Place, Novato - $10

- CONSTANTINE T. DE AZEVEDO to ANTONIO LAWRENCE etal
  Land in Sausalito - $500

- Sausalito Land & Ferry Co. to ANTONIO LAWRENCE etal
  Lot 25, Blk 43, Sausalito Land & Ferry Co. - $180

- Estate of WILLIAM GARZOLI to ROSA GARZOLI etal
  Undivided 1/3 700 acres - Distribution

Superior Court
- G.A. FERGUSON vs. His Creditors
  Final account received, exam of insolvent debtor set for February 28

- OHM vs. OHM
  Set for March 1

EVA N. GREGG vs. Her Creditors
Adjudged insolvent, meeting of creditors set for March 22
Sheriff appointed receiver in bond of $1,000

O.C. RAWKINS vs. C.I. JACOBS etal
Default of defendant entered

F.W. SPENCER vs. V. NEALE
Demurrer to answer overruled

Estate of W. LOSEE
Decree assigning estate to widow of deceased ordered

Estate of WILLIAM DORR
Final account of executor settled, estate distributed

Estate of FLORIMEL E. RUSSELL
Sale of real estate ordered, Bond $500

C.A. BOLAND vs. County of Marin
Motion for a nonsuit granted

Mere Mention
San Rafael, February 20 - Two more cases of smallpox at Paperville were reported this morning. Engineer GEDDING, the first afflicted, died Saturday and was buried in the hills back of the old sealskin tannery. It is supposed that the first cases were contracted by the men while sorting the rags, etc., used in the paper factory. Quarantine regulations are being strictly enforced, and every precaution is being taken to prevent the spread of the pestilence.

Mr. NEIL WILLIAMS left San Rafael for Arizona last week.

Miss W.M. HEYWOOD is in San Rafael on a visit to her sister, Miss EMMA FANNING.

Mr. CHARLES STRATTON intends to enter into the poultry industry near Willow Springs.

An Unknown Suicide
On Tuesday, Coroner EDEN held an inquest on the BODY of a man who was found dead in the brush near Belvedere with a bullet hole in his head and a pistol grasped in his right hand. No one has identified the body, and the coroner's jury gave the verdict of suicidal death. The corpse was interred at the Poor Farm.

Born
OBITZ – In San Rafael, February 21, 1893, to the wife of JACOB OBITZ, a son

McCAMISH – In San Rafael, February 9, 1893, to the wife of H.F. McCAMISH, a son

Marin Journal
Thursday, March 2, 1893

Superior Court
Estate of JAMES M. DONAHUE, deceased
Sale of railroad stock to Messrs. SMITH and FOSTER
42,060 shares for $850,500 confirmed

Estate of JANE LA PAGE, deceased
Decree of due and legal notice to creditors ordered

EVA N. GREGG vs. Her Creditors
Certain personal property exempt from execution set apart to insolvent

OLIVER vs. OLIVER
Set for hearing March 8th

Estate of JAMES M. DONAHUE, deceased
Motion of T.C. VAN NESS in regard to attorney fees of CHARLES F. HANLON
Laid over to March 13th

Estate of E.E. ADAMS, deceased
Motion of attorney for estate laid over to March 6th

GEORGE W. FOX vs. SUSAN FOX
Motion to open default and judgment submitted

Estate of JAMES M. DONAHUE, deceased
Compromise of LIPPITT matter submitted
Ordered that executors dig up and cut into wood trees on orchard in Ukiah

Estate of H.J. VAN DYKE, deceased
Letters of administration issued to ARTHUR CROSBY, bond of $100

AMANDA TANN vs. Patent Brick Co.
Demurrer submitted

J.A. ROY vs. N.P.C.R.R. Co.
On trial

Mere Mention
R.B. LOUDON, who has been very ill with pneumonia for several weeks, was in town last Saturday.

ROY BARNEY is now in a business college in San Francisco.

A license was issued last week by County Clerk BONNEAU authorizing the marriage of FRED L. MOORE of Fresno, to Miss HANNAH L. CALAHAN of San Francisco.

Mr. WHITNEY, once in the employ of Wells Fargo & Co. in their office in San Rafael, and afterwards promoted to service on the road, has again been advanced, this time to run as far as Omaha.

Mr. HUDSON SMYTH of Stockton, formerly a student at the Mt. Tamalpais Military Academy, was in town on Friday last, and attended the reception given by the academy in the evening.

Mr. SIMPSON of San Francisco will shortly occupy the house on 5th Street next to the residence of Mr. T.J. CROWLEY. Mr. SIMPSON has been residing in San Rafael for sometime past, occupying the cottage belonging to Mr. HANSEN on D Street.

HIRAM NOTT, who lives on the mesa beyond Bolinas, had a horse fall on him last Sunday morning. It was thought at first that his leg was broken. A San Rafael physician was called who pronounced the supposed fracture only a bad sprain, but will lay Mr. NOTT up for several weeks.

Town Talk
Miss HOAG, sister of the Editor of the Petaluma Imprint, is visiting Mrs. W.J. WICKMAN.

The engagement is announced of Miss PAULINE SCHILLING of San Francisco to FREDERICK H. BAUER of Fruitvale, Alameda County.

CHARLES LAUFF of Bolinas, who suffered a stroke of paralysis a few weeks ago, is still very ill. He has not yet recovered the use of his limbs.

Notice to all Creditors
    In the matter of ANGUS McDONALD and W.F. PASCOE, Insolvent Debtors
    Must appear before court on March 27, 1893
    Dated February 21, 1893
                      THOMAS S. BONNEAU, Clerk

Marin County Tocsin
Saturday, March 4, 1893

Assignees Sale of Real Estate and Personal Property
In matter of insolvency of ANGUS McDONALD and WILLIAM F. PASCOE
Sale to be held Saturday, March 11, 1893
Lot of land situated in Oakland, Alameda County
All outstanding book accounts of McDonald & Pascoe business
Date March 3, 1893

FRANK HEALY
Assignee of Estates of Insolvents

Local News

GEORGE LARSEN, of the Pt. Reyes life saving station crew was drowned last Wednesday by the upsetting of a surfboat. Coroner EDEN left yesterday to investigate the matter.

The Rev. J.K. HARRISON, formerly of Santa Rosa and now Home Missionary Superintendent, will conduct the services of the First Congregational Church of San Rafael, corner of B and Third Streets, next Sunday morning at 11 o'clock.

ENOS and LACERDA opened the Bellevue last Tuesday in the first class shape guaranteed by the firm. The stock is as choice as the best San Francisco wholesalers could furnish and the attendance is to correspond.

Execution at San Quentin

The first execution under the new law took place at San Quentin yesterday, the sufferer being an Indian by the name of JOSE GABRIEL. He was convicted of a brutal double murder committed in San Diego County. According to the representative of the Tocsin, who was present, the uncanny proceeding went off without a hitch and with commendable coolness and skill on the part of the officers in charge. At the appointed hour, three strings were cut by as many guards. One of the cords held the trap in place, but the guards did not know which one it was. The Indian met his fate with the stolidity of his race, walking carelessly to the scaffold, and seeming perfectly indifferent to his awful surroundings. The doctors examined the body after it was cut down, and found the neck broken. Death must therefore have been painless. Sheriff HARRISON and a number of others from San Rafael witnessed the execution.

Board of Supervisors
Liquor licenses were granted:
- FRANK RODGERS & Co. – Nicasio
- LACERDA & ENOS – San Rafael
- C. FLORES & M.V. AVILLA – Sausalito
- PETER ANDERSON – Bolinas
- CHARLES OZANN – Tiburon
- JUAN DE ROMERO – Novato
- M.D. DUTRA – Novato
- CHARLES T. THOMPSON – Tomales
- SILVEIRA & LAWRENCE – San Rafael

Real Estate Transfers

MILLARD F. HUDSON and wife to DONALD Y. CAMPBELL
Lots 17, 160, 165, & 167, Subdv. 2 & 3
Lot 162, Lot 2, Blk 1; Lot 18, Blk 2; Subdv 1
Lot 146, Tamalpais Land & Water Co. - $10

EDITH PENMAN to GEORGE PENMAN
Lot 25, Reservoir Hill Place, Novato -$10

JOHN W. MACKAY etal to JOHN PARETO etal
Lot in Picnic Valley tract, San Rafael - $400

ARTHUR A. MARTIN to FLORENCE MOULTON
Lot 24, Tamalpais Land & Water Co., Map 2 - $5

J.F. CURTIS to ADELINE CHURCH
Lot 34, EDWARD HARRISON's tract, Old Sausalito - $10

S.M. AUGUSTINE to JOHN N. McDONALD
Lot 24, Miller's addition to San Rafael - $10

Home & Farm Co. to JOSEPH GAMBETTI
Lots 13, 14, 15, Blk J, Novato - $10

Lease
W.H. JEWELL and wife to CHARLES F. ROBINSON
Jewell Stables, Fourth & B Streets, San Rafael, 5 yrs - $75 per month

Died
BEATON – In Taylorville, Marin County, February 20th, JOHN J. BEATON, a native of Prince Edwards Island, aged 26 years.

Married
BROWN-MINER – In South Berkeley, February 9th, by Rev. J.D. FOSTER, WILL W. BROWN to ELLA F. MINER, both of Marin County

Notice to Creditors
    Estate of CATHERINE COLLINS, deceased
    September 12, 1892
                      EDWARD EDEN, administrator
                      E.B. MAHON, Attorney for administrator

Marin Journal
Thursday, March 9, 1893

    Superior Court
        J.A. ROY vs. N.P.C.R.R. Co.
        Jury trial in favor of the plaintiff
        Sum of $4500 with interest

        Estate of CATHERINE COLLINS, deceased
        Decree of due and legal Notice to Creditors ordered

        Estate of JAMES M. DONAHUE, deceased
        Sale of watch, over one week

Town Talk
Miss IVY SHAVER returned home last week very ill.

Miss GUNN of Kelseyville, Lake County, is visiting her sister, Miss EMILY GUNN.

Capt. J.D. BOWLAND, of San Francisco, has rented the cottage on E Street lately purchased from Mr. WILLIAMS by JOHN SHINE.

Mere Mention
Mr. GEORGE FRANETTA, formerly of San Rafael, is now filling a first-class position in a large wholesale house in Central America.

Local News
Miss KENNEDY, a graduate of the California Kindergarten School, San Francisco, has opened a kindergarten school under the Mahon Hotel, where she is prepared to receive young children and teach them according to the best and most improved kindergarten methods. Miss MURRAY is the able assistant.

Estate of PETER MORRISSEY, deceased
    Petition to Sell Real Estate
                      EDWARD EDEN, administrator

JOHN PERCY STUART is a resident of Oregon. Some years ago he married LUCY VIRGINIA SMITH of San Francisco. After a few years of domestic happiness, domestic warfare ensued which resulted in a separation and divorce. In due time, each felt sorry for the separation, and resolved to forgive and forget. Consequently they appeared before the county clerk last week, obtained a license and were re-married on Saturday.

Letter List

BATISTA, B.	ALVARADO, J.
DEALY, E.V.	AVENS, --
GLIDMACHER, L.	HURD, M.
HUBARK, J.	HUTCHINSON, W.S.
JACOBY, S.	KAHAN, W.
LaPRANKY, J.	LAWTON, M.A.
LEAVY, W.	McGINNES, Rev.
PIERCE, W.	POWERS, M.
STORY, --	SMITH, H.
SMITH, J.	WERLEFF, F.

Real Estate Transfers

JOSEPH BERTRAND and wife to G.F. OCHS
Land at intersection of San Geronimo Creek and Olema Road - $10

W.A.S. NICHOLSON and wife to THEO. E. TODTMANN
Sub 4, Lot 146, Tamalpais Land & Water Co. - $10

Married

CAESAR-SCHNEIDER – At St. Joseph's Church, San Francisco, February 1893, by Rev. HUGH LAGAN, JOSEPH SILVESTER CAESAR to Miss ANNIE SCHNEIDER, both of San Rafael.

Marin County Tocsin
Saturday, March 11, 1893

A.B. THOMSON
    Dry Goods Store
    San Rafael

Mare Found
Came to my premises February 23, 1893, a roan mare, swaybacked, tip of tail cut, shod all around, no visible brand.
                R.C. HART
                Ross Valley

Local News
Mrs. OSGOOD has leased her tract at San Anselmo to MEHL & KLEIN

The latest addition to the list of Town Officers is E. GARDNER for Recorder.

Mr. and Mrs. SPENCER have returned to Marinita Park, San Rafael, after an absence of over eight months. In the meantime, Mrs. SPENCER has visited her daughter in Sweden, friends in England, and her parents in New Jersey.

Superior Court
    Estate of CATHERINE COLLINS, deceased
    Decree of due and legal Notice to Creditors

    Estate of E.E. ADAMS, deceased
    Will admitted to probate, letters issued to GROVE ADAMS

    Estate of JAMES M. DONAHUE, deceased
    Continued to March 13th

G.A. FERGUSON vs. His Creditors
Insolvent examined

W.M. OLIVER vs. O.L. OLIVER
Divorce proceedings, Tried and submitted

JULIA LEONARDA vs. F.S. AZEVEDO
Tried and submitted to Court

Real Estate Transfers
Belvedere Land Co. to ROBERT B. PHILLIPS
Lot 25, Block 7, Belvedere - $10

Belvedere Land Co. to ROBERT S. WHEELER
East ½ of Lot 1, Block 3 - $10

WILLIAM P. GERLACH and wife to GEORGE GERLACH
Lot 3, block 8, Sunnyside - $10

GEORGE HYATT and wife to MANUEL D. SILVA
Lots 4 & 5, block G, Novato - $20

PIERCE J. ELLIOTT to WILLIAM FLANAGAN
Portion of Lot 5, Block 15, Tomales - $10

GALEN BURDELL to Marin County
Right of way from Pt. Reyes and Olema Road

ALBERTO S. MAGNES to J.E. SHOOBERT
Lots 1 & 2, block 11, Sausalito Bay & Land Co. - $5

ROBERT S. WHEELER and wife to E.J. BENJAMIN
East ½ of Lot 1, Block 8, Belvedere - $10

GEORGE R. SANDERSON to CHARLOTTE H. SANDERSON
Villa lots 119 & 120, block 21, Old Sausalito - Gift

Sausalito Bay Land Co. to F.B. WASHINGTON
Villa lots 121, block 21, Old Sausalito - $10

M.C. DUDLEY to P.H. RUDDICK
Lot 8, block I, Coleman's addition, San Rafael - $5

Marin Journal
Thursday, March 16, 1893

Superior Court
Estate of JAMES M. DONAHUE, deceased
Confirmation of sale of watch, motion for counsel fees

P.M. BERKHART vs. MARY CULLEN etal
Demurrer dropped from the calendar to be restored on notice

E. SCHWIESAU vs. T.J MAHON etal
Demurrer of T.J. MAHON submitted

G.W. FOX vs. SUSAN FOX
Judgment of August 4, 1893, vacated and set aside

AMANDA TANN vs. Patent Brick Co. etal
Demurrer overruled of S.F. & N.P.R.R. Co., 20 days to answer

Estate of JANE LA PAGE, deceased
Final account settled and estate distributed as prayed

E. DuBOIS vs. L.B. COLEMAN
Judgment for plaintiff for foreclosure of mortgage, sum of $1,957.79 and costs

L. OHM vs. E. OHM
Set for trial on March 15th

S. HANSON vs. CHARLES HANSON
Set for March 17th

O.C. HAWKINS vs. CHARLES I. JACOBS etal
Foreclosure, judgment for plaintiff in sum of $3,800

JULIA LEONARDA vs. F. AZAVEDO
Judgment for defendant

Letter List

BAPTISTE, A.	BROWN, C.B.
CLARK, F.L.	ELLIS, J.V.
ENOS, T.	FRAZER, S.J., MD
INGRAM, P.	MOYLE, N.
MORSE, KATE	NEEDHAM, --
SASTKOWSKE, F.	ROSE, J.P.
THURN, --	SEARS, A.S.
WHITE, J.T.	VESTRY, B.
WESSON, R.S.	WILSON, J.H.
WALKER, W.J.	WELSH, Ed

Foreign

TEIXERA, J.A.	MESA, --
SILVEIRA, J.	VICTORINO, J.
CANEEREAO, CATH	BETTENCOURT, A.
EGERA, M.	IGNACIO, J.
MOIMS, M.	MINEIS, C.

City Election
Candidates
  Trustees
        E.W. McCARTHY – coffee merchant in San Francisco
        S.P. MOORHEAD – member of board of town trustees
        H. SLOSSER – retired furniture manufacturer
        HENRY GIESKE – grocery in San Rafael
        W.P. MILLER – real estate and insurance
        M. HERZOG – butcher and capitalist
        JOHN SHEEHY – member of board for number of years
        C.A. ZINKAND – owns considerable real estate
        J. PETERSEN – prominent builder and contractor

  City Marshall
        JOHN LUCAS – present incumbent
        JOHN HALEY – present nightwatchman
        J.P. DAVENPORT
        W.H. JEWELL
        JOHN ALDERMAN
        Mr. JOHNSON – Pioneer Mill & Lumber Co.

  Treasurer
        R.W. JOHNSON – present incumbent
        J.L.G. ARMSTRONG – Wells Fargo agent

Police Judge and Recorder
    J.M. JONES – supported by Ex-Justice DUFFICY
    GRATTAN PERRY – insurance agent
    Justice of Peace GARDNER – proved to be a good worker

Board of Education
    Mr. HANSEN
    Dr. JONES
    Mr. STRATTON
    Mr. CROWLEY
    Mr. BURTCHAELL

Mere Mention
H.A. GORLEY is confined to his bed with a severe attack of asthma.

Mr. FRED WALTERS, one of our former news dealers, is in town.

Mr. HARRIS, agent for the Singer Sewing Machine, has rented Mr. SAULTRY's cottage on Ross Street.

Mr. LOUIS WERTZ, formerly a resident of San Rafael, was in town Sunday, visiting his numerous friends.

Mrs. BARKER has leased her flat on D Street for the summer to Mr. and Mrs. COHEN of San Francisco.

The marriage license of Dr. ALFRED BRANDON, formerly of San Rafael, and Miss MILLIE BULLARD of West End has been issued.

Mr. STRATTON, formerly of San Rafael, now of Shellville, Sonoma County, passed through town Tuesday on his way to San Francisco.

The primary department of the Novato School opened last Monday. Miss CARRIE SHANE of San Francisco, who taught at the Franklin district school last term, is installed as teacher.

Mr. A.H. STINSON, formerly a resident of San Rafael, and once a prominent dairyman of Marin County, was in San Rafael last week for a few days. He was the guest of C.S. BARNEY.

Mr. JOHN W. BARNEY, who has been for the last 5 years stationed in the eastern states in the U.S. service, has lately returned, and is now in San Rafael on a visit to his brother, Mr. C.S. BARNEY.

Miss K. O'NEIL has opened dressmaking parlors in the Miller building near the post office, and is prepared to do any work in her line in a superior manner.

Town Talk
Mrs. TIERNEY of Tomales is rapidly improving in health.

Mr. E. BUTLER of Petaluma is spending this week in San Rafael.

Mrs. HAAS has rented one of Mr. ZINKAND's new flats on B Street.

J.W. COCHRANE has bought a lot on the corner of Nye and Fifth Ave.

Mr. KNAPPENBACH has rented the BUNDY cottage, near West End.

Capt. MIAS dropped dead of heart disease in SCOWN's store at Novato yesterday.

Miss DORA SEEHIND, sister of Miss KNAPPENBACH, will shortly return to her home in Munich.

Mr. HENRY PETERSON, a San Rafael boy, is occupying a position in a drafting office in Los Angeles.

Mr. JOSEPH CAESAR, who is now residing in San Francisco, was in town last week on a visit to friends.

Mrs. CLAYTON has returned to her home in Oregon after paying her daughter, Mrs. CHARLES DuBOIS, a short visit.

A young man named KLOSE, stopping at the Liberty Ranch on Tuesday, broke his shoulder blade. A San Rafael physician was called and attended to the little sufferers injuries.

Mrs. CORBALEY has rented the OLIN cottage on Mission Street.

ROBERT GRAHAM has leased the OLIN cottage on Laurel Place.

Mrs. RALEIGH of Portland, OR, has rented the ROSE cottage on Laurel Place for a year.

DAVID BASSETT, a former resident of this county, but now of Petaluma, was in town last Thursday.

Mr. S. JEWELL and wife of Sonoma County passed through San Rafael Friday on their way to San Francisco.

Mr. DeLONG of Novato is hard at work practicing for the next singles tennis tournament, which will be held on the courts of the Hotel Rafael this spring.

The engagement is announced of Miss RUBY FLINT of Sacramento, and J.F. HUGHES of Salem, OR. Miss FLINT is a granddaughter of Mrs. I.R. JEWELL of Chileno Valley.

Accident
On Saturday last, twin sons of Mr. M. HART of San Rafael, and a son of Mrs. FORD, formerly of this place, but now of San Francisco, while hunting, dropped a spark into an exposed old fashioned powder flask causing its contents to explode. One of the boys was slightly injured by being cut with a piece of the tin, and all were more or less powder burned.

Mr. GEORGE F. FANNING has returned to San Rafael after a protracted stay in Petaluma.

Recommendations for life diplomas have been issued by the County Board of Education in favor of Miss FLORIDE GREEN, Miss K.C. BATCHELDER, Miss LOUISE CLUVER, and Mrs. L.E. REYNOLDS. Ten years of successful teaching is one condition necessary for a life diploma.

Real Estate
    Dr. W.J. WICKMAN
    NW corner of Fourth & E Street

    Dr. and Mrs. JONES to ARCHIE McALLISTER
    Lot on Laurel Street near Belle Avenue

Marriage Licenses
    JOHN SHERWOOD, 54, to Miss JOSEPHINE AVERY, 52, San Francisco
    LUDWIG B. MAISON, 35, San Francisco, to Miss MARY M. BEER, 28, San Francisco
    EDWARD A. SINCLAIR, 22, Oakland, to Miss ANNIE F. LUBMENSON, 18, Oakland
    D. FRANZIOLI, 31, Chileno Valley, to Mrs. ROSA GARZOLI, 33, Chileno Valley
    H.W. MORGAN, 35, San Francisco, to Mrs. ELLA MULLIGAN, 23, San Francisco

Born
CONNOLLY – In San Rafael, Sunday, March 12, 1893, to the wife of M. CONNOLLY, a daughter.

Marin Journal
Thursday, March 23, 1893

    Superior Court
        SARAH HANSEN vs. CHARLES HANSEN
        Suit for divorce, Judgment for defendant

        E.SCHWIESAU vs. T.J. MAHON etal
        Demurrer overruled, 10 days for defendant to answer

Estate of JAMES M. DONAHUE, deceased
Sale of Lot 10, Wright Ranch confirmed
Sale of office furniture confirmed
Application to lease Litton Springs property, over 2 weeks

Local News
Miss FANNIE HAWKINS of San Rafael, who has been holding a position in San Francisco for some time past, left for Chicago on Tuesday last. Miss HAWKINS has become the treasurer of the educational exhibit from California, and as such expects to remain in Chicago for the time during the fair.

Marriage Licenses
JOHN H. MYERS, 45, San Francisco, to CLARA M. SALSBERG, 29, San Francisco
ANTONIO BOSSI, 30, San Rafael, to ROSI CADRA, 27, San Rafael
JAMES McDONALD, 29, Novato, to MARY SNEE, 22, San Rafael

Real Estate
JOHN O.B. SHORT and wife to MARY F. DE FIENNES
NE Ross and Glenn, Short's Addition, San Rafael - $10

WILLIAM E. JAMES and wife to CARL A.A. ROLEN
Ptn Lot 2, block 7, Sausalito Land & Ferry Co. - $1500

Letter List

BROWN, M.A.	BOYD, H.C.
CLARK, F.L.	SWANSON, A.
DAYTON, E.	FREDERICKSON, --
FRAGER, S.J.	FITZPATRICK, WILLIAM
HAMMOND, L.	EMMETT, R.
HYIEL, H.J.	HENRE, J.
MAHONEY, L.	McKINNEY, J.C.
McKEE, S.	O'POPE, GEORGE
POND, M.S.	SEET, WILLIAM
STACK, THOMAS	WRIGHT, W.

Died
STEINECKE – At Cypress Villa, San Rafael, March 18, 1893, Mrs. SOPHIA STEINECKE, age 60 years.

Estate of SOPHIA ZELLAR, deceased
Otherwise known as SOPHIA STEINECKE
Notice for Publication of Will
Dated March 22, 1893
E.B. MARTINELLI, attorney for Petitioner
JOHN F. JORDAN, letters testamentary
THOMAS S. BONNEAU
Clerk
By JOHN L. GREER
Deputy Clerk

Mere Mention
GEORGE HARDING has completed his new blacksmith shop on 4th Street.

Mrs. CORBALEY has rented the OLIN Cottage on Mission Street.

ROBERT GRAHAM has leased the OLIN Cottage on Laurel Place.

Mrs. RALEIGH of Portland, OR, has rented the ROSE Cottage on Laurel Place for one year.

DAVID BASSETT, a former resident of this county, but now of Petaluma, was in town Thursday.

Mr. S. JEWELL and wife of Sonoma County, passed through San Rafael Friday on their way to San Francisco.

Mrs. DeLONG of Novato is hard at work practicing for the next singles tournament, which will be held on the courts of the Hotel Rafael this spring.

The engagement is announced of Miss RUBY FLINT of Sacramento, and J.F. HUGHES of Salem, Oregon. Miss FLINT is a granddaughter of Mrs. I.R. JEWELL of Chilano Valley.

Marin County Tocsin
Saturday, March 25, 1893

Born
BRADLEY – In Tiburon, March 18, 1893, to the wife of THOMAS BRADLEY, a son.

J.M. BASSFORD, Jr.
    Agent for Cabinet Kitchen Co.
    Marin County

WILLIAM A. SCOTT
    Fire Insurance
    San Francisco

JOHN L. GREER
    Marin County Abstract Co., Searcher of Records
    San Rafael

Sheriff's Sale
    Superior Court
    O.C. HAWKINS vs. CHARLES I. JACOBS, ELLA JACOBS, and MORRIS FEINTUCK
    Foreclosure
    Land in San Rafael on Hayes Street
    Filed March 17, 1893
    Sale to be held Saturday, April 8, 1893 at Courthouse in San Rafael
        HENRY HARRISON, Sheriff
        By T.J. FALLON, Undersheriff

Sheriff's Sale
    Superior Court
    ELISHA DuBOIS vs. LUTHER B. COLEMAN, NELLIE NOONAN, JOHN DOE, JANE DOE, and RICHARD ROE
    Foreclosure
    Land in San Rafael on Bayview Street
    Filed March 15, 1893
    Sale to be held Tuesday, April 18, 1893 at Courthouse in San Rafael
        HENRY HARRISON, Sheriff
        By T.J. FALLON, Undersheriff

Receiver's Sale
    Superior Court
    Insolvency of EVA N. GREGG
    Land at corner of 4th and E Streets, and personal property
    Files March 17, 1893
    Sale to be held Wednesday, March 22, 1893
        HENRY HARRISON, Receiver

Superior Court
    MATILDA SHEEK vs. WILLIAM SHEEK
    Divorce
    Must appear before within 10 days of summons
    Filed April 21, 1891
    JAMES W. COCHRANE, Attorney for plaintiff
        THOMAS S. BONNEAU, Clerk

Local News

BOB GRAHAM, of the N.P.C. has just returned from a trip to Oregon.

M.C. DUFFICY has retired as a candidate for Town Recorder, in favor of J.M. JONES.

GEORGE HARDING is building a blacksmith shop on his lot on the corner of 4th and Cijos Streets.

The San Rafael Druids presented their Treasurer, EDWARD EDEN, with a handsome badge last Monday night.

A steam schooner for the Bolinas trade is being built in San Francisco by Capt. MADSEN, O.B. LAUFF and others. It will be ready for service in the Spring.

J. FRANETTA has leased a fine house to C.C. STEVENSON, Jr., now in the BARSTOW cottage, to be built at once on the southeast corner of Fifth and H Streets.

Mrs. THOMAS MARTIN, a resident of Tiburon, died suddenly there last Wednesday. Coroner EDEN held an inquest, which showed the cause of death to be heart disease.

Mr. J.F. MANNEY has withdrawn his name for the office of Town Trustee.

Poisoned

Last Tuesday, an Italian by the name of ARBINI, and a fellow countryman, who have been working for Mr. J.F. FUGAZI, found what they supposed to be mushrooms, growing on the San Rafael Hill and proceeded to construct a savory dish of the same. It was freely partaken of and a cat and dog were also allowed to have a sample of the good thing. A short time thereafter, the entire quartet, the animals as well as the humans, were seized with agonizing cramps and other symptoms of irritant poisoning. Dr. WICKMAN was hurriedly sent for, who, after wrestling with his patients for several hours and invoking the aid of heroic remedies, had the satisfaction of bringing them out of imminent danger. The dog and the cat, in the meantime, were left to their own resources, and when Dr. WICKMAN turned his attention to them, he found that both had been gone to that better world.

Superior Court
    GEORGE FRITCH etal vs. PHILIP GRETHEL etal
    Demurrer withdrawn, defendant allowed 10 days to answer
    Name A. LAWRENCE substituted for JOHN DOE

    W.F. WHEATLEY vs. ISAAC HARRIS
    Motion of change of venue granted

    AMANDA TANN vs. Patent Brick Co. etal
    Continued to March 27th

    W.W. ELLIOTT vs. Tamalpais Land & Water Co.
    Motion for new trial argued and submitted

Real Estate Transfers
    CHARLES HANSON to SARAH E. HANSON
    Villa Lot 11, Miller Park Place, Novato - gift

    W.H. DAVIS to FRANK FOSTER
    Lot 1, Block J, Novato - $10

    J.W. ATHERTON to Home and Farm Co.
    Right of way - $1

    Mrs. PETER RUSH to Home & Farm Co.
    Right of way - $10

    MANUEL MAURICIO to MAGGIE R. MAURICIO
    Lot of First Street, near C Street, San Rafael - Gift

KARL O. KOEHLER etal, by Sheriff, to VINCENT H.E. KOEHLER etal
Lot on Bayview Street, near D, San Rafael - $1,010

ELLA W. NICHOLS to JAMES W. COCHRANE and wife
Lot on corner of Fifth and Nye Streets, San Rafael - $10

ELLA W. NICHOLS to LOUISE N. WILKINS
Lot on fifth and Nye Streets, San Rafael - $10

American Land & Trust Co., to FRITZ GOERL
Lot 6, Block H, Larkspur - $10

American Land & Trust Co. to T.C. COOGAN
Lots 5, 7, & 8, Block I, Larkspur - $10

Wealth in Tatters

For several years, a forlorn, poverty stricken looking old woman has sat on one of the benches on the Courthouse grounds whenever the season permitted. Her face was wrinkled and weather beaten as if the storms of a hundred years had buffeted her, and her clothes were little more than a conglomerate of worn out rags, that any self-respecting beggar would have been ashamed of. She was such a heartbreaking spectacle of loneliness, desolation and want that almost everyone who saw her was filled with compassion. Not a few would gladly have contributed financially to gladden her joyless life, but the old woman never indicated a desire for favors or recognition. She was indifferent to attempts at acquaintance, and no matter what was going on around her, she sat as impassive as a sphinx, gazing into the vacancies of space.

She was a German, and her name was SOPHIA STEINECKE ZELLAR. Her residence was the Albion House and there last Saturday she died. For several years, the old lady had suffered from sudden and acute attacks that threatened her life. On the afternoon of the above day, she was found dead on the floor of her room, having evidently fallen from the chair on which she had been sitting. When it came to settling her affairs this week, the surprising fact was brought to light that the venerable woman, whose appearance had so often excited the emotion of pity, was in fact a person of property, having very nearly $40,000 in gold coin in the bank. Her Will was filed for probate this week, and two San Rafael ladies, who were kind to the deceased, come in for large legacies. Mrs. J.F. JORDAN, proprietress of the Albion House, is bequeathed $20,000, and a German lady by the name of ROSALIE VATER is remembered to the extent of $10,000.

Nominations Complete

City Trustees – E.W. McCARTHY, H.C. GIESKE, W.J. MILLER, S.P. MOORHEAD, HY. SCHLOSSER, JOHN SHEEHY, J. PETERSEN, M. HERZOG, and C.A. ZINKAND

Board of Education - W.F. JONES, J.S. STRATTON, THOMAS HANSEN, T.J. CROWLEY, P.T. BURTCHAELL, J.J. SCHNEIDER, and W.J. WICKMAN

Marshall – JOHN LUCAS, JOHN HEALY, O. ALDERMAN, W.J. JOHNSON, J. ALLISON, W.H. JEWELL, and J.P. DAVENPORT

Assessor – W.F. DOUGHERTY, WALTER WALSH

Treasurer – R.W. JOHNSON, J.L.G. ARMSTRONG

Recorder – E. GARDNER, J.M. JONES, and GRATTAN PERRY

Marin Journal
Thursday, March 30, 1893

Real Estate Transfers
JOHN W. MACKAY etal to SILAS S. WOODWORD
Lot in Picnic Valley, San Rafael - $400

OLNEY HIBBARD to JANE T. DOWLING
Lot 6, Block 4, Tamalpais Land & Water Co. - $2,100

JANE T. DOWLING etal to ESTHER J. WHITE
Lot 6, block 4, Tamalpais Land & Water Co. - Gift

Mere Mention
Mr. AL BOHM of San Francisco was in San Rafael Friday evening to answer to his name at inspection drill.

Mr. MARTIN JOHANSEN has taken to crutches for a short time having cut himself badly in the right leg while using a knife.

Mr. YOUNG of San Rafael will soon open a cobbler's shop in the vacant store adjoining Thomson's dry goods store on Fourth Street.

County Clerk THOMAS S. BONNEAU returned on Sunday from a two-weeks trip to San Diego, where he went on business and for the health of his wife.

C.F. HANLON and wife will pass the summer again in San Rafael. The climate here is beneficial to Mrs. HANLON, and her husband is thinking very strongly of building here and establishing a permanent home.

GEORGE HARDING has completed his new blacksmith shop on Fourth Street.

Mr. J.F. MANNEY has withdrawn his name from the candidates for City Trustees.

Marriage Licenses
    BENJAMIN B. LEE, 37, San Rafael, to Mrs. ALA L. FETHEROFF, 27, San Rafael
    FRANK L. HARLOW, 24, Alameda to Miss MARGARET G. HAMB, 20, Alameda

Superior Court
    Estate and Guardianship of FRANK M. MAZEAS, minor
    A.G. SCOWN appointed guardian

    W.M. OLIVER vs. O.L. OLIVER
    Divorce granted to plaintiff

    P.A. DE FRIEZE vs. E. QUINT, admx
    Demurrer overruled, 20 days to answer

    Estate of PETER MORRISSEY, deceased
    Notice to Creditors ordered entered

    Estate of GEORGE TILGHMAN, deceased
    Partial distribution ordered

    Estate of JAMES M. DONAHUE, deceased
    Confirmation of sale of watch denied

    EVA GREGG vs. Her Creditors
    H. SCHLOSSER appointed assignee in bond of $1000

    H.C. ACKLEY vs. A.S. ASHBRIDGE
    Demurrer overruled, 3 days to answer

    McDONALD & PASCOE vs. Their Creditors
    Application for discharge of McDONALD, laid over one week

    Estate of JAMES M. DONAHUE, deceased
    Application of partial allowance of counsel fees, continued 3 weeks
    Executors to file their accounts, pay creditors claims

    JOHN A. ROY etal vs. N.P.C.R.R. Co.
    Motion to relax costs, continued until motion for new trial

Letter List
ALLEN, H.H.	BURNS, M.
BOYD, J.D.	BRETZEL, --

CLARK, A.C.	HILL, G.F.
HOFER, F.	LOIS, B.
MULLER, L.	MOLLER, S.L.
McFARLAND, C.	REYES, M.M.
MALLORY, M.	SWIFT, K.
SEWELL, C.	WINNIGAR, G.H.

Mere Mention
ARCHIE C. McALLISTER has resigned his position as superintendent of the Poor Farm. JAMES BRADLEY was appointed.

Mr. CHARLES STRATTON was in town last week. He is at present stopping at Ukiah.

Mr. F. LEGAULT has rented the O'BRYEN cottage on the corner of H Street and Culloden Ave.

Marin County Tocsin
Saturday, April 1, 1893

    Referee's Sale
        Superior Court
        THOMAS JEFFERSON BIGGINS etal vs. CATHERINE PRUNTY etal
        Land in Rancho Punta de Quentin
        Auction to be held April 25, 1893, at Courthouse, 1 p.m.
        Dated March 31, 1893
                JAMES TUNSTEAD
                Referee

    Notice to Creditors
        Estate of E.E. ADAMS, deceased
        Dated March 10, 1893
                GROVE ADAMS
                Executor of last Will

P. CRANE
        Proprietor, Royal Billard Hall
        San Rafael

JOHN McNAMARA
        Gardener
        Sausalito

W.T. SALE
        Home Furnishings
        San Rafael

Notice to Creditors
        Estate of HENRY J. VAN DYKE, deceased
        Dated March 17, 1893
        HEPBURN WILKINS, Attorney for Administrator
                ARTHUR CROSBY
                Administrator of Will

    Summons
        Superior Court
        JENNIE DIMOCK vs. FRANK H. DIMOCK
        GEORGE C. SARGENT, plaintiff's attorney
        Divorce
        Dated March 6, 1893
                THOMAS S. BONNEAU
                Clerk

Insolvent
>Superior Court
>SILAS S. SIMPSON, Insolvent debtor
>>F.M. ANGELLOTTI
>>Judge

Superior Court
>Estate of THOMAS OXNARD, deceased
>Final account approved and estate distributed

>Estate of LOUISE A. OXNARD, deceased
>Final account approved and estate distributed

Marin Journal
Thursday, April 6, 1893

>Died
KURTZ – In San Rafael, April 1, 1893, EUGENE KURTZ, aged 41 years.

Mere Mention
Twenty-five members of the local fire department attended the funeral of the late chief of the San Francisco fire department. Chief HUGHES was one of the pall-bearers. The departed Chief SCANNELL gave to the San Rafael department, its first hose cart and hose, and he always felt great interest in the welfare of the department of this city.

Our School Teachers

School	Teacher
Aurora	Miss MINNIE JOY
American Valley	Mrs. J.H. JENKINS
Bay	Miss M.C. JOHNSON
Black	Miss K.A. CHANDLER
Bolinas	R.G. COTTER
Chileno Valley	Miss NELLIE KIRK
Clark	Miss MAGGIE J. LOWDEN
Dixie	Miss ADDIE McDONNELL
Eastland	W.H. HENDERSON
Estero	Miss CLARA RODGERS
Fairfax	Miss MAZY BOYD
Franklin	Miss SADIE C. CHENEY
Garcia	Miss L.C. McALLEP
Halleck	Miss MAE NEYCE
Laguna-Joint	Miss MAGGIE KEATING
Lincoln	Miss LENA CLUVER
Marshall	Miss MAY MOORE
Nicasio	Miss FLORENCE GALLOWAY
Novato	Miss FRANCES A. PETERS
	Miss CARRIE E. COLLINS
Olema	Miss SABRA A. FINCH
Pierce	Miss LOUISE CLUVER
Pt. Reyes	Miss EDNA M. NELSON
Reed	Miss MATILDA HAUSS
Richardson	JAMES B. DAVIDSON
	Miss CARRIE FIEDLER
	Miss ANNIE FARRELL
	Miss JENNIE FARRELL
Ross Landing	Miss E.T. MAHONEY
San Antonio	Mrs. ELLA McPHAIL
San Geronimo	Miss M.A. CRITTENDEN
San Jose	Miss MARION G. PARKER
San Rafael	C.S. SMYTH, Principal
	CHESTER WETMORE
	Miss L.M. McLEAN
	Miss BELLE C. BROWN

	Miss ALICE A. GATES
	Miss MARY FARRELL
	Miss K.C. BATCHELDER
	Miss FLORIDE GREEN
	Miss E.H. NICHOLS
	Miss E.J. DUFFICY
	Miss BESSIE McALLISTER
San Quentin	Miss GEORGIANA SCOTT
Sausalito	Miss CLARA B. SMYTH
Salmon Creek	Miss NELLIE O'ROURKE
Tocaloma	Miss ANNIE L. HORNSBY
Tomales	E.M. COX
	Mrs. L.E.S. REYNOLDS
Tiburon	Miss BERTHA E. LEEDS

Letter List

BAUR, C.	HUNTER, E.T.
MITTON, R.	MARVIN, I.F.
MORGAN, W.H.	McCORMACK, J.P.
ROBERTS, J.H.	REED, C.H.

Marriage Licenses
ANTONIO SIMONTACCHI, 31, Nordon, Ventura Co., to FRANCESCA PIANTANIDA, 20, San Rafael
OSCAR MAYER, 29, Oakland, to MARY BOYSEN, 18, Oakland

Superior Court
H. GREGG vs. EVA GREGG etal
Assignee substituted in place of H. HARRISON, receiver

W.W. ELLIOTT etal vs. Tam Land & Water Co.
Motion for new trial denied unconditionally

Estate of WILLIAM SEET
E. EDEN appointed administrator

PRESTON & McKINNON etal vs. EMILY F. LIBBEY etal
Motion for new trial granted

Re-application of ANGUS McDONALD for discharge from incompetence
Granted

Mere Mention
EUGENE KURTZ, the baker, of the firm STEINMETZ & KURTZ, has been ill some time, but on Saturday night last, he was attacked by a hemorrhage and died very suddenly. The funeral occurred on Monday and was largely attended.

SALVADOR PACHECO has sold the ranch beyond Fairfax, which he bought from Mrs. BRESSON, to a syndicate of 30 people from San Francisco, who will camp on the ranch during the summer. The price paid was $12,000. There are 600 acres in it.

ARCHIE C. McALLISTER has resigned his position as Superintendent of the Poor Farm. JAMES BRADLEY was appointed to fill the position.

Mr. J.F. FRANETTA is erecting two cottages on his lot on the corner of Fifth and H Streets.

Mr. CHARLES STRATTON was in town last week. He is at present stopping at Ukiah.

Mr. F. LEGAULT has rented the O'BRYEN Cottage on the corner of H Street and Culloden Avenue.

Mr. A. CHEDA comtemplates erecting a number of cottages on the McVANNER lot, northeast corner of Third and A Streets, adjoining the wood and coal yard.

Sudden Death

On Saturday afternoon, Attorney E.B. MARTINELLI was summoned by telegraph to Petaluma on account of the sudden and severe illness of his father, L. MARTINELLI, who for some years has resided on a ranch at Lakeville some miles from Petaluma. It seems that the elder MARTINELLI, while driving on the road between Lakeville and Petaluma, was suddenly stricken with a stroke of apoplexy. He was removed to the residence of Mr. CY WHITE near where he was taken ill, and medical attendance was summoned. He died however, Sunday night, never having regained consciousness. Mr. MARTINELLI was well known in this county where he resided for years, and where he still owns a large ranch near Nicasio. He was a man of considerable means and highly respected. He leaves a wife and several children who have the sympathy of the entire community in their sudden and severe bereavement.

Marin County Tocsin
Saturday, April 8, 1893

Real Estate Transfers

Estate of ASA C. NICHOLS to ELLEN W. NICHOLS
Grantors interest in lot at corner of Nye and Fifth Streets, San Rafael – by distribution

MICHAEL W. KEOGH to E.C. RUST
Lot 17, block 7, Old Sausalito - $10

W.R. HEARST to Sausalito Land and Ferry Co.
Lots 62 & 63, block B, Sausalito Land and Ferry Co. - $10

EMIL DE GHETALDI to ADOLPH B. SPRECKELS
Portion of Lot 1, block 9, Sausalito - $10

METTIE M. JONES to KATE McALLISTER
Lot on Laurel Street, San Rafael, $10

W.P. HAROLD and wife to GEORGE E. BILLINGS
Portion of Lot 207, Tamalpais Land and Water Co. - $10

Belvedere Land Co. to EDWARD N. HARMON
Lot 17, block 3, Belvedere - $10

WALTER POWELL etal to JAMES M. STREETEN
Portion of tide land, block 7, Sausalito Land and Ferry Co. - $10

Marin County Water Co. to DAVID WARDEN
Lot adjoining Reservoir Tract, San Rafael - $10

SARAH E. HANSON to MAX ARNO THEILIG
Villa lot 11, Miller Park Place, Novato - $10

JAMES M. STREETEN to LOUIS JOHNSON
Portion tideland, block 8, Richardson's Bay - $10

Sausalito Bay and Land Co. to MARGARET LONG
Villa lot 41, block 19, Sausalito Bay and Land Co. - $10

FRANK E. ADAMS to CATHERINE BULLIS
Lot 4, block 28, San Rafael - $10

LEE HIBBARD to PETER J. SULLIVAN
Portion of lot 1, block 9, Tamalpais Land and Water Co. - $10

Local News

Mrs. L. GULDAGER, of Tomales, one of the old and respected residents of that section, passed away last Wednesday.

Mr. GEORGE McMILLAN, a first class photographer, will open a gallery in the Tunstead Building, on or about April 12th.

Capt. McALLISTER will build a residence on his lot on Laurel Place for his future home, and hopes to have it ready for occupancy shortly after he retires from the Poor Farm superintendency.

The grocery store of GEORGE KOHLHOFF on the corner of Fourth and F Streets was closed last Saturday night, the proprietor turning his establishment into a wholesale agency for Buffalo Beer.

The San Francisco papers announce the death of HENRY C. HYDE on Thursday last, who for many years resided in San Rafael with his family in the house now occupied by Judge MORROW. The deceased left this town on the death of his young son several years ago, but still retained a large circle of friends and acquaintances here who will hear of his death with sorrow.

Markmanship
The Marin County Schuetzen Club had their prize range shooting at the park last Sunday. The competition was open to all comers and the interest was sufficient to attract all the crack marksmen of the State. A handsome sum was netted by the Club after defraying expenses. The following is the score, 100 being the possible maximum:
- 1st prize – JOHN UTSCHIG, 97
- 2nd prize – A. STRECKER, 94
- 3rd prize – D.W. McLAUGHLIN, 93
- 4th prize – WILLIAM GLINDERMAN, 92
- 5th prize – F. KUHNLE, 91
- 6th prize – Dr. ROGERS, 91
- 7th prize – F.O. YOUNG, 90
- 8th prize – GEORGE HELM, 90
- 9th prize – F. KUHNLE, 90
- 10th prize – P. JACOBY, 90
- 11th prize – ENGE, 89
- 12th prize – O. BURMEISTER, 88
- 13th prize – E. HOVEY, 88
- 14th prize – F. ATTENGER, 87
- 15th prize – J.F. ROBINSON, 87
- 16th prize – J.E. KLINE, 87
- 17th prize – JOHN JONES, 87
- 18th prize – A. GEHRET, 86
- 19th prize – H.B. BROWN, 85
- 20th prize – H. SCHRODER, 83
- First Bulls-eye forenoon – F. KUHNLE
- Last Bulls-eye – D.W. McLAUGHLIN
- First Bulls-eye afternoon – WILLIAM HAHN
- Last Bulls-eye – P. JACOBY
- Best 5 tickets – A. STRECKER
- Second 5 tickets – JOHN UTSCHIG
- Most Rings – F. KUHNLE
- Most Bulls-eye – F. KUHNLE

Board of Supervisors
1. Accepted resignation of A.C. McALLISTER as Superintendent of the Marin County Poor Farm. There were 6 aspirants for the vacant position: MERRIT ROBINSON, HERBERT RING, A. TIMONY, H.J. LUCAS, HORACE DAILY, and JAMES BRADLEY. JAMES BRADLEY won with a unanimous vote. His wife will serve as matron.
2. The coyote scalp returns were canvassed and the following persons were declared entitled to State bounty for scalps: H. DALESSI, L. GIOLI, B.B. JOHNSON, Z. LEWIS, S.L. MYERS, J. MAILLIARD, T.B. ROY.
3. Permits to obtain liquor licenses were granted as follows: H. CASSOU, GEORGE E. HAMILTON, THOMAS H. NICHOLS, ROBERT McQUARRIE, all of San Rafael
4. The allowance of $10 per month for the support of CHARLES WRIGHT and wife was increased to $17.50.
5. The sum of $8.50 a month was allowed for the support of Mrs. M. NELAN of Tomales.

6. The following persons were chosen on the County Board of Education: C.S. SMYTH, J.B. DAVIDSON, BELLE C. BROWN, MAGGIE LOWDEN

The Late Mrs. ZELLAR
The case of the late Mrs. SOPHIA ZELLAR, who lived in San Rafael in apparent poverty, but who subsequently turned out to be worth in the neighborhood of $40,000, was not as bad as the Tocsin painted it. The old lady was utterly regardless of external appearances, and it is true that her clothes appeared to have come out of the Ark. But otherwise she denied herself nothing. She had the best room at the Albion House, and anything at her meals that suited her appetite, and was otherwise mindful of her material comfort. The deceased was in all respects as happy as age and infirmity would permit, notwithstanding her old clothes. Mrs. JORDAN, proprietress of the Albion House, was assiduous in her disinterested attention and to the constant kindness to Mrs. ZELLAR. She was remembered handsomely in her Will. The kind-hearted landlady has many acts of benevolence to her credit. She has often kept penniless boarders through long spells of sickness, cared for them as well as if she expected to be paid for it, and buried them at her own expense when they died. Her friends are more than pleased to see her reap a handsome reward for the exercises of these virtues. The German lady, Mrs. VATER, who is the other principal heir, comes by her good fortune through kindly offices to the deceased, inspired by compassion for her apparently desolate condition.

Death of LOUIS MARTINELLI
Mr. E.B. MARTINELLI was warned by telegram last Saturday of the sudden and probably fatal illness of his father, LOUIS MARTINELLI, at his home in Lakeville, Sonoma County. He immediately hastened hither and arrived just in time to see his parent before the last flicker of life went out. Death resulted from a stroke of apoplexy. He had visited Petaluma on Saturday afternoon and while there had complained of pains in his head, but attended to his business as usual and started for home. As he neared White's residence at Lakeville, he evidently realized that the spell was coming on, for he turned his team against the fence and put the brake on. He was noticed by two men who happened to be walking along at the time and they came up just as he fell against the dashboard. He was carried into the residence of J.H. WHITE and Dr. REED was hastily summoned, but he pronounced the case hopeless. The sufferer lingered until early on Sunday evening. The deceased was a native of Switzerland, and was one of the first of that nationality to settle in this section of the country, where they now form so important an element. Like most of his countrymen, Mr. MARTINELLI applied his energies to the dairying industry, at which he was predominantly successful. He succeeded in building up a large fortune, possessing extensive landed interests in both Marin and Sonoma counties. Personally, Mr. MARTINELLI was universally esteemed and respected for all the qualities that should adorn a good citizen. The funeral took place last Wednesday from the family residence and was attended by many sorrowing friends from the neighborhood and adjacent counties.

Marin Journal
Thursday, April 13, 1893

Winners of the Election
Trustees
EDWARD W. McCARTHY, WILLIAM J. MILLER, STANLEY P. MOORHEAD, JOHANNES PETERSON, HENRY C. GIESKE
Board of Education
P.T. BURTCHAELL, THOMAS HANSEN, W.F. JONES, W.J. WICKMAN, JOHN S. STRATTON
Assessor
W.F. DOUGHERTY
Marshall
JOHN E. HEALY
Treasurer
ROBERT W. JOHNSON
Recorder
EDWIN GARDNER

Distribution of Monies Paid in Estate of JAMES M. DONAHUE, deceased
Mrs. SUSAN LOWE, aunt - $10,000
ELLEN MAGUIRE, aunt - $10,000
J.F. BURGIN - $5,000
MARY JANE WHITE, nee MAGUIRE - $5,000
OLIVE MAGUIRE, godchild - $25,000

SUSANNAH MAGUIRE - $5,000
LAURA MAGUIRE - $5,000
THOMAS GODFREY MAGUIRE Jr. - $5,000
THOMAS DONAHUE - $10,000
S.G. MURPHY, as guardian of JOHN HENRY VON SCHROEDER - $5,000
S.G. MURPHY, as guardian of JEANNETTE VON SCHROEDER - $5,000

Death of J.G. KITTLE
JONATHAN G. KITTLE, the senior member of the firm of Kittle & Co., died at 5:30 p.m. Sunday at the Hotel D-Augerot on Eighteenth Street and Fifth Street, New York. The cause of his death has not been determined, although three physicians were in attendance for some time previous to his demise. When he left San Francisco for the East on September 28 last, there were no visible signs of any malady, but about 4 months ago, and attack of severe illness precipitated the disorders from which death resulted. Mr. KITTLE was about 64 years of age and married. His wife, who was a daughter of General L.H. ALLEN, and 4 children survive him. The family residence is at Ross Station, where the deceased merchant kept up a magnificent establishment, in keeping with his wealth and commercial position. He was a member of the Union Club in San Francisco. Nothing has yet been decided as to the date of the funeral, but the body will undoubtedly be brought to California for interment.

Public Administrator's Sale
    Estate of PETER MORRISSEY, deceased
    Sale to be held Tuesday, May 9, 1893 on premises
        All of Lot 15, part of Lot 14
        Both in Block 17, Tomales
Filed April 10, 1893
                            EDWARD EDEN, Administrator

Mere Mention
Mrs. J.D. TUCKER and her daughter, Miss HENRIETTA TUCKER, of Petaluma, visited San Rafael last week.

The Grand Parlor of Native Sons' meets on the 26th in Sacramento, and on Monday night, Dr. GEORGE F. RODDEN and ARTHUR SCOTT were elected delegates to that body from the San Rafael parlor.

A Spanish woman died on the 4th instant at the County Hospital. She had reached the remarkable age of 104 years. Her name was CHRISTIANA ERUTIA. Some of the Spanish population say she was over 140 years old.

It is rumored that Mr. ANTONE DE BORBA, of Novato, contemplates shortly to erect another creamery at that place in addition to the one already in operation there. Mr. DE BORBA controls several large dairies in the vicinity of Novato, and is at present one of the largest suppliers of milk to the Novato Creamery.

PETER SWIEFEL, a German, and a member of the Salvation Army, was married on Tuesday evening to Miss FLORENS CHEVERS, an ex-member of the Army.

Miss CARRIE COLLINS, who is filling the position of teacher of the primary school at Novato, is in San Rafael this week attending the teachers' institute. She is the guest of Mr. C.S. BARNEY.

Superior Court
    Estate of PETER MORRISSEY, deceased
    Sale of real estate ordered

    Estate of SOPHIA ZELLAR, deceased
    Opposition to probate of Will filed

    Estate of JAMES M. DONAHUE, deceased
    Decree distributing legacies ordered

    Estate of JEAN M. MAZEAS, deceased
    A.G. SCOWN appointed administrator

People and Co. vs. JEREMIAH SHINE etal
Motion of T.J. CROWLEY laid over to next week

H. GREGG vs. EVA N. GREGG etal
Motion of E.B. MARTINELLI laid over one week

Estate of EUGENE KURTZ, deceased
All papers in said estate ordered transferred to San Francisco

Estate and guardianship of JUDITH MAZEAS
Mrs. SCOWN appointed guardian in bond of $3,000

ROSA EMILY SILVA vs. ANTONIO MACHADO SILVA
Decree of divorce ordered

Marriage Licenses
    GEORGE H. WHEELER, 31, Oakland, to MINNIE F. LYNAS, 18, Oakland
    CHARLES M. MOORE, 25, Temescal, to MARY DOLAN, 21, Oakland
    WALLACE S. BRACKETTE, 34, Oakland, to ANNIE D. WESTFALL, 20, Oakland
    PETER SWIEFEL, 38, San Rafael, to FLORENS CHEVERS, 36, San Rafael

Letter List

CHITTENDEN, G.E.	DANIELS, J.
FRANKS, --	FRICKE, C.
KENDALL, J.	KNIGHT, E.
KOENIG, A.	MINAMI, F.

Real Estate Transfers
    WALTER POWELL etal to JAMES M. STREETEN
    Portion lots 7 & 8, New Sausalito - $10

    ALEX R. BECKER etal to ARNOLD BECKER
    Lots 15, 16, 17, block 21, Golden Meadow - $10

    ARNOLD BECKER to J.D. SPRECKELS and Bros.
    Lots 1 & 2, block 24, and lot 47, block 23, Golden Meadow - $10

    ARNOLD BECKER to J.D. SPRECKELS and Bros.
    Lots 15, 16, 17, block 21, Golden Meadow - $10

    Sausalito Bay and Land Co. to LORING P. RIXFORD
    W 30 Feet of lots 8, 9, and 10, block 14, Old Sausalito - $10

    FREDERICK A. WHEELER to CHARLES W. FAY
    Ptn. Lot 27, plan of lots near San Rafael - $10

    B.T. MILLER to MARY S. CORNWELL
    113.4 acres, ptn. of Rancho Nicasio - $10

    PETER J. SULLIVAN to MARY SULLIVAN
    E ptn. Lot 1, block 9, Tamalpais Land Co. – Gift

    CYRUS R. SARGENT to WOOD CHRISTIESON and Co.
    Lot 12, block 54, Coleman's addition, San Rafael - $10

    CHARLES M. COLE etal to HETTIE B. WICKMAN
    NW corner 4th Street and E Street, San Rafael - $10

    Tamalpais Land and Water Co. to SARAH J. SCHULTZ
    1 acre south and west of Cascade Drive and Marion Ave - $500

Tamalpais Land and Water Co. to HARRY R. WILLIS
Lot 294, Tamalpais Land and Water Co. - $800

May Inherit a Fortune
Mrs. THOMAS S. BONNEAU stands a good chance of inheriting a round $1,000,000. It seems an ancestor of hers in 1733 obtained a grant of land on which Trinity Church and other buildings in the heart of New York now stand. In 1777 the land was leased for 99 years. In 1832 fire destroyed all the city records, and 2 years later the possessors began selling the land. Very recently the records of the lease were found, and the descendants began the work of having their claim recognized. On this coast there are only 8 heirs, and their share of the estate is estimated at over $1,000,000 each. Several lawyers who rank in the front rank of the legal profession have interested themselves in the case, and all are confident of a judgment in favor of the EDWARDS heirs. Among these are various members of the MEEKER family of Sonoma County, of which family Mrs. BONNEAU is a member. Mr. and Mrs. BONNEAU are expecting to soon start for the East to look after the interests of the heirs on this coast.

Marin County Tocsin
Saturday, April 15, 1893

Local News
C. GROSJEAN was down from Healdsburg this week, looking after his San Rafael interests.

STEPHEN RICHARDSON is a candidate for night watchman, to succeed JOHN HEALY, who will assume the duties of Marshall next week.

Col. THOMAS RYAN, telegrapher of the U.S. Lighthouse at Pt. Reyes, spent a portion of his annual furlough in San Rafael this week.

Mr. and Mrs. E. SCHWIESAU have invited their friends to their crystal wedding, which they will celebrate at Hayes Hall on the evening of May 9th.

District Attorney COCHRANE will leave for the East early in May to attend to urgent business connected with the estate of his wife's uncle. He will be absent for about 6 weeks.

Mr. P. SECONDINO has leased the Hayes' Tract, near San Rafael, and will make it a picnic and camping resort. Dance platforms and other necessary buildings are being rapidly constructed.

J.C. HOOVER, the candy magnate of Fourth and B Streets, is in the swim for the Spring business. His specialties are ice cream soda, and ice cream for families.

The HINIKER Brothers, connected with the great slaughtering establishment at Baden, have rented a stand in the new Wilkins building on Fourth Street. They will open a first class market there in about 10 days.

Died
BOYLE – In San Rafael, April 12, 1893, at the residence of her son, HENRY BOYLE, JANE BOYLE, a native of Londonderry, Ireland, aged 77 years.

Sheriff's Sale
  Superior Court of San Francisco
  JOSEPH E. SHAIN against L. DU JARDIN
  Sum of $486.50
  Sale of personal property to be held Monday, April 17, 1893 at Courthouse
  Dated San Rafael, April 7, 1893
         HENRY HARRISON, Sheriff
         By T.J. FALLON, Deputy Sheriff

Notice to Creditors
  Estate of PETER WEBER, deceased
  Vouchers must be presented at Executrix residence
  Dated San Rafael, February 10, 1893
         ANNE WEBER
         Executrix of Will
  HEPBURN WILKINS, Attorney for Executrix

Marin Journal
Thursday, April 20, 1893

Superior Court

People and Co. vs. J. SHINE etal
Over one week

J. SCHNELL vs. Sausalito Land and Ferry Co.
Continued to May 1st

Estate of JAMES M. DONAHUE, deceased
Motion for counsel fees, over one week

R.E. SILVA vs. A.M. SILVA
Decree of divorce granted

Estate of ANTON ELMERICH
Final account settled and distributed

H.J COLLIN vs. J. McCOMB etal
Motion to dismiss over one week

J.W. MIDDLETON vs. J. McCOMB etal
Motion to dismiss over one week

AMANDA TANN, admx. Etal vs. Patent Brick Co. etal
Demurrer of amended complaint overruled, 20 days to answer

GEORGE W. FOX vs. SUSAN FOX
Notice of motion for alimony and counsel fees, 10 days to present to authorities

H.R. GREGG vs. EVA N. GREGG etal
Laid over one week

Tamalpais Land and Water Co. vs. J.H. McINNES
Cause submitted

Marriage Licenses

E.E. SHOTWELL, 32, Ross Valley to Miss EMMA DOHERTY, 30, Ross Valley
CHAUNCEY A. PARMARLEE, 25, San Francisco, to Miss CHRISTINA KELLERAN, 31, San Francisco
WILLIAM S. MOSSON, 29, Olema, to MARY JOSEPHINE BRESSON, 20, Fairfax
ELMER E. BATCHELDER, 32, Oakland, to Miss ANNA RYAN, 35, Oakland

Letter List

ADAMS, HOLLY	BOREN, P.
BROWN, --	BARRETT, A.
BUTTERFIELD, L.H.	CYPHUS, C.
FISHER, M.	GREY, W.
GOODRUM, M.	HALLORAN, O.
KELLEHER, L.	LOWENFIELD, B.
LAMERROW, J.	McCOLLOUGH, J.
McKEE, S.	OTTUAL, J.
REED, Mrs. G.B.	SPONEY, J.B.
STOCKER, M.	SPENNEY, CHARLES
SMITH, J.M.	TANFORAN, F.
TOLAND, D.	VALENCIA, V.
WELCH, E.M.	VALENCIA, T.
WELSH, J.	WOOD, B.

Foreign

RESENDES, A.T.	NILSON, O.

Real Estate Transfers

Tamalpais Land & Water Co. to JOHANNA CUDWORTH
Lot 14, block 6, Tamalpais Land & Water Co. - $300

Tamalpais Land & Water Co. to JOHANNA CUDWORTH
Lot 13, block 6, Tamalpais Land & Water Co. - $10

Home and Farm Co. to MARY P. GOMEZ
Lot 8, block C, Lot 12, Reservoir Hill Place, Novato, $297

WILLIAM EDWARD to PASQUINUCCI MENOTTI
Lot 62, Edward Harrison Map, Old Sausalito - $10

ELLA C. POND to ARNOLD BECKER
Lots 35, 36, 37, 38, 40, 41, block 24, Golden Meadow, San Rafael - $10

ARNOLD BECKER to S. FOSTER
Lot 35, 36, 37, 38, 40 and 41, block 24, Golden Meadow, San Rafael - $10

DAVID THRASHER to W.R. FAIRBANKS
Lots 1, 2, 3, 4, block 24, Tomales - $10

M.W. KAIN and wife to W.O. BROWN
Lots 1, 2, 3, 4, 5, 6, 7, 8, 9, 10, Kain's addition to San Rafael - $10

DAVID WARDEN and wife to Marin County Water Co.
Right of way over land conveyed to Moore to Warden etc. - $10

ZALIE J. ELLIOTT to JACOB GARDNER
6 ½ acres beginning at C.M.P. 181 etc. - $10

JACOB GARDNER and wife to WILLIAM N. SHELLEY
5.09 acres, Rancho Corte Madera del Presidio etc. - $10

JOSEPH A. BAXTER by sheriff to A.B. CASE
Lot 10, block B, Coleman's addition - $175

JOHN KNELL to BARBARA KNELL
Lots 7 & 8, block 7, Belvedere
Lot 10, block 9, & lot 158, Tamalpais Land & Water Co. – gift

Town Talk
Mr. B.C. ROOS, who has been connected with the local Gas & Electric Co. for 5 years, is now occupying a position with the CA Electric Light Co. in San Francisco. He left yesterday with his family.

Marin County Tocsin
Saturday, April 22, 1893

Notice to Creditors
Estate of JEAN M. MAZEAS, deceased
Dated April 21, 1893
HEPBURN WILKINS, Attorney for Administrator
ADOLPH G. SCOWN, Admr.

Notice for proving Will
Estate of JONATHAN G. KITTLE, deceased
Monday, May 8, 1893, in Superior Court
Dated April 21, 1893
MYRICK & DEERING, Attorneys for Petitioner
THOMAS S. BONNEAU, Clerk
By D.T. TAYLOR, Deputy Clerk

Auction Sale
> Estate of JAMES McM. SHAFTER, deceased
> Thursday, May 18, 1893, at Courthouse
> Ranch known as North Bend Ranch – 333 acres
> Ranch known as Riverside Ranch – 12 ½ acres
> Ranch known as Olema Ranch – 300 acres
> > JAMES TUNSTEAD, Real Estate Agent

Local News

FRANK MAZZA, an old and respected resident of this County, died suddenly at his ranch near Nicasio last Wednesday.

Mr. J.G. EASTLAND will build a $25,000 house in Mill Valley this season, by far the handsomest residence yet constructed in that growing town.

Mr. V.A. REY, of the prominent printers supply firm of Palmer & Rey, is the latest addition to the population of Belvedere.

A KAPPENMAN is negotiating for the rental of the New England Villa and will probably be its proprietor this season. He will undoubtedly make it a success.

Miss GREGG, the popular proprietress of The Cedars Boarding House in San Rafael, has opened a like establishment in Chicago, where visitors to the World's Fair from this section will be welcomed.

Mr. W.D. KELLY was appointed Postmaster at Tiburon last week, and is the first local Democrat to be remembered.

Runaway Accident

ANTHONY CRIMMINS, a well known farmer of the San Anselmo Valley, and RAMON VALENCIA, met with a serious runaway accident yesterday afternoon. They were nearing the Junction, about a quarter of a mile east of the station, when an approaching train terrified the horses and caused them to run away. A sudden lurch of the wagon hurled CRIMMINS head long to the ground, and VALENCIA followed a second later. RAMON grasped the lines from CRIMMINS hand as he fell and hung on like a thoroughbred until knocked senseless. His clothes and even shoes were torn to tatters. Assistance came promptly and Dr. WHITE was hurriedly brought from San Rafael. VALENCIA's injuries did not seem to be serious, and he soon recovered sufficiently to take his seat in a buggy and be driven home. CRIMMINS case, however, was far more serious. The physician looked very grave as he examined him, and said that it was difficult to forecast the results of the injuries as yet. It looked as if there was a serious concussion of the brain. CRIMMINS lies at the Central, where he receives every attention.

Board of Town Trustees
Officers appointed:
> Library Trustees
> > V. NEALE, C.P. POMEROY, A. BOYEN, L. HASKELL, J.W. COCHRANE
> City Attorney
> > E.B. MARTINELLI
> City Engineer
> > GEORGE L. RICHARDSON
> Nightwatchman
> > WILLIAM DWYER, S. RICHARDSON
> Pound Keeper
> > D. BEGLEY
> Engineer of Pump Works
> > D.S. SOUTHWICK
> Fire Steward
> > GEORGE FITZROY
> Standing Committees
> > Sewers & Drainage
> > > MOORHEAD & GIESKE
> > Finance
> > > MILLER & GIESKE

Streets
PETERSON & MILLER
Fire Department
MOORHEAD & GIESKE

Real Estate Transfers
FREDERICK S. TAYLOR to KATE R.E. TAYLOR
Lot 19, block 1, Sunnyside – Gift

Estate of ANTON ELMERICH to JOSEPHINE ELMERICH
Portion of lot 2, block 17, San Rafael – Distribution

JAMES SIBLEY and wife to JAMES TUNSTEAD & HEPBURN WILKINS
Lot on corner of Clark and Fourth Street, San Rafael - $5

G.B. PEPPER to LeROY G. HARVEY
159.68 acres of tideland on Bolinas Bay - $5

JAMES M. STREETEN to ZALIE J. ELLIOTT
Portion of tideland, blocks 7 & 8, Sausalito - $10

O.C. MILLER etal to REBECCA LEVY
Villa lot 25, Campbell tract, Sausalito - $10

A LAWRENCE etal to MANUEL MANSEBO
Lot 16, block 10, Sausalito Land & Ferry Co. - $1

Sausalito Land & Ferry Co. to MANUEL MANSEBO
Land in Sausalito Land & Ferry Co. - $10

JOHN W. MACKAY etal to WILLIAM BABCOCK
7.75 acres, William Street & Mountain View - $8,000

JAMES W. FOSS to FREDERICK S. TAYLOR
Lot 19, block 1, Sunnyside - $10

JACOB GARDNER and wife to WILLIAM N. SHELLEY
Land at Rancho Corte Madera - $10

JOSEPH A. BAXTER, by Sheriff, to A.B. CASE
Lot on Petaluma Ave., San Rafael - $175

JOHN KNELL to BARBARA KNELL
Lots 7 & 8, block 7, Belvedere
Lot 10, block 9, & lot 158, Tamalpais Land & Ferry Co. – Gift

ELLEN TUMELTY to HELEN M. LAKEMAN
Portion of lot 9, Tamalpais Land & Water Co. - $10

Marin Journal
Thursday, April 27, 1893

Real Estate Transfers
Sausalito Land & Ferry Co. to ANTONIO S. BETTENCOURT
Lot 12, block 27, Sausalito Land & Ferry Co. - $10

S.A. PACHECO and wife to JACOB STADFELD
800 acres as partitioned to DOMINGA BRESSON, ptn. Of Sais Rancho - $10

Marriage Licenses
ARTHUR E. WELLINGTON, 24, San Francisco, to Miss ANNA E. BOOLE, 22, Ross Valley
TAYLOR DICKSON, 44, Philadelphia, PA, to Miss JEANNIE GRIFFITH, 30, Ross Valley

A German Club

Something over 40 of our German citizens have formed a German-American Club. The name of the club has not yet been definitely decided upon as yet. The place of the meeting is the old Masonic Hall. The officers elected last Saturday were: W. HAHN, President; W. HERZOG, Secretary; E. FAUST, Treasurer.

Letter List

AQUINN, M.	DeMANUEL, E.T.
DUARTE, A.	FARQUHASSON, R.
GENSEN, H.	HOLLAND, N.
JANSEN, J.	JONES, MARY
JOHNSON, S.	MAXON, G.W.
RUNFELDT, M.A.	ROBERTS, J.M.
STEFFINS, E.J.	STRAND, G.B.
STEINWOOD, E.A.	STONE, J.
SVENSON, A.	TOOFRY, J.
TAYLOR, T.	TERRY, B.F.
TWILIA, M.	ZINCKE, E.

Foreign

OLIVEIRA, S.M.	ZABIANA, M.S.
FREITAS, J.T.	NILSON, O.
ALOMADA, A.P.	DIAZEN, A.F.
DEL GROSSO, L.	THOMAS, J.J.
BACCI, G.	DA SILVA, M. DE S
BRAZIL, J.J.	SIMONI, P.
AZEVEDO, F.S.	BATTISTA, Z.G.

Rev. C.H. EMERSON

LUTHER EMERSON, the foreman of the Journal Office, has been receiving a visit from his parents, Rev. C.H. EMERSON, and his wife. Mr. EMERSON is a Presbyterian clergyman from the Pope Valley, Napa County. He is much pleased with the many beauties of San Rafael. Mr. EMERSON, though a man of 75 years, has the vigor and mind and body possessed by the average man of 60 years. In former years he was greatly interested in politics, as he is even to this day. In Massachusetts he was a prominent Whig.

Town Talk

GEORGE McMILLAN, the photographer, has rented one of the Hunnewell Cottages on Third Street.

Marin County Tocsin
Saturday, April 29, 1893

Real Estate Transfers

ALBERT S. SHOBERG to SOPHIA SHOBERG
Lot on northeast corner of Fourth and Irwin Streets, San Rafael - $10

ALBERT S. SHOBERG to Pioneer Mill and Lumber Co.
Lot on southeast corner of Fourth and Irwin Streets, San Rafael - $10

JOHN W. FERRIS to P.W. RIORDAN
Portions of sections 2, 5, 10, and 11, township 2, range 6 W, 250 acres - $10

LOIS A. PECKHAM to MAURICE WINDMILLER
Lot 9, Tamalpais Land & Water Co. - $1,000

FRANK AMIOT and wife to JOSEPH LAURIANO
Fraction of block 23, Sausalito Land & Ferry Co. - $200

Sausalito Bay & Land Co. to CRESS UNGER
Lot 42, block 19, Sausalito Bay & Land Co. - $10

JOHN O.B. SHORT and wife to DELIA WALL
Lot 28, block A, Short's addition, San Rafael - $10

Tamalpais Land & Water Co. to FANNIE M. PEARSON
Lot 296 - $10

Tamalpais Land & Water Co. to JOHN W. BUTLER
Lot 291, Tamalpais Land & Water Co. - $800

Death of J.G. McMULLIN
Many residents of Marin County were deeply shocked last Thursday when they read the account in the city papers of the probable suicide of JAMES G. McMULLIN in San Francisco. The young man was born and raised at Bolinas and had a large circle of acquaintances. He was one of the numerous sons of our Marin County farmers who have gone to San Francisco and achieved success there. Mr. McMULLIN chose a mercantile career, for which he had a natural aptitude. He rose rapidly and at the time of his death was senior partner in a large dry goods firm. The city papers have given full reports of his death – how he wandered around a tough part of the city until a late hour at night, evidently very sick, how he was finally conveyed to a boarding house, where he died in convulsions. The case is one of the deepest mystery. No possible incentive to suicide is apparent. The deceased was in good health, was prosperous, and his domestic relations apparently very harmonious. Yet the facts of the case seem to point irresistibly to the conclusion that the young man took his own life. Mr. McMULLIN was only 32 years old.

Death of HIRAM AUSTIN
The news comes to the Tocsin office of the death of HIRAM AUSTIN, at Placerville, El Dorado County, where he moved after leaving San Rafael 7 or 8 years ago. The old gentleman had continued the practice of the profession of civil engineering there, had been elected County Surveyor, and we believe his circumstances of late years have been fairly comfortable.

The deceased was one of the most noted characters around Marin County in the early days. He was universally known as the "Professor", partly because he had never been one, and partly for the same reasons that induce some people to apply that title to the editor of this paper. From way back in the early fifties, down to the time when he left this section, he held the office of County Surveyor with only one or two breaks in the succession. He either conducted or was connected with about all the important surveys upon which much of the titles to property rights in Marin depend, and it is safe to say that he made acquaintances in a professional way with every acre in the county. His bulk was enormous, and on the slightest exertion, he blew and wheezed worse than a sperm whale. In the early days, when work was abundant, and the compensation of Surveyors about anything they chose to ask, AUSTIN must have made a bucketful of money every year. It did him no good, however. He had contracted the lavish habits that characterized young California, and when he had money in his pocket, his greatest concern seemed to be to find the easiest and most expeditious way of getting rid of it. A large circle of amiable friends stood always ready to help him out in this line and between all hands they made such a success of it, that even in the heyday of his fortunes, he was constantly pursued by a horde of creditors, lived in a hovel, cooked for himself, and was suspected of doing his own washing. His utter recklessness in business matters and some other shortcomings, often exasperated those who had dealings with him, and by many he was harshly judged. It is true that he was a kind hearted man, with many amiable qualities, and in most matters had a more correct standard than many whose weaknesses never led them into the follies that blighted AUSTIN's career.

After he had lived in San Rafael for some years, it was discovered that he had made for himself a little private history before he came to the Pacific Coast. His true name was found to be ERASTUS SPELLMAN. He had married early in life, but the attempt had proved a failure and a separation had followed. When he drifted westward, for some reason he sought to sink his old identity and assumed the name of HIRAM AUSTIN, which he clung to until the end notwithstanding the fact that everyone knew his true name.

Singularly enough, the pair who had found the married state unsupportable in the springtime of life, were reunited when the frosts and snows of their December had bleached their hair, and furrowed the cheeks of the aged couple. Old Mrs. AUSTIN (or SPELLMAN) came to San Rafael to join her venerable husband about two years before he left for Placerville. The union during their declining years seemed very happy, time probably having taught them the valuable lesson of mutual forbearance. They lived together until the end of the old Surveyor came a few days ago.

Superior Court
    Estate of SOPHIA ZELLAR, deceased
    Continued to May 1st

    J.A. ROY etal vs. the N.P.C. R.R. Co.
    Motion to relax costs set for May 1st

People vs. JEREMIAH SHINE
Motion for new trial argued and submitted

H.J. COFFIN and J.W. MIDDLETON vs. JOHN McCOMB
Motion to dismiss dropped from calendar

McDONALD & PASCOE vs. Their Creditors
Account of Assignee settled

Born
WALL – In San Rafael, April 21, 1893, to the wife of JAMES WALL, a daughter.

FRONK – In San Rafael, April 27, 1893, to the wife of GEORGE FRONK, a daughter.

PREZZI – In Tomales, April 15, 1893, to the wife of H. PREZZI, a son.

Died
DeVALIN – In San Rafael, April 20, 1893, Mrs. E.E. DeVALIN, wife of W.H. DeVALIN, aged 50 years.

Local News
J.P. LACERDA has sold his interest in the Bellevue to his partner, ALECK ENOS.

Information is wanted of the whereabouts of CHARLES SARTORI, late of Tomales.

Olema Items
Mrs. WILLIAM CLEIR, late of this place, but now of Oakland, is visiting friends about here this week.

ANDY CRANDALL of Lompoc, son of Judge W.O.L. CRANDALL, is here on a brief visit.

Marin Journal
Thursday, May 4, 1893

Real Estate Transfers
DONALD Y. CAMPBELL to OSCAR H. SCHNEIDER
NW Throckmorton Ave. and Cornelia Ave., Mill Valley - $10

OSCAR H. SCHNEIDER to DORA L. SCHNEIDER
NW Throckmorton Ave. and Cornelia Ave., Mill Valley – Gift

State of California to JOHN W. FERRIS
Patent for 186.56 acres, portion Sec 3 & 11, T 2, N R 6 W

JOHN W. FERRIS to P.W. RIORDAN
Patent for 186.56 acres, portion Sec 3 & 11, T 2, N R 6 W

Mere Mention
J. FRANETTA's new cottage is fast approaching completion.

Mr. JAMES HOGG of San Francisco has rented the SUMMERFIELD cottage.

Miss PEARL SCUDDER of Petaluma is visiting Mrs. S. BURDELL of Burdells.

Mrs. ANNIE CARMODY of Sausalito was granted a license to marry TEIPHIL STOZYNSKE, also of Sausalito.

Mr. F.K. ZOOK, chief engineer of the broad gauge railroad, has rented the JOHNSON house on Petaluma Ave.

J.R. SWIFT and JOHN P. DAVENPORT have entered into partnership in the house painting, wallpapering, etc. business and have opened a shop on Fourth Street.

Found Dead

Monday morning the coroner received a dispatch from Sausalito stating that the body of a man was lying in the hills back of the Wildwood Glen picnic grounds. The coroner immediately hastened to Sausalito and found the remains of a badly decomposed body, probably having lain there for at least 4 to 5 months. Tuesday morning, F. EGED of San Francisco identified the remains as those of his friend J. WILTSPIEL, who formerly worked on Montgomery Street. WILTSPIEL had a brother in the city, but refused to come over and give the remains a decent burial. They were interred yesterday by the coroner in the potter's field.

Wedding Anniversary

Mr. and Mrs. W.F. DOUGHERTY celebrated their 16th wedding anniversary at their residence last Wednesday evening. A few of the most intimate friends of this popular couple were present, and after the usual congratulations were received, all proceeded to enjoy themselves to the full.

Superior Court

    G.W. FOX vs SUSAN FOX
    Debt allowed $10 per month for alimony

    People vs. JEREMIAH SHINE etal
    Court to proceed to arraign the defendants

    Ex parte J.R. GERMAINE, on habeas corpus
    Writ to be dismissed and prisoner remanded to custody at San Quentin

    Estate of JAMES M. DONAHUE, deceased
    Motion for counsel fees laid over one week
    Application of widow and child for partial distribution of property laid over one week

    W.H. MAHONEY vs. M.W. KAIN
    Appeal dismissed

    JACOB SCHNELL vs. Sausalito Land & Ferry Co.
    Demurrer argued

    M. MURRAY vs. C.H. BYRNE
    Case dismissed

    J.A. ROY vs. N.P.C.R.R. Co.
    Motion to retax costs argued, costs reduced

    Estate of CATHERINE COLLINS, deceased
    Final account and distribution set for hearing May 15

    Estate of SOPHIA ZELLAR, deceased
    Continued for trial July 6

    Estate of C.H. BYRNE, deceased
    Decree of distribution granted

    JAMES I. TAYLOR vs. His Creditors
    Order of Adjudication entered
    HENRY HARRISON appointed assignee – bond $2,000

Town Talk

On Sunday last, Mr. JAMES CHRISTIANSON received a visit from his brother-in-law, Mr. J. McCARTHY, of San Francisco.

Mr. COIT, of COIT & ELLIOTT, is putting up a fine house on G Street, near Fourth Street.

Marin County Tocsin
Saturday, May 6, 1893

Insolvent Debtor
> Superior Court
> JAMES I. TAYLOR
> Creditors must appear before court June 12, 1893
> > F.M. ANGELLOTTI, Judge

Local News
Mr. T.E. HAMILTON will open in a few days a first class resort near the Narrow Gauge Depot.

J.F. BERTRAND, of Tocaloma, has been seriously ill at the French Hospital, but is now on the road to recovery.

Mr. and Mrs. WILSON of New Hampshire, and Mr. and Mrs. HATCH, of Washington DC, have been the guests of Mrs. W.H. ABBOTT, of Olema.

District Deputy Grand Arch, M.J. MULHERN, installed the following officers of Mt. Tamalpais Grove No. 58, U.A.O.D. last Tuesday evening: W.J. BOYD, Noble Arch; M. McNAMARA, Vice Arch; W.F. DOUGHERTY, Secretary; W.C. HICKEY, Treasurer; P.H. COCHRANE, Conductor.

A KAPPENMAN has rented the New England Villa and is busily engaged in fitting it for the accommodations of the public. He proposes to make the establishment an ideal family resort, where everyone will feel fully at home, sit down every day to three first class meals, and have rational means of amusement always at hand.

Real Estate Transfers
> Land Improvement Co. to SALVADOR A. PACHECO
> Lot on Petaluma Ave., San Rafael - $10
>
> Belvedere Land Co. to JANE COOP
> Lot 11, block 40, Belvedere - $10
>
> JOHN SYLVA etal to ANTONIO LAWRENCE
> Lot 6, block 16, Sausalito Land & Ferry Co. - $10
>
> JAMES B. MACKIE to EMILY ISABELLA MACKIE
> Lot 9 & 10, block 1
> Lot 33, 119, 120, Tamalpais Land & Water Co. – Gift
>
> HEPBURN WILKINS and wife to LEON A. LANCEL
> Lot on Fifth Street, San Rafael - $10
>
> JOHN O.B. SHORT and wife to MARTINI MARTELLI
> Lot 20, block A, Short's Addition to San Rafael - $10
>
> Estate of JOHN WARD WILSON to CHARLOTTE S. WILSON
> 623.46 acres of Rancho Laguna De San Antonio – Distribution

Marin Journal
Thursday, May 11, 1893

Real Estate Transfers
> Tamalpais Land & Water Co. to PARKER MERRILL
> Lot 13, block 1, Tamalpais Land & Water Co. - $400
>
> JAMES TUNSTEAD etal to GRACE ROWLAND
> Lot 4, block 5, Short's addition to San Rafael - $10

Mere Mention
Mr. GEORGE BUTLER of Petaluma is in San Rafael this week at work on the addition now being made to the Catholic Church.

Miss HENRIETTA CANTELL of Petaluma was in San Rafael Friday evening attending the Mt. Tamalpais Military Academy reception. She was the guest of Miss OLIVE SARTORI of West End.

RICHARD J. MAGEE of Nicasio has been ill a long time, and had tried to lessen his pain by taking morphine. Last Sunday he took an overdose and shortly after died. The coroner's jury rendered a verdict of accidental death as above. The funeral took place at Petaluma last Tuesday, and was well attended by the Native Sons and many friends of the deceased.

T.J. CROWLEY and family leave for the East and Europe shortly. They will be absent a number of months, and it is hoped the trip will result in benefiting Mr. CROWLEY'S health.

A large number of friends attended the crystal wedding anniversary of Mr. and Mrs. E. SCHWIESAU at Hayes Hall on Tuesday evening. No couple in town is more popular or better liked than Mr. and Mrs. SCHWIESAU, a fact which was proved on this occasion. There was beautiful music from the city.

Marriage Licenses
>THOMAS SMITH, 27, Oakland, to Miss KATE CARECHELLOW, 26, Berkeley
>MAX HENRY MILLER, 29, San Francisco, to Miss LEZA CATHERINE PLETTE, 17, San Rafael

Superior Court
>JOHNSON vs. HENRY ROWSON
>Continued indefinitely
>
>FITCH vs. GRETHEL
>Continued to June 2
>
>Estate of J.G. KITTLE, deceased
>Will admitted to probate
>HARRIET De WITT KITTLE appointed admx., without bonds
>
>JULIA LEONARDA vs. F.S. De AZEVEDO etal
>Continued to June 12
>
>Estate of JAMES M. DONAHUE, deceased
>Third annual account of executors continued to May 12
>Petition for partial distribution continued to May 15
>
>Estate of J.M. MAZEAS, deceased
>Final account of special administrator settled, allowed, and approved

Letter List

BARTLETT, G.H.	BERTRAND, L.
BROWN, E.	BRANDT, H.
CHAIS, P.	DICKMAN, T.
DONAHUE, R.	DICKINSON, J.H.
ELLIS, C.L.	FROST, J.
FULLER, M.	FREASE, A.
GEDGE, J.	HOBART, R.D.
HADLER, J.	HOLBZ, M.
HYDE, A.S.	HILL, WILLIAM H.
JOHNSON, A.	KELLY, R.
KELLY, Mrs. L.	LENT, C.H.
MALONEY, R.	MULLER, R.
McCULLOUGH, J.	NELSON, A.
OWENS, W.W.	SWEENEY, L.
STALOW, J.	SMITH, A.C.
SMITH, WILLIAM	THOMAS, H.
YOUNG, WILLIAM E.	VALENCIA, A.
VEILLER, S.	WATTS, J.
WILEY, G.E.	WRIGHT, CHARLES

Died
MAGEE – In Nicasio, May 7, 1893, R.J. MAGEE, aged 26 years.

DEAN – In Belvedere, May 7, 1893, Mrs. ISABELLA DEAN, aged 53 years.

Born
KLEIN – In San Rafael, May 6, 1893, to the wife of C. KLEIN, a daughter.

Marin County Tocsin
Saturday, May 13, 1893

Wanted
    Information on Mrs. ANN FEENEY, deceased
    Need birthplace, maiden name, next of kin, places of residence
    Late widow of MATTHEW FEENEY
    For many years a resident of Bolinas
Dated May 12, 1893
                              EDWARD EDEN, Public Administrator

Notice to Creditors
    Estate of JONATHAN G. KITTLE, deceased
                      HARRIET De WITT KITTLE
                  Executrix of Will
Dated May 10, 1893

Mere Mention
T.J. CROWLEY and R. MAGNES will represent our local Knights of Pythias at Nevada City next week.

Death of W.I. MORGAN
    W.I. MORGAN, the well known real estate man and President of the Belvedere Land Co., was called into eternity on Tuesday last, under conditions that will never be understood by those who knew the man and were cognizant of the circumstances of the case. The facts seem plain enough and appear to point conclusively to suicide. During the afternoon of the day in question, he retired to a closet in the neighborhood of his business office, and a few minutes later the report of a pistol startled his employees who ran to his assistance only to find the gentleman struggling in the agonies of death with a bullet through his head. It was shown that he had also purchased a quantity of strychnine. Nothing could be more manifest, seemingly than that the deceased had knowingly taken his own life.
    On the other hand, many friends of Mr. MORGAN combat the suicide theory with all the earnestness of conviction and argue that the gentleman's death must have been the result of accident. They point out forcibly that all the elements that usually lead to self-extinction were absent in his case. His financial circumstances were more than comfortable, his health excellent, and his domestic relations of the most harmonious kind. Besides, he was ambitious, sanguine, full of hope for the future, and of a buoyant disposition that made light of ordinary set back – just the kind of man who usually clings strongest to existence. The suspicious circumstances of the purchase of the pistol and strychnine, is also explained satisfactorily enough. On account of a feud with a man called PAFF, which had taken an ugly turn, it appears that the Belvedere Directors had insisted the day before on his arming himself for defense. As to the strychnine, it is shown that a friend had just advised him to buy it to kill gophers. The deduction from these facts, that the fatal shot must have been accidentally fired while deceased was handling the pistol, seems very plausible, although it will probably never meet with acceptance by more than a few friends. The death of the President will cut no figure in the affairs of the Belvedere Land Co. All the wild newspaper talk incident to the tragedy of the involved condition of the Company's affairs, is entirely incorrect. It was never on a better basis.

Local News
GEORGE E. RING has written from Boston, and he has had enough of the Eastern climate, and wants to be back in Marin.

Mrs. CATHERINE BULLIS gives legal notice required by law that she will apply for deeds for two pieces of realty bought by her for delinquent taxes.

The Will of the late J.G. KITTLE was admitted to probate last Monday by the Superior Court. It disposes of a large estate, which will probably reach a million dollars. The entire property goes to the widow.

The Late HIRAM AUSTIN
A short time ago, the Tocsin noted the death of ex-county Surveyor HIRAM AUSTIN, and made somewhat extended mention of the deceased. The article was certainly not written in an unfriendly spirit. We had none but kind recollections of the old gentleman, and had no desire to stir up a different feeling in others. The widow of the deceased has, however, taken deep exception and writes a bitter letter of complaint to this office. Among other things that she specially demurs to is the mention of the circumstance of his assuming the name of HIRAM AUSTIN, his veritable title being FESTUS SPELLMAN. Every old time resident of the county believed this to be the fact, although we do not know upon what evidence. Mrs. AUSTIN states that there is no foundation for the story. Her husband's true name was HIRAM SPELLMAN AUSTIN, and nothing else. We gladly give space to her version of it.

Real Estate Transfers
    Tamalpais Land & Water Co. to DORA L. SCHNEIDER
    Lot 281, Tamalpais Land & Water Co. - $1,000

    Tamalpais Land & Water Co. to CARL ALBERT FORSELL
    Lot 86, Tamalpais Land & Water Co. - $400

    Land Improvement Association to S.A. PACHECO
    Lot on Petaluma Ave., San Rafael - $10

    MARY H. JAMES to WILLIAM KING
    Portion of Block 7, Sausalito Land & Ferry Co. - $10

    R.F. WELCH and wife to ROBERT L. COLEMAN
    Lot 15, block 54, Coleman's addition to San Rafael - $10

    Sausalito Bay Land Co. to JOHN BRUCE
    Lot 1, block 19, map 8, Sausalito Bay Land Co. – 410

    WARREN DUTTON to County of Marin
    Lot 4, Tomales Cemetery - $25

The Marin Homestead Association, organized last Monday night at Hayes Hall, San Rafael, with a membership of 26. The following officers were elected: President, F. MURRAY; Vice-President, J. ALBERTI; Secretary, T. HOCK; Treasurer, F. MEHL; Auditor, JULIUS BUTHMAN. The object of the association is to buy, sell, and hold real estate on the co-operative plan and is based on the operation of other successful institutions.

GEORGE SCOTT, the bright young son of W.A. SCOTT won easily in the competition examination last week and is the County's candidate for a seat in the Examiner's Fair car. He still has to meet the successful candidates of six other counties and the outcome is still doubtful as all stand very high. The Marin County boy passed a splendid examination notwithstanding the fact that he was badly handicapped by a recent illness that gave him no opportunity for special preparation.

Marin Journal
Thursday, May 18, 1893

Mere Mention
The funeral of Mr. RICHARD MAGEE of Nicasio took place at Petaluma under the auspices of the Native Sons parlor. He was buried at Cypress Hill Cemetery. Many friends and acquaintances came from Nicasio to offer the last tribute to the dead.

LOUIS HERBERT SCHARRER, of San Francisco, aged 40 years, obtained a license on Monday to marry MARY BOWIE, also of San Francisco, aged 45 years.

Mr. W.N. SELKIRK, editor of the Petaluma Weekly Courier, has sold out his interest in the paper to his partner, Mr. MICHAELSON, and will soon move to San Francisco where a business situation has been offered him.

The San Rafael Band
On Monday night the members of the San Rafael Brass Band serenaded Mr. A. KAPPENMAN at the New England Villa that has just opened. The Band recently elected officers as follows: GEORGE MURRAY, leader; WILLIAM ARMSTRONG, business manager and secretary; S. EDEN, treasurer. The band is composed as follows: GEORGE MURRAY, E flat coronet; S. EDEN, 1st flat cornet; FRED SCHOENEMAN, 1st alto; WILLIAM O'BRIEN, 2nd alto; D.M. SCHNEIDER, 1st tenor; Z. HERZOG, baritone; BEN MURRAY, E flat bass; M. JOHANSEN, snare drum; F. BUSTIN, bass drum.

Town Talk
Miss ANNIE MILLER's cottage on Latham Street has been rented to Mrs. J.P. EKLUND o f San Francisco.

A Missing Man Found
Washed Ashore at Gravelly Beach
On Monday evening Coroner EDEN brought from Lime Point, the remains of a man which had been washed ashore on Gravelly Beach. They were badly decomposed, having been in the water a long time. A description of the remains was sent to the city papers and appeared in print Tuesday morning. A woman named Mrs. JULIA McGOWAN read the description, and on coming to San Rafael, identified the remains as those of her husband, who had been missing since December 8th. The features were unrecognizable, but Mrs. McGOWAN positively identified the watch found in the pocket and the clothes he wore. She testified that the deceased had no enemies who would have instigated his death, but that he had been sun-struck some years ago, and that since then he was a little out of the head at times. He was last seen by a teamster in San Francisco, as he went onto the Sausalito boat. The remains were taken to the city, where the widow lives at 230 Clara Street.

Real Estate Transfers
    DENNIS CULLENAN to ROBERT L. COLEMAN
    Lots 14 & 15, block 54, Coleman's addition to San Rafael - $20

    Tamalpais Land & Water Co. to EDWARD H. MICHELS
    Lot 282, Tamalpais Land & Water Co. - $1,000

    Sausalito Bay Land Co. to MARY H. JAMES
    Lot 15, block 10, Old Sausalito - $10

    Sausalito Bay Land & Ferry Co. to WILLIAM R. HEARST
    Lot 55 & 56, block B, Sausalito Bay Land & Ferry Co. - $10

    Sausalito Bay Land & Ferry Co. to WILLIAM R. HEARST
    Lot 53, 54, & 100, Block B, Sausalito Bay Land & Ferry Co. - $1,400

    BRIDGET LYNCH to MARY TALBOT
    Lot 8, plat of lots San Anselmo - $10

Letter List
ALEXANDER G.	CRITTENDEN, C.N.
CHARRAS, J.	CAYESTRI, A.
CRESALIA, M.	GARCIA, D.
HILTS, R.J.	KOGMINSKY, H.
NELSON, M.	PETERSON, A.S.F.
O'MARA, M.	SCOTT, --
STARKEY, E.	

Superior Court
    R.W. JOHNSON vs. ROBERT FURLONG
    Argument submitted and taken under advisement

    THOMAS BIGGINS vs. CATHERINE PRUNTY etal
    Hearing of report of referee set for Monday, May 22nd

    HERBERT GREGG vs. EVA N. GREGG
    Dropped from the calendar to be restored on notice

Estate of JAMES M. DONAHUE, deceased
Accounts of executors settled and allowed
Allowance of counsel fees, $13,000 to C.F. HANLON, $1,300 to HEPBURN WILKINS

DANIEL SLINKEY vs. C.H. HARRISON
Dropped from calendar to be restored on notice

Estate of CATHERINE COLLINS, deceased
Final account of administrator settled and allowed
Petition for distribution continued until June 12th

P.N. BERKHART vs. MARY CULLEN
Demurrer to amended complaint argued and submitted

Marin County Tocsin
Saturday, May 20, 1893

Local News
JOHN PACHECO left last Saturday for a visit to the Bartlett Springs.

Letters have been received from District Attorney COCHRANE showing his safe arrival in North Stockholm, NY.

GEORGE BARGATE, ex-President of the Belvedere Land Co., is again connected with that corporation as a general manager.

Mr. KANEEN, Superintendent of the San Rafael Gas & Electric Light Co., has recovered from his recent severe illness completely and is again attending to his duties.

THOMAS R. RYAN, U.S. telegrapher at the Pt. Reyes Lighthouse, has been transferred to the meteorological department and will henceforth observe the elements from the top of the Mills Building in San Francisco.

Assessments in the order of Chosen Friends must be paid hereafter to W.F. DOUGHERTY, at the Courthouse, he having succeeded A. KAPPENMAN, whose new duties on the hotel line compelled him to retire as secretary.

It is not generally remembered that JOHN DAGGETT, the new Superintendent of the Mint, was once a resident of San Rafael. Most prominent men have lived here at one time or another. Mr. DAGGETT lived in the Holman Cottage way back in the seventies, and was then a man of large fortune. After staying in San Rafael a season or two, Mr. DAGGETT left to embark in new mining enterprises.

Real Estate Transfers
JUSTA GARDELLE to G.B. GROSIGLIA
Portion of lot 3, block 2, Picnic Valley Tract - $5

G.B. GROSIGLIA to JUSTA GARDELLE
Portion of lot 3, block 2, Picnic Valley Tract - $5

GEORGE HUNNEWELL and wife to JOHN H. MERRILL
Lot on south side of Third Street, San Rafael - $10

JOHN W. MACKAY etal to RICHARD MERRY
Lot on San Rafael road - $400

Home and Farm Co. to JOHANNA ESSNER
Lot 9, block F, Novato - $10

GUSTAV F. OCHS and wife to Indianapolis Furniture Co.
Lot near San Geronimo - $10

FREDERICK G. KNELL to P.W. RIORDAN
Part of lot 158, Tamalpais Land & Water Co. - $20

HERMAN LOFSH to KATRINA NEWMAN
Lot on south side of Fourth Street - $10

JACOB STADFELD and wife to Fairfax Villa Co.
800 acres of MANUELLA M. SAIS Tract, entire capitol stock of Co.

Wanted
Information as the whereabouts of CHARLES SARTORI, a young man of light complexion, age 28. He disappeared from Mr. WOODWORTH's Ranch, near Tomales, on April 18th last for parts unknown. Anyone who has any information will please send word to
J.B. CAUZZA
Tomales, CA

Marin Journal
Thursday, May 25, 1893

Mere Mention
Mr. FRED KRUTZ has opened his hotel, the Buena Vista, at Mill Valley.

On Sunday, two teams of 10 each, from Companies B and D had a rifle shoot, in which Co. D won by 8 points, and fine dinner was thrown in Schuetzen Park. The score of the local team was as follows: Capt. ELLIOTT, 36; SCHOENEMAN, 44; DAVENPORT, 38; VANDERBILT, 36; N. ELLIOTT, 37; S. EDEN, 34; F. MULHERN, 38; J. MULHERN, 39; P. TREANTON, 37; A. BOYEN, 42.

JAMES CUSICK of San Francisco was arrested on Monday for kidnapping his 4 year old boy from near the residence of Mrs. MAGUIRE, his grandmother, near the narrow gauge depot. CUSICK is a ball player and lives in San Francisco. He claims that the mother of the boy is in Chico, and that the child should not be under her control at all. He was arrested in Sausalito, and gave bonds for his appearance before Judge RODDEN on Saturday for preliminary examination.

Mr. T.J. JUKES of San Francisco is again reinstated at the Willow Camp Hotel at Easkoot's.

Mr. WILL LONDON, a San Rafael boy, and one who will be remembered by those who attended the public school here 7 years ago, is now residing in Petaluma, where he has a position in the American Hotel.

CROFTS – McDONALD Wedding
Invitations are out for the wedding of Mr. FRANCIS E. CROFTS and Miss EFFIE McDONALD at the First Presbyterian Church on the 31st instant. Mr. CROFTS filled the position of teacher of English, Latin and Mathematics in the High School here from the time it was put in operation until he was offered a better position in the San Francisco Boys' High School, which he still holds, and his great ability as a teacher is acknowledged by all who knew him. Miss McDONALD is the daughter of Rev. JAMES McDONALD, formerly pastor of the church in which she will be married, and is well known and liked by all the older residents of San Rafael. It is hoped that the married life of the young couple will be of the happiest.

Superior Court
Estate of PETER MORRISSEY, deceased
Sale of real estate confirmed

T.J. BIGGINS etal vs. CATHERINE PRUNTY etal
Referree's report and sale confirmed

Estate of MARY SYLVA, deceased
A LAWRENCE appointed administrator in bond of $200

R.W. JOHNSON vs. ROBERT FURLONG
Writ of mandate ordered

K.C. BATCHELDER vs. ROBERT FURLONG
Demurrer sustained

Insane
A young man named HENRY PENDLETON, who has been working for FRANK BURRIS of Ross Valley, was adjudged insane last Saturday by the County Board of Commissioners and taken to Napa by Sheriff HARRISON. PENDLETON had been injured on the head some time ago and the injury affected his brain. He believed the spirits were talking to him all the time.

Marin County Tocsin
Saturday, May 27, 1893

Superior Court
Estate of WILLIAM G. MILLS, deceased
Notice for publication of Will
Monday, June 12, 1893 at 10:30 o'clock in Courtroom
Application of JULIET W. MILLS for letters testamentary
Dated May 24, 1893
HAVEN & HAVEN, Attorneys for Petitioner
THOMAS S. BONNEAU
Clerk

Superior Court
Estate of MELVINA C. COBB, deceased
Petition of HENRY ALFRED COBB, Executor
To mortgage certain real estate
Dated April 26, 1893
F.M. ANGELLOTTI
Judge

Partnership Dissolved
Notice that I have sold my interest in the business of ENOS & LACERDA to my partner, ALECK ENOS, who will collect all accounts and be responsible for all debts of the late firm.
J.P. LACERDA

Insane
A rather sad and rather mysterious case of insanity came before Judge ANGELLOTTI last Thursday. The individual was brought up from Sausalito by Constable CREED. Less than two months ago, a woman calling herself HESTER A. DRAKE settled there, renting a comfortable furnished cottage. She lived quite alone, but appeared to be in fairly prosperous circumstances, purchasing liberally and meeting all her obligations promptly. She seemed to be a woman of culture and education, who had spent her life on Easy Street and had retired to a country town to end it accordingly. Not a soul knew her and during her six weeks residence in Sausalito, no one visited her. It was not long before she manifested strong symptoms of insanity. It was not of a dangerous kind to others, or apparently to herself, and the spectacle of the old woman seemingly without a friend in the world and now even bereft of reason, aroused only sentiments of pity for her awful position. Nevertheless, it was not considered safe or humane to allow her liberty and she was accordingly examined before the Lunacy Commission, adjudged insane and sent to the Napa Asylum. A considerable quantity of personal property was found in the residence, but only 50 cents in money, and a Savings Bank book showing a deposit of $17. It is thought that she must have other property elsewhere.

Local News
Mr. A. MONTGOMERY has donated $2,500 to the building fund of the Presbyterian Church.

The Superior Court confirmed last Monday the sale of the PRENTY Home Tract to ROGER JOHNSON, a San Francisco attorney.

Miss MAMIE PESCH, niece of Mrs. E. SCHWIESAU, and Miss MARTHA JACKSON, will spend the summer with Mrs. SCHWIESAU in San Rafael.

JOSEPH JENKINS of Tomales and Miss MAUD MOORE, the popular postmistress of the same place, were married in Santa Rosa May 23rd. Mr. JENKINS has a wide circle of friends who wish him much prosperity in his matrimonial undertaking.

New Dry Goods Store
Mr. J. SILBERSTEIN, a merchant of many years standing and experience, will open a dry goods store in the new Wilkins building on Fourth Street about June 12th.

Real Estate Transfers
    ROBERT L. COLEMAN to JANE A. HADDEMAN
    Lot 15, block 54, Coleman's addition to San Rafael - $550

    ROBERT L. COLEMAN to CHARLES B. SHAVER
    Lot 14, block 54, Coleman's addition to San Rafael - $550

    Home & Farm Co. to OSCAR CONRADSON
    10 acres of land, Novato - $10

    Sausalito Land & Ferry Co. to GEORGE QUARRES
    Lot 9 & 10, block 43, Sausalito Land & Ferry Co. - $225

    GEORGE A. GINN to DANIEL O'CONNELL
    Lot 7, block 33, Sausalito Land & Ferry Co. - $10

    BELLA F. SWISHER to FREDRICK C. KECK
    Villa lot 223, block 13, Sausalito Bay & Land Co.

    O.C. MILLER etal to C.T. BAKER
    Lots 3, 4, 5, 6, & 7, Campbell Tract, Sausalito - $10

    ANTONIO BARAZILI to JOHN E. BETTENCOURT
    Lot on Fourth Street, near Tamalpais Ave., San Rafael - $5

    ADOLPH KOENIG and wife to A.H. BROWN
    Lots 11 & 12, block J, Novato - $10

    THOMAS CAIN to SARAH CAIN
    Lot on Second Street, near B, San Rafael – gift

    GEORGE H. WINTERBURN and wife to WILLIAM WRENCH
    Portion Winterburn Tract, Old Sausalito - $10

    Sausalito Land & Ferry Co. to FREDERICK G. KNELL
    Portion block 32, Sausalito Land & Ferry Co. - $10

    Estate of PETER MORRISSEY to CAUZZA & HOLLAND
    Lot 15, and portion lot 14, block 17, Tomales - $455

Superior Court
    THOMAS BIGGINS etal vs. CATHERINE PRUNTY
    Referee's sale of real estate confirmed

    PETER N. BECKHORT vs. MARY CULLEN etal
    Demurrer of defendant sustained

Died
ZINKAND – In San Rafael, May 21, 1893, Mrs. SOPHIA ZINKAND, beloved wife of CHARLES A. ZINKAND, a native of Germany, aged 47 years.

Marin Journal
Thursday, June 1, 1893

Items of Interest

HEPBURN WILKINS has rented his last store to J. LOPEZ for a restaurant.

Mr. ABRAMS of San Francisco is erecting a two-story residence at Belvedere.

On Decoration Day, Mr. FRIES moved in the DODGE house, and Mr. KOHLBERG into the ADAMS house.

CORY HAWKINS arrived in town on Tuesday after an absence of two months greatly improved in health.

Mrs. DONAHUE, proprietress of the Sonoma House at Tiburon, is putting up three new cottages at that place.

Mrs. E. HASSETT will do sewing by the day or week; children's and ladies' dresses stylishly made.

Captain H.A. GORLEY was among the California Volunteers who attended the Decoration Day services at the Presidio as the guest of the GEORGE A. THOMAS post.

Mr. JENKINS and Miss MOORE, both of Tomales, were married last Wednesday. Miss MOORE is the postmistress as that place, and is well liked by all who know her.

Mr. PAUL JONES lately graduated from the Lincoln Grammar School of San Francisco.

Mr. JEFFERSON THOMPSON, a Marin County boy, is playing with Stockwell's stock company at Stockwell's theatre. Though new in the business, Mr. THOMPSON's natural qualifications make him an actor from which much may be expected when a little time has given him the experience needed.

Mr. J.M. FLIAT, a former talented school teacher of this county, and now employed in the naval office, San Francisco, was in Novato and vicinity on Sunday, and in San Rafael on Monday.

HESTER A. DRAKE, a woman who has been renting a cottage at Sausalito for some time, and who has lived entirely alone, was brought here by Constable CREED, adjudged insane on Thursday last, and taken to Napa. She seemed to have no friends, and her history is unknown. But little money was found, although it is believed she was not in destitute circumstances.

Dr. BURDELL left California last week to join his family in Europe. His daughter, MABEL, aged 18, has entered upon a course of study in one of the leading educational establishments of Berlin.

GILBERT McDONALD, formerly of this place, is manager of the racetrack in Petaluma. His daughter, LILLIE, is married to the manager of Hon. J.G. FAIR's ranch in Sonoma County.

JAMES NUGENT, a famous exterminator of wild animals, is now employed as gardener and general utility man on the premises of the Rev. Father O'NIEL.

Among the enterprises lately begun in Novato, may be mentioned the new creamery of ANTONE De BORBA on Deer Island, and the manufacture of concentrated milk by the American Condensed Milk Co., organized as follows: President, F.H. GREEN of the Millbrae Dairy; Vice-President, Hon. F.C. DeLONG; General Manager, F.D. SMITH; Secretary and Treasurer, F.C. DeLONG.

The recent death of Mrs. A.D. SCOTT, a most estimable lady and a universal favorite, has cast a gloom over the entire community.

The family of Mr. OLBERS, since leaving Novato, have been called to mourn the death of two children by diphtheria.

A one-armed youth named STEELE, for several years a pupil in Bates Academy, San Rafael, has recently, by the death of his mother, fallen heir to several thousand acres of land in Santa Cruz County.

Real Estate Transfers
  Calvary Presbyterian Church to WILLIAM R. PEPPER
  Corner at NW of Morse Landing on County Road

Mt. Tamalpais Cemetery to CHARLES A. ZINKAND
Lot 13, Sec M, Mt. Tamalpais Cemetery - $210

GEORGE M. YOUNG and wife to ALEX McKINNON
Lot 24, block 21, Golden meadow, San Rafael - $10

FRANK DeLONG to Home and Farm Co.
Part of Novato Rancho as in deed of lease to Home Farm Co. - $10

Home and Farm Co. to H.P. HAUPTMANN etal
Lot 20, Div. C, Home and Farm Co. lands - $10

LOUIS H. BONESTELL and wife to JAMES BROWN
14.21 acres, Redhill and Ross Landing near Peter Smith's store

Decoration Day
Decoration Day passed off very quietly. There was no celebration, and the only exercises were the decorating of the soldiers' graves. Coroner EDWARD EDEN was in charge. The list of decorated graves includes the following:
   Old Cemetery
      Mexican veterans – FRANK HANNA and Judge HUGHES
   Tamalpais Cemetery
      General AMES, Mr. UPTON, D.I. BASCOM, JAMES DAILEY, Dr. KIRKUP, PETER CHANCEY, and General ALLEN.
   Catholic Cemetery
      H. BLINK, J. ROSLETT, and P. COURTNEY
   Private citizens
      Dr. TALIFERRO, WILLIAM LUCAS, JAMES STUTT, JOHN REYNOLDS, VAL DOUB, JOHN LYNCH, and JAMES MAKIN.

A few members of the Grand Army who reside in San Rafael attended this service in body. They were Capt. H.A. GORLEY, Capt. BOLAND, T. CURREY, GEORGE ATCHLEY, GEORGE KENDALL, and Sheriff H. HARRISON.

Letter List

DEL GROSSE, A.	EVANS, H.
HASKELL, N.	HENNESSEY, F.D.
JOHNSON, F.H.	KRATZER, G.
LAMB, M.	KAUGER, E.
MALORE, J.	MANN, A.
MALORE, J.H.	MATHER, E.
McJOHNSTONE, D.	NIELSON, H.
RICE, W.H.	ROBERTS, J.
REED, J.	RHONE, L.
RODEY, M.A.	SAWLET, G.
SULLIVAN, --	SWANSON, A.
WALLACE, WILLIAM	WARD, E.
WELSH, A.	WALKER, J.P.

               Foreign

GARDELLE, C.	LUBRANT, L.
VICTORINO, V.J.	DeSOUSA, J.A.
DeBRUN, J.M.	MARZONI, P.
GRACIA, F.R.	TUBAINI, L.
ORLOZA, L.	SILVA, A.
CORREIA, A.V.	

High School Graduates

AUGUSTINE, WINIFREDE	SEIBEL, FRED
HULBE, MARTHA	SARTORI, OLIVE
DONAHOE, REBECCA	RYAN, LIZZIE
MOORE, ARTHUR	

Novato School District
Graduates of the Novato School district are making good records for themselves. CLARENCE ATHERTON is in the employ of one of the leading business houses on Batter Street in San Francisco. EUGENE CONNELL is bookkeeper for a firm in Contra Costa. GEORGE DeLONG is entering upon his second year at the Stanford University. LEWIS HAVEN is with the well known firm of Lilienthal & Co., San Francisco. HUGH GALLAGHER is about to graduate from one of the leading educational institutions of Oakland. ACTON HAVEN is at Heald's Business College. TONY BROWN is chief engineer at the Deer Island Creamery. FLORENCE DeLONG has just graduated from the Denman grammar school. JOSEPH FAGGIANO is taking lessons from Mr. LIBBEY, master mechanic and builder. FLORA KYNOCH has graduated from the Petaluma grammar school.

The schooner Solferino is tied up at the Novato landing, having made her last voyage under Captain FRANK. One day the captain, after dining with some friends in Novato, lay down to rest and wakened not again. The schooner California, under Captain LEON, replaces the Solferino, making weekly trading trips between Novato and the city.

New Dry Goods Store
Mr. J. SILBERSTEIN, who has had a long and successful experience as a merchant, will open a dry goods store in San Rafael soon.

Wedding Bells for CROFTS – McDONALD
The marriage of FRANCIS CROFTS to EFFIE McDONALD was held yesterday. The Presbyterian Church was well filled with the friends of the young couple. The bride is the daughter of J.S. McDONALD, the missionary. She stands among her friends for her amiability, her many accomplishments, and her true nobility. The ushers were WILLIAM HEWITT, Mr. BRUNE, Mr. SKYBARKER, of San Francisco, and Mr. W.S. POND of San Rafael. The best man was LLEWELYN F. HASKELL, and the bridesmaids were Miss MATTIE HEVENS of Oakland, Miss LAURA M. WILLIAMS of San Francisco, Miss ANNIE PARK BARSTOW of San Rafael, and Miss GRACIE McDONALD, sister of the bride. The officiating clergymen were Rev. JAMES S. McDONALD, and Dr. NOBLE, pastor of the church. After spending a short honeymoon, the couple will reside in San Francisco, where Mr. CROFTS is a successful instructor.

Marin County Tocsin
Saturday, June 3, 1893

Local News
M.J. CONWAY has bought the interest of his brother in the plumbing business formerly carried on by them jointly.

P. LE CORNEC killed a large cinnamon bear in Ross Valley last Thursday near the residence of Mrs. J.S. PORTEOUS. The animal was a monster of its kind and attracted much attention when brought into San Rafael. It is shrewdly surmised that this bear was the celebrated Ross Valley lion.

H. WILKINS has rented the remaining business stand in his new block to H. LOPEZ, who will open it next week as a first-class restaurant.

In Memoriam
Nicasio Parlor in response to death of RICHARD J. MAGEE
       FRANK W. TAFT
       CHARLES A. REDDING
       THOMAS IRVING

Public School Promotion
Eighth Grade – C.S. SMYTH, teacher
 MILLIE DOUGHERTY, HESTER FISH, RUTH MORGAN, GERTRUDE OGE, MARY OGE, MERCEDES PACHECO, JENNIE SAUNDERS, JULIA SMITH, ELLA WALKER, JAMES BEGLEY, BERT BURTCHAELL, GEORGE HANSEN, IVER MASTRUP, GEORGE OLIVER, RALPH PRESCOTT, OREY SHORT, GEORGE SCOTT
Seventh Grade – Miss BROWN, teacher
 DAVID ALDERMAN, SAMUEL BARCLAY, CARL DRAHM, EDDIE DAVENPORT, MARCIA DOUGHERTY, MAY CLIFFORD, CARSON HANSEN, WILLIE HEARN, GEORGE HERZOG, FANNIE HARRIS, SADIE HALE, NELLIE JAMIESON, FRED MURRAY,

MARGARET McDONALD, LENA NICHOLS, EVA SALE, EDITH STRATTON, FANNIE TURNER, EDDIE WATSON, WILLIAM ZINKAND

Sixth Grade – Miss GATES, teacher

EMMA BRIGGS, GRACE BARNARD, EMMA HAAS, EDITH JONES, SADIE LUNNY, PHEBE MACKENZIE, ELLA MAHONEY, ABBIE McKENZIE, LULU MILLER, ANTOINETTE MONDON, ADELINE TABOR, JULIA THARPE, GARF BARSTOW, PETER BEGLEY, MELVILLE DOLLAR, WILLIE EASTMAN, WALTER ELLIOTT, EDWIN GARDNER, DELMORE GARDNER, FRITZ GOERL, VIVIAN HOXIE, JOE KEENE, MERREL KEEFER, LOUIS LAVIOSA, MALCOLM MACKENZIE, HARRY PETER, WILLIE SCOTT, ARTHUR STUDLEY, FRED WILLIAMS

Fifth Grade – Miss MARY FARRELL, teacher

EMMA BOYEN, CHARLES CORBALEY, REGINALD CLIFFORD, DANIEL FLANAGAN, LOUISE FERRY, ELEANOR GRANDIDO, LOUISE GREFFOZ, HENRY HANSEN, ALICE HARRISON, ADA JORGENSON, PATTIE KANEEN, EDDIE KANEEN, THEODORE MASTRUP, HENRY MONDON, ETTA McQUARRIE, WILLIAM NELSON, EDWARD OLSON, MINNIE PETERSEN, GRACE PETERSEN, OLIVIA PETERSEN, LEWIS PETERSEN, LAURA ROOS, EMILE RONBERG, KITTIE SALE, LENA SALME, ERSILIA SARTORI, BERTHA SMYTH, SADIE SCOTT, CHARLES SCOTT, ROBERT WARDEN, AGNES WATSON, JAMES WATSON, IDA ZIERENBERG

Fourth Grade – Miss BATCHELDER, teacher

GRETA AUGUSTINE, NELLIE BOWEN, BERT BURTCHAELL, FRANK BIGELOW, CARLTON CURTIS, STANLEY DOLLAR, ED De METZ, BESSIE FORSE, PERRY FURLONG, ARTHUR FURLONG, FREDERICK GODDARD, JOHN GARRISON, DIANA JORGENSEN, MAMIE KNITTEL, BERTHA KAPPENMAN, WILLIE KING, GRACE LIVINGSTON, GRACE MOORHEAD, JAMES McDERMOTT, MARTHA NICHOLS, MABEL PRESCOTT, MINNIE PETERSEN, MAUDE REYNOLDS, KATIE RYAN, MAMIE RYAN, LEONE ROBINSON, SUSIE SMITH, ADA SECOMBE, ESTHER SHREVE, CHRISTINE SEIBEL, DON SEIBERT, ZEKIE SMITH, EDWARD SAIS, ZELMA WALKER, HUGH WALKER, ALBERT WALKER, CLARA GROSSMAN

Third Grade – Miss GREEN, teacher

ALVA BEACH, GEORGE DAY, SHERMAN DOUGHERTY, HALLIE GIBNEY, CONRAD GOERL, FRANK HAAS, STAFFORD HAMM, SIDNEY HERZOG, HOWARD MACKENZIE, JAMES McKENZIE, FRANK MURRAY, ROY PRESCOTT, JOHN SHEEHY, RAYMOND SHAVER, GEORGE VRANG, ALICE WHITE, MARIE ABEILLE, PAULINE BAILEY, IRIDE CHEDA, MINNIE FOX, VESTA GULDE, ELEANOR JONES, ETHEL MARCHANT, LAURA McBRYDE, BERNICE McCLELLAN, KATE SARTORI, OLETA SHIELDS, LOTTIE SORENSON

Second Grade – Miss NICHOLS, teacher

LEROY ACKLEY, BERTIE ALDERMAN, AL BLUMENTHAL, HENRY BOYEN, LILLIE CORDES, ROBERT CURREY, NED DAY, NATHAN FOX, ALICE GODDARD, JACOB GOERL, FRED HAAS, WOLDEMAR HAMM, OLIVIA JACOBS, KATIE JORGENSEN, JOE KAPPENMAN, EMILE LAVIOSA, FLORENCE MAGEE, ETHEL MAXWELL, BLANCHE McCLELLAN, IRVING MAGNES, JEANETTE MONDON, HOMER MORDOFF, HAROLD MOORHEAD, WILLIE MURRAY, WILLIAM MURRAY, JEAN RASMUSSEN, LOTTIE REYNOLDS, SADIE SECOMBE, HATTIE SMITH, HARRY SMITH, LAURA SARTORI, GEORGE TAYLOR, FRIEDA VOGEL, ANNIE WHITE, GEORGE SURRIENBURG

First Grade – A Division – Miss McALLISTER, teacher

FLORENCE BLUMENTHAL, CLARA CORDES, CHRISTINE CORTI, GRACE DOLLAR, EVA ALDERMAN, ROSA MORRIS, VIOLET McBRYDE, JESSIE PROUDFOOT, ETHEL ROBINSON, BELLA SMITH, FANNY SHANK, MARTHA SALE, WILLA SALE, GERTIE SAUNDERS, JENNIE WHITE, MARTHA WHITE, THOMAS H. BOLAND, MAYNE CORBIN, RAY DUFFY, WILLIA FLANAGAN, CARL GULDE, WALLACE LIVINGSTON, LOUIS LAVIOSA, LAWRENCE MAXWELL, WILLIE MARCHANT, JOHN MACKEN, JOE REILLY, FRANK SHANK, WILLIAM SHANK, ALFRED SAIS, MANUEL TABOAS, RALPH TANNER, GUY THOMPSON

First Grade – B Division – Miss DUFFICY, teacher

ARTHUR ANDERSEN, CLAUDINA ALBUGAZIO, JUANITA BAILEY, WILLIE BARR, HAROLD CLIFFORD, HARRY CORDES, MAY DOLLAR, MAY DRISCOLL, IRENE FOX, W. GRANDJEAN, PAUL GROSSMAN, LEONIE HERZOG, NETTIE HAAS, HENRY HALEY, HANNAH KAPPENMAN, CONSTANCE KNITTEL, AUGUSTINE LANG, AMELIA LAVIOSA, LILLIE McCLELLAN, ETHEL MOORE, THOMAS McBRIDE, CAMILLE MIRANDER, WILLIE OGE, ALEXANDER PLETTE, VICTOR RAMOS, JAMES

RASMUSSEN, HARRY ROBERTS, ROY SEIBERT, MORTON VRANG, FRANCO TABOAS, CLIFFORD THAYER, CELESTINE WALKER, LOTTIE WRIGHT, GEORGE WALSH, WILLIE SMITH

Real Estate Transfers

DANIEL O'CONNELL to JAMES V. COLEMAN
Lot 7, block 33, Sausalito Land & Ferry Co. - $10

JAMES TUNSTEAD etal to EMMA E. GREYSON
Lot 16, block 55, Coleman's addition to San Rafael - $5

J.O.B. SHORT and wife to DAVID WARDEN
1.2 acres in Short's addition, also right of way - $10

EDWARD EDEN, admr. To J.B. CAUZZA etal
All lot 15 and part of lot 14, block 17, Tomales - $455

ELIZA A. TYRRELL to D.P. BELKNAP
Contract for sale of lot on west side of San Carlos Ave, Sausalito - $1600

Born
CONRADSON – In San Rafael, May 31, to the wife of OSCAR CONRADSON, a son

Married
CROFTS – McDONALD – In San Rafael, May 31st, 1893, by Revs. McDONALD and NOBLE, FRANCIS E. CROFTS of San Francisco, to Miss EFFIE McDONALD of San Rafael

HARRY SMITH
    Proprietor, Marin Boat House
    Point Tiburon

Marin Journal
Thursday, June 8, 1893

Letter List

BISSELL, A.	BURTON, Mrs. C.F.
CHILDRENS, HON.	CURTIS, A.R.
DAVIDSON, CHARLES	GORDON, D.S.
HAZE, --	HARNEY, F.
HIGGINS, D.	KERR, J.
KELLEY, J.	

Marriage Licenses
J.J. LENNON, 27, San Francisco, to EMILY C. LENHART, 26, Mill Valley
JOHN CAREW, 27, San Francisco, to NELLIE V. WARRINGTON, 25, San Francisco

Items of Interest
Mr. PICKET of Arizona is in San Rafael on a visit. He is a guest of Mr. ROBERTSON of the south side.

Mr. FRED GRAVES, who has been employed in Smith's drug store for some months past, left San Rafael Tuesday for San Diego.

Messrs, KEENE, CHARLES SMITH, and others who attend Hastings College of Law in San Francisco, are now enjoying a well earned rest during the summer months.

Miss EDITH STRATTON, who has been staying with her uncle, Mr. STRATTON of the south side, left San Rafael on Monday the 29th on her way to her home in Arizona.

GEORGE MILLER leaves town on Saturday for Shasta where he will enter the employ of the Shasta Lumber Company. His many friends will be sorry to have him leave town, but wish him every success.

Letter from Switzerland
Former resident and dairyman of this county, who after acquiring a competence here by industry and economy, returned to his old home in Switzerland to spend his last days near the mountains and valleys of his boyhood days. In his letter he says:

"I left San Rafael in 1873, and, I know that many of my old friends there have passed away. But I believe there still remains alive my old friends W.J. MILLER and CHARLES BARNEY, and also H.F. TAFT in Nicasio, to whom please present my best regards. I am now old and feeble, the father of 6 children, all alive and in good health. Very soon some of them will come to Marin County to try and better their conditions. In the Journal, I read with regret of the death of my first cousin, L. MARTINELLI. I feel much bereaved. I send my best wishes to all my old friends."

Yours very respectfully,
PLACIDO GARZOLI

Local Brevities
Hon. JAMES I. TAYLOR is now studying law with the expectation of being admitted to the Bar next fall.

Mill Valley Times is the name of the new paper devoted to Mill Valley and vicinity. FREDERICK F. RUNYON is the editor. Success to him and his enterprise.

Real Estate Transfers
FRANK M. PIXLEY and wife to WILLIAM HENRY YATES
4.5 acres at Corte Madera Station - $300

American Land & Trust Co. to ELLEN E. McCORMICK
Lot 10, block I, Larkspur - $10

Superior Court
Estate of JAMES M. DONAHUE, deceased
Matter of petition for guardian continued to June 12
Also matter of partial distribution of estate

Estate of C. COLLINS, deceased
Ordered that commission issued to take testimony

Estate of HENRY MILES, deceased
Final account settled and estate distributed as prayed for

Estate and guardianship of ALMA JOSSLYN
ARTHUR MARTIN appointed guardian

GEORGE FRITCH etal vs. PHILIP GRETHEL etal
On trial

Marin County Tocsin
Saturday, June 10, 1893

Local News
Miss NELLIE BUNN leaves for Texas on June 19th.

J.D. BRAVO has broken ground for a building on his lot, corner of Fourth Street and Tamalpais Ave.

HOUSTON JONES, late of San Rafael, and Miss REYNOLDS of Healdsburg, were married at that place last Saturday.

Real Estate Transfers
Tamalpais Land & Water Co. to CHARLES J. REILLY
Lot 173, Tamalpais Land & Water Co. - $1200

A MARTINELLI etal to E. MAGGETTI etal
Lot of land at Marshall - $10

JOSE M.T. BETTENCOURT to MANUEL T. BEIRAO
Lot 7, block 16, Sausalito Land & Ferry Co. - $500

MANUEL SILVA and wife to MANUEL T. BEIRAO
Lot 5, block 191, Sausalito Land & Ferry Co. - $65

WENDELL EASTON etal to ROSA K. HUG
Lot 6, block 3, Sunnyside Tract - $10

J.S. McCUE and wife to S.R. GRIFFIN
Lots 5, 6, 7, block 3, McCue Pixley Tract, Corte Madera - $10

Tamalpais Land & Water Co. to H.H. WAINRIGHT
Land adjoining Tamalpais Land & Water Co. - $1,000

Estate of WILLIAM A. BIRCH to LAURA S. WHITE
Lots 47, 50, 76, & 77 & SE ½ subdivision 1, Lot 75, Tamalpais Land Water Co. – distribution

WENDELL EASTON etal to ELLEN COLLURS
Lots 34 & 35, block 2, Sunnyside tract - $10

CHARLES R. CHITTENDEN and wife to GEORGE A. GINN
South 22 feet of lot 22
All of lots 23 & 24, Block A, Sausalito Land & Water Co. - $50

Dissolution of partnership
E.S. CHEDA
ATTILIO C. MARTINELLI
Marshall, June 1, 1893
                    MARTINELLI & CHEDA

Marin Journal
Thursday, June 15, 1893

Marriage Licenses
JAMES MITCHELL, 33, San Francisco, to Miss MAGGIE NOLAN, 29, San Francisco
EDWARD P. VANDERCOOK, 29, Oakland to VIVIAN PEARL ELLIOTT, 20, Oakland

Superior Court
Estate of JAMES M. DONAHUE, deceased
H. WILKINS appointed guardian ad litem of ISABEL DONAHUE, minor child

EVA GREGG vs. Her Creditors
Account of receiver set for Monday June 19th

Estate of WILLIAM G. MILLS, deceased
Will admitted to probate, letters ordered issued to J.W. MILLS

PRESTON & McKINNON vs. EMILY F. LIBBEY
Set for trial July 25th

Estate of CATHERINE COLLINS, deceased
Distribution of estate continued to July 25th

Belvedere Land Co. vs. CHARLES PAFF etal
Motion to vacate injunction granted without prejudice

JULIA LEONARDA vs. F.S. DE AZEVEDO
Justification of sureties

J. SCHNELL vs. Sausalito Land Co.
Demurrer overruled – 15 days to answer

JAMES I. TAYLOR vs. His Sureties
M.F. COCHRANE appointed assignee in bond of $2,500
Examination set for Monday, June 26th

GEORGE FRITCH etal vs. PHILIP GRETHEL etal
On trial

Real Estate Transfers
   Estate of GEORGE FREDSON to ESTHER C. FREDSON
   Lot at San Quentin – distribution

   JOHN W. MACKAY etal to City of San Rafael
   Lot on S side of Second Street, E of Lindaro Street - $100

   FRANCES OAKES to RUDOLPH & LOUISE SCHMITT
   Lot 3, Division B, Rancho de Novato - $10

   MAX A. THEILIG to OTTO LANG
   Villa lot 11, Mahlstedt Park Place, Novato - $10

   GEORGE A. HUNNEWELL and wife to JOHN H. MERRILL
   Lot on S side 3rd Street, ptn. Of block 40, San Rafael - $10

   HENRY KNITTEL etal to HARRY HARRISON
   Ptn block 13, Shorts addition to San Rafael - $10

Letter List

BURKE, T.	BRIONES, J.
CARLSON, T.	FLOOD, A.
D'AREY, E.	HANSON, C.
HAYES, J.	KELLER, O.
JOSEPH, M.	MINER, MARY
MORGAN, H.	NORTON, C.
McGLERRON, E.	O'BRIEN, D.F.
NILSON, C.	PERRY, P.
OLSEN, C.H.	POWERS, T.
PETERSEN, L.	REY, C.
POWELL, S.G.	SPINNEY, C.
PANCOAST, G.F.	STINELL, A.
VAUGHN, GEORGE	WESTERBERG, H.
STOLP, O.	WARD, C.W.

Local Brevities
Mr. FRANK FAIRBANKS of Petaluma was in town Tuesday morning.

Miss EDITH WELCH of San Francisco is visiting Miss EMMA FANNING.

Miss IVY JONES and Miss HATTIE HOXIE have returned from Healdsburg where they attended the wedding of HOUSTON JONES, son of J.M. JONES of San Rafael. Miss JONES was bridesmaid at the occasion.

Mr. WINNIE GOSSAGE of Petaluma is staying at Tiburon, where he will remain for about two months, being employed on Angel Island, where some new government buildings are being erected.

Delinquent Tax List 1892
   AMOS, JOHN
   AMARAL, JOSEPH B.
   ACKERSON, WILLIAM W. – admr. of Estate of C.H. ACKERSON
   BALES, GEORGE E.
   BIGGINS, THOMAS J.
   BIGGINS, JAMES

BOAS, JUDAH
BOOMER, MARY J.
BOTHIN, J.C.
BRENNAN, JOHN H.
BROWN, CHARLES
BROWN, S.H.
BUNKER, H.C., CHARLES D., EDWARD A.
BUTLER, GEORGE E.
CAPLICE, EDMUND
CHEVERS, HELEN F.
CHAPPARI, G.
CHICK, DONALD A.
CLARK, JOHN, GORDON, ESTELLA
COLEMAN, Mrs. C.M.P.
COULTER, GEORGE
CRAIG, ANNIE C.
CRIMMINGS, P.J.
CROCKARD, HUGH
CONNELL, MORRIS
CURLETT, WILLIAM
CURRY, JOHN
DAVER, KOSEN EDWARD
DUNN, JOHN
DUFFEY, THOMAS J.
FEENEY, JOHN B.
FISHER, JOHN
FEINTUCK, MORRIS
FRITCH, GEORGE
GAMBONI, G.
HALDEN, EDWARD B.
HANSON, H.T.
HALEY, J.
HAWKINS, O.C.
HERZOG, M.
HOBART, R.D.
HUTCHINSON, FERNANDE
IBS, GEORGE
JEWELL, Mrs. JULIA S.
LAND, C. EVANS
LAVADA, JOSEPH
LEOPOLD, C.M.
LEWIS, A.C.
LEWIS, MARY E.
LOWE, J.A.S.
LYMAN, A.J.
LUDOLPH, WILLIAM
MacDONOUGH, JOSEPH
MACHADO, MANUEL F.
MALLON, PATRICK, Estate of
MALLON, HONORA M.
MARDEN, EMMA F.
MARKS, FRANK B.
MARION, WASHINGTON
MATTHEWS, E.S.
McCUE, HENRIETTA
McELNAY, JOHN
MEYER, DAVID
MILLER, CHARLES E.
MIRANDA, S.
MONTGOMERY, A.
MORRIS, JOHN
MORRIS, Mrs. SALLIE

OTIS, GEORGE
SHAUNESSY, M.M.
PEARCE, GEORGE
PERILLAT, A.
PERRY, KATE
REY, J.J.
RICHARDS, EMMA
RITCHIE, WILLIAM
ROBERTS, GEORGE F.
ROSENTHAL, JOSEPH
ROSENTHAL, MARCUS
ROSS, M.L.
SCHNELL, JOHN
SHATTUCK, D.D.
SHELTON, J.
SHEERIN, DAVID
SILVIUS, HERMAN T.
SMITH, GEORGE W.
STEVENS, Mrs. T.J.
STONE, PETER V.
STRITTMATTER, JACOB
SUTCLIFFE, JULIA ANN
TIBBEY, EMILY F.
WALKER, HUGH
WALTERS, JULIA H.
WHEELER, HAROLD
WHITTEL, GEORGE W.
WILSON, CARRIE E. LADD
WOODS, E.
YELMORINI, MARIA
YOUNG, GEORGE M. and wife
ZOLEZI, P.

Personal Property
AZEVEDO, M.S.
AZEVEDO, F.S.
ACKLEY, C.F.
ALDERMAN, O.
BECKER, LOUIS
BERNSTEIN, JULIUS
CABRAL, JOHN
CORDA, JOHN
DE LA MONTANYA, H.
ESCALLIER, V.
ENGEL, JOHN G.
EDEN, E.
FREITAS, M.S.
FAIS, A.B.
FURGESON, G.A.
FORTUNE, W.R.
GAY, CHARLES A.
GREEN, W.A.
HYMANS, Mrs. F.
HAM, A.L.
HEATHCOTE, B.
JELLET, S.J.
LONG, R.H.
MANUEL, JOSEPH
MARSHALL, LOUIS
MARTIN, JAMES
McMILLAN, R.J.
MORGAN, P.B.

    NOBLE, Mrs. C.J.
    O'CONNOR, Mrs. CATALINA
    OSTERMAN, Mrs. S.
    PERRARI, JOHN
    PETERSON, A.F.
    ROBERTS, GEORGE F.
    SCOTT, GEORGE
    SEVEN OAKS, Mrs. J.
    SOLDATE, M.A.
    SOUZA, ANTONIO
    STARRETT, J.F.
    VALENCIA, Mrs. C.C.
    YELMORINI, A.

Marriage
JONES-REYNOLDS – In Healdsburg, June 1?, 1893, by Rev. LOWE, HOUSTON JONES, son of J.M. JONES of San Rafael, to Miss BERTHA REYNOLDS of Nebraska.

Marin Journal
Thursday, June 22, 1893

Items of Interest
On Friday last, JOHN SCHIPPERS, one of the old pioneers, passed away at Bolinas after a long illness.

Mr. FAGAN has nearly completed the large addition to his building on C Street, and it will soon be opened as a hotel and boarding house.

A MARTINELLI, formerly storekeeper at Marshall, and who was bought out by the MAGGETTI Bros., is now conducting a general merchandise store at Petaluma.

Miss NELLIE BUNN and Mrs. GEORGE BUNN left San Rafael last Monday morning for Texas.

On Wednesday, June 7, 1893, Mr. JOHN COULTER, father-in-law of Mr. FRANK JACOBS, passed away after a severe illness. The funeral was largely attended by the friends of the deceased and his family.

J.D. BRAVO is erecting a large two-story hotel and boarding house on the corner of 4th Street and Tamalpais Avenue. G. VRNWINK & WILLIAM CARMON of Petaluma are the contractors.

M. GILLIGAN, who formerly conducted the Central Hotel, and who is now a prominent shoeman of Nevada, was in town last week. He still regards San Rafael as the best residence city in California, and in due time will return here for permanent residence.

Mr. CHARLES BACH of San Francisco is erecting a 2 ½ story residence in Ross Valley.

Mrs. SHELTON has left San Rafael for Kansas, where she will remain for some time at the home of her parents.

Mrs. Capt. LEES, mother of FRED LEES, the recently appointed license collector of San Francisco, is stopping at Mrs. JORDAN's.

Mr. CORNWELL is completing a new residence at Nicasio on the property he purchased some time ago from BERNARD MILLER.

Mr. McDONALD, the blacksmith of Nicasio, lost his little child from diphtheria last Saturday. Mr. McDONALD is the successor of Mr. CORNWELL.

Local Brevities
Mrs. GEORGE ATKINSON, who has been in San Francisco lately on account of her health, is reported to be greatly benefited by the change and treatment received.

R.P. TROY has been recommended by the powers that be, to the position of assistant cashier of the custom house.

A volunteer fire department has been organized in Mill Valley. The officers are A.H. WHEELER, president; J.D. HARRIES, Secretary; GEORGE HUNT, Treasurer.

Killed by a train
FREDERICK JORGENSEN, aged 14 years, a resident of Sausalito, met with a terrible death at Sausalito last Saturday. He was in the act of getting on a train while it was in motion, and in some unaccountable manner was thrown to the ground, striking the track in such a manner as to throw him partly under the cars. The train stopped as soon as possible, but not until several cars had passed over the unfortunate boy. Death was instantaneous. Coroner EDEN removed the remains to the morgue where an inquest was held in accord with the above facts.

Superior Court
  EVA N. GREGG vs. Her Creditors
  By Consent laid over one week

  Estate of FRANCISCO MAZZA, deceased
  LUIGI MAZZA appointed guardian of J.J. MAZZA, bond of $25

  Estate of JAMES M. DONAHUE, deceased
  Sale of Lapidee Street property confirmed
  Matter of partial distribution of property to widow and child – on trial

Died
SCHIPPERS – In Bolinas, June 16, 1893, JOHN SCHIPPERS, aged 72 years.

COULTER – In San Rafael, June 7, 1893, JOHN COULTER, aged 69 years.

Marin County Tocsin
Saturday, June 24, 1893

  Estate of JOHN A. THOMPSON, deceased
    Publication of proving Will
    Monday, July 10, 1893 at 10:30 a.m.
    Superior Court
    Application of HANS JACOB OLSEN, for letters of testamentary
    June 19, 1893
    HAVEN & HAVEN, attorneys for Petitioner
      THOMAS S. BONNEAU, Clerk

  Estate of CHARLES BROSIN, deceased
    Petition for sale of real estate to pay debts
    MORITZ MEYER and SIMON C. SCHEELINE, executors
    June 23, 1893
      F.M. ANGELLOTTI, Judge

  Notice to Creditors
    Estate of WILLIAM G. MILLS, deceased
    June 23, 1893
    HAVEN & HAVEN, Attorneys for Petitioner
      JULIET W. MILLS, Executrix

Local News
The Will of JOHN SCHIPPERS, deceased, has been filed for probate. The bulk of his little property is left to WILLIAM BETTEN and Mrs. JOHN SEBREAN, both of Bolinas.

The Pacific Coast dispatches give a very brief account of the shooting of GEORGE W. PARKER, in a saloon row at Ukiah last Monday night. The deceased lived many years in San Rafael, where he carried on the business of jeweler. He was peaceable enough when in the normal state, but while under the influence of liquor, he was quarrelsome and considered by some rather an unsafe man to fool with. The dispatch states the Coroner's jury returned a verdict of justified homicide.

JAMES CUMMINGS, one of the old residents of Marin County, passed away at Sausalito last Thursday, after a very brief illness. He was one of the ill fated settlers on the Reed Ranch, at the time when it was believed to be government land. After spending a lifetime in litigation, he was finally ejected in his old age and spent the last few years in poverty.

Superior Court
> Estate of LOUIS MAZZA, deceased
> Estate assigned to widow
>
> GEORGE FRITCH etal vs. PHILIP GRETHEL
> Testimony closed, argument set for Saturday, June 24th
>
> G.A. FERGUSON vs. His Creditors
> Sale of book accounts confirmed
> Final account of Assignee M.F. COCHRANE allowed
> Pro rata to creditors of 15 cents on the dollar ordered

Real Estate Transfers
> Sausalito Land & Ferry Co. to ARTHUR C. BRIGGS
> Lot 15, block 23, Sausalito Land & Ferry Co. - $10
>
> Home and Farm Co. to DAVID MYERS
> Land on north bank of creek at SE corner of Davidsons - $10
>
> SIDNEY V. SMITH and wife to ANTONE BOREL
> 108.98 acres of Punta de Quentin Rancho
> 5 acres on E side of Bald Hill, also right of way - $5
>
> J.W. SPERRY to JOHN J. ROSS
> Lot 4 of Sperry's subdivision of portion of block 2, Sausalito Land & Ferry Co. - $10
>
> J.W. SPERRY to THOMAS RYAN
> Lot 5 of Sperry's subdivision of portion of block 2, Sausalito Land & Ferry Co. - $10
>
> F.C. DeLONG to HENRY PIERCE
> Novato Rancho and all grantor's property
> Assignment for benefit of creditors
>
> Home & Farm Co. to WILLIAM W. SCHMITT and ANNIE SCHMITT
> Lot 8, division B, Rancho de Novato - $10
>
> J. MARIANO ROMA to GEORGE H. WINTERBURN
> Lot on W line of Front Street, S of line between Old and New Sausalito - $10
>
> GEORGE W. WINTERBURN to J. MARIANO ROMA
> Portion of Winterburn's tract, Old Sausalito - $10
>
> CARL F. AHLBERG and wife to MARY E. HART
> Lot 16, block 2, Tamalpais Land & Water Co. - $10
>
> JOHN COULTER to OLIVIA COULTER
> Lots 8, 9 & 10, subdivision lot 6, block 4, townsite of San Rafael – gift
>
> HENRY LOOMIS to EMMA FANNING
> Lot on N line of Harcourt Street - $10
>
> CHARLES S. WIELAND to ALBERT G. WIELAND
> Subdivisions 5, 6, 7, Edwards-Harrison Tract, Old Sausalito - $10
>
> JAMES TUNSTEAD, Referee etal, to ROGER JOHNSON
> Portion of Punta de Quentin Rancho - $5,200

Tamalpais Land & Water Co. to JULES FLEURY
Portion of lot 1, block 5, Tamalpais Land & Water Co - $300

CAROLINE MONDON to JACOB BLUM
Lot on NE corner of Petaluma Ave and Fourth Street, San Rafael - $7,250

Marin Journal
Thursday, June 29, 1893

Real Estate Transfers
F.C. DeLONG to HENRY HARRISON, Sheriff
General assignment for benefit of creditors

Sausalito Land & Ferry Co. to PIERCE J. ELLIOTT
Lot J, Block 28, Sausalito Land & Ferry Co. - $10

Superior Court
JAMES I. TAYLOR vs. His Creditors
Continued to July 18th

People vs. E.T. RICHARDSON
Information filed arraignment set for Monday, July 3rd

People vs. NARCISSE PETRI
Assault with deadly weapon, set for July 3rd

Application of AMBROSE BIERCE, habeas corpus
By consent laid over to July 5th

Estate of C. COLLINS, deceased
Over 2 weeks, final distribution set for July 10th

Estate of JAMES M. DONAHUE, deceased
Hearing of Montgomery compromise laid over to July 5th

EVA N. GREGG vs. Her Creditors
Account of receiver set for Friday, June 30th

Estate of PETER MORRISSEY, deceased
Final account of E. EDEN, public administrator, estate distributed

Married
DAVIS-SNELL – In San Francisco, June 21st, by the Rev. Dr. DILK, JOHN DAVIS to Mrs. E.L. SNELL, both of San Rafael

Accident
On Monday, Mrs. J.M. JONES went to Lakeport in response to a telegram announcing the serious illness of her sister, Mrs. ISAAC MILLER, who in some way, met with a severe accident which threatens her life.
Mrs. IVY JONES returned from Petaluma on Monday.
Later – It is learned that Mrs. MILLER fell from a ladder while picking cherries and broke her collarbone, besides sustaining other internal injuries. Her condition is said to be critical.

Marin County Tocsin
Saturday, July 1, 1893

Estate of CHARLES BROSIN, deceased
MORITZ MEYER & SIMON C. SCHEELINE, executors
Sale of real estate
June 23, 1893
F.M. ANGELLOTTI, Judge

Estate of MELVINA C. COBB, deceased
    HENRY ALFRED COBB, executor
    Permission to mortgage real estate to pay debts
    April 24, 1893
                  F.M. ANGELLOTTI, Judge

Summons
    JESSIE E. BARNETT vs. JOSIAH BARNETT
    Divorce on grounds of extreme cruelty
    Must appear before Superior Court
    Custody of minor child WILLIAM J. BARNETT to plaintiff
    May 27, 1893
                  THOMAS S. BONNEAU, Clerk
                  By D.T. TAYLOR, Deputy Clerk

Notice
    My wife, SOPHIA FITZROY, has deserted me and is now living separate and apart from me, and that I will not be responsible for her support and will not pay any bills or debts contracted or incurred by her.
    June 15, 1893
                    G. FITZROY

Local News
 T.J. CROWLEY is reported to be much improved in health by his visit to the Adams Springs in Lake County.

Miss AGGIE STOWELL, late of San Rafael School department, who has been located in San Bernardino for some time, is visiting friends in San Rafael.

Real Estate Transfers
    Sausalito Land & Ferry Co. to PIERCE J. ELLIOTT
    Lot J, block 28, Sausalito Land & Ferry Co. - $10

    Estate of PATRICK CARBERRY to FRANK WEIGAND
    Tract 21, Blucher Rancho – distribution

Marin Journal
Thursday, July 6, 1893

    Abandoned Children at St. Vincent's Asylum
        MULLINS, JOHN – 13 years
        COLL, FRANK – 11 years
        HYDE, JOHN – 12 years
        McGURK, FRANK – 10 years
        JOSEPH, HARRY – 9 years
        LAWRIE, WILLIAM – 10 years
        FORSATI, JAMES – 9 years
        ROSCELLI, ATTILO – 9 years
        MINOR, GEORGE – 11 years
        McSWEENEY, JAMES – 12 years
        JENKINS, JOSEPH – 12 years
        WATERS, MICHAEL – 9 years
        LYDON, JAMES – 8 years

Board of Supervisors
    County Aid of $10 awarded to Mrs. ANNA MAGEE and her 2 children
    County Aid of $10 awarded to Mrs. PABLO SANDOVAL and her 5 children
    J.E. SLINKEY of Sausalito was granted license to sell liquor
    MAGGETTI & CHEDA of Marshalls were granted license to sell liquor
    J.H. BRICKWIEDEL of San Rafael was granted license to sell liquor

Diplomas Awarded for San Rafael schools

GERICKE, AGNES	Clark District
MARTIN, LINDA	Chileno Valley District
BLOOM, POLDINA	Chileno Valley District
SHAFTER, HELEN	Garcia District
MYERS, MARY	Garcia District
NELSON, WALTER	Garcia District
BAIN, KITTIE	Dixie District
SUTTON, MINNIE	Novato District
GALLAGHER, NELLIE	Novato District
VONSEN, KATIE	San Antonio District
NISSON, LENA	San Antonio District
JONES, LENA	San Antonio District
CRONAN, JOHN	San Antonio District
O'CONNELL, NORA	Tiburon District
GULDAGER, WILLIAM	Tomales District
TREANOR, MARY	Tomales District
LEWIS, J.	Richardson District
BEIRAO, MANUEL	Richardson District
HEALEY, WILLIAM	Richardson District
RYAN, MAGGIE	Richardson District
RYAN, NORA	Richardson District

City School Matters
The following teachers were re-elected:

McALLISTER, Miss	First grade, A
DUFFICY, Miss E.	First grade, B
NICHOLS, Miss E.H.	Second grade
GREEN, Miss F.	Third grade
BATCHELDER, Miss KATE	Fourth grade
FARRELL, Miss M.	Fifth grade
GATES, Miss A.A.	Sixth grade
BROWN, Miss B.C.	Seventh grade
McLEAN, Miss L.M.	Eighth grade

Mr. MORTON was elected janitor.

Born

TREANOR – In San Rafael, July 3rd, 1893, to the wife of W. TREANOR, a son

JEPHSON – In San Rafael, July 3rd, 1893, to the wife of T.P. JEPHSON, a daughter

Real Estate Transfers

 J.B. FAGGIANO to RICHARD R. CONNELL
 13.80 acres, portion of Rancho San Jose
 1.39 acres, portion of Rancho San Jose - $10

 LOUIS A. DeVOTO to Home & Farm Co.
 Strip of land, Division A, Rancho de Novato for highway - $10

 Estate of GEORGE ZIMMERMAN to LOUISA ZIMMERMAN
 Grantors Tomales Ranch and personal property – distribution

Superior Court

 EVA N. GREGG vs. her Creditors
 Final account of receiver laid over to July 5th

 CHARLES NORTON vs. his Creditors
 Adjudged insolvent – meeting of creditors set for August 7th

 JAMES I. TAYLOR vs. his Creditors
 Final account of receiver settled

G.R. GREGG vs. EVA N. GREGG
Demurrer sustained without leave to amend

People vs. E.T. RICHARDSON
Defendant plead guilty to grand larceny – sentenced to San Quentin – 3 ½ years

Marriage Licenses
EDWARD TOJETTI, 38, San Francisco to CATHERINE CLARK, 2-, San Francisco
MAX A. THEILIG, 3-, Novato to RUTH A. MERRILL, 2-, Novato

Letter List

GRANT, M.W.	HAYES, J.
MELZER, J.	McINTOSH, A.
NUTTING, L.B.	PERRY, J.E.
REGAN, J.C.	RICHARD, A.
REYNOLDS, T.	RICHARD, H.
SMITH, A.	ZULOTTI, --
ARMAND, E.	ADAMS, W.S.
AHEN, C.	AUSTIN, E.
BOYD, JESSIE	CHAMBERS, S.
CUSP, M.	DAVIS, Mrs. W.G.
ELLIOTT, E.M.	GRAVES, P.A.
GOIRS, F.	GALLAGHER, --
HAMMOND, --	HAGGER, H.
HOLLAND, A.	HACKER, L.
LUNDBARK, J.	JOHNSON, --
MENVILLE, --	MARLANE, G.
McMAHON, GEORGE	MULLER, --
OHLMANN, E.	NIELSEN, H.
PIPIN, E.	REILLY, G.
PENROSE, T.	ROBERTSON, L.
REATZ, L.	TUGINAN, A.
THOMAS, L.	WILSON, R.
THOSOPH, M.	WALSH, M.
WHITE, R.T.	WEBERBECK, E
BROWN, H.	BULOTTI, V.
BROWN, JOSEPH	COLLINS, C.S.
CARAZEAN, --	EUSLU, F.
HAMMOND, J.	HANSEN, M.
KENNEY, S.	LEWIS, ED
LeCOUNT, --	MILBURY, W.
MARINDA, M.	McCABE, N.
NEAL, R.W.	O'REILLY, T.
SAGE, E.	SWEENEY, --
WILSON, J.W.	

Marin Journal
Thursday, July 13, 1893

Items of Interest
Mrs. SEVEN OAKS is now successfully running a boarding house in Chicago on Kimbark Ave., near the fair grounds.

Mr. COX, teacher of the Tomales School, has accepted a fine position in Sonoma County, and the Tomales School will be presided over this term by Mr. J.A. NOWELL, a graduate of Palo Alto.

Local Brevities
ROY BARNEY is clerking for JOSSA & DuBOIS in the absence of Mr. JOSSA.

G.W. LONGLEY, a prominent citizen of Olema, was in town on Tuesday.

J.C. GIBSON, the Bolinas merchant and postmaster, was in town Tuesday.

Dr. JONES passed Sunday in Cloverdale visiting his parents, who reside there.

The family and friends of R. MAGNES gave that gentleman and his wife a celebration on Sunday night, it being the occasion of their tin wedding.

Judge PHINNEY of Bolinas was in San Rafael on Monday.

Board of Supervisors
    JOHN DIAS of Larkspur was granted license to sell liquor

Two New Teachers
    Mr. FRANK DUNNE will act as principal
        Taught last year at Mt. Tamalpais Military Academy
        Graduated of University of California at Berkeley with high honors
    Mr. FREDERICK K. HAZZARD will act as vice-principal
        Graduated from State Normal School at Los Angeles
        Graduated from University of Pacific at Santa Clara
        Was principal of Grammar School at Norwalk at Los Angeles
        Age 26, and has a family

Tomales Letter
Mr. and Mrs. DICKENSON of Bakersfield are spending the summer in Tomales.

Miss LILLIE BUTTNER of San Francisco is spending a few weeks in Tomales, the guest of Mrs. VAUGHN.

Mrs. TRAVIS NORMAN, of Dixon, is spending a few weeks in Tomales, the guest of Miss NELLIE KIRK.

Mr. J. PHILLIPS and wife of San Francisco, are spending a month with the latter's mother, Mrs. E. GRIFFIN.

Our most worthy citizen, Mr. T.J. ABLES, who with his wife has been in Southern California for many months for their health, have returned much improved. Mr. ABLES will resume his place in the bank.

Among the miracles and wonders of this life, is the case of our highly esteemed lady friend, Mrs. WILLIAM TIERNEY, whose recovery to health is remarkable. She has borne more suffering than any 10 ordinary persons do. We want to thank Dr. LAGON of San Francisco, and Dr. WICKMAN of San Rafael.

Mr. LANDGRAF, the reliable jeweler, will move this week into his new and cozy cottage on First Street.

Died
BURNS – In San Miguel, July 9, 1893, FRANK J. BURNS, aged 33 years.
    Mr. BURNS was editor and proprietor of the San Miguel Messenger. He leaves two children and a wife, nee Miss ELIZABETH EHMAN of Sausalito. He was a brother of Mrs. J.S. NASH, Mrs. T.C. FITZGERALD, Miss EMMA BURNS, and J.F. BURNS.

Shot to Death
About 3 o'clock Monday morning, at the ranch of PETER BOLLA, 3 ½ miles southwest of Petaluma, a deplorable accident occurred through the careless handling of fire arms which resulted in the sudden death of a young Swiss. A party of friends had been invited to the ranch, and those present had been feasting and dancing throughout the night and were just preparing to leave for home when a shot was fired outside the house. Presently another shot was heard, and it was learned that the disturbance was caused by MISUNIO GHIDOSSA, an employee of the ranch, who fired the gun "just for fun". A moment later a horrible discovery was made. Lying upon a table under a tree, within 17 feet of the spot from which GHIDOSSA fired, was the form of a young Swiss boy, SILVIO CORDA, aged 13, covered with blood and in the throes of death. The lad was borne into the house, and laid on a bed, and a messenger was dispatched to Petaluma for a doctor, who responded promptly, but to no purpose, as the boy was dead when the doctor arrived.

Superior Court
    Mr. BRENNFLECK vs. J. SHINE etal
    Set for trial September 5th

People vs. NARCISSE PETRI
Simple assault – fined $20

R.A. BIERCE, habeus corpus
Set for hearing July 31st

EVA N. GREGG vs. her Creditors
Final account of receiver settled

Estate of JAMES M. DONAHUE, deceased
Compromise of Montgomery claim

Estate of CATHERINE COLLINS, deceased
Over 2 weeks

Estate of J.A. THOMPSON, deceased
Will admitted to probate
Letters testamentary ordered issued to J. OLSEN

Estate of JOHN SCHIPPERS, deceased
Will admitted to probate
Letters testamentary ordered issued to HARRY BRETTEN

CHARLES HARLAN etal vs. their Creditors
Over one week

GEORGE FRITCH etal vs. P. GRETHEL etal
Judgment for plaintiff in accordance with opinion

Marriage Licenses
- L. GREENWALD, San Francisco, to MABELLE S. THOMPSON, 22, San Francisco
- C.S. PASTORI, 37, Fairfax, to ADELE PUERERI, 23, San Francisco
- E.L. JACOBS, 25, San Francisco, to MABEL EDDY, 23, Mill Valley

Letter List

CHADWICK, F.R.	EARL, WILLIAM
FAURE, F.	KOCH, H.
KRATZER, G.	KUPRION, C.
KEYES, F.	MOORE, S.E.
MOLINE, A.J.	McBENNA, A.
NESBIT, J.	ROGERSON, F.
STAMFELDE, A.	SMITH, J.H.
WEBERBECK, E.	WILLIAMSON, P.
WISE, E.B.	WIGGIN, CHARLES
WIARD, G.E.	

Born
CHRISTIESON – In San Rafael, July 1, 1893, to the wife of J.P. CHRISTIESON, a son

CAESAR – In San Rafael, June 28th, to the wife of J.S. CAESAR, a daughter.

Marin Journal
Thursday, July 20, 1893

Real Estate Transfers
JAMES M. STREETEN to CHARLES MATSEN and wife
Bolinas and Olema Road at Skyline - $10

Sausalito Land & Ferry Co. to ANTONE BOREL
Southerly ptn. Lot 4, Sausalito Rancho - $10

J.W. MACKAY etal to Cal Schuetzen Club Park & Building Assn.
35.12 acres Schuetzen Park Tract - $1,536

MARY & WILLIAM TALBOT to BRIDGET LYNCH
Ptn. Lot 8, near San Rafael - $10

LOUIS L. DUNBAR to JENNIE M. DUNBAR
Lots 23, and 24, block 1, Belvedere – gift

JAMES BLOOM and wife to JOSEPH BLOOM
Tracts of land on Olema Creek, Tomales and Bolinas Rancho - $20

SARAH CAIN to THOMAS CAIN
Lot on S line of Second Street and B Street - $10

J. GLOVER SMITH to ANNIE PARDEE SMITH
Lot 3, block 15, Sunnyside tract – gift

J.S. McDONALD and wife to PEMBROSE W. JONES
Lot on N line Clayton Street W of Welch Street - $10

WENDELL EASTON etal to WILLIAM A. RICHARDS
Lot 10, block 13, Sunnyside tract - $10

Belvedere Land Co. to LOUIS L. DUNBAR
Lots 23 and 24, block 1, Belvedere - $10

Items of Interest

Mr. JOHN W. BARNEY of San Francisco was in town last week on a visit to his brother, Mr. CHARLES S. BARNEY.

Mr. EDWIN DICKSON of the White Ranch, returned from a protracted stay in the vicinity of Ukiah on Monday last. He was accompanied by his uncle, Mr. GEORGE DICKSON.

SAM GARDNER has been elected chief engineer of the Mill Valley volunteer fire department, J. BUNDY 1st assistant, FRANK MILLER 2nd assistant, and Messrs. NIELSON, LOUIS JONES, and CHARLES CLAPP have been chosen as trustees.

Tomales Letter
Miss KITTIE HUNDLY of San Francisco is visiting the Misses HOLLAND.

Mrs. ATWATER of San Rafael is visiting her daughter, Mrs. ABLES, at present.

Letter List

ALEXANDER, N.P.	BROWNE, D.
BEEDY, J.	BILLO, GEORGE
BORAU, Mrs.	CRAFTS, C.W.
DE VEECHI, P.	GRAY, F.
HYMAN, A.B.	HARRISON, F.
HELLER, M.	JANSON, O.
JACOBS, E.	KIMBALL, W.E.
KELLOGG, W.J.	LAMSON, --
LONG, LULU	LICHTENSTEIN, D.
MULLEN, F.	NELSON, CHARLES
OTT, CHARLES	PORTLEY, MAY
ROBINSON, Mrs. J.	RICE, CLARA
SULLIVAN, M.	SAWYER, ED
WIARD, G.E.	WERLEN, F.
WEILLY, O.F.	

Death of J.C. GIBSON
On Thursday last, Mr. J.C. GIBSON, the pioneer resident and merchant of Bolinas, passed away after a brief illness, caused by a complication of liver troubles. Mr. GIBSON was one of the best known and most highly respected men in the community. He was full of public spirit and as a supervisor of his district years ago, was the occasion of many improvements being made which aided materially in the development and prosperity of this county. He was instrumental in the building of the road from here to Bolinas – a work then of the greatest importance. The funeral occurred on Saturday and was largely attended, many being present from a distance. Rev. J.S. McDONALD, formerly pastor of the San Rafael Presbyterian Church, conducted the funeral services which were very impressive. The interment occurred at Bolinas. In the death of Mr. GIBSON, his townsmen have lost an estimable and enterprising citizen, and the family a loving and indulgent father.

A Wedding
Mr. CHARLES PASTORI, the popular host of Fairfax, on Wednesday last, took unto himself a charming bride in the person of Miss ADELE PUERERI, of San Francisco. Judge RODDEN performed the ceremony, after which the guests partook of an elaborate wedding breakfast, after which Mr. and Mrs. PASTORI left for Coronado on their honeymoon trip.

Superior Court
    MARTHA BUCKELEW vs. ANNIE McGARIN
    Default of defendant ordered entered
    Judgment for plaintiff for restitution and possession of premises

    People vs. LEE DOON
    Time for execution set for Friday, September 1st

    HENRY SCHLOSSER, admr. vs. P.T. BURTCHAELL
    Judgment for defendant

    Estate of ISAAC SHAVER, deceased
    Order for lease of real estate set for August 5th

    Estate of WILLIAM DORR, deceased
    Passed

    Estate of CORNELIUS MURRAY, deceased
    Account of executors settled and approved – estate distributed

    Estate of DAVID RING, deceased
    Letters of administration ordered issued to M. MURRAY

    CHARLES HARLAN vs. their Creditors
    Over one week

    JAMES I. TAYLOR vs. his Creditors
    Continued indefinitely

Died
GIBSON – In Bolinas, July 13th, 1893, Mr. J.C. GIBSON

Marriage Licenses
    GEORGE BLIEL, 40, Pleasanton, to Miss CLINE ELIZABETH SAPIN, 23, Alameda
    HENRY LAMPMAN, 62, San Francisco, to Mrs. ELIZABETH ELLEN FOWLER, 30, San Francisco

Marin Journal
Thursday, July 27, 1893

At Tomales
RALPH WOODWORTH, son of our most worthy citizen, Mr. A. WOODWORTH, returned Friday last from Harvard College, having graduated with high honors. We predict for this young man, a bright future, as he is known for his energy and brightness.

Mr. and Mrs. J. PHILLIPS, who have been spending several weeks among their friends here, returned to their home in San Francisco Monday, where Mr. PHILIPS is engaged on the Morning Call.

Conductor J.C. McDANIELS has purchased a home near Petaluma, paying a good round sum of $100 per acre, which speaks well for the enterprising conductor.

CHARLES BURREY of the Sausalito News was on our streets Monday in the interest of the News. Mr. BURREY is a rustler, but he is like the preacher in one respect, and that is, he can't please everybody.

Mr. H.B. HARRINGTON is a special agent for the Pacific Coast Savings Society.

School Notes
There are a few changes among the teachers, as follows: Mr. NOWELL succeeded Mr. COX at Tomales; Mr. COX taking the grammar school principalship at Santa Rosa; Miss EMMA BROWN succeeds Miss JOHNSON at the Bay School at Bolinas; Miss H.L. JEWELL succeeds Miss LOUISE CLUVER in the Pierce District, the latter teacher succeeding her sister, Miss LENA CLUVER, lately married, in the Lincoln District; Miss ADELAIDE E. GRAHAM will teach in the San Geronimo School; succeeding Miss M.A. CRITTENDEN, who is to teach in the new district school at San Anselmo. Mrs. ANGELINA CERINI has been elected school trustee and district clerk. Mrs. CERINI and Mrs. C.C. VALENCIA at Novato, are the only lady trustees in the county.

Sudden Death
Dr. F.J. WHITE Found Dead in His Office
An Able Physician and a Popular, Large-Hearted Man is Suddenly Taken Away
The community was deeply shocked on Tuesday evening by the announcement that Dr. F.J. WHITE had suddenly died in his office in the Gordon block about 8 o'clock. An inquest was held Wednesday morning at which it was determined that he had died of a clot to the heart that had traveled to the brain causing instant death.
Dr. F.J. WHITE had been a resident of this county over 7 years, during which time he had established his reputation as a skillful physician and a man of great generosity and large-heartedness. For some time he had been County Physician.
He came here from Nevada, where he had remained some years as a successful practitioner, but which place he left in order to give his family the advantages of San Rafael's superior climate.
During the war, he was rated one of the most skillful surgeons in the confederate service, and he was on active duty at the front for a long period, being finally captured and held many months in a Northern military prison. He was a Mason of excellent standing, and a general favorite among all classes on account of his genial, kindly nature, and his readiness to ever answer to the responses of the needy and destitute. Few men occupy a larger place in the hearts of the community.
The Dr. leaves a widow, but no children, these having been taken away in early childhood. The blow which has fallen on Mrs. WHITE is doubly severe, owing to its suddenness, and she has the heartfelt sympathy of the entire community.
The funeral services will be held at the home of the deceased today, Thursday, at 3 o'clock, Rev. E. E.A. HARTMAN officiating. The interment will take place at Tamalpais Cemetery under Masonic auspices.

Local Brevities
Mrs. MARSHALL J. KINNEY of Astoria has rented the CROWLEY house on Fifth Ave.

Mr. WILLIAM STEVENS, once a resident of San Rafael, but now living in San Francisco, is encamped near Liberty's.

WILLIAM HICKEY leaves in a few days for a month's visit with his parents at Stockbridge in Western Massachusetts. Mr. HICKEY has been absent from his home over 14 years.

Mr. W.G. YOUNG, who was lately engaged in the shoe business here in San Rafael, and wife, left town last Monday for San Francisco where they will make their future home.

Superior Court
    R.W. JOHNSON vs. R.T. COTTINGHAM
    Judgment for plaintiff

JENNIE DIMOCK vs. F.H. DIMOCK
Divorce not granted. Time given to present authorities

GEORGE W. FOX vs. SUSAN FOX
Judgment for defendant with costs and alimony

Real estate and guardianship of HUGH A. BOYLE Jr.
CARMELITA N. BOYLE appointed guardian

Estate of JANE LA PAGE, deceased
Administrator discharged

T.B. VALENTINE vs. M.M. DEFFEBACH etal
Case set for argument on August 31st

R.W. JOHNSON vs. R. FURLONG
Opinion filed, judgment for plaintiff

Estate of CATHERINE COLLINS, deceased
Over for two weeks

Estate of S.R. BROWN, deceased
Decree due and legal notice to creditors ordered

Estate of CHARLES BROSIN, deceased
Sale of real and personal property ordered

Estate of F.C. SHUFELDT, deceased
Over one week

Estate of JAMES M. DONAHUE, deceased
Further hearing of partial distribution

G. ZUMINI vs. His Creditors
Adjudged insolvent, meeting for creditors set for August 28th

PRESTON & McKINNON vs. EMILY F. TIBBEY etal
Verdict for plaintiff

Real Estate Transfers
OLIVE DRAKE to IGNAZIO SARTORI
Lot 5 and Raymond lot, Forbes Reserve, San Rafael - $10

GEORGE MASON and wife to PETER WILLIAMS
Ptn. Lot 1, Short addition to San Rafael - $10

RALPH BROWN to EMMA FANNING
Lot on SE corner C and Second Streets, San Rafael - $10

Sausalito Bay Land & Ferry Co. to J. LOWDER and wife
Lot 1 & 2, block 3, Sausalito Bay Land & Ferry Co. - $10

A.S. BETTENCOURT to MANUEL CONSTANT
Ptn. Lot 1, block 68, Sausalito Land & Ferry Co. - $10

J.C. GIBSON to LOUISA J. SJOGREN
Ptn. Grande Vista Tract, Bolinas - $75

Home and Farm Co. to JOHN A. SWANSON
10.81 acres Home & Farm Lands, division A - $10

Sausalito Bay Land Co. to DAVID NEWELL
Lots 20 and 21, block 59, Sausalito Bay Land Co. - $10

HORACE W. BALL to CLARA A. BALL
Lot 5, block 5, Belvedere – gift

Home & Farm Co. to ARTHUR SEMLER
Lot 3, Sunnyside Place, Novato - $10

Estate of J. McM. SHAFTER to JAYNE J. SHAFTER
The Olema Ranch 300.60 acres, order confirming sale - $12,600

Home & Farm Co. to MANUEL D. BRONCE
11.65 acres Home & Farm Co. lands - $10

Estate of CORNELIUS MURRAY to CATHERINE MURRAY etal
368.16 acres ptn of Nicasio Rancho
508.57 acres ptn of Nicasio Rancho – distribution

MARY A. FORBES to IGNAZIO SARTORI
Lot 5 and Raymond lot, Forbes Reserve, San Rafael - $5

Tamalpais Land & Water Co. to OTTO E. FALCH
Sub. 2, lot 228, Tamalpais Land & Water Co. - $100

JOHN W. MACKAY etal to Pioneer Mill & Lumber Co.
Lot on E line of Irwin Street and Fourth Street, San Rafael - $1

JOHN W. MACKAY to JEAN B. GUINTRAND
Lot on SW corner of San Rafael and San Quentin Road and Picnic Ave. - $1,000

Born
CLARK – In San Rafael, July 18th, to the wife of J.H. CLARK, a daughter.

PACHECO – In San Rafael, July 19th, to the wife of A.F. PACHECO, a daughter.

Marriage Licenses
    VINCENT RANDIT, 32, San Francisco, to Miss LIZZIE RATIGAN, 25, Sausalito
    FRANCIS AUGUSTUS MUNDT, 24, San Francisco, to Miss CLARA LEONTINA MAYER, 23, San Francisco
    ARTHUR WHEELER, 30, San Francisco, to MINNIE L. DEMPSEY, 31, San Francisco
    WILLIAM HANNA, 33, San Francisco, to JULIA CLANCY, 31, San Francisco

Letter List

ALLEN, W.	BOGGINHAN, A.
BIGBY, J.	CONLY, M.
CONNELL, N.	FISCHER, E.A.
HAYES, Mrs. M.	HEALY, K.
JONES, B.	JORDAN, ED
McCUNE, L.	PERRY, J.
REYNOLDS, T.	RUSSELL, M.
SPENCE, F.	SARMENTO, M.T.
WEST, G.	WEBERBECK, E.

Died
WHITE – In San Rafael, July 25, 1893, Dr. F.J. WHITE, aged 54 years.

FARLEY – At Pt. Reyes, July 7, 1893, BENJAMIN THOMAS FARLEY, youngest child of Mr. and Mrs. JAMES H. FARLEY.

Marin County Tocsin
Saturday, July 29, 1893

Order to Show Cause
    Estate of ISAAC SHAVER, deceased
    HARRIET B. SHAVER, Executrix
    Order to lease lands known as the New England Villa
    Application by A. KAPPENMAN for 4 years and 9 months
    July 15, 1893
                                  D.J. MURPHY
                                  Judge Superior Court

Notice to Creditors
    Estate of JOHN A. THOMPSON, deceased
    HAVEN & HAVEN, Attorneys for Petitioner
    July 12, 1893
                                  HANS JACOB OLSEN
                                  Executor of Will

Notice to Creditors
    Estate of JOHN SCHIPPERS, deceased
    JAMES W. COCHRANE, Attorney for Executor
    July 10, 1893
                                  HENRY BETTEN
                                  Executor of Will

Notice to Creditors
    Estate of WILLIAM G. MILLS, deceased
    HAVEN & HAVEN, Attorneys for Executrix
    June 23, 1893
                                  JULIET W. MILLS
                                  Executrix of Will

Insolvency
    Matter of CHARLES NORTON, an Insolvent Debtor
    Creditors must appear before court August 7, 1893
    June 30, 1893
                                  F.M. ANGELLOTTI
                                  Judge of Superior Court

Local News
J.B. RICE will sell his livery stable at Larkspur at public auction and move his business base elsewhere. Marin County will regret to lose the genial JOSEPH.

TOM ELLIOTT, late of Wells Fargo & Co's Agency at San Rafael, was in town this week. He is now running on an express route in Oregon, but is very weary of the climate and surroundings up North and heartily anxious to be given a route somewhere near his old home. He is as healthy and handsome as ever and looks like one on whom the cares of life did not rest heavily.

Superior Court
    JENNIE DIMOCK vs. F.H. DIMOCK
    Further hearing continued to July 31st

    M. EICKHOFF vs. M. EICKHOFF
    GEORGE EICKHOFF appointed guardian of HENRY & EDWARD EICKHOFF

    People vs. G.W. BEERMAKER
    Time to plead extended to August 31st

Real Estate Transfers
    JAMES TUNSTEAD and wife to GEORGE HUNNEWELL
    Lot in San Rafael - $10

H.M. HALL to LAURA L. WHITE
Lot 48, Tamalpais Land & Water Co. - $10

LOVELL WHITE and wife to EDWARD L. HEUTER
Portion of lot 47 & 50, Tamalpais Land & Water Co. - $10

THOMAS MAGEE etal to ALBERT ROULLIER
Portion of lot 44, Tamalpais Land & Water Co. - $10

Marin Journal
Thursday, August 3, 1893

Local Brevities
Mr. WILLIAM LOFTUS of Petaluma was in town last week.

Drop into R.T. MULLIGAN's new barber shop, next to Thomson's, for a first-class shave or haircut.

Hon. C.L. ESTEY, ex-assemblyman and brother of Hon. T.H. ESTEY of Nicasio, has been visiting in the county recently. His home is in San Diego.

School Trustee Appointments
    Bolinas district – W.W. WILKINS, GEORGE RUNKEL, CHARLES McKEE
    Black district – P.F. SCILACCI
    Chileno Valley district – D.S. FRAZIER, CHARLES MARTIN, JAMES BLOOM
    Eastland district – S.R. GARDNER, CHARLES K. GRAHAM
    Pierce district – W.D. EVANS, CHARLES MOLTZEN, C. HULBE
    Pt. Reyes district – W.D. SKINNER, P.H. CLAUSSEN, J.R. REEVES
    Reed district – J.J. REED, J.P. REED, JUSTO VIDAL
    Ross Landing district – FRANK J. MURRAY
    San Antonio district – J. VONSEN, E.P. NISSON, HENRY EHLERS
    Tiburon district – E.B. LEEDS, J.O. CONNELL

Items of Interest
Capt. J.C. EDGAR and wife of San Quentin are at Cazadero.

Mr. G. ABBINK of Petaluma who has been here for some months past, has returned home.

Dr. W.K. VANCE, a physician of Sonoma City, has been looking over San Rafael with a view to locating here.

Mrs. J. ESCALLE of Corte Madera will shortly leave for Paso Robles to try the medicinal virtues of the famous springs there.

Dr. H.O. HOWITT, a prominent and rising young physician of San Francisco, is thinking very seriously of locating here on account of the superior climate of San Rafael, which he hopes will prove beneficial to the health of his family.

Mr. WILLYE, a substantial rancher of Contra Costa County, has been visiting his daughter, Mrs. P. SCHUETZEN of Coleman's addition. Mr. WILLYE, who is a man of advanced years, sustained considerable injuries about two weeks ago by falling from a load of hay, compelling him to take an enforced vacation.

Tomales Letter
Mrs. HEMINWAY of Petaluma is in camp with friends at Dillon's beach.

Miss HANNAH GRAVES of Alameda was the guest of Miss HOLLAND on Sunday.

LOUIS GULDAGER Jr. went to San Francisco Friday with a carload of very fine cattle.

Miss JESSIE EDMINSTER of San Francisco spent last week in Tomales among friends.

Dr. C.C. BAKER of Napa was upon our streets one day last week looking up a new field of labor.

Mrs. W.H. DARDEN etal of Petaluma are camped on the famous Dillon Beach for a couple of weeks.

B.J. HILDEBRAND of San Francisco is spending a few weeks in Tomales, the guest of A. GERICKE, Esq.

Dr. URBAN moved to town this week where he will be located permanently to attend all calls. He comes recommended to our people, who will support him.

Notice to Creditors
> Estate of SOPHIA ZELLAR, deceased
> Also known as SOPHIA STEINECKE, deceased
> August 2, 1893
> JOHN F. JORDAN
> Executor of Will

Additional Locals
Mr. BRUCE and family of Balfour, Guthrie & Co., have taken the MORRIS cottage on Fifth Avenue, through Wood, Christieson & Co.

Mr. VALENTINE BURRY and his sister, Miss MAMIE BURRY of San Francisco, were in San Rafael last Sunday. They were the guests of Mrs. FARRELL.

Mrs. MORRIS and her son, ROY, left San Rafael last Tuesday on their way to Portland, OR, where they will join Miss MAY MORRIS, who started the day previous.

Cupid TAYLOR, at the courthouse, who has made so many hearts happy, issued papers last Saturday authorizing THOMAS F. McDONALD of San Francisco, age 21 years, to marry MARY HELENSCHILD of San Francisco, aged 19 years.

Superior Court
> People vs. W.W. BOWERS
> Information filed by District Attorney for libel
>
> People vs. A. BIERCE
> Libel, over one week
>
> Estate of F.C. SCHUFELDT, deceased
> Over two weeks
>
> Estate of HENRY MILES, deceased
> Decree of final discharge
>
> Estate of W.H. PATTEN, deceased
> Final account settled and distribution made
>
> Estate of J.C. GIBSON, deceased
> Letters of administration issued to R.E. GIBSON, bond of $6,000
>
> SLINKEY vs. HANNON
> Defendant to withdraw demurrer, 20 days to answer
>
> R.W. JOHNSON vs. R.T. COTTINGHAM
> Judgment for plaintiff
>
> Estate of SOPHIA ZELLAR, deceased
> Will admitted to probate, letters testamentary to J.F. JORDAN

Letter List
ADAMS, L.	ADAMS, D.
CHAMBERS, J.P.	COWELL, HARRY
FAGAN, JAMES	FELLMANN, L.

GAMET, P.	GARCIA, I.
HOLTZ, G.	HENNESSEY, ---
KELLER, J.	KIFLY, HATTIE
LAWLER, M.	LYNCH, ---
LIVINSTON, A.	MILLER, ETTA
MILLER, A.	WALKER, M.

Died

BARBER – In Stockton, July 23, 1893, CARRIE E. BARBER, daughter of HYLAND E. and HATTIE ATHERTON BARBER, aged 9 months.

PAULSEN – At Pt. Bonita, July 28, 1893, KARMEN PAULSEN, a native of Denmark, aged 23 years.

FAGUNDES – At Fairfax, August 2, 1893, CLARA FAGUNDES, aged 18 months.

Marin County Tocsin
Saturday, August 5, 1893

    Notice to Creditors
        Estate of DAVID KING, deceased
        July 27, 1893
        HEPBURN WILKINS, Attorney for Administrator
                MICHAEL MURRAY, Admr.

    Sheriff's Sale
        JOEL F. HILLS, Admr. of Estate of SANFORD M. HILLS, deceased
        Vs.
        F.W. RUSSELL, FRANK E. HILLS, JOHN DOE, and F.W. RUSSELL, Executor of the Will of FLORIMEL E. RUSSELL, deceased
        Foreclosure on land in Sausalito
        Filed in office of Marin County Recorder January 13, 1893
        Offered for sale Monday, August 28, 1893 at Courthouse
                HENRY HARRISON, Sheriff
                T.J. FALLON, Under Sheriff

    Executor's Sale of Real Estate
        Estate of CHARLES BROSIN, deceased
        To be sold August 22, 1893
        Land in San Rafael
        Filed July 28, 1893
                MORITZ MEYER
                SIMON C. SHEELINE
                Executors of Estate of CHARLES BROSIN, dec.

Died
EVANS – At Santa Margarita, August 3, 1893, HARRY EVANS, a native of County Wexford, Ireland, aged 74 years. Funeral from St. Raphael's church on Sunday, August 6th, at 1 p.m. o'clock.

W.K. VANCE MD
    Physician and Surgeon
    San Rafael (lately occupied by Dr. WHITE)

GEORGE McMILLAN
    Photograph Gallery
    San Rafael

A.B. THOMSON
    Dry Goods, Linen Goods
    San Rafael

Local News
R.P. TROY left last Thursday for Washington, the scene of his new labors.

HARRY EVANS, an old farmer of San Rafael township, died at his home near the County Poor Farm last Thursday. The deceased was a native of County Wesford, Ireland, aged 74 years.

Dr. WICKMAN has been informally directed by the majority of members of the Board of Supervisors to perform the public duties formerly discharged by Dr. WHITE as County Physician.

Primary Election
The primary election in Sausalito was held Wednesday. The following results were:
    For Trustees
        J.H. DICKINSON, J. RICHARDS, JOHN SCHNELL, C.H. HARRISON, and J.W. SPERRY
    Town Clerk
        D.H. SCHULTZ
    Treasurer
        S.S. FIEDLER
    Marshal
        RICHARD GARRITY

German School
The German residents of San Rafael have organized to maintain a school for instruction in the German language. M. HERZOG was chosen President.

Marin Journal
Thursday, August 10, 1893

Tomales News
FRED WOODWORTH, attorney at law in the city, visited his parents here Saturday, and spent Sunday at the beach, returning Monday to his office.

Mrs. McGINNIS and sister of San Francisco are visiting Mrs. P. GALLAGHER.

Mrs. STEWART of San Francisco, formerly a resident of Tomales, spent last week here with her sister, Mrs. P. BURNS.

The many and numerous friends will feel much grieved to learn of the death of Miss LENA McALLEP, who formerly resided here. She had been afflicted some time, though her death was not expected. We all extend our deepest sympathy to her bereaved family.

A branch representing $60,000 of the Pacific Coast Savings Society, has been established in Tomales. The officers are P. CARROLL, President; M.L. MURPHY, vice-president; W.H. VAUGHAN, Secretary; J.B. CAUZZA, Treasurer; and Agent Appraisers, P. TUNZI, W.H. EVANS, A. LAFRANCHI, A. GIACOMINI, and C. MALTZEN. Mr. W.V. HARRINGTON, special agent, we give credit for organizing this branch.

Mr. ROUKE, a millionaire and wholesale merchant of New York City, in company with the chief of police, Mr. DONAHUE, of the same city, spent several days here last week visiting the former's sister, who is a resident of Tomales. The gentlemen were taking a tour of the continent, having visited many cities in California.

Items of Interest
Mr. ROBERT DUREE of Petaluma was in San Rafael on Wednesday.

Miss CAMILLA LUND of San Francisco was in San Rafael last week, the guest of Miss OLIVIA LEAVENWORTH.

FRANK HEALY is booked for a good place in the mint, although the appointment has not yet been made.

Found Dead
DAVE FRAZIER was found dead in his cabin at the head of Tomales Bay on Tuesday. The body when found was much decomposed and had been dead some time. Coroner EDEN went to Olema yesterday morning to hold an inquest.

Real Estate Transfers
Belvedere Land Co. to JOHN C. PELTON Jr.
Lot 18, block 2, Belvedere - $10

ISAAC JESSUP to L.F. DUNAUD
6.52 acres, portion of Jessup Tract, San Rafael - $10

M.R. MILLER to MAGDALENA R. MILLER
Villa lot 31, Block 18, Sausalito Bay & Land Co. – gift

JAMES W. SPERRY and wife to CHRISTOPHER BECKER
Portion of Sperry Tract, Sausalito - $10

J.B. GIACOMINI and wife to Nicasio Grove No. 42, U.A.O.D.
Lot in Nicasio - $10

ISAAC JESSUP to HENRY EICKHOFF
Portion Jessup Tract, San Rafael - $10

LOUIS VESARIA to HARRIETTE L. VESARIA
Lots 4, 5, 6, & 7, Block N, Larkspur – gift

Tamalpais Land & Water Co. to F.B. WASHINGTON
Lot 174, Tamalpais Land & Water Co.

Home & Farm Co. to AGNES MILLMEISTER
Lot 27, Reservoir Hill Place, Novato - $10

HANS B. VOGEL to CHARLES SCHLADITZ
Lot on S line Fourth Street and Ida Street - $10

Home & Farm Co. to ARTHUR SEMLER
Lot 3, Sunnyside Place, Novato - $10

JAMES A. TUNSTEAD and wife to GEORGE A. HUNNEWELL
Portion of Block 51, San Rafael - $10

LOVELL WHITE and wife to WILLIAM RIEGER and wife
Portion of lot 47, Tamalpais Land & Water Co. - $10

H.H. HALL to LAURA M. WHITE
Portion of lot 48, Tamalpais Land & Water Co. - $10

LOVELL WHITE and wife to ERNEST L. HUETER
Portion of lot 47, Tamalpais Land & Water Co. - $10

T. MAGEE etal to ALBERT ROULLIER
Portion of lot 44, Tamalpais Land & Water Co. - $10

WENDELL EASTON etal to ANTOINETTE TONINI
Lot 11, block 13, Sunnyside Tract, - $10

Superior Court
Estate of ISAAC SHAVER, deceased
Hearing continued to August 12

People vs. A. BIERCE
Over one week

C. NORTON vs. His Creditors
Over one week

JENNIE DIMOCK vs. F.H. DIMOCK
Action dismissed

Tamalpais Land & Water Co. to J.H. McINNES
Demurrer overruled

Estate of CATHERINE COLLINS, deceased
Decree of distribution

Estate of THEODORE MUNDT, deceased
Final account settled and estate distributed

Estate of M. L'AMOUREAUX, deceased
Final account settled and approved

Estate of S.R. BROWN, deceased
Final account settled and estate distributed

M.W. EICKHOFF vs. M. EICKHOFF
Demurrer argued and submitted

Died
GEARY – At Ross Valley, August 5, 1893, WILLIAM W. GEARY, aged 39 years, 10 months, and 9 days.

Marin County Tocsin
Saturday, August 12, 1893

Sheriff's Sale
JOSEPH SHAIN vs. JOSEPH McNAMARA
Sum of $74.70 awarded to plaintiff
Sale of personal property Saturday, August 19, 1893
Dated August 12, 1893
HENRY HARRISON, Sheriff
T.J. FALLON, Deputy Sheriff

Adjudication of Insolvency
In the matter of FRED KRUSE, an Insolvent Debtor
All creditors must appear before court Monday, September 11, 1893
Dated August 10, 1893
H.S. HERRICK, Attorney for Insolvent
F.M. ANGELLOTTI, Judge of Superior Court

Local News
CHARLES BUKER was thrown from his horse last Wednesday evening and suffered a fracture of the collarbone.

Dr. H.O. HOWITT, a San Francisco practitioner of high standing, has engaged offices in the Wilkins Block on Fourth Street.

Dr. MANSFIELD, resident physician at San Quentin Prison, was thrown violently from his buggy last Tuesday. He was dashed against the rough side of a barbed wire fence, and sustained painful though not serious injuries.

Real Estate Transfers
ELLA C. POND to CHARLES H. DWINELLE
Lot 6, Block 24, Golden Meadow, San Rafael

Estate of SAMUEL R. BROWN to MARY A. & BELLE C. BROWN
4 acres beginning at east gate post of Brown's house and lot of land, Larkspur - $10

Estate of THEODORE MUNDT to F.A. MUNDT etal
Portion of Red Hill Tract, Punto Quentin Rancho – distribution

D.W. HAYES to E.A. HAYES
Lots 225, 211, 212, Tamalpais Land & Water Co. – gift

Belvedere Land Co. to JOHN C. PELTON
Lot 18, Block 2, Belvedere - $10

Home & Farm Co. to N.F. BARNUM
Portion of Lot 3, Home & Farm Co. land - $10

From Sausalito
J.W. COLEMAN, a barber, lately in the employ of JACQUES THOMAS, died last week in San Francisco

Fatal Accident
      Coroner EDEN was notified last Thursday evening that an unknown man was lying dead at the foot of White's Hill on the San Rafael road. He at once hastened to the place designated and found the information to be correct. The dead man had evidently met his end by driving his vehicle over a steep pitch near the foot of the hill which has long been a menace to travel. The hillside falls away from the roadway here almost perpendicularly for not less than 50 feet to the creek bottom. The accident must have occurred about 3 o'clock as the unfortunate man was seen driving westward near the foot of the hill about that hour. It is also evident that careless driving, in some way, must have been the cause of the casualty, for it was plain that there had been no runaway, as the horse was entirely uninjured and remained standing patiently only a few feet from the dead man.
      A search of the deceased's effects disclosed nothing to indicate his identity. There will, however, be no difficulty in locating him. He had in his pocket two unopened letters, one addressed to Mrs. A.R. HAMILTON, the other to the estate of JAMES McM. SHAFTER, postmarked San Francisco, which he evidently was conveying to Olema to Mrs. HAMILTON. In addition he had a miscellaneous cargo of articles in his top buggy representing the usual purchases of odds and ends for a large ranch and including flower seeds, rooted plants, a rubber hose, carriage wrenches, and several other tools together with a lot of unopened packages, seemingly done up in a store. It is almost certain therefore that the dead man was an employee of the Shafter estate, who had been sent by Mrs. HAMILTON to San Francisco to make sundry purchases and obtain any mail that might be waiting for her at that point.
      The deceased was a man of about 60 years of age or upwards, 5 feet 8 inches high, short gray hair and mustache, and complete set of false teeth. His dress indicated that he was a farmhand. Death undoubtedly resulted from a fracture of the skull.
Later
As we go to press, Olema has been heard from. As suspected, the deceased was a servant of Mrs. HAMILTON, MICHAEL McCLOSKY by name. He was an old employee of the SHAFTER family, and Mrs. HAMILTON expressed deep grief when she heard of his unfortunate end. She at once started for San Rafael to take charge of the remains.

Marin Journal
Thursday, August 17, 1893

Tomales Letter
Mrs. Dr. REARDON, from Oroville, is spending a week with her parents here, Mr. and Mrs. HOLLAND.

JAMES W. KEYES, attorney, of San Francisco, spent Sunday here with his mother, Mrs. KEYES, returning Monday afternoon.

Miss EMMA TURNER, now living in the southern part of the State, is up on a visit to her parents, Mr. and Mrs. O. TURNER.

Miss M. KENNEDY, who has been spending the past 6 weeks here with her friends, Mr. and Mrs. BUCHANAN, returned Monday to her home in Sacramento.

HORACE ABLES, son of our townsman, returned this week from an extended trip in the East, having visited Chicago and other prominent cities, also spending a few weeks in Moberly, MO, with a sister who resides there.

Items of Interest
JOE McNAMARA, a grocer and saloon keeper of Larkspur, has been attached and closed up. His goods will be sold by the sheriff next Saturday.

JOSEPH RAWLINGS, a prominent rancher of Reed's, is reported to be very ill.

Mrs. O.W. GROVE of Atwater, San Joaquin Valley, sister-in-law of Dr. GROVE, is visiting the family of the latter.

W.W. GEARY, who died so suddenly last week at Ross Valley, came to his death from blood poisoning, caused primarily from the bite of a small black spider on the hand. The hand and arm swelled up to alarming proportions, blood poisoning set in, and death ensured in about 4 days. The attending physician was Dr. GROVE.

Petaluma Courier
The funeral of WILLIAM REDDING of Nicasio, son of Mr. and Mrs. W.C. REDDING, occurred Monday, the remains being brought to Petaluma for burial in Calvary Cemetery. The deceased was a very popular young man of high standing in the community. Besides other relatives, he leaves a wife and many friends to mourn his loss.

Died
KERR – In San Francisco, August 13, 1893, EARL T. KERR, a native of San Francisco.

Marriage Licenses
    A.N. AITKEN, 23, San Francisco, to GERTRUDE WILSON, 20, Alameda
    CARL MATSEN, 21, Bolinas, to BELLE BONNEY, 25, Bolinas

Superior Court
    Estate of ISAAC SHAVER, deceased
    Order granted to lease property

    People vs. A. BIERCE
    Over one week

    People vs. W.W. BOWERS
    Over one week

    AMANDA TANN, admx. Etal vs. Pat. Brick Co. etal
    Set for trial September 12th

    CHARLES HARLAN et ux vs. Their Creditors
    Application for discharge set for meeting August 29th

    Estate of FRANKLIN .J. WHITE, deceased
    Letters of administration ordered issued to MARY V. WHITE

    Estate of SIDNEY F. BOYLE, deceased
    CARMELITA N. BOYLE appointed administrator

    Estate of W.G. MILLS, deceased
    Sale of interest of partnership for $7,500, confirmed

    Estate of F.C. SCHUFELDT, deceased
    Petition for letters dismissed for want of jurisdiction

    People vs. W.B. WINN
    Charge – libeling G.W. MONTALON, information as filed

Real Estate Transfers
    Tamalpais Land & Water Co. to JOHN REA
    Ptn. Lot 23, Tamalpais Land & Water Co. lands - $10

HENRY N. McCHESNEY to ELIZA J. McCHESNEY
Corner of lots 115, 116, Tamalpais Land & Water Co. - $1,000

JOHN O.B. SHORT and wife to LOUISA BORELLA
Lot on east line South C Street, South of Bay View Street - $10

Letter List

ABEL, C.	BUBAC, A.H.
BAPTISTE, F.	HANSEN, J.
CUNNING, I.	HERZOG, A.
CULBERTSON, S.	HARDING, C.
GARCIA, B.	JOHNSON, J.
HAMMOND, L.G.	JACOBS, S.
KOUTZ, T.	MILLER, J.
MORRIS, B.F.	MILLER, BILL
MOORE, H.H.	MARTENS, DICK
MYER, E.	MULLER, E.
MAGEE, ---	McGREW, W.H.
McKENNA, P.	ORDWAY, W.F.
JORGENSEN, A.	PURVIS, J.P.
PETSCH, M.	RODGERS, M.
RODY, M.	RICHARDSON, D.
ROSNER, E.M.	SAVAGE, J.
SMITH, A.	SNOOK, S.

Marin County Tocsin
Saturday, August 19, 1893

Born
PIXLEY – At Corte Madera, August 17, 1893, to the wife of FRANK PIXLEY Jr., a daughter.

Local News
Mr. C.S. SMYTHE has been recently elected Principal of the Hollister High School, a very satisfactory position and a better one than he recently held in the San Rafael School.

The Board of Supervisors met yesterday, and granted liquor licenses to the following:
 CHARLES KUNZ and JOHN PACHECO – San Rafael
 McMILLAN and MESA – Sausalito
 RUDOLPH KOHN – San Rafael

P. GALLAGHER, who has conducted an extensive quarry business at Novato for some years past, filed his petition in insolvency last Tuesday. The failure of his business puts a number of workmen out of employment.

Real Estate Transfers
 CHARLES DWINELLE to SARAH SPAULDING
 Lot 6, block 24, San Rafael - $250

 Estate of BARBARA KADEL to MARY M. KADEL
 Lots 2 and 3, block 24, Sausalito Land & Ferry Co.

 Estate of C.H. THON to MARGARET THON
 Lot 10, tidelands of Richardson's Bay

 San Francisco Theological Seminary to WENDELL EASTON etal
 Exchange for water rights, Sunnyside tracts

 PIERRE FORTIN to Fortin Brick Co.
 Water lots at Oak Point, San Rafael - $10

 Tamalpais Land & Water Co. to JOHN REA
 Portion of lot 23, Tamalpais Land & Water Co. - $1,200

EVELINE PICKERING to JOHN CURLEY
Portion of lots 1 and 2, block A, Coleman's addition, San Rafael - $10

SARAH W.I. TAYLOR to Anglo California Bank
Lot at southeast of McCrea lot, San Rafael
Lot on B Street south of 2nd Street, San Rafael - $5

Marin Journal
Thursday, August 24, 1893

Tomales Notes
Miss MABEL HOLLAND, who lives now in the city, visited her parents here Saturday.

Mrs. E.J. CALLOU visited her parents, Mr. and Mrs. J.L. FALLON, of San Francisco, last week, returning Saturday.

DAVE CASTRO of Pt. Reyes, who recently joined the Odd Fellows, was present Saturday night at their meeting here.

Marriage Licenses
G.E. ELMQUIST, 28, Oakland, to Miss IDA AXEN, 26, Oakland
G. LAFRANCHI, 34, San Rafael, to Miss M. CALLESTRO, 18, San Rafael
LOUIS C. PLETTE, 18, San Rafael, to ANETA NORIEL, 17, San Rafael

Letter List

ANDERSON, I.	BAKER, F.
BURKE, ---	BROOKS, ---
BOWDEN, M.	CONLEY, G.H.
COFFIN, JOE	CARSON, H.
DAVIS, Dr. H.H.	DE ST. GERMAIN, ---
FAUST, E.	JOHNSON, HILDA
NATHAN, A.	O'CONNOR, ---
ORDWAY, W.F.	PHILLIPS, M.
POWYLE, H.	QUINN, I.
KENNEDY, N.	RILEY, K.A.
SHEARER, L.W.	SMITH, ANNIE
SMITH, W.H.	TAYLOR, ---
THROCKMORTON, I.W.	VAN SICKLE, C.
TAYLOR, G.	WAGNER, E.
WILKINS, B.L.	

Born
GULDAGER – In San Rafael, August 22, 1893, to the wife of GEORGE M. GULDAGER, a daughter

RANDESON – At Olema, August 18, 1893, to the wife of J.D. RANDESON, a son

SILACCI – At Pt. Reyes, August 14, 1893, to the wife of P. SILACCI, a son

ELLIOTT – At San Rafael, August 14, 1893, to the wife of WILLIAM ELLIOTT, a son

RICHARDSON – In San Francisco, August 20, 1893, to the wife of G.L. RICHARDSON, a son

Superior Court
M.W. EICKHOFF vs. MAGDALENA EICKHOFF
Demurrer sustained – 20 days to answer

A BIERCE on habeus corpus
Over one week

People vs. W.B. WINN
Libel – over one week

People vs. G.W. BEERMAKER etal
Motion to dismiss granted

People vs. W.W. BOWERS
Motion to dismiss granted

Estate of PETER WEBER, deceased
Account settled – estate distributed

GEORGE W. FUTCH etal vs. P. GUTHEL etal
Plaintiff's motion to amend findings denied
Defendant's motion to retax plaintiff's costs granted

JULIA E. BELL etal vs. Sausalito Land & Ferry Co.
Motion to retax plaintiff's costs granted

Real Estate Transfers
    Home & Farm Co. to ADAM STEWART and wife
    Lots 6 and 7, Block C
    Lot 13, Reservoir Hill Place, Novato - $10

    JAMES W. SPERRY to V.C. DUFFIELD
    Lot 9, Sperry tract, Sausalito - $10

Marin Journal
Thursday, August 31, 1893

Death of C.E. MALLON

This community was greatly shocked on Monday by the announcement of the death of Mr. CHARLES E. MALLON. Mr. Mallon was ill only a few days, he having been taken with a hemorrhage on Wednesday last while sitting in the office of Constable GANNON. He went home and suffered a worse hemorrhage than before, losing a large quantity of blood. This so weakened his system, that he could not rally, but became delirious, sinking steadily, until the end came on Monday afternoon.

Mr. Mallon was one of the best known young men in the county, his genial ways making him a general favorite. He has filled the office of Clerk of San Rafael, and as Deputy Sheriff and Constable. He has been connected with a large number of important legal proceedings in this county. He was well educated, and his talents were appreciated especially by newspaper men who were always glad to receive contributions from his pen.

He married Miss HONORA BIGGINS, who is greatly prostrated by the sudden demise of her husband, who has never manifested any tendencies toward weakness of the lungs. Four young children are left to mourn the loss of a father. On Wednesday, a mass was celebrated in the Catholic Church, after which the remains were taken to the city for interment.

Death of T.J. BOWERS
Former Superior Judge of Marin County

A great many people in this county on Monday heard with sorrow the announcement of the death of Ex-Judge T.J. BOWERS, formerly of San Rafael, and recently of San Francisco, where he died at his residence, 1825 Hyde Street, on Saturday.

He was born in Nashville, TN, in 1828, where he studied law and was admitted to the bar. He came to California in 1850, and settled in Nevada County for a time, removing from there to Sierra County in 1854, where he practiced law until 1868, when he was appointed Chief Justice of Idaho by JOHNSON. He presided in that until relieved of the position in the year following by a change in the administration, when he returned to this state and settled in Marin County. Here he was District Attorney for three successive terms, and upon the adoption of the new constitution in 1879, was elected Superior Judge, and upon the expiration of his term in 1884, he came to San Francisco and practiced law there up to the time of his death.

Last year, Judge BOWERS was a candidate for the nomination for Superior Judge on the Democratic ticket, and subsequently was before the people for a police judgeship, but was unsuccessful in both instances.

He was one of the leaders in the movement known as the Butte County compromise in 1865 when the Democratic party was divided into two factions. He was involved instrumentally in which harmony was restored in the party ranks.

He was a leading Mason, and had held high and frequent office in the lodges of that order, which had charge of the funeral exercises from the Masonic Temple on Tuesday at 1:30 o'clock.

Heart failure, which he had long anticipated, was the cause of death. He arose Saturday morning feeling comparatively well, but was soon compelled to return to his bed and the end came shortly afterward.

Local Brevities
HUGH WALKER of the Central Hotel has been attached, and is going through insolvency proceedings.

LOUIS R. CARRIGAN and ADA MAUD RODDEN will be married at the residence of the bride's father next Monday morning. There will be a reception in the afternoon.

Marriage Licenses
  JOHN A. STEEN, 24, Sacramento, to Mrs. ANNIE STEEN, 26, Sacramento
  CHARLES J. DOWD, 29, Mill Valley, to Miss EMMA KRATZENSTEIN, 29

Superior Court
  People vs. W.B. WINN
  Libel – over two weeks

  People vs. A. BIERCE
  Libel – plea not guilty

  WILLIAM LEARY vs.. JAMES FAGAN
  Motion to dismiss granted

  M. HERZOG vs. J.M. TERRY
  Judgment for plaintiff

  Estate of M. COBB, deceased
  Account settled and estate distributed

  H. WALKER vs. His Creditors
  Sheriff appointed receiver in bond of $250

  CHARLES HARLAN etux vs. Their Creditors
  Continued to September 5th

Real Estate Transfers
  WARREN DUTTON and wife to CORDELIA OSBORNE
  Lot 13 and W ½ lot 14, Block 15, Tomales - $125

  W.H. DAVIES and wife to FRANKLIN P. BALL
  Lots 7 and 8, Block H, Novato - $10

  FRANKLIN P. BALL and wife to M.E. ESSNER
  Lots 7 and 8, Block H, Novato - $10

  JOHN DOUGHTY to EDWARD C. BARTLETT
  E part of lot 43 and 44, Block A, Sausalito Land & Ferry Co. - $3,000

  A.C. McALLISTER and wife to ELIAS C. LUND etal
  Lot on E line of Looten's place S of Fourth Street - $10

  FRANK G. WATERHOUSE and wife to M.M. SIBREAN
  Lot 3, Grande Vista tract - $250

  JAMES TUNSTEAD etal to ROSA C. GREEN
  Lot on SW corner 3rd and Irwin St., San Rafael - $10

  Home and Farm Co. to J.T. ANDERSON
  Ptn. Lot 11, Division C, Novato Rancho - $10

JOHANNA REDMOND to MARY E. REDMOND etal
Redmond Ranch, Marin County – Gift

Estate of PETER WEBER to ANNIE WEBER
207.47 acres on N line of Alice Street – Distribution

SARAH SPAULDING to C.H. DWINELLE
Lot 9, block 24, Golden Meadow, San Rafael - $280

C.H. DWINELLE to HARRY FRANCES
Lot 6, block 35, Golden Meadow, San Rafael - $150

ELIAS C. LUND and wife to JENNIE LYONS
NW corner of H.C. LUND lot, San Rafael - $10

Letter List

BERI, W.	BOWEN, M.
BLASINGAME, J.A.	BARNETT, A.
BACON, F.E.	CAMLIN, T.J.
CYPHERS, C.	EDEN, B.
GRANGE, C.	GONZALES, N.
HOOPER, C.A.	KEELER, J.B.
LAWTON, G.F.	METZ, A.
LOFSTROM, I.	MORAIS, M.
PIERCE, M.	PETERS, J.A.W.
ROBINSON, A.T.	SCHAFER, BECKIE
SHAFTER, R.B.	SCHLOPER, Dr.
SUTTON, ---	JOHNSON, ---
VICTORINO, J.	JESSARICH, T.M.
WATKINS, E.	VALESQUEZ, I.M.
WRIGHT, M.M.	WHITE, A.

Died
MALLON – In San Rafael, August 28th, CHARLES E. MALLON, beloved husband of HONORA M. MALLON, and son of the late PATRICK MALLON, a native of San Francisco, aged 30 years, 3 months, and 1 day.

Marin Journal
Thursday, September 7, 1893

Local Brevities
W.H. SMITH and son have sold out their drug business here and will locate near St. Helena where they purchased a $14,000 fruit ranch and nursery.

Mr. JOSEPH G. ZUMINI, lately of Valley Ford and now of Tomales, was in town yesterday on business connected with his new hotel enterprise at Tomales. Mr. ZUMINI has leased the Keyes Hotel and will open it at once as a first class hostelry.

Born
COCHRANE – In San Rafael, September 4, 1893, to the wife of P. COCHRANE, a daughter.

Tomales Letter
Mrs. GRAHAM, who formerly resided in Tomales many years since, is now spending a while here visiting her friends.

Mrs. Dr. RIORDAN, after spending three weeks here with her parents, Mr. and Mrs. HOLLAND, returned to her home Sunday at Oroville.

Mr. MELZER OSBORNE, formerly a Marin County Supervisor, and now a mine owner of Arizona, is in Tomales on a visit to his many friends.

Dr. D.E. VAUGHAN, a brother of our station agent, and who has been in Humboldt County for awhile, is stopping for a few days in Tomales.

Mrs. HALL of Stoney Point died Sunday. She was the mother of our most estimable friend, Mrs. A. WOODWORTH, to whom we extend our deepest sympathies in her terrible loss. Mrs. HALL, having recently erected a very fine house, had only been in it for a few weeks. She was estimated to be worth a half million dollars.

JOHN GUAY, the wide-awake liveryman, is putting up a new business house adjoining his stable.

A Brilliant Wedding

On Monday, LOUIS R. CARRIGAN of the wealthy San Francisco firm of Dunham, Carrigan, & Co., was united in marriage to Miss ADA MAUD RODDEN, one of the most beautiful and accomplished young ladies of San Rafael, and one of the most successful instructors in the San Francisco Normal School. Miss RODDEN graduated from this college two years ago, but was immediately called to fill one of the most responsible positions in that institution on account of the high abilities she displayed in those qualifications required to make a successful normal school instructor.

She is not only a teacher, but a musician as well, and her beautiful contralto voice has delighted many an audience, both here and in San Francisco. Besides her ability as a vocalist, she also plays the piano and violin with rare skill, and these and other accomplishments joined to an amiable and unselfish disposition, have made her a general favorite in any circle where circumstances may have placed her.

The wedding took place at the home of the bride's father, Judge G.W. RODDEN, on the corner of Bay View and Marin Streets. WILLIAM CARRIGAN, brother of the groom, acted as best man, the maid of honor being Miss EDNA RODDEN, the sister of the bride. The ceremony was performed by Rev. Father McQUAID of the San Rafael Catholic Church.

The wedding ceremony and breakfast was witnessed only by relatives, who were: Mr. and Mrs. GEORGE RODDEN, Dr. and Miss EDNA RODDEN, Mrs. HUNT, and Mrs. BELLINGHAM (aunt and grandmother of the bride), Mr. F. LUX, Dr. F. WILLIAM LUX, Mrs. BRAGG, Messrs. GEORGE and A.L. LUX, Rev. Father McQUAID, Rev. Dr. NOBLE and his wife, Mr. ANDREW CARRIGAN and wife, Miss CARRIGAN, Mr. WILLIAM CARRIGAN, Messrs. JOHN and CLARENCE and Master JOSEPH CARRIGAN, Mrs. EDWIN HARRIS, and Miss GRANT, and Mr. and Mrs. W.C. KIRKOTERS.

Letter List

AHERD, A.	BOSSERMAN, C.H.
AYERS, BIRDIE	HELLER, M.
CONKLIN, E.	KAMOOL, ---
JANSON, A.	LE COUNT, ---
MURBACH, A.	MORRIS, ---
McDONALD, A.	NORDEN, L.
ROSME, E.	RESCH, M.R.
REAKLE, J.	SHAFFER, R.E.
SHORB, S.	SILVERMAN, J.
SCHMIDT, R.	WATKINS, E.
RYAN, M.	WALLIS, H.B.

Foreign

BELGARI, G.	BERDUGO, G.
GIACOMINI, T.	MELANO, A.
NIPPERT, L.	PORTO, DAL
PALOGGI, A.	SODRE, M.V.
SPALETTO, E.	FLOUAN, W.

Married
CARRIGAN-RODDEN – In San Rafael, September 4th, 1893, by Rev. Father McQUAID and Rev. W.B. NOBLE, LOUIS R. CARRIGAN of San Francisco to Miss ADA MAUD RODDEN of San Rafael.

Died
KENNEDY – In San Rafael, September 1, 1893, MARY ELLEN KENNEDY, a native of Benecia, aged 27 years.

LEON – At the County Hospital, September 2, 1893, F.G. LEON, a native of Chile, aged 87 years.

Marin County Tocsin
Saturday, September 9, 1893

Superior Court

Estate of C. MURRAY, deceased
Decree of Final Distribution ordered

Estate of HENRY EVANS, deceased
Will admitted to probate
Letters testamentary issued to MARIA L. LUCAS

Estate of W.W. GEARY, deceased
JAEMS E. WALSH appointed Administrator, bond $5,500

People vs. Sausalito Land & Ferry Co.
Set for trial for October 17, 1893

P.A. DE FRIEZE vs. LEANDER QUINT
Demurrer to answer overruled

CHARLES HARLAN et uxor vs. Their Creditors
Further hearing continued to September 18th

P. GALLAGHER vs. His Creditors
Petition to set apart certain personal property submitted and taken under consideration

Real Estate Transfers

J.L. BRADBURY to M.A. HAYCOCK
Lots 14 and 15, Block 2, Belvedere - $2,500

MINDORA L. BERRY to JENNIE T. DAVIS
Lot 12, Block 7, Belvedere - $5

R. BULLIS and wife to Marin County
Right of way for road on Pt. San Pedro - $352

Estate of J. McM. SHAFTER, deceased
Order confirming sale of Olema Ranch to P.J. SHAFTER - $12,600
Order confirming sale of Riverside Ranch to C. RIGHETTI - $8,000

J.D. SAUNDERS to JAMES TUNSTEAD & HEPBURN WILKINS
Lot corner of Tamalpais Ave. and Fifth Street, San Rafael, correcting former deed

JAMES TUNSTEAD and wife to Marin County
Right of way over ranch near Pt. Reyes Station - $175

ELLEN FORD to Marin County
Right of way over ranch on Pt. San Pedro Road - $352

Indianapolis Furniture Co. to G. KLEINCLAUS
Two lots on San Geronimo Creek - $10

C.E. BASEBE to ROSA BASEBE
Lots 6 and 11, Block T, Larkspur - $10

Belvedere Land Co. to Miss JENNIE T. DAVIS
Lot 12, Block 7, Belvedere - $10

Local News

W.E. ZANDER, formerly manager of the Hotel Rafael, is one of the sufferers of hard times. He has filed his petition in insolvency in San Francisco.

W.H. SMITH has exchanged his fine drug establishment for a ranch at St. Helena, and will give possession to the new proprietors about October 1st. The people of San Rafael will regret to lose the gentleman, who stands in high favor here with everyone.

We are sorry to note the financial difficulties of another old resident of Marin County, D.L. HAYDEN. The gentleman was more or less involved by the DeLONG failure, and the present unparalleled condition of the money market did the rest. Under ordinary conditions, Mr. HAYDEN could have carried the load and met his obligations, but with things as they are, he had no recourse, save to face the situation.

Notice to Creditors
    Estate of HENRY EVANS, deceased
    September 4, 1893
    E.B. MAHON, Attorney for Executrix
                             MARIA L. LUCAS
                             Executrix of the last Will

Marin Journal
Thursday, September 14, 1893

    Local Brevities

Mr. O.W. GROVE, of San Joaquin Valley, brother of Dr. GROVE, visited the latter the first of the week.

Mr. JAMES A. PENDERGAST, once a prominent rancher at Pt. Reyes, now in business in San Francisco, was in San Rafael on Saturday and Sunday last.

Mr. KELLY, who is one of the pioneer lodgers of Mrs. JORDAN's Hotel, the Cypress Villa, will start for the eastern states in about a month, where he expects to remain.

Mrs. COIT returned this week from an extended visit with relatives and friends in England. She had a most delightful visit, and returns to San Rafael in the best of health and spirits.

Mrs. E. GRIFFIN is with her daughter, Mrs. PHILLIPS, in the city for a few days.

JAMES SOLDATI made a shipment of 1600 pounds of butter this week off his ranch.

Mrs. MARY DILLON, who has been spending a week with her father, Mr. IRVIN, returned home Saturday.

JOE SOLDATI has sold his interest in the ranch to his brother JAMES SOLDATI, and has moved to Pt. Reyes.

Letter List

ADAMS, G.	ANDREW, B.
BUCHANAN, A.	BUYERS, ---
BELLOW, J.M.	BREEN, WILLIAM
BORBECK, H.E.	CLARK, J.B.
DENNIS, M.E.	ENGLEFIELD, ---
FLINT, N.	FREMONT, M.
FISH, S.	GRADY, M.
HOGAN, J.E.	HOATMESTER, A.K.
HOVELAND, J.L.	JOHNSON, A.
JEWELL, B.	JOST, M.
KRAMER, J.H.	KERLOOR, J.G.
KOCH, H.	KIRMAN, J.
LYNN, W.	LOUHEED, C.
LARSEN, M.A.	MILLER, E.C.
NOBLE, H.H.	PALACHI, G.
PETERSEN, J.	PLARITZ, F.V.
ROBINSON, C.J.	RICHARDSON, R.
SMITH, J.H.	WALSH, J.H.
WALLISER, T.	WHITE, M.V.

The Supervisors
    Liquor Licenses were awarded to
        MARIE PERILLAT – Ross Landing
        ANDREW NICHOLS – Sausalito
        ANTONIO BOSSI – San Rafael
        J.P. LACERDA – San Rafael
        G. ZUMINI – Tomales
        JOHN KENNEDY – Ignacio
    Appointed County Physician
        Dr. W.J. WICKMAN

Funeral
The funeral of Mrs. BRADY took place here Thursday last. Mrs. BRADY has resided for the last 4 years at Sausalito. The funeral services were conducted by Rev. Father VALENTINI. A large number of dear friends and acquaintances were present to listen to the touching remarks of the priest. Mrs. BRADY was the wife of the late EDWARD BRADY, and formerly resided in Tomales, where she reared a family of children, of which 4 survive her, viz: Mrs. H. COLLINS, Miss MAGGIE, JOHN E., and JAMES BRADY. The two boys are bright and energetic conductors on the N.P.C. Railway. A large crowd of Tomales friends had congregated at the depot to meet the funeral train, and went in the long procession to the church.

Marin County Tocsin
Saturday, September 16, 1893

    Notice to Creditors
        Estate of FRANKLIN J. WHITE, deceased
        August 18, 1893
                MARY V. WHITE
                Administratrix of estate

    Notice to Creditors
        Estate of JOHN C. GIBSON, deceased
        August 8, 1893
        HEPBURN WILKINS, Attorney for Administrator
                RICHARD E. GIBSON
                Administrator of estate

    Notice to Creditors
        Estate of SYDNEY F. BOYLE, deceased
        August 31, 1893
        HEPBURN WILKINS, Attorney for Administratrix
                CARMELITA N. BOYLE
                Administratrix of estate

    Notice to Prove Will
        Estate of JOSEPH RAULINO, deceased
        August 31, 1893
        HEPBURN WILKINS, Attorney for Petitioner
        Application by CAROLINA B. RAULINO for letters testamentary
                THOMAS S. BONNEAU, Clerk

    Adjudication of Insolvency
        Matter of HUGH WALKER, an Insolvent Debtor
        August 28, 1893
                F.M. ANGELLOTTI
                Judge of Superior Court

Local News
LACERDA and VIERRA are the new proprietors of the German Hotel

WILLIAM T. BUTTERWORTH has opened a harness shop at 731 Fourth Street.

Mr. TOGNAZZI, of Olema, died there suddenly last Tuesday from a stroke of apoplexy.

JAMES ROY, of San Geronimo, is lying dangerously ill at the residence of DAVID WARDEN in San Rafael.

The creditors of FRED KRUSE met at the Courthouse last Monday and elected J.F. SCHLINGMAN, of Mill Valley, assignee.

MYLES O'DONNELL, of the Sausalito News, has retired from the scene of his former triumphs, and is now located in Contra Costa County.

A dairyman by the name of GIACOMINI, while returning from Petaluma to his home in Marin County on September 8th, was thrown from a runaway team and instantly killed.

A tennis tournament at the Hotel Rafael ended last Saturday with brilliant playing. Miss HOOPER, formerly of San Rafael wrested the lady championship of the Coast from Miss MORGAN, and the HARDY brothers defeated Messrs. DeLONG and STETSON in the doubles.

FRANK SUTTON has been appointed to a position in the Custom House by Collector WISE, and is now on duty. Mr. SUTTON, besides being an old resident and a respected citizen, has been one of the most faithful and unselfish party men in Marin County. Everybody seems pleased that his modest and untiring services have been fitly recognized.

The little 2 year old daughter of District Attorney COCHRANE is desperately ill, and hovering between life and death. Every resource of medical science is being exhausted to save the poor little sufferer, but at present her condition is extremely critical. There is a universal hope that Mr. and Mrs. COCHRANE may be spared the threatened desolation of their home.

Died
WINSLOW – In San Rafael, September 15, 1893, Mrs. MARGARET WINSLOW, aged 72 years, 9 months and 3 days.

Superior Court
    People vs. W.B. WINN
    By consent, continued to September 25th

    F. KRUSE vs. His Creditors
    J.F. SCHLINGMAN elected assignee by creditors – bond $1,000

    AMANDA TANN vs. The Patent Brick Co. etal
    Continued to October session

Real Estate Transfers
    HONORA M. MALLON to THOMAS J. BIGGINS
    Lot on east side of E Street south of Third Street, San Rafael - $5

    THOMAS J. BIGGINS to GUSTA HERZOG
    Lot on east side of E Street south of Third Street, San Rafael - $10

    GUSTAV SCHRODER and wife to ADOLPH BARKAN
    Lots 308, 309, and 310, Tamalpais Land & Water Co. - $10

Marin Journal
Thursday, September 21, 1893

Death
The death of Mrs. WILLIAM O.L. CRANDALL of Olema has left a lasting impression upon the minds of the old and young. Mrs. CRANDALL did her whole duty, shirked no part of it, sought out the sick, nursed them to health and strength, never asked if the disease was infectious or contagious. A devout Methodist, she did everything to establish good. She was a Sunday school teacher for 19 years, helping establish the only Sunday school in this valley up to the present time. The funeral service was read by Rev. Mr. MAYNE in the Methodist Episcopal Church.

Was it Murder

Coroner EDEN held an inquest on Tuesday over the head that was found near Sausalito on September 14th enclosed in a wire netting. LAURA ALLEN and W.K. DeJARNATT of Colusa positively identified the head as that of Miss ADDIE GILMOUR of Colusa, who conducted a millinery establishment there with Miss ALLEN. It seems that Miss GILMOUR came to San Francisco about three weeks ago to buy a stock of millinery for her store at Colusa, and obtained permission from F. TOPLITZ of 571 Market Street to trim the hats at his store. She was last seen alive on September 4th. She roomed at the Elmer House in San Francisco. Miss ALLEN and Mr. DeJARNATT identified the head by its shape, hair and teeth. Dr. WICKMAN is inclined to the belief that the head shows marks of the dissecting room, and is the head of a man about 40 years old. A few days ago, portions of a woman's body was washed ashore near Alameda. It is possible the head and portions of the body found belong to the same woman. No record can be found of the death of Miss GILMOUR.

Tomales Letter

Miss EDITH KEYES is spending a week with her aunt, Mrs. TUNSTEAD, at San Anselmo.

E.H. KOWALSKY, a commission merchant of San Francisco, spent Sunday last in our town.

Miss LULU HUFF spent last week with her parents at Hamlet, returning to the city Saturday.

Mrs. J. BUCHANAN left Tuesday of last week for a months visit to her son at Sacramento who is U.S.M. messenger out of that city.

We are sorry to note the death of Mrs. A.P. GAVER, the wife of the well known capitalist of Valley Ford, and who is also a large stockholder and director of the Tomales Bank. Mrs. GAVER was only sick 4 days in confinement. She was before marriage, a Miss CUNNINGHAM, from near Santa Rosa, and all through her life she was a model lady, and to know her was to love her. She was a devoted wife and a loving mother. She had only been married about 5 years and leaves a little girl about 3 years of age and an infant boy of but a few hours. The funeral took place Sunday last at Bloomfield, where numbers of her relatives and friends paid their last earthly respects.

Real Estate Transfers

    Estate of J. McM. SHAFTER to EDMUND BROWN
    Lot 14, Block 17, Inverness - $125

    FRANK S. DUARTE and wife to EDWIN BEARN
    Portion of Block 4, Tomales - $10

Letter List

BAMBER ---	BARONE, BELLE
BOGGENBARE, A.	CURTIS, C.W.
HEALY, M.	LAWTON, G.W.
KENNEDY, N.	MACKIN, J.
MURPHY, M.	MERCER, EDWIN
MULLER, B.	McINTOSH, A.
MOSSOP, W.S.	REYNOLDS, JAMES
ROSE, A.	SARATTE, JON
SYLVESTER, A.	WELSH, M.
TACHIRIA, ---	WINSTEDT, H.
WALKER, W.J.	

                    Foreign

COPA, M.	BELGERI, G.
RODRIGUES, J.M.	BRAZIL, A.M.
PALOGGI, A.	BROOKS, J.T.

Superior Court

    CHARLES HARLAN etux vs. Their Creditors
    Opposition discharge of insolvents overruled

    Estate of JAMES M. DONAHUE, deceased
    Widow and child for partial distribution denied

P. GALLAGHER vs. His Creditors
H. HARRISON elected assignee in bond of $1,000

Estate of JOSEPH RAULINO, deceased
Will admitted to probate, CAROLINA RAULINO appointed executrix

A.F. BRANCO vs. J.E. BETTENCOURT
Default entered, Judgment for plaintiff

Born
VRANG – In Ross Valley, September 19, 1893, to the wife of Mr. VRANG, a daughter.

DAVENPORT – In San Rafael, September 18, 1893, to the wife of Lt. J. P. DAVENPORT, a daughter.

Died
WOLF – In San Rafael, September 17, 1893, LESTER WOLF, aged 2 years.

WINSLOW – In San Rafael, September 15, 1893, Mrs. MARGARET WINSLOW, aged 72 years, 9 months, 2 days.

CRANDALL – In Olema, September 15, 1893, Mrs. DOLLIE MARIA CRANDALL, aged 76 years, 11 days.

JEPSON – In San Rafael, September 15, 1893, MARGARETH FRANCES JEPSON, aged 2 months.

RAEDANIDA – In San Rafael, September 13, 1893, GANGICHA RAEDANIDA, aged 1 month and 25 days.

ROY – In San Rafael, September 20, 1893, JAMES ROY, of San Geronimo, aged 58 years, 5 months.

TOGNAZZI – In Olema, September 13, 1893, PETER TOGNAZZI, a native of Switzerland, aged 41 years.

Marriage Licenses
    J.R. HADDEN, 21, Oakland to Miss FLORA HOLTON, 21, San Francisco
    EUGENE G. GREUET, 22, San Francisco, to Miss JESSIE McMANUS, 21
    JOAS SILVEIRA AVILLA, 27, Sausalito, to Miss MARY TERRIS, 16, Sausalito

Local Brevities
Mr. PEACOCK, of the firm PEACOCK & DuBOIS, will occupy Mr. STALFORD's Cottage on Bayview Street shortly.

Mr. WILLIAM P. BEGGS of San Francisco was in San Rafael last Sunday on a visit. He was the guest of C. ROY BARNEY.

The 2 year old daughter of D.A. COCHRANE, who has been very ill from pneumonia, is now out of danger and on the road to rapid recovery.

Mr. A.H. STINSON of San Jose was in San Rafael last week. He was the guest of CHARLES S. BARNEY.

Marin County Tocsin
Saturday, September 23, 1893

Local News
GEORGE AGNEW & J. BUSTIN have formed a partnership in the express business. Transferring, heavy hauling, etc. attended to.

Dr. W.K. VANCE has been appointed Medical Examiner of the Druid's Grove, San Rafael, also of the Northwestern Mutual Life Insurance Co., in succession to Dr. F.J. WHITE, deceased.

Coroner EDEN had a pleasant task last Wednesday in the matter of certifying to the bones of a dozen Chinese convicts buried in the prison cemetery at San Quentin, whose considerate friends wished to ship them to the Flowery Kingdom.

Mystery Solved

The mystery of the head that was found on the beach near Sausalito, has been solved. Through a chain of remarkable circumstances, it is practically certain that it is a part of the body of Miss ADDIE GILMOUR, a milliner of Colusa, that she was murdered, and that her slayer was a physician by the name of E.F. WEST, now in custody. Dr. WEST is a professional abortionist. It is believed that the unfortunate young woman was lured to his house by one of the advertisements that disgrace the San Francisco papers, that she there submitted to a criminal operation at his hands, and died from the effects of it. Dr. WEST then came up with the idea of cutting up the body and disposing of it. The main facts have been admitted to by the Dr.

Real Estate Transfers

> WILLIAM N. SHELLEY and wife to MICHAEL O'BRIEN
> Land on north line of County Road from Alto to Eastland - $10
>
> MARTHA PATTERSON etal to JOHN C. SPENCER
> Lots 1 and 2, Block 2A, Tamalpais Land & Water Co. - $10
>
> JAMES TUNSTEAD etal to SUSIE A. ROCHE
> Lot on south side Fifth Street east of Tamalpais Ave., San Rafael - $10
>
> Sausalito Bay Land Co. to BERTHA LABORDE
> Lot 15, Block 14, Old Sausalito - $10
>
> JOHANN C. GIESKE etal to CHARLES S. BARNEY etal
> Lot 2, Block 27, Townsite San Rafael - $10
>
> CHARLES S. BARNEY etal to J.C. GIESKE etal
> Lot on East B Street north of Second Street - $10
>
> HARRIET B. SHAVER, admx. To HENRY CASSANS
> Lot on south side Fourth Street east of Ida Street, San Rafael - $450
>
> HENRY CASSANS to G.B. DONDERO
> Lot on south side Fourth Street east of Ida Street, San Rafael - $10
>
> Belvedere Land Co. to FLORENCE C. MOORE
> Lots 11 and 12, Block 3, Belvedere - $10

Marin Journal
Thursday, September 28, 1893

Drowned While Drunk

On Tuesday Coroner EDEN held an inquest over the remains of the Swedish sailor, JOHN QUIST, who was found on the beach at Sausalito on Saturday last. The testimony showed that the night before, QUIST was very drunk in the saloons of Sausalito, and about midnight, when the saloons were shut up, was left to wander by himself. He was a sealer, and had come to Copper Island on the schooner Mattie Dwyer. After his companions left him, he probably wandered down to the beach, influenced by an unconscious desire to go on board his schooner anchored in the bay. Becoming drowsy, he lay down on the beach, the tide came up, and the poor wretch was drowned. The body was buried yesterday by the Coroner in the poor farm cemetery.

The funeral of Mr. JAMES ROY of Nicasio, who died last week from inflammation of the stomach, was held last Saturday from the Presbyterian Church and was largely attended, Rev. Dr. NOBLE officiating. The deceased was widely known and eminently respected, he being one of the ROY brothers, comprising two of the most enterprising and successful ranchers in Nicasio township. The deceased was unmarried. The remains will be taken back to Vermont for interment.

Miss KITTIE HUNDLY, who has very pleasantly spent the summer here with the Misses HOLLAND, returned to her home Friday last in Oakland.

Removed to San Rafael
Dr. W.K. VANCE has stepped into the vacancy of physician caused by the death of our popular physician. Dr. VANCE comes from Anglo-Irish stock, and received his early training at Wesley College, in Dublin. In 1868 he entered Apothecaries' Hall, and matriculated at the Royal Irish University, winning a scholarship in literature and ancient classics. After three years at the University, a fourth term was passed in Royal College of Surgeons, Dublin. A fifth course was taken out in London, at several hospitals, also microscopy, and surgery was studied at Cook's Laboratory. The Dr. became a resident Medical Officer of Wandsworth Provident Dispensary, London, an institution boasting a clientele of 4,000 members. He desires to be considered a practitioner of rational medicine and surgery. He has delivered several lectures in the Sonoma High School upon literary and scientific subjects.

Local Brevities
H.P. BOSTWICK is the happiest man in town now. It's a fine boy of 9 pounds which his wife presented him Thursday last.

Another happy man in town is our local butcher, Mr. ED BEAN, whose wife presented him with a son last Sunday morning.

HORACE ABLES left Friday last for Ontario, CA, where he enters school for a term.

It is said that we are now assured of another physician in the person of Dr. SPEDDING, who we believe has bought out Dr. STEPHEN.

ALEXANDER MONTGOMERY has donated $50,000 for the erection of a beautiful chapel at San Anselmo in connection with the Theological Seminary. A.W. FOSTER will have charge of the erection of the building and beautifying the grounds.

A Model Guardian
A guardian's account was filed in Superior Court this week. The guardian, NATHAN H. STINSON, is a former resident of this county, now residing in San Jose. The name of the ward is ARCHIE A. UPTON. In 1880, Mr. STINSON received form the Estate of JAMES W. UPTON, $2,526.20. The interest on this at 6% to September 1, 1893, was $2,373.70, making a total of $4,899.90. The ward is his step-son, and since the time he was appointed guardian, Mr. STINSON has charged himself with all the interest on the money received by him, and has also expended large sums for the support and education of young UPTON, who has completed a course of study at Ann Arbor. Mr. STINSON had defrayed all fees in the matter of guardianship, and turned over the $4,899.90 to his step-son.

Miss MINNIE HEALY, for the past 15 months in the dry goods store of H.A. GORLEY of this place, has accepted a situation of the same character in the dry goods establishment of J.J. O'BRIEN & Co. in San Francisco.

Rev. J.H. GARDNER, a Presbyterian clergyman, has rented the BUNDY house near the West End depot.

Mrs. F.J. WHITE has rented her house unfurnished to Mr. LOUIS BLANKENHORN of San Francisco for one year.

Mr. RICHARDSON, the chemist for the new drug firm of INMAN & Sons, has rented the BARSTOW cottage on Fourth Street.

Superior Court
    JESSIE E. BARNETT vs. JOSIAH BARNETT
    Default of defendants entered

    Estate of MARY SILVEIRA, deceased
    Notice to Creditors ordered

    Estate of A.H. UPTON, deceased
    Final account of guardian settled and guardian discharged

    P. GALLAGHER vs. His Creditors
    Certain property set apart for insolvent

FRED KRUSE vs. His Creditors
Amt. of keepers and sheriffs fees - $130, Attorney fees - $39

Estate and guardianship of M. and R. RAULINO
Over till Friday

County of Marin vs. R. FURLONG & Co. vs. M. BLUMENTHAL
Demurrer set for hearing

Marriage Licenses
GEORGE THOMSON, 21, Oakland to MATTIE WRIGHT, 28, Oakland
CLYDE N. BROWN, 21, Petaluma, to JANE FRANCES BOYD, 16, San Rafael
FRED J.R.M. TREWEEK, 32, San Francisco, to MARY M. FAIRBANKS, 24, San Francisco
ALONZO PRITCHARD, 21, Oakland, to Miss JENNIE C. WRIGHT, 18, Oakland

Letter List

BRUTON, J.	COLANN, M.
DEMERY, L.	HARNING, D.B.
KUNZ, J.	KLETZ, A.
MULLEN, A.	MEREDITH, G.
McKENNA, P.	PACHECO, V.
POWELL, B.G.	ROGALLE, A.
RUSSELL, M.	WEISLLI, E.
TILDEN, CHARLES	WOLF, A.

Married
BROWN-BOYD – In San Rafael, September 26, 1893, by Rev. Father McQUARRIE, CLYDE N. BROWN of Petaluma, and JANE FRANCES BOYD, of San Rafael

Born
ALBUGAZIO – In San Rafael, September 22, 1893, to the wife of DAMIAN ALBUGAZIO, a daughter.

WALL – In San Rafael, September 24, 1893, to the wife of J.H. WALL, a daughter.

Died
SHEEHY – In San Rafael, September 22, 1893, VERONICA DARLING SHEEHY, daughter of Ex-Trustee JOHN SHEEHY, aged 5 years and 8 months.

HEWITT – In San Rafael, September 21, 1893, ISABELLA HEWITT, aged 87 years.

QUIST – At Sausalito, September 24, 1893, JOHN QUIST, a native of Sweden, aged 85 years.

Marin County Tocsin
Saturday, September 30, 1893

Local News
H.B. VOGEL, one of our old citizens, has left San Rafael, having purchased the interest of C.H. DEXTER in the San Rafael Yacht Club bar and restaurant.

VERONICA SHEEHY, the 5 year old daughter of JOHN SHEEHY Esq., died last Friday after a long and painful illness. She was a bright, loveable little child, and her loss is keenly felt by her parents, who have the earnest sympathy of their many friends.

Notice of Co-Partnership
Business to be known as ATWATER & CRIMMINS
EDWIN L. ATWATER & HENRY CRIMMINS
September 28, 1893
THOMAS S. BONNEAU
Clerk

Marin Journal
Thursday, October 5, 1893

Death of WALTER SHORT

On Thursday, WALTER E. SHORT, oldest son of O.B. SHORT, passed away at his home at San Anselmo, after a lingering illness from slow consumption. The deceased was one of the most estimable young men of the county, and the large attendance at the funeral was a slight index of the esteem in which he was held. He was a native of this county, his father having been a resident of this county for over 40 years. The remains were brought to the Catholic Church, where a mass was celebrated, after which the long procession wended its solemn way out to the Catholic Cemetery, where all that was mortal of the beloved son, brother, and friend, was laid to rest.

Under the Sod

The head and mutilated portion of the body of ADDIE GILMOUR were removed last week from the morgues of this and Alameda County to Colusa by the father and sister of the poor girl, whose horrible death and mutilation has so shocked the people of California. Last Sunday, the funeral over the remains was held in Colusa, and was very largely attended, the girl having hosts of friends, who condoned her errors in view of her awful fate.

Items of Interest

Larkspur Inn has closed for the season. Proprietors HEPBURN & TERRY have had a hard time of it, and have gone to San Francisco there to engage in the hotel business.

Mr. KELLY, who has been in San Rafael so long for the benefit of his health, leaves next Tuesday for Massachusetts, where he will remain unless the weather and climate prove too trying.

T.J. JUKES, the lessee of Willow Camp at Bolinas beach, was in town this week. Mr. JUKES' lease has run out, and he has not yet decided whether or not he will renew it for the reason that there is much doubt as to the building of the proposed narrow gauge train from Sausalito to the beach. If the road is built, Mr. JUKES does not want to renew his lease.

Tomales Letter

J.H. KNARSTON of Oakland was in town this week, a guest of M.L. MURPHY.

Mr. McMAHAN, who formerly resided in Tomales, and who has been living in Petaluma for a few years past, has returned to his old home and says Tomales is good enough for him.

Injured by Explosion

WILLIE BEACH, aged 7 years, met with a serious accident Monday afternoon which may cause the loss of both his eyes. He and several other boys were playing with a can of powder, which in some unaccountable manner, exploded, burning Beach's hands and face in a horrible manner.

BROWN-BOYD Nuptials
Petaluma Imprint

A quiet wedding took place in San Rafael yesterday, at which CLYDE N. BROWN of this city, and Miss JANE FRANCES BOYD were the high contracting parties. Only a few of the near relatives of both parties were present, and the news will be a great surprise to many Petaluma friends of the groom. Mr. BROWN was formerly the Petaluma correspondent of the Santa Rosa Democrat, and is a well known amateur musician.

Real Estate Transfers

JOHN T. LAND to J.C. WEIGHTMAN
Lots 3, 4, 13, & 14, Block 2, Sausalito Bay Land C0. - $800

JAMES TUNSTEAD etal to HENRY DALESSI
Lot on Fourth Street, west of Clark Street, San Rafael - $10

H.A. COBB, Exec. to MANUEL CONSTANT
Ptn. Block 8, Sausalito Land & Ferry Co. - $10

MANUEL CONSTANT to JOSE S. AVILLA
Ptn. Block 8, Sausalito Land & Ferry Co. - $10

Tamalpais Land & Water Co. to WILLIAM TERRY
Lot 84, Tamalpais Land & Water Co. - $400

Builder's Contract
ALEX MONTGOMERY with WILLIAM BARR
Memorial Chapel at San Anselmo - $17,500

ALEX MONTGOMERY with McKAY & McKENZIE
Memorial Chapel at San Anselmo - $14,500

First Presbyterian Church of San Rafael with WILLIAM BARR
Church building, corner E and Fifth Street - $11,500

First Presbyterian Church of San Rafael with McKAY & McKENZIE
Church building, corner E and Fifth Street - $12,500

JOHN T. COCHRANE with S.P. MOORHEAD
Cottage, corner C and Bayview Streets - $1,515

Marriage Licenses
THOMAS F. LOWNEY, 24, San Francisco to MARY MYERS, 26, San Francisco
C.B. HARTON, 38, San Francisco, to MILLIE BYERS TIBBEY, 22, Sausalito
DENNIS FAY, 40, Tehama County, to Miss MARY BUCKLEY, 38

Superior Court
M. GILLIGAN vs. H. WALKER etal
Judgment entered in favor of plaintiff
T.B. VALENTINE vs. JESSIE O. DEFFEBACH etal
Leave granted to withdraw defendants demurrer
Interlocutory degree ordered

Estate of JOHN GIACOMINI, deceased
JAMES BLOOM appointed administrator

E. WORMOUTH vs. J. GARDNER etal
Demurrer to amend complaint withdrawn

A.P. HOTALING vs. D. PARRISH
Demurrer overruled

People vs. WINN
Plea of not guilty entered

Letter List

BROOKS, J.F.	BRANDT, M.
BEST, D.	CROKER, A.
FOX, C.J.	HENLEY, F.
JOHNSTON, ---	JOHNSON, H.
KELLY, J.G.	LEARY, J.G.
MULLER, ---	MOGOLLO, F.M.
MILLER, A.	McKAY, ALEX
NELSON, E.	PHILLIPS, M.
ROSECRANS, W.S.	SULLIVAN, M.
THOMAS, G.W.	WHITE, W.J.

Born
SHELLY – In Greenbrae, September 30, 1893, to the wife of WILLIAM N. SHELLEY, a son

Died
SHORT – In San Anselmo, September 28, 1893, WALTER E. SHORT, aged 33 years, and 3 days, a native of San Rafael

Brevities

LEE HAKES, son of D. HAKES of Valley Ford, is now on a visit to his father. The young man was once an employee of the N.P.C., but now holds a position down in Utah as a station agent.

It is reported that JACK GANNON and DAN TAYLOR will shortly start for Chicago to look up GEORGE DICKSON and bring him home. A letter from Chicago states that GEORGE has lost his heart over the dancing girls in the Midway Plaisance. The report cannot be true, as GEORGE is too old a bird now to be caught in any way such as that. A good many girls have tried it, but GEORGE always skips away in time.

Marin County Tocsin
Saturday, October 7, 1893

Notice to Creditors
Estate of WILLIAM W. GEARY, deceased
October 5, 1893
JAMES E. WALSH, Admr.

Notice to Creditors
Estate of JOSEPH RAULINO, deceased
HEPBURN WILKINS, Attorney for Executrix
September 18, 1893
CAROLINA B. RAULINO, Executrix

Notice to Proving Will
Estate of BELLA F. SWISHER, deceased
JAMES W. COCHRANE, Attorney for Petitioner
October 3, 1893
D.T. TAYLOR, Deputy Clerk

Notice to Creditors
Estate of JOHN GIACOMINI, deceased
October 3, 1893
JAMES BLOOM, Administrator

Local News
Owing to the retirement of HUGH WALKER from the Central Hotel, that establishment is temporarily closed. Several parties are negotiating a new lease, and it will probably re-open in the course of a couple of weeks.

P. McDERMOTT has re-opened the Mulberry Restaurant. The best meals are served in town at popular prices.

A.L. HAM has sold the business of the San Rafael Express to Messrs. FITCH & CARROLL, of Oakland. They are old hands at the trade, Mr. FITCH having been for years the manager of the Whitney Express.

Board of Supervisors
Accepted resignation of F.F. PLANK as Constable of Tomales township

Granted licenses to sell liquor:
M. O'BRIEN – Alto Station
J. LAWDER – Sausalito
J.M. & J.P. SILVA – Novato

Real Estate Transfers
MARIA O. CRANDALL to WILLIAM O.L. CRANDALL
10.89 acres in Village of Olema - $10

JOHN W. MACKAY etal to S.F. & N.P. Railway Co.
Lot southeast corner of Petaluma and Mountain View Ave., San Rafael - $1

MARY M. KADEL to CORNELIUS O'LEARY
Lots 2 & 3, Block 24, Sausalito Land & Ferry Co. - $10

E.J. & H.M. McCHESNEY to FLORENCE HARRIES
Portion of lot 116, Tamalpais Land & Water Co. - $10

WOOD, CHRISTIESON & Co. to SYLVESTER PARKS
Lot 12, Block 54, Coleman's Ave., San Rafael - $10

Superior Court
E. WARMOUTH vs. J. GARDNER etal
Demurrer to amend complaint withdrawn

HUGH WALKER vs. His Creditors
M.F. COCHRANE appointed assignee

F.C. DeLONG etal vs. HENRY PIERCE
Tried, argued and submitted

Born
SHREVE – In San Rafael, September 19, 1893, to the wife of E.D. SHREVE, a son.

Marin Journal
Thursday, October 12, 1893

Local Brevities
Judge ANGELLOTTI has refused to allow the setting aside of FRANK C. DeLONG's estate as a homestead.

Superior Court
FOX vs. FOX
Application for alimony continued for 8 weeks

P. GALLAGHER vs. His Creditors
Application of GALLAGHER to set aside one horse, harness, and wagon denied

Oakland Iron Works vs. A.R. TUCKEY
Motion to strike out costs and motion to dismiss denied – cause for trial set

Marriage Licenses
WINTLER WOOD, 21, Novato, to IDA MAY BAYLES, 19, Oakland
F.A. HOLTON, 24, Oakland, to ADELLA L. BRAY, 21, Oakland
LOUIS F. GILMORE, 35, San Francisco, to Mrs. MINNIE GILMORE, 25, San Francisco
L.J. HARRISON, 35, Sausalito, to LAURA P. MASON, 25, Sausalito
FRANK J. HALL, 28, Pt. Reyes, to Miss JENNIE FLANAGAN, 18, San Rafael

Tomales Letter
CHARLES T. THOMPSON is the proud father of a fine baby girl, born last week. He is now on a visit to the city on business.

Dr. J.J. STEPHEN has sold out his practice here to Dr. SPEDDING, who comes well recommended. Dr. STEPHEN with his family and "the dogs" left for San Francisco Saturday.

All acquaintances of Mr. McADAMS, who was very well known in Tomales, will read with sorrow of his death. He was a man who worked hard for the good of the dairymen and who contracted the machinery for the Fallon creamery. He had built a fine creamery in Humboldt County where he died a few days since of pneumonia.

Items of Interest
Mr. ED MONDON, now of Los Angeles, was in San Rafael last week on a short visit.

The supervisors have granted Mrs. HOWARD of Marshall an allowance of $10 a month.

Mr. HENRY PETERSON has returned to San Rafael to remain, after a protracted stay in Los Angeles.

Real Estate Transfers
> JOHN McNAMARA and wife to E.H. SHOEMAKER
> Part of Lot 32, Block A, Sausalito Land & Ferry Co. - $10
>
> ISAAC JESSUP to JOSEPH ARBINI
> Portion of Jessup tract - $10

Death of an old Pioneer
On Thursday last, THOMAS SHAW, an old man of 75 years of age, died at the County Hospital, of which institution he had been an inmate for a long time. He was well known in this county, having been here since 1854. He was a printer, and was employed by the Journal, the first paper published by this county, when it was established in 1861. He has worked at odd jobs around town since the memory of almost the oldest inhabitant.

Died
SHAW – At the County Hospital, October 7, 1893, THOMAS SHAW, a native of Maryland, aged 75 years.

Letter List

ANDERSON, J.	BOYNE, A.
BENSON, J.	BEMEUDERFER, C.
DOMINGO, M.	GRIN, ---
GENGENBACH, ---	GEDERSEN, H.N.
JOHNSSON, ---	KENMAN, I.
MAHAR, J.	McGOVERN, P.
NIELSON, H.	O'MALLEY, A.
PETERSON, A.	RAEDVIDA, ---
SCHENGLE, A.G.	SMITH, J.
SMITH, J.H.	THEDERMAN, ---
DE SILVA, ---	DE SOUZA, M.

Marin County Tocsin
Saturday, October 14, 1893

Real Estate Transfers
> Home & Farm Co. to S.S. ROBISON
> 3 acres of Davidson's lot, Novato - $10
>
> JAMES W. SPERRY to ALFRED NILSON
> Lot 3, Sperry's subd. Block 2, Sausalito Land & Ferry Co. - $10
>
> Estate of ALFRED GROSS to LOUISA GROSS
> 6 acres on N side Ross Landing Road – distribution
>
> PAYNE J. SHAFTER to SAMUEL J. HOPKINS
> Allotment P, Subdivision Shafter Ranch at Olema - $10
>
> JAMES DONALDSON to ANN S. ROSS
> 57.25 acres - $5

Local News
F. FIEDLER, the well known Sausalito businessman, died in San Francisco last week, after a long and painful illness.

The wedding of Lt. FECHTELER of the U.S. Navy and Miss MAUD MORROW, daughter of Judge MORROW, will be solemnized next Monday at the residence of the bride's parents.

At the annual meeting of the Marin Central Labor Union last Monday night, the following officers were elected for the ensuing term: President, THOMAS BOLAND; Vice President, FRITZ IHLE; Recording Secretary, WILLIAM J. BOYD; Financial Secretary, T. HOCK; Treasurer, J. ALBERTI; Sergeant-at-Arms, F.T. BAILEY; Trustees, M. O'BRIEN, D.E. BAKER, J.W. BAGGI.

Mrs. THOMAS FLANAGAN was returning home last Wednesday from San Francisco when her husband boarded the car and approached her in a threatening manner. The woman is in mortal dread of the fellow, who is a desperate and dangerous man. Terrified by his menacing appearance, she fled screaming through the car and jumped off while it was at full speed, sustaining very serious injuries, from which she is slowly recovering. FLANAGAN's anger with his wife was because she has consented against his wishes to the marriage of her daughter to a highly respectable young man.

Superior Court
>F.C. DeLONG vs. HENRY PIERCE, assignee
>Judgment for defendant, assignee

>D.L. HAYDEN vs. his Creditors
>J.Q.A. HAVEN appointed assignee

>W.F. TIERNEY vs. His Creditors
>H. HARRISON appointed assignee

Board of Supervisors
>Liquor licenses granted:
>>J.D. BRAVO – San Rafael
>>A BOSSI – San Rafael

Married
HALL-FLANAGAN – In San Rafael, October 11, 1893, FRANK J. HALL of Pt. Reyes, and Miss JENNIE FLANAGAN, of San Rafael

Marin Journal
Thursday, October 19, 1893

Brilliant Wedding
The wedding of Lt. FECHTELER of Albatross to Miss MAUD MORROW was a most brilliant affair, and was witnessed by a large number who represented the beauty and culture of this county and San Francisco. The wedding occurred in St. Paul's Church on Monday at 12:30 o'clock, Rev. E.A. HARTMAN officiating. Miss BATES, a professional decorator, had transformed the sanctuary into a floral grotto or conservatory. Miss ELEANOR MORROW was maid of honor, and the bridesmaids were Miss RUGER and Miss McKENNA. FRANK FECHTELER, of New York, brother of the groom, was the best man. The ushers were Lt. LOUD of Boston, and Lt. RAMSEY and Ensigns WILSON and SHOEMAKER. The wedding breakfast was celebrated after the ceremony at the home of Judge MORROW. The music at the church was rendered by Dr. POWERS and his wife who played selections on the organ and violin.

Marriage Licenses
>FRANK FECHTELER, 36, San Rafael, to Miss MAUD MORROW, 20, San Rafael
>DANIEL J. RYAN, 41, Novato to BERTHA C. REDMOND, 30, Novato
>HENRY W. WHITELAW, 31, Stockton, to ETTA L. LEWIS, 28, San Gabriel

Found Dead
On Monday evening, word was brought to Coroner EDEN that a BODY was lying in the creek along the railroad track near the Patent brickyard. On Tuesday morning, the Coroner and his secretary, WALTER WALSH, started for the locality, but could not drive any nearer to it than two miles. With the assistance of some men who happened along, the body was carried to the wagon in a box and brought to town where an inquest was held Wednesday evening. The corpse was that of an old man at least 70 years of age, and well dressed, the underclothing being homemade. A silver watch, still running, lay on the bank of the creek, together with a hat, overcoat, and undercoat near it. The man was of medium height, and weighed about 120 pounds. His teeth are nearly gone. The sum of $4.25 was found in his pocket. No papers of any description were found, and his identity remains a mystery. The man was seen walking along the track the day of his death. It is either a case of suicide or else the old man laid down on the bank to rest and fell into the creek in a fit or while asleep.

Town Talk
Mr. DAVIES, formerly of San Rafael, but now residing in Los Angeles, was in San Rafael last week on a visit to his mother.

Mr. OSCAR FITCH, formerly of the Oakland Express Co. has bought out the express business of Mr. HAM. Mr. FITCH is an experienced man in the business and a rustler as well.

Tomales Letter
Mr. MORTON, a prominent farmer near Tomales, is reported being very sick with pneumonia with small hopes of his recovery.

Mrs. CHARLES PETERS of Santa Ana, has been spending several weeks with her daughter, Mrs. O. TURNER. She departed for her home Monday.

JAMES L. FALLON, formerly a resident of Tomales, but now of San Francisco, is spending a week here with his daughter, Mrs. E.J. CALLAN.

J.J. BUCHANAN, U.S. messenger of Sacramento, was called to his father's bedside here this week, the latter fell unconscious at an early hour Saturday afternoon, and up to this writing has not revived and little hope is entertained for his recovery.
Later:
Mr. BUCHANAN has died having been in an unconscious state since 5 o'clock Saturday afternoon without ever showing any indications of regaining consciousness, and apparently from the first, he was as though not suffering. He died at 3:35 Wednesday morning. The end came peacefully and without a struggle. His funeral will take place here at 2 p.m. Thursday.

Superior Court
  M.W. EICKHOFF vs. M. EICKHOFF
  Demurrer overruled

  Estate of ANNIE BRADY, deceased
  Letters of administration issued to J.E. BRADY

  Estate of JAMES ROY, deceased
  Over until October 30th

  CATHERINE GALLAGHER vs. H. HARRISON
  Set for trial October 23rd

  JAMES I. TAYLOR vs. his Creditors
  Demurrer sustained with leave to amend

  A.P. HOTALING vs. D. PARRISH
  Set for October 17th

  People vs. BIERCE and WINN
  Over for the term

  Estate of A. FORBES, deceased
  Continued to October 23rd, E. MARTINELLI appointed to examine accounts

  E. WORMOUTH vs. PETER GARDNER etal
  Motion for new trial argued and submitted

Marin County Tocsin
Saturday, October 21, 1893

  Dairy for Sale
    At Reed's Station
    Property same as heretofore used and possessed by JOSEPH RAULINO, JOHN ENOS SILVA, and MANUEL RODGERS as co-partners.
    Property for sale to dissolve partnership due to death of JOSEPH RAULINO
    October 18, 1893
        JOHN ENOS SILVA
        MANUEL RODGERS

Auction Sale
> Estate of HUGH WELKER, insolvent
> Personal property
> To be held Saturday, October 28, 1893
> > M.F. COCHRANE, Assignee

Local News

Messrs. FITCH & CARROLL have completed the purchase of the business of the San Rafael Express and are now in charge.

NEIL McISAACS has purchased a portion of the Olema Ranch, adjoining his tract lying between Tocaloma and the village of Olema.

J. SILBERSTEIN & Co. are about to remove to San Francisco, and are offering great bargains in dry goods.

FRANK PERARA, of Novato, has been adjudged insolvent by the Superior Court.

Mr. JOHN BUCHANAN, one of the old residents of Tomales, died there on Wednesday morning of this week from the effects of injuries to the head, received by a fall. Deceased was one of the jurymen drawn for the term of the Superior Court next Monday.

JAMES V. KELLY, one of the old original Tocsin compositors, returned from the East this week after a 2 years' absence from San Rafael. Mr. KELLY has been located in Chicago, and had a case in one of the big newspaper offices there, but he finally concluded that California was the only place fit to live in. He says he would rather die forthwith than face another Chicago winter.

MORROW - FECHTELER

The wedding of Lt. FECHTELER, of the U.S. Navy, and Miss MAUD MORROW, daughter of Judge W.W. MORROW, on Monday last, was a brilliant social event. The numerous Army and Navy officials were in full uniform and the assemblage included nearly every noted name in California.

Real Estate Transfers
> JAMES MARSHALL etal to Marin County
> Right of way over grantor's lands near Marshall Station - $200
>
> Tamalpais Land & Water Co. to ADA TURRELL
> Lot 193 - $1,600
>
> ADA TURRELL to HELEN R. DAVIDSON
> Lot 193, Tamalpais Land & Water Co. – gift
>
> JOHN W. MACKAY etal to MARCUS & JOSEPH ROSENTHAL
> Lands in Ross Valley - $5
> Portion of villa lots near San Rafael - $11,368
>
> WILLIAM T. COLEMAN and wife to GEORGE A. HUNNEWELL
> Lot on south side of Fourth Street, near Tamalpais Avenue - $10

The engagement is announced of Miss MINNIE FITZGERALD and EARLINGTON TRAXLER, both of San Rafael. The wedding will take place some time in December.

Auction Sale
> Personal Property of Mrs. T.J. O'BRYEN, San Rafael
> > GEORGE D. SHEARER
> > Public Auctioneer

P. McDERMOTT has re-opened the Mulberry Restaurant in San Rafael.

BURGESON Brothers, a well known firm of concrete men, have established themselves in San Rafael.

Died
MURPHY – In San Rafael, October 19, 1893, MARY M. MURPHY, dearly beloved mother of HANNAH MURPHY, Mrs. J.H. ROBERTSON, and the late Mrs. JAMES HUNTER and JOHN MURPHY, a native of Bandon, County Cork, Ireland, aged 79 years.

Marin Journal
Thursday, October 26, 1903

Unknown Dead
The BODY found last week at Lime Point remains unidentified. No clue was found to establish his identity.

The Supervisors
LUTHER E. MOORE was appointed constable of Tomales township.

BENNETT-BIXBY
The Santa Cruz Surf recently contained a full account of the wedding of FRANK P. BENNETT, son of Mrs. C.M. BENNETT of San Rafael, to Miss LELIA E. BIXBY, one of the most lovely and popular young ladies of Santa Cruz. The wedding occurred in the First Baptist Church, which was crowded with the friends of the contracting parties. Mr. BENNETT is an active young businessman of exemplary habits, and has recently purchased a pretty home in Santa Cruz whither he will take his bride on their return trip from their honeymoon.

Items of Interest
Miss MATTIE AUGUSTINE, formerly a teacher in the public schools of this county, and a sister of the cashier of the HOTALING bank, has recently been married in the East.

Superior Court
> Estate of WILLIAM DORR, deceased
> Administrator discharged
>
> SLINKEY vs. HARRISON
> To be set in November
>
> Estate of F. FIEDLER, deceased
> Letters issued to S.S. FIEDLER – bond $10,600
>
> Estate of E.A. STEMPLE, deceased
> Final account settled and estate distributed
>
> Estate of A. BEAN, deceased
> Account settled and estate distributed

Real Estate Transfers
> JAMES TUNSTEAD and wife to HENRY F. BRUNS
> Portion of Red Hill tract, adjoining THEODORE MUNDT
> Portion on Olema Road - $10
>
> Tamalpais Land & Water Co. to VAN LEER EASTLAND
> Lots 175, 176, 183, 184, 185, Tamalpais Land & Water Co. - $10
>
> Home & Farm Co. to S.S. ROBISON
> 3 acres, beginning at SE corner of Davidson's lot, Novato – $10
>
> JAMES W. SPERRY to ALFRED NELSON
> Lot 3, Sperry's map, Subdv. Block 2, Sausalito Land & Ferry Co. - $10
>
> Estate of ALFRED GROSS to LOUISA M. GROSS
> 6 acres, N line of Ross Landing to San Rafael road
> Punta de Quentin Rancho – distribution
>
> P.J. SHAFTER to SAMUEL J. HOPKINS
> Portion SHAFTER Ranch near Olema known as allotment P - $10

JAMES DONALDSON to ANN S. ROSS
57.25 acres, by prison grounds in Coleman's addition - $5

Swift Lumber & Improvement Co. to PATRICK SWIFT
4.95 acres, Atkinson tract, portion of Punta da Quentin Road - $10

FERNANDE HUTCHINSON to MANUEL CONSTANT
Portion Block 8, Sausalito Land & Ferry Co. - $10

JOAQUIN DE SOUZA SOARES to JOHN FOSTER SILVA
4th and Grand Ave, San Rafael - $10

JOSE M. HOMAN to MANOEL S. DE SOUZA
Lot 8, Block 66, Sausalito Land & Ferry Co. - $100

CORNELIUS O'LEARY to MARGARET O'LEARY
Lots 2 & 3, Block 24, Sausalito Land & Ferry Co.
S ½ Lot 14, N ¼ Lot 13, Block 16, Sausalito Land & Ferry Co. – Gift

Tomales Letter
Dr. K. URBAN has moved into his cozy cottage.

Miss SARAH CASSADAY of Petaluma spent Thursday last with friends here.

Mrs. GRIFFIN went to the city Tuesday morning to visit her daughter, Mrs. J.S. PHILLIPS.

Town Talk
Mr. E. DuBOIS will ship today, to his ranch on Grizzly Island on the Sacramento River, two dozen Bolinas quail, the object being to breed them on the island.

Born
STRONG – In San Rafael, October 22, 1893, to the wife of E.B. STRONG, a son.

WALSH – In San Rafael, October 23, 1893, to the wife of WALTER WALSH, a son.

Died
BURY – In San Rafael, October 22, 1893, Miss MAMIE BURY, aged 24 years.

Marin County Tocsin
Saturday, October 28, 1893

Superior Court
Estate of WILLIAM DARR, deceased
Discharge of Administrator from liability

SLINKEY vs. HARRISON
Set for trial for November – jury

County of Marin vs. J.A. McNEAR
Trial set for November 13th

Estate of F. FIEDLER, deceased
Letters issued to S.S. FIEDLER

Estate of E.A. STEMPLE, deceased
Account of administratrix settled and estate distributed

JAMES D. TAYLOR vs. His Creditors
Continued to October 31st

Estate of A. BEAN, deceased
Account settled and distributed

Estate of A. FORBES, deceased
Final account settled and estate distributed

Tamalpais Land & Water Co. to J.H. McINNES
Jury dismissed, continued to November 27th

CATHERINE GALLAGHER vs. H. HARRISON, assignee
Verdict for $450

C.S. BARNEY vs. C.F. LARSEN
Verdict for $18.47

Local News
F.S. AZEVEDO is again on the streets after his late severe illness.

H. HARRISON, assignee of P. GALLAGHER, will sell a valuable horse at public auction at Novato next Sunday.

Mr. HIRAM NOTT and Miss CHARLOTTE MATSEN, two well known young residents of Bolinas, were married by Rev. J.S. McDONALD last Wednesday. Quite a number of friends from Bolinas witnessed the ceremony.

Death of JAMES BLOOM
We learn with regret as we go to press, that JAMES BLOOM, of Chileno Valley, has been stricken down by the hand of untimely death. The fatal disease was pneumonia, and its progress must have been terribly rapid, for only last Saturday Mr. BLOOM was in Petaluma a well man. On the Thursday following he died. The deceased was of Swiss parentage, and was an early settler of Marin County. He had a large private fortune invested in real estate in Marin, Sonoma, and San Diego counties. He was a gentleman of the highest character, and enjoyed the confidence and friendship of everyone who knew him. The funeral will take place in Petaluma today at 11:30.

Real Estate Transfers
    Home & Farm Co. to ANTONIO S. LOPES
    10.10 acres, corner of Block T, Chase Street in Novato - $10

    JULIA R. HAMILTON, admx, to CANDIDO RIGHETTI
    Riverside farm, 124 acresd, portion of GARCIA Rancho - $8,000

    Estate of ALEX BEAN to EMMA JANE BEAN
    80 acres known as ALEX BEAN Ranch, Tomales township – distribution

    Estate of ELIZA ANN STEMPLE to LEONARD S. STEMPLE etal
    Portion of STEMPLE Ranch, Tomales township – distribution

    SAMUEL J. HOPKINS to PAYNE J. SHAFTER
    Allotment P. SHAFTER Ranch, Olema - $10

    MARCUS ROSENTHAL etal to MARGOT HENERMANN
    Portion lot 5, villa lots near San Rafael - $1,200

    ANTHONY TIMONY and wife to PATRICK D. CONNOLLY
    Lot 24, Block B, Coleman's addition - $10

    LADISLAO MARTINEZ and wife to ALEXIS GAUDARO
    Portions of OHM Ranch, San Rafael township - $10

    Home & Farm Co. to MANUEL S. PEREIRA
    10.29 acres, Cherry Street and Railroad Ave, Novato - $10

AARON CALIN to J.A. & M.A. SILVA
Lot 2, Block 13, Tamalpais Land & Water Co. - $1,500

A.E. MINTIE to LOTTIE C. MINTIE
Lot 17, Edward Harrison tract, Old Sausalito - $10

F.A. MUNDT etal to F.B. LATHAM
4 acres, portion of Red Hill tract - $5

F.B. LATHAM to ALICE LATHAM
4 acres, portion of Red Hill tract – gift

WILLIAM N. SHELLEY etal to MICHAEL O'BRIEN
Eastland and Alto Road near station, Corte Madera Rancho - $10

JAMES C. SHAFTER etal, by Sheriff, to CANDIDO RIGHETTI
Riverside Ranch, 124 acres, portion of GARCIA Rancho - $6,897.39

Born
CORNELL – At Novato, October 26, 1893, to the wife of RICHARD CORNELL, a son.

BANCROFT – In San Francisco, October 14, 1893, to the wife of W.B. BANCROFT, twin sons.

Marin Journal
Thursday, November 2, 1893

The Palace
J. LOPEZ has opened a new restaurant in the Wilkins block.

A Sad Telegram
A telegram was received Thursday by Mrs. ALBERT HOWE of South Fourth Street calling her to Ogden, UT, to the presence of her dying husband, who it is believed cannot survive. Mr. HOWE has been very ill for the past 4 months from a complication of troubles. About a month ago, he was taken by his son to Ogden, expecting the change would be beneficial, but apparently he has steadily failed and has not long to live. His son, HARVEY HOWE, formerly telegraph operator at West End, San Rafael, is stationed at Ogden in the same capacity. The wife left immediately on receipt of the telegram accompanied by her little daughter.

Items of Interest
Mrs. E.M. HINCKLEY will open a cooking school in San Rafael about November 14th.

Mr. and Mrs. LOUIS CARRIGAN, having returned from their honeymoon, will take up residence in San Francisco.

Mr. JOHN SILVA will open a new saloon at Novato this week.

FRED HAYES of Petaluma, who is attending the Military Academy here, visited home Thursday.

ALEXANDER MONTGOMERY, the capitalist, and the generous donor of the funds used in the erection of the San Francisco Theological Seminary at San Anselmo, is lying in very critical condition at his residence in San Francisco. Mr. MONTGOMERY's illness is of a dropsical nature.

Tomales Letter
Mr. EUGENE MORTON died last Thursday morning, his funeral taking place here Friday, and was largely attended.

It is reported that WILLIAM HENSHAW, who has been sick for some time past, had died. We are glad, however, the report proved to be a mistake. Mr. HENSHAW is not dead, but very sick, having been poisoned with oysters some two months since. He is the only heir of Mr. PAT HENSHAW, who is reputed to be worth half a million.

The death of Mr. JAMES BLOOM occurred Thursday night, and the funeral was Saturday. Mr. BLOOM was a native of Switzerland, and had been in this State for many years, where he had accumulated wealth of some half a million or more. He owned a fine ranch in Marin County, where he had just finished a fine house. He also owned 10,000 acres of land in Santa Clara County, and 4,000 acres in San Diego County. His brother, JOE BLOOM, who is a resident of Olema, and who takes quite an interest in politics, is interested in some of the above tracts. Mr. BLOOM leaves a large family and multitude of friends to mourn his loss.

Letter List

ALVAREZ, J.	BRADBURY, ---
BERRY, Mrs. T.	BORNECKE, L.
CLARK, M.	DOLLY, H.
ERVING, J.C.	FRANKLIN, M.
GILWERT, N.N.	HOWARD, F.
LAKE, NELLIE	MORTON, J.
McLATTAN, C.	SNYDER, ---
SHARON, F.	ZINCKE, WILLIAM
WINDER, ED	WINSTEDT, H.
ATKINSON, J.R.	BRADLEY, GEORGE F.
COX, E.M.	BROWN, ---
CARY, KATIE	CLARK, MARY
FIGEL, JOS.	FINEER, H.M.
GARCIA, F.	HUNTER, E.F.
HAMMOND, JANE	KOLLING, C.E.
KEELER, J.B.	MORAN, M.
O'MALLEY, A.	PATTISON, J.H.
RIVAS, J.	STEFFINS, E.J.

Died
BLOOM – At his home in Chileno Valley, October 26, 1893, JAMES BLOOM, aged 52 years, a native of Canton Ticino, Switzerland.

Married
NOTT-MATSEN – In San Rafael, Wednesday, October 25, 1893, by Rev. J.S. McDONALD, Mr. HIRAM NOTT to Miss CHARLOTTE MATSEN, both of Bolinas.

Born
DUFFY – In San Rafael, October 27, 1893, to the wife of P.E. DUFFY, a son.

CORNELL – At Novato, October 26, 1893, to the wife of RICHARD CORNELL, a son.

LUND – In San Rafael, October 31, 1893, to the wife of E.C. LUND, a son.

Marriage Licenses
HIRAM J. NOTT, 30, Bolinas to Miss CHARLOTTE MATSEN, 17, Bolinas
JOE J. WILLIAMS, 28, Petaluma, to Mrs. ANNIE S. McFARRELL, 22, Victoria, BC

Superior Court
BRESSON vs. BRESSON
Set for November 1 at 10 a.m.

Estate of JAMES A. ROY, deceased
Hearing for letters of administration – over until November 13

Estate of JAMES M. DONAHUE, deceased
Application for family allowance – over one week

JAMES I. TAYLOR vs. his Creditors
Set for Wednesday, November 15

Marin County Tocsin
Saturday, November 4, 1893

Died
McCAMISH – In San Rafael, October 31, 1893, CHESTER B. McCAMISH, son of W.F. and WINNIE McCAMISH, aged 2 years, 3 months, and 25 days.

Local News
Mrs. R.M. KEARNEY, an old resident of San Rafael, died in San Francisco last Monday.

Mr. A. WOODARD has purchased the interest of H. CRIMMONS, in the grocery business of ATWATER & CRIMMINS.

JAMES HAYES had an arm badly fractured last Tuesday through undue familiarity with the business end of a mustang.

Mrs. ANNIE BURTCHAELL, mother of P.T. BURTCHAELL, and sister of JAMES TUNSTEAD, of San Rafael, died last Tuesday at her residence in San Francisco. The deceased lady had warm friends in Marin County who esteemed her for her many amiable and unselfish traits, and who will sincerely lament her loss.

Real Estate Transfers
P.J. SHAFTER to S.J. HOPKINS
Lot in Bear Valley - $10

WILLIAM T. COLEMAN etal to Marin County
Right of way for a public road over the McCue Hill, in Sausalito township

J.O.B. SHORT etal to L. MARTINEZ etal
Lot on South Fourth Street, San Rafael - $10

P.J. SHAFTER to NEIL McISAACS
113.50 acres, part of Olema Ranch - $100

JANE BLAIN etal to T.B. ROY
All their right, title and interest in the estate of JAMES ROY, deceased

JULIA R. HAMILTON, admr. to P.J. SHAFTER
The Olema Ranch, near Olema, containing 300.60 acres - $12,600

VAN LEER EASTLAND to ALICE L. EASTLAND
Lots 175,176,177,178,179,180,181,182,183,184,185, Mill Valley - $10

G.A. NAGEL to Pioneer Mill & Lumber Co.
Lots 4 & 5, Block W, Larkspur

P.J. SHAFTER to H.H. ATWATER
Lot in Bear Valley - $10

Marin Journal
Thursday, November 9, 1893

Died
HOWE – In Ogden, UT, November 4, 1893, Mr. A.S. HOWE, of San Rafael.

BURTCHAELL – In San Francisco, October 31, 1893, Mrs. JOHN BURTCHAELL, mother of P.T. BURTCHAELL, and sister of JAMES TUNSTEAD, and THOMAS TUNSTEAD.

Real Estate Transfers
ALEXANDER ROY etal to THOMAS B. ROY
Real estate at Nicasio township - $8,000

G.B. DONDERO to ANTONIO ARBINI
Lot 4th Street and Ida Street, San Rafael - $10

Estate SARAH GEARY to EMMA GEARY etal
16.74 acres on Ross Landing Road

Letter List

CRANE, V.T.	DAYTON, E.
DARCY, P.M.	DAVIS, S.P.
DELPOINTI, A.	EBELE, H.
MORROW, A.J.	McKAY, A.
McALLISTER, L.	LIVEEN, Mrs.
MORSE, Mrs.	PETERSON, A.
RESCH, M.	RAMOS, J.B.
ROSE, A.	RUSSELL, M.
ROSME, W.E.	TREE, TREEDA
SYLVESTER, A.	TAYLOR, WILLIAM

Foreign

UHELDI, LUF	CANDIDA, M.
SIMONI, P.	JOAQUIN, J.
PETO, J.	ALVAREZ, J.
BITTER, J.S.	GIOVIANNI, G.
ROSELLI, ANDRES	COSTELLO, G.

Superior Court
LUCA BONETTI vs. BARBOLINA M. BONETTI
Decree of divorce in favor of plaintiff

Estate of JAMES M. DONAHUE, deceased
Continued to November 13th

Estate of JAMES M. DONAHUE, deceased
Ordered that executors pay to BELLE W. DONAHUE $15,500 family allowance

JOHN SILVA vs. FRANK PERARA
Plaintiff appointed receiver – bond $500

Estate of JOHN SCHIPPERS
Decree of due and legal notice to creditors ordered

Local Brevities
Mr. H.P. CARR visited San Rafael on Monday.

United in Marriage
On Wednesday, November 1, 1893, the Rev. J.S. McDONALD united in marriage, Mr. ROBERT L. DUNCAN of Santa Rosa and Miss FANNY ROBERTSON of San Rafael. Miss ROBERTSON is well known and liked by all the young people of town, and this time has stolen a march on her friends, as none knew, up to the time when the pair were wed.

Death of ALEXANDER MONTGOMERY
ALEXANDER MONTGOMERY, the capitalist, died at his residence in San Francisco last Saturday evening. His death had been expected for some time, and resulted from dropsy. Mr. MONTGOMERY was one of the pioneer settlers of California, coming here in 1849, when the gold fever was at its height. A large portion of his princely fortune, which is estimated at about $3,000,000, will go to the Presbyterian Theological Seminary at San Anselmo, which he has so richly endowed in the past with large sums. He gave the magnificent sum of $250,000 towards the erection of the handsome stone buildings now occupied by that institution, adding $50,000 about a month ago for the erection of a chapel for the same institution. About a month ago, he gave a neat sum toward the erection of the new Presbyterian Church in San Rafael, now under construction. He leaves a wife and 2 daughters, who are the only relatives in this country with the exception of 4 cousins who live in Brooklyn, NY. His wife is said to be perfectly satisfied with the Will.

Town Talk
G.A. FERGUSON, a former San Rafael grocer, visited the town on Saturday. He is located in Alameda at present.

Mrs. F.J. WHITE, widow of the late Dr. WHITE, departed Tuesday for Marshall, Michigan, which will be her future home.

Tomales Letter
We regret to note the death of Mr. WILLIAM HENSHAW, who was referred to last week. His funeral took place Saturday last in Petaluma.

CHARLES F. TURNER was presented with a boy by his wife on Sunday morning November 5th. Both are doing well.

Mrs. W.H. VAUGHN presented to her husband on November 1st, a 9 pound boy.

Marriage Licenses
    ROBERT L. DUNCAN, 30, Santa Rosa, to Miss FANNY J. ROBERTSON, 29, San Rafael
    RICHARD CARR, 22, San Francisco, to Miss ELEANOR O'BRIEN, 22, San Francisco

Mrs. JOHN BURTCHAELL
A commitment service was held at Cypress Lawn Cemetery on Sunday, when the body of Mrs. JOHN BURTCHAELL was taken from the vault to the tomb chosen as her last resting place. The regular funeral services were held in St. Luke's Episcopal Church on Wednesday last, and the service on Sunday was that of the Reformed Episcopal Church on Polk Street. The deceased lady came to this coast from Newark, NJ, and at one time figured prominently. She had 5 brothers when the war broke out, and she urged them to join the fight for the Union. They enlisted in the Third and Ninth New Jersey regiments. Three were wounded in the Battle of Bull Run, the eldest, WILLIAM BURTCHAELL, dying of his wounds. The other two men were able to go to the front again, one finding death at Antietam, and the other at Petersburg. Two out of five brothers escaped injury. Mrs. BURTCHAELL lived in this State for upwards of 20 years. She was a native of Carlow, Ireland, and her maiden name was DORA TUNSTEAD. She was a sister of ex-sheriff TUNSTEAD of Marin County, and of THOMAS TUNSTEAD, who resides in San Francisco. Nine children, all doing well, survive her. So less than 27 of her relatives followed her to the grave. She was 59 years of age.

Marin County Tocsin
Saturday, November 11, 1893

Died
HAACK – In San Rafael, November 6, 1893, N. HAACK, aged 61 years.

SALM – In San Rafael, November 9, 1893, MARTIN SALM, aged 60 years, 7 months, and one day.

Local News
NICHOLAS HAACK, an old German resident of San Rafael died Wednesday at his residence here.

WILLIAM ROBERTSON, otherwise known as "Roxie", fell from a scaffolding on the Methodist Church and suffered a compound fracture of the ankle joint. The injury is a very severe one, and will confine the patient to his room for some weeks to come, if it does not leave permanent lameness.

THOMAS P. BOYD, reporter of the Superior Court, is to be a lawyer.

Death of MARTIN SALM
MARTIN SALM, an old resident and respected citizen of San Rafael, died last Wednesday night from the effects of blood poisoning, the result of a slight wound in the hand. The hurt was received while working on the Methodist Church addition, and was in itself a mere trifle, but pus was absorbed from a slight suppuration of the injured part, and critical phases of blood poisoning ensued, under which the patient rapidly sank. The funeral will take place today under the auspices of the Ancient Order of Workmen.

Superior Court
    Estate and guardianship of JOSEPHINE NEIMEYER
    Both applications for letters of guardianship denied

DOMINGA BRESSON vs. JOSEPH BRESSON
Decree of divorce granted

Marin Journal
Thursday, November 16, 1893

Letter List

BRADLEY, G.F.	ADAMS, WILLIAM
BEMENDERFER, C.	CRIDER, J.W.
COX, E.M.	CLARK, M.
CAREY, Mrs. K.	CARLTON, MARY
CAREY, Miss K.	FOSTER, F.
FIGEL, JOS.	FINGER, H.M.
FRONK, GEORGE G.	GORDON, A.
GARCIA, F.	GRAYHAM, W.R.
HOWARD, GEORGE	KOHLBERG, M.S.
KEELER, J.B.	LAWTON, M.A.
LEWIS, P.	MAGEE, J.
LINDQUIST, M.	MARSHALL, L.
MICTICKER, JOS.	MORAN, M.
WARDEN, A.L.	MURPHY, L.J.
McCARTHY, M.	MACKENZIE, JANE
OLDAM. A.	PRATT, E.W.
PATTERSON, W.J.	PAINTER, R.
RIVAS, J.	REDFIELD, O.F.
RAY, H.H.	STOUT, M.
SCOTT, W.P.	SCOTT, H.T.
WYMAN, L.S.	SCOTT, J.E.
WINSTEDT, H.	SMITH, E.H.
SMITH, S.H.	

Born

SWIFT – In San Rafael, Tuesday, November 14, 1893, to the wife of J.R. SWIFT, a son.

TURNER – In Tomales, November 4, 1893, to the wife of THAD TURNER, a son.

RILEY – At Pt. Reyes Station, November 2, 1893, to the wife of JOHN RILEY, a daughter.

DEAS – In San Francisco, November 4, 1893, to the wife of Dr. W.B. DEAS, formerly of Olema, a son.

Real Estate Transfers

Tamalpais Land & Water Co. to GUSTAV F. SCHRODER
4 acres, Map 2, Tamalpais Land & Water Co. - $10

NICHOLAS HAACK to HELENA HAACK
Lot on Clayton Street and Welch Street, San Rafael - $10

GEORGE REYNOLDS to WILLIAM WHITMORE
3/10 acre San Anselmo Road and Lagunitas Road
1.9 acres Arroyo, San Anselmo - $900

Pioneer Paper Mill Co. to JAMES I. TAYLOR
7.3 acres, Jewell tract - $1

Home & Farm Co. to MARGIE A. OLIVER
Lots 3,4,5,6, Block D, Novato - $10

GUSTAV SCHRODER to LOUISE SCHRODER
Lot 5, block 4, Tamalpais Land & Water Co. – Gift

LADISLAO MARTINEZ etal to Marin County
Right of way over grantor's lands for highway - $25

Pioneer Paper Mill Co. to SARAH W.I. TAYLOR
4 acres, N.P.C.R.R., south of old mill - $10

S.S. TILTON and wife to WALTER M. TILTON
17 acres, Home & Farm Co. tract, Novato - $1

Pioneer Paper Mill Co. to W.P. TAYLOR
5.43 acres, San Rafael and Olema Road - $200

WILL BROOKS to San Rafael Gas & Electric Light Co.
Lot on 3rd Street and A Street - $400

DAVID MORTON and wife to Marin County
Right of way over grantor's lands for highway - $25

Estate of JOHN SCHIPPERS to MARTIN FARRELL
1/5 acre Olema and Bolinas Road - $800

Superior Court

Estate of B.F. SWISHER, deceased
Will admitted to probate

Estate of JOHN SCHIPPERS, deceased
Sale of real estate confirmed

Estate of JAMES M. DONAHUE, deceased
Over until November 15th

Marin County vs. J.A. McNEAR etal
Demurrer sustained, 10 days to file amendment to complaint

CATHERINE GALLAGHER vs. H. HARRISON
Motion to retax costs argued and granted

E. WORMOUTH vs. JACOB GARDNER
Motion for new trial granted

Estate of JAMES ROY, deceased
Letters of administration granted to E. EDEN

Marriage Licenses
WILLIAM KEARNEY, 21, San Francisco to Miss JENNIE FORREST, 19, San Francisco
MARANNO JOSE GOMES, 26, San Rafael, to FRANCISCA MARIA DE ROZA, 18, Sausalito
WILLIAM HILTON, 43, San Francisco, to AMELIA C. ROCKFORD, 46, San Francisco

Marin County Tocsin
Saturday, November 18, 1893

Real Estate Transfers
D.U. MYERS to J. MITCHELL
20 acres in Tomales township - $10

ELIZA A.R. CRANE to JOHN MITCHELL
27.43 acres in Tomales township - $10

Tamalpais Land & Water Co. to GUSTAV F. SCHRODER
4 acres in Mill Valley - $10

HENRY BETTEN, Exec., to MARTIN FARRELL
Estate of JOHN SCHIPPERS, land at Bolinas - $800

Estate of STEMPLE to JOHN MITCHELL
292.41 acres in Tomales township - $17,364.60

R.R. CONNELL to MARY SCOWN
1/3 interest in 391.46 acres in SCOWN Ranch, Novato – love and affection

Sausalito Land & Ferry Co. to EDGAR M. WILSON
Lots 20 & 21, Block 11 ½, Sausalito Land & Ferry Co. - $10

Notice to Creditors
    Estate of BELLA F. SWISHER, deceased
    November 15, 1893
    JAMES W. COCHRANE, Attorney for Executors
                        F.C. KECK, Executor
                        E.S. GREER, Executor

Notice for Proving Will
    Estate of EUGENE MORTON, aka OWEN MORTON, deceased
    Publication of Will
    December 4, 1893
    Filed November 13, 1893
    JAMES W. COCHRANE, Attorney for Petitioner
    Application by ELLEN CATHERINE MORTON for letters testamentary
                        THOMAS S. BONNEAU, Clerk

Notice for Proving Will
    Estate of JAMES BLOOM, deceased
    Publication of Will
    December 11, 1893
    Filed November 14, 1893
    LIPPITT & LIPPITT, Petaluma, Attorney for Petitioners
    Application LUCIA M. BLOOM, & ADOLPH J. BLOOM, for letters testamentary
                        THOMAS S. BONNEAU, Clerk

Notice for Proving Will
    Estate of MARTIN SALM, aka MARTIN SALME, deceased
    Publication of Will
    December 4, 1893
    Filed November 14, 1893
    JAMES W. COCHRANE, Attorney for Petitioner
    Application of P.E. DUFFY for letters testamentary
                        THOMAS S. BONNEAU, Clerk

Local News
The many friends of WILLIAM D. ENGLISH in Marin County, were delighted at his appointment as Surveyor of the Port of San Francisco.

THOMAS P. BOYD passed through the Supreme Court ordeal last Tuesday with flying colors, and is now a blooming barrister. Auditor and Recorder BENSON will be the next applicant for such honors.

Mr. and Mrs. HERZOG announce the engagement of their daughter, JENNIE HERZOG, to HARRY M. LICHTENSTEIN, of San Francisco.

Dr. MARY A. MORGAN M.D., an accomplished physician of the homeopathic school, has rented the Herzog house on Fourth Street, near Shaver Street, and will commence the practice of medicine forthwith. The lady comes with the highest letters from such eminent gentlemen as Dr. BREYFOGLE, Dr. DAVIS, and others. In addition to general practice, Dr. MORGAN will use her residence as a sanitarium for special cases. The lady is a daughter of Dr. P.B. MORGAN, formerly of San Rafael.

With Dr. MARY A. MORGAN is Frau VON MANDERSCHEID, a most skillful pianist and teacher of the German language. The lady has taken the normal course in Germany, and has testimonials from Mrs. CARMICHAEL CARR and other leading artists.

Mrs. E.M. HINCKLEY will give regular lessons in cooking at the residence of Mrs. HOYT, Laurel Place, every Tuesday morning at 9 o'clock. The first meeting was held last Tuesday, and proved very interesting indeed. Among those attended, were Mesdames, FOSTER, SCOTT, CURTIS, BIGELOW, WINTERINGHAM, JONES, BRUNER, FARRELL, and HOYT.

Recovering
The many friends of WILLIAM ROBERTSON will be pleased to learn that he is rapidly recovering from the severe injuries he received a couple of weeks ago. The nature of his hurt was a compound fracture of the ankle joint.

Druids Public Installation
The public installation of the officers of Mt. Tamalpais Grove, No. 58, U.A.O.D. came off on last Friday evening as announced. The following named officers installed were:

    M. McNAMARA – A.A.
    P.H. COCHRANE – V.A.
    W.F. DOUGHERTY – Secretary
    P.D. CONNOLLY – Treasurer
    C.L. COULTER – Con.
    CHARLES KUNZ – I.G.
    SAM BELLAMY – O.G.

Tomales Letter
Attorney F. WOODWORTH visits us frequently. He will soon open a branch office at Fowler's Store, in Valley Ford.

JOSEPH BOSSONI returns from Switzerland next week.

Marin Journal
Thursday, November 23, 1893

Real Estate Transfers

Estate of CHARLES STEMPLE to ELIZA A. STEMPLE
27.4 acres, part of estate – Distribution

FRANK S. DUARTE and wife to ALBERT D. GLOVER
Land in Tomales - $10

ALBERT B. GLOVER and wife to JOHN W. GAVER
40 acres on Marin County line - $1,900

Superior Court

HUGH WALKER vs. his Creditors
Exempt property set apart

D.L. HAYDEN vs. his Creditors
Exempt property set apart

FRANK PERARA vs. his Creditors
Exempt property set apart

JESSIE E. BARNETT vs. JOSIAH BARNETT
Decree of divorce granted

JAMES TAYLOR vs. his Creditors
Dropped from calendar to be entered on notice

AMANDA TANN, Admx vs. Patent Brick Co. etal
Further hearing November 23rd

JOHN SILVA vs. FRANK PERARA
Judgment for plaintiff ordered

Notice to Creditors
Estate of JAMES ROY, deceased
Filed November 15, 1893
EDWARD EDEN, Admr.

Marin County Tocsin
Saturday, November 25, 1893

Local News
Mrs. JAMES SAUNDERS is suffering from a severe case of inflammatory rheumatism.

A.L. HAM and Capt. MINOTT are about to open a wood, coal, and grain business at the narrow gauge depot.

The Journal fixes the value of the estate of the late MARTIN SALME at $112,500.

The BODY of the old man found near the Patent Brickyard about a month ago, has been identified by the clothes kept by Coroner EDEN as a former resident of Petaluma.

Judge DUFFICY's son, GEORGE W. DUFFICY, who is well remembered in San Rafael, was one of a class of 30, who graduated from the College of Pharmacy in the University of California. Mr. DUFFICY stood third in his class.

M. DOLCINI arrived in San Rafael yesterday morning before daybreak and left on the 6:15 a.m. train for the city. He told men at MURRAY's livery stable that he had received news of the death of his brother in a runaway accident at Santa Barbara, and he was hastening to that place.

Real Estate Transfers
F.G. WATERHOUSE etal to Mrs. SARAH DUGGAN
Lots 22 & 23, Granda Vista tract, Bolinas - $500

Sausalito Land & Ferry Co. to S.F. DE SOUZA
Lot 1, Block 73, New Sausalito - $10

SARAH W.I. TAYLOR to Anglo California Bank
4 acres near Paper Mill site - $5

Superior Court
Estate of ANN FEENEY, deceased
Annual account of administrator approved

Estate of JAMES M. DONAHUE, deceased
H.P. WOOD, JOHN FRANETTA, & FRANK JACOBS appointed appraisers

Born
PHELPS – At Sausalito, November 20, 1893, to the wife of CHARLES PHELPS, a daughter.

OTTON – In San Rafael, November 23, 1893, to the wife of HEDLEY OTTON, a son.

LAKIN – In San Rafael, November 23, 1893, to the wife of J.J. LAKIN, a daughter.

Marin Journal
Thursday, November 30, 1893

Died
COLEMAN – In San Francisco, November 22, 1893, WILLIAM T. COLEMAN, formerly of San Rafael, aged 89? Years and 9 months.

STETSON – In San Francisco, November 22, 1893, MARIA STETSON, wife of J.B. STETSON, aged 52 years and 11 months.

Death of WILLIAM T. COLEMAN

Probably in no other section of California was the death of WILLIAM T. COLEMAN felt so keenly as in San Rafael. The sad intelligence reached here through the evening papers of Wednesday, November 22, 1893, and on every side were heard expressions of regret. The immediate cause of death was ascribed to heart failure, though it was known that for many months past, the citadels of strength of the deceased were fast giving way to the inroads of the destroyer. Close friends of Mr. COLEMAN say that his health has steadily failed since his business reverse in 1888.

San Rafael owed much to Mr. COLEMAN. He was the Nestorian of her public enterprises, and his popularity here was unbounded. His property interests in and around San Rafael were large. He built the Marin County waterworks, pushed the incorporation through successfully, and was instrumental inducing many enterprises to be inaugurated here, notably the S.F. & N.P. railroad and the Hotel Rafael.

The chapters of his life's history during his residence in California furnish largely to the history of the State, which without them would be incomplete.

The funeral took place on Saturday at 11 o'clock from the family residence on Fillmore Street and Pacific Avenues. At the house at the appointed hour, there was an unusual gathering of merchants of San Francisco, save the Examiner, and besides the merchants, men of other callings, who had been glad to call WILLIAM T. COLEMAN friend, assembled to be present at the offering of the last tribute to the dead and to express sympathy to the mourning survivors. While the company within the house was made up mostly of men whose names are marked in business life, yet many women, friends of the COLEMAN's in social life, were there too, to give their tears and their condolences. Through the rooms was the fragrance of violets, the blossom that was the favorite of Mr. COLEMAN of all the flowers. Over the coffin, which rested in the main drawing room, was a fall of violets, placed there by Mrs. COLEMAN. Clusters of the same flowers were placed around the room.

Town Talk

FRANK JACOBS, who has been undergoing a lengthly siege of rheumatism, is seen upon the streets occasionally, wearing a beard that would have made the patriarch Abraham envious.

A Floater Identified

On October 21st last, Coroner EDEN was notified that a BODY had washed ashore at Lime Point, this county. He went to the Point and held an inquest on the body, which was considerably decomposed, and bore no marks or means of identification. He, however, made a minute record of description, to aid if possible in identifying the unfortunate at some future time, and the body was buried in the potter's field. Last Saturday, a man giving his name as BERNARDINO ANSENIO, living in San Francisco, called at the coroner's office, and by reading over the minutes made by Coroner EDEN, was able to identify the deceased as those of JOHN ROLINEO, a native of the Azores, aged 26, and a sailor by occupation, enabling the coroner to have marked one more nameless grave in the potter's field.

Marriage Licenses

CHARLES FILIPPINI, 24, to KRYSTIE NILSON, 24, both of Pt. Reyes Station

Superior Court

County of Marin vs. M. BLUMENTHAL and JERRY ADAMS
Ordered that Defendant's demurrer be overruled

AMANDA TANN vs. Patent Brick Co. etal
By consent case not closed

MARION LISK vs. D.A. LISK
Decree of divorce granted

F.W. SPENCER vs. VINCENT NEALE etal
Set for trial January 3rd

A.C. DIGGINS vs. T.J. MAHON etal
Set for trial Wednesday, December 19th

E. SCHWIESAU vs. T.J. MAHON etal
Set for trial Wednesday, December 19th

Estate of PEDRO SAIS, deceased
Hearing of application to lease property set for December 18th

F. PERARA vs. his Creditors
By consent over one week

Estate of JOHN GIACOMINI, deceased
H. STEITZ appointed administrator, bond $3,000
Sale of some personal property ordered

People vs. SYDNEY SPENCER
Arraigned and sentenced to one year in state prison

Letter List
- BOYER, ---
- BERTRAM, F.W.
- CALDWELL, Dr.
- DUGGAN, M.
- PADRET, N.
- SHEELS, H.
- SMITH, J.N.
- WEEKS, F.L.
- LEWIS, E.
- COSTELLO, ELIFIA
- DORE, M.
- HENRY, A.S.
- GLEESON, T.D.
- SMALL, A.
- SANCHEZ, N.
- SMITH, W.
- WEST, JOHN C.

Marin County Tocsin
Saturday, December 2, 1893

Sheriff's Sale
JOHN SILVA vs. FRANK PERARA, HENRY HARRISON, Receiver of the Estate of FRANK PERARA, an Insolvent Debtor, and ANTONIO NUNES
Sale of 16 horses
Sale to be held at courthouse December 18, 1893
                    HENRY HARRISON, Sheriff

Application of Insolvency
Matter of SEVERINO J. SOARES, an Insolvent Debtor
HENRY HARRISON, Receiver of the Estate
All creditors must respond by January 8, 1894
Filed November 29, 1893
                    F.M. ANGELLOTTI
                    Judge of Superior Court

Notice of Co-Partnership
ABNER L. HAM, San Rafael
JAMES P. MINOTT, San Rafael
Business known as HAM & MINOTT
Filed November 28, 1893
                    JAMES W. COCHRANE
                    Notary Public

Sheriff's Sale
R.K. PATTRIDGE vs. THOMAS E. SUTCLIFFE and H. WYATT
Judgment of foreclosure
Land for sale in Woodward Valley, Sausalito
Sale to be held at courthouse December 26, 1893
                    HENRY HARRISON, Sheriff
                    By T.J. FALLON, Undersheriff

Local News
JOE MARSHALL, a lunatic living near Novato, was arrested and brought to San Rafael yesterday.

Messrs. CLEARY and TRACHNEY are putting the Central Hotel into first class shape throughout, and it will open next week.

GEORGE BOWEN, the possessor of the fine kit of burglar's tools, who was captured last week, was sentenced to serve 100 days in the County Jail.

The Sausalito News conveys the information that J.J. SCHNEIDER is very ill. None of his acquaintances here were aware of it. He is around and attending to business just as if he was well.

A.B. MORETTI & Co. have leased the BOYEN business stand on Fourth and F Streets, and have opened a first class grocery store there.

Departure of a Good Citizen
We regret to announce the departure of J.F. BIGELOW from San Rafael. The gentleman has managed the extensive MACKAY & FLOOD interests here for the past 4 years, and has fairly earned the good will and esteem of our citizens. Mr. BIGELOW has represented the most advanced progressive ideas, favoring improvements of all kinds, but at the same time showing consideration for those who could ill afford to meet the heavy demands of street and sidewalk assessments, even once going to the extent of inducing his principals to meet a part of the expenses to place on the shoulders of the needy. Mr. BIGELOW will be succeeded by Mr. WALSH, now private secretary for Mr. J.L. FLOOD, who we trust will prove as courteous and public spirited as his predecessor. The retirement of the present manager is made imperative by reason of his exhaustive labors as Vice-President of the Nevada Bank, but later on he hopes to make San Rafael again his place of residence.

Real Estate Transfers
    T.J. MAHON to ELLEN HYAMS
    Lot on B Street S of Second Street - $10

    Home & Farm Co. to ROSE M. WHITE
    11.87 acres, subdv. 3, Lot 13, div. B - $10

    ANTON MILLER to BARBARA DESCHLER
    Part of lot D, Block 29, Sausalito - $50

Marin Journal
Thursday, December 7, 1893

    Superior Court
        People vs. PATRICK RICE
        Set for Monday December 11th

        W.N. SHELLEY vs. E. WORMOUTH
        Demurrer withdrawn

        FRANK PERARA vs. his Creditors
        Assignee appointed
        Petition to set aside personal property one week

        CHARLES PASTORI & RIZZINI vs. their Creditors
        Hearing set for December 18th

        Estate of JAMES M. DONAHUE, deceased
        Matter of drinking fountain submitted for briefs

        Estate of A. PERILLAT, deceased
        Settled and account distributed

        G.W. FOX vs. SUSAN FOX
        Order to show cause dismissed

Estate of EUGENE MORTON, deceased
Will admitted to probate
Letters testamentary ordered issued to ELLEN C. MORTON, bond $400

Estate of MARTIN SALME, deceased
Will admitted to probate
Executor P.E. DUFFY in bond of $2,500

GREGG vs. GREGG
Set of Wednesday, December 6th

Letter List

BRIGGS, A.	CARLETON, J.M.
CASSANS, H.	FLOPS, A.
HOAG, D.A.	LUNEY, K.M.
McCLURE, D.	PIERCE, W.
RILEY, J.	SHEPPARD, E.
WRIGHT, J.L.	RYAN, A.

Notice of Dissolution of Co-Partnership
EDWIN L. ATWATER has bought interest of HARRY CREMMINGS
Filed October 30, 1893

Notice of Co-Partnership
Dairymen JOSEPH RAULINO, JOHN ENOS SILVA, & MANUEL RODGERS
At Reed's Station
Partnership has been dissolved due to death of JOSEPH RAULINA
Filed December 4, 1893

Lease of Real Estate Ordered
Estate of PEDRO SAIS, deceased
Parcel of Rancho Canada De Herrera, containing 20 acres
Filed November 27, 1893
F.M. ANGELLOTTI, Judge of Superior Court

Items of Interest
The engagement is announced of Miss REDMOND of Nicasio to Mr. H. LUCAS of Happy Valley.

ORA SMITH, a brakeman on the narrow gauge road, had his hand badly cut in some manner while on duty Sunday, and is in consequence taking an enforced vacation.

Town Talk
The little daughter of L. PETERSON of South Fourth Street, who has been ill for sometime past is improving.

The funeral of the little daughter of Mr. and Mrs. PATTARINA, aged 1 year and 1 month, took place last Saturday at San Anselmo.

Marriage Licenses
JOHANNES NELSON, 36, to ALICE JANE MERCER, 26, both of San Rafael

Marin County Tocsin
Saturday, December 9, 1893

Notice of Co-Partnership
Firm name JENKINS & FAIRBANKS
JOSEPH LEE JENKINS, Tomales
WILLIAM R. FAIRBANKS, Tomales
December 5, 1893
ANDREW L. FISHER
Justice of the Peace

Local News

JOE MARSHALL, an insane man, was committed to Napa Asylum by Judge ANGELLOTTI last Friday.

Real Estate Transfers

Home & Farm Co. to JOSEPH RALSTON
62.10 acres, lot 15, Div. B, Novato - $10

IRWIN C. STUMP to PHOEBE A. HEARST
102 acres, near Fairfax Station, Austin Reserve tract - $10
1,231.77 acres, adjoining above tract to west - $10

A.B. MORETTI and wife to Marin County
Right of way through tract of land on Pt. San Pedro - $125

JOHN A. BROWN and wife to F. KAUFMAN
Lot in Jessup tract - $10

FRANK M. PIXLEY and wife to CORNELIUS STAGG
1 acre, Corte Madera Station – no consideration

CORNELIUS STAGG to JOSEPHINE OLDIS
1 acre, Corte Madera Station – no consideration

Estate of J. McM. SHAFTER to JOHN J. GALLAGHER
331 acres, tract known as North Bend Ranch, near Olema - $9,000

Estate of J. McM. SHAFTER to Mrs. KATE JOHNSON
Undivided 100 acres, Inverness tract - $5,000

W.H. MILLER to H.C. ACKLEY etal
Lot 9, block 13, Mill Valley - $10

Sausalito Land & Ferry Co. to FRANCES JACKSON
Lot 38, block 59, New Sausalito - $10

Marin Journal
Thursday, December 14, 1893

Letter List

BAAR, S.	CAREY, JAMES
BANFLEMO, M.	DAVIS, M.
COLTON, ---	DAVIS, Rev.
DONNELLY, D.	FOLLETT, L.A.
EARL, W.E.	GORDON, A.
LOVIE, F.	MINOR, E.
MAY, J.	OSS, I.
RATO, F.	RICHARDSON, THOMAS
GARCIA, JOE	

The COLEMAN Will

About $60,000 is to be disposed of by the Will of WILLIAM T. COLEMAN. His two sons, ROBERT L. COLEMAN and CARLETON COLEMAN, are each to receive $3,000. The Catholic Orphan Asylum near San Rafael and the Protestant Orphan Asylum of San Francisco have each been remembered. The Union Trust Co. of San Francisco is the executor and sole trustee. Eighty per cent of the income is set aside for the use of the widow, CARRIE M.P. COLEMAN. The petition for probate shows that Mr. COLEMAN was 69 years of age, Mrs. COLEMAN 65 years, CARLETON C. COLEMAN 34 years, and ROBERT L. COLEMAN 23 years.

It is rumored that JAMES B. BURDELL of Rancho Olompali will soon start a creamery in San Antonio township.

Suicide at Tomales

The death of ROBERT LANDGRAF, the jeweler, at Tomales last Saturday, from a pistol shot inflicted by his own hands, was the termination of a life worn out with care and sickness. For many years the deceased, who was a man long past middle age, has borne up under a load of ill health that finally became too heavy to bear. He had been confined to his bed for several weeks past. On Saturday afternoon, he called his wife to his bedside, and expressed a desire to give up, asking her to go to a neighbor nearby with the request to come and assist him to arise. Upon returning soon after being accompanied by the neighbor, the lifeless body of her husband met her horror-stricken gaze, and a revolver was close at hand. Friends had been expecting his death for some time, though none suspitioned he contemplated suicide.

The deceased knew he had no chance to get well. He has suffered with an internal cancer of the breast, also with a running sore on the leg, which has baffled the skill of eminent physicians on both hemispheres. He had crossed the Atlantic on 13 different occasions in quest of medical assistance, all without avail. Inflammation of the lungs added its complications during his last illness.

The deceased conducted a small watch repairing establishment in Tomales. A number of years ago, he was located in San Rafael in the same business. He came here from New York many years ago, where he was connected with the famous jewelry firm, Tiffany & Co. He owned a small cottage at Tomales, built upon leased land, and a small amount of personal property. He was a man greatly respected wherever known.

Local News

Among those who graduated last week from the Cooper Medical Institute at San Francisco were CHARLES H. SARTORI and AGNES WALKER of San Rafael. Both acquitted themselves excellently well, and stood high in their studies. Dr. SARTORI expects to take a post-graduate course in the leading medical college of London, England.

Town Talk

Mr. JERRY SHINE of San Anselmo is ill with pneumonia.

Real Estate Transfers

Tamalpais Land & Water Co. to GUSTAV PAGE
Lot 192, Map 2, Tamalpais Land & Water Co.

Tamalpais Land & Water Co. to WILLIAM TERRY
Lot 33, map 2, Tamalpais Land & Water Co. - $400

WILLIAM H. MILLER to HENRY C. ACKLEY etal
Lot 9, block 13, Tamalpais Land & Water Co. - $10

JOHN W. MACKAY etal to JAMES E. WALSH
Lot on SW corner Belle Avenue and Walnut Streets, San Rafael

Marriage Licenses

ADAM NEUMANN, 53, Santa Rosa, to ANNA WIRKAN, 39, Petaluma
ANTONE C. MUHLBEYER, 32, to Miss BERTHA KLENHAMMER, 19, both of San Francisco

Superior Court

Estate of JAMES M. DONAHUE, deceased
Order confirming sale of real estate and personal property

H. GREGG vs. E.N. GREGG
Struck from calendar

The People vs. PATRICK RICE
By consent, time to plead over one week

Estate of JAMES BLOOM, deceased
Will admitted to probate
Letters ordered issued to LUCIA M. BLOOM and ADOLPH BLOOM

Estate of JAMES ROY, deceased
Application for letters of administration denied

Notice to Creditors
>   Estate of JAMES ROY, deceased
>   Filed November 15, 1893
>   E.B. MAHON, Attorney for Administrator
>   EDWARD EDEN, Administrator

Marin County Tocsin
Saturday, December 16, 1893

Died
MORRIS – In San Rafael, December 14, 1893, JAMES MORRIS, aged 49 years, a native of Ireland, Sheriff of Eureka County, NV.

Local News
JAMES W. COCHRANE is preparing plans for a $50,000 residence, which he will erect shortly on his lot on the corner of Fifth and Nye Streets.

Judge PENNIE, the pioneer who passed away in San Francisco last Friday, was a property owner of this county and had many friends here. He at one time had charge of the State Prison at San Quentin.

Real Estate Transfers
>   ANSON P. HOTALING and wife to RICHARD LYNCH
>   Lots 7 & 8, Block 4, Larkspur - $265
>
>   RICHARD LYNCH to BESSIE LYNCH
>   Lots 7 & 8, Block 4, Larkspur – love and affection
>
>   Tamalpais Land & Water Co. to J.H. McINNES
>   Lots 7 & 8, Mill Valley - $10
>
>   J.W. MACKAY etal to JAMES E. WALSH
>   Part of block 4, Coleman's addition - $10
>
>   Estate of A. PERILLAT, to MARIE PERILLAT
>   Lots on corner of Fifth and C Street
>   Lot at Ross Landing – distribution

Marin Journal
Thursday, December 21, 1893

>   M.F. INMAN
>   PRATT C. INMAN
>   Druggist and Chemists
>   San Rafael

Born
BURGLE – To the wife of EUGENE BURGLE, Thursday, December 17, 1893, a son.

Died
BEEMAN – At Mill Valley, December 14, 1893, WILLIAM BEEMAN, aged 75 years.

MORRIS – In San Rafael, December 14, 1893, JAMES MORRIS, aged 49 years.

Letter List

BUTLER, J.	BURRIS, H.
BUNNELL, J.S.	BRANDT, C.
CHAMBERS, J.P.	CAREY, JAMES
CARPENTER, G.	COSTA, E.H.
DALTON, H.	HAMILTON, M.
HARTZELL, I.W.	HESTER, A.W.
JOHNSON, T.B.	LOUGHAD, H.W.
KINNAN, J.	LELFEHULT, F.

LEWIS, L. LAWTON, M.A.
LEWIS, M. MORRIS, E.B.
QUERKE, --- RODD, M.E.
TREE, T.

Superior Court
> Estate of H.N. CROOK, deceased
> Final account settled and estate distributed
>
> Estate of M.J. O'CONNOR, deceased
> Account of trustees set for February 26, 1894
>
> People vs. PATRICK RICE
> Submitted and taken under advisement, motion to set aside denied
>
> Estate of PEDRO SAIS, deceased.
> Application to lease property denied
>
> Estate of J.A. THOMPSON, deceased
> Account settled and distributed
>
> PASTORI and RIZZINI vs. their Creditors
> Set for Wednesday, December 27
>
> A.C. DIGGINS vs. T.J. MAHON etal
> Tried and submitted on brief
>
> E. SCHWIESAU vs. T.J. MAHON etal
> Case tried and submitted on brief

Town Talk
Mrs. GEORGE HARDING and children left last week for the east, to be absent on a visit of a year or more. Mr. HARDING accompanied them as far as Sacramento.

Marriage Licenses
> WILLIAM REUBEN ROGERS, 27, Sonoma, to ANNA WEYL, 22, Sonoma
> GEORGE M. McDONALD, 24, Hollister, to Miss EFFIE G. PRESCOTT, 24, San Rafael

Marin County Tocsin
Saturday, December 23, 1893

Local News
WILLIAM J. MILLER was appointed Postmaster of San Rafael by the President last Wednesday. The gentleman is one of the old and respected citizens of Marin, and his success gives satisfaction, not only in San Rafael, but to hundreds of friends throughout the county. Mr. MILLER will take charge of the post office about the middle of January.

CHARLES MARTIN, the wealthy landowner of San Antonio, was in San Rafael this week.

Coroner EDEN left yesterday for Bolinas, in response to a telephone announcing that a BODY had been found on the beach there.

Professor C.S. SMYTHE, who has been teaching in the Hollister High School for the past term, is spending his vacation in San Rafael.

GORDON BAECHTAEL, formerly a clerk with Grosjean & Co., spent several days in San Rafael this week, visiting his many friends here. Mr. BAECHTAEL is now a prosperous merchant of Willits, Mendocino County.

Tomales
Miss N. KIRK closed her school in Chileno Valley and is at home for the winter.

Mrs. REYNOLDS will teach in Tomales next term. The Trustees could not do without her as she is so bright and popular.

Estate of MICHAEL J. O'CONNOR, deceased
    Notice to all parties interested in the trust in the Will ordered to appear
    FANNY C. O'CONNOR, MARY STONE O'CONNOR, FANNY STONE O'CONNOR, SARAH A. O'CONNOR, CHARLES F. O'CONNOR, ELLIE O'CONNOR VALLETTE, MAGGIE K. O'CONNOR, JOHN F.K. O'CONNOR, SARAH O'CONNOR GRIFFIN, FANNY O'CONNOR KRUMPEL, AGNES K. O'CONNOR, THOMAS D. O'CONNOR, MARY O'GORMAN, MICHAEL J. O'CONNOR, JOHN A. O'CONNOR, JAMES C. O'CONNOR, ANGELA O'CONNOR, WILLIAM O'CONNOR, and ANN W. O'CONNOR
    Must appear before Superior Court February 26, 1894
    A.H. LOUGHBOROUGH, Attorney for Trustee
                THOMAS S. BONNEAU, Clerk

Marin Journal
Thursday, December 28, 1893

    Superior Court
        FRANK PERARA
        Order setting aside personal property

        People vs. PATRICK RICE
        Plea "not guilty"

        Estate of H.A. BOYCE, deceased
        Demurrer overruled, 10 days to answer

        Estate of CHARLES BROSIN, deceased
        Sale of real estate confirmed

        D.L. HAYDEN vs. his Creditors
        Continued 2 weeks

        EMANUEL BEHM vs. FRANK PERARA
        Judgment for plaintiff

    Real Estate Transfers
        Home and Farm Co. to MARY P. NASON & MAGGIE C. STRAND
        80.26 acres, Lots 9 & 10, Divn C, portion of Rancho de Novato - $10

        JOHN P. STANLEY to SAMUEL WEBSTER
        196.89 acres, known as Stone Ranch, partly in Sonoma and Marin Counties - $7,000

        CANDIDO RIGHETTI and wife to AQUILINE RIGHETTI
        124 acres, Riverside farm, portion of Garcia Rancho - $10

        JESUS M. SAIS to MARTIN PETERSEN
        65.7 acres near Fairfax Station

Died
DENNERY – In San Rafael, Sunday, December 21, 1893, WINIFRED DENNERY, aged 23 years, wife of LEON DENNERY.

Town Talk
Father LAGAN returned from his European trip Tuesday.

Mrs. EVA GREGG has returned from Chicago. She is contemplating starting a boarding house.

Mr. C.T. THOMPSON, a highly respected citizen of Tomales, died at that place on Monday, December 18. His funeral was largely attended.

Mrs. T.C. O'CONNOR, who has been making an extended stay in Paris, France, has started homeward, and is now spending a season in New York City.

ROBERT DICKOW and CHARLES KURTZ, of the firm DICKOW & KURTZ, bakers, have dissolved partnership, Mr. DICKOW retiring from the business which will be conducted by Mr. KURTZ, who will receive monies due the firm and pay all bills.

PIO LAFRANCHI, nephew of Mr. I. SARTORI, and well known in this county, will participate in the rendition of the opera "Martha" at the Grand Opera House in San Francisco in January. The opera will be given for the benefit of the proposed Italian Hospital. Mr. LAFRANCHI has a magnificent bass voice, which has been heard with pleasure in many a parlor concert.

Court Rafael, No. 8032, A.O.F. of A., elected officers for the ensuing year at its meeting last night at Odd Fellows' Hall as follows:
- Chief Ranger – JAMES W. COCHRANE
- Sub Chief Ranger – JOSEPH J. MURRAY
- Financial Secretary – W.J. BOYD
- Recording Secretary – WILLIAM EDEN
- Senior Woodward – P.E. O'BRIEN
- Junior Woodward – N. EMHOFF
- Senior Beadle – M. MADSEN
- Junior Beadle – JOSEPH BARROWS
- Trustee – E. BURGLE
- Doctor – W.F. JONES
- Druggist – J. WOLFE

Letter List

ALDERMAN, L.	ACKLEY, H.C.
BASSI, M.	BECKENDORF, B.
COOLEY, M.	COURAN, J.
FERDINANDO, C.	COSTA, A.
HURLEY, K.	HOGAN, J.F.
LAWTON, T.D.	JONES, O.E.
MAXWELL, A.	MORGANSEN, M.
PETERSEN, C.	PALMER, J.
RUSSELL, J.	STEVENS, M.
SANCHEZ, F.	SALMON, ---
XAVIER, P.	TULLY, M.
WRIGHT, J.L.	WILSON, S.
RUSSELL, K.	

Foreign

MIRAELL, C.	FIGORA, L.
DES NEVOS, M.F.	CANDIDO, N.
COPA, M.	AGOSTINO, F.

Dissolution of Partnership
Business known as DICKOW & KURTZ
DICKOW is retiring
KURTZ will continue
Filed December 24, 1893

ROBERT DICKOW
CHARLES KURTZ

MARIN COUNTY NEWSPAPERS 1894

Marin Journal
Thursday, January 4, 1894

Superior Court
   LEVI HENDRICKS vs. D.L. HAYDEN etal
   Demurrer withdrawn

   Estate of W.E. HOLLOWAY, deceased
   Final account and distribution set for trial January 3, 1894

   AMANDA TANN vs. Patent Brick Co.
   Set for January 7, 1894

   PASTORI and RIZZINI vs. their Creditors
   Further hearing continued to January 10, 1894

   F.W. SPENCER vs. V. NEALE etal
   Defandants motion for non-suit denied

Deaths in San Rafael
The following deaths occurred in San Rafael from January 1, 1893 to January 1, 1894:
   January 4, 1893 - Mrs. EMMA H. BELL, 64 years
   January 25, 1893 – HIRAM TOWNE, 62 years
   February 5, 1893 – MARY SILVA – 8 months, 24 days
   February 8, 1893 – Mrs. CATHERINE ENOS – 50 years
   March 13, 1893 – NORMAN A. LULL, 53 years
   March 13, 1893 – Mrs. SOPHIA S. ZELLAR, 60 years
   April 1, 1893 – EUGENE KURTZ, 41 years
   April 15, 1893 – Mrs. JANE BOYLE, 77 years
   April 20, 1893 – Mrs. SOPHIA ZINKAND, 47 years
   June 23, 1893 – LEE CHUNG LOW, 39 years
   June 28, 1893 – MATHEW HART, 43 years
   July 4, 1893 – MICHAEL LAWLER, 74 years
   July 18, 1893 – JOHN KEIGHO, 21 years
   July 25, 1893 – F.J. WHITE M.D., 55 years
   August 13, 1893 – EARL T. KERR, 31 years
   August 28, 1893 – CHARLES MALLON, 30 years
   September 1, 1893 – LEE DOON
   September 2, 1893 – MARY KENNEDY, 26 years
   September 12, 1893 – BAILEY KINNEY, birth
   September 13, 1893 – JOSEPH PACDANEDA, 1 month, 5 days
   September 15, 1893 – MARGARETH JEPSON, 3 months
   September 20, 1893 – JAMES ROY, 55 years
   September 21, 1893 – VERONICA SHEEHY, 5 years
   September 21, 1893 – ISABELLA HOWITT, 87 years
   October 22, 1893 – MARY E. BURY, 24 years
   October 19, 1893 – Mrs. MARY MURPHY, 79 years
   October 31, 1893 – CHESTER McCAMISH, 2 years, 3 months
   November 6, 1893 – NICHOLAS HAACK, 62 years
   November 9, 1893 – MARTIN SALME, 58 years
   November 29, 1893 – H.T.W. PETERSON, 54 years
   December 14, 1893 – JAMES MORRIS, 49 years
   December 24, 1893 – Mrs. W. DENNERY, 23 years

Causes of death – 10 from consumption, 9 from heart disease, 1 from cancer, 2 from brain disease, 1 from apoplexy, 1 from whooping cough, 1 from legal execution, 1 from diphtheria, 2 from old age, 1 from cysts, 1 from blood poisoning, 4 were infants, 11 were strangers.

Educational Notes

Several changes will occur in other districts. Mr. HENDERSON will retire from Mill Valley, Miss NEYCE from Halleck, and Miss CHENEY from Franklin. Miss M.J. LOWDEN, who has taught the Clark School for several years, has resigned her position to be married on the 4th instant.

EUGENE BURGLE
    Practical Gardener
    San Rafael

WILLIAM SALE
    Furniture
    San Rafael

THOMAS CURREY
    Harness and Saddles
    San Rafael

DICKOW & KURTZ
    French Bakery
    San Rafael

J.P. CHRISTIESON, Manager
    Pioneer Mill and Lumber Co.
    San Rafael

A.B. MORETTI & Co.
    Groceries
    San Rafael

HANSEN & LUND
    Lumber
    San Rafael

WOOD, CHRISTIESON & Co.
    Real Estate
    San Rafael

GEORGE McMILLAN
    Photograph Gallery
    San Rafael

PETER BRUNN
    Boots & Shoes
    San Rafael

JOHN BROOKS
    Shoe Shop
    San Rafael

GEORGE HARDING
    Horseshoer and Hoof Expert
    San Rafael

H. IVERSON
    Rock Paving Co.
    San Rafael

Dr. H.B. DAVISON
    Physician and Surgeon
    San Rafael

Dr. K. URBAN
 Physician and Surgeon
 Tomales

Dr. W.K. VANCE
 Physician and Surgeon
 San Rafael

Dr. H.O. HOWITT
 Physician and Surgeon
 San Rafael

Dr. MARY A. MORGAN
 Physician, San Rafael Sanitarium
 San Rafael

Professor F. DIETZ
 Vocal and Piano instruction
 San Rafael

J.P. ROBERTS
 Plain and Ornamental Plaster
 San Rafael

H. CASSOU, Proprietor
 Hotel de Paris
 San Rafael

MEHL & KLEIN
 Meat Market
 San Rafael

KINSELLA & JOHNSON
 Stoves
 San Rafael

W.B. WINN
 Editor of Marin Journal
 San Rafael

SCHNEIDERS
 Boot polishing
 San Rafael

A.B. THOMSON
 Dry Goods
 San Rafael

R. SWIFT
J.P. DAVENPORT
 House Painters
 San Rafael

JOHN WHITE
 Contractor and Builder
 San Rafael

CHARLES S. BARNEY
 Real Estate and Insurance
 San Rafael

SAUNDERS & JACOBS
    Plumbers
    San Rafael

GEORGE F. RODDEN
    Dentist
    San Francisco

JOHN L. GREER
    Marin County Abstract Co.
    San Rafael

E.B. MARTINELLI
    Attorney
    San Rafael

GEORGE M. DODGE
GEORGE L. RICHARDSON
    Civil Engineers
    San Rafael

WILLIAM N. ANDERSON
    Meats
    San Rafael

M. BLUMENTHAL & Co.
    Meats, Vegetables
    San Rafael

P.E. DUFFY
    Carriage Shop
    San Rafael

INMAN & Sons
    Druggists
    San Rafael

GROSJEAN & Co.
    Groceries
    San Rafael

DAVID NYE
    Attorney
    San Rafael

HAM & MINOTT
    Coal and Wood
    San Rafael

MILLIGAN's
    Shaving Parlor
    San Rafael

W.F. DOUGHERTY
    Search and Notary
    San Rafael

Miss J. KRAENBUHL
    Music and Piano lessons
    San Rafael

Mrs. M. COIT
Millinery
San Rafael

Marin County Tocsin
Saturday, January 6, 1894

Died
CASE – In Saucelito, January 4, 1894, ARLO V. CASE, aged 28 years.

DIXON – In San Francisco, entered into rest, January 1, 1894, Mrs. MARIAN DIXON, mother of Mrs. A.C. McALLISTER, Mrs. JOHN E. BURRESS, Mrs. GEORGE FETHERSTON, and Miss BESSIE DIXON, aged 78 years and 6 months. (Peterboro, Ontario, and San Jose papers please copy)

Tomales News
THOMAS G. ABLES, nephew of the well known cashier of the Tomales Bank, was kicked by a horse at that place last Saturday evening and received injuries that may prove fatal. The vicious brute struck him full on the forehead as he was entering a stall, and the iron horseshoe tore away nearly an inch square of the skull. The sufferer was unconscious for an hour. He recovered sufficiently to walk into the house. His condition is now critical, but the doctors hope to pull him through.

Superior Court
E. BEHM vs. F. PERARA
Submission set aside

Real Estate Transfers
Home & Farm Co. to HENRIETTA BOWMAN
Lots 1, 2, & 3, Subd. Lot 17, Div C, containing 36.75 acres - $10

WILLIAM EDWARD to HOWARD HAVENS
Certain lots in EDWARDS-HARRISON tract

Estate of CHARLES BROSIN to J.H. McDONOUGH
Lot in Glen Park tract, San Rafael - $10

Sausalito Bay Land Co. to ANTONIO PEREIRA
Lot on Main Street, Crescent Ave., Sausalito - $10

Masonic Installation
Marin Lodge, No. 191, F & AM, installed the following officers:
THOMAS S. BONNEAU – W.M.
JAMES SAUNDERS – S.W.
W.F. JONES – J.W.
F.J. JACOBS – Secretary
B.W. STUDLEY – Treasurer
WILLIAM ELLIOTT – S.D.
J. BETTENCOURT – J.D.
WILLIAM K. FLICK – Tyler
JAMES T. McLEAN – Marshall
S.M AUGUSTINE – Steward
W.G. CORBALEY – Steward

Marin Journal
Thursday, January 11, 1894

Local Brevities
Mr. AMES is transforming the old unused schoolhouse at the foot of E Street into a dwelling.

It is rumored that JAMES B. BURDELL of Rancho Olompali will soon start a creamery in San Antonio township.

Card of Thanks
> San Antonio, Marin County, December 29, 1893
> Mr. JOHN VONSEN, donated a lot to build new schoolhouse
>> A.C. MATHESON
>> B MACK Jr.
>> E.P. NISSON
>> H. EHLERS
>> WILLIAM JONES

Annual Meeting
> California Schuetzen Club Park and Building Association
>> O. BURMEISTER, Secretary

Local Brevities

R. CONSTANTINI, a crazy foreigner, was found yelling on Fourth Street Wednesday morning at 4 o'clock by Watchman JAMES HEALY, and was landed in the town jail after a desperate struggle. This is not his first disturbance.

PETER WILLIAMS is putting up a fine two-story house on the corner of First and E Streets. In the Spring, he will put up another. PETER now has 7 houses in town, but will make it an even dozen before the year is out.

Marriage Licenses
> HENRY HOFF, 28, Oakland to Miss N.E. CONTERNO, 23, Oakland
> F.E. DOYLE, 23, San Francisco to Miss H.W. COOK, 22, San Francisco
> P.D. CONNELLY, 30, San Rafael to Miss MARY E. KERRIGAN, 25, San Rafael

Real Estate Transfers
> Estate of CHARLES BROSIN to J.H. McDONOUGH
> Order confirming probate, lot 3, block J, Coleman's addition to San Rafael - $1200
>
> Estate of CHARLES BROSIN to J.H. McDONOUGH
> Lot 5, block J, San Rafael
>
> JAMES TUNSTEAD and wife to GEORGE A. HUNNEWELL
> Lot on W Irwin Street, San Rafael - $10
>
> ISAAC JESSUP to JOSEPH ARBINI
> Ptn. Of Jessup tract, San Rafael - $10

Superior Court
> SPENCER vs. NEAL etal
> Under advisement
>
> Estate of A.H. DODGE, deceased
> Letter issued to E. EDEN
>
> Estate of D.L. HAYDEN, deceased
> Account of receiver settled
>
> Estate of S.J. SOARES, deceased
> Over one week
>
> TAYLOR vs. BELLRUDE
> Set for January 22, 1894
>
> AMANDA TANN, Admx. Vs. Patent Brick Co.
> Defandant's motion for a new trial taken under advisement

Letter List
ADAMS, R.	COSSA, ----
CARPENTER, L.G.	CRANE, C.M.

CONNOLLY, A.	DUPERYRAUX, B.
DORE, M.	GONZALES, J.
KUNIS, J.	LOW, J.
MULLEN, J.	NEWLANDS, M.
OSBORNE, W.H.	POWERS, THOMAS
PERSSON, L.O.	PADRET, N.
RUSSELL, A.	De RAMOS, A.E.
SHEEHAN, ----	STEWART, R.F.

Born
DALESSI – In San Rafael, January 6, 1894, to the wife of H. DALESSI, a son.

Marin County Tocsin
Saturday, January 13, 1894

Local News
J.J. O'REILLY has been appointed a guard of the Midwinter Exposition.

C.A. ZINKAND has returned from Europe and will probably settle in his handsome San Rafael residence.

Night Watchman JAMES H. HEALY and Miss CLARA SCHOENEMAN were married quietly last Wednesday evening.

M.C. DUFFICY was examined by the Supreme Court last Tuesday, and admitted to practice as an Attorney at Law. Mr. DUFFICY will open an office in San Rafael.

G. PROTESTI, an Italian vegetable gardener of Picnic Valley, was thrown from a delivery wagon last Wednesday and suffered a fracture of the leg. The limb was set by Dr. WICKMAN and the patient is doing well.

THOMAS P. BOYD had moved is law office to San Francisco, and is now with J.C. McKEE, at 419 California Street. He will, however, do court reporting here, and when not occupied with reporting, will practice law in San Francisco.

J. ESCALLE, we understand, was arrested for selling wine in Sausalito without a municipal license, and was duly convicted by the local Justice. Presumably he was selling his own wine, and if so the proceeding was utterly illegal, as no license can be exacted from a man engaged in selling articles grown or produced by himself.

Mr. P.D. CONNOLLY, one of the popular and promising young men of San Rafael, and Miss MARY E. KERRIGAN, were married last Wednesday morning in the Catholic Church, Father LAGAN officiating.

SAM SIMARD, the Superintendent of the Remillard Brick Co., at Greenbrae, died at his home last week after a long and painful illness. Mr. SIMARD, about two months ago, feeling a little stronger, went to Santa Barbara for his health. His health rapidly declined, and he was brought home to die. He was a prominent member of the Odd Fellows, Druids of Pleasanton, Court Estrella 7905, A.O.F,, of San Rafael. He was buried at Mountain View Cemetery, Oakland. He was married a year ago to Miss MAUDE MANN of San Quentin. ED REMILLARD will take charge of the yard.

Mt. T.G. ABLES, who suffered terrible injuries when kicked by a vicious horse, has improved.

Improvements in San Rafael
Thirty seven new buildings were constructed in San Rafael during the year 1893. The names of the builders are:

J.W. COCHRANE	Mrs. BURNS
T.B. BELL	J.D. BRAVO
P. WILLIAMS	Mrs. SEIBEL
H. WILKINS	J. STAFFORD
P. RYALL	GEORGE HARDING
J. HUNNEWELL – 3	J. WALL
Mrs. COIT	A BORELLA
Mr. DAVIS	F. MEHL

CHEDA & Co. – 2
I.H. PARKS
A.C. McALLISTER
Mr. De FIENNES
W. DREYPOLCHER
J. FRANETTA
J. PETERSEN – 2

MARTIN SALME
G. MORELLO
J. PERATA
F. GEIGER
HANSEN & LUND – 2
P.D. CONNELLY

Real Estate Transfers
    A.B. CASE to HUGH G. TODD
    Lot 19, Block B, Coleman's addition to San Rafael - $525

Died
SHELLEY – In San Rafael, January 11, 1894, SAMUEL GILMAN SHELLEY, youngest son of Captain W.N. and FRANCIS SHELLEY, a native of Marin County, aged 3 months and 12 days.

BYERS – In San Rafael, January 9, 1894, ANNIE E. BYERS, beloved daughter of the late Captain JOHN and ELLEN BYERS, and beloved and only sister of Mrs. LIZZIE J. THOMAS and the late ROBERT J. BYERS, a native of San Francisco, age 25 years.

Notice to Creditors
    Estate of MARTIN SALME, aka MARTIN SALM, deceased
    JAMES W. COCHRANE, Attorney for Executor
    Filed December 14, 1893
                      P.E. DUFFY
                      Executor of Estate

Notice to Creditors
    Estate of EUGENE MORTON, aka OWEN MORTON, deceased
    JAMES W. COCHRANE, Attorney for Executor
    Filed December 20, 1893
                      ELLEN CATHERINE MORTON
                      Executrix of Estate

Notice to Creditors
    Estate of JAMES BLOOM, Deceased
    LIPPITT & LIPPITT, Attorneys for Executors
    Filed Petaluma, December 21, 1893
                      LUCIA M. BLOOM
                      ADOLPH J. BLOOM
                      Executors of Will and Estate

Next Grand Jury
W.M. ANDERSON
H.B. BASS
E. DuBOIS
E.C. LUND
A.C. McALLISTER
M. MURRAY
M. O'CONNOR
GEORGE T. PAGE
WILLIAM PATTEN
H. SCHLOSSER
J.O.B. SHORT
F. SEIBEL
D. SUTHERLAND
W.P. TAYLOR
A.P. TOWNE
D. WARDEN
GEORGE E. WILSON
H.A. COBB
PETER DEAN

GEORGE E. RING
J. SCHNELL
J.E. SHOOBERT
HANS NIELSON
A.G. SCOWN
J.R. SWEETSER
G.W. GRINTER
A. INGERMANN
B.G. MORSE
W.J. DICKSON
T.H. ESTEY
E. GALLAGHER
P.H.C. CLAUSSEN
G. CODONI
GEORGE MASON
F. MILLER
L. BONETTI
D.B. BURBANK
W.R. FAIRBANKS

CHARLES FORREST	H. GULDAGER
J.T. HARMES	O. HUBBELL
A. LAWRENCE	M. KIRK
R.D. MAGEE	CHARLES MARTIN
J.J. REED	JOHN VONSEN

Trial Jurors for Superior Court

P. DADO	Tomales
C.J. DOWD	Sausalito
A.C. McLEOD	Sausalito
THOMAS HENNESSEY	San Rafael
A. INGERMANN	Bolinas
C. CHISHOLM	San Rafael
B. HEILFRON	Nicasio
L. FILIPPINI	Tomales
F.W. HOLLAND	Tomales
T.J. STEELE	Sausalito
P. SMITH	San Rafael
S.B. CUSHING	San Rafael
L. MARTINELLI	Nicasio
M. JENSEN	Tomales
M. BENSON	San Rafael
J.B. RICE	San Rafael
J.B. BURDELL	Novato
HENRY BETTEN	Bolinas
DAVID DOUGLASS	Tomales
SALVADOR PACHECO	San Rafael
M. BURREIAS	Sausalito
W.D. FREEMAN	Tomales
A.F. PETERSON	San Rafael
JOHN BEISLER	Bolinas

Marin Journal
Thursday, January 18, 1894

Notice to Creditors
Estate of AIRMET H. DODGE, deceased
E.B. MAHON, Attorney for Administrator
Filed January 11, 1894
EDWARD EDEN
Administrator of Estate

Seven Lives Lost
Total Collapse of a Bridge
A terrible accident occurred on the narrow gauge road at the Austin Creek Bridge near Cazadero on Sunday night. By means of a breaking bridge, 7 men have lost their lives: WILLIAM F. BREMER, Clerk of the Cazadero Hotel; THOMAS COLLISTER, Locomotive Fireman; FRANK HART, of the Hotel, and brother of W.F. HART of the Examiner; R.H. SABINE, the Railroad Agent; THOMAS GOULD, Postmaster; JOHN RICE, Engine Wiper; A.C. BRIGGS, Engineer. WILL BROWN, the Conductor, is the only man who escaped death. Thus far only two bodies have been recovered.

Local Brevities
Mr. EUGENE BOST of Merced is visiting Mrs. BARCLAY on E Street.

Mrs. FARRELL and family of D Street, contemplate moving to San Francisco to live.

Mr. FRED FIELD, who was formerly station agent at the Ross Station, was in San Rafael last Saturday.

Mr. S. MARTINEZ is erecting a house on the lot on South Fourth Street which he purchased lately from Mr. J. SHORT.

Mr. and Mrs. CLYDE N. BROWN (nee BOYD), who have been visiting relatives and friends returned to San Francisco last Sunday.

Mr. JAMES CRANE left San Rafael last Tuesday on the James Peabody as a seal hunter. Mr. CRANE is an experienced hand at shooting seal, and it is expected that he will return home with a goodly number of pelts to his credit.

Town Talk
Mr. HUNNEWELL is erecting a two story house on the east side of Irwin Street near the broad gauge depot.

Marriage Licenses
    STEPHEN T. FLYNN, 30, Oakland, to Miss LUCY SMITH, 23, Bolinas
    J.M. MORAS, 24, San Rafael, to Miss MARIA DOS ANGOS MORAS, 21, San Rafael
    A.M. FRANCISCO, 27, San Rafael, to MARIANNA J. DA SILVEIRA, 22, San Rafael

Abandoned Children
The following Orphans and Abandoned Children have been received in St. Vincent's Asylum since October 1, 1893.

Orphans	Age
HUGH DOUGHERTY	11 years
VINCENT CULATTO	8 years
CHARLES PAGANINI	9 years, 7 months
FRANCIS GLEESON	9 years
MARTIN MULLEN	9 years
FRED SCHMEIRER	10 years, 5 months
MARSTON SMITH	10 years, 3 months
MANUEL MARTINEZ	12 years
MICHAEL KENNEDY	11 years
WILLIAM DOYLE	13 years
PATRICK KIELY	9 years, 10 months
THOMAS KIELY	8 years, 6 months
JOHN KIELY	7 years, 4 months
RICHARD JAMES MOONEY	11 years
EUGENE KILLEN	10 years, 4 months
THOMAS KILLEN	8 years, 1 month
HARRY WALLACE	11 years, 4 months
MICHAEL WALLACE	10 years, 3 months
JOHN CLARK	10 years, 4 months
JAMES CLARK	9 years, 3 months
HARRY CLARK	7 years, 7 months
WILLIAM FITZGERALD	12 years
PETER NEVIN	---
BAPTISTE ROUCHETO	9 years, 7 months
WILLIAM STORLIM	9 years, 4 months
WILLIAM SANDERS	9 years
JOHN CASSIDY	10 years, 9 months
JAMES IVIEN	---
FRANCIS CONRAD	12 years, 2 months
JOHN CUNLIFFE	10 years, 8 months
Abandoned	
CHARLES McKEEL	13 years

Items of Interest
E. SCHWIESAU will have his new rock crusher in working order this week when the work on re-surfacing Fourth Street will commence.

JOHANNES PETERSON, the builder and contractor, has opened an office under the Central Hotel. His son, HENRY PETERSON, is associated with him in business and is also an agent for the celebrated Victor bicycle.

Superior Court
> People vs. JAMES TAYLOR
> Arraignment set for Wednesday, January 17th

> Estate of J.G. KITTLE, deceased
> Partial distribution

> Estate of J. GIACOMINI, deceased
> Hearing on confirmation of sale

> PASTORI and RIZZINI vs. their Creditors
> Order to show cause dismissed

> Estate of MARIA L. VELASCO, deceased
> Application of Dominican College for distribution to them of $1,000 under the Will
> Argued and submitted

> S.J. SOARES vs. his Creditors
> Sheriff appointed assignee, no bonds

> Estate of ROBERT LANDGRAF, deceased
> Letters of administration issued to JOSEPH NORDMAN, bond of $700

> Estate of HENRY EVANS, deceased
> Petition for sale of personal property set for hearing Monday January 22nd

> Estate of DAVID RING, deceased
> Account settled and distributed

> AARON SHAVER vs. R.M. KEARNEY etal
> Decree of foreclosure

Father McCUE, formerly assistant at St. Rose's Church in San Francisco, has been appointed rector of the parish of Novato in place of Rev. CHARLES E. O'NEILL, whose health will not permit him to attend to his duties.

Rev. J. McQUAID of San Rafael has been assigned to Holy Cross parish in San Francisco, and Rev. E. DEMPSEY, a newly ordained priest, will take Father McQUAID's place here.

Marin County Tocsin
Saturday, January 20, 1894

Local News
STEPHEN CALHOUN BOWERS, the philosopher of the Sausalito News, spent yesterday in San Rafael.

ISIDOR DAUS, a well known and wealthy resident of San Rafael, died at his residence here last Wednesday morning.

The names of M.J. MULHERN and M. ROBERTS were omitted from the Grand Jury list selected by Judge ANGELLOTTI last week.

Several San Rafael ladies nearly died of a broken heart last Wednesday night. These catastrophes were almost precipitated by the marriage of handsome MILES J. CONWAY which took place that evening. MILES has long been a favorite here with the fair sex, and it was hoped that some daughter of San Rafael might capture his affections. A San Franciscan, however, won the day. Mrs. CONWAY's name was Miss KATE M. HEALEY. The wedding took place very quietly in San Francisco, only relatives and a very few friends being present.

Real Estate Transfers
> MARY P. NASON to MAGGIE C. SHAND
> Lots 9 & 10, containing 80.26 acres - $10

Home and Farm Co. to FRED & LIZZIE LIND
Part of lot 8, Div. C, Home & Farm Co. tract - $10

J.C. WEIGHTMAN to CLARA I. LONG
Lots 3, 4, 13, 14, Block 2, Sausalito Bay & Land Co. tract - $800

Marin Journal
Thursday, January 25, 1894

Superior Court
People vs. T.J. JUKES
Set for hearing January 29th

Estate of JOHN GIACOMINI, deceased
Over one week

People vs. PAT RICE
Continued for session

Estate of HENRY EVANS, deceased
Continued

People s. JAMES P. LAWLER
Arraigned, time to plead set

M.M. EICKHOFF vs. M. EICKHOFF
Set for trial February 16th

M. BRENNFLECK vs. J. SHINE
Over for the term

Marin County vs. L. TOMASINI
Over for the term

H.W. TAYLOR vs. J.S. BELLRUDE
Set for hearing February 6th

DANIEL SLINKEY vs. C.H. HARRISON
Judgment for defendant

Marriage Licenses
PAUL F. RECEKER, 42, San Francisco to S. LOUISE CAMEHL, 22, San Francisco

Town Talk
Professor LUCA BONETTI of Millerton was in town last week.

Miss H.B. DAVIS of Ross Valley will be married soon to Mr. G.J. BECKER.

It is rumored that Mr. WILLIAM JEWELL contemplates starting a real estate and insurance office in San Rafael.

The large windmill on the premises of GEORGE E. WILSON, near Forbes Avenue, was blown down and badly wrecked during the wind of last week.

Mr. ED CUMMINGS, one of the early settlers in Marin County, is lying in a very critical condition at the County Farm. He is not expected to recover.

Mr. P.J. SHERIDAN's new house in Coleman's addition is now almost completed. Mr. SHERIDAN expects to bring his family here sometime this spring.

The following Marin County young ladies and gentlemen have graduated from Heald's Business College, during the past year: BENJAMIN H. GRAVES, JOSEPHINE DUFFICY, MARY H. MONDON, San Rafael; ACTON HAVEN, Novato; SILVIA CODONI, J.J. CODONI, Tocaloma; JOSEPH LEWIS, Sausalito.

District Deputy GEORGE F. RODDEN installed last Monday evening, the following officers of Mr. Tamalpais Parlor No. 64, N.S.G.W.S: S. HERZOG, President; C.H. BENSON, Vice-President; THOMAS P. BOYD, 2nd Vice-President; W.J. BOYD, 3rd Vice-President; JOHN F. SCHNEIDER, Financial Secretary; ROY SHAVER, Marshall; FRANK MULHERN, Inside Sentinel; A.J. CHICK, Outside Sentinel. The retiring President, STEPHEN EDEN, was presented with a magnificent badge in token of the esteem in which he is held by the members of the Parlor.

On Monday morning, a young man named ERNEST RUSSELL, started from the landing below the broad gauge depot in an old dilapidated catboat, intending to sail to Oakland. BERT WALS, of this place, intended to accompany him on the trip, but at the last moment concluded he would not as the craft was very old and rotten. RUSSELL was seen to pass through Raccoon Straights late in the afternoon. That was the last seen of him until Tuesday afternoon, when his boat was discovered near Tiburon, bottom up, with its occupant gone. No news has been heard from the missing youth, and undoubtedly he was drowned in the bay.

Funeral of Engineer BRIGGS
The funeral of Engineer BRIGGS, who met his death by the fatal accident at Austin Creek last week, took place here on Friday at St. Paul's Episcopal Church, and was attended by a large number of the friends of the deceased. Rev. HARTMAN preached a touching sermon. Mr. BRIGGS was a resident of Sausalito, and leaves a widow and 3 children. His remains were interred in Mt. Tamalpais Cemetery at this place.

Born
WINN – In San Rafael, January 21, 1894, to the wife of W.B. WINN, a son.

Married
CONWAY-HEALEY – In San Francisco, January 18, 1894, at the residence of the bride's parents, on Leavenworth Street by Rev. Father RYAN, M.J. CONWAY of San Rafael, to Miss KATIE M. HEALEY of San Francisco.

Died
DAUS – In San Rafael, January 18, 1894, ISIDOR DAUS, a native of Germany, aged 52 years, and 9 months.

Notice of Proving Will
    Estate of ISIDOR DAUS, deceased
    BENJAMIN HEALEY, Attorney for Petitioner
    Application of SUSAN SAUS for letters testamentary
    Filed January 20, 1894
                THOMAS S. BONNEAU, Clerk
                By D.T. TAYLOR, Deputy Clerk

Real Estate Transfers
    Estate of JONATHAN G. KITTLE to HARRIET De WITT KITTLE
    Decree of distribution, lands in Ross Valley

    Estate of DAVID RING to MICHAEL MURRAY etal
    Land in West side of C Street, San Rafael

    HUGH CROCKARD, by tax collector to S. FOX
    Lots 184, 186, 194, 195, Tidelands in Sausalito - $3.53

    JOHN AMOS, by tax collector to S. FOX
    Lot 22 ½, Sec 15m Township 9, 4 acres, San Rafael - $1.35

    A.B. CASE to HUGH G. TODD
    Lot 19, block E. Coleman's addition - $4.25

    ABNER S. MANN and wife to AUGUSTA W. AMES
    Portion Lot F, plat of lands in San Anselmo Valley - $10

AUGUSTA W. AMES and PELHAM W. AMES to WORTHINGTON AMES
Lot on west side of Wordsworth Avenue in Ross Valley - $10

Marin County Tocsin
Saturday, January 27, 1894

Born
BOTTARINI – At San Anselmo, January 20, 1894, to the wife of CHARLES BOTTARINI, a son.

ADAMS – At San Anselmo, January 21, 1894, to the wife of W.L. ADAMS, a son.

Died
ABLES – In Tomales, January 22, 1894, T.G. ABLES, a native of Ohio, aged 29 years.

BUCHANAN – In San Francisco, January 20, 1894, HENRIETTA J. BUCHANAN, daughter of E.Y. BUCHANAN, a native of Marin County.

Certificate of Co-Partnership
MAGGETTI & CHEDA
Filed January 17, 1894, Marshall
SILVIO J. MAGGETTI, Marshall
ELVEZIO S. CHEDA, Marshall

Local News
JOHN JULIAN, for many years a resident of Marin County, has been appointed Postmaster of the City of El Paso, Texas.

Assignee HARRISON gives notice that he will sell the leasehold interest of P. GALLAGHER, insolvent, in the Penn's Grove quarry.

Dr. HAMPTON, who formerly lived in Tomales township, near the Sonoma line, died suddenly in Arizona last Wednesday, as he was returning home from a prolonged tour of the United States and Europe.

Death of THOMAS TUNSTEAD
Last Saturday afternoon, THOMAS TUNSTEAD called to see his friend, T.D. RIORDAN, the well known attorney. Not finding him in, he laid down on a lounge and fell asleep. He was awakened not long after and started to leave. While descending the flight of stairs, he fell heavily and tumbled headlong to the landing, where he was found helpless and scarcely conscious. An examination proved that the spinal cord was fractured, and but little hope of recovery remained. The patient sank rapidly and passed away Thursday.
There is ample and positive evidence that he was absolutely sober at the time, though it is probable that he was suddenly attacked by vertigo while descending the stairs, as he had lately been subject to severe onsets of this disorder.
Mr. TUNSTEAD had a wide circle of friends in Marin County, and held a high place in the esteem of all who knew him. He was as generous and warm-hearted a man as ever lived, and deserved fully the many kind and sympathetic expressions that his sad end have called forth. He was a brother of ex-Sheriff JAMES TUNSTEAD, and an uncle of the BURTCHAELL brothers, of San Rafael and Larkspur.

Death of T.G. ABLES
The condition of T.G. ABLES was so improved last week, that we believed he was on the road to recovery. A sudden change for the worse set in, however, and the patient sank rapidly, passing away at an early hour on Monday. The untimely end of Mr. ABLES is a most distressing incident of the new year. He was a young man of exemplary habits and fine prospects, and had his life been spared, would have achieved a successful career. He had just rented a ranch in Tomales, risking all he was worth in the venture, and this investment must prove nearly a total loss, leaving his little family, now about to be increased, practically without support. The greatest sympathy is expressed for the widow in her heavy bereavement.

Real Estate Transfers
ELLA F. PARK to First Presbyterian Church of San Rafael
Lot on northwest corner of Fifth and E Street - $5

Renton Coal Co. to A.M. SIMPTON
Tideland lots in Richardson's Bay

A.M. & P.W. AMES to ABNER S. MANN
7 ½ acres near Ross Station - $10

Home & Farm Co. to LILLIAN A. PARKER
Lots 1 & 2, Novato, containing 20.7 acres

Home & Farm Co. to E.E. NORDLING and wife
Part of lot 8, Div. C, Novato, 15.35 acres - $10

Home & Farm Co. to A.H. TETTERBERG
Part of lots 7 & 8, Novato, containing 12 acres - $10

Marin Journal
Thursday, February 1, 1894

Marriage Licenses
JAMES M. MUNEO, 26, San Rafael, to Miss MARIA C. MARES, 20, San Rafael
G.J. BECKER, 27, San Francisco, to Miss HATTIE B. DAVIS, 24, Marin County
LOUIS A. GOSS, 25, Oakland, to Miss ANNIE V. COMMONN, 18, Alameda
ANTONIO F. SOUZA, 28, San Rafael, to JULIA LEONARDA, 20, San Rafael

Superior Court
Estate of M.L. VELASCO, deceased
Application of Dominican College for partial distribution denied

Estate of HENRY EVANS, deceased
Dismissed

Estate of ARTHUR JACKSON, deceased
Over one week

People vs. JAMES P. LAWLER
Over one week

Estate of JOHN GIACOMINI, deceased
Sale of personal property confirmed

People vs. THOMAS J. JUKES
Over two weeks

Estate of W.E. HOLLOWAY, deceased
Over one week

Town Talk
M.J. MILLER's commission as postmaster of San Rafael has arrived from Washington, and he will assume charge of the office today.

ROXIE ROBERTSON has recovered sufficiently from the effects of the severe fall he had last November to be about some.

TEMPLE SMITH of Santa Rosa is attending school at the Tamalpais Military Academy.

Mr. HENRY STEIZ of Petaluma was in San Rafael Monday.

Mrs. F.A. ANGELLOTTI of San Francisco was in San Rafael last Tuesday.

Marin County Tocsin
Saturday, February 3, 1894

Local News

PETER TRAINOR formerly connected with the Broad Gauge ticket office, died last Thursday at Healdsburg, of consumption.

LEE SING, a Chinaman, was hanged at Sam Quentin yesterday. This is the second execution at the State penitentiary under the new law.

The wedding of Mr. G.J. BECKER and Miss HARRIET B. DAVIS, daughter of J.B.F. DAVIS of Ross Valley took place last Wednesday at the residence of the bride's father. Rev. C.L. MILL officiated.

The body of young SABINE, the last of the victims of the Austin Creek horror, was recovered this week. The funeral took place at Petaluma last Thursday, and was attended by a number of members of Tamalpais Parlor, N.S.G.W., which sent a beautiful floral emblem.

Mr. W.J. MILLER and his son GEORGE MILLER took charge of the San Rafael Postoffice last Wednesday. Mr. and Mrs. BARSTOW retired gracefully from the field of the labors they have discharged so efficiently, but are giving the new Postmaster a helping hand over the hard places.

The DeLONG Estate

HENRY PIERCE, assignee of F.C. DeLONG, has filed with the County Clerk, a statement of the business transacted by him since he came into possession of the great Rancho de Novato property. The document shows that the receipts from July 1, 1893, to January 1, 1894, were $33,185.92, and the disbursements were $30,848.85, leaving a balance of $2,237.07. Of the receipts, $16,037.93 represented sales of fruit, and there are still 6,500 boxes of apples and 25,000 gallons of vinegar on hand. The remainder of the receipts were from sales of milk and from other sources. The total indebtedness of the estate reaches the figure of $729,645.82.

Real Estate Transfers

    HARRIET DE WITT KITTLE to LUCIA HAMILTON KITTLE
    Tract of land in Ross Valley, land of JONATHAN G. KITTLE, dec. – love and affection

    Home & Farm Co. to REUBEN SMALL
    11.11 acres, Novato, Part of lot 11, div. B - $10

    MARY A. TUNSTEAD to HEPBURN WILKINS
    Lot on corner of Fourth and A Streets, San Rafael - $5

    HEPBURN WILKINS to JAMES TUNSTEAD
    Lot on corner of Fourth and A Streets, San Rafael - $5

    Tamalpais Land & Water Co. to BERTHA M. KELLOGG
    Lot 186, Mill Valley - $1,200

    Tamalpais Land & Water Co. to A. BARKAN
    Part of the "Reserve", Mill Valley - $750

    A PEDROTTI to A. HOWE
    Lot in village of Olema - $375

    LAURA L. WHITE etal to OTTO E. FALCH
    Subd. 1 & SE ½ of Subd. 2, Lot 76, Mill Valley - $10

    J.W. MACKAY and J.L. FLOOD to JOHN F. BIGELOW
    Part of block 14, Coleman's edition to San Rafael - $10

    J.A. WORMOUTH to J.A. McNEAR
    351.30 acres on Pt. San Pedro - $7,000

Marin Journal
Thursday, February 8, 1894

Local News

Mrs. J.D. TUCKER of Petaluma was in San Rafael last week on a visit to her father, Mr. GEORGE F. FANNING.

Superior Court

    AMANDA TANN vs. Patent Brick Co. etal
    Judgment for defendants

    People vs. JAMES P. LAWLER
    Set for Monday February 12

    Estate of E.I. SUMARD, deceased
    Set for Monday, February 12

    Estate of E.W. HOLLOWAY, deceased
    Set for Monday, February 12

    Estate of ARTHUR JACKSON, deceased
    Estate distributed

    Estate of HENRY EVANS, deceased
    Estate distributed

    Estate of C.T. THOMPSON, deceased
    WILLIAM VANDERBILT appointed administrator, bond $200

Marriage Licenses

    HARRY EDWIN ALLEN, 21, San Francisco, to ELIZABETH S. HAGON, 22, San Francisco
    JOHN F. CANNON, 21, San Francisco, to Mrs. FRANCES D. STEWART, 20, San Francisco

Letter List

ANDERSON, Mrs. M.M.	ANDERSON, ALICE
ALDERMAN, Mrs.	BROWN, Mrs. C.G.
BERTRAM, F.W.	BROWN, Mrs. Dr.
BOYD, G.D.	BARRY, W.M.
CANNARA, FRANK	

BODY

JOHN MORGAN, keeper of the Lime Point reservation, found the remains of a man in the water Monday morning. The deceased was badly decomposed, having been in the water about 3 weeks. His height was 5 feet 8 inches, weight 160 pounds, age 25 to 30 years. He wore striped casimere pants, white flannel underclothing, white cotton shirt with red stripes running around, and no shoes or socks. Coroner EDEN was notified and held an inquest.
Later:
On Wednesday, a man came over from San Francisco and identified the remains at the morgue as those of his brother, PATRICK WATERS, who was drowned while attempting to swim from one vessel to another.

Real Estate Transfers

    Home & Farm Co. to E.E. NORDLING
    Portion lot 8, Div C, Rancho de Novato - $10

    Home & Farm Co. to AUGUST H. ZETTERBERG
    Portions of lot 7 & 8, Div. C, Rancho de Novato

    Sausalito Land & Ferry Co. to ALICE M.M. WALL
    Portion of lot 2, block 68, Sausalito Land & Ferry Co. - $10

    DAVID MEYER by Tax Collector to ROBERT L. COLEMAN
    Lots 289 & 290, Section 38, Sausalito - $5.65

    CARRIE L. OSGOOD etal to H.A. AMES and wife
    Lot 1, Angellotti's addition to San Rafael

Died
SAUL – At St. Vincent's Orphan Asylum, February 4, 1894, OTTO SAUL, aged 9 years.

Marin County Tocsin
Saturday, February 10, 1894

Real Estate Transfers
Tamalpais Land & Water Co. to ELLEN M. DOMETT
Lot 7, Block 2 - $550

Tamalpais Land & Water Co. to BERTHA M. KELLOGG
Lot 280, Mill Valley - $10

MARGARET & GEORGE DAWSON to A.H. WINN
Lots 4, 5, 6, Subd. Q & R, San Anselmo Valley - $10

Sausalito Bay Land Co. to LAURA E. BRIDGEMAN
Lots 19 & 20, block 16, Old Sausalito - $10

JOSEPH ALMY, County Judge, to BENJAMIN S. BROOKS
Block 29, San Rafael town site - $12.50

Home & Farm Co. to JOHN A. SWANSON
Lot 3, div. A, Novato - $10

JOHN A. SWANSON to CHARLES PETERSON
Lot 3, div. A, Novato - $10

EMMA E. DOMETT to CHARLES LUNARNTY
Lots 7 & 8, block 2, Mill Valley - $10

Town Talk
JOSEPH HOXIE of San Rafael is very ill. His trouble began with an ordinary bone felon on a finger, which usually causes only a little inconvenience. Blood poisoning has set in, and the patient is in a very precarious way.

Marin Journal
Thursday, February 15, 1894

Marriage Licenses
CHARLES WILLIAMS, 27, San Francisco, to MAMIE DURAN, 23, San Francisco
CHARLES M. CHASE, 68, San Francisco, to Mrs. KATE BOWLEY, 48, San Francisco
I ROUTSTEIN, 26, San Francisco, to CELIA HAMBURG, 23, San Francisco
H.G. SOHNCKE, 38, Oakland, to MARY A. SULLIVAN, 33, Oakland

Born
AGNEW – In San Rafael, February 9, 1894, to the wife of GEORGE AGNEW, a son.

DE BORBA – In Novato, February 11, 1894, to the wife of ANTONE DE BORBA, a daughter.

HEYWOOD – In San Rafael, February 7, 1894, to the wife of WALTER M. HEYWOOD, a son.

LAKE – In San Rafael, February 9, 1894, to the wife of H.W. LAKE, a son.

Local Brevities
HOP SING has opened a first class laundry on E Street between First and Second Streets, San Rafael.

Miss MAY COOK of San Francisco, is in San Rafael visiting Mr. C.S. BARNEY.

Miss LANHAM of San Francisco was in San Rafael last week on a visit to her mother. She was the guest of Mr. C.S. BARNEY.

Town Talk

I. ROUTSTEIN of San Francisco was married yesterday to Miss CELIA HAMBURG of San Francisco by Rev. J.S. FISHER.

The firm of ATWATER and WOODWARD, grocers, has dissolved partnership, Mr. WOODWARD retiring. The business will continue under Mr. ATWATER.

THOMAS S. ARCHER is now chief clerk in the postoffice, ably assisted by Miss GREEN.

Dr. CAROLYN M. McELROY, dentist, has opened an office in the Wilkin's block. She is a graduate of Ann Arbor University and is thoroughly competent in her chosen profession.

Mr. A. THEYER has opened a new gun and locksmith shop in the Odd Fellows' building.

Superior Court

Estate of JAMES MURPHY, deceased
Final account settled and estate distributed

Estate of W.E. HOLLOWAY, deceased
Over one week

Belvedere Land Co. to CHARLES PAFF
Set for February 14

Estate of E.T. SIMAND, deceased
MAUDE SIMAND appointed administratrix - bond $5,750

Estate of ISIDOR DAUS, deceased
Continued to first Monday in March

Estate of J.A. MURPHY, deceased
PATRICK MURPHY appointed administrator – bond $600

Estate of M.L. VELASCO, deceased
Order to Dominican College appeal made

Estate of B.L. PACHECO, deceased
Account settled and estate distributed

People vs. J.P. LAWLER
Plea entered, not guilty – Set for trial February 21

WILLIAM TIERNEY vs. his Creditors
Insolvent discharged

Letter List

BERTRAM ---	BISMARK, HARRY
BUTLER, Mrs. GEORGE	BYRNES, MARY
CASTRO, Mrs. LOUISA	CHARLES, Miss MABEL
GEOGHABEN, T.	FURLONG, Miss MARJORIE
HOWARD, Mrs. TERESA	HINES, THOMAS
HARVEY, Miss A.	HYDE, Mrs. GEORGE
NEUMANN, JULIUS	MARSHALL, Mrs. LOUIS
REED, Mrs. G.W.	RAMOS, A.E.
ROGGENLAN, ADOLF	

Marin County Tocsin
Saturday, February 17, 1894

Real Estate Transfers
  Home & Farm Co. to THEODORE REICHERT
  Lot 3, Franklin Place, Novato - $10

  JOHN F. LONG to CLARA I. LONG
  Lots 3, 4, 13, 14, block 2, Old Sausalito - $1,400

  Home & Farm Co. to CHARLES A. JACOBSON
  19.5 acres, Novato, part of lot 7, div. C - $10

  Home & Farm Co. to A.G. IVERSON
  19.5 acres, Novato, Novato - $10

  B.M. KELLOGG to ALICE L. EASTLAND
  Lot 186, Mill Valley - $10

  P.E. & JULIA DUFFY to JULIA MULLEN
  Lot 8, block A, Coleman's addition - $10

  GEORGE BARGATE and wife to Belvedere Land Co.
  Lot 4, block 5 - $10

  Estate of B.L. PACHECO, deceased
  Estate distributed to A.F., JUAN, & G. PACHECO, & CATALINA VALENCIA

  WARREN DUTTON to MARY E. THOMPSON
  Lot 21, block 16, Tomales - $50

  Estate of ARTHUR JACKSON, deceased
  Estate distributed to C.R., MARY LOUISA, & E.W. JACKSON, lots in Sausalito

  Estate of M.L. VELASCO, deceased
  Estate distributed to GUMESCINDO, JUAN & A.F. PACHECO, & CATALINA C. VALENCIA

  Belvedere Land Co. to GEORGE BARGATE
  Lot 35, block 3, Belvedere - $10

Born
CHAIX – In San Francisco – February 13, 1894, to the wife of ADRIEN CHAIX (nee MARCHANT), a son.

Notice to Creditors
  Estate of J.A. MURPHY, deceased
  JAMES W. COCHRANE, Attorney for administrator
  Filed February 12, 1894
      PATRICK J. MURPHY
      Administrator of estate

Notice to Creditors
  Estate of SAMUEL T. SIMARD, deceased
  Filed February 12, 1894
      P.N. REMILLARD
      Administrator of estate

Notice of Proving Will
  Estate of CHARLES ARTHUR OZANN aka ARTHUR CHARLES OZANN, dec.
  LOUISE N. OZANN, application for letters testimentary
  THOMAS V. O'BRIEN, Attorney for Petitioner, San Francisco
  Filed February 15, 1894
      THOMAS S. BONNEAU
      Clerk

Marin Journal
Thursday, February 22, 1894

Local Brevities
Dr. WICKMAN will soon join the ranks of the cyclers.

Town Talk
Mr. HENRY JEPSON, who has been down with a long fever, is recovering slowly.

HENRY McMANUS, who sustained a broken thigh as a result of a runaway about three months ago, is now able to take slight exercise outside.

Miss JENNIE HERZOG and Mr. HARRY LICHTENSTEIN will be married a week from Sunday in San Francisco at the synagogue. They will then take the steamer for Honolulu where they expect to remain some weeks.

A Sudden Death
JACOB OBITZ died on Tuesday at his residence after an illness of less than two days. The deceased has been in the meat business in this town for many years, and by his social nature, had a large circle of friends and acquaintances. He was taken ill on Sunday afternoon with pneumonia, and though medical attendance was at once secured, he was unable to shake off the disease with its accompanying complications, and he died about noon on Tuesday. The suddenness of his death was a great shock to the community, as on Saturday he was at his place of business as usual and seemed to be in perfect health.

Funeral Notice
To the members of San Rafael Lodge, No. 24, A.O.U.W.
You are respectfully requested to attend the funeral of our late Brother JACOB OBITZ, deceased, on Thursday, February 22, 1894, in the Masonic Hall building, at 9 o'clock a.m. By order of the Lodge.

Letter List

AMARAL, J.M.	ADAMS, E.C.
ANDERSON, JOHN	ALEXANDER, F.
BAPTISTE, Mrs. ANNA	BIGELOW, Mrs. F.W.
BURNS, Mrs. ELLEN	BRIGGS, Mrs. ARTHUR C.
BRESACK, Miss PORTIA	BROWN, Dr.
BUNDY, JESSIE E.	BOILNAN, Miss L.
BIBBY, AUGUSTA	BIBBY, MARY
CRISANTI, G.	CUNNINGHAM, R.
CHRISTENSEN, MARTIN	CUITER, CHARLES E.
CARPENTER, Miss GRACE	DAWFERY, Miss GRACE
DUTTON, Miss ERMINA	DAVIS, Rev. Mrs. W.W.
DELANEY, Mrs.	DUFFY, W.
DONZEL, A.J.	EWALD, Miss LIZZIE
ENGEL, J.G.	

Superior Court
MORSE KAHN vs. J.B. FAGGIANO
Judgment for plaintiff

Estate of ISIDOR DAUS, deceased
SUSAN DAUS appointed administratrix, bond $4,000

H.R. GREGG vs. EVA N. GREGG
Judgment for plaintiff

Estate and Guardianship of J.B.C. ALVARADO
Letters of Guardianship issued to MARY A. BOND, bond of $100

JOSEPH BOUQUET vs. ESTELLE MINESINGER
Judgment for plaintiff in sum of $640

Estate of GEORGE LARSEN, deceased
Over one week

Estate of W.E. HOLLOWAY, deceased
Over one week

People vs. JAMES P. LAWLER
Plea of not guilty withdrawn and plea of guilty entered
Friday fixed for time of sentence

Belvedere Land Co. vs. CHARLES PAFF
Set for trial March 13

M. COLLUM vs. WILLIAM VANDERBILT etal
Judgment for plaintiff

County of Marin vs. ROBERT FURLONG
Demurrer of defendant sustained

Marin County Tocsin
Saturday, February 24, 1894

Real Estate Transfers
AMANDA HAHN to JOHN KUNNEMANN
Lot in Old Sausalito - $10

AMELIA C. SAVAGE & WENDELL EASTON to J.E. DOOLITTLE
Lots 26 & 27, block 1, Sunnyside tract

GEORGE H. WINTERBURN to J.F. ROOT
Lot in Old Sausalito - $10

DOMINGA BRESSON to GEORGE E. DICKSON
10.628 acres near Fairfax - $10

GEORGE E. DICKSON to DOMINGA BRESSON
Lot on Welch Street, San Rafael - $10

Born
LONGLEY – In Bolinas, February 12, 1894, to the wife of C.J. LONGLEY, a daughter.

Died
OBITZ – In San Rafael, February 20, 1894, JACOB OBITZ, aged 48 years and 18 days.

Sheriff's Sale
MICHAEL CALLAN vs. WILLIAM VANDERBILT, Administrator of the estate of CHARLES T. THOMPSON, deceased, MARY E. THOMPSON & WILLIAM F. BASSETT, defendants
Order of sale under decree of foreclosure
Land in Tomales
Sale to be held at courthouse March 19, 1894
    HENRY HARRISON, Sheriff
    By T.J. FALLON, Undersheriff

Sheriff's Sale
HERBERT R. GREGG vs. EVA N. GREGG, widow, HENRY SCHLOSSER, Assignee of the Estate of EVA N. GREGG, an Insolvent Debtor
Order of sale under decree of foreclosure
Land in san Rafael
Sale to be held at courthouse March 19, 1894
    HENRY HARRISON, Sheriff
    By T.J. FALLON, Undersheriff

Sheriff's Sale
> JOSEPH BOUQUET vs. ESTELLE MINESINGER
> Order of sale under decree of foreclosure
> Land in San Rafael
> Sale to be held at courthouse March 19, 1894
>> HENRY HARRISON, Sheriff
>> By T.J. FALLON, Undersheriff

Notice of Proving Will
> Estate of CAROLINE V. JOHNSTON, deceased
> EDWIN L. GRIFFITH applying for letters of administration
> Filed February 19, 1894
> GEORGE W. TOWLE Jr. – Attorney for Petitioner
>> THOMAS S. BONNEAU, Clerk

Notice to Creditors
> Estate of CHARLES T. THOMPSON, deceased
> Filed February 21, 1894
>> WILLIAM VANDERBILT, Administrator

Local Brevities

Mrs. LIBERTY, the leasee of the Lagunitas Ranch, has sold out to A. BAROFOLDI, who is a nephew of HENRY DALESSI, who will continue the summer resort business, which was so popular under the late tenant. Her many friends will regret to learn that Mrs. LIBERTY will leave Marin County and locate elsewhere.

Coroner EDEN held an inquest last Saturday on the body of HENRY ARK, a San Quentin convict, who died suddenly.

Marin Journal
Thursday, March 1, 1894

Local News

Mrs. LIZZIE McDONALD of San Francisco will teach the Pt. Reyes district school next term in Miss NELSON's place, whom sickness prevents from filling the position.

Mrs. COAN-HAMBLY and Mrs. NELLIE PAULL CARROLL have opened a music studio at New England Villa, cottage No. 1. They will teach voice culture, piano and violin.

Letter List

AHERN, Mrs.	ALLEN, Mrs. H.H.
BROWNING, I.	BUTTERWORTH, Mrs. EMMA
COLLAPY, G.M.	DINSMORE, PAUL
DELZE, A.C.	EASTMAN, Mrs. MARY
FROHMAN, L.	FLICK, Miss LENA
HOYER, S.	GRAVES, WILLIAM
LAWLOR, J.P.	LUZ, INO
MADDEN, JAMES	MESSER, W.T. Jr.
PERSON, OLA	MAILLIARD, JOHN WARD
RYAN, Miss LENA F.	RIPPERT, FIRMIN
TOBIN, ROY J.	SHILLING, AMIR
TERRA, M.M.	

Superior Court
> People vs. JAMES P. LAWLER
> Defendant sentenced to 18 months at San Quentin
>
> R.S. STARR vs. JESSIE BUNDY etal
> Set for March 2
>
> J.R. RICE vs. GEORGE MURPHY etal
> Demurrer overruled

Estate of M. J. O'CONNOR, deceased
Second account of trustee settled

Estate of GEORGE LARSEN, deceased
W.H. ABBOTT appointed administrator, bond of $200

Estate of A.C. BRIGGS, deceased
Mrs. BRIGGS appointed administratrix, Bond of $550

R.A. WILKE vs. L.J. JOHNSON
Motion to substitute attorney granted

Estate of W.E. HOLLOWAY, deceased
Over one week

JOSEPH ALBERTI et ux vs. J.D. BRAVO
Set for trial March 2

Real Estate Transfers
A RIGHETTI & G. TOMASINI to County of Marin
Right of way of Pt. Reyes and Marshall Road - $200

Belvedere Land Co. to GEORGE BARGATE
Lot 35, block 3, Belvedere Land Co. - $20

WILLIAM H. JEWELL and wife to LIVIO H. CHEDA
Lot 13, block 1, Sunnyside tract - $30

MICHAEL W. KEOUGH to TIMOTHY ELLSWORTH
Lot 20, block 9, Old Sausalito

Marin County Tocsin
Saturday, March 3, 1894

Sheriff's Sale
PRESTON & McKINNON (A Corporation), WILLIAM CHASSELS, ARTHUR W. HOBSON, and THOMAS VAN TASSELL
Vs.
EMILY F. TIBBEY, EDNEY S. TIBBEY (her husband), A.E. GRAHAM & H.C. MOORMAN, doing business under the firm name of GRAHAM & MOORMAN, JOHN DOE (a corporation), RICHARD ROE, JOHN ROE, JAMES BLACK, FRANK GREEN, THOMAS WHITE, JOHN WHITE, JAMES DOE, THOMAS ROE, FRANK HOE, and JOHN HOE
Decree of foreclosure
Land in Town of Sausalito
Land to be sold at courthouse March 26, 1894
HENRY HARRISON, Sheriff
By T.J. FALLON, Undersheriff

Local News
Mrs. DAVID NYE has sold her San Rafael residence on Sixth Street to the widow of the late DAVID SCANLAN, chief of the San Francisco Fire Department of San Francisco. Price $6,600.

Mrs. M.J. O'CONNOR and family have returned from Europe and spent the day in San Rafael this week.

Mr. HUGH TODD will immediately commence the erection of a fine two-story residence on the lot he recently purchased on Petaluma Ave.

Mrs. ARCHER, of Tomales, was brought down from there last Wednesday to be examined on a charge of insanity. Dr. JONES and Dr. DuBOIS investigated her case, and ordered her kept at the Poor Farm a week to await developments.

Death of GEORGE BUNN

GEORGE BUNN, one of the old settlers of Marin County, passed away at his residence on Fifth Street, San Rafael, two days after his return from a prolonged visit to Hembrie, Crockett County, Texas, where he had a large cattle ranch about 90 miles from a railroad. On the journey northward, he contracted a severe cold, which settled into a case of acute pneumonia. The old gentleman was really in a dying condition when he reached San Rafael, and though a joy of being once more at home caused him to rally a trifle, it was only the flicker of a candle before the flame went out. Mr. BUNN came to California in 1852, and settled in Tomales in 1857. He owned a very handsome ranch property there, which he disposed of about 10 years ago, at the time of his coming to San Rafael. He then intended to pass the balance of his life in the leisure that he had fairly earned, but his natural energy would not permit of inaction, and he soon became heavily interested in a Texas investment that kept him busy till the day of his death. The deceased was a man of sterling character and blameless life, and though not given to social relaxations, had many friends who sincerely mourn his loss. The funeral takes place today from the Presbyterian Church at 1:30 p.m.

LICHTENSTEIN-HERZOG

The wedding of Mr. HARRY M. LICHTENSTEIN, the well-known capitalist, and Miss JENNIE HERZOG, daughter of M. HERZOG of San Rafael, will take place tomorrow at Shireth Israel Synagogue, San Francisco. A number of invitations have been extended to friends of the young couple and a large and fashionable audience will witness the ceremony. The finest choir in San Francisco will furnish the wedding music for the occasion. Mr. and Mrs. LICHTENSTEIN will receive after the ceremony, at Armory Hall, corner of Ellis and Polk Street, where an elegant wedding breakfast will be served.

Real Estate Transfers

MAUDE M. BOOLE to FRED W. BOOLE
Lot 2, block 5, Belvedere Land Co. - $5

ANDREW P. GAVER etal, Trustees M.E. Church, Valley Ford, to S. LOBENSTEIN
3 acres of land in Tomales township - $280

A.J. BLANEY to S. LOBENSTEIN
3 acres of land in Tomales township - $280

Estate of WILLIAM GARZOLI, deceased
Distribution to ROSA GARZOLI, widow, and his minor children, ROSA, ARNOLDO, CORRENO, and BELARDO GARZOLI, according to law
Land in Marshall, Rancho Laguna de San Antonio, and Sonoma County

Belvedere Land Co. to J.H. & MARY KEEFE
Lot 26, lot 7, Belvedere - $10

LIZZIE McDERMOTT to PATRICK McDERMOTT
Lot on SE corner of Fourth and B Streets – love and affection

CARRIE M.P. COLEMAN to ROBERT L. COLEMAN
Lots 4, 5, 7, 10, 11, Block I, Coleman's addition to San Rafael - $10

T.E. TODHUNTER to CHARLES LIMARUTY
Sub 4 of Lot 146, Tamalpais Land & Water Co. - $10

Estate of T.H. INK, deceased, to HARRIET J. INK
220 acres of ranch set apart to widow as homestead

Marin Journal
Thursday, March 8, 1894

Local Brevities

Mr. CRONE of the Pine Lumber Co. of San Francisco has moved into Mr. PETER WILLIAMS' house on Bayview Street.

ED GREAVER, formerly connected with M. BLUMENTHAL's market, has accepted a position with HINIKER Bros.

Dissolution of Partnership
> LANG Brothers & Co.
> C.O. CAHOON has sold interest to LANG brothers
> Filed February 12, 1894
>> LANG Brothers & Co.

Order of Adjudication of Insolvency
> Matter of ANGELO GIACOMINI, an insolvent debtor
> HENRY HARRISON, Sheriff appointed to be receiver of property
> Filed March 6, 1894
>> F.M. ANGELLOTTI
>> Judge of Superior Court

S.C. BOWERS has severed his connection with the Sausalito News as it's editor. Mr. BOWERS is an excellent writer and his loss will be severely felt by the News.

A Brilliant Wedding
The wedding of Mr. HARRY M. LICHTENSTEIN, a successful young businessman of San Francisco, and Miss JENNIE K. HERZOG, a most charming young lady of quiet manners, but well educated, observing, and accomplished, a genial favorite among her acquaintances, took place at the Jewish Synagogue in San Francisco. Six ushers preceded the wedding party, followed by RITA BLUMENTHAL, and several little boys and girls. These were followed by 5 bridesmaids and their partners, after whom came Mr. Z. HERZOG, a brother of the bride, who acted as groomsman. Then came the groom and his mother, then Miss JULIA HERZOG as maid of honor, then the bride and her father, and last the bride's mother on the arm of the groom's father. The honeymoon will be in Monterey, and upon their return they will reside in San Francisco.

Superior Court
> JOSEPH ALBERTI etal vs. J.D. BRAVO
> Judgment for plaintiff
>
> People vs. T.J. JUKES
> Judgment of justice court affirmed, remitter ordered issued to court
>
> Estate of W.E. HOLLOWAY, deceased
> Over one week
>
> Estate of ANN FEENEY, deceased
> Order that commission issue, continued 4 weeks
>
> Estate of C.A. OZANN, deceased
> Letters testamentary issued to LOUISE N. OZANN
>
> S.J. SOARES vs. his Creditors
> Homestead set apart to insolvent
>
> Estate of ISIDOR DAUS, deceased
> Over 2 weeks
>
> E. WORMOUTH vs. J. GARDNER
> Submitted on briefs

Marriage Licenses
> S.P. LIEBRECHT, 24, San Francisco, to FLORENCE A. HEGAN, 23, San Francisco
> ALBERT S. CONNER, 27, San Francisco, to ANNA R. WORMCASTLE, 26, San Francisco

Letter List

ANDERSON, Miss MARY	ATKINS, Mrs.
BRAMNER, Miss	BERTRAM, F.W.
BROWN, G.A.	BROWN, G.
BROWN, Mrs.	BONNEL, Mrs.
BURROWS, FRANK D.	BRYEN, Mrs. T.
BRIGGS, AUGUST	CHAMBERS, Mrs. EMMA

CUMPTON MD, S.C.	CROWELL, Miss K.M.
DAVIS, Mrs. WILLIAM W.	DAVIS, Dr. W.K.
DUNON, JOHN	DUNBAR, Capt. JOHN
FORD, Mrs. EDWIN	FRITZ, GEORGE L.
FLANAGAN, Miss MAGGIE	HEYWOOD, Mrs. LOU
HASSETT, E.L.	HALL, JAMES
MORROW, ANDREW J.	MALONEY, M.R.
MURPHY, Miss MAGGIE	MOYLE Sr., Mrs.
MORGAN, Miss ELLA	MAGEE, Mrs. JAMES
MINOR, D.K.	MASSEY, A.
MANNHEIMER, M.	MEEKER, Rev. B.C.
MURPHY, I.J.	MORTIMER, E.E.
METZLER, Mrs. ANNA	LIND, Mrs.
LUX, ---	LEVY, Mrs. EUGENE W.
LEVY, Mrs. EUGENE W.	McAULAY, JOHN E.
McCUE, J.	RAMOS, ANNA E. DE
RING, HERBERT E.	SAVAGE, Mrs. C.
STONE, PETER V.	

Real Estate Transfers

JAMES P. CHRISTIESON etal to GARRET VINWINK
Lot 18, block B, Coleman's addition to San Rafael - $10

JAMES D. SAUNDERS and wife to WILLIAM H. SAUNDERS
Block 33, Town of San Rafael on Fifth and Nye Streets

JOHN D. BRAVO to MADDALENA BRAVO
NE corner of Tamalpais Ave and Fourth Street, San Rafael – gift

Sausalito Land & Ferry Co. to ANTONE BOREL
Portion of block 57, Sausalito Land & Ferry Co. - $1

ANTOINE BOREL to Sausalito Land & Ferry Co.
Portion of Borel tract adjoining Block 57 - $1

BENJAMIN F. LYFORD, by admx, by sheriff, to CHARLES C. & HENRY C. JUDSON
616.51 acres ptn. Rancho Corte Madera del Presidio, except 190.8 acres sold to PATRICK MALLON etal - $8,832.25

Notice

I will not pay any debts contracted by my son, LELAND L. LIBERTY.
Filed San Rafael, February 27, 1894
                    M.J. LIBERTY

Marin County Tocsin
Saturday, March 10, 1894

Born
COCHRANE – In San Rafael, March 2, 1894, to the wife of JAMES W. COCHRANE, a daughter.

BARTLETT – In Tiburon, February 28, 1894, to the wife of GEORGE BARTLETT, a daughter.

Married
LICHTENSTEIN-HERZOG – In San Francisco, March 4, 1894, by Rabbi NEITO, HARRY M. LICHTENSTEIN of San Francisco, to Miss JENNIE K. HERZOG of San Rafael.

Died
BUNN – In San Rafael, March 2, 1894, March 2, 1894, GEORGE BUNN, aged 74 years.

Local News
Miss C.B. BASSETTE is about to start a millinery establishment in Tomales.

J.N.E. WILSON, of Ross Valley, has left for a visit to his mines in Mexico.

J.L.G. ARMSTRONG, formerly W.F. & Co. agent at San Rafael, has bought the market business of the late J. OBITZ, on Fourth Street. He will conduct it in first class style and expects a big patronage.

Mrs. ARCHER, late of Tomales, was committed to the Napa Asylum last Wednesday by Judge ANGELLOTTI. A few days before, she had been placed in the County Hospital to await developments, but had rapidly become so violent that it was found necessary to convey her at once to a regular asylum.

PETER PRUNTY, one of the old and well known residents of Marin County, passed away last week in San Francisco. The deceased has long been in failing health, and his death was no surprise to those acquainted with his physical condition. Mr. PRUNTY was formerly engaged in an extensive brick manufacturing business, in connection with Messrs. BIGGINS and MALLON. The firm had a very successful career for many years, during most of which the deceased was in full control. As a businessman and private citizen, Mr. PRUNTY was alike respected by a large circle of acquaintances.

Real Estate Transfers
W.J. OSGOOD to CAROLINE L. OSGOOD
San Anselmo Station tract
Also lots 1,2,3,4,5,6,9,13,14,15,28, Osgood's addition - $5

Sausalito Land & Ferry Co. to PETER GOMEZ
Southeast part of Lot 1, block 28, Sausalito - $10

Sausalito Land & Ferry Co. to EDWARD FLAHERTY
Lot 32, block 27, Sausalito - $10

E. WORMOUTH to Tamalpais Land & Water Co.
Right of way at Mill Valley - $75

S.J. SOARES to MORRIS BLUMENTHAL
Lot corner Clayton & Welch Streets, San Rafael - $10

Superior Court
J.S. SHEARMAN & S. CAMM vs. A.S. SPENCE
Demurrer submitted, set for trial March 27

People vs. KEIGHO
M.C. DUFFICY appointed to defense, arraignment set for March 12

Marin Journal
Thursday, March 15, 1894

Born
LOVEJOY – In San Rafael, March 12, 1894, to the wife of W.H.L. LOVEJOY, a son.

Married
BRUNN- MASTRUP – In San Rafael, March 11, 1894, by Rev. J.S. FISHER, PETER C. BRUNN to MARIA C.S. MASTRUP, both of San Rafael.

Died
GULDAGER – In San Rafael, March 13, 1894, RUTH E. GULDAGER, aged 6 months and 19 days.

Marriage Licenses
CYRUS L. LUCAS, 21, Oakland, to SUSIE BUNKER, 18, Oakland
EMANUEL EDWARDS, 26, San Francisco, to LILLIE FLANAGAN, 18, San Francisco
HENRY TELLERSON, 33, Oakland, to MARY ANDERSON, 28, Oakland
MAX LINDAUR, 31, San Francisco, to MARY E. BLAKE, 29, San Francisco
PETER C. BRUNN, 35, San Rafael, to MARIA C.S. MASTRUP, 20, San Rafael
HARRY C. NEWMAN, 34, San Francisco, to MARY E. LEDGETT, 19, San Francisco
MILTON FRESHWATERS, 49, San Francisco, to ANNIE BIBER, 19, San Francisco

County Directory
Member of Assembly – JAMES H. WILKINS
Superior Judge – F.M. ANGELLOTTI
Sheriff and Tax Collector – T.S. BONNEAU
Clerk – THOMAS J. FALLON
Treasurer – E.B. MARTINELLI
Recorder – CHARLES E. BENSON
Assessor – IRA H. PARKS
School Superintendent – ROBERT FURLONG
Surveyor – GEORGE L. RICHARDSON
Coroner & Public Administrator – E. EDEN
Supervisor, 1st District – WILLIAM BARR
Supervisor, 2nd District – RICHARD KINSELLA
Supervisor, 3rd District – JACOB GARDNER
Supervisor, 4th District – GEORGE W. BURBANK
Supervisor, 5th District – A.G. SCOWN

City Directory
City Trustees – E.W. McCARTHY – President
    HENRY SCHLOSSER, M.J. MULHERN, WILLIAM J. MILLER, J. PETERSEN
City Clerk – JOHN T. BUSTIN
Assessor – W.F. DOUGHERTY
Marshall – JOHN E. HEALY
Attorney – EDWARD H. BOYEN
Treasurer – R.W. JOHNSON
Recorder – E. GARDNER
Engineer & Street Superintendent – G.L. RICHARDSON
Poundkeeper – D. BEGLEY
School Directors – Dr. W.F. JONES, President
    THOMAS HANSEN, Secretary
    P.T. BURTCHAELL, Dr. W.J. WICKMAN, J.S. STRATTON
Library Trustees – VINCENT NEALE, President
    ALBERT N. BOYEN, Secretary
    C.P. POMEROY, JAMES W. COCHRANE, CHARLES H. FISH

HOBART-WILLIAMS
The engagement of the rich W.S. HOBART of San Francisco and the beautiful society belle, Miss HANNAH NEIL WILLIAMS of San Rafael, is announced, and the marriage is anticipated as soon as the Easter joys shall dispel the somber tints of Lent. The fair bride elect is a great favorite in her little home city as is also her sister, Miss JULIETTE WILLIAMS. Both are beauties, vivacious and cordial. The wedding will take place at the residence of Mr. and Mrs. ROBERT E. NEIL, grandparents of the bride, in San Rafael, and will be one of the most notable social events that has ever occurred on the coast.

Assessor's Work
Mr. PARKS has appointed the following deputies:
    J.L. GREER – Office Deputy
    E. GARDNER – San Rafael
    J.E. CREED – Sausalito
    THOMAS FOTTRELL – Mill Valley
    WILLIAM LEWIS – Tiburon
    CHARLES NOTT – Bolinas
    CHARLES LONGLEY – Olema
    QUINTO CODONI – Pt. Reyes
    ARNOLD MARTIN – San Antonio
    L.R. TAFT – Nicasio
    LOUIS DeVOTO – Novato

Novato
Mr. HATCH has a large number of men and teams engaged in plowing up the DeLONG orchard. Among the ploughmen are WILBUR HAYDEN, IRVING JOHNSON, HUGH GALLAGHER, FRANK GALLAGHER, and scores of other young ranchers.

Mr. BEN HEILFRON has been appointed road overseer for Nicasio, and Dr. WILLIAM LANDO has charge of bridge repairs between Novato and Ignacio.

JOSE DE BORBA, a young son of ANTONE DE BORBA, was kicked in the jaw by a horse last week. The jaw was badly fractured together with the loss of 4 teeth. The lad received the necessary surgical assistance from Dr. KUSER who has taken up permanent residence in Novato.

Ex-constable BOB FAGGIANO is on the sick list, along with STEVE PORCELLA, the blacksmith.

It is rumored that Mr. SAMUELS is to have the Novato postoffice.

Mrs. MARY (REDMOND) ZICOVICH of San Jose visited her home in Novato last week.

AIDEN SUTTON of San Francisco spent last week at his old stomping ground in Novato.

JAMES NUGENT is acting as substitute mixologist at ESSNER's Hotel.

RICHARD KEATING of Bouldin Island spent last Sabbath with his family in San Francisco.

Miss MAGGIE KEATING reopened her school in Chileno Valley last Monday.

Supervisor SCOWN is improving his orchard by setting out new trees of choice variety. Mrs. SCOWN, who has been suffering for a long time with rheumatism of the hands is slowly improving.

Mr. A. TIMONY's chicken ranch at Santa Margarita is proving a grand success.

CLARENCE ATHERTON paid a flying visit to his Novato home with the force constructing the Valley Railroad. Mr. and Mrs. E.P. MATTESON of San Francisco were also guests at the ATHERTON Ranch.

Santa Margarita and Happy Valley
Supervisor BARR is making great improvements on the county road. He is assisted by P. MORAN, D. GAFFNEY, and H. LUCAS.

Miss NELLIE BAIN has again resumed the teaching of the Larkspur School.

The Dixie School has opened with Miss McDONNELL of Alameda as teacher.

Superior Court
    Estate of MARY JONES, deceased
    Final account settled and estate distributed

    Estate of M.J. LAUFF, deceased
    Final account settled and estate distributed

    Estate of F. OSTINI, deceased
    Final account settled and estate distributed

    M.F. COCHRANE assignee, vs. W.P. TAYLOR etal
    Demurrer submitted

    T. HANSON etal vs. S. JOHNSON etal
    Demurrer sustained

    C.C. LEROY vs. S. JOHNSON etal
    Demurrer sustained

    E. SCHWIESAU vs. ANNA GEIGER
    Set for trial March 31

    J.J. O'CONNOR vs. J.E. SLINKEY etal
    Demurrer overruled

Estate of M.W. SAIS, deceased
Refused settlement of account, assigned estate to minor heirs
Denied petition to mortgage property

P. MULVANEY vs. JAMES MARSHALL
Suit for value of crop – judgment for plaintiff

Real Estate Transfers
    MARY V. WHITE to EMMA H. JORDAN
    Lot on Sixth Street, San Rafael - $10

    BARBARA KNELL to ANNA A. CAPPELMANN
    Lot on Alcatraz Avenue, Mill Valley - $10

    Sausalito Land & Ferry Co. to LAURA HARRISON
    Lot on Water Street, Sausalito - $10

    MAMIE R. HARRISON to LAURA HARRISON
    Lot on Berkeley Ave., Sausalito - $5

    LeROY G. HARVEY to EMILY A.P. SMITH
    Pepper Island, in Bolinas Bay - $10

    SIDNEY B. CUSHING etal to HARRIET R. CUSHING
    Southerly portion Lot 125, Tamalpais Land & Water Co., Map 2 - $10

    HARRIET R. CUSHING to SIDNEY B. CUSHING etal
    Right of way for sewer in land last above described - $10

    LIZZIE E. BATHURST to MARGARET CURREY etal
    Lot on Latham Street, San Rafael - $800

    CHARLES H.W. KOERNER to GEORGE A. HUNNEWELL
    Lot on D Street, near Taylor Street, San Rafael - $10

Marin County Tocsin
Saturday, March 17, 1894

Born
HANLAN – In San Rafael, March 11, 1894, to the wife of W. HANLAN, a daughter.

McDONALD – In San Rafael, March 14, 1894, to the wife of ANGUS McDONALD, a son.

Journalistic Changes
Mr. WINN has retired from the management of the Tocsin. He has worked here for 2 years. Mr. WINN will be replaced by Mr. S.F. BARSTOW, the Nestor of the profession in this county. The Tocsin welcomes him back.

Local News
Mrs. GREGG has rented the Hotel Bella Vista in Mill Valley. Under her able management, it will again become both popular and profitable.

C.S. KANEEN, son of the Superintendent of the electric light works, had an upset while riding on a bicycle this week, and suffered a fracture of one of the small bones of the arm.

Real Estate Transfers
    P.J. SHAFTER to JOSEPH BLOOM
    Right of way for water - $10

    Tamalpais Land & Ferry Co. to CAROLINE SELIGMAN
    Lot 2, block 10 - $200

Tamalpais Land & Ferry Co. to C.W. BEALS
Subd. 1, lot 134 - $2,000

S. FOX to Mrs. S.N. MORRIS
¼ of tideland lots 184, 185, 194, 195 - $10
½ of tideland lot 22 ½, Sec 15, containing 6 acres - $10

W.F. McALLISTER to County of Marin
Right of way for Pt. San Pedro Road - $588

GEORGE W. HENDRY to VALENTINE HERNANDEZ
Part of Sec 16 & 21, T 2, containing 75.64 acres - $10

T. ELLSWORTH to L.R. ELLSWORTH
Lot 20, block 7, Old Sausalito - $10

Will Contest
The Will of the late BELLA F. SWISHER is to be contested by her surviving sister. The deceased was a somewhat eccentric old lady, rather given to speculating on the mysterious and abstract side of things, who lived at the time of her death in Sausalito. Outside of her spiritualistic leanings, however, she was universally considered an unusually level headed person, with plenty of caution and business thrift. The charge brought by the contesting relative, is that the deceased was unduly influenced by one F.C. KEEK, a spirit medium, who worked upon her mind to his advantage, and the disadvantage of her relatives. The trial of the case is set for April 2nd.

Superior Court
Estate of HENRY EVANS, deceased
Final discharge of executrix granted

Estate of BELLA F. SWISHER, deceased
Continued to April 2, 1894

People vs. THOMAS KEIGHO
Demurrer to indictment ordered, trial set for March 22nd

Estate of C.V. JOHNSTONE, deceased
Will admitted to probate, E.L. GRIFFITH appointed administrator, bond $40,000

Estate of JOHN GIACOMINI, deceased
Account settled and estate distributed

Estate of JACOB OBITZ, deceased
Mrs. J. OBITZ appointed administratrix, bond $1,300

J.B. RICE vs. GEORGE MURPHY etal
Dismissed

Belvedere Land Co. vs. CHARLES PAFF etal
Continued to March 21st

Marin Journal
Thursday, March 22, 1894

Local Intelligence
The engagement of Miss ALICE DECKER and our Senator ELLIOTT McALLISTER has been announced.

Mrs. CHARLES H. FISH has gone to Dr. BURKE's sanitarium in Oakland. She has been very ill a long time, and went across the bay to a bed.

The town of Novato boasts of an addition to it's commercial enterprises. This time it is a harness factory which has been opened by Mr. ROBERTS, formerly of San Francisco.

Large additions have been made to the BIGELOW house, opposite Hotel Rafael, which will soon be occupied by Mr. WALSH, manager of the MACKAY-FLOOD property in San Rafael.

News was received in Petaluma Thursday to the effect that A.M. BARNES of Ventura, who formerly resided in Petaluma, had died at his home several days before. He lived for many years with his family in Petaluma, where he was highly esteemed, leaving about 6 years ago. He leaves a widow, a son, and a daughter to mourn his loss.

R. MAGNES will take a summer trip to Poland, the scene of his early life.

Mr. J.B. BURDELL of Rancho Olompali has just finished building a creamery on San Antonio Creek, near the county line, and it is expected that the machinery will be in place and things in running order inside a couple weeks more. A shipping station will be established in Hicks Valley, and the ranchers in that quarter will thus be enabled to take advantage of the separators.

Mr. and Mrs. WILLIAM McKENZIE of Kansas City arrived in San Rafael last Friday and will take up residence in this vicinity. Mr. McKENZIE is a brother of E. McKENZIE, one of the contractors on the new Presbyterian Church.

Real Estate Transfers
> F.C. KECK to JAMES W. COCHRANE
> Villa lot 223, block 13, Old Sausalito - $10
>
> WENDELL EASTON etal to J.W. FOSS
> Lot 30, block 4, Sunnyside tract - $10
>
> D.L. HAYDEN, insolvent, to D.L. HAYDEN
> Decree setting aside homestead, lot 4, Franklin Place, Novato
> Also lots 3, 4, 6, Mahlsteadt Park Place, Novato
> Also villa lot 5, Miller Park Place, Novato Ranch
>
> MICHAEL HAGERTY and wife to BARNARD ROURKE
> Lots 1, 2, 3, block 18, Tomales - $10
>
> J.W. MACKAY etal to PAUL H. ECKELMAN
> 1 acre on N line Mission Street - $10
>
> WILLIAM LEVISTON etal to JAMES TUNSTEAD & HEPBURN WILKINS
> Portion of SUSAN WRIGHT tract in D Street - $3000
>
> GEORGE E. OTIS and wife to H.S. BRIDGE
> E ½ Sec 10, T 1 - $50

Letter List

ADAMS, WILLIAM J.	ATWELL, JOHN
ABRAMS, MELVILLE S.	BARBARA, JOAQUIN
BRIGGS, AUGUST	COLLUT, Mrs. ELVINA
CROWELL, Miss K.M.	CONRAD, J.H.
CORBIN, Mrs. WILLIAM	CHRISTIESON, MARKS
CONWAY, Miss MAGGIE	FOX, THOMAS H.
FISHER, M.C.	FUCHS, HUGO
FORBES, Miss E.	GUINTRAND, JEAN B.
HOWARD, WILLIAM C.	HAYS, Mrs. E.B.
KING, ARMIA RAMOS	LeMAR, L.
LAUGHLIN, LESTER	MORGAN, Miss LAURA
McGUIRE, Mr.	McCARTHY, CHARLES
SHATTUCK, D.D.	SAVELL, WILLIAM B.
SCHOONMAKER, JAMES B.	

Superior Court
> Estate of ANNIE BRADY, deceased
> Account settled and estate distributed
>
> Estate of ISIDOR DAUS, deceased
> Probate continued 2 weeks
>
> Estate of JAMES A. ROY, deceased
> T.B. ROY to file partnership account March 23

Marin County Tocsin
Saturday, March 24, 1894

Local News
Ex-Editor WINN has accepted a position in San Francisco.

DENNIS DONOHUE Jr. has purchased a lot on the corner of Grand and Belle Avenues and will soon build a residence on it.

R.B. LOUDON has announced that he will be an aspirant for the Democratic nomination for County Clerk. The gentleman is an excellent businessman and should have a strong backing, both in the Convention and before the people.

Superior Court
> Belvedere Land Co. vs. CHARLES PAFF
> Continued to March 30
>
> People vs. KEIGHO
> Verdict of not guilty

Real Estate Transfers
> J.W. FOSS to M.T. DANNER
> Lot 20, block 7, Sunnyside - $10
>
> HONORA M. MALLON to M. HERZOG
> Lot E Street between Second and Third Streets, San Rafael - $10
>
> J.W. FOSS to Trustees of San Anselmo School District
> Lot 9, Block 8, Sunnyside - $10
>
> W. EASTON etal to Trustees San Anselmo School District
> Lot 11, block 8, Sunnyside - $10
>
> ELLA A. ELLSWORTH to DAN EUSTACE
> Lot 20, block 7, Old Sausalito - $10
>
> Home & Farm Co. to L. CANTEL
> Lots 2 & 3, Block B
> Lots 4 & 5, Block J, Novato - $10
>
> LUCY H. THAYER to THEO. C. TODTMANN
> Subd. 1, Lot 161, Mill Valley - $1500
>
> THOMAS BIGGINS etal to H.M. MALLON
> Lot on E Street, near Third, San Rafael - $5
>
> H.C. CAMPBELL etal to THEO. E. TODTMANN
> Subd, 1, Lot 161, Mill Valley - $1

Died
McCONNELOGUE – In San Rafael, March 16, 1894, Mrs. CATHERINE McCONNELOGUE, aged 80 years, a native of Ireland, aunt of Mrs. P. BRESSNAN.

WALLS – In San Rafael, March 20, 1894, ELEANOR LOUISE WALLS, daughter of Mr. and Mrs. BERT WALLS, aged 11 months and 26 days.

Probably Dead

JAMES FAGAN, the owner of the Fourth Street building occupied by the Salvation Army, and other San Rafael property, appears to be dead, although his demise was never officially announced. Some time ago, a San Francisco paper detailed the circumstances of the wretched death of an old man miser in the city. From the similarity of the names and the general description, many surmised that the individual referred to was FAGAN. However, the name was not exactly the same. Since then, circumstances seem to indicate that he has actually died. No one has seen him for a long period, and his regular visits here have been discontinued. But most significant of all is the fact that the remittances of rent by the Salvation Army remain uncalled for at the Wells Fargo office in San Francisco. This was not the way FAGAN did things, and it is practically certain that he is no longer in the land of the living.

Marin Journal
Thursday, March 29, 1894

Letter List

ADAMS, W.S.	ALDERMAN, OSCAR
BARR, F.H.	BATTEN, G.C.
BAILEY, F.T.	CHAMBERS, Miss EMMA
COOPER, Mrs. MARY	COFFIN, Miss
CARRIGAN, L.	CONENDT, A.L.
DUNBAR, L.	EDWARDS, Mrs. LEGNIA
FRONK, EDW. B.	FOX, BERNARD E.
FRONK, GEORGE G.	FILIPPO, PINGITORE
HYNE, ROBIN	HOPKINS, Miss GERTRUDE
HARRISON, ROBERT	HATCH, Miss HELEN
HAMMEL, PETER P.	JOHNSON, Mrs. F.D.
JOHNSON, EMMA B.	KIRKHOPE, WILLIAM
JOHNSON, Miss MAY	McPHERSON, Miss KATIE
KELLEY, FRANK	NUNES, Mrs. RITA
MACULY, W.	RUTHERFORD, THOMAS W.
ROOS, Miss LAURA	RANZONI, L.
ROBINSON, FRANKLIN	RUEF, JOHANN
ROMER, CHARLES	TAYLOR, Mrs. D.
TURNER, Mrs. A.E.	TURNER, Miss FANNIE
THOMAS, Dr. H.B.	

Local Brevities

The BIGGINS property, 190 acres, was sold to Referee TUNSTEAD last Monday, to Mrs. PRENTY, for $15,000.

ARTIE W. SMITH came down from his father's ranch in St. Helena to pay San Rafael a visit. ARTIE is looking well and displays a well sunburned cheek.

Mr. and Mrs. R. MacGREGOR THOMSON of San Francisco have taken a cottage here for the summer. Mr. THOMSON is the genial bookkeeper for Levi Strauss & Co.

Mr. SAMUEL STOY paid San Rafael a visit last Sunday. Mr. STOY has been in Oregon for some time in the interest of the London and Lancashire Insurance Co., for whom he is a field man.

The nominations for town officers of Sausalito on file show an extensive list of candidates.
Trustees
H.J. CRUMPTON, J.H. DICKINSON, GASTON DOMERGUE, JOHN T. HARMES, C.H. HARRISON, D.T. HUGHES, O.C. MILLER, WILLIAM McMILLAN, JOHN RICHARDS, JOHN SCHNELL, E.D. SPARROW, J.W. SPERRY, E. STAHL, P.S. WILSON

Clerk
CHARLES H. DEXTER, N. METZLER

Treasurer
JOHN BRODERICK, A. LAWRENCE, F.D. LINDSLEY
Marshall
JOHN D. CRAMER, JOHN E. CREED, JOHN HANSON, J.S. SUSAVILLA

Novato
FRANCIS SUTTON is on duty in the appraiser's office.

PATRICK GALLAGHER is building a new road to Rush's Landing.

Mrs. ESSNER, wife of the proprietor of the Novato Hotel, is very ill.

Miss MINNIE SUTTON, a graduate of the Novato Grammar School, has entered the San Rafael High School.

E.P. MATTESON, formerly of this place, has been promoted to an $1800 clerkship in the auditing department of the San Francisco customhouse.

Professor E.E. ENLOW, late principal of the Novato Public School, since entering his duties as inspector of the customhouse, has made a number of important arrests. He is generally assigned to duty at the gangplank of the China steamers.

Mrs. M.E. SHANE of San Francisco was in Novato last Sunday on a visit to her daughter, Miss CARRIE COLLINS.

Marin County Tocsin
Saturday, March 31, 1894

Superior Court
E. WORMOUTH vs. JACOB GARDNER etal
Demurrer sustained

A.D. REMINGTON vs. F.C. DeLONG
Demurrer overruled

San Francisco Lumber Co. vs. WILLIAM O'CONNOR etal
Demurrer overruled

J.S. SHEARMAN vs. A.S. SPENCE etal
Continued to April 10

Estate of S.T. SIMARD, deceased
Family allowance of $75 per month granted widow
Household furniture set apart to widow

J. PAFF vs. Belvedere Land Co.
Taken under advisement

Notice for Publication of Will
Estate of JAMES B. ABLES, deceased
Application of SAMUEL M. AUGUSTINE & THOMAS B. ABLES for letters
Filed March 27, 1894
HEPBURN WILKINS, Attorney for Petitioner
THOMAS S. BONNEAU, Clerk

BARNEY REILLY, an old resident of San Rafael, who has long been in ill health, passed away yesterday morning. The funeral takes place tomorrow.

Died
REILLY – In San Rafael, March 30, 1894, BERNARD W. REILLY, aged 48 years and 7 months. Funeral Sunday at 2 o'clock from the Catholic Church.

Local Brevities

District Attorney COCHRANE convicted CHARLES FISCHER, the confederate note artist, before Justice RODDEN last Tuesday and the scamp was given a sentence of 100 days in the County Jail.

L.C. KEYES did a land office business last year planting fancy sidewalk trees in San Rafael. He contracted to replace any that might die, and he is now here to meet his obligations. He wishes to request all parties who have dead trees send him word and he will promptly plant others.

Mrs. JAMES ABLES, of Tomales, sister-in-law of District Attorney COCHRANE, is lying at death's door and nothing short of a miracle can save her. Mrs. COCHRANE hurried to the bedside of her sister early this week, and Dr. WICKMAN was summoned by telegraph on Thursday. A tragedy in real life is represented in this sad event. At the opening of the year, everything promised well for young JAMES ABLES and his happy little family. About two months ago, the father received fatal injuries from the kick of a vicious horse, and now his heartbroken widow is preparing to follow him into the mysterious land beyond this life. Three little children, one of them only a few days old, are left to face the world alone.

He Liveth

JAMES FAGAN is not dead. On the contrary, he is very much alive. The gentleman was in San Rafael last Wednesday, and created considerable consternation among those who believed him under the daisies. Coroner EDEN informed the alleged corpse that he ought to be ashamed to be on the streets.

Real Estate Transfers

JAMES W. FOSS to M.T. DANNER
Lot 27, block 1, Sunnyside - $10

MARIE DE SOUZA to G.A. HUNNEWELL
Lot 25, Gordon's tract of Short's addition, San Rafael - $10

G.A. HUNNEWELL to MARIE DE SOUZA
Part of block 51, San Rafael - $10

MARY A. MAGGARY to JAMES F. LOGAN
East part of lot 1, block 4, Mill Valley - $10

LILLIE A. ROCCATAGLIATA to MARY ROCCATAGLIATA
Lots 12 & 13, block 9, Sunnyside tract – love and affection

CAROLINE L. OSGOOD etal to RICHARD BULLIS
Lot 6, and part of lot 5, Angelotti's addition to San Rafael

J. ROSENTHAL etal to JOSEPH MALATESTA
Lot at Ross Landing – 410

J. McDONOUGH to E.A. ENGELBERG
Lot 76, 77 & 78, Block B, New Sausalito - $10

E.A. ENGELBERG to San Francisco Yacht Club
Lots 76, 77 & 78, Block B, New Sausalito - $10

J.C. DICKSON etal to T. SHAY
Lot 6, Block A, Coleman's addition to San Rafael - $10

Marin Journal
Thursday, April 5, 1894

Married

TOBIN-SIMS – In San Rafael, March 28, 1894, by Rev. Father LAGAN, JOHN TOBIN and Miss ALICE SIMS, both of San Geronimo.

MACKIN-BRALLEY – In San Rafael, April 4, 1894, by Rev Father LAGAN, ANDREW MACKIN and Miss MAGGIE BRALLEY, both of San Rafael.

DWYER-O'SULLIVAN – In San Rafael, March 28, 1894, by Rev. Father LAGAN, JOHN DWYER and Mrs. CATHERINE O'SULLIVAN

St. Vincent's Orphans

The following Orphans and Abandoned Children have been received in St. Vincent's Asylum since January 1, 1894:

Orphans

VRASIUS DEMETRIATAS	7 years, 5 months
FRED GARAGHTY	9 years, 8 months
JOSEPH GARAGHTY	11 years, 10 months
STEPHEN FERREA	11 years
JOSEPH BROPHY	12 years, 9 months
NICHOLAS BROPHY	8 years, 6 months
JAMES MULLIGAN	13 years
CHARLES OLIVIA	12 years, 4 years
FERDINAND HYNES	13 years
JAMES DANIELS	10 years
WILLIAM DANIELS	7 years
JOHN HARTWELL	12 years
JAMES HARTWELL	11 years
GEORGE HARTWELL	8 years
AUGUST OMAN	8 years, 2 months
JOHN FLYNN	11 years, 4 months
GEORGE HARCOURT	11 years
JOSEPH RAWLINGS	9 years, 9 months
THOMAS CONNELL	11 years, 9 months
RICHARD CONNELL	10 years, 1 month
JOSEPH BRUCE	14 years
EDWARD GLEESON	11 years, 3 months
JAMES SANFORD	9 years, 3 months
ARTHUR SANFORD	7 years, 3 months
JOHN COLLINS	8 years
FRANCIS McGURK	10 years
EDWARD ALVERSON	7 years, 7 months
JAMES MORAN	12 years, 7 months
ERNEST MARTINEZ	10 years, 3 months
HENRY KELLEGREN	11 years
RUSSELL SMITH	8 years
ALI POULET	12 years
ABEL POULET	10 years

Abandoned

JESSIE WALKER	7 years
IVAN LINSCOTT	8 years, 11 months

Notice to Creditors
    Estate of CAROLINE V. JOHNSTON, deceased
    Filed March 27, 1894
                    EDWIN L. GRIFFITH
                    Admr. of Will and Estate

Local Intelligence
Mrs. H.A. HOWE has been appointed School Census Marshall for San Rafael District.

Mr. and Mrs. OSCAR V. WALKER have went out cards announcing the marriage of their daughter, HELEN WALKER, to CHARLES FOX TAY.

Mr. SCHLOSSER is moving the last of the old buildings on the Cedars lot, Fifth and E Streets, to Fourth and Petaluma Avenues, where they will be transformed into stores.

Mr. B.K. BURKE has retired from the position of secretary of the Mt. Tamalpais Academy, and will be succeeded by Mr. JONES, brother of Dr. JONES. Mr. BURKE will return East.

The wedding of G.W. SINGLEY and Mrs. LUCY A. WILKINS was celebrated last Thursday evening at the residence of the bride. The ceremony was performed by Rev. Dr. MACKENZIE in the presence of the friends and relatives of the couple. The house was beautifully decorated will rare plants and flowers and a delicious menu was served.

S.F. Chronicle

M.H. ALLEN died in Sacramento a few days ago. He will be remembered as a former citizen of San Rafael and a long popular engineer on the narrow gauge. He was a large heavy man, and having been injured in a railroad accident, suffered by the jar of the engine, which made his occupation deleterious to his health. One of his two sons died a short time before him, his widow being now doubly bereaved. The family have many friends here.

JOHN TOBIN and Miss ALICE SIMS were joined in wedlock last week. Mr. TOBIN is the station agent at San Geronimo, and his fair bride is the daughter of Mr. and Mrs. CHARLES SIMS. ANDREW MACKIN and Miss MAGGIE BRALLEY were married yesterday. Both happy couples have hosts of friends, and we give warm congratulations.

Lt. DWIGHT E. HOLLY arrived last week and entered upon his duties at Mt. Tamalpais Academy. His appointment to this institution was a very high compliment, but one such officer being allowed to the coast and a number of other large schools actively competing, and it must give the Academy unique advantages as a military school. It carries with it a complete supply of arms, ammunition, and U.S.A. equipments. Lt. HOLLY's family is still in the East, but will join him later.

Superior Court

Estate of ROBERT LANDGRAF, deceased
Estate set aside for family

Estate of H.J. VAN DYKE, deceased
Account settled and estate distributed

Estate of C.A. OZANN, deceased
Estate assigned to widow

ZOE M. HARRISON vs. F.A. HARRISON
Judgment by default

SHERMAN vs. SPENCER etal
Demurrer overruled

L.J. CAMM vs. A.S. SPENCE etal
Demurrer overruled

R. CHAPMAN vs. WILLIAM H. JEWELL
Application dismissed

A GIACOMINI vs. his Creditors
Exempt property set apart

People vs. CHARLES MANNING
Continued for the session

People vs. PATRICK RICE
Set for jury trial April 30th

AMELIA V.R. PIXLEY vs. North Pacific Coast Railroad
Stricken from calendar by consent

Marin County vs. LOUIS TOMASINI
Stricken from calendar

T.B. VALENTINE vs. W.D. KELLY
Set for trial April 17th

T.B. VALENTINE vs. S. McDONOUGH
Set for trial April 17th

M.W. EICKHOFF vs. MAGDALENA EICKHOFF
Set for trial April 17th

Marin County vs. J.A. McNEAR
Set for trial April 30th

Marin County vs. M. BLUMENTHAL
Set for trial April 30th

C.B. RAULINO exec. vs. MANUEL RODGERS etal
Set for trial May 8th

A DA ROSA vs. MANUEL RODGERS etal
Set for special jury trial April 18th

Matter of MICHAEL ALICARN on habeus corpus
Writ dismissed and prisoner remanded

Letter List

ANDERSON, LEO
ADAMS, Mrs. W.L.
BRESACK, Miss PORTIA
BROWN, S.H.
BOWN, M.
BAUMSTARK, BEN
BARKER, ANNIE E.H.
CHRISTOFFER, NIELS
CROFTS, Mrs. M.L.
CARTER, Miss MARY
DUMOND, Miss ANNIE
DUFF, Mrs.
DUPTRY, Mr. J.
DAVIS, J.
FIFE, GEORGE S.
GARCIA, JOE
GUMPEL, CLIFFORD A.
HOLMBERG, GUS.
HOCK, DIANA
HEANY, T.U.
HURST, H.C.
HARRIGAN, MARY
HOPKINS, WILLIAM E.
JAMES, Miss HATTIE
KISER, Mr.
KULER, Mrs. J.B.
LOWENFIELD, BERNARD
LANDER, NELSON A.
LEONARD, M.S.
MARION, WASHINGTON
MACULY, Mr. W.
MORLEY, W.I.
MAURRI, MAT
MORGAN, J.C.
MORNS, M.J.
MAGEE, JAMES
MASSEY, A.
MAHONEY, ---
NELSON, ALFRED

ADAMS, E.C.
ADAMS, GROVE
BURGESS, WILLIAM
BOOMER, MARY J.
BOWMAN, ELLA
BROWN, Mrs. WILLIAM
CUTTER, Mrs. S.C.
CARROLL, Mrs. E.H.
CORBIN, Mrs. WILLIAM
DECKER, VON DE GEORGE
DUREE, CHARLES
DEARBORN, Miss ISABELLE
DWYER, WILLIAM
DREYPOLCHER, FREDERICK
FREUD, EMILY
GOLTICK, MARIANO
HYDE, Mrs. H.C.
HAMILTON, Mrs. ALICE
HALENBASH, HENRY
HASKELL, L.F.
HOWE, Mrs.
HENNESSEY, THOMAS
JOHNSTON, MARY
KELLY, GEORGE
NEUMAN, JULIUS
LAWTON, Mrs. U.A.
LeFRANKY & BULOTTI
LEARY, WILLIAM
MAMSCHEIMER, Mr. U.
MAHAR, Mrs. J.
MAXWELL, Mrs. H.J.
MITCHELL, THEODORE
MINVIELLE, Miss DENISE
MORININI, JOE
MAHONEY, M.
MURPHY, MARY
METZLER, Miss ANNA
NIELSEN, HEINRICH
NOE, VICTOR

NEPPERD, LOUIS
McGILLIARY, G.O.
McGUIRE, Mrs.
McGILLIWIG, ANNIE
PLASTER, GEORGE
PERRY, FRANK
PRETZELS, Mrs.
ROBBINS, Mrs. THOMAS G.
RICHARDS, C.O.
REOUBEOIS, Monsieur
TILGUMAN, W.P.
VELANTIN, Mrs.
SMITH, S.L.
SMITH, BLANCHE
SPERRY, Mrs. E.
SULLY, MINNIE
WOOD, DAVID
YOUNG, EMILY
ZANIKE, WILLIAM
PALIDINI, ASSUNTO

McCLOSKY, ---
McMANUS, HENRY
McCLOSKEY, Mrs. A.
PATEZAN, JAMES
PICKERING, Mrs. EVERLINE E.
ROBBINS, Mr.
RIXON, Mr. HARRY
RICHARDS, C.O.
TALBOT, Mrs. A.P.
UPSHAIN, BENJAMIN P.
VATER, ROSALIE V.R.
SMITH, Miss SUSIE
SMITH, MANUEL
SEDGWICK, A.V.
WOOD-HALL, MARY C.
WRIGHT, Mrs. JAMES L.
XAVIER, PAULINO
JOAQUIN, JOSE ANTONIO
SLACK, Miss ELIZA
De AZEVEDO, FRANCISCO S.

Real Estate Transfers

Estate H.N. COOK, deceased to EDITH COOK etal
Decree of distribution, lot 3, block 4, Belvedere

J.C. DICKSON and wife to JULIA MULLEN
Lot 5, block A, Coleman's addition – 410

O.C. MILLER etal to N.R.K. YOUNG
Lot 9, and portion of lot 10, Campbell tract, Old Sausalito - $10

Belvedere Land Co. to EDWARD J.N. HARRISON
Lot 44, block 3, Belvedere - $10

Belvedere Land Co. to V.J.A. REY
Lots 28 and 29, block 3, Belvedere - $10

GEORGE F. ROBERTS and wife to JAMES TUNSTEAD & HEPBURN WILKINS
Lot on NW corner of Irwin and Third Streets, San Rafael - $10

JOSEPH MacDONOUGH to EMIL A. ENGEL
Lots 76, 77, and 78, block B, Sausalito Land & Ferry Co. - $10

J.C. DICKSON and wife to TIMOTHY SHAY
Lot 6, block A, Coleman addition to San Rafael - $10

SARAH W. TAYLOR to M.T. DANNER
Portion of lot 2, Block 1, Sunnyside - $10

Marin County Tocsin
Saturday, April 7, 1894

Local News
Mr. JAMES TAYLOR of Los Gatos, a former resident of San Rafael, was here visiting Tuesday.

Prof. C.S. SMYTHE, principal of the Hollister High School, was home for a short visit this week.

Mr. C. GROSJEAN has disposed of his interests in Healsburg and will probably return to San Rafael.

The City Board of Education has selected Mrs. H.A. HOWE as Census Marshall of San Rafael.

ONE FARRELL has been chosen by the residents of Ross Valley as a peace officer to succeed C.L. FOSTER.

The engagement of Senator ELLIOTT McALLISTER and Miss DECKER of San Francisco, has been announced.

Accident
JAMES DOWNEY, a young man in the employ of the Electric Light Co., was run down by the noon local from San Francisco at the crossing of Second and B Streets, and escaped death by little short of a miracle. He was driving one of the wagons of the Company at a rapid rate, and seems to have been unconscious of the approaching train until it was almost on him, when it was too late to make even an effort to escape. The young man was hurled 40 or 50 feet and was picked up in unconscious condition, bleeding profusely from several severe scalp wounds. He was also suffering more or less from shock, and he showed symptoms of grave cerebral injury. Yesterday he was thought to be out of serious danger. Young DOWNEY is related to Superintendent KANEEN by marriage and was temporarily filling the place of his son, who is laid up with a broken arm.

Real Estate Transfers
>JAMES & MARY TUNSTEAD to H. WILKINS
½ interest in lot on NW corner of Irwin and Third Streets - $10

>CLARA I. LONG to KITTY W. COLE
Lots 3, 4, and 13, block 2, Old Sausalito

>Estate of HENRY J. VAN DYKE
Lot on NW corner of B and Fifth Streets, San Rafael
Distributed to HENRIETTA VAN DYKE & DARWIN G. EATON

>REBECCA S. McDONALD to DAVID WARDEN
¼ acre adjoining the Moore tract, San Rafael - $10

>P.H. KELLY to MARIE PAULE DONOHOE
Lot 24, Marinita Park tract - $1,400

Board of Supervisors
1. The resignation of CHARLES L. FOSTER as Poundmaster of District 1 was received and filed.
2. The order appointing Dr. McDONALD heath officer of Sausalito was rescinded.
3. H.A. COBB and FRANK SUTTON were appointed to represent Marin County at the Sportsmen's Convention.
4. The resignation of J. MOONEY as Poundmaster of District No. 4 was received and filed. J.B. MAHAR was appointed Poundkeeper of said District to fill the vacancy.
5. J.A. NOWELL was appointed a member of the Board of Education, vice Miss MAGGIE LOWDEN, resigned, and Miss BELLE C. BROWN was likewise appointed to succeed self.
6. Liquor licenses were granted as follows:
   >WATSON & ENOS – San Rafael
   MARTIN PETERSEN – San Rafael
   R.M. BRIARE – Larkspur
   F. GIRTH – El Campo
   C.H. DEXTER – Sausalito
   NATALIE OZANN – Tiburon

Born
SCOTT – In San Rafael, April 1, 1894, to the wife of ROBERT SCOTT, a son.

STERN – In San Rafael, April 4, 1894, to the wife of CHARLES K. STERN, a son.

Marin Journal
April 12, 1894

>Local Intelligence
TOM SMITH left last Thursday to take a position in Vacaville, where he will remain for some little time.

Mrs. Dr. WHITE has returned from the East, where her health was not good, and is stopping in San Francisco.

Mr. JEAN ESCALLE will open Limerick Hall at the Corte Madera vineyard on the 21st instant. A large crown is anticipated.

Miss HALL has been engaged as assistant teacher in the receiving room of the San Rafael public school, in which Miss McALLISTER, with 80 scholars, has had too hard work.

Mrs. C.H. FISH was lately taken to Lytton Springs, bearing the journey well and appearing to improve in health after arriving there. But on Tuesday last, Mr. FISH received a telegram from Miss ALICE FISH to come up, that her mother was very sick. Mr. FISH left here on the evening train for Santa Rosa, intending there to take livery and reach Lytton's as soon as possible. Meanwhile friends of the family here are very anxious.
Later: We learn that after Mr. FISH left, another telegram was received that Mrs. FISH is better.

Clerk BONNEAU went to Sebastopol Monday on a sad errand, to attend the funeral of his brother-in-law, FRANK KAUFMAN, who died in Stockton.

Novato
EUGENE CONNELL of Novato was one of the candidates at the recent examination for night inspector held by the San Francisco Custom House authorities.

JOSEPH FAGGIANO of this place is learning the carpenter trade under the direction of School Director DUNN of San Francisco.

GEORGE DeLONG is meeting with great success in supplying pure milk to the citizens of San Francisco from the Novato dairies. The excellent quality of the milk causes an increased demand for it. JOHN SWEETSER supplies the young contractor with a goodly supply of the lacteal fluid.

Letter List
BEAN, JAMES
EMHOFF, NIC
FRENCH, ALICE
KOERNER, CHARLES
LINDSLEY, C.F.
O'BRIEN, MOLLIE
OSBORNE, Dr. O.E.
PETERSEN, MARIE
PERRY & RAMOS
VON METZER, Mrs. E.
VINING, EVERETT A.
ZINDELAR, Mr.

BROWN, GEORGE
FULTON, Mrs. J.
HILL, Mrs. MARY
KOPP, P.F.
LADATO, MARY
OXNARD, Mrs. R.
OKI & HARUKNEH
PERTELCHICK, JOS.
QUICK, Mrs.
VAN PALVEREN, W.E.J.
WILLIAMS, J.E.

Died
FOLEY – In San Rafael, April 9, 1894, MARY E. FOLEY, native of Brooklyn, NY, aged 43 years.

ANDERSON – At the County Hospital, April 7, 1894, ANDREW ANDERSON, a native of Denmark, aged 79 years.

Superior Court
J.B. RICE vs. G. MURPHY etal
Judgment for plaintiff and costs against defendant – VARNEY & WALLIS
Suit over the Larkspur School lot purchase

Estate of ANN FEENEY, deceased
Account settled and estate distributed

A GIACOMINI, insolvent
A.J. BLOOM elected assignee, bond $1,000

HENRY W. TAYLOR vs. J.S. BELLRUDE
Defendant allowed 5 days to file brief

Marin County Tocsin
Saturday, April 14, 1894

Local news
Captain R.C. HART's house, near Ross Station, was burned to the ground yesterday afternoon.

GEORGE D. SHEARER will hold an auction sale of horses at the corner of Petaluma Avenue and Fourth Street next Friday, April 20th at one o'clock. Great bargains can be secured.

SAM STOY, the representative of the London and Lancashire Insurance Co. at Portland, OR, spent last Sunday in San Rafael, visiting many friends here.

CHARLES E. BURREY has resumed the management of the Sausalito News, after an absence of several weeks in Southern California. Mr. BURREY never actually retired from his duties on our contemporary, but was merely taking a much needed rest.

School Census Marshalls

Aurora	W.R. FAIRBANKS
American Valley	Miss D. ROBERTSON
Bay	Miss A.E. BROWNE
Black	QUINTO CODONI
Bolinas	Miss JANE C. STEELE
Chileno Valley	Miss MAE FRAZIER
Clark	Miss N. GERICKE
Dixie	Miss NELLIE MADDOCK
Eastland	PETER GARDNER
Estero	Mrs. MARY A. PIEZZI
Fairfax	Mrs. H. DALESSI
Franklin	Miss ANNIE DILLON
Garcia	S.H. HARDMAN
Halleck	H. SIEMSEN
Laguna	Mrs. ISABEL OFFUTT
Marshall	Mrs. S. RISCIONI
Nicasio	Miss E.K. McISAAC
Novato	FRED W. SWEETSER
Olema	Miss EDNA MUSCIO
Pierce	Miss MAY L. WAMBOLD
Pt. Reyes	D.C. CUNNINGHAM
Reed	Miss MATILDA DEFFEBACH
Richardson	GEORGE W. SIMPTON
Ross Landing	JAMES L. MURRAY
San Antonio	CARL PLOW
San Geronimo	Mrs. C.H. SIMES
San Jose	RAMON PACHECO
San Rafael	Mrs. H.A. HOWE
San Quentin	GEORGE A. CONLEY
Sausalito	Miss M.J. BROWN
Salmon Creek	Miss NELLIE HESKETH
Tocaloma	W.H. HEALION
Tomales	Mrs. D.B. LAWTON
Tiburon	Miss BERTHA LEEDS

Superior Court
P.N. BERKHART vs. MARY CULLEN etal
Demurrer sustained

Estate of BELLA F. SWISHER, deceased
Continued for one week

Estate of JAMES ROY, deceased
Citation ordered discharged

Real Estate Transfers
E.M. & M.H. HARMON to Belvedere Land Co.
Lot 17, block 3, Belvedere - $10

OLIVIA A. & SUSAN E. GORDON to JAMES TUNSTEAD & H. WILKINS
Part of the Susan Wright tract, San Rafael - $5
Lot on South C Street, San Rafael - $5

THOMAS MAGEE etal to AUGUST C. HINZ
Lot in Mill Valley - $2,000

JOSEPH TRAVERSI to M. TOMASINI
Undivided ½ interest in 3 parcels of land in Nicasio, 681.68 acres - $10

Marin Journal
Thursday, April 19, 1894

Pt. Reyes
H. CLAUSSEN, our Pioneer dairyman is perhaps the happiest man to be found here just now, owing no doubt to the fact that he has lately become the father of a bouncing young daughter. They speak in the highest praise of Mrs. Capt. BROWN who attended Mrs. CLAUSSEN during her late illness. The people in this entire neighborhood should be grateful to this lady who on many occasion has left her family and gone forth to care for the afflicted.

Letter List

ALLEN, Mrs. H.	AHERN, JAMES B.
BAYER, G.E.	BERNSTEIN, J.
BATTEN, G.C.	CARTER, Miss U.
CLEMENTINA, MES. V.	CAVERAL, JOSE
DELANEY, Mrs.	DUNN, JOHN
GOODILL, J.M.	GUERIN, FELIX
GOULDE, Miss JULIA	HAMDT, JOHN
HILL, GEORGE F.	JOHNSON, ALFRED
JOAQUIN, JOHN	KENDALL, JOHN
KELLERICA, THOMAS	LAMBERT, HUGH
KEINER, HERMAN	MARDEN, A.L.
LENAN, ELLA	MILLS, Mrs. W.G.
MIRANDA, Mrs. S.	MURRAY, J.D.
MENKEN, U.E.	PATTEN, WILLIAM
NICOLAYSEN, ---	SMITH, Mrs. S.
PORTATTA, Mrs.	SMITH, J.R.
SCHUELER, JOHN	STONE, PETER V.
SEIBERT, Mrs.	SPONY, Monsieur J.W.
SCHERBE, Miss B.	SHILLING, ANNIE
STEWART, JOHN	STONE, O.C.
SLANCER, Mrs.	STEFFINS, Captain
SHELLEY, Mrs. W.N.	SCHOONMAKER, CYRUS
STOWELL, E.H.	SHEARS, Mrs.
SPOOR, Mrs. H.C.	SCHMIDT, RICHARD
SLAYTON, Miss E.	SIMPSON, RICHARD S.
WINSE, Mrs. M.	SHAW, Mr.
WELCH, E.M.	SAVELL, WILLIAM B.
WILSON, Mrs. A.E.	SINCLAIR, A.U.
WILLIAMS, Mrs. L.N.	WARRON, ROBERT
WILSON, CARRIE E.L.	WILLIAMS, Miss A.N.
WETMORE, CHESTER	WELCH, E.M.
WILSON, S.M.	

Died
FARRELL – In San Rafael, April 14, 1894, Mrs. JANE FARRELL, aged 56 years.

Born
ACKLEY – In San Rafael, April 12, 1894, to the wife of M.D. ACKLEY, a son.

CLAUSSEN – At Pt. Reyes, March 14, 1894, to the wife of HENRY CLAUSSEN, a daughter.

Novato
A sale of 25 acres of Black Point land to Mr. MASON was negotiated by Agent MACKIN last week.

RICHARD KEATING, formerly of Novato, has 250 acres sown with barley on Boulder Island in the Sacramento River, with the prospect of a big crop, and a big price for it.

Mr. LEEK, of this place, aged 72 years, was married last week to a comely young Portuguese woman after a brief acquaintance. On Saturday evening, the aged benedict was treated to a lively party. Mr. LEEK responded by treating his tormentors to a liberal supply of firewater.

Local Intelligence
DAVID NYE has taken a position at the narrow gauge depot.

Mrs. SHENTON has returned to San Rafael last month with a husband.

P.J. SULLIVAN will be hung at San Quentin at 11 o'clock tomorrow, for wife murder.

Mrs. JANE FARRELL suffered a stroke of paralysis a short time since, and on Saturday last she peacefully passed away. She was the relict of the late JOHN FARRELL, and mother of the Misses FARRELL, so well known on the roll of our efficient teachers. The funeral took place Monday, when the number and richness of the floral offerings attested the esteem in which the deceased and her family were held.

Mr. WILLIAM BROWN, of San Francisco, who will be remembered by the frequenters of Willow Camp. Bolinas, as a partner of Mr. JUKES, the hotel proprietor at that place, has bought out Mr. JUKES' interest in the business, and will have charge of the hotel this year at the beach. Mr. BROWN is well liked, and considering the increasing popularity of Willow Camp, should do a rushing business there this year. He is already on the grounds preparing for his summer trade.

Death of JAMES BIGGINS
A gruesome story comes from San Francisco Saturday of the death by suicide, of JAMES BIGGINS. As it said that he owned property in San Rafael, it was feared that deceased might be JAMES BIGGINS, as it proved. The young man died of a pistol shot discharged in his mouth, and ranging up through his head. He lived at 3 Everett Street. A man named Mr. MITCHELL was in the room with him when the shot was heard. He ran out and called a doctor. A policeman went to the room, opened the door of a narrow closet, and the dead body of BIGGINS fell into the room, a pistol which had rested on his lap falling with him. It was not easy to determine whether he died by his own hand or by that of MITCHELL. The latter said BIGGINS went into the closet; then he heard a shot, and at once ran for the doctor. BIGGINS was dissipated, but he had means, and no reason for suicide can be surmised, while robbery might be the motive for the murder. MITCHELL was arrested, and later discharged after an inquest was held.

Superior Court
    FELIZ A. SILVEIRA vs. MANUEL De M. SILVA etal
    Submitted and taken under advisement

    J.S.S. NEARMANN vs. A.S. SPENCE etal
    Amendments filed and case submitted

    Estate of R. LANDGRAF, deceased
    Decree of final discharge

    Estate of ISIDOR DAUS, deceased
    Over two weeks

    Estate of BELLA F. SWISHER, deceased
    Over two weeks

    E. SCHWIESAU vs. E. FLAHERTY
    Five days to file briefs and demurrer

    Estate of WILLIAM SEET, deceased
    Final account settled

    Estate of JAMES B. ABLES, deceased
    Letters issued to S.M. AUGUSTINE, bond $500

    Estate of CHARLES E. MALLON, deceased
    Letters issued to HONORA MALLON, bond $100

    S.N. MORRIS vs. ELLA C. POND
    Demurrer overruled

    S.N. MORRIS vs. A. BECKER
    Demurrer overruled

    ZOE HARRISON vs. F.A. HARRISON etal
    Judgment for $380 rents to stand

Marin County Tocsin
Saturday, April 21, 1894

    Notice of Sale
        Estate of CHARLES MEYER, deceased
        Sale to be held Monday, May 7, 1894
        Land in Larkspur
                      MARY MEYER
                      Executrix of Estate

    Auction Sale
        Property of P. GALLAGHER, insolvent
        Leasehold interest in basalt quarry at Roberts' Ranch, Penngrove, Sonoma Co.
        Sale to be held Monday, April 30, 1894
        Filed April 20, 1894
                      HENRY HARRISON
                  Assignee of said insolvent

Murder or Suicide
The death of JAMES M. BIGGINS, well known in San Rafael, came to his death last Friday under circumstances that indicate suicide, although there are some who believe that the unfortunate young man was foully dealt with. BIGGINS was rooming at the time at a lodging house on Everett Street, San Francisco, together with several companions who, like himself, were addicted to the inordinate use of opium. It is known that he had a considerable amount of money the day before, and the money is missing. An inquest was held and the verdict was suicide, but there are those who probably will never know if it was murder or suicide.

Local News
SULLIVAN, the wife murderer, was quietly eliminated from the land of the living yesterday at San Quentin Prison. This is the third execution held there under the new law.

Mr. MARCUSE, a well known San Francisco man, has leased the store in the Wilkin's block, formerly occupied by J. SILBERSTEIN, and will open a wholesale liquor establishment there about May 1st.

The Board of Supervisors met last Monday and granted liquor licenses to J.J. GAFFNEY, Tiburon; H.O. ADAMS, Tiburon; and Mrs. EMMA SCHAER, San Rafael.

The residence of Mrs. CLAUDIANOS, on Second Street, caught fire from a spark of a passing locomotive last Sunday and narrowly escaped destruction. The blaze was noticed by neighbors and promptly extinguished while in the incipient stage.

The fine residence of J.M. SHOTWELL, near Ross Station, was burned to the ground last Sunday afternoon, together with the greater part of its contents. The fire had reached considerable headway when discovered, and all efforts to stay its progress were fruitless, even when the devout congregation of San Anselmo Chapel threw its influence and exertions into the scale.

Real Estate Transfers

J.F. BIGELOW to DENNIS DONOHUE
Lot 55, Coleman's addition to San Rafael - $10

J.O.B. SHORT to E. SCHWIESAU
Part of block 5, Short's addition to San Rafael - $10

W. DUTTON etal to MARY E. THOMPSON
Lots 22 & 23, block 16, village of Tomales - $50

W. DUTTON etal to CHARLES W. THOMPSON
Lot 76, Tomales Cemetery - $25

JAMES W. FOSS to KATE R.E. TAYLOR
Lot 19, block 1, Sunnyside

DONALD Y. CAMPBELL to MARY E. ROBERTS
Lot 18, block 2, Eastland - $10

Home & Farm Co. to LEON GREENBERG
Lot 7, block I, Novato - $10

R.H. McDONALD to Pacific Bank
Block 27, New Sausalito - $10

H.C. CAMPBELL & T.B. KENT to THOMAS MAGEE & LOVELL WHITE
Tract in Mill Valley – Reconveyance

E.H. KOWALSKY to Marin County
Right of way for Pt. Reyes and Marshall Road - $550

Tamalpais Land & Water Co. to CLARA MERSEBACH
Subdivision 3 of lot 140, Mill Valley - $1,000

Marin Journal
Thursday, April 26, 1894

Real Estate Transfers

ALLEN M. SUTTER and wife to ARTHUR PAGE
Portion block 1, Belvedere - $10

Estate of JAMES McM. SHAFTER, deceased to Estate of KATE JOHNSON, deceased
Order confirming sale of undivided 10 acres of Inverness tract

JOHN H. BRENNAN and wife to J. GAMBETTI
Lot 16, block J, Novato - $100

Home & Farm Co. to MARION MATTONI
Lots 4 & 5, block H, Novato - $150

Home & Farm Co. to JOHN CABRAL
Lot 13, block H, Novato - $10

GEORGE E. BUTLER and wife to WINFIELD S. DAVIS
Land on south side Lagunitas Road in Ross Valley - $10

ALEXANDER ROY etal to THOMAS B. ROY
All interest in Estate of JAMES ROY, deceased

Born
CROFTS – In San Francisco, April 20, 1894, to the wife of F.E. CROFTS, a daughter.

CRISANTI – In San Rafael, April 16, 1894, to the wife of GERALAMO CRISANTI, a daughter.

PLETTE – In San Rafael, April 22, 1894, to the wife of LOUIS PLETTE, a son.

KLEIN – In San Rafael, April 23, 1894, to the wife of CHRISTIEN KLEIN, a son.

MARILLA – In San Rafael, April 23, 1894, to the wife of MICHAEL MARILLA, a daughter.

Died
BEISLER – In Bolinas, April 24, 1894, JOHN BEISLER, aged 67 years and 3 months.

Local Intelligence
Mrs. SHIELDS has sublet the house she occupies on D Street to Mrs. FELTON of Alameda.

Mr. and Mrs. MURRAY, recently of Idaho, have taken a house on D Street. Mr. MURRAY is contemplating the purchase of a fruit ranch.

FRANK S. JOHNSON last week took Mrs. CHARLES DORE to be his bride, and the couple are at the Hotel Coronado, while the beautiful Johnson Villa in Marinita park is taking on new graces to welcome them when they come home.

Mrs. MORRIS has rented her house for 4 months to Mr. MARCUSE. She will leave for Old England with her daughter, Miss MAY, next month.

Another trimmer of the electric lamps is crippled. Last Saturday, FRED JACOBSON, at the gas works, slipped, striking his hand against a dynamo, and fracturing the small bone of his arm.

Rev. J.S. FISHER will soon join the ranks of the local cyclists, having recently become an adept.

Miss SHOTWELL and Mrs. TOURGEE were married in St. Paul's Church, San Rafael, last week. The bride's trousseau was lost a few days before by the fire which destroyed her father's house. But there are more things than trousseaux in a pair of loving hearts, and the marriage chimes had no note of discord.

This summer will give San Rafael an inning of society people. We have never seen Mr. BRENNAN more confident of a big season for the Hotel Rafael; Mrs. JORDAN and Mrs. KAPPENMAN are equally sanguine for the Cypress and the New England Villas.

BIRDY HAWKINS was in San Rafael last week on a visit. Miss HAWKINS is taking a course in the State Normal at San Jose, from which she will graduate in about a year.

Suicide at Valley Ford
On Monday afternoon, JOHN CURRY of Valley Ford committed suicide by shooting himself through the head. He kept the Valley Ford Hotel, and lately been doing something in the way of dealing in stock. On that day, FRANK EMERSON of this city, arrived at Valley Ford in the afternoon with a drove of hogs, which CURRY proposed to buy. He did not have sufficient money to make the purchase, and on application to the Valley Ford Bank, failed to get it. He then wanted his wife to join him in a note to get the required money, which she declined to do, saying that dealing in stock was a losing business. This seemed to have completely upset his reason, for soon after he called his children about him and bid them goodbye, and then, placing the muzzle of the revolver in his mouth, he fired the fatal shot. The deceased was a native of Ireland, and leaves a wife and 8 children. The funeral took place Thursday at Tomales.
Petaluma Argus

The execution of SULLIVAN took place Friday at San Quentin Prison. This man killed his wife because she left him, unable to endure his cruelty any longer. He was a savage. He purposely covered his hands with blood from the wounds of his defenseless victim. It took 2 years to finally hang him.

J.J. SCHNEIDER and E.B. MARTINELLI are delegates to the Grand Parlor, N.S.G.W. at Eureka, now in session.

Death
JULIUS BERNSTEIN is well remembered in San Rafael. About 3 years ago, he was proprietor of the store in which H. KELLNER now is, selling about the same line of goods. He had a wife and numerous children living in the rear of the store. He appeared a clever man, intelligent and affable. Business went poorly with him, and we believe he retired from it under attachment. He went to Petaluma, and soon after to Oakland. Then came the news that he died by suicide, leaving his family $9,000 in life insurance. He had disappeared from Oakland and from his family. Now comes the Examiner, saying that he is very much alive in Detroit. That his family, ostensibly leaving here for Berlin, stopped in Detroit, and are with him, enjoying his company as much as if he had never been dead, nor even suicidal. Effort was made to collect the life insurance, but none has ever been paid, although the supposed widow has enjoyed the interest on one policy of $2,000, from the B'nai B'rith order. He was also a Workman, and had $5,000 in the Endowment Rank, I.O.O.F. We should never have thought him a man who would try so mean a scheme to raise the wind.

Additional Local
Mr. ALLAN LEE is suffering with a stubborn neuralgia, a relic of sciatica, which prostrated him a few weeks ago.

The wedding of Miss CHARLOTTE LICHTENBERG and Mr. VIEL of Alameda took place yesterday at the home of the bride, Mr. WILLIAM LICHTENBERG, Marinita Park, San Rafael.

Coroner EDEN was notified Tuesday that a Chinese INFANT was found in the bay at Angel Island, and he brought the body here, a boy about 3 months old. An autopsy disclosed no evidence of violence or foul play, and a verdict of death from natural causes was given. Coroner EDEN asked the Chinese consul what he should do with the body, and was told to bury it.

Superior Court
    A DE ROSA vs MANUEL RODGERS & J.E. SILVA
    Trial – judgment for plaintiff for $613.30

    A.D. REMINGTON vs. F.C. DeLONG
    Ten days stay of sale from April 19th

    H.W. TAYLOR vs. J.S. BELLRUDE
    Motion to strike out costs of bills of court granted

    Estate and Guardianship of WILLIAM GARZOLI etal, minors
    Account of Guardian settled

    E. WORMOUTH s. J. GARDNER etal
    Demurrer to second defense and cross complaint sustained
    Demurrer to third defense overruled

    A GIACOMINI vs. his Creditors
    Trial account of receiver allowed and settled

Letter List
- BACON, Mrs. F.C.
- BENGSTON, O.V.
- BEGGS, TOM J.
- BALDES, RAFAEL
- BRAZIL, P.
- CONTREAS, Mrs. J.
- DUFFY, T.J.
- FOSS, J.W.
- FUGITA, Y.
- KOEHLER, VINCENT H.E.
- MANNNING, Miss MINNIE
- MAHONEY, T.V.
- METZLER, ANNA
- NICOLASSEN, J.
- PARKER, HENRY
- PRULLEY, Mrs. A.
- PASTORIA, Mr.
- PEARSON, LEWIS

GALINDO, BENEDICTO	REDINGTON, Mrs. L.C.
HEIDEL, J.	STANDLEY, ANNIE E.
HEIDEL, THOMAS	

Marin County Tocsin
Saturday, April 28, 1894

Local News

ALECK PRATT, formerly reporter of our Superior Court, together with his brother FRED PRATT, visited San Rafael yesterday.

JOHN BEISLER, an old resident of Bolinas, died suddenly at his home there last Monday. Deceased had been ailing for some weeks. He was a widower and leaves 2 small children.

The Fireman's Fund Insurance Co. has brought suit against HARRIET INK, administratrix of the Estate of T.H. INK, deceased, to foreclose a mortgage on a large tract of land in Nicasio township, commonly known as the "Ink Ranch", containing about 2500 acres.

Much surprise and regret was expressed by the many friends of Miss BESSIE LICHTENSTEIN at the announcement of her sudden death this week. Last Sunday she was in San Rafael, apparently full of life and health, visiting her connections by marriage, the HERZOGs. Four days later she was dead. The fatal disease was pneumonia in its most severe form. She was a graduate of the Dominican College of San Rafael.

The corner stone of Montgomery Memorial Chapel was laid yesterday at Sunnyside. Mrs. MONTGOMERY, daughter of the deceased capitalist, officiated and the ceremonies were simple but effective. Dr. LANDON, Professor of Practical Theology, delivered the principal address, which was a most thoughtful and scholarly effort.

JULIUS BERNSTEIN, who founded the Royal Billiard Parlor, to which Col. GANNON succeeded and which is now operated by PETER CRANE, the Home Missionary, is reported to be alive in Detroit notwithstanding the fact that elaborate accounts of his suicide were published in the San Francisco papers sometime ago. The object of JULIUS in withdrawing himself from the public view in this sensational manner was the outgrowth of a thrifty desire to beat sundry institutions out of about $10,000 of insurance money.

Real Estate Transfers

C.S. HOLMES etal to Holmes Investment Co.
Lots 16 & 17, block 2, Belvedere - $10

Mt. Tamalpais Cemetery to MARY SALM
Lot 2, Section L - $109.50

J.M. ROMA etal to London & San Francisco Bank
Lot in Old Sausalito - $10

American Land & Trust Co. to MARY E. BARIGHT
Lot 18, block 10, Larkspur - $10

ROBERT DICKSON etal to JAMES COFFIN etal, Trustees San Anselmo Schools
Lot 10, Block 8, Sunnyside tract - $10

Died

LICHTENSTEIN – BESSIE LICHTENSTEIN, beloved daughter of M.H. and T. LICHTENSTEIN, aged 19 years and 6 months.
Funeral from 2318 Clay Street, San Francisco, Sunday, April 29, 1894

Marin Journal
Thursday, May 3, 1894

Local Intelligence

Mr. MARCUSE, who has opened a liquor store in one of Mr. H. WILKIN's store buildings, has taken Mr. HERZOG's house on D Street.

Mr. JOSEPH SPEAR Jr., and Mrs. T.E. DOUGHERTY had a quiet wedding and wedding breakfast with a few friends at Father LAGAN's rectory Tuesday.

The engagement of Mrs. KATE PERRY of San Anselmo and Mr. J.E. BYRNE is announced, and the Examiner adds that Linda Vista, Mrs. PERRY's home for several years past, will be retained and extensively improved.

Letter List

AVERY, Mrs. R.J.	MORROW, ANTON
BLANCHARD, Rev.	REED, Mrs. J.J.
BRAZIL, BENJAMIN	REED, Miss J.
CROWNE, MARIA	SPENCER, Mrs. A.
FURNANCE, NORA	STEEL, FRED
GRORBELL, Mr.	McARTHY, J.
KENDALL, JOHN	LANGUETIN, M.E.

Superior Court

S. SCHWIESAU vs. E. FLAHERTY
Demurrer sustained

County of Marin vs. GEORGE P. McNEAR
Dropped from calendar

Estate of ISIDOR DAUS, deceased
Contest dismissed, Will admitted to probate, letters issued to SUSAN DAUS

People vs. PATRICK RICE
Continued for session

County of Marin vs. M. BLUMENTHAL
Set for trial June 5th

Estate of BELLA F. SWISHER, deceased
Continued one week

Estate of JAMES M. BIGGINS, deceased
HONORA M. MALLON appointed administratrix, bond $3,500

A.D. REMINGTON vs. F.C. DeLONG
Motion to recall execution denied

Married
POLSEN-HARVEY – In San Rafael, April 29, 1894, by Rev. J.S. FISHER, CHARLES A. POLSEN, of Pt. Bonita, and ALICE HARVEY of San Rafael.

SPEAR-DOUGHERTY – In San Rafael, May 1, 1894, JOSEPH S. SPEAR Jr. and Mrs. ANNIE BAPTIST DOUGHERTY, both of San Francisco

Marin Journal
Thursday, May 10, 1894

Mr. MAGNES has contemplated a trip to his old home in Poland, his special purpose to see his old mother, who was in poor health. He had made all arrangements for his departure, to start last Monday, when he received the sad news that his mother was dead. This was the only link that bound him to his native land, and he has abandoned the journey.

Novato
Miss JENNIE LEIS has returned to San Rafael from a two week's sojourn with her sister, Mrs. KOENIG.

W.N. HART has been appointed postmaster at Cazadero, vice T.J. GOULD deceased.

Matter of Insolvency
> GOTTARDO GUIBBINI, an Insolvent Debtor
> HENRY HARRISON, Sheriff appointed Receiver
> Filed May 8, 1894
>> F.M. ANGELLOTTI
>> Judge of Superior Court

Local Intelligence

O.M. BRENNAN has resigned the management of the Hotel Rafael, and is succeeded by J.A. CLOUGH, manager for several years of Del Monte.

Mr. GEORGE S. GRAHAM has assumed the management of the Saratoga Springs Hotel, one of the inviting resorts of Lake County, kept by Mr. WARFIELD of the Hotel California, San Francisco. Mr. GRAHAM is one of the best hotelmen on the coast, and Mr. WARFIELD is fortunate in securing his services. Mrs. GRAHAM will go there with her husband for the season, which is a loss to San Rafael, where her wide circle of friends will deeply regret her absence.

Mr. C.E. WILLARD, in a private note from the East, expresses a tender recollection of old friends in San Rafael, and confesses to a strong drawing in his heart backward to his home of 20 years ago. Speaking of great men who have passed away within the year, he mentions Gov. STANFORD, and particularly WILLIAM T. COLEMAN, for whom he had a great admiration. And looking further back, he recalls VAL DOUB, JOHN REYNOLDS, U.M. GORDON, Judge BOWERS, JAMES MILLER, ISAAC SHAVER, and others.

Mrs. F.T. MEAGHER died at her home in San Rafael Tuesday night last, and her funeral will take place at the Presbyterian Church at 11:30 a.m. this day, Thursday. Mrs. MEAGHER was a lady of many accomplishments and high character, and leaves a wide circle of friends here and in the bay cities. Her early home was in Pleasant Ridge, a fine suburb of Cincinnati, OH, and she was a granddaughter of General CARTER of Kentucky.

Mrs. P. PRYOR of San Francisco is visiting her son, J.H. PRYOR. She is accompanied by Miss FANNIE LEITSCH of Shasta.

Real Estate Transfers
> CAROLINE E. NYE to MARY E. SCANLIN
> Lot 2, block 35, San Rafael townsite - $10
>
> MOLLIE J. McNIGHT to CHRISTOPHER LEEK
> Half interest in lots 19, 20, & 21, block G, Novato – 410
>
> S. SUSSMAN to M.E. O'SHAUGHNESSY
> Lot 41, Mill Valley, map 1 - $10
>
> Estate of J.J. REY to JANE REY
> Lots in Belvedere, Sausalito and another county
>
> S. GAMBONI to CHARLES MARTIN
> 350.20 acres in San Antonio township - $10
>
> Belvedere Land Co. to EDGAR M. WILSON
> Lot 33, block 7, and lot 21, block 8 - $10
>
> M. ROSENTHAL etal to CHARLES BACH
> Lot 12 on plan of Villa lots, Ross Valley - $10
>
> JAMES TUNSTEAD, referee, to CATHERINE PRUNTY
> 190.88 acres, rancho Corte Madera - $15,000
>
> HONORA M. MALLON to CATHERINE PRUNTY
> Quit claim to 190.88 acres, rancho Corte Madera

CATHERINE PRUNTY to HEPBURN WILKINS
Undivided ½ interest in 190.88 acres, rancho Corte Madera - $10

W.T. COLEMAN to VINCENT NEALE
Lot 14, block 24, Golden Meadow, San Rafael - $1

VINCENT NEALE to NINA R. SPENCER
Lot 14, block 24, Golden Meadow, San Rafael - $1

J.W. MACKAY etal to THOMAS McHUGH
Lot 7, 8, 9, 10, block 47, Lomita Park, San Rafael - $10

Sausalito Bay Land Co. to EMILY L. PERLEY
Lots 84 & 85, block 29, South Sausalito - $10

Superior Court
THOMAS J. BIGGINS etal vs. CATHERINE PRUNTY etal
Referee's report approved and sale confirmed

Application of W.M. CARNAHAN for writ of habeas corpus
Writ denied and prisoner remanded

Estate of BELLA F. SWISHER, deceased
Continued to two weeks

S.N. MORRIS vs. A.R. BECKER etal
Demurrer overruled

M. HERZOG vs. J. PRINGLE
Set for trial May 22nd

VIALE vs. MAHAR
Set for trial May 17th

Letter List

BURRELL, Mrs. P.F.	HASS, Mrs. WILLIAM
BOYD, Mrs. LAURA J.	HEILMAN, Mrs. I.W.
BLOWER, E.J.	HEATH, Mrs. RICHARD
BROWN, J.A.	BROWN, AMELIA
BANNON, JANE	BANNON, CATHRINE
HARVEY, Mrs.	HUNT, ---
BYERS, ROBERT	HAYNE, R.T.
BUTLER, ADELINE	HANKINS, Mrs. MARY P.
BENNETS, JOHN	METZLER, Miss ANNA
BASKER, ANNIE H.	MELHUS, GUGRI
BARBER, Mrs. H.E.	MEEKER, M.
BURGESS, WILLIAM	MORSCHEIMER, A.
CRAGEN, Mrs. R.W.	MACK, Mrs. A.
CONWAY, Miss MALANA	MORRIS, Mrs. E.B.
CLARK, Miss A.M.	NOLTHING, WILLIAM
CHASE, Miss BERTHA C.	McALLMEY, Mrs.
CLYNE, Mrs.	O'CONNELL, JOHN
DOMINGO, JOS.	OLSON, CHARLES
FORTUNE, Mrs. WILLIAM	RING, BYRON
FULTON, Mrs. J.	REGAN, Mrs. J.C.
GOULDE, JULIA	RICHARDS, C.O.
GOODMAN, ---	RAWLINGS, JOE
GROSH, Mrs. E.T.	WILLIAMS, CLARA P.
GROENWOLD, Mrs. L.	WALSH, JEFF
GILFILAN, WALTER A.	WILLIAMS, LUCY N.
GOSS, MARY	ZELLAR, JOSEPH
HANDON, MAUDE	ZINCKE, WILLIAM

VICTORINO, V.J.

Died
MEAGHER – In San Rafael, April 10, 1894, Mrs. LIZZIE IRENE MEAGHER, wife of FRANK T. MEAGHER, and mother of RALPH BRIGGS, a native of Cincinnati, OH, aged 45 years. Funeral will take place at the Presbyterian Church, San Rafael, at 11:30 a.m. this day (Thursday). The remains to taken by the 12:45 Donahue train to San Francisco, for interment in Odd Fellows' Cemetery.

FRAJSRTADT – In Przedburg, Poland, April 12, 1894, Mrs. CHAJA F. FRAJSRTADT, mother of ROBERT MAGNES of San Rafael, and MOSES MAGNES of Hayward, aged 60 years.

Marin Journal
Thursday, May 17, 1894

Local Intelligence
Mr. GEORGE S. GRAHAM declined the management of the Calistoga Springs Hotel, and has taken an engagement with Mr. BRENNAN at the Pleasanton, San Francisco.

Superior Court
C.B. RAULINO, executor vs. MANUEL ROGERS & J.E. SILVA
Trial commenced and continued to May 16th

Estate of HENRY N. HOWE, deceased
Will admitted to probate, JUANA D. HOWE appointed executrix

VIALE vs. MAHAR
Reset for trial May 23rd

Real Estate Transfers
Home & Farm Co. to EMMA E. DOTTERS
26.25 acres at Novato - $10

Home & Farm Co. to LUCY JOHNSON
8 acres in lot 6, Division C, Novato - $10

HENRY HARRISION, Sheriff to ELISHA DuBOIS
Lot on Bayview Street, San Rafael - $4,000

Tamalpais Land & Water Co. to ARTHUR M. BROWN
3 acres in Tamalpais Land & Water Co. lands - $900

Belvedere Land Co. to REGINALD D. BRAY
Lot 28, block 3, Belvedere - $10

H.C. CAMPBELL to AUGUST REUSCHE, Jr.
Part of lot D, Sausalito Rancho - $10

Mrs. S.W.I. TAYLOR to JOS. S. DARNER
Lots 22 & 23, Sunnyside - $500

MARY H. JAMES etal to RICHARD B. KELLOGG
Lot 15, block 10, map 3, Sausalito Bay Land Co. - $10

H. FRANCES to H. LACY
Lot 6, block 24, Coleman's addition to San Rafael - $10

JACOB GARDNER to HARRIET R. CUSHING
Part of Section 29, township I, North R 6 W - $10

HARRIET R. CUSHING to JACOB GARDNER
Portion of Blythdale tract - $10

Married

TORRE-SALINA – In San Rafael, May 13, 1894, by Justice RODDEN, JOHN TORRE and MODESTA SALINA, both of Eureka

PALM-DICK – In San Rafael, May 3, 1894, by Rev. J.S. FISHER, CHARLES W. PALM and NELLIE M. DICK, both of Los Angeles

GREAVER-KENNY – In San Rafael, May 11, 1894, by Rev. Father LAGAN, EDWARD GREAVOR to Miss ELLA KENNY, both of San Rafael

Marin County Tocsin
Saturday, May 19, 1894

Notice to Creditors
Estate of GEORGE LARSEN, deceased
H. WILKINS, attorney for Administrator
Filed May 18, 1894
W.H. ABBOTT, Administrator

Local News
Mr. HUGH TODD has brought his family from Petaluma and moved into his new residence on Petaluma Avenue.

Real Estate Transfers
Home & Farm Co. to BENJAMIN HEALY
Lots 20 & 21, Reservoir Hill tract - $10

R. McF. DOBLE to MARIANA S.R. SOUZA
Subdivisions 1,2,3, of lots Q and R, San Anselmo villa lots - $900

JOHN SHEEHY to WINIFRED J. SHEEHY
Residence lot on Mission Street, San Rafael – love and affection

Superior Court
EICKHOFF vs. EICKHOFF
Tried and submitted on briefs

In the matter of R.T. MILLIGAN, on habeus corpus
Petitioner ordered, discharged

Died
RODGERS – In San Rafael, May 18, 1894, FRANCIS ROGERS, native of Cornwallis, Nova Scotia, aged 54 years and 3 months.
Funeral Monday, May 21, 1894, at St. Raphael's Church

Marin Journal
Thursday, May 24, 1894

Letter List

ADAMS, J.B.	LOUIS, J. Jr.
ADAIR, HANNAH	LEWIS, Mrs. BENJAMIN
BUCKER, CARRIE	LACK, MICHAEL
BERRY, Mrs. M.F.	MILLS, CHARLES
BRUSON, A.	MURPHY, JOS.
BUHNE, Mrs. A.H.	MARTINEZ, D. FRANCISCO Sr.
BROWN, Mrs. J.	MAYER, LOUISE
BAXTER, H.B.	MORININI, JOSEPH
BONAM, J.B.	MAHAR, JOHN B.
BARNES, H.H.	MAHAR, JAMES
BIRD, MABEL	McGILLAWEY, ANN
BROWN, GEORGE	McGLOCKEN, JACK
BOYLE, Miss HUGH	McFARLAND, Mrs. J.

BRIGGS, AUGUST	PAGE, Mrs.
BETHUNE, ELLA	PHILPOTT, Mrs. HATTIE
BLANDING, WILLIAM	PARKS, Mrs. L.F.
BENGTON, B.W.	PERRY, FRANK
BULTER, Miss J.	PARKS, B.F.
BLANDING, Mrs. GORDON	PIERCE, W.
BENNARD, CHARLES	PEDERSON, H.
BUNKER, H.C.	POWERS, HARRY
BOYD, NELLIE	SCHEREER, PAUL
CARROLL, DENNIS	STEVENS, Mrs. ELLA
ENGSTROM, Miss A.S.	SULLIVAN, P.
FULTON, Mrs. J.	SHAW, THOMAS
HUTCHINSON, Mrs. H.L.	SULLIVAN, CON.
HAYS, C.B.	SHARKEY, JOHN H.
JOHNSTON, Miss MARY	STOWELL, E.H.
KRAMER, Miss	SPONY, JOHN B.
KAHN, LEWIS	SARGENT, ATIGLIA
KRIEGEL, EDWARD	WELSH, E.M.
KNOX, GEORGE R.	WILSON, A.C.
LANTHUM, Dr. E.P.	WHITE, F.J.
LOW, JENNIE	WHEELER, F.A.
LATHAM, Mrs. F.B.	VAN WIC, Miss A.
BULLOTTI, VERGILLO	MILTON, R.
BRAZIL, A.	MIRANDA, S.
CALLAGHAN, Mrs. FRANCIS	MORININI, JOE
CIVIANNO, JOSE	NEVEZ, MANOEL F.
DACEY, JAMES	ROSSEFALLE, MAGNESEN
DAVES, Mrs. W.W.	RODRIGUES, JOAN M.
DIXON, Mrs. FRANK	RUSSELL, Mrs. A.D.
DAILEY, MICHAEL	RODDY, KATE
DIVIER, CHARLES	REGAN, Mr. & Mrs. J.C.
DOLA, Miss J.M.	SHIELDS, Mrs. J.
GASPAR, JOSE CARDOZA	SMITH, Miss MARY
GORDI, F.L.	SIMPSON, LORETTA
HENDLEY, Miss INETH	SALAZAR, J.U.
JOSEPH, U.	TAYLOR, FREDERICK W.
KALENDER, F.H.C.	TERRY & MATTOS
KELLY, LEWIS	RWIEFEL, POTTER
KEELER, Mrs. J.B.	ZAPATA, MARIA VILA DE

Born

CASSOU – In San Rafael, May 21, 1894, to the wife of H. CASSOU, a daughter.

VON SEIBOURJ – In San Rafael, May 14, 1894, to the wife of OTTO JOS. VON SEIBOURJ, a son.

Died

EMERSON – In Santa Barbara, May 14, 1894, PERCY W. EMERSON, aged 23 years and 11 months.

GALLAGHER – In San Rafael, May 17, 1894, BERNARD GALLAGHER, native of County Derry, Ireland, aged 33 years.

Real Estate Transfers

    American Land & Transfer Co. to MINNIE C. SADLER
    Lot in Block I, Larkspur - $10

    ALFRED E. WHITAKER to LIZZIE BRISTOWE
    Villa lot 19, Sausalito - $10

    Sausalito Land & Ferry Co. to MARGARET M. HANNON
    NE part of SE half of lot 2, Block 27, Sausalito - $10

Local Intelligence
Miss JULIETTE and HANNAH WILLIAMS and Miss KATE TOWLE will leave tomorrow for the East to spend a year.

Professor HYATT, formerly of San Rafael, is principal of the Yreka Schools.

Coroner EDEN exhumed three bodies of children from the old San Rafael Cemetery last week for removal to Olema. This makes 4 removals lately. If nothing better can ever be done, this slow process will in the course of ages clean out the old burial place, and allow it to be changed into some more appropriate use.

PERCY EMERSON, son of D.W. EMERSON, former resident of San Rafael, died at his home in Santa Barbara on the 14th instant. He has frequently visited here from the south and kept up his friendship with former acquaintances. He was a very fine young man, and his family is in deepest sorrow for his early death.

Found Dead
BERNARD GALLAGHER, Merchant, Drowned
On Thursday of last week, BERNARD GALLAGHER, of the grocery firm of CONVERY & GALLAGHER, disappeared, and his friends became very apprehensive that some evil might befall him. He had shown signs of aberration of the mind, which led his friends to keep a watch upon his movements, but on Wednesday, the 16th, he went down to San Quentin, where his actions were so peculiar that acquaintances tried to bring him home on the cars, but he would not come. He would not speak, and did not appear to notice anything going on about him. Finally they got him to come home in the cab of the last engine from San Quentin. When it arrived here, ANDREW DONNELLY, of the gas works, a cousin of his, took him home and cared for him. He seemed suspicious of everybody, very reticent and restless. The next day, Thursday, he disappeared, and all search for him was unavailing, until Tuesday morning last, Mr. CRIMMINGS, driving on a toll road to San Quentin, he discovered the body of the unfortunate man dead in the creek just below the island. He notified the Coroner, who brought the body to the morgue, and yesterday morning held an inquest. The funeral will take place at 10 a.m. this day, Thursday.

Superior Court
    JOS. VIALE vs. J.B. MAHAR
    Partially argued and submitted on briefs

    People vs. ROSA TEIXEIRA
    Continued one week

    S.N. MORRIS vs. A.R. BECKER etal
    Demurrer of ARNOLD BECKER overruled

    Estate of JOHN BEISLER, deceased
    Will admitted to probate, letters issued to JOHN HENRY BEISLER

    E. DUTRA vs. M. DUTRA
    Counsel fees and expenses $50 allowed

    Estate of JOHN SCHIPPERS, deceased
    Final account settled and estate distributed

    Estate of BELLA F. SWISHER, deceased
    Application to mortgage property dismissed

Additional Local
Miss VERONICA A. DUFFICY has received a diploma for the classical course of the Boys' High School of San Francisco, which admits her to the State University without examination.

Mr. W.A. MARSHALL, son of the late S.A. MARSHALL, who was the owner of a number of rich ranches throughout Marin County, was in San Rafael last Tuesday on business.

Mr. W.C. POND was here this week, and returned Monday to Seattle. Mrs. POND has gone to Auburn, where she expects to be joined by her husband, now at Topeka, KS.

Local Brevities
Miss FLORIDE GREEN has resigned from the public school, and will leave San Rafael for the big city – a loss to the school and regret to the lady's many friends here.

Marin County Tocsin
Saturday, May 26, 1894

 Notice to Creditors
  Estate of JAMES MICHAEL BIGGINS, deceased
  HEPBURN WILKINS, Attorney for Administratrix
  Filed May 4, 1894
     HONORA MARGARET MALLON
     Administratrix of Estate

 Notice to Creditors
  Estate of JAMES B. ABLES, deceased
  HEPBURN WILKINS, Attorney for Administrator
  Filed May 2, 1894
     SAMUEL M. AUGUSTINE
     Administrator of Will and Estate

 Notice of Proving Will
  Estate of JOHN BEISLER, deceased
  Application by JOHN HENRY BEISLER for letters testimony
  Date set for Proving Will
  JAMES W. COCHRANE, Attorney for Petitioner
  Filed May 4, 1894
     THOMAS S. BONNEAU, Clerk

Local News
Mrs. ANDERSON, a woman recently employed by P. TROY as a house servant, was adjudged insane by Judge ANGELLOTTI and committed to the Napa Asylum.

CHARLES F. PETERSON, of the Hotel Rafael, had a sudden and severe attack of illness last Wednesday night and has left for San Francisco for treatment.

The residence of foreman WALLACE at Larkspur was destroyed by fire last Tuesday evening. The building was of an inexpensive description and the loss was well covered by insurance.

JAMES DOWNEY, who was so severely injured by a passing train at the Second and D Street crossing, has sued the North Pacific Coast Railroad Co. for $50,000. DELMAS & SHORTRIDGE are his Attorneys.

Mr. CHRISTOPHER CHISHOLM located the woman guilty of inserting an advertisement in the Examiner reflecting on his daughter and on last Saturday procured her arrest. She was a discharged domestic, JENNIE ELLIS, by name. The prisoner, when locked up and confronted with the evidence of her guilt, broke down completely, and made a full confession. Her sorrow and repentance seemed so genuine that Mr. CHISHOLM, with a leniency greater than deserved, asked that she be released on her own recognizance. She was accordingly discharged from custody.

Graduation Exercises
San Rafael High School graduates are:
 Miss EDNA RODDEN of San Rafael
 Miss MARY PETER of San Rafael
 Miss AGNES RITCHIE of Sausalito
 Mr. GEORGE HARLAN of Sausalito
 Mr. BENJAMIN BOSQUI of Ross Valley

Real Estate Transfers
 DILLWYN PARRISH by HENRY HARRISON, Sheriff, to ANSON P. HOTALING
 The FISHER property, Ross Valley – Sheriff's deed

JULIA S. HAMILTON etal to J.J. PRENDERGAST etal
Undivided 100 acres in Inverness tract, Pt. Reyes - $5,000

Estate of MARY BRADY, deceased
Lot in village of Tomales, distributed by Court to MARY ALICE COLLINS, JAMES BERNARD BRADY, JOHN E. BRADY, and MAGGIE AGNES BRADY, share and share alike, order of the court

Tamalpais Land & Water Co. to ELLEN KELLY
Lot 283, Mill Valley - $1,000

News from the Sealers
JAMES WATSON received a letter this week from his half brothers, WILLIAM and HENRY CRANE, who shipped with the sealing fleet this year. They have had a rough experience. While off the coast of Northern Asia, they encountered a terrific storm that dismantled the vessel and every timber in it. The crew was kept at the pumps for days together and with all their efforts were barely able to keep the ship from foundering. Finally, when hope had almost been abandoned, a favorable turn in the weather enabled them to reach Hakodadi, in Japan, where they still were recuperating. The letter confirms the report of DAN FLAHERTY's death.

ISRAEL KASHAW, one of the very old residents of Marin County, died last Sunday at St. Luke's Hospital. He was about the first settler in the neighborhood of Tiburon and took up there the tract known as "Peninsular Island", afterwards called "Kashaw's Island", and later, to suit the fastidious taste of the present occupants, "Belvedere". The tract was then supposed to be Government land, but the courts finally included it in the Corte Madera del Presidio grant. Deceased, however, still held waterfront and tideland property in this county of considerable value.

Superior Court
M. HERZOG vs. JAMES PRINGLE
Judgment for plaintiff

C.B. RAULINO etal vs. MANUEL ROGERS etal
Testimony taken

Date for Proving Will
Estate of HENRY NATHANIEL HOWE, deceased
Application of JUANA B. HOWE for letters testamentary
J.P. RODGERS, Attorney for petitioner
Filed April 25, 1894
                                THOMAS S. BONNEAU, Clerk
                                By D.T. TAYLOR, Deputy Clerk

Notice to Creditors
Estate of JOHN BEISLER, deceased
Filed May 25, 1894
                                JOHN H. BEISLER, Executor

Marin Journal
Thursday, May 31, 1894

Local Intelligence
Mrs. GEORGE B. WILLIAMS of Petaluma, 87 years of age, mother of the better half of the editor of this paper, went to the residence of her son, GEORGE R. WILLIAMS, in Oakland, last week, to have a cataract removed from her eye. She had gradually lost her sight until she was blind. The operation was successful and the aged matron and her friends are rejoiced that she can see again. She suffered no shock or injury from the operation.

FRED WOODWORTH, Esq., gave us a pleasant call last Saturday. He has a growing law business and attends to it with pleasure and devotion.

Miss LILLIAN SLINKEY, daughter of Brother SLINKEY of the News, made a successful debut in opera on the 11th instant, and received highest praise from the most exacting critics.

Superior Court
> C.B. RAULINO vs. MANUEL RODGERS etal
> Continued on account of illness of H. WILKINS, attorney for plaintiff
>
> Estate of G. BELGERI, deceased
> Account settled and estate distributed
>
> People vs. ROSA TEIXEIRA
> On July calendar
>
> GOTTARDO GUIBBINI vs. his Creditors
> Over one week
>
> Estate of J.G. KITTLE, deceased
> Final account settled and estate distributed

Real Estate Transfers
> Tamalpais Land & Water Co. to CHARLES LIMARUTY
> Subd. 4 of lot 140, Tamalpais Land & Water Co., Map 2 - $10
>
> Belvedere Land Co. to JOSEPH BRITTON
> Lots 8 & 9, Block 40; Block 53; and lots 7 & 8, Block 31, Belvedere - $10
>
> E.C. BEASLEY to JOHN DE LACY
> Part of lot 12, block 4, Sausalito Land & Ferry Co. lands - $10

Death of ALLAN LEE

After an illness of several weeks, Mr. ALLAN LEE passed away at an early hour last Wednesday morning. Although he had passed the allotted span of life, he retained great vigor of body and mind, and could not recognize the necessity of adapting his activities to his age. He felt young, and as a man feels so is he. Hard work and exposure brought on sciatica, and this left complications which proved too much for his strength, and he is gone.

Mr. LEE was a native of Ayreshire, Scotland, which he left when a young man for Canada. In 1859 he came to California, and in 1871 he located in San Rafael, and bought from Mr. PLATT the gas machine, which in a primitive way, was giving us light. He soon found this too slow, and in his progressive way outlined and started a more satisfactory plan for lighting the town, and the work grew on his hands into the elaborate system which we now enjoy. Thus he became a prominent factor in the material progress of the place, and has always been a leader in enterprises of advancement. Subsequently his brother-in-law, the late J.O. ELDRIDGE, became interested with him in the gas works, and that interest is still retained by the family.

Mr. LEE was a good man and a good citizen. He took a lively interest in every project to promote the general wealth, and was always a wise counselor and generous promoter in local enterprises. He was a pleasant companion, affable, considerate, and honorable in all relations in life. He will be greatly missed.

Scholars Promoted

First to Second Grade – EDWINA J. DUFFICY, teacher
> FORREST ACKLEY, JOHN BETTENCOURT, FLORENCE BLUMENTHAL, CLARA CORDES, CHRISTINE CORTI, GRACE CARPENTER, GRACE DOLLAR, RAY DUFFY, IRVING FURLONG, JAMES FLANAGAN, CHARLIE KAPPENMAN, MINNIE KOHLER, GRANVILLE MAYHEW, WILLIAM NORIEL, HARRY ELMERICH, ARVILLA PARKS, ETHEL ROBINSON, MARTHA SALE, WILLA SALE, WILLIE SAIS, HAZEL SCOTT, GUY THOMPSON

Promotions
> CHARLES BUKER, EDWARD GRANDJEAN, WILLIE FLANAGAN, WILBER JAMES, WALLACE LIVINGSTON, WILLIAM MARCHANT, VIOLET McBRYDE, ROSA MORRIS, MAUD MORGAN, STELLA MORGAN, TOMMY PETERSEN, JESSIE PROUDFOOT, JOE REILLY, ALBERT SAIS, PHILIP SEABEL, JEAN WHITE, MARTHA WHITE, MANUEL TABOAS, ALFRED WRIGHT

Second to Third Grade – E.H. NICHOLS, teacher
Honorary

      GRACE DAVENPORT, HELEN HUNTER, LILLIE McCLELLAN, EMILY SAUNDERS, KATIE JORGENSEN, WILLIE BARR, HARRY CORDES, HAROLD CLIFFORD, CLARENCE McCARTHY, WILLIE OGE, HARRY ROBERTS, CLIFFORD THAYER, BERNHARDT SCHMIDT, HARRY HALEY

Promoted
      ARTHUR ANDERSON, WALTER GRANDJEAN, PAUL GROSSMAN, HARRY OBITZ, EUGENE FERRAN, ALFRED FERRAN, IRENE FOX, HIRREL DAVIS, JUANITA BAILEY, LEONIE HERZOG, HANNAH KAPPENMAN, AUGUSTINE LANG, JAMES RASMUSSEN, GEORGE WALSH, AMELIA LAVIOSA, CONSTANCE KNITTEL, LOTTIE WRIGHT, MAY DOLLAR, EMMA HOAG, JOSIE BRESSON, EDITH AGNEW

Third to Fourth Grade
Honorary
      ALFRED BLUMENTHAL, LILLIE CORDES, NED DAY, RALPH ELLIOTT, LEROY ACKLEY, WOLDEMAR HAMM, JOE KAPPENMAN, WILLIE MURRAY, SADIE SECOMBE, IRVING MAGNES, EDDIE WHITE

Promoted
      LOIS CORBALEY, GEORGIE DOODY, OLIVIA JACOBS, LOTTIE LUNT, FLORENCE MAGEE, BLANCHE McCLELLAN, LOTTIE REYNOLDS, LAURA SARTORI, HELEN SCOTT, HATTIE SMITH, ANNIE WHITE, HENRY BOYEN, ROBERT CURREY, NATHANIEL FOX, CLARENCE FURLONG, JACOB GOERL, EMILE LAVIOSA, HAROLD MOORHEAD, HOMER MORDOFF, WILLIAM MURRAY, HERBERT SEIBEL, HARRY SMITH

Fourth to Fifth Grade – KATE C. BATCHELDER, teacher
Honorary
      IRIDE CHEDA, ALECK CURLETT, CHARLES CLARKE, GEORGE DAY, SHERMAN DOUGHERTY, MINNIE FOX, STAFFORD HAMM, ELEANOR JONES, BERNICE McCLELLAN, JAMES McKENZIE, ETHEL MARCHANT, ANNA OWEN, HARRY RALEIGH, KATE SARTORI, OLETA SHIELDS, ED SAIS, ALEC WHITE, CLARA GROSSMAN

Promoted
      PAULINE BAILEY, GEORGE DUNAND, VESTA GULDE, MILLIARD GROVE, SIDNEY HERZOG, LAURA McBRIDE, FRANK MURRAY, ROY PRESCOTT, AGNES REILLY, RAYMOND SHAVER, WILBUR THAYER, TOM FINLAYSON, HELEN SUTHERLAND, BERTHA MORGAN

Haven't taken the examination
      ALVA BEACH, LOTTIE SORENSON, JOHN SHEEHY, GEORGE BLANKENHORN

Fifth to Sixth Grade – Miss MARY FARRELL, teacher
Honorary
      BERT BURTCHAELL, JANET DOLLAR, BESSIE FORSE, HARRY FLETCHER, CHARLES GRANDJEAN, MARIN CROVE, JOHN JAMIESON, MAMIE KNITTEL, BERTHA KAPPENMAN, GRACE LIVINGSTON, MABEL PRESCOTT, MAMIE RYAN, RENA ROCHE, LEONE ROBINSON, WALTER ROBERTS, ADA SECOMBE, ESTHER SHREVE, ZELMA WALKER, GRACE WEST

Promotions
      FRANK BIGELOW, CARLTON CURTIS, EDWARD DUNAND, EDWARD DE METZ, EDWARD EDEN, FREDERICK GODDARD, DIANA JORGENSEN, EDDIE JESSUP, DAVID KIRWAN, MARIO LAVIOSA, GRACE MOORHEAD, WALTER McCARTHY, MINNIE PETERSEN, MAUDE REYNOLDS, KATIE RYAN, WALTER REDMOND

Seventh to Eighth Grade – BELLE C. BROWN, teacher
Honorary
      WILLIAM SCOTT, JULIA THARPE, BESSIE HAMM, LULU MILLER, SADIE LUNNY

Promotions
      GARF BARSTOW – honorary in English, arithmetic, geography, and science
      GRACIE BARNARD – honorary in English, arithmetic, and geography
      ALICE CHAPPALEAR – honorary in English, arithmetic, and science
      MAURICE DUNAND – honorary in English, arithmetic, geography, and science
      MARY DOLLAR – honorary in English, grammar, geography, and science
           (advanced from sixth to seventh during the year)
      MELVILLE DOLLAR – honorary in English, arithmetic, geography, and science

WILLIAM EASTMAN – honorary in English, arithmetic, grammar, geography, and science
EDWARD GARDNER – honorary in arithmetic, geography, and science
WILLIAM ELLIOTT – honorary in English, arithmetic, geography, and science
DELMORE GARDNER – honorary in English, geography, science, and history
FRITZ GOERL – honorary in English, arithmetic, geography, science, and history
JAMES HALEY – honorary in arithmetic, geography, and science
VIVIAN HOXIE – honorary in English, arithmetic, geography, and science
HARRY PETER – honorary in English, arithmetic, geography, science, and history
ARTHUR STUDLEY – honorary in English, arithmetic, geography, and science
MAMIE FRANETTA (special) – honorary in English, geography, and science

Lists of promotions from sixth to seventh, and eighth to the high school, and high school promotions are not yet made out. They will be given next week. Promotions from the receiving class to first grade will not be made until later.

Parochial Commencement
St. Raphael School
Miss A. GLEASON, Miss M. O'BRIEN, Miss K. KINSELLA, Miss M. OLIN, Miss M. FLAHERTY, Miss A. DUFFICY, Miss R. CHADDICK, Miss N. MURRAY, Miss K. REDMOND, and Master F. O'TOOLE.

Letter List

BIGELOW, E.P.	CHALEWEES, Miss A.
BAILEY, H.F.	DENISTON, Miss MAGGIE
BOYLE, H.	DONNELLY, ALICE
CHAMBERS, J.P.	FRENCH, ALICE
CONNELLY, Mrs. T.	HILL, MARY
CALLENDER, CHARLES H.	HASKELL, G.S.
CLARK, HELENA	McGROTH, Miss MAGGIE
COFFIN, JAMES	SHEEHAN, JEREMIAH
COLWELL, JESSIE	SMITH, ALONZO C.
CROWELL, HAROLD W.	SMITH, Mrs. G.B.
CHECK, DONALD A.	TANNER, R.
COFFIN, JAMES A.	TANJLE, HOMER
CLARKE, EDW. G.	WALSH, EMMET
CHAMBERS, JOHN P.	WRIGHT, WHITAKER

Born
McNEAR – In Petaluma, May 29, 1894, to the wife of GEORGE P. McNEAR, a daughter.

Died
CAESAR – In San Rafael, May 28, 1894, Mrs. ANNIE CAESAR, daughter of J.J. SCHNEIDER. Funeral from the residence of Mrs. SCHNEIDER at 9:30 this day Thursday.

McNAMARA – In Petaluma, May 29, 1894, Mrs. McNAMARA, formerly of Nicasio, sister of THOMAS CURRY, of San Rafael.

LEE – In San Rafael, May 30, 1894, ALLAN LEE, beloved husband of SARAH A. LEE, aged 75 years 11 months, and 19 days.
Funeral Friday, June 1st, at 11 o'clock a.m. at late residence. Interment private.

Marin Journal
Thursday, June 7, 1894

Superior Court
E.W.S. VAN SLYKE vs. GRATTON PERRY
Set for trial July 10th

Estate of F.J. WHITE, deceased
Final account settled and estate distributed

Estate of IRENE MEAGHER, deceased
Letter of administration issued to FRANK T. MEAGHER, bond $7,000

G. GUIBBINI vs. his Creditors
Exempt property set apart for insolvent

RUSSELL CHAPMAN vs. WILLIAM H. JEWELL
Motion to set aside order dismissing appeal denied

S. PACHECO vs. S. FOX
Argued to file briefs

Application of DAN KINCAID for writ of habeas corpus
Writ denied and prisoner remanded

Local Intelligence
Dr. LAKIN, well known here, and who is practicing in Petaluma, was in town last Sunday on a visit.

The engagement is announced of Dr. HENRY S. WAGNER of San Francisco and Mrs. MARION WISE, daughter of the late HALL McALLISTER.

The death of Miss KATIE HAM, which occurred Wednesday night of last week, was a crushing blow to her fond parents, A.L. & ELLEN HAM, and a deep bereavement to a large circle of friends. Just past 18, native of here, where all her brief years were spent, she was a happy, cheerful spirit, with a gift of song that made her life seem like a constant melody and won the affection of a large circle of friends. Her religious experience was exceedingly bright and sunny, and her resignation to death, which she plainly foresaw, is great comfort to those who mourn her loss.

Mr. RALPH WOODWORTH may not come home during this season's vacation. At the Harvard Law School, RALPH rooms with BURLEY, a nephew of ex-Governor BURLEY of Maine, and he has agreed to go home with him to see the big timber fields of the Far East; so, unless the two young men should conclude to take in the Mid-Winter Fair in addition to the above, RALPH will not come home. A year ago, Mr. WOODWORTH graduated from Harvard College with high honors and the A.B. degree. He is now closing his first year of learning, and has two years more to stay there.

State Shoot
Company D, Fifth Regiment, Make a Fine Shoot
On Sunday last, Company D held the first of two shoots for State decorations, and made a record of which they are justly proud. For the year 1894, 78 men participated, and 48 ment made the required percentage. The scores of the 50 men are as follows:
Priv. F.B. MOULTON 46, Priv. J.P. MULHERN 45, Corp. A.E. SCOTT 43, Sergt. T. KERRIGAN 43, Sergt. S. EDEN 43, Lieut. T.J. MURRAY 42, Sergt. A.N. BOYEN 42, Priv. J. DAWSON 42, Priv. GEORGE IVERSON 42, Priv. J.S. WHITNEY 42, Priv. P. BAILEY 41, Capt. W. ELLIOTT 41, Priv. F.J. JACOBS 41, Priv. H. IVERSON 40, Priv. A.A. SMITH 40, Priv. J.F. ROBINSON 39, Priv. SCHOENEMAN 39, Priv. CLARK 39, Priv. H. FRITZ 39, Priv. L. PLETTE 39, Corp. TREANTON 39, Corp. F. VANDERBILT 39, Priv. J.F. BUSTIN 39, Priv. WEST 38, Priv. BUTTERWORTH 38, Priv. T.J. FALLON 38, Musc. SCHLOSSER 38, Lieut. DAVENPORT 38, Priv. F. MULHERN 38, Priv. ARCHER 37, Priv. D. MARTENS 36, Sergt. GREY 36, Musc. JOHANSEN 36, Priv. M. REILLY 35, Priv. DAWLEY 35, Priv. VANDERBILT 34, Priv. J. BEGLEY 34, Priv. E. SMITH 33, Priv. DONOHUE 34, Priv. N. ELLIOTT 33, Priv. ARMSTRONG 31, Corp. BARROWS 31, Priv. J.J. MURRAY 31, Priv. BAPTISTE 31, Priv. F.J. BUSTIN 30, Priv. W. MULCAHY 30, Priv. BRICKWIEDEL 30, Priv. STOLPH 36, Priv. LE CORNEC 29, Priv. HERZOG 29.

Additional Local
E.B. MARTINELLI made a flying trip to Lakeville, Sonoma County, last Sunday to visit his brother, who lives at that place.

After a brief illness, Mrs. ELLEN McNAMARA, an old and highly respected lady, died early Tuesday morning at her home in this city. Her death was a perfect shock to her family, for although unwell for a few days, she was not considered in any immediate danger. The deceased was 68 years of age and a native of Ireland. On Wednesday the remains were taken to San Francisco for burial in the Calvary Cemetery.
Petaluma Argus

Is He Dead?

There is reason to believe that JOHN DIXHEIMER has answered the last roll call. A letter sent to him from the Masonic Lodge has come back marked "dead". No notification has been received here direct, either by friends of Uncle JOHN, or by the lodge, but answers to the inquiries are daily expected.

Scholars Promoted

In addition to the names given last week, the following promotions to grammar school are:

From Sixth to Seventh Grade

Honorary

    EMMA BOYEN, MARY ROSS, AGNES WATSON, R. CLIFFORD

Promoted

    CLARA CRUMPTON, honorary in English, geography, and botany
    LOUISE GREFFOZ, honorary in English and botany
    ALICE HARRISON, honorary in English and botany
    ADA JORGENSEN, honorary in English, geography, botany, grammar, and history
    PATTIE KANEEN, honorary in English, geography, science, and grammar
    OLIVIA PETERSEN, honorary in English, and botany
    LENA SALME, honorary in botany
    SADIE SCOTT, honorary in English, arithmetic, geography, and botany
    KITTIE SALE, honorary in English and arithmetic
    ERSILIA SARTORI, honorary in English, geography and botany
    BERTHA SMYTH, honorary in English, geography, and botany
    ALICE WILKINS, honorary in English, arithmetic, geography, botany, and history
    C. CORBALEY, honorary in English, botany, and history
    H. HANSEN, honorary in English, arithmetic, botany, grammar, and history
    E. KANEEN, honorary in arithmetic, and botany
    E. KAPPENMAN, honorary in English and botany
    J. KEANE, honorary in English, grammar, and history
    WILLIAM NELSON, honorary in English, arithmetic, geography, and botany
    E. OLSEN, honorary in English, arithmetic, geography, and botany
    L. PETERSON, honorary in English
    C. SCOTT, honorary in English
    J. WATSON, honorary in botany
    R. WARDEN, honorary in geography, and botany
    W. KING, honorary in English, and botany
        (advanced into Fifth during the year)
    O. SMITH, honorary in botany
        (advanced to Sixth during the year)
    Z. SMITH, honorary in botany
        (advanced to Sixth during the year)
    I. PACHECO, honorary in English

Eighth Grade to High School

Honorary

    AMY FURLONG, LENA HAMM, WILLIE JAMIESON, EVA SALE, SADIE HALE, FANNIE HARRIS, MARGARET McDONALD, FANNIE TURNER

Promoted

    SAM BARCLAY, honorary in English, arithmetic, geography, and botany
    RALSTON CURTIS, honorary in English, arithmetic, geography, science, and history
    EDWARD DAVENPORT, honorary in English, arithmetic, geography, and science
    CARL DRAHM, honorary in arithmetic, geography, and history
    CARL HANSEN, honorary in arithmetic (failed in botany)
    WILLIAM HEARN, honorary in English, geography, botany, and history
    GEORGE HERZOG (failed in grammar)
    EMMET MANN, honorary in English, arithmetic, geography, and history
    HENRY REGAN, honorary in English, arithmetic, geography, and history
    SADIE BAILEY, honorary in English, geography, and botany
    MARCHIE DOUGHERTY, honorary in english, arithmetic, and botany

High School Promotions

Junior to Middle

Honorary
> JENNIE SAUNDERS, BERT CORBALEY, MARGARET SMITH, MARGARET SMITH, IDA LEAGUE, HESTER FISH, GERTRUDE OGE, DORA BOYEN, GEORGE SCOTT, FRED WHITE, MAZIE CROWLEY, LEONORA RYAN, MARY OGE, ALICE McALLISTER, MARTHA RICHARDSON

Promotions
> ELLA WALKER, MAGGIE DEASY, WALTER NELSON, SABINA KENNEY

Middle to Senior
Honorary
> ELIZABETH EDMEADS, ROBERT STEDMAN, GRACE MILLER

Promoted
> RAYMOND PRESCOTT, BERTHA WOSSER, AGNES HARRISON, MAUD STOCKER, MARY SMITH, H.F. HAMADA, JOSIE RICHARDSON, ERNEST JACKSON

Special
> MAGGIE MURRAY, FRANCES CRISP

Letter List

AVILLA, SHERRY	COOK, Mrs. J.
BARLOW, THOMAS E.	ELLIOTT, ADAM G.
BYRNE, Miss MARY	HEAD, Mrs. ROSE
BEALE, L.L.	KAISER, JACOB
BROWN, J.	KIRCKER, Miss JOHANNA
BORBA, MARIANA	KELLY, Miss SALLY
BRUCE, WILLIAM	SMITH, Mrs. CORA B.
CROWELL, Miss K.M.	STEARNS, Miss MARY
CARDER, Mrs. KATE	WOODWORTH, Miss M.
CRAIG, Mrs. A.G.	WALKER, Mrs. LIZZIE

Real Estate Transfers
> Home & Farm Co. to MANUEL S. MATHEWS
> Lots 49, 50, 51, & 52, block J, town of Novato - $10
>
> Belvedere Land Co. to FRANK UNCH
> Lots 29 & 30, block 6, Belvedere - $10
>
> HUGH COLLINS etal to FRANCIS McPHILLIPS
> 1 acre in Tomales - $10

Marin County Tocsin
Saturday, June 9, 1894

Local News
Mr. JAMES B. BURDELL is a candidate of the Republican nomination for Supervisor of the Fifth District. The young gentleman has great interests in the district, and is capable, energetic, and an excellent businessman.

Tomales Tidings
Last Tuesday evening, the marriage was held of WILL MURPHY and Miss JOSIE FAUCRAULT. It was performed by Rev. J. ROGERS. JENNIE O'CONNOR was the bridesmaid, and the groom was attended by his brother, M.L. MURPHY, who was best man, and LOUIS FAUCRAULT and ALBERT GULDAGER.

Another wedding took place on Tuesday at noon, the contracting parties being Miss DELL TURNER and WILLIAM IRVIN, son of JOSEPH IRVIN, one of our old pioneers. The ceremony was performed by Rev. Mr. LEUDGEON of Bloomingdale.

Miss KATE HUNDLY of Oakland is the guest of Miss MAE HOLLAND.

Mrs. CONROY of San Jose is visiting her daughter, Miss MAE HOLLAND.

Born
KOHLHOFF – In San Rafael, June 7, 1894, to the wife of GUSTAV KOHLHOFF, a daughter.

Real Estate Transfers
    J.D. BOWLAND and wife to H. WILKINS & JAMES TUNSTEAD
    Lot 4, block 5, San Rafael - $10

    Estate of FRANKLIN J. WHITE
    Lot at head of B Street, San Rafael, distributed to widow, order of court

    J.M. ROMA to London & San Francisco Bank
    Part of Winterburn tract, Sausalito - $10

    MARY MEYER to J.A. MILLER
    Lot 9, block H, Larkspur - $300

    J.A. MILLER and wife to C.B. STONE
    Lot 9, block H, Larkspur - $10

    Belvedere Land Co. to CHARLES O. PERRY
    Lots 32 & 33, and W ½ of lot 1, Block 3, Belvedere - $10

Marin Journal
Thursday, June 14, 1894

    Real Estate Transfers
        GEORGE PENMAN to GEORGE SAMMY
        Lot 25, Reservoir Hill Place, Novato, 10.03 acres - $10

        ELLIS M. SWAIN to HATTIE E. SWAIN
        Lot D, portions of 19, 20, 21, & 22, block 6, Richardson Ranch – Gift

        JOSEPH M. SHOTWELL to MARIANNE TOURGEE SHOTWELL
        Lot in Ross Valley – gift

        ELISHA DuBOIS to GERALAMO CRISANTI
        Lot on South C Street, near Taylor, San Rafael - $10

        GEORGE A. CRALL to LOUIS LEVY
        Part of lot 5, block 30, Sausalito Land & Ferry Co. Lands - $1,850

        American Land and Trust Co. to JERUSHA M. WALLIS
        Lots 8 & 21, block 10, Larkspur - $10

        FRITZ SHUEMAN to S.F. & N.P.R.R. Co.
        Lot on the line of the San Rafael and San Quentin Railroad - $5

        HUGH COLLINS to J.E. BRADY etal
        1 acre in Tomales - $10

    Estate of ALLEN LEE, deceased
        Time appointed for proving Will
        Filed June 12, 1894
        H. WILKINS, Attorney for Petitioner
        Application of SARAH A. LEE for letters testamentary
                      THOMAS S. BONNEAU, Clerk
                      By D.T. TAYLOR, Deputy Clerk

    Superior Court
        Estate of B. GALLAGHER, deceased
        Letters issued to ANDREW CONNOLLY, bond $1000

        G. GUIBBINI vs. his Creditors
        H. HARRISON appointed assignee, bond $400

The People vs. DAN KINCAID
Burglary – arraigned and plead not guilty

Local Intelligence
News is received of the total loss of several sealhunting vessels in the Japan seas, among which it is feared was the ship "Rattler", on which was CHARLES ALMY of San Rafael, for whose fate grave apprehensions are felt.

To the great regret of a wide circle of friends, Professor ANDERSON has severed his connection with the Mt. Tamalpais Military Academy and will go to Alameda. Professor ANDERSON and his family will be greatly missed.

Dr. AIKEN, convicted of illegal use of the mails in connection with a malodorous medical practice, was taken to San Quentin Prison Friday last, and died during his first night there. Coroner EDEN held an inquest on the remains, and the jury returned a verdict of suicide by poison. It appears that the deceased carried life insurance for $30,000, which will be jeopardized by the verdict of suicide.

Additional Local
Among the bequests of the late Mrs. ELLEN C. McNAMARA is $1,000 to Father CLARY of Petaluma.

Local Brevities
FRED B. McKINNON, second son of the late HUGH McKINNON and Mrs. B.G. MORSE of Bolinas, died in San Francisco on the 11th instant. He was a fine young man and loving son, and will be universally missed in Bolinas.

Died
McKINNON – In San Francisco, June 11, 1894, FREDERICK BUTLER McKINNON, son of the late HUGH McKINNON and Mrs. B.G. MORSE of Bolinas, aged 23 years, 2 months, and 22 days.

Married
SHAVER-HURLEY – In San Rafael, June 12, 1894, by Justice GARDNER, AARON SHAVER and ANNIE J. HURLEY

MURPHY-FAUCRAULT – In Tomales, by Rev. J. ROGERS, WILLIAM MURPHY and Miss JOSIE FAUCRAULT, both of Tomales.

Delinquent Tax List 1893
    AZEVEDO, F.S. & Co. – Fairfax
    AMARAL, A.S. – Dixie
    AZEVEDO, A.S. – Dixie
    ANDERSON, STEPHEN – Tiburon
    BELLO, C.S. & Co. – Eastland
    BERNARDO, M. & Co. – Eastland
    BUTLER, M. – Point Reyes
    BAREUCHI, CHARLES – Garcia
    BACOLLIO, A. – Novato
    BOTTINI, BATISTA – Fairfax
    BOGIANO, D. – Fairfax
    BURTEN, B. – Tiburon
    BEYRIES, VICTOR – Tiburon
    BRIDGE, H. – Eastland
    BETTENCOURT, M.A. – Eastland
    BORGES, MANUEL & Co. – Reed
    CORREA, JOHN ENOS – San Geronimo
    COSSA Bros. – Lincoln Valley
    CHEVAL, JOS. – Novato
    COOKSON, H. – Tiburon
    CARPENTER, E.S. – Tiburon
    DOMINGO, JOS. – Dixie
    DELCROIX, Mrs. J. – Tiburon

DUNBAR, Dr. L.L. – Tiburon
DOWD, CHARLES – Eastland
DORSEY, J.W. – Tiburon
ENRIGHT, THOMAS – Tiburon
ERVING, A.M. – Tiburon
FRANZI, A. – Point Reyes
FOSTINO, ANTONIO & Co. – Ross
GUELMINI, G. – Tocaloma
GIACOMINI, G. – Lincoln
GOGGIN, E.W. – Tiburon
GAY, C.A. – Eastland
GARDNER, PETER – Eastland
HOEFT, GEORGE – Point Reyes
JUKES, T.J. – Bolinas
HOOPER, K. – Tiburon
KATEN, JOHN – Clark
KLOSE, A.H. – San Quentin
LEWIS, CANBY – Nicasio
LEWIS, WILLIAM C. – Tiburon
MALTOS, A. & Co. – Eastland
MASON, CLINTON – Richardson
MASON, JOHN – Richardson
MARTINELLI, S. – Point Reyes
MACHADO, ANTONIO – Point Reyes
MAGGETTI, LOUIS – Nicasio
McLAUGHLIN, J. – San Antonio
McNAMARA, J. – Sausalito
McDONALD, Mr. – Tiburon
McCUE, HENRIETTA – Eastland
OWIEN, P. – Tiburon
OZANN, A. – Tiburon
O'CONNOR, Mrs. W. – Tiburon
O'CONNELL, J. – Tiburon
PETERS, HENRY – Laguna
PETRONI, M. – Lincoln
PEIREIRA, FRANK – Novato
PERRY, Mrs. KATE – San Anselmo
PETER, ANTONE – Reed
ROOT, E.M. – Tomales
RICE, J.B. – Sausalito
RIZZOLI, R. – Salmon Creek
SOUZA, J.J. & Co. – Eastland
SILVA, M. & Co. – Eastland
TAYLOR, JAMES I. – Tocaloma
TORRA, M. – San Jose
VALENCIA, Mrs. C.C. – San Jose
ZUMINI, Mr. – Bay
NIZZOLI, Mr. – Bay
RIORDAN, P.W. – Garcia
RITCHIE, WILLIAM – Sausalito
ROCHEFORT, PAUL – Eastland
ROSS, MARIE – Eastland
SHUCK, Mrs. McL. - Sausalito
SUTCLIFFE, D.D. – Sausalito
FRITCH, GEORGE – Sausalito
BOTHIN, J.C. – Sausalito
SWISHER, BELLA F. – Sausalito
SUTCLIFFE, THOMAS E. – Sausalito
SANDERSON, CHARLOTTE H. – Sausalito
SHELTON, J. – Laguna
SUTCLIFFE, JULIA ANN – Eastland
SCHNEIDER, O. – Eastland

SWAIN, ELLIS M. – Eastland
STEARNES, ELIZA A. – Eastland
SMITH, GEORGE F. – Eastland
SPALDING, J.D. – Tiburon
TAYLOR, Mrs. SARAH I. – Richardson
TEVIS, WILLIAM S. – Tiburon
TUCKEY, MATILDA R. – Belvedere
VATER, ROSALIE A. – Ross
WORMOUTH, J.A. – San Rafael
WORMOUTH, E. – Richardson
WILSON, PETER S. – Richardson
WHEELER, HAROLD – Richardson
WORMOUTH, E. – Eastland
WINSLOW, Mrs. E.J. – Reed
WALSH, MAGGIE – Eastland

San Rafael

ALEXANDER, CHARLES O.
BAYLEY, NORA F.
CROCKETT, J.B.
DONOVAN, JAMES & CATHERINE
HOYT, C.A.
IRWIN, ESTELLE
JOHNSON, A.S.
LYNCH, MARGARET
MIRANDA, S.
MONTAGUE, H. DE LA
MONTEITH, GEORGE W.
MILLS, MINNIE B.
McALLISTER, W.F.
PINKARD, BELLE E.
PORTER, ROBERT
STONE, PETER V.
SARGENT, ELIZABETH R.C.
STINSON, A.H.
SARGENT, C.R.
SIBLEY, JAMES
DE SOUZA, MARIA E.
STRAUSS, LEVI
STIMPSON, J.S.
TOWNSEND, ALICE C.
VAN DYKE, J.H.
YOUNG, GEORGE M. & wife
WISE, H.E.

Letter List

BRIZARD, HENRY F.   KELLOGG, LANSING
CANTWELL, Mrs. J.C.   PARKER, HARRY
GRANT, MARY   PERKINS, S.H.
HEMICHSON, DOROTHY   ROBINSON, Mrs. KATE
HARRIS, C.F.   RILEY, MARY
HILL, MARY   TALBOT, Mrs.
JEROME, CHRIS   WALKER, WILLIAM
KRAGEN, Mrs.   WALLACE, H.M.

Foreign

ANGELINETTA, PABLO   HIBBEN, Miss
VON GUNTEN, Miss B.   BRIGGS, Mrs. L.

Marin County Tocsin
Saturday, June 16, 1894

Notice to Creditors
>	Estate of BERNARD GALLAGHER, deceased
>	M.C. DUFFICY, Attorney for Administrator
>>		ANDREW DONNOLLY, Administrator

Order to Show Cause
>	Estate of BELLA F. SWISHER, deceased
>	F.C. KECK and E.S. GREER, Executors of Will and estate
>	Filed June 12, 1894
>>		F.M. ANGELLOTTI, Judge

Local News

J.R. WALSH, of San Rafael, fell off a moving train at Cheyenne last week while on the way East and suffered a fracture of the collarbone.

Miss CHRISTINA HOCK of San Rafael made her debut at Mme. COURSEN-ROECKEL's Musicale last week in San Francisco. The young lady is quite an accomplished vocalist.

Our two newly married couples, Mr. and Mrs. DAVID CHARLEBOIS and Mr. and Mrs. AARON SHAVER, were recipients of a complimentary serenade, given by their friends.

Mr. JOSEPH ALBERTI, the dry good merchant, has opened the William Tell House. He will run the house as a first class mechanics boarding and lodging house.

Real Estate Transfers
>	MARY A. VOGEL to AGATHA VOGEL
>	3.119 acres, near San Anselmo - $10
>
>	C.A. GRAHAM and wife to KATE F. SCHETZEL
>	Lots 3, 4, 5, & 6, block 2A, Mill Valley - $10
>
>	JOHN RICHARDS to W.J. THOMAS
>	Part of block 10, near Sausalito - $800

People's Party Club

A People's Party Club was organized last Sunday at the City Hall, San Rafael. The following gentlemen were elected officers:
>	L.F. HASKELL – President
>	JAMES A. McKAY – Vice President
>	CHARLES DuBOIS – Secretary
>	JOHN PACHECO – Treasurer
>	County Committee
>>		L.F. HASKELL, JAMES A. McKAY, CHARLES DuBOIS, F.T. BAILEY, T. HOCK, San Rafael
>>		A.H. WHEELER, Mill Valley
>>		THOMAS A. McGOVERN – Bolinas
>>		BEN HEILFRON – Nicasio

Notice to Creditors
>	Estate of LIZZIE IRENE MEAGHER, formerly LIZZIE IRENE BRIGGS, deceased
>	JAMES W. COCHRANE, attorney for Administrator
>	Filed June 7, 1894
>>		FRANK T. MEAGHER, Administrator

Died

MURPHY – At Tamalpais Station, June 13, 1894, EDWARD W. MURPHY, son of EDWARD MURPHY, aged 18 years, 10 months, and 20 days.

GREEN – In San Rafael, June 13, 1894, LOTTIE GREEN, daughter of CHARLES GREEN, aged 10 months.

SHAVER-HURLY

Uncle AARON SHAVER was quietly married by Justice GARDNER last Tuesday night to Miss ANNIE HURLEY and the event has been the sensation of the week. There is somewhat of a disparity between the ages of the contracting parties, the bridegroom being 71, and the bride 25. Some people are inclined to criticize the old man's action, but the Tocsin is not one of them. We think AARON did the correct thing. There is no reason why old men should not have as good a right to get married as young men. Certainly they do not make anymore worse botch work out of the job of matrimony than their more youthful contemporaries. In the present case, it was a matter of advantage on both sides. Neither party wasted much sentiment, but the bride, who is a good cook, good housekeeper, good woman, and nearly as close as AARON himself, wanted a home and old AARON wanted someone to take care of him. Both have got what they were looking for and are satisfied. The public should be satisfied also.

Marin Journal
Thursday, June 21, 1894

Superior Court
Estate of ANNIE MARIA SCOTT, deceased
Decree of final discharge

Estate of A.H. DODGE, deceased
Final account settled and estate distributed

Estate of GEORGE BUNN, deceased
Continued to June 26th

Real Estate Transfers
Tamalpais Land & Water Co. to WILLIAM TERRY
Lot 85, portion of lot D, Sausalito Rancho - $450

MARY L. SHUCK to FLORENCE SYLVA
Lot 5, block 129, Sausalito Land & Ferry Co. - $10

Additional Local

Dr. HENRY L. WAGNER, a physician of San Francisco, is said to be going to London about the middle of July, partly for the purpose of performing an operation on the throat of HENRY IRVING, whom he attended in the United States. The trip will also be the physician's honeymoon, it is reported, on his marriage to Mrs. MARION WISE, daughter of the late HALL McALLISTER.

Letter List

AUCALBITER, A.	GILBERT, CLIFFORD A.
ANDERSON, W.W.	GOSS, Miss MARY
BIRD, MABEL	JOHNSON, EMMA B.
BEGGS, F.	KYSER, Miss L.D.
BEALE, L.L.	LAFTRONN, ANNA
BROWN, Mrs. W.W.	LUNDQUIST, WILLIAM
BENZEN, L.P.	MADDEN, JAMES
BROWN, FLORA	MELVILLE, Mrs. G.A.
BRIGGS, A.	MINAND, F.
BEEDLE, W.H.	MARINI, V.A.
CALLOPY, Mr.	MACKLE, JAMES B.
CHAPMAN, HARVEY W.	MALE, L.
CROCKETT, HENRY	MAHONEY, MICHAEL
CLARKE, Mrs. EDWARD G.	VON RETZER, CARL
DAVIS, G.W.	STOWELL, E.H.
DAVIS, W.	SARRY, Mrs. M.E.
EASTING, J.M.	LEWIS, M.
EUSTACE, D.F.	VIGREANIE, Miss C.
FOLEY, RICHARD	VERRUDER, Mrs. R.
FULTON, Mrs. J.	WILSON, A.C.
GALLAGHER, HARRY	RICHARD, Mrs. F.E.

Died
VAN ARSDALE – In San Francisco, June 15, 1894, at her late residence, 2233 Washington Street, NELLIE VAN ARSDALE, beloved wife of W.W. VAN ARSDALE, a native of Tomales, aged 35 years, 5 months, and 10 days.

McKENNAN – In San Francisco, June 11, 1894, FREDERICK BUTLER McKENNAN, son of the late HUGH McKENNAN and Mrs. B.G. MORSE of Bolinas, aged 23 years, 2 months, and 22 days.

Marin County Tocsin
Saturday, June 23, 1894

Summons
> WALTER WALSH vs. J.D. LAWTON
> Judgment for $138.28
> J.D. LAWTON must appear within 5 days and pay fine
> Filed February 13, 1893
>
> E. GARDNER, Justice of Peace

Local News
Mrs. SHOBERG has sold the Cosmopolitan Hotel to San Francisco parties.

Mrs. BRADLEY of Tiburon, is suffering from a complicated case of measles that threatens the gravest results.

We are glad to announce that Mrs. ANTONE GUGLIELMINA has been able to return to her home at Tocoloma, restored to perfect health and also with a bouncing boy. Dr. WICKMAN was hastily summoned a short time ago to render services to her at Tocoloma, when he found it imperative to have her removed to St. Mary's Hospital with all due haste, in order that her life and that of another might be spared. Next afternoon she willingly submitted to have the rare operation known as caesarian section performed upon her, which was done by Dr. WALTER THORNE, assisted by Dr. W.F. McNUTT, Dr. WILLIAM WATT KERR, and Dr. W.J. WICKMAN. The operation was successfully performed. The patient was snatched from the grave, and her courage and her motherly instincts were rewarded in the happy possession of a fine boy.

Fatal Accident
ALPHONSE BRESSON, a young man about 19 years, whose father keeps a public house at Fairfax Station, was thrown from the cars last Thursday near Callott's brickyard and was instantly killed. Exactly how the fatal accident occurred is not known, but it is almost certain that he was hurled from the rear platform of the train by one of those sudden lurches due to taking sharp curves at a high rate of speed, with which those who travel on the line are so familiar on passing Callot's. The body of the young man was not discovered immediately. When found, life was extinct and an autopsy showed that death must have resulted instantly. The skull was fractured near the base of the brain, and it seemed probable that the neck was broken also. An inquest was held on the unfortunate young man, and a verdict of death from accidental causes was rendered.

Marin Journal
Thursday, June 28, 1894

Local Intelligence
CHARLES ALMY, for whose safety much anxiety has been felt, has been heard from. He had arrived at Hakodadi all safe, and the "Rattler" had made a winning catch.

Superior Court
> Belvedere Land Co. etal vs. CHARLES PAFF
> Judgment for plaintiff
>
> F.A. SILVEIRA vs. M. DeM. SILVA
> Order of submission set aside, case placed on July calendar
>
> W.F. GOAD, executor etal vs. S.T. TAYLOR etal
> Demurrer overruled, 12 days to answer
>
> A GIACOMINI vs. his Creditors
> Account approved and distribution of money ordered

Fireman's Fund Ins. Co. vs. H.J. INK, administrator etal
Dismissed as to fictitious defendants
Foreclosure in favor of plaintiff for $27,030

Died
BRESSON – In San Rafael, by accident, June 23, 1894, ALPHONSE BRESSON, a native of Fairfax, in this township, aged 18 years and 17 days.

Born
CARRIGAN – In San Francisco, June 23, 1894, to the wife of LOUIS R. CARRIGAN, a son.

LAVIOSA – In San Rafael, June 24, 1894, to the wife of LOUIS LAVIOSA, a daughter.

Real Estate Transfers
    HENRY KNITTEL to P.H. PETERSEN
    Lot on Bayview Street, San Rafael - $10

    ISAAC JESSUP to FREDERICK H. DEAKIN
    Lot in Jessup tract, San Rafael - $10
    Triangular lot on Fourth Street and the railroad, San Rafael - $200

    FRANK HEALY, late sheriff, to THOMAS M. QUACKENBUSH
    3.172 acres in Jessup tract, deed to correct previous deed

Marin County Tocsin
Saturday, June 30, 1894

Local News
JAMES WATSON has sold his interest in the Bellevue, and will open a restaurant and bar in the Sale building, San Rafael.

P.D. CONNOLLY has purchased the interest of his brother, M. CONNOLLY, in the sample rooms in Tunstead's building.

R. MAGNES bought the old building formerly occupied by Mr. PETER's tailoring establishment and has moved it on his lot on Fourth Street near Cijos Street.

The Sausalito News Sold
The Sausalito News has been sold to Messrs. J.H. PRYOR and F.W. PARSON, who will take possession of the property today.

Real Estate Transfers
    G.T. PAGE etal to G.A. HUNNEWELL
    Lot 2, block 47, San Rafael - $10

    JOHN THOMAS and wife to WILLIAM SUTHERLAND
    Lot 14, block 14, South Sausalito - $10

    Sausalito Bay Land Co. to WILLIAM SUTHERLAND
    Lot 14, block 14, South Sausalito - $5

    J.W. MACKAY and J.L. FLOOD to JOELLA G. CORNWELL
    Lots 3, 4, & 5, block 5, Lomita tract

    HENRY B. WOOD to J.F. GARVEY
    Lots 16, 17, & 23, Novato - $10

    Tamalpais Land & Water Co. to OSCAR H. SCHNEIDER
    Sub 2, lot 285, Mill Valley - $1000

Board of Education
Teacher's certificates were granted this week:
- Grammar Grade on State Normal School Diplomas
    - MAY WAMBOLD, ROSE L. ROBERTSON, RICHARD I. WALSH, BERTHA HALL
- Grammar Grade on Certificate from city and county of San Francisco
    - Miss MAGGIE CURRAN
- Grammar Grade on examination
    - E.C. HOUSTON
- Primary Grade
    - LOUISE A. KOCH, Mrs. A.H. SMITH, Mrs. E.C. HOUSTON, Miss ANNA GERICKE
- Certificates renewed
    - Miss KATE A. CHANDLER, Miss NELLIE KIRK, Miss CARRIE COLLINS, Miss KEATING, Miss MARGARET SMYTHE, Mrs. J.S. MARTINELLI

Marin Journal
Thursday, July 5, 1894

Marin Lodge I.O.O.F. will install new officers next Monday evening. They are:
- P.H. RASMUSSEN – N.G.
- CHARLES JENSEN – V.G.
- ALBERT BOYEN – P.G.
- ROBERT SCOTT – Secretary
- D. SUTHERLAND – Treasurer
- Minor officers – D. MARTENS, H. PETERSEN, P. BRUNN, P.M. JORGENSEN, NEIL CHRISTOPHERSON, JESSE GRAY and L. EMERSON
- Trustees – J. PETERSEN, E.C. LUND, A.C. McALLISTER

Local Intelligence
Rev. J.S. FISHER returned last week from Los Angeles, where he was called by the illness of his son.

FRANK I. KINGWELL and FRED F. RUNYON are making a bright little paper of the Record in Mill Valley.

WILLIAM J. BOYD and M. MULHERN returned last week from Santa Cruz, where they had been in attendance to the grand lodge of the U.A.O.D. as delegates from San Rafael. They report an enthusiastic meeting on this flourishing order. J. BUTHMAN was also a delegate.

The following officers have been elected by the local parlor of Native Sons:
- C.H. BENSON – President
- THOMAS BOYD – 1st vice president
- W.J. BOYD – 2nd vice president
- B.L. DAVIS – 3rd vice president
- F.M. ANGELLOTTI – treasurer
- GEORGE B. KEEN Jr. – financial secretary
- W.F. MAGEE – recorder
- ROY B. SHAVER – marshall
- E.B. MARTINELLI – historian
- A.E. SCOTT, GEORGE F. RODDEN, LOUIS A. HUGHES – trustees

J.E. PELLOW of Sierra City, representing a fraternal insurance association, was here Friday and Saturday of last week.

R. KINSELLA and THOMAS BOYD were delegates to the Y.M.I. in session in San Francisco last week.

Court Estrella, No. 7906, A.O.F. elected new officers last Thursday as follows:
- R. SCOTT – chief ranger
- P. FORTIN – sub chief ranger
- A HINIKER – financial secretary
- J. WEST – recording secretary
- E. EDEN – treasurer
- J.J. LAKIN – junior woodward
- J.P. LACERDA – senior woodward

        F. SYLVA – junior beadle
        W.H. DOWNING – senior beadle
        Dr. WICKMAN – physician

Superior Court
        PETER N. BERKHART vs. MARY CULLEN etal
        Judgment for plaintiff in sum of $103.10

        Oakland Iron Works vs. A.R. TUCKEY
        Judgment for plaintiff in sum of $82.65 and costs

        J. VIALE vs. J.B. MAHAR
        Judgment for plaintiff

        Estate of F.B. McKENNAN, deceased
        Letters ordered issued to B.G. MORSE – bond $300

        Estate of B.F. SWISHER, deceased
        Over one month

Died
KUSCHE – In Ross Valley, July 1, 1894, EARNEST KUSCHE, son of AUGUST KUSCHE and wife.

REDMOND – At the Poor Farm, Marin County, July 2, 1894, TIMOTHY REDMOND, aged 55.

HELLINGS – In Mill Valley, June 30, 1894, DESAREE HELLINGS, aged 14.

Marin County Tocsin
Saturday, July 7, 1894

    Sheriff's Sale
        Fireman's Fund Ins. Co. vs. HARRIET JANE INK, admr. Estate of T.H. INK, dec.
        HARRIET JANE INK, VICTRIX BERRI, E. BERRI, RICHARD ROE, JOHN DOE
        Foreclosure
        Property in Rancho Soulajule – 2434 acres

Local News
GEORGE GREEN, a sailor, fell from the rigging of the British Ship Rohane last Monday and was drowned. The body was not recovered.

GREGORY HARTE, a prominent businessman and former resident of San Rafael, was in town this week after an absence of 8 years in the East.

Dr. WAGNER, the eminent specialist, and Mrs. MARION WISE were quietly married last Thursday. They will start for a trip to Europe as soon as the strike permits.

Real Estate Transfers
        ELLEN M. TEN BROECK and A.H. TEN BROECK to PHINEAS F. FERGUSON
        Lot 6, block 14, Mill Valley - $10

        Sausalito Bay Land Co. to WILLIAM N. KETCHUM
        Lot 14, block 8 and westerly ½ of alley E of said lot, now legally closed - $10

Marin Journal
Thursday, July 12, 1894

    Mr. CARPENTER, who has been managing Wells Fargo & Co.'s office here in San Rafael, has been detailed for work at another part of the system. Mr. MILLER, who has been in the company's employ near Santa Rosa, will take charge of the San Rafael office.

Abandoned Children

The following Orphans and Abandoned children have been received in St. Vincent's Asylum since April 1, 1894:

Orphans Name	Age Years	Months
SETTARO, FERNANDO	9	8
GOUDY, WILLIAM	13	
CULVER, CHARLES	9	
ALCARAZI, JOE	10	3
ALCARAZI, DANIEL	7	9
KOUSE, WILLIAM	11	
RAAB, CHARLES	11	
SHEA, JOHN	-	
REILLY, WILLIAM	10	3
CUNNINGHAM, ALOYSIUS	10	9
GILL, EUGENE	9	8
GILL, WALTER	13	
RHODES, JESSIE	8	
CONNOLLY, JAMES	11	5
STROBEL, JAMES	10	4
CRUZ, ALFRED	12	
BRADY, PETER	8	3
PEPE, JOSEPH	8	
HURDLE, EDDIE	9	
CROWLEY, JOHN	13	5
CROWLEY, WILLIAM	13	5
HARRIS, JOHN	13	
NEWBERRY, WILLIAM	8	
RYAN, CHARLES	8	
CARROLL, HENRY	9	
BUELNA, OCTAVIA	12	
McKINNEY, WILLIAM	10	9
COLLINS, JOHN	12	5
WEINER, AXEL	8	1
CONNELLY, JAMES	12	4
O'KEEFE, ROBERT	12	1
MARTINEZ, JOSE	7	
CULLIE, WILLIAM	12	7
CAHILL, JAMES	13	
PANCHARD, RALPH	11	
OLIVIA, ATTILO	10	9
RIDGE, THOMAS	13	
SHEA, FRANCIS	10	7
NORTON, JOHN	8	6
ROKIE, ATTILO	7	
ESTELITA, MICHAEL	11	10
HOFFEY, JAMES	10	4
ROACH, DAVID	11	6
Abandoned Children		
FLEISHER, OSCAR	9	8
FLEISHER, HERMAN	10	11
TETCOVITCH, BLAS	10	

Notice to Creditors
    Estate of ARTHUR C. BRIGGS, deceased
    E.B. MARTINELLI, attorney for admx.
    Filed July 6, 1894
                      CASSIE BRIGGS, Admx.

Mr. G.E. HINIKER of Hickman, Stanislaus County, brother of A. and J. HINIKER of this place, registered at the Central Saturday, remaining until Tuesday.

Notice to Creditors
> Estate of FREDERICK BUTLER McKENNAN, deceased
> E.B. MARTINELLI, attorney for admr.
> Filed July 6, 1894
>
> BENJAMIN G. MORSE, Admr.

Notice to Creditors
> Estate of GEORGE GUNN, deceased
> HEPBURN WILKINS, attorney for admx.
> Filed June 27, 1894
>
> FRANCES E. BUNN, Admx.

Local Intelligence

GEORGE D. SHEARER has been appointed Deputy United States Marshall for this district.

Mr. JOHN ROBERTSON is still critically ill. He has had surgical operations on his foot and leg, which has somewhat relieved him, but his life hangs in the balance.

Golden Star Rebekah Lodge, I.O.O.F., will install new officers at their next regular meeting, July 19, as follows:
> Miss SOPHIA SHOBERG – noble grand
> Mrs. E.C. LUND – vice grand
> Mrs. P. BRUNN – secretary
> Mrs. VRANG – treasurer

Death of WALTER WALSH

WALTER WALSH, of the prominent hardware house of Scott & Co., passed away about 6 p.m. Tuesday. His death was not unexpected, for he had suffered long, though with great fortitude, from Bright's disease. His disposition was very genial, and his vivacity and high spirits never forsook him. He was an exempt and active member of the Fire Department, a member of the Labor Union, and of San Rafael Lodge, No. 24, A.O.U.W. The hall of the Fireman is draped in mourning to his memory. The funeral will take place from the residence on D Street, at 9:30 a.m. today, and from the Catholic Church at 10 o'clock, and will be attended by the three societies named.

Coroner EDEN last Thursday brought to San Rafael the body of JOHN F. GRANT, drowned on the 4th at Belvedere. Deceased was tipped over in a boat in company with his son-in-law, JOHN DUNCAN. The latter swam ashore, but GRANT went down, and perished before help could reach him. The body was recovered by dragging. The inquest developed these facts, and the body was taken to the city for burial.

The body of a man was found on Thursday in the water at Lime Point, and brought here by Coroner EDEN. The body was kept preserved with fluid until Saturday, when it was identified by Mrs. REED, sister of the deceased, as JOHN TUHER of San Francisco, a carriage painter. He was drowned on the night of the 4th, but the circumstances of his death beyond this is unknown. The remains were taken to San Francisco.

A sailor on an English ship off Sausalito was drowned last Tuesday. He was scraping the ship's side from a staging when he fell into the water and sank before a boat could reach him. His BODY has not been found.

Mr. GEORGE POND, a former resident of San Rafael, has been appointed manager for the Mutual Life Insurance Co. of New York for the territory within the boundaries of Washington and Oregon.

The presentation of the watch to RICHARD McGREAVY, by the Sausalito News, was announced to take place last evening at the El Monte Hotel. The prize, a gold watch, to the man who received the greatest number of votes as the most popular man in Marin County, was won by Mr. McGREAVY.

Real Estate Transfers
> J.W. MACKAY etal to HELENE R. DALY
> 17.394 acres on Sims Street and San Quentin County Road, San Rafael - $10
>
> H. HARRISON, sheriff, to FRANK E. HILLS
> Tract in Sausalito - $3,774.46

W.O. BROWN to CHARLES GRASS
Lots 1 to 10, Kain's addition to San Rafael

H.W. KAUFMAN to PARKER MERRILL
Portion of lot D, Richardson Rancho - $625

Born
CRON – in San Rafael, July 11, 1894, to the wife of CHARLES L. CRON, a son.

Died
WALSH – In San Rafael, Julu 10, 1894, WALTER A. WALSH, husband of MARY A. WALSH, and brother of ARTHUR and CARRIE SCOTT, aged 37 years. Funeral on Thursday from the residence, Third and D Streets, services at Catholic Church at 10 a.m.

Superior Court
Estate of P.H. WEBER, deceased
Continued for one week

Estate of PIETRO ROSSINI, deceased
Final account settled and estate distributed

Estate of LIBBIE CRITTENDEN, deceased
Estate distributed

Estate of ALLEN LEE, deceased
Will admitted to probate, letters issued to Mrs. S.A. LEE

J. DeWITT ALLEN vs. H.M. ANTHONY etal
Submitted and taken under advisement

F.C. DeLONG vs. HENRY PIERCE
Defendant's motion for change of venue argued and submitted

DUTRA vs. DUTRA
Order to show cause dismissed

ELISHA DuBOIS vs. ELIZA DuBOIS
Demurrer sustained, 10 days to answer

E.W. VAN SLYKE vs. GRATTAN PERRY & D.F. NYE
Tried, 5 days allowed NYE to file points and authorities

Marin County Tocsin
Saturday, July 14, 1894

Born
BOLAND – In San Rafael, July 12, 1894, to the wife of THOMAS BOLAND, a son.

Local News
A.B. MURRAY, the popular conductor of the North Pacific Coast Railroad Co., has retired after years of service. The gentleman is a mechanical genius, and having patented a number of promising inventions, has determined to devote his entire time to introducing them.

W.R. MELVILLE, of Mill Valley, clerk of the Bank of California, has disappeared mysteriously. When last heard of he left Sausalito in a skiff, which has since been found in a shattered condition on the Belvedere shore. This would indicate to most minds that the missing man was drowned, but his friends seem to have their own reasons for believing that he is well. His accounts with the bank are said to be perfectly alright.

A mechanic by the name of O'HARA, a resident of San Francisco, fell from the roof of a house at Mill Valley on which he was at work on Wednesday last, and received injuries from which he soon died. Coroner EDEN held an inquest which determined that the casualty was purely accidental.

Real Estate Transfers

    T.B. VALENTINE to S.F. & N.P.R.R Co.
    Right of way over land in Sausalito township - $10

    Sausalito Land & Ferry Co. to J.A. & W.H. HANNON
    Lot 3, block 27, New Sausalito - $1000

    J.A. & W.H. HANNON to CATHERINE HANNON
    Lot 3, block 27, New Sausalito – love and affection

    H.W.E. KAUFMAN and wife to AARON ROBINSON
    Lot 7, block 1, Mill Valley - $625

    AARON ROBINSON to PARKER MORRILL
    Lot 7, block 1, Mill Valley - $625

    R.McF. DOBLE and wife to ANNIE W. LUNDSTROM
    Lot 7, block A, San Anselmo Valley - $750

Marin Journal
Thursday, July 19, 1894

School Notes
Miss CARRIE L. FIEDLER has resigned position of first assistant of the Richardson district (Sausalito) schools. She is taking a course in the State University. Her successor will be Miss FLORENCE C. GALLOWAY, who has been teaching the Nicasio School. Mr. E.C. HOUSTON succeeds J.A. NOWELL as principal of the Tomales School. The late principal thinks of returning to Stanford University. Garcia district (Olema) reopened last Monday, Miss L.C. McALLEP continuing in charge. Miss NELLIE R. GALLAGHER will teach the Nicasio School.

Local Intelligence
Mr. FRED MILLER, Wells Fargo agent, and wife are residing at the Cypress Villa.

Mrs. FRED MILLER, wife of Wells Fargo agent, is a crack shot with the rifle. At a shooting tournament held at the Cypress Villa recently, in which 12 people participated, Mrs. MILLER carried off the honors of the day, and beat the second best by five points.

Rev. J.S. FISHER is improving slowly from his paralytic shock, and his friends hope to see him about soon.

J.S. WHITNEY, who fractured his cheekbone on the evening of July 4th by falling from a hammock, has about recovered.

Mr. JOHN TACKNEY of Sacramento came down last Saturday by boat, and is visiting his brother, M. TACKNEY, of the Central Hotel.

W.W. PERCIVAL of Healdsburg has taken a position in the Wells Fargo office here. Mr. PERCIVAL recently graduated from a Santa Rosa College, and was the winner of a gold medal in the oratorical contest at the commencement exercises.

Mr. D.O. KELLOGG, who is an extremely heavy man, at Bolinas last Saturday, broke through the wharf and snapped the big bone in his leg. He took a carriage and returned home, where Dr. WICKMAN attended him, and he is doing well.

Prof. J.L. WILLIAMS, who was awarded the medal for the best decorative penmanship at the Midwinter Fair, is registered at the Central Hotel.

Board of Supervisors
FELICIANA DARCE was allowed $10 a month from the hospital fund.

JAMES WATSON was granted a permit for a liquor license.

Superior Court
    J. DE WITT ALLEN vs. H.M. ANTHONY etal
    Demurrer of HENRY PIERCE to be submitted on briefs

    Estate of J.M. MASEAS, deceased
    Sale of vessel confirmed

    FRANK C. DeLONG vs. HENRY PIERCE
    Change of venue granted

    Estate of JOHN SCHIPPERS, deceased
    Decree of final discharge

Letter List

CUPID, SAMUEL	HOLM, CHARLES
EARL, WILLIAM E.	HOWARD, Mrs. CARRIE
GOSS, MARY	HENDLEY, C.
GOMEZ, ANTONE	HASS, CHARLEY
HINES, Miss MARY	HATTROUN, Miss
HAYDEN, Mrs. M.	HELM, WILHELM
HOSKINS, OTTO	JOHNSON, MARTIN
HOOPER, J.G.	JOHANSSOM, Madame
HAAS, EMMA	LIMBERG, J.
HAMMEL, PETER P.	MORGAN, Mr.
HAGEISBEEN, LEONARD	MYERS, CHARLES W.
HASBRAM, K.J.	OSMENT, Miss DELIA
HAMERSCHLAGER, J.B.	STEFFINS, Mrs.
HUMBOLDT, W.B.	STEFFINS, Capt.
HAYDEN, Mrs.	SEIBEL, Mrs.
HAMILTON, G.E.	STOCKMEYER, Mrs. D.
HEARST, MARY	SULLIVAN, Mrs. J.
HAYES, J.	STEFERT, LOUISE
HAYDEN, Justice	

Superior Court
    Estate of OWEN MORTON, deceased
    Decree of legal notice to Creditors entered

    Estate of P.H. WEBER, deceased
    Matter continued one week

    Estate of C.B. RAULINO, dec. vs. MANUEL ROGERS etal
    Judgment for plaintiff for $2,415.48

    Estate of ISIDOR DAUS, deceased
    Account for special administrator settled
    Personal property set apart to administratrix

    Estate of P.H. WEBER, deceased
    Matter continued one week

    Estate of F. FIEDLER, deceased
    Final account settled and estate distributed

    Estate of BELLA F. SWISHER, deceased
    Decree of legal notice to Creditors entered
    Real estate in Sausalito ordered sold

    CHARLES FORBES etal vs. M. ZELLERBACH
    Judgment for plaintiff

MELOCENE W. EICKHOFF vs. MAGDALENA EICKHOFF
Judgment for defendant with costs

Marin Journal
Thursday, July 26, 1894

Letter List

ARBINI, DOMENICO	FOX, BERN E.
ALLEN, H.P.	FELT, Miss CORNELIA
ALLEN, Mrs. E.M.	GOUZENNE, J.
ALBINI, GUISEPPI	GUMPEL, MICHAEL
ALDERMAN, OSCAR	GUINTRAND, JEAN B.
BROOKS, Capt. JAMES	GIRVIN, Mrs. R.
BRUNNER, R.	GREEN, CHARLES
BATES, HARRY S.	GRAVES, Mrs. EMMA C.
BOETZEAR, C.	HEARN, A.
BOWEN, MICHAEL	HASTINGS, Mrs. ROBERT P.
BARKER, Miss R.	HAHN, Mrs. F.J.
BUSTUDE, Miss	HAYDEN, Mrs.
BORBECK, E.	HENDLEY, CHARLES B.
BECCIO, A.	JENNINGS, C.B.
BULIN, Miss SAL	JOHNSON, E.
COARCH, JOHN	KRAMER, Miss S.
CONNELL, R.R.	LEWIS, Mrs. G.H.
CANNON, Miss MAMIE	LEARY, WILLIAM
CLARK, Mrs. B.	LARSEN, A.
CAPLAIN, Miss HANNAH	MILLER, Miss ANNIE
CLOSE, Mrs. B.	MASON, S.
CLARK, Miss HELENA	MORSE, W.H.
CONTEHUEN, Miss MARIE	MASTINGS, Madame R.
CANTELEN, Miss MARIE	MURPHY, Mrs. JOHN W.
CONLEY, Miss ADA	MASUDA, Mr.
DICKSON, Miss MARIAH H.	NAPPENBACK, HENRY
DOW, GEORGE A.	SCHMIDT, Mrs. R.
DELLAVEN, JOSIE D.	STEWART, H.M.
DANVERKOSEN, R.	THATCHER, Mrs. E.S.
EMERY, Miss CORDELLA	WARREN, Miss RITA
WILSON, J.N.	WILSON, J.H.

Born
GULDAGER – In San Rafael, July 25, to the wife of GEORGE GULDAGER, a daughter.

Married
DE FIENNES-BISHOPP – In Sacramento, July 23, 1894, RUDOLPH H. DE FIENNES of San Rafael and Miss LILLIAN BISHOPP of Sacramento.

Local Intelligence
Mr. KUTTNER, an old time San Francisco tobacco merchant, is making San Rafael his home. Mr. KUTTNER has heart trouble and was advised to try our mild climate. He is much improved, and has concluded to reside here permanently.

Mrs. SHUTE of the Mt. Tamalpais Military Academy teachers' corps has left us to take the vice principalship of the Hayward High School, of which Prof. GAMBLE is principal. Mrs. SHUTE is an accomplished, agreeable and successful teacher, and her loss will be felt in our academy.

Marin County Tocsin
Saturday, July 28, 1894

Local News
A.J. BARCLAY is about to open a civil engineering and surveying office in San Rafael.

The Will of SOPHIA ZELLAR, who died in San Rafael a little over a year ago, is about to be contested in the Superior Court of San Francisco.

Dissolution of Co-Partnership
    Poultry business in Bolinas
    G.B. PEPPER retiring
    Filed July 25, 1894
                                G.B. PEPPER
                                W.R. PEPPER

The many San Rafael friends of Miss MARGUERITE WALLACE were shocked to learn of her sudden and untimely death which occurred in San Francisco day before yesterday. Deceased was the daughter of Judge W.T. WALLACE and sister of Mrs. J.M. DONAHUE, at whose house in San Rafael she was a frequent visitor. Miss WALLACE was a beautiful and accomplished woman who excited admiration everywhere, and the end of her young life seems like one of the things that should not be.

Superior Court
    Estate of OWEN MORTON, deceased
    Decree of legal notice to Creditors entered

    Estate of P.H. WEBER, deceased
    Matter continued one week

    Estate of C.B. RAULINO, dec. vs. MANUEL ROGERS etal
    Judgment for plaintiff for $2,415.48

    Estate of ISIDOR DAUS, deceased
    Account for special administrator settled
    Personal property set apart to administratrix

    Estate of P.H. WEBER, deceased
    Matter continued one week

    Estate of F. FIEDLER, deceased
    Final account settled and estate distributed

    Estate of BELLA F. SWISHER, deceased
    Decree of legal notice to Creditors entered
    Real estate in Sausalito ordered sold

    CHARLES FORBES etal vs. M. ZELLERBACH
    Judgment for plaintiff

    MELOCENE W. EICKHOFF vs. MAGDALENA EICKHOFF
    Judgment for defendant with costs

    County of Marin vs. H. BLUMENTHAL etal
    Continued by consent

    People vs. THOMAS RILEY
    Information for burglary filed

    FRANK PERARA vs. his Creditors
    Insolvent discharged

    WILLIAM R. HEARST vs. JOHN DOE BROOKS etal
    Demurrer overruled, 3 days to answer

Real Estate Transfers
    Home & Farm Co. to GEORGE PENMAN
    Lots 11, 12, 13, 14, 15, Garden Place tract, Novato - $10

J.O.B. SHORT and wife to FRANK ENCH
Tract in Short's addition, adjoining San Rafael Brewery property - $10

J.H. HUNTER to CHRISTINA E. HUNTER
Lot on D Street near Third Street, San Rafael – love and affection

DONALD E. CHICK to JAMES TUNSTEAD
Lot 5, block 3, Sunnyside - $10

Marin Journal
Thursday, August 2, 1894

Born
POMEROY – In San Rafael, July 21, 1894, to the wife of C.P. POMEROY, a daughter.

Died
STEVENSON – In Wrights, CA, July 27, 1894, JANE HAIGHT STEVENSON, beloved wife of C.C. STEVENSON Jr., aged 33 years, 3 months, and 22 days.

Letter List

AZAVEDO, JOAS	MAXWELL, HARRY
ANDERSON, W.W.	MORRIS, ANNA
ABEL, FRED	MILLER, Mrs. E.M.
AHERN, JAMES B.	MULLER, Mrs. HENRY
BRIMS, Miss ALMA	McGEARY, JOHN
BUTTERWORTH, Mrs. EMMA	McCAFFERY, BURT
BARRETS, ROBERT	McCOY, Dr. J.C.
OSTAERA, TONEY	McREA, J.G.
DAVIS, JOHN	O'NEIL, LENA
DOWNEY, JAMES	OSGOOD, JAMES
DOWDEN, JOHN	O'BRIEN, Mrs.
DAVIS, Mrs. ANDREW M.	OLSON, CHARLES
DAVIS, Mrs. W.W.	POWERS, W.
EARL, W.E.	REGAN, J.C.
EMHOFF, NIC	REED, J.
FERDINAND, H. CARMATI	RYAN, M.J.
GRETCHEN, Miss	POWELL, Mrs. R.C.
GREGORY, ELISE	SCHLOSSER, Mr.
HOLITE, ANTONIO	SMITH, MAY
LYONS, Mrs.	SMITH, J.G.
LASSEN, JOHN	SEARS, BEN
LACY, Miss N.	SAUDMAN, KATE
MURPHY, Mrs. CARRIE	SAUDMAN, JENNIE
MATHESON, A.E.	SHERWOOD, H.M.
MORRIS, ROLAND S.	LIVER, OTTO
MURPHY, Miss	TERRY, Mrs. M.

Foreign

MORININI, JOE   PIE, PIGOZZI

Superior Court
People vs. JESUS NAVARRO
Mayhem, arraignment set for Monday, August 6th

Estate of M.L. VELASCO, deceased
Executors discharged

Estate of P.H. WEBER, deceased
Continued one week

Estate of JOHN GRIFFIN, deceased
Continued one week

Estate of B. GALLAGHER, deceased
Order for sale of personal property

Estate of CHARLES BROSIN, deceased
Sale of real estate confirmed

Estate of B.L. PACHECO, deceased
Decree of final discharge of executors entered

E. SCHWIESAU vs. WILLIAM CAESAR
Demurrer argued and submitted, under advisement

J. DeWITT ALLEN vs. H.M. ANTHONY
Demurrer overruled, 10 days to answer

Estate of FREDERICK KRUSE, deceased
Account of assignee settled

Local Intelligence
Coroner EDEN was summoned yesterday by telephone from Sausalito to come for a BODY found in the water at Gravel Beach, and he had not yet returned when this paper went to press.

Mrs. C.C. STEVENSON Jr. went to the Santa Cruz mountains last week, hoping to find relief in the change of air, but her vitality was exhausted, and Friday night, in the arms of her husband, she fell asleep to wake no more. The steady advance of a pulmonary complaint had prepared her husband and friends for the worst, but it is not true. Affection cannot be reconciled by death. Death may be expected, but the shock of his awful presence is not lessened. The family left are a husband and two young children, to whom the loss is measureless, and in the East, the parents and brothers and sisters of the deceased. Mrs. STEVENSON also filled a large place in the social and philanthropic activities of our city, and a wide circle of friends are bereaved, whose tender sympathies go out to the stricken family. The remains were brought home, and the funeral took place Monday afternoon, Rev. Dr. NOBLE and Mr. CROSBY officiating.

Real Estate Transfers
    HENRY HARRISON, sheriff, to A.C. HAWKINS
    Lot on Hayes Street, near Latham, San Rafael - $491.27

    Sausalito Bay Land Co. to MANUEL FERNANDEZ
    Lots 11 & 12, block 15, South Sausalito - $10

    WILLIAM McALESTER to Marin County
    Right of way for road - $588

    FRITZ SCHUEMANN to Marin County
    Right of way for road - $5

    TELFER CHRISTOPHER to AUGUST MAYER
    Lot on H Street, near Forbes Avenue, San Rafael - $10

    CHARLES MARTIN to JEREMIAH RESPINI
    585.97 acres in Bojourquez Rancho - $100

    JEREMIAH RESPINI to CHARLES MARTIN
    585.97 acres in Bojourquez Rancho
    Deed of partition

    G. MORETTI to JEREMIAH RESPINI
    Undivided half of 134.40 acres in Rancho Tomales
    And 237.80 acres, part of Rancho Balsa de Tomales
    No consideration mentioned

J. HALEY by Sheriff HARRISON to GEORGE L. RICHARDSON
Tract of tidelands in San Rafael - $19.71

JOSEPHINE BLOOM to ULYSSES BLOOM
1/6 interest, 700 acres in Bloom Rancho, Chileno Valley - $1000

Fatal Accident
ANGUS BATHURST met death on the rail at Tomales Monday last. He was conductor of a freight train on the N.P.C. Railway, and as he was slowly moving his train at the station, his foot slipped, he fell upon the rail, and the wheel caught him, crushing his side. His ribs were broken, his head severely injured, and has had internal injuries. The poor man lived in great suffering three hours and a half. Mr. BATHURST had been 13 years on the road, and for 9 years, has had the same run. He leaves a wife and two children at Tomales. He said the accident was carelessness on his own part, and no one else is to blame, and at his own request no inquest was held. His body was taken to Oakland for burial. Deceased was a Canadian, 41 years of age.

St. Vincent's
Rev. Father CROWLEY will retire from the management of St. Vincent's Orphan Asylum for boys. The change will take place about the middle of this month when the Christian Brotherhood will assume charge. Father CROWLEY will return to the superintendence of the Youths Directory in San Francisco which he left to come here.

Marin County Tocsin
Saturday, August 4, 1894

Notice to Creditors
Matter of ANGELO GIACOMINI, insolvent debtor
Court date September 3, 1894
Filed August 3, 1894
THOMAS S. BONNEAU, Clerk

Real Estate Transfers
JAMES ARCHIBALD etal to CHARLES MARTIN
238 acres, part of Rancho Balsa de Tomales - $100

Home & Farm Co. to GEORGE KNOX
27 acres, part of lots 6 & 7, division C, Novato - $10

ERNESTINE KRELING to F.W. KRELING
Undivided ½ of villa lot 12, Coleman's addition, Petaluma Avenue tract

Home & Farm Co. to F.T. NASON and wife
26.24 acres, part of lot 23, division C, Novato

Home & Farm Co. to F.J. COPE and wife
24.01 acres, division C, Novato - $10

C.I. JACOBS, by Sheriff, to O.C. HAWKINS
Lot on Hayes Street, San Rafael - $101.27

JAMES TUNSTEAD to Ross Improvement Co. (a corporation)
28.446 acres, San Anselmo Valley - $10

L.C. MINTIE to A.E. MINTIE
Lot 17, Edwards Harrison tract, Sausalito - $10

Born
ROBERTS – In San Rafael, July 19, 1894, to the wife of J.P. ROBERTS, a daughter.

HYAMS – In San Rafael, August 1, 1894, to the wife of FRANK HYAMS, a son.

Marin Journal
Thursday, August 9, 1894

Died
HAACK – In San Rafael, August 5, 1894, HELENA HAACK, aged 68 years and 4 months.

Novato
Mrs. A. TIMONY, who has been under treatment for a time in St. Mary's Hospital, San Francisco, is at her home in Santa Margarita, and is improving in health. This will be good news to her many friends.

Mr. NEWCOMBER, for a long time one of the prominent teachers in Marin County, had been appointed principal of the public schools at San Fernando, CA. His regret at leaving his old stamping ground is moderated somewhat by the fact that his salary will be increased by 25% more than the wages here, which shows that he is appreciated in his new field of usefulness.

STEVE PINCHELLO, blacksmith at Novato, who was bitten by FOSTER's dog last week, is getting along finely. He is able to be about and will resume work in a few days. When PINCHELLO dismounted from his horse in front of FOSTER's residence, the dog sprang at him and bit him quite severely, lacerating both hands and legs. Mrs. FOSTER and daughter came quickly to his rescue and dragged the dog off. At FRANK FOSTER's direction, the blacksmith procured a gun from the house and killed the dog.

Local Intelligence
The son of WILLIAM BABCOCK, who was thrown from his horse on the 4th of July last, is in critical condition. Four physicians have been in attendance, and have removed a piece of bone from his forehead. He was getting along nicely until a few days ago. The doctors think he must have been kicked in the forehead by the horse after he fell.

Local Intelligence
J.J. PENNYPACKER, a veteran publisher, died in Oakland Tuesday, aged 80. He was one of the early day printers of Petaluma, eccentric, and outspoken, but a general favorite.

GEORGE ANDERSON has turned the tables on San Rafael as a sanitarium. He left us in poor health last year, took in the Fair and went to Iowa. He is now in Dubuque, in good health, the husband of MINNIE GRIFFIN, and in a good business.

Marin County Tocsin
Saturday, August 11, 1894

Real Estate Transfers
J.R. LITTLE etal to NELLIE BEDELL
Part of Cobb's 1 acre lot, Edwards Harrison tract, Sausalito - $5

H.J. & MARY J. DE FIENNES to CHARLES FISH
Lot on corner of Ross and Glen Streets, San Rafael - $10

J.O.B. SHORT and wife to W.A. MILLER
Lot on Reservoir Road, San Rafael - $10

W.A. MILLER to MARY J. DE FIENNES
Lot on Reservoir Road, San Rafael – 410

G.A. HUNNEWELL and wife to W.G. HUNNEWELL
North ½ of lot 25, Gordon's tract, San Rafael - $120

G.A. HUNNEWELL and wife to ADDIE C. HUNNEWELL
South ½ of lot 25, Gordon's tract, San Rafael - $10

Tamalpais Land & Ferry Co. to CHARLES A. WAINWRIGHT
Lot in Mill Valley, bounded by Ethel Avenue and Jones Street, Foot Alley - $800

Tamalpais Land & Water Co. to P.T. FERGUSON
Lots 10, 11, & 12, block 10, Mill Valley

W. DUTTON and wife to P. MULVANEY
Part of lot 2, block 15, Tomales - $10

Superior Court
People vs. JESUS NAVARRO
Writ of habeus corpus dismissed and prisoner remanded
Arraigned and plea of not guilty entered

Estate of FRED McNAMARA, deceased
Administrator discharged

T.B. VALENTINE vs. M.M. DEFFEBACH
Hearing set for Tuesday, September 4th

Estate of JACOB OBITZ, deceased
Legal notice to creditors given
Homestead ordered set apart to widow

Estate of JOHN GRIFFIN, deceased
Contest of final account of administratrix continued to August 30th

Estate of P.H. WEBER, deceased
Letters of administration ordered issued to DENNIS DONOHUE Jr.

ELISHA DuBOIS vs. ELIJAH DuBOIS
Demurrer overruled, 5 days to answer

ELLEN ESCALLE vs. North Pacific Coast Railroad Co.
Tried and taken under advisement by the Court

Local News
J.B. CAUZZA, the well known merchant, has been appointed Postmaster at Tomales.

THOMAS VAUGHN, who has been sojourning in Oregon for a couple of years, has returned to San Rafael.

The ANTON MORELLA, who was killed this week while deer hunting near the Sonoma line, was not a resident of San Rafael, as reported.

Marin Journal
Thursday, August 16, 1894

Local Intelligence
A 7 year old son of Marshall HEALY had his leg broken on the train Sunday. With other boys, he jumped on the cars at the junction, and was hanging over the platform playing his foot up and down, when he was caught in the cattle guard and hauled off.

The 12 year old son of Dr. GROVE sustained a broken wrist last Tuesday.

The engagement is announced of Miss ALICE DAVIS, daughter of J.B.F. DAVIS of Ross Valley, and FRANK RICHARDSON of Menton, formerly of San Francisco.

R.P. TROY reached home from Washington last Monday.

Mr. and Mrs. J.F. JORDAN accompanied their daughter PEARL JORDAN to Santa Rosa last Thursday. She is attending Miss CHASE's seminary at that place.

HARRY McFARLAND, an inmate of the St. Vincent Orphan Asylum, while playing last Thursday afternoon, fell from a bench and broke his arm at the elbow. The little fellow was brought to the office of Dr. WICKMAN, who attended him.

Mr. A. MARTINELLI, a merchant of Petaluma, was in town last Tuesday. He has bought the business formerly owned by JERRY ADAMS of Olema. Mr. MARTINELLI was at one time a resident of this County, and we are happy to welcome him home again.

JOSEPH LANINI, a rancher of Bolinas, while riding a spirited horse recently, was violently thrown against the horn of the saddle, sustaining internal injuries from which he died on last Tuesday. He leaves a widow and a child two months old.

Born
De ROSA – In San Geronimo, August 13, 1894, to the wife of ROQUE De ROSA, a son.

Married
KRENKEL-SPENCER – In San Rafael, August 13, 1894, by Rev. J.S. FISHER, GUSTAV W. KRENKEL and Miss CLARA A. SPENCER, both of Oakland

CARRINGTON-HILDRETH – In San Rafael, August 11, 1894, by Justice GARDNER, BARTINE HARRINGTON and Miss ALICE L. HILDRETH, both of Oakland.

N.S.G.W.
The officers of Tamalpais Parlor No. 64, were installed by District Deputy STEPHEN EDEN last Monday evening. They were:
- Past president – S. HERZOG
- President – C.H. BENSON
- 1st vice president – T.P. BOYD
- 2nd vice president – GEORGE H. DeVALIN
- 3rd vice president – B.L. DAVIS
- Marshall – R.F.B. SHAVER
- Financial Secretary – G.B KEANE
- Recording Secretary – W.F. MAGEE
- Trustees – A.E. SCOTT, G.F. RODDEN
- Inside sentinel – A.G. CHICK
- Outside sentinel – E.C. WINDER

Letter List

ADAMS, Mrs. E.E.	HERBERT, A.
BRIMS, ALMA	HAHN, F.F.
BROOKS, Capt. JAMES	JAMES, IDA
BRUMER, ROBERT	KELLY, M.
BECKHUSON, Miss M.	McNAMARA J.H.
DICKINSON, Miss M.	McDONALD, J.A.
ENGERMANN, Mrs. Capt.	NICHOLS, CHARLES C.
ELLIOTT, Mrs. THOMAS	OSTERMAN, Mrs. M.
FOOMBERG, Mrs. J.M.	PETERSEN, MATHILDA
GANNON, DENNIS	RICHARDSON, M.
GRIFFITH, Mrs. E.	SMITH, S.
GENSWINDT, Mrs. M.	SCHMIDT, JOHN
HEATH, Mrs.	SCHNEIDER, ANNIE
HOWARD, Mrs. S.D.	VAN BALVERON, W.E.J.
HENDLEY, CHARLES	WILLIAMS, MAY
HANSEN, N.B.	WATSON, HENRY
HOLMBERG, AUGUSTUS	

Marin County Tocsin
Saturday, August 18, 1894

Real Estate Transfers
Belvedere Land Co. to JESSE C. LOHSE
Lot 14, block 3, Belvedere - $10

Belvedere Land Co. to EMMA E. HALL
Lot 13, block 3, Belvedere - $10

Sausalito Bay Land Co. to MARY SMITH
Lots 14 & 47, block 19, Sausalito Bay Land Co.

Home & Farm Co. to H.B. WOOD
Lots 16, 17, & 23, Reservoir Hill Place - $10

Estate of W.T. COLEMAN, dec. to Sausalito School District
Undivided ½ acre, lot at Larkspur for school site - $250

SUSAN A. SCHULTZ to E.K. BEEMAN
Lots 17 & 18, block 6, Mill Valley – love and affection

Home & Farm Co. to MARGARET K. SMITH
10.6 acres on Black Point - $10

MACK WEBER to O.C. MILLER
Villa lots 176 & 177, block 35, Sausalito Bay Land Co. - $10

Sausalito Bay Land Co. to LOUIS THORS
Lots 230 & 231, Old Sausalito - $10

LOUIS PETERSEN to LUDWIG JOCKERS
Lot on corner of South Fourth Street and Glen Street, San Rafael - $10

T.J. MAHON to P. KING and wife
Lot on corner of First and B Streets, San Rafael - $10

Superior Court

Estate of SOPHIA ZELLAR, deceased
Continued to August 20th

Estate of JAMES BLOOM, deceased
Continued to August 20th

B.F. LYFORD vs. C.E. CHRISTIANSON
Continued to August 20th

B.F. LYFORD vs. J.M. DULIP
Continued to August 20th

Estate of R.W. OSGOOD, deceased
Final account settled and decree of distribution ordered

C.V. MANNER vs. A. CRAWFORD
Cause transferred to Circuit Court

Married
GILL-DAWSON – In San Rafael, August 15, 1894, by Rev. J.S. FISHER, WILLIAM L. GILL to Miss LENA B. DAWSON.

LATRONEL-ROSE – In San Rafael, August 13, 1894, by Justice RODDEN, JOHN P. LATRONEL to Mrs. ADENA ROSE.

Local News
Col. JERRY ADAMS, who has for years held an iron grip on the mercantile interests of Olema, has disposed of his business to A. MARTINELLI of Petaluma. Mr. ADAMS will not leave us, as he has considerable interests in the neighborhood still, and he has also signified a willingness to serve the people as Sheriff for the next four years.

Fatal Accident
FRED GEIGER, proprietor of the new Enterprise Bakery and Confectionary on Fourth Street, opposite Masonic Hall, will open up for business next Tuesday.

We just learned the sad news of the accidental shooting of the son of WILLIAM CURLETT of San Rafael. The unfortunate youth was hunting deer on Tamalpais and was shot through both legs by his companion. We were able to gather no further particulars except that the boy who did the shooting, whose name was PRESCOTT, was almost beside himself with grief and terror.

Child Drowned
A little boy, OSCAR S. LARSON by name, fell into the water at Tiburon last Thursday and was drowned. His parents lived near the water's edge and he probably walked out on one of the neighboring wharves or trestles and fell overboard. The first that was known of the accident was when a couple of railroad employees saw the body floating past the railroad bridge to the west of the slip. One of them immediately swam out and recovered it, and every method of restoration was attempted but life was extinct. The Coroner summoned a jury and a verdict of accidental drowning was rendered.

Marin Journal
Thursday, August 23, 1894

Died
CURLETT – In San Rafael, August 17, 1894, WILLIAM A. CURLETT Jr., son of WILLIAM and CELIA CURLETT, a native of San Francisco, aged 18 years and 11 months.

SEASE – At Sausalito, August 21, 1894, NICHOLAS J. SEASE, aged 11 years, 2 months, and 3 days.

Born
FURLONG – In San Rafael, August 16, 1894, to the wife of ROBERT FURLONG, a son.

Novato
FRANK SUTTON of Novato and ANTHONY TIMONY of Santa Margarita are in attendance at the State Democratic convention in San Francisco, also C.B. SMYTHE of Hollister, late principal of the San Rafael public school. The Professor is looking remarkably well.

Local Intelligence
EDWARD H. BOYEN, after a highly creditable examination has been admitted to the bar, and is practicing with W.H. LINFORTH, and in connection with H.H. HIGHTON.

Mr. GEORGE R. WORN of San Anselmo is making an active and telling canvass for the Republican nomination for sheriff. It is but a week since he decided to become a candidate, yet he has already interviewed nearly the whole county. He is candid, manly, outspoken, and energetic, and makes friends. He belongs to the pioneer WORN family, son of GEORGE A. WORN, and has always lived in Ross Valley. He is in the real estate business, and this is his first political aspiration.

Accidental Shooting
Our community was plunged in gloom last Friday afternoon by the intelligence that young WILLIAM A. CURLETT Jr. had met his death by accident while hunting on Mt. Tamalpais. When the full facts were known, they brought no relief; the poor lad had received an accidental shot, and had died where he fell. RALPH PRESCOTT and he went out Thursday, and camped on the "Potrero". Next morning they were early on the trail of game, but Mr. LE CORNEC, seeing them, forbade their hunting where they were, and they started for camp. RALPH was behind. He swung his rifle over his shoulder, the muzzle to front, when a twig discharged it, and the shot struck CURLETT in the leg. It entered below the knee from behind, and was found close to the surface above the knee in front, severing arteries, from which he bled to death. Dr. WICKMAN said he could only have been saved by binding the leg tightly above the knee. RALPH called young BICKERSTAFF and tendered what aid he could. Both the lads had much hunting experience, and were very expert, and WILLIAM was noted for excelling as a rider and in many sports. He was a boy of great promise, son of WILLIAM CURLETT, the architect, whose family is bereaved beyond expression by the dreadful occurrence.

Local Brevities
W.M. TILTON has sold his 17 acre fruit place at Novato to Mr. ROSE of San Francisco for $6,000. It has good improvements, and the price was very low, even for these hard times.

Letter List
        ARGALL, Mrs.   McELWEE, ---

BELLONDE, J.S.	McDONALD, D.
COLWELL, JESSIE	O'CONNOR, Mrs. M.C.
CARROLL, MIKE	OXNARD, Mrs. ROBERT
DIXON, Mr. FRANK	O'DONALE, C.
DOMINGO, JOE	PATTEN, WILLIAM
DONOVAN, M.	PETERSON, MICHAEL
DIAS, Mr.	BRAZIL, Mr.
EVANS, A.F.	STONE, Miss H.
FOX, PATRICK	SAUNDERS, WILLIAM H.
FARNUM, J.	DE SOUZA, Mrs. GEORGE
GEOHOGAN, L.	TEBI, FRED
KREMER, JOHN	THOMAS, Rev. J.S.
KELLY, Mr.	THOMAS, Dr. H.B.
LUNEY, KATE M.	TETIQUES, Mr.
MORRIS, ROWLAND	WHYTE, Mrs.
MENKEN, E.	WELLS, Miss

Additional Local
Misses LENTZ and FREYSCHLAG will open a kindergarten in San Rafael. Both of the young ladies have diplomas to teach and are experienced in kindergarten work.

Drowned
Little OSCAR S. LARSON was drowned at Tiburon last Thursday. He was but 4 ½ years old. In company with a playmate he had gone fishing, against his father's orders, and the first that was known of the accident was the discovery of the body in the water, close to shore, by a railroad man. The child was a native of Denmark, and his father is a bus driver.

Real Estate Transfers
> Home & Farm Co. to AUGUSTA SVENSON
> Part of lot 11, division B, Novato

> JOHN E. SCHOOBERT to ALBERTO S. MARQUESS
> Lot on Third Street, Sausalito - $5

Marin Journal
Thursday, August 30, 1894

Died
PERRY – In San Rafael, August 28, 1894, GRATTAN PERRY, beloved son of RISTEOME and MARGARET L. PERRY, and husband of ADELA DOWNING PERRY, aged 42 years, 9 months, and 14 days.

BRIGGS – In San Rafael, August 26, 1894, AMELIA BRIGGS, beloved mother of JOHN and WILLIAM BRIGGS, a native of Germany, aged 58 years and 11 months.

Married
HICKEY-KING – In the Catholic Church, San Rafael, by Rev. Father LAGAN, August 22, 1894, WILLIAM C. HICKEY and Miss NORA KING, both of San Rafael.

Local Intelligence
Mrs. GEORGE BUNN started for Texas Monday to attend to business affairs.

J. SHAVER has gone to Mendocino County, where he has taken up some public lands.

Mrs. BRIGGS, mother of JOHN BRIGGS, proprietor of the gardens by that name, died on Sunday.

Mr. FRANK E. WOOD and Miss F.S. MATHIN, both of Oakland, were married by Judge RODDEN on August 23, 1894.

JACOB SCHLOSSER of San Rafael is doing Europe on a wheel. He has traveled the world over, and still likes it, and may visit all quarters of the globe on his present outing, if he does not tire of the wheel.

GRATTAN PERRY died Monday night. He was a son-in-law of Mr. HENRY DOWNING, and leaves a widow and one son to mourn his loss. He was a brilliant and agreeable man, but has long suffered from pulmonary trouble.

A sheet and pillow case party walked in on Mr. WILLIS NOBLE Tuesday evening, who will return to Stanford University next week.

BRUNN-JONES
Mr. C.D. BRUNN and Miss EDITH A. JONES were married in Berkeley on August 22nd. The bridegroom has spent several summers in San Rafael, where he has many friends, who wish him and his fair bride many happy years of wedded concord.

HICKEY-KING
Mr. WILLIAM HICKEY and Miss NORA KING were united in marriage last Wednesday by Rev. Father LAGAN, the ceremony taking place in the Catholic Church. The happy couple have many warm friends here, with whom the Journal heartily unites in best wishes.

Superior Court
    Estate of ELLEN O'KEEFE, deceased
    Administrator discharged

    Estate of ANTONIO PEDRANTI, deceased
    Administrator discharged

    Estate of SOPHIA ZELLAR, deceased
    Continued one week

    E.F. TIBBEY vs. A.H. GRAHAM
    Demurrer withdrawn

    Estate of GUISEPPI LOUINI, deceased
    CARLO PETER appointed administrator – bond $6000

    Estate JOHN T. JAMES, deceased
    Account settled and estate distributed

    Estate of B. GALLAGHER, deceased
    Continued to August 29th

    GOTTARDO GUIBBINI vs. his Creditors
    Accounts of receiver and assignee settled and fees allowed

    Estate of JOHN GRIFFIN, deceased
    Annual account partially heard and continued to September 3rd

Real Estate Transfers
    J.W. NORTHUP to CORNELIUS TOOHEY
    Lot in Eastland – $10

    Tamalpais Land & Water Co. to GEORGE LEONARD
    Lot 150, map 2 - $800

    Tamalpais Land & Water Co. to J.W. NORTHUP
    Part of lot 232, map 2 - $600

    MARY HAYES to Marin Central Labor Union
    Lot corner Third and D Streets, San Rafael - $950

    WILLIAM W. ACKERSON etal to GEORGE E. ACKERSON
    Lot adjoining the McCREA tract, San Rafael - $10

WALTER M. TILTON etal to HENRY ROSE
550 acres in Rancho Novato - $10

CAROLINE L. OSGOOD etal to S.H. CHEDA
Lot 28, Angellotti's addition to San Rafael - $10

FREDERICK G. KNELL to BARBARA KNELL
Lots in Larkspur – love and affection

Additional Local
HENRY SCHMIEDELL, one of the most respected, oldest, and wealthiest citizens of San Francisco, died last Saturday morning at the Hotel Rafael. Death resulted from a stroke of apoplexy, which overtook the deceased on Thursday.

A German Lutheran Church was organized at Odd Fellows' Hall, San Rafael, 8th instant, by Rev. Mr. UNGARTH. The officers selected were:
    Trustees - HENRY GIESKE, WILLIAM SCHNEIER and CHARLES VOGEL
    Secretary – CHARLES VOGEL
    Treasurer – Miss WEINGARTH
    President of ladies society – Mrs. VOGEL

Marin Journal
Thursday, September 6, 1894

Died
BRUN – In San Rafael, September 3, 1894, Mrs. MARIA BRUN, aged 54 years.

Born
DONNELLY – In San Rafael, September 2, 1894, to the wife of ANDREW DONNELLY, a daughter.

Notice for Proving Will
    Estate of HELENA HAACK, deceased
    EDWARD H. BOYEN, attorney for Petitioner
    Filed August 13, 1894
        THOMAS S. BONNEAU, Clerk

Notice to Creditors
    Estate of PETER H. WEBER, aka JOHN PETER HENRY WEBER, deceased
    E.B. MAHON – attorney
    Filed August 30, 1894
        DENNIS DONOHUE Jr., Admr.

Local Intelligence
HUGH WALKER, who has been laid up several weeks at Camp Taylor with an abscess on a limb, is recovering. He has been confined to his bed and room about six weeks.

ANDREW GROFF, a painter from East Oakland, fell through a skylight at Bate's academy Monday, while painting, and broke his arm and leg, besides sustaining internal injuries.

Mrs. WILLIAM BASSETT, of Tomales, died at Litton Springs last Monday, where she had gone in the hope of improved health. The funeral took place yesterday from her late home in Tomales.

The wedding of Miss EDITH FORBES, daughter of Mrs. ALEXANDER FORBES, and Mr. EDGAR A. NEARNE of England, will take place next Wednesday at the home of the bride's mother in San Francisco.

C. CLEMMER, formerly at Schneider's, opened a barbershop in the Parisian house building stand, formerly occupied by S. FOX. Mr. CLEMMER is an adept tonsorialist and invites his old friends and a host of new ones to give him a call.

Superior Court
    Estate of BERNARD GALLAGHER, deceased
    Account of surviving partners to be filed in ten days.

E. DuBOIS vs. E. DuBOIS
Demurrer overruled, motion to strike out denied, 2 days to answer

County of Marin vs. ROBERT FURLONG
Demurrer overruled, motion to strike out denied, 15 days to answer

Estate of SOPHIA ZELLAR, deceased
Continued two weeks

Estate of HELENA HAACK, deceased
Will admitted to probate, letters testamentary issued to GERTRUDE WUTH

Estate of JOHN GRIFFIN, deceased
Continued one week, sale of bank stock ordered

A GIACOMINI vs. his Creditors
Insolvent ordered discharged

People vs. RICHARD DONAHUE
Murder, September 11 set for arraignment

THOMAS B. VALENTINE vs. J.O. DEFFEBACH etal
New partition of lands ordered

Real Estate Transfers
JAMES TUNSTEAD to FRANK R. BELL
Lot on Marin Street, San Rafael – $10

Town Talk
Rev. Dr. SMITH, successor to Dr. NOBLE in San Diego, was stricken with apoplexy in the pulpit last Sunday and died in a few hours.

Letter List

ALEXANDER, CHARLES O.	LORCH, CHARLES
ANDERSON, LEO	MICHELS, KATIE
ALDEN, Mrs. C.E.	McKENZIE, Mrs. ROBERT
ARNOLD, Mrs. W.L.	MISSIT, ANNIE
ARGALL, Mrs.	MURRAY, B.
BROOKS, Capt. JAMES	MUNDT, T.
BULOZ, MARIANNE	MOORE, CHARLOTTE
BROWN, Mr.	MURPHY, Mrs. D.C.
BORLE, Mr.	MAKIN, JAMES
BETTACKER, JAMES	NELSON, CHARLES
BARKER, Mrs. D.	McCARTHY, HARRY A.
CUTTER, Mrs.	McDONALD. S.J.
CROVER, Mrs. E.	McBRIGHT, JOSEPH
CLOSE, Mrs.	O'SHEA, HENRY
COHEN, Miss C.	POWERS, THOMAS
FARLEY, Miss	PATTEN, WILLIAM
FELT, CORNELIA	RIDITER, Mrs. FRITZ
HOLMBERG, AUGUSTUS	STEWART, W.K.
HENIGAN, HATTIE	SMITH, J.C.
HESS, E.L.	SALLING, Miss E.
HOURIHAN, ANNIE	STACK, JOSEPH
INGELKEN, Miss M.	SCHMIDT, Mrs. R.
JOHNSON, Mrs. S.S.	STEELE, JAMES
JOHNSON, J.	VOGEL, Miss A.
JOHNSTON, Mrs. W.B.	WEST, J.A.
KUNTRY, CHARLES	WILER, JOE
KITTLE, WILLIAM	WELSH, CATE
KITTLE, Mrs. N.	WILLIAMS, ANNIE

KAUPF, C.	WALL, Mrs. WILLIE
LENNAN, MEARY	YOUNG, HARRY
LAUDE, Mrs.	ZINGLER, Mrs. ED

Marin Journal
Thursday, September 13, 1894

Born

ESCALLIER – At Tamalpais, September 9, 1894, to the wife of MAURICE ESCALLIER, a daughter.

MOORHEAD – In San Rafael, September 12, 1894, to the wife of S.H. MOORHEAD a daughter.

COCHRANE – In San Rafael, September 6, 1894, to the wife of P.H. COCHRANE, a daughter.

Died

BABCOCK – In San Rafael, September 6, 1894, WILLIAM F. BABCOCK, son of WILLIAM and the late HELENA BABCOCK, aged 11 years and 4 months.

RESIGA – In San Rafael, JOSEPHINE RESIGA, daughter of the late ELLEN and FRANK RESIGA, sister of Mrs. P.H. COCHRANE and JOHN RESIGA, a native of San Francisco, aged 20 years.

GRAHAM – In this city, September 8, 1894, CLARA AUGUSTA GRAHAM, beloved wife of W.G. GRAHAM, a native of Pilston, Maine, aged 53 years, 3 months, and 28 days.

Local Intelligence

WILLIE BABCOCK died of his injuries last Thursday. He was a lovely lad, the only son of his father, whose heart was bound up in him.

Miss JOSEPHINE RESIGA passed away after a lingering illness last Sunday. She was a very estimable young lady, and had many warm and sincere friends, who deeply deplore her early death.

The death of Mrs. W.G. GRAHAM, which occurred at her San Francisco home Friday last, brought sorrow to a large circle of friends in San Rafael, her former home. She was the mother of Mrs. AZEL FISH, Miss NELLIE GRAHAM, and Mr. GEORGE S. GRAHAM, and never was filial love more perfect and tender than theirs, and there is an added sadness for the family in the absence of the elder daughter, Mrs. FISH, who is in the East, with her husband. The interment took place in San Rafael.

The New England Villa, formerly run by Mr. A. KAPPENMAN, has changed hands. The good will and furniture of the hotel have been bought by Mr. M. O'CONNOR. The trade was consummated Saturday, but Mr. O'CONNOR will not take possession until the 15th of this month. Mr. O'CONNOR is well and favorably known as a hotel man and understands the business in all its branches. He will make but few changes, as the hotel was thoroughly renovated and newly furnished a few months ago.

Letter List

ALEXANDER, Mr.	LEVARI, JOHN MARLE
ANDERSON, THEODORE	MERCER, EDWIN
AYERS, Mrs. A.D.	MURBACH, A.
BRUNS, Mr.	MONAGHAN, KATE
BUSINI, Mr.	MARKHAM, J.
BROOKS, Capt. JAMES	MULHERN, M.J.
BARTLETT, Miss	McCAFFONAY, B.
CHAPMAN, HENRY W.	OWEN, J.W.
CONCUSING, Mrs.	OWEN, WILLIAM
CLOSE, BESSIE	PORT, Mr.
CONWAY, MALANA	PERRY, Mr.
DAVIS, H.E.	PRAETZEL, Mrs. C.
DOYLE, THOMAS	RASMUSSEN, K.
DENN, NELLIE	RICHARDS, Miss
DAVIDSON, Mrs. M.	RILEY, CHARLES
ELLIOTT, THOMAS	REYNOLDS, Miss C.E.
ERICKSON, EMIL	RODDEN, Mrs.
EICKHOFF, Mrs. HENRY	ROSS, FRANK E.

ELLSWORTH, MAGGIE
FARRELL, MARY
GRIFFITH, Mrs.
GALENTINE, P.W.
LOWENFIELD, BERNARD
LABOURDETTE, PIERRE
LOGAN, T.O.
LILLEY, MICHAEL

SLEVIN, BESSY
TREFILE, Dr. SIMEON D.
WILSON, Mrs.
WALSH, Mrs.
WILLIAMS, ANNA
YOUNG, W.G.
ZINCKE, --

Town Talk
Mrs. R. DE FIENNES of Sacramento is visiting her relatives in San Rafael.

Superior Court
People vs. RICHARD DONAHUE
Continued one week

H. FLOYD vs. E.B. STRONG
Default set aside, 10 days to answer

Estate of JOSEPH RAULINO, deceased
Final account submitted, taken under advisement

Estate of JOHN GRIFFIN, deceased
Contest withdrawn and executrix account settled

Real Estate Transfers
J. McM. SHAFTER to VINCENT BELLMAN
Lot 30, block 15, at Inverness - $5

Mason Malt Whisky Distilling Co. to SAMUEL L. LESZYNSKY
Lots 5, 6, 15, & 16, block 72, Sausalito Land & Ferry Co. - $10

WENDELL KASTON etal to EMMA RICHARDS
Lot 7, block 13, Sunnyside tract - $10

Marin Journal
Thursday, September 20, 1894

Married
CLEMMER-CURREY – In San Rafael, September 15, C. CLEMMER and Miss MAGGIE CURREY, both of San Rafael.

DE LONG-SCHUTZ – In San Rafael, September 15, by Justice RODDEN, CHARLES DeLONG of Denver, CO, and MATILDA SCHUTZ of San Rafael.

Born
JONES – In San Rafael, September 15, 1894, to the wife of Dr. W.F. JONES, a son.

RYAN – In Novato, September 15, 1894, to the wife of DANIEL RYAN, a son.

RODGERS – In Novato, September 15, 1894, to the wife of JAMES RODGERS, a son.

Superior Court
W.F. GOAD, exec. etal vs. SARAH W.I. TAYLOR etal
Judgment for plaintiff

Estate of SOPHIA ZELLAR, deceased
Continued for 3 weeks

M. TUNZI vs. I.L. TUNZI
Demurrer overruled for want of prosecution

DEFFEBACH vs. DEFFEBACH
Set for October 16th

E.F. TIBBEY vs. A.W. GRAHAM
Demurrer submitted on briefs

P.N. BERKHART vs. MARY CULLEN etal
Motion for new trial denied

Local Intelligence
The engagement is announced of Mrs. BELLE DONAHUE and R.H. SPRAGUE, marriage set for October 11th.

Miss BERTHA HALL has resigned as teacher of the fifth grade of the San Rafael School, and is succeeded by Miss WEEK. There were two BERTHA HALLs in the school, BERTHA and BERTHA M.; the former one is the one who has resigned.

The 6 year old son of JOHN BIRMINGHAM, a police officer in San Francisco, is lying at the Central Hotel, suffering with a broken arm, the result of a fall from a horse last Monday. Mr. BIRMINGHAM had been taking an outing with his son in Ross Valley when the accident occurred.

Mr. J.E. LAYNG of the U.S. Smokeless Powder Co. nearly lost his life Tuesday by the loss of blood from a varicose vein. He became so weak that he had difficulty in calling help. Dr. GROVE was summoned just in time to save his life.

A man named EDWARD McGEE died in San Francisco last Thursday. He had traveled a short time before on the S.F. and N.P. Railroad, and on the trip, had made some disturbance, in the course of which he was injured, and when he died, his friends set up that he was kicked by the brakeman and was mortally injured. The brakeman proved to be ALPHONSO MILLER. The facts appear that the man, intoxicated, made himself obnoxious in the car, and MILLER tried to quiet him. They had a struggle, in the course of which McGEE was hurt in the side.

Mrs. JAMES H. McNABB of Petaluma, wife of our brother of the Argus, and sister of Judge SCUDDER, died at her home on the 8th instant. She was a woman of rare gifts of mind and heart. The light of her home and the sweet influences of her beautiful life were felt throughout the community in which she lived.

CHARLES CLEMMER and Miss MAGGIE CURREY were united in marriage by Rev. E.A. HARTMANN in the Episcopal Church last Sunday afternoon at 3 o'clock. The groom was attended by the bride's brother-in-law, Mr. F.A. CARMICHAEL, and the bride by her sister, Mrs. F.A. CARMICHAEL. Mr. CLEMMER is a well known young man of this place. His bride is a bright and agreeable young lady, and the numerous friends of the couple wish them much happiness.

Novato
Miss NINA MURPHY, who has been visiting relatives in Novato, returned to her home in Stockton on Saturday last.

Mr. GEORGE OLIVER is spending his vacation with relatives in Crescent City, El Dorado County.

Mrs. A.G. SCOWN is confined to her bed with a severe attack of rheumatism.

GEORGE DeLONG, a Novato boy, was one of the champions at the late tennis tournament in San Rafael.

Mrs. MEAD and her daughter MAMIE MEAD, have returned to their home in Minnesota after a most enjoyable visit with friends and relatives in this place.

THOMAS SUTTON has gone to Bouldin Island.

Board of Supervisors
Ordered that $5 each per month be allowed to the 5 children of CAROLINA RAULINO.

Accepted resignation of C.H. ELLISON as County Surveyor and appointed GEORGE L. RICHARDSON to take his place.

Liquor licenses were granted to G. ZUMINI, A. & O. MARTINELLI, M.D. CONNELLY, and SILVA & SILVA.

The contract for feeding prisoners was let to H. CASSOU.

Suicide
Our people were exceedingly pained to learn last Thursday that JOHN D. BRAVO had committed suicide. His body was found a little below San Rafael, near the S.F. and N.P. Railroad, with a fatal pistol shot through his head. Near the body was found a note. Mr. BRAVO was in easy circumstances, and happy in his family. He had lately built a hotel near the Donahue Depot, the care and cost of which may have worried him and possibly affected his mind. His widow is heart-broken, and his many friends are greatly shocked by the terrible tragedy.

Marin County Tocsin
Saturday, September 22, 1894

Real Estate Transfers
WILLIAM ALFONSO MILLER to MARY F. DE FIENNES
Lot on Reservoir Hill, San Rafael - $10

JOSEPH M. JEWETT to C. BECKER
Part of block 8, Sausalito Bay Land Co. - $10

J.L. LYON to W.A. SCHROCK
Lot 4, block H, Coleman's addition to San Rafael - $10

LENA M. DUNARD to ISAAC JESSUP
Lots in Jessup tract, San Rafael - $10

OLLEY HIBBARD to PETER J. SULLIVAN
Lot 1, block 9, Tamalpais Land & Water Co. - $10

GEORGE T. PAGE etal to GEORGE HUNNEWELL
Lot on Fourth Street, between Tamalpais and Petaluma Ave, San Rafael - $10

Marriage Licenses
HENRY SMITH, 31, to NETTIE WILLIAMSON, 20, both of San Francisco
CHARLES DeLONG, 30, of Denver, CO, to MATILDA SCHUTZ, 20, of San Rafael
MICHAEL NOLAN, 27, of San Francisco to MARY COLLINS, 23, of Oakland

Born
WISE – In San Rafael, September 18, 1894, to the wife of H.E. WISE, a son.

Died
QUINN – In Oakland, September 16, 1894, beloved son of JOHN T. and MARY J. QUINN, aged 1 year, 3 months, and 6 days.

Local News
Mrs. JOHN BURNS is very ill.

District Attorney, JAMES W. COCHRANE is still confined to his home by illness.

WILLIAM HAHN has sold his bakery business to PHILIP VOGEL of San Francisco. Mr. HAHN will take a rest for the present.

JAMES W. KEYES, nephew of JAMES TUNSTEAD, is an aspirant for Police Court Judge of San Francisco. The young gentleman has our best wishes for success.

Miss LILY SHERWOOD, sister of Miss H.M. SHERWOOD of Oakland, is making weekly visits to San Rafael for the purpose of giving lessons on the mandolin and guitar.

Marin Journal
Thursday, September 27, 1894

Superior Court

Estate of JAMES B. ABLES, deceased
Decree that due notice to Creditors has been published

Estate of JOHN T. JAMES, deceased
Executors discharged

People vs. RICHARD DONAHOE
Continued one week

Estate of BERNARD GALLAGHER, deceased
Surviving partner examined as to account, and matter dismissed

Real Estate Transfers

A.P. HOTALING to H. WILKINS etal
Strip on south C Street - $20

Tamalpais Land & Water Co. to WILLIAM STEEL
Lands of Tamalpais Land & Water Co. - $10

J.O.B. SHORT to DELIA WALL
Lot on south C Street, San Rafael - $10

LOUIS JOHNSON to GASTON DOMERGUE
Lot on Pine Street, Sausalito – $10

EDGAR M. WILSON etal to DAVID A. McLEAN
Lot 21, block 8, Belvedere - $10

EDGAR M. WILSON etal to NEIL A. McLEAN
Lot 33, block 7, Belvedere – $10

I.G. WICKERSHAM to HERMAN CHURCH
126.40 acres, Rancho Laguna de San Antonio - $7,584

Sausalito Land & Ferry Co. to H.A. COBB Jr.
Lot on Sacramento Avenue, Sausalito - $10

M.G. SILVA to ANTON J. SEBASTIAN
Lot in Tomales - $500

M.G. SILVA to ANDREW NICKLES
Lot in Sausalito - $10

M.G. SILVA to A. COBB Jr.
Lot in Sausalito - $10

ALBERT H. GLOVER to JOSE H. SILVEIRA
Lot in Tomales - $10

ALBERT N. BOYEN to A.B. MORETTI
Lot SE corner Fourth and F Streets, San Rafael - $10

S.S. SOUTHWORTH to MARY J. SOUTHWORTH
Lots 46, 47, & 48, Granda Vista - $10

CHRISTOPHER LEEK to MOLLIE J. McKNIGHT
Undivided half interest in lots 19, 20, & 21, block G, Millers map of Novato - $10

E.D. JONES to Sausalito Land & Ferry Co.
Lot 2, Sausalito Grant - $500

Local Intelligence
ELLERY B. MOORE has gone to Spokane, WA, where he has a fine opening in the real estate business.

Miss BELLE GORLEY, of Uniontown, PA, is visiting her uncle, Capt. GORLEY, and will make a tour of the state. She is charmed with the beauties of San Rafael.

Mr. GEORGE A. WORN last week submitted to a serious operation, the removal of a tumor from his neck, and we are glad to say that it was very successful, and he is doing well, with every prospect of speedy recovery.

Mr. GILLIGAN has returned with his family to make his home in San Rafael. He is at present in the hack business. He will make himself felt in business circles, and is always ready to help with any public enterprise, and his many friends welcome him back with pleasure.

Miss ELLA E. CURTIS passed away Monday evening, after long suffering from a baffling illness. Her mother, sister, and brother are heartbroken. Mr. PETER McGOVERN, a retired merchant, uncle to the deceased, has been for many weeks a watcher by her bedside. A father could not have been more devoted, and his brother, FRANK McGOVERN, has been equally kind. The funeral takes place today (Thursday) at the Catholic Church at 10:30 a.m.

Mrs. ALVIN B. ABBOTT, formerly a resident of Olema, and a sister of our townsman, Mr. H.T. DAILEY, died at her home in Aurora Grande on the 9th instant. Mrs. ABBOTT is well remembered in this county in the early days, when she and her family were conspicuous as worthy promoters of all that was best for the substantial growth of the new community, and where that influence for good is still gratefully felt.

A serious accident occurred last Monday afternoon at Fortin's brickyard at Point San Pedro. While some men were working at the claybank, about a ton of clay fell on P. CANDOLFI and H. MILANO. P. CANDOLFI sustained a compound fracture of the right leg, had 3 ribs broken, his nose broken, and his eye injured. He has been working at the yard for several years, and saved his money, as he intended to return to Italy soon, having sent his wife and children there a short time ago and intending to follow them next month. H. MILANO was injured, but nothing serious.

Died
ABBOTT – At Aurora Grande, San Luis Obispo County, September 9, 1894, Mrs. ALVIN B. ABBOTT, sister of H.T. DAILEY, formerly of Olema, aged 60 years.

CURTIS - In San Rafael, September 24, 1894, Miss ELLA ELIZA CURTIS, elder daughter of Mrs. ELIZABETH and the late LOOMIS CURTIS, aged 28 years.

BYRNES – In San Rafael, September 23, 1894, Mrs. BRIDGET BYRNES, aged 55 years.

Town Talk
Dr. A.S. TUCHLER, formerly of San Francisco, has opened an office in the Hayes building.

Mr. T.N. ALEXANDER has left Tiburon, where he was assistant storekeeper, and gone to Glen Ellen as station agent.

Mrs. BRIDGET BYRNES, relict of JOHN BYRNES, and mother of WILLIAM CONNOLLY, passed away last Sunday. Mr. CONNOLLY was expected home, but did not arrive in time for his mother's funeral.

Letter List

ARMSTRONG, JOHN
AITKEN, J.
BUELER, CECILIA
BALL, F.F.
BIRRILLIER, L.
BRIEL, Mrs. A.
BRONSON, ANDREW
BELLAMY, SAM

HOBBS, F.F.
HASSLER, MARGRETHA
KENNELLY, MARY
LAMPLOUGH, CECIL A.
LOWNEY, NELLIE
MOORE, J.C.
MEYER, EDWARD
MURPHY, Mrs. J.

BYERS, Miss A.
CARZALLERAS, ---
CHAPMAN, HARVEY W.
CORBIN, Mrs. WILLIAM
DAVIS, Mrs. T.J.
DIAS, ---
BRAZIL, ---
DAVISON, D.V.
FORBES, Madame
FISCHER, Mrs. EMIL
FISHER, A.M.
GRETCHEN, ALMA
GRIFFIN, JOHN
GAFFNEY, MILLER
GRACE, M.N.
HOLLENBERG, GUS

O'MALLEY, DICK
PETERS, HERRMANN
PETRELLI, MICHELE
SMITH, SUSIE
SCHOELLAMER, A.M.
SENOMEC, MONT LUIGI
WILLIAMSON, JOHN A.
WILLIAMS, ANNIE
WILLIAMS, MARY
WILLIS, J.A.
WHITMORE, W.
WILE, R.E.
WURTENBERG, FLORA
WELSH, MAGGIE
ZANIOL, M. NATALE

Marin County Tocsin
Saturday, September 29, 1894

Superior Court
People vs. JESUS NAVARRO
Set for trial November 19th

J.C. DICKSON vs. HANS IVERSON
Judgment entered for plaintiff

M. TUNZI vs. I.L. TUNZI
Default of defendant entered, judgment for plaintiff

Married
BRADY-BUCKLEY – In San Rafael, September 24, 1894, by Rev. Father LAGAN, JAMES B. BRADY of Sausalito, and Miss CATHERINE BUCKLEY of San Rafael.

Local News
JAMES B. BRADY, conductor on the Narrow Gauge, and Miss KATIE BUCKLEY, of San Rafael, were married last Monday in the Catholic Church.

M. GILLIGAN, proprietor of the Central Hotel block, has returned to San Rafael, after eexperiencing considerable bad luck in Virginia City, his late residence. Mr. GILLIGAN is at present engaged in the hacking business.

Real Estate Transfers
Sausalito Land & Ferry Co. to H.A. COBB, Jr.
Lot 15, block 111, New Sausalito - $10
Lot W, Map J, Sausalito Heights – $10

EVA GREGG by Sheriff to H.R. GREGG
Lot 18, Marinita Park tract, San Rafael - $722.03

Land & Improvement Co. to PETER C. BRUNN
Lot on Petaluma Avenue, south of Laurel Street

S.M. AUGUSTINE and wife to ALBERT N. BOYEN
Lot 20, Miller's addition to San Rafael - $10

MARY McELNAY to M. HENNESSEY
Lot 6, Miller's addition to San Rafael - $10

CHARLES HANSON to OTTO LANG
Villa lot 11, Mahlstadt Place, town of Novato - $195

Belvedere Land Co. to DeLANCEY STONE
Lot 26, block 2, Belvedere - $10

Marin Journal
Thursday, October 4, 1894

Abandoned Children

The following Orphans and Abandoned Children have been received in St. Vincent's sylum since July 1, 1894:

Orphans	Age Years	Months
SLATER, GEORGE	7	6
MAKER, THOMAS	11	9
SKIFFINGTON, MATTHEW	11	10
SIMMONS, JOSEPH	11	1
BAKER, WALTER	8	3
SHARKER, GROVER	8	8
JORDAN, CIRIANO	7	1
CRUZ, ALEXANDER	11	7
PERALTA, MANUEL	11	6
LYON, ROBERT	11	-
MADERA, RAYMOND	10	9
HAGON, NUMA	13	-
HAGON, JULIUS	9	6
DEMPSEY, JOSEPH	10	4
MOORE, JOHN	10	4
WHELAN, FRANCIS	9	11
FURLONG, WILLIAM	12	4
DOLE, RAYMOND	9	7
DOLE, CHARLES	7	9
NILES, EDWARD	13	4
BRANNAN, JAMES	10	-
REGLAY, GEORGE	11	8
ALLEN, ARTHUR	10	-
IDAL, ROBERT	12	-
CONANT, RUSSELL	9	-
SPECULA, JOHN	12	-
ROONEY, JAMES	14	4
KEARNY, JOHN	10	3
RAMUS, JOHN	9	-
GILER, JOHN	8	11
GRAS, CELESTINE	12	11
GRAS, LEON	9	9
CURLEY, JOHN	11	4
O'LEARY, WILLIAM	8	-
SCHULTZ, HARRY	8	-
ALPHONSE, ADOLPH	11	-
ALPHONSE, LOUIS	10	-
McCLOSKEY, HUGH	12	-
MURPHY, LAWRENCE	-	-
MURPHY, PATRICK	-	-
Abandoned		
MANN, ARTHUR	10	-
WELLS, CLARENCE	10	-

Local Intelligence

Mr. SAMUEL McCURDY of Bolinas was in San Rafael Monday, and went from here to visit his sister, Mrs. McMULLEN, who is sick in Oakland.

Miss A.A. GATES returned from Santa Cruz this week, and resumed her labor in the public school, having had a furlough for the forepart of this term.

PETER WILLIAMS has sold his house on the corner of Taylor and Bayview Streets to Mr. C.L. CRONE, Secretary of the Pacific Pine Lumber Co. of San Francisco.

Dr. W.B. NOBLE, of San Rafael has been added to the teaching force in the department of Greek of the San Francisco Theological Seminary at San Anselmo.

GEORGE FRANETTA is home from Guatemala, and will remain 3 weeks. He went down there as a clerk, and has now created a business house, and is buying goods on his own account. He is hale, hearty and happy, and his visit is a joy to himself and his family and friends.

Born
MACKENZIE – In San Rafael, September 27, 1894, to the wife of E. MACKENZIE, a son.

BRAUNING – In San Rafael, September 30, 1894, to the wife of JOHN BRAUNING, a daughter.

McGUIRE – In San Rafael, September 27, 1894, to the wife of FRANK McGUIRE, a daughter.

LOUDON – At Tamalpais Station, September 28, 1894, to the wife of ROBERT B. LOUDON, a son.

Superior Court
    Estate and Guardianship of R.W. BRIGGS
    F.T. MEAGHER appointed guardian, bond $1100

    THOMAS REICHERT vs. MOLLIE REICHERT
    Divorce granted

    Estate of JAMES ROY, deceased
    First account of Administrator settled

Letter List

AYADOUX, MARIE	JOACHIM, LAURENT
BECKTEL, H.W.	KELLY, Mrs. J.S.
BROWN, GRACE	KATON, W.H.
BARBIE, ANNIE	KENNY, J.P.
BARNUM, PETER	LUNDBARK, JOHN
CASE, F.	MAYER, LOUISE
CODONI, G.A.	NEEL, J.F.
DOMINGO, JOSE	RAY, MILAN
EBELE, HENRY	ROBERTS, J.F.
EISTNER, CHARLES E.	RILEY, MARY
ESCOBAR, J.M.	SMITH, FRANCIS L.
FISHER, A.	SMITH, FANNY
GORDON, WILLIE A.	TANNEBAUM, B.
GRAVES, WILLIAM	WALSH, Mrs. KATE
HARRIDGE, JOHN	WALLS, Mrs.
HUFF, A.	WITKE, ALBERT
HECKEL, HAVIER	WHITTENBURG, Mrs. W.
HILL, CHARLES S.	WALLACE, A.D.
	WILLIAMS, Mrs. MARY

Real Estate Transfers
    THEO. REICHERT to J. DALZIEL BROWN
    4.94 acres in Novato - $10

    American Land & Trust Co. to BENJAMIN G. LATHROP
    Lots 2 & 3, block 4, Larkspur - $10

    American Land & Trust Co. to GEORGIANA A.M. WRIGHT
    6 lots in block 16, Larkspur - $10

Marin County Tocsin
Saturday, October 6, 1894

Real Estate Transfers

J.W. MACKAY etal to E. SCHWIESAU
Lot on Grand Avenue near Linden Lane, San Rafael - $10

EMMA C. PIXLEY to M.F. PIXLEY
Lot at Corte Madera – love and affection

W.J. TABOR to MARY E. TABOR
South part of lot 2, block 3, Short's addition, San Rafael – love and affection

H.R. GREGG to J.W. & M.F. COCHRANE
Lot 81, Marinita Park tract - $10

Mrs. P.T. BURRELL to S.M. AUGUSTINE
Lots 25 & 26, Miller's addition - $10

GEORGE A. HUNNEWELL and wife to JAMES TUNSTEAD
Lot on Fourth Street, near Tamalpais Avenue – $10

W.A. MILLER to C.H. FISH
Lot in Short's addition to San Rafael - $10

MARY MULCAHY etal to ANNIE CONNOLLY
Lot on Third Street, near Cijos Street, San Rafael - $10

ULYSSES BLOOM to L. & A.J. BLOOM
Half interest in JAMES BLOOM Home Ranch, San Antonio, 718.08 acres - $15,000

Land & Improvement Co. to H.M. DAVIS and wife
Lot on east line of Petaluma Avenue near Mission Street - $10

A.J. LYMAN by Sheriff to JERRY ADAMS
Lots 25 & 28, block 15, Inverness – tax deed

MANUEL CONSTANT to J.S. ROZA
East part of lot 1, block 68, Sausalito - $10

Marin County Tocsin
Saturday, October 6, 1894

Local News
A boy by the name of E. MULHERN fell from a roof where he was playing in Ross Valley last Thursday and broke both arms.

An UNKNOWN corpse was picked up on the beach at Sausalito last Wednesday morning and is now at the morgue awaiting further identification.

Rev. A.S. GIBBONS, a well known and talented clergyman, has succeeded Rev. J.S. FISHER as pastor of the Methodist Church of San Rafael.

Marin Journal
Thursday, October 11, 1894

Local Intelligence
HANS NIELSON of Ignacio is building a new residence for himself on the ranch he leases from GUMESINDO PACHECO.

The firm of THOMPSON & JENKINS, of Tomales, has been dissolved, Mr. JENKINS retiring. The business will hereafter be conducted by Mr. THOMPSON who is a very successful and popular businessman.

Letter List

ANDERSON, Mrs. MAREN	JACOBUS, IDA
ANDERSON, Dr. J.P.	MORTON, NELLIE
BYERS, Miss A.	MAYLE, Hon. J.W.
CLEARWATER, DANIEL	McDONALD, Mrs.
DOHERTY, Mrs. P.E.	NILSON, JOHN
DAVIDSON, Dr. H.S.	SEARS, LAURA
	ZWIEBEL, PETER

Marin County Tocsin
Saturday, October 13, 1894

Superior Court

People vs. R. DONAHUE
Continued to October 15th

Estate of L.A. BASSETT, deceased
Letters of administration issued to WILLIAM BASSETT – bond $900

DuBOIS vs. DuBOIS
Trial set for October 29th

Estate of J.M. BIGGINS, deceased
Account settled and estate distributed

Estate of J.B. ABLES, deceased
Account settled and estate distributed

Estate of B.F. SWISHER, deceased
Property ordered sold

Local News
A surprise party was given at Hall Raphael last Wednesday evening to Mr. and Mrs. H.C. GIESKE, it being the 20th anniversary of their marriage. Several costly gifts of china were presented to the happy couple. A banquet was served and dancing was continued until early in the morning.

COLEMAN-BURDELL
Mr. JAMES B. BURDELL received a cable message last Saturday announcing the marriage of his sister, Miss MABEL BURDELL to Capt. JOHN COLEMAN. The ceremony took place in Dublin, Ireland. The bridegroom was in California several years ago and met Miss BURDELL at her father's house in Marin County. These are all the particulars that could be gathered concerning this interesting event.

Democratic Ticket Nominees
Assemblyman – JAMES H. WILKINS
Sheriff – HENRY HARRISON
County Clerk – ROBERT B. LOUDON
Assessor – H.A. COBB
Auditor & Recorder – JOHN L.G. ARMSTRONG
District Attorney – JAMES W. COCHRANE
Treasurer – TOM FALLON
School Superintendent – Dr. JAMES BLACKLEDGE
Coroner & Public Administrator – RICHARD BULLIS

Real Estate

JAMES TUNSTEAD and wife to G.A. HUNNEWELL
Lot at Fourth and Irwin Street, San Rafael - $10

MARY A. & BELLE C. BROWN to EMMA C. PIXLEY
1/3 of an acre near Larkspur - $10

W.H. SAUNDERS to M. HERZOG
Lot 114, Fifth Ave. and D'Hierry Street - $10

Estate of PHILIP BELL, dec. to CATHERINE BELL etal
Lot 8 & 9, and part of lot 7, New Sausalito – decree of distribution

OLIVIA A. & S.E. GORDON to G. DOMERGUE
Lot 8 and part of lot 9, New Sausalito - $1

J. LAURIANO to G.V. METZGER
Lot 8 and part of lot 9, New Sausalito - $1

G.V. METZGER etal to G. DOMERGUE
Lot 8 and part of lot 9, New Sausalito - $10

Terrible Accident
A most distressing accident, that may have fatal results, occurred last Thursday afternoon, the victim being NATHAN STRAUSS, nephew of M. HERZOG of San Rafael. The young man was out hunting in a buggy with a son of P. McDERMOTT, and when near the foot of White's Hill, attempted to lift his gun from under the seat. As he did so, the weapon was discharged, the shot tearing a ragged hole through his right shoulder. That it did not prove immediately fatal was almost miraculous, for several vital points were barely missed. Young McDERMOTT drove his injured friend to San Rafael where he arrived in a state of terrible prostration from loss of blood and shock. He was attended by Dr. WICKMAN and Dr. JONES, who pronounced the wound desperate but not necessarily fatal. The latest accounts, we regret to say, are not very encouraging, although hope is still held out. It is now feared that the left lung of the sufferer is seriously injured.

Republican Candidates
    Assemblyman – General JOHN H. DICKINSON
    Sheriff – THOMAS H. NICHOLS
    District Attorney – E.B. MARTINELLI
    Assessor – IRA PARKS
    County Clerk – THOMAS S. BONNEAU
    Auditor & Recorder – C.H. BENSON
    Coroner & Administrator – E. EDEN
    Surveyor – GEORGE L. RICHARDSON
    Treasurer – S.P. MOORHEAD
    Superintendent of Schools – ROBERT FURLONG
    Auditing Committee – GEORGE MASON, W.P. TAYLOR, H.L. SEARLES, J.T. HARMES
    Supervisors – 1st District – WILLIAM BARR, 5th District – HANS NIELSON
    Justices
        San Rafael – E. GARDNER, G. RODDEN
        Sausalito – G.W. SIMPTON, THOMAS FORTRELL
        Point Reyes – W.O.L. CRANDALL, H. CLAUSSEN
        Novato – J.Q.A. HAVEN, S.J. DAVIDSON
        Nicasio – P.F. SCILACCI
    Constables
        San Rafael – J. GANNON, JESSIE CALDWELL
        Sausalito – JOHN E. CREED
        Tiburon – PETER OWLER
        Point Reyes – TOM IRVING, PETER REINHOLDT
        Novato – L.A. DeVOTO
        Nicasio – CHARLES FILIPPINI

People's Party Ticket
    Assemblyman – JOHN GILROY
    Sheriff & Tax Collector – EUGENE W. SMITH
    County Clerk – LLEWELLYN F. HASKELL
    Treasurer – ELISHA DuBOIS
    Auditor & Recorder – A. KAPPENMAN
    Assessor – A.H. WHEELER
    Superintendent of Schools – E.C. HOUSTON
    Surveyor – GUS D. AVERY
    Supervisor, 1st District – TOBIAS HOCK

Supervisor 5th District – MICHAEL BUTLER
Justice of Peace – Tiburon – SAMUEL McDONOUGH
CONSTABLES – Tiburon – A.J. MARRIOTT
San Rafael – ANGUS McDONALD
San Rafael – JOHN GREEN

Marin Journal
Thursday, October 18, 1894

Local Intelligence

Capt. KELLEHER has returned to his San Francisco home, and the BARSTOW cottage near Fourth and F Street, is now for rent.

FRED H. CARROLL returned from the East last week where he has been filling a baseball contract, playing with the Grand Rapids nine, and is now looking after his interests in the express business.

T.R. RYAN came up this week from Arizona, and is at the Central Hotel, in very poor health. He was formerly in charge of the telegraphic service at the Point Reyes lighthouse where he contracted severe pulmonic trouble.

Dr. J.F. VANDERLIP and G.G. VANDERLIP of San Francisco, have opened up dental parlors at Fourth and C Streets, San Rafael.

Married

SWAN-SMALL – In San Rafael, October 25, 1894, by Rev. A.S. GIBBONS, JABEZ SWAN and Miss MAMIE SMALL, both of San Francisco.

Born

WICKMAN – In San Rafael, October 15, 1894, to the wife of Dr. W.J. WICKMAN, a daughter.

Died

CHAPMAN – Entered into rest, in San Rafael, October 12, 1894, RUSSELL CHAPMAN, father of Mrs. GEORGE H. POWERS, in his 83rd year.

Real Estate Transfers

JOHN S. DIAS to A. BRAZIL
Lot 12, block C, Larkspur - $10

R.E. BYERS to L.A. LANCEL
Lot on Latham Street, San Rafael - $463

Home & Farm Co. to HENRY B. WOOD
Lot 2, block J, Novato - $10

Home & Farm Co. to JOHN C. WOOD
Lot 1, block J, Novato - $10

CARRIE E. WILSON to OTTO LEEGE
Lot in Ross Valley - $10

Belvedere Land Co. to ADDIE C. CHERRY
Lot 13, block 7. Belvedere - $10

RICHARD MERRY to DELIA KENNEDY
Lot on San Quentin Road, near Eva Street - $10

FERDINAND STARK to ELLA M. BROWN
Lot 21, block 2, Richardson Rancho - $10

Letter List

BRIGGS, Mrs. E.E.
BOWEN, FRED
JACKSON, ANNIE
LANDERS, Mrs. JOHN E.

COLEMAN, W.P.	LARSEN, C.F.
COHEN, B.	MOORE, R.J.
CASSEN, ANDREW	MORGAN, SAM
CLEARWATER, D.D.	MINOR, D.K.
COHEN, Miss B.	MILLER, Miss A.
CONLEY, WILLIAM P.	MARCUSE, Mrs. B.M.
CONNELLY, MARY	SMITH, ETHEL S.
DANS, Rev. WILLIAM	SMART, G.T.
DOMINGO, MAMIE	SANCHEZ, Mrs. NELLIE
DOYLE, JAMES	SCHWERIN, Mrs. R.P.
FUJITO, T.	STEWART, Miss
FRIES, ELLEN	STEENSHORN, J.
HANKMAN, FRANK	THOMPSON, Mrs. J.E.
HALLERON, O.	THOMAS, D.

Marin County Tocsin
Saturday, October 20, 1894

Local News
NATHAN STRAUSS is recovering rapidly from the effects of the accident which so nearly cost him his life.

The notice for the trustees sale of the DeLONG estate, appears today. The day of the sale is fixed for November 13th.

Fatal Accident
JOSEPH HOMES, a Portuguese, employed in the railroad shops at Sausalito, met a terrible death there last Saturday. He was working in the pit of the big flywheel, which was revolving rapidly, when in some mysterious manner he was caught by the flying machinery. The wheel made several revolutions before the horror stricken companions of the victim succeeded in stopping it, and when it came to rest, HOMES was a shapeless mass of crushed flesh and bones. Coroner EDEN took charge of the remains and held an inquest.

Superior Court
Estate of J.C. GIBSON, deceased
Legal notice to Creditors given

JACOB GARDNER vs. E. WORMOUTH
Demurrer sustained, 15 days to amend

MARY M. DEFFEBACH vs. JESSIE O. DEFFEBACH etal
Documentary evidence introduced by plaintiff

Belvedere Land Co. vs. N. BICHARD
Commission ordered issued

J.S. SHEARMAN & J.L. CAMM vs. A.S. SPENCE
Judgment for plaintiff SHEARMAN $918.81, CAMM $277.80

HENRY FLOYD vs. E.B. STRONG
Testimony taken

Real Estate Transfers
O.C. MILLER to AMELIA KANNGEISER
Lot 5, and south ½ lot 6, Sausalito Bay Land Co. - $10

Marin Journal
Thursday, October 25, 1894

Sale of Dairy Fixtures
Next Wednesday at the CORWALL Ranch, San Antonio, Sheriff HARRISON will sell at auction, all the dairy fixtures and stock of M. & L. PETRONI, insolvents.

Real Estate Transfers
> MARIA REY SANDER etal to JANE ANN REY
> Various tracts in San Francisco, Contra Costa, and Marin Counties - $10
>
> DENNIS DONOHUE to ELIZA R. DONOHOE
> Lot in Golden Meadow tract, San Rafael – love and affection
>
> WARREN DUTTON to JOHN L. PFEIFFER
> Lot in Tomales - $10
>
> FRANK FOSTER to STEPHEN PORCELLA
> Lot 1, block J, Novato - $10

Superior Court
> People vs. RICHARD DONAHUE
> Murder at San Quentin, plea not guilty, set for trial November 19th
>
> People vs. TONG KI
> Murder, H.C. GRANT, attorney, arraigned, set for plea October 29th
>
> Estate of B. GALLAGHER, deceased
> Decree that legal notice to Creditors given
>
> GEORGE L. WHITE vs. J.E. CREED
> Demurrer overruled, 10 days to answer

Letter List

BRUNS, H.F.	POWERS, HARRY
BRIGGS, Mrs.	RAISCH, Mrs. A.J.
BUTTERWORTH, EMMA	ROBINSON, SARAH F.
BULLARD, Mrs.	SCHMIDT, Mr. R.
BISHOP, Mrs. L.A.	STEFFINS, Mrs. N.
CLARK, ETHEL L.	SONLAE, J.
DOWDEN, JOHN	WATSON, JOHN
DAVIDSON, Dr. H.B.	WILSON, Mrs. JOHN A.
KOSHLAND, Mrs. M.C.	MARIA, JACK

Marin County Tocsin
Saturday, October 27, 1894

Local News
MARTIN SALME of this place graduated with high honors from Hastings College last Monday.

E. BARNARD, for many years a resident of our city, was in town this week. He is residing in Humboldt County.

Mr. COLE CHAPMAN has opened a purchasing agency and special messenger office between San Rafael and San Francisco, office B Street near Second, San Rafael.

Mrs. J. BRESSON leaves for Contra Costa County on the 1st instant to be absent for several months.

Mr. DOLLORES, who committed suicide in a San Francisco lodging house last week, was well known here. He was the defendant in a lawsuit brought by one of our well known businessmen on an endorsed note for $500, which was alleged the direct cause of his rash act.

GEORGE PAGE of the well known PAGE Ranch in Sonoma County, is about to open a large hay and feed store near the broad gauge depot. Mr. PAGE raises all of his hay on his large ranches, and will ship it here and store it in warehouses to be sold.

Superior Court
> Estate of JOHN GIACOMINI, deceased
> Administrator discharged

Belvedere Land Co. vs. N. RIEHARD etal
Set for November 8th

JOHN DeWITT ALLEN vs. H.M. ANTHONY etal
Set for trial December 4th

M. DEFFEBACH vs. JESSIE O. DEFFEBACH etal
Plaintiff attorney directed to prepare findings

HENRY FLOYD vs. EDWARD B. STRONG
Argued and submitted

Estate of JOHN GRIFFIN, deceased
Continued to October 30th

Real Estate Transfers

ALICE ACKLEY to JOHN O.B. SHORT
60 acres of land in Butterfield Valley, Marin Co. - $10

JOHN O.B. SHORT etal to S.H. CHEDA
Block B of Short's addition, San Rafael - $10

AMANDA SMITH to LAURA M. McBRYDE
Lot of land at Ross Landing and Sausalito Road - $300

S.C. BIGELOW etal to O.C. MILLER
Lot of land in Coleman tract, San Rafael - $10

Home and Farm Co. to MANUEL S. MATHEWS
Lot 53 & 54, block J, town of Novato - $10

HENRY C. CAMPBELL etal to BARBARA KNELL
Lots 9 & 10, block 9, Tamalpais Land & Water Co. - $10

BARBARA KNELL etal to CARROLL G. CAMERON
Lots 9 & 10, block 9, Tamalpais Land & Water Co. - $10

Marin Journal
Thursday, November 1, 1894

Letter List

BARRELO, ROBERT
BARKER, Mrs. W.
DIECKMAN, P.
FRAZER, MANUEL C.
GOLDSTONE, Mrs. OLENIA
HASS, CHARLEY
MORRIS, Miss ANNA
RICHARDS, Mrs.
SHAND, DAVID O.
SMITH, Miss CLARA A.

TAYLOR, ANDY
TURNER, FRANK
WILSON, Mrs. JOHN
WILSON, Miss ETTIE S.
WILLIAMSON, J.P.
WELCH, MYRTLE
WALSH, Mrs. SARAH
WEST, J.A.
WITKE, ALBERT
WEBER, Mons. IGNAZ

Died

HOPKINS – At his home in Ross Valley, October 24, 1894, Commodore WILLIAM EVELYN HOPKINS, United States Navy (retired). Born at page Brook, Clark County, VA, January 10, 1821. (All Virginia papers please copy.)

EASTMAN – At Corte Madera, October 30, 1894, Mrs. HARRIET A. EASTMAN, a native of Portland, Maine, wife of WILLIAM H. EASTMAN, and mother of Mrs. JAMES S. McCUE, aged 78 years.

WINANS – In San Rafael, October 25, 1894, Mrs. EMELINE F. WINANS, a native of New York, aged 85 years, 5 months, and 15 days.

MAGNESON – In Ross Valley, October 25, 1894, Mrs. BERTHA MAGNESON, a native of Norway, aged 76 years, 10 months, and 2 days.

Superior Court
    Matter of estate of MAURIZIO PETRONI, as surviving partner of the partnership firm of MAURIZIO PETRONI and LOUIS PETRONI
    Order of Adjudication of Insolvency
    Filed October 20, 1894
                F.M. ANGELLOTTI, Judge

Local Intelligence
MANUEL BOLINI, employed on JOHN DAVIS' Ranch, was dragged by a horse Sunday last and severely injured.

S.C. BOWERS is no longer writing for the Herald. He has a rare gift with the pen, and we shall be sorry to lose him from the editorial corps.

NATHAN STRAUSS is so far recovered from his gun injury as to be out a little for exercise, but is probable that his arm may be permanently weakened.

Mrs. EMELINE F. WINANS, an old and much esteemed resident of San Rafael, passed away last Thursday at the great age of 85 years. She was a sister of Mrs. MOORE of San Diego and of DANIEL OLDS, who has made his home with her of late, and Aunt to Mrs. GEORGE MASON. The remains were taken to Petaluma for interment by DAVID WINANS, stepson to the deceased.

Miss AGNES WALKER, M.D., started on Monday for a six months visit to New York where she expects to pursue her medical studies. It will be remembered that this young lady graduated with distinction at the Cooper Medical College last year, and since then she has been gaining experience as an intern at the Children's Hospital and Maternity Home on Sacramento Street, San Francisco. We wish her all kinds of good fortune and a safe return home.

Real Estate Transfers
    PETER SULLIVAN to MARY J. SULLIVAN
    Lot in Mill Valley - $10

    Sausalito Land Co. to D.P. BELKNAP
    Lot in South Sausalito - $10

    D.P. BELKNAP to JOSEPH M. SHOTWELL
    Lot in South Sausalito - $10

Superior Court
    E. SCHWIESAU vs. W. CAESAR etal
    Set for November 15th

    People vs. TONG KE
    Over one week to plead

    Estate of J.C. GIBSON, deceased
    Accounts settled, and decree of distribution

    Estate of JAMES ROY, deceased
    Final account settled, decree of distribution

    ANSON P. HOTALING vs. SUSANNE CATHERINE GREFFOZ
    Decree of foreclosure for $3,045.59

    ELISHA DuBOIS vs. ELIJAH DuBOIS
    On jury calendar for November 19th

Marin County Tocsin
Saturday, November 3, 1894

    Real Estate Transfers

        B TOOHEY etal to GEORGE KANZIE etal
        Part of lot 242, Mill Valley - $10

        MARY TREANOR to MARY A.C. TREANOR
        Lot on Treanor Street, San Rafael – love and affection

        Home & Farm Co. to P.L. EARHART
        Lot 14, Novato, containing 34.42 acres - $10

        MARION BELKNAP etal to S.C. BIGELOW etal
        Lot 1, division 1, Old Sausalito - $2500

        P.J. SULLIVAN to MARY J. SULLIVAN
        Part of lot 1, block 9, Mill Valley - $10

        WARREN DUTTON to HENRY C. DONNELL
        W ½ Lot 6, Tomales - $10

        H.C. CAMPBELL etal to GEORGE KANZIE
        Lots 232 & 233, Mill Valley

        ALEX LEWTHWAITE to CATHERINE W. COOK
        Lots 32 & 33, block 2, Sunnyside tract - $400

        CORNELIUS TOOHEY to GEORGE KANZIE
        Lots on map 2, Tamalpais Land & Water Co. - $10

    Publication of Will
        Estate of EMELINE F. WINANS, deceased
        Application of LESLIE B. McMURTRY for letters testamentary
        Filed October 31, 1894
        HEPBURN WILKINS, attorney for petitioner
                THOMAS S. BONNEAU, Clerk
                By D.T. TAYLOR, Deputy Clerk

Local News
HOUSTON JONES has returned from a visit to Fresno County in fine health and spirits, the latter due to the fact that he believes he has made a valuable mineral discovery.

FELL-BOWERS
Miss ANNIE BOWERS, daughter of Hon. S.C. BOWERS, will be married today at the residence of her parents to Mr. THOMAS FELL of San Francisco. The bride is an old favorite among her friends of San Rafael and Sausalito, and her loss to the social circle will be felt by many friends. The groom is a rising young businessman of the city who has already reached the important position of head salesman in a wholesale hardware store, and who will certainly reach the top of the ladder before he is through.

Marin Journal
Thursday, November 8, 1894

    Letter List

ARGALL, Mrs.	MORRIS, Mrs. IGNACIO
BURKE, Mrs. JOHN	MADRUGA, SAMUEL P.
BACKER, Mrs. ROSA	MOORE, Mrs. CHARLOTTE
BORBECK, E.	McBRIDE, M.
CHABOT, Mrs. RENI	McGRATH, JOHN
DEYONY, Mrs.	ONSTOTT, JOHN

GLOVER, Mrs. E.	O'HALLORAN, Mr.
HANSON, B.	PERCY, Mrs.
HICKEY, WILLIAM C.	ROBERTS, JOE
HAMMOND, P.S.	RANLIN, H.
HOLLENBERG, GUS	REYNOLDS, ANNIE M.
HANSEN, LOUIS	PARLOR, TALIAFERRO
HOWELL, SADIE	STERLING, HENRY
HEALY, J.	SCHREEVES, Mrs. F.
KINGSBURG, Mrs. EDITH	WATSON, MARVIN
KIRKHOFF, CLAY	WILLIAMS, ECK
KARE, THOMAS	WARE, Mrs. S.
FOX, THOMAS H.	WALTERS, Mrs.
FOX, ED	VAN WIE, Miss N.
FORTUNE, WILLIAM	YATES, W.H.
FLETCHER, Mrs. C.H.	ZENGLAR, ED

Notice to Creditors
    Estate of LAURA A. BASSETT, deceased
    HASKELL & MEYER, attorneys for estate
    Filed October 17, 1894
                WILLIAM BASSETT, Admr.

Marin County Tocsin
Saturday, November 10, 1894

    County Winners of Election
        Assemblyman – JAMES H. WILKINS, D.
        Sheriff – HENRY HARRISON, D
        County Clerk – THOMAS S. BONNEAU, R
        County Treasurer – STANLEY P. MOORHEAD, R
        District Attorney – E.B. MARTINELLI, R
        Auditor and Recorder – J.L. ARMSTRONG, D
        Assessor – I.H. PARKS, R
        Superintendent of Schools – ROBERT FURLONG, R
        Surveyor – GEORGE L. RICHARDSON, R
        Coroner – EDWARD EDEN, R

Local News
HENRY ACKLEY of the firm of Ackley Bros., has moved to Lake County where he is engaged in farming.

E.C. OVERMAN, editor of the Petaluma Daily Imprint, gave the Tocsin a friendly call last Thursday.

District Attorney COCHRANE will open law offices in the Wilkin's building on Fourth Street upon the expiration of his term as District Attorney.

Mr. GEORGE SHINE, for many years a resident of San Rafael, returned after an absence of four years in Mexico. He is employed with the Mexican Railway Co. and is here on a visit to his home.

Real Estate Transfers
    ELIAS C. LUND etal to RICHARD and CATHERINE MERRY
    Part of block 51, city of San Rafael - $10

Superior Court
    Estate of J.C. GIBSON, deceased
    Order of final discharge entered

    Estate of PETER CLANCY, deceased
    Letters of administration issued to E. EDEN

    Estate of GERTRUDE BODIN, deceased
    Continued to November 12th

Estate of M. PETRONI, insolvent
Order setting apart personal property

Matter of RUDOLPH KOHN, insolvent
Continued to November 12th

R. BULLIS vs. M.J. GALLAGHER
Continued to November 12th

Marin Journal
Thursday, November 15, 1894

Real Estate Transfers
H. HARRISON, tax collector, to H. ZOPF
Lot 1, block 2 - $240

S.P. WEEKS to GEORGE RUNKEL
¼ acre land in Bolinas - $5

Died
LAUFF – In Bolinas, November 5, 1894, Mrs. MARY J. LAUFF, wife of CHARLES LAUFF, aged 62 years.

Superior Court
MARY HARDING vs. GEORGE HARDING
Notice of motion for alimony set for hearing November 16th

Belvedere Land Co. vs. NICHOLAS BIRCHARD
Set for trial November 20th

HENRY FLOYD vs. E.B. STRONG
Judgment for defendant

G.W. MONTEITH vs. his Creditors
Over one week

EMILY F. TIBBEY vs. A.W. GRAHAM etal
Demurrer sustained and 5 days to answer

Estate and Guardianship of GEORGE W. BEISLER
JOHN BEISLER appointed guardian, bond $1000

Notice to Creditors
Estate of PETER CLANCY, deceased
Filed November 10, 1894
EDWARD EDEN, Admr.

Local Intelligence
Mr. JOHN ROBERTSON, who has been long confined by illness, was out on election day.

Dr. BURDELL and wife reached their home in Novato Friday last, after a long and agreeable jaunt abroad.

Mr. ED WINTER, the accommodating assistant at the broad gauge depot, has been transferred to the company's office at Front and Vallejo, San Francisco – a superior position, with a corresponding raise of salary.

Letter List
AGESTINHO, MANHOLL
AMES, Mrs. PELHAM
ANDREWS, Mrs. J.H.
BOOLE, M.
BRIGGS, Mrs. M.
ESTUDILLO, LOU
McGRASS, Mrs. M.
NORMAN, JOHN
PRIDA, JOS.
PEGETTI, S.R.
PUCKHABEN, H.C.
RYLAND, Mrs. MARY A.

ECKELS, S.
HANSEN, H.
HANSEN, ELIZABETH
KEELER, LAURA
KENNEDY, BRIDGET
STINE, Mrs.
SCHMERDT, Miss BABETTI
STENCIL, Miss A.
TEIXEIRA, MACHEDA
TENIR, MARTIN
WEST, Mrs. EMMA J.

Marin County Tocsin
Saturday, November 17, 1894

Local News

GEORGE and ED NELSON have opened up a blacksmith, wagon, and horseshoeing shop at the old corner, Third and C Streets, where they are prepared to do all kinds of blacksmithing and repairing at short notice.

The sale of the DeLong Ranch, under foreclosure of trust deed, by the San Francisco Savings Union, took place last Tuesday. The property was bought in for $275,000 by W.S. GAGE, a well known businessman of San Francisco, and a considerable creditor of Mr. DeLONG. It is understood that he represents the syndicate of creditors formed to take up the estate, as the last means of realizing on their claims. It is believed that the big ranch will now be cut up and offered for sale in small subdivisions. If so, it will start a boom in Northern Marin.

Real Estate Transfers

H. KNITTEL etal to C.L. CRON
Part of block 13, Short's addition to San Rafael - $10

W.P. HARRISON to ANNIE HENDRY
Lot in Belvedere tract - $10

CHRISTY ANN McCALLAM (unmarried) to CHRISTY ANN McCALLAM (widow)
Strip of land on east side of lot 8, block 4, Mill Valley - $10

METTIE M. JONES etal to AUGUSTUS F. FECHTELER
Lot on corner of Belle Avenue and Irwin Street, San Rafael - $10

Home and Farm Co. to ANTONIO G. NUNES
Lot 30, block B, Novato - $10

THOMAS DALY to HANNAH M. PARKIN
Part of lot 10, block 7, Short's addition to San Rafael - $10

ANNIE HENDRY to W.P. HARRISON
Part of lot 12, block 6, Belvedere - $10

Belvedere Land Co. to MINDORA F. BERRY
Lot 11, block 7, Belvedere - $10

J.O.B. SHORT etal to S.H. CHEDA
Block C, Short's addition to San Rafael - $10

Superior Court

B. GALLAGHER vs. his Creditors
Final account of receiver submitted and taken under advisement

Estate and guardianship of GEORGE W. WAGNER
Application for partition of real estate granted

Estate of GERTRUDE BODIN, deceased
M.F. COCHRANE appointed administrator

People vs. P. RICE
On motion District Attorney, charge dismissed

People vs. RICHARD DONAHUE
Continued to next jury term

People vs. JESUS NAVARRO
Continued to next jury term

People vs. ROSA TEIXEIRA
Charge dismissed

JULIA S. HAMILTON, admx estate of J. McM. SHAFTER, dec. vs.
J.J. PRENDERGAST & BENJAMIN BANGS, exec. of estate of KATE JOHNSON, dec. etal
Judgment for partition ordered by Court, according to consent of parties

E. SCHWIESAU vs. WILLIAM CAESAR etal
Dismissed on motion of plaintiff

Marin County Tocsin
Saturday, November 24, 1894

Local News
C.F. LARSEN, late of the Summit House, has bought the business of the Cosmopolian Hotel, and will reopen it on December 1st under the name of Larsen's Villa. The gentleman has had great experience as a caterer and will undoubtedly conduct the Villa in splendid style.

Hon. THOMAS J. GEARY leaves for the East next Friday evening, December 30th. On his return from the short term of Congress, he will probably practice law in San Francisco, making San Rafael his residence.

Superior Court
Estate of J.M. BIGGINS, deceased
Estate settled and administrator discharged

Estate of E.F. WINANS, deceased
Probate of Will continued to November 26th

GEORGE W. MONTEITH vs. his Creditors
Application to set apart homestead continued to November 26th

Estate of ISIDOR DAUS, deceased
H. WILKINS appointed attorney to represent absent heirs

ELISHA DuBOIS vs. ELIJAH DuBOIS
Continued to November 26th

B.F. LYFORD vs. C. CHRISTENSON etal
Set for trial December 20th

R. KOHN vs. his Creditors
Continued to November 26th

MARY HARDING vs. GEORGE HARDING
Divorce granted

Died
THOMAS R. RYAN, late telegrapher at the Point Reyes lighthouse, ended his long illness at the home of the family at Novato on December 17, 1894. The deceased was a bright young man and gave promise of a successful career. His constitution, however, gave way under the harsh climate of Point Reyes, and of late he had been a hopeless invalid.

Died
JOHN R. BRIGGS, one of the proprietors of Briggs' Gardens, San Rafael, passed away last Thursday afternoon. He had been in failing health with lung trouble for several years past, and for months only his grit and determination kept him alive. Mr. BRIGGS was an excellent businessman and popular with everyone.

Terrible Suicide

Coroner EDEN was summoned last Thursday to examine into the details of a weird and awful case of suicide, which occurred in San Antonio township, near the northern limit of Marin County. The victim was MARY EVANS, wife of ALEXANDER EVANS, a farmer. The lady had on several occasions exhibited evidences of mental infirmity and once had been an inmate of Napa Asylum. For several days before her tragic end, her conduct had been a trifle erratic, but as such symptoms were of common occurrence, nothing special was thought of it. On the fatal morning, she performed her household duties as usual, and her husband and son left for their tasks. Shortly after, the son, who was ploughing a field, noticed a column of fire and smoke dashing about the house. Ignorant of the cause but fearful of some awful occurrence, he rushed home and discovered the still burning remains of a human being on the ground. Without further inquiry, he sought the neighbors, and an examination proved that the charred body was that of Mrs. EVANS. She had evidently poured a can of kerosene over her clothes and then ignited them.

Real Estate Transfers

M. HERZOG and wife to GEORGE SCOTT
Part of block 33, San Rafael - $10

JAMES M. STREETEN to LeROY G. HARVEY
5 acres of land at Bolinas - $10

GEORGE HARDING to MARY HARDING
Lot on southeast corner of Fourth and Cijos Streets - $10

MARY E. TABOR to GEORGE APPLETON
S part of lot 2, block 3, San Rafael – no consideration

MARY LAUGHLIN to Mrs. W.R. FAIRBANKS
Lot 30, Tomales - $10

Born
DAVIS – In San Rafael, November 20, 1894, to the wife of HENRY M. DAVIS, a son.

McCAMISH – In San Rafael, November 20, 1894, to the wife of WILLIAM F. McCAMISH, a son.

PARETO – In San Rafael, November 20, 1894, to the wife of G. PARETO, a son.

FOLKER – In Mill Valley, November 19, 1894, to the wife of GEORGE N. FOLKER, a daughter.

Married
WHEELER-ARMSTRONG – In San Francisco, November 14, 1894, by Rev. Dr. E.ER. DILLE, ALBERT H. WHEELER, of Mill Valley, and Miss ANNIE M. ARMSTRONG.

MYERS-KELLY – In San Francisco, November 20, 1894, H.A. MYERS, of Mill Valley, to Miss KATE KELLY.

LEIALE-FEREIRA – In Eastland, Marin County, November 17, 1894, by Rev. Father VALENTINI, MANUEL LEIALE and MARY FEREIRA.

Died
RYAN – At Novato, November 17, 1894, THOMAS RYAN, a native of Connecticut, aged 31 years.

Marin Journal
Thursday, November 29, 1894

Born
HAHN – In San Rafael, November 21,1894, to the wife of WILLIAM HAHN, a son.

Died
HAHN – In San Rafael, November 23, 1894, infant son of Mr. and Mrs. WILLIAM HAHN.

BRIGGS – In San Rafael, November 22, 1894, JOHN BRIGGS, beloved husband of HATTIE BRIGGS, father of EMMA BRIGGS, and son of the late GUSTAV and EMELIA BRIGGS, a native of Breslau, Germany, aged 40 years and 21 days.

Superior Court
    ELISHA DuBOIS vs, ELIJAH DuBOIS
    Set for trial November 28th

    Belvedere Land Co. vs. NICHOLAS BICHARD
    Set for trial December 4th

    M. PETRONI vs. his Creditors
    H. HARRISON elected assignee by the Creditors, bond $2000

    Estate of E. WINANS, deceased
    Will admitted to probate, letters issued to L.B. McMURTRY without bonds

    G.W. MONTEITH vs. his Creditors
    Motion to set apart homestead continued to December 17th

    Estate of ISIDOR DAUS, deceased
    Property set apart as homestead to widow

Local Intelligence
Mr. J.F. BOYD and family have returned from their Danville Ranch home to San Rafael.

Mr. and Mrs. ROBERT LACEY, parents of Mrs. SEIBEL and Mrs. ROLLS, celebrated their golden wedding Friday last.

Mrs. Dr. THOMAS F. RUMBOLD died Sunday last. Dr. RUMBOLD's family spent last summer in the L'AMOUREAUX house, Petaluma Avenue. Mrs. RUMBOLD suffered a long time with cancer.

E.B. MARTINELLI, esq., has filed his bond as District Attorney and taken the oath of office. His sureties on the bond are H. SCHLOSSER, J. FRANETTA, J.F. JORDAN, and J. PETERSEN.

JOHN BRIGGS died at his home, Brigg's Gardens, San Rafael, Thursday last. Deceased was a prominent member of the O.C.F., and a man whom everybody liked. His father and mother both died here within the past 2 years. He leaves a widow and two children. His funeral, which took place Sunday, was very largely attended.

Coroner EDEN last week recovered the body of a man from the bay near Angel Island. He kept the cadaver at the morgue until Monday morning, when it was buried unidentified, and if marked at all, the grave will simply bear the inscription "UNKNOWN". The man had been a long time in the water, was dressed like a seaman, and nothing was found to give a clue to his identity.

Sixty Years Married
The descendants of Mr. and Mrs. GEORGE B. WILLIAMS of Petaluma will today, at their house, observe Thanksgiving, and at the same time, celebrate the 60th wedding anniversary of the hale old couple, which occurred last week. The commemoration was deferred, that the two occasions might be blended in one reunion. The 50th wedding anniversary was celebrated 10 years ago, but Mr. and Mrs. WILLIAMS are still strong in body and young in spirit. Among the guests today will be 4 generations, embracing 7 grandchildren, and 8 great grandchildren of the old people. They will come from San Francisco, Oakland, San Rafael, and Santa Rosa. The wife of the Journal man is a daughter of the house.

Town Talk
Mr. W.A. SELKIRK, formerly editor of the Petaluma Courier is now on the San Bernardino Sun, of which he is part proprietor.

Letter List
    BROWN, M.A.   LUIZ, A.

CONNELLY, Mrs. M.
CANDIDO, UMBELINA
DAVISON, Dr. H.B.
DARUI, EDVARDO
DIONEY, L.H.
ETTOBART, MARY
GRAHAM, Miss A.E.T.
GRAY, Mr.
HUME, W.O.
KIRSCHNER, Miss H.
WILLIAMS, Miss M.J.

LYMAN, Mrs.
MURRAY, MAY
MULLER, KETEKA
MOORE, A.A.
McARTHY, MARY M.
McMULLEN, JOSEPH
PRINGLE, MAMEY
SMITH, Mrs. G.F.
SPERRY, J.W.
WALSH, E.G.

Marin County Tocsin
Saturday, December 1, 1894

Local News
T.B. MACKINDER, editor of the St. Helena Star, was in San Rafael this week, and gave the Tocsin office a call.

Attention is called to the notice of auction sale of valuable personal property belonging to the estate of the late Mrs. KATE JOHNSON.

Sheriff's Sale
SARAH N. MORRIS vs. ELLA C. POND, ARNOLD BECKER, S. FOSTER, and the City of San Rafael
Decree of Foreclosure
Sale December 17, 1894
Land in San Rafael

HENRY HARRISON, Sheriff
By T.J. FALLON, Undersheriff

Real Estate Transfers
A GAUDARD and wife to PIERRE MONTMAYEUR
2 lots on Point San Pedro adjoining W.F. McAllister tract - $500

Sausalito Land & Ferry Co. to CHARLES ANDERSON
Lots 7 & 8, block 74, New Sausalito - $475

JAMES BROWN etal to ANGELO SOLDAVINI
Lot on C Street near Second Street, San Rafael - $690

HANNAH LAWSON to CHARLES W. LAWSON
All of lot 6, division B, Novato - $10

J.O.B. SHORT to G.A. BORELLA
Lot on Bayview Street, near South C Street, San Rafael - $10

ISABEL H. OFFUTT to LYDIA J. WALKER
Lots 51, 52, 53, 54, of the Walker Villa tract - $10

MARY M. DEFFEBACH to H. WILKINS & CATHERINE PRUNTY
Right of way over tract of marshland at Alto Station - $5

G.A. HUNNEWELL to H. WILKINS
Lot on N line Fourth and Tamalpais Avenue, San Rafael - $10

HENRY HATTON to ELINOR D. PRATT
Lots 61, 62, 64, and 65, Golden Meadow tract - $5

H. WILKINS and wife to JAMES TUNSTEAD
Lot on Irwin Street and Third Street, San Rafael - $10

E.A. RONBERG to MARTIN JOHANSEN
Part of lot 32, Angellotti's addition to San Rafael - $10

Marin Journal
Thursday, December 6, 1894

Born
BARR – In San Rafael, Thanksgiving, November 29, 1894, to the wife of Supervisor-elect, WILLIAM BARR, a daughter.

Married
BLOCK-HARLAN – In San Rafael, December 5, 1894, by Rev. Dr. GIBBONS, THOMAS R. BLOCK, and Mrs. OLIVE M. HARLAN, both of Elmherst, CA.

Died
MILLER – In San Rafael, December 2, 1894, NELLIE MILLER, aged 23 years and 6 months.

Publication of Will
    Estate of ISIDOR DAUS, deceased
    Order to show cause to mortgage real estate
    Filed December 5, 1894
    BENJAMIN HEALEY, attorney for Executrix
    SUSAN DAUS, Executrix
                    F.M. ANGELLOTTI, Judge

Local Intelligence
The marriage of Mr. RICHARD POWER and Miss CARRIE GROVER, daughter of Mr. and Mrs. JOHNSON GROVER, of Colusa, formerly of Petaluma, is announced to take place December 18th.

Miss NELLIE MILLER died last Sunday. She was a graduate of our High School, and teacher of the Olema School, which closed two weeks ago. She was consumptive and no doubt in her ambition to assist her family, she overtaxed her strength. A few days ago her father, DANIEL MILLER, a railroad carpenter, hurt his finger. He neglected it, and was stricken with tetanus, and was very low when his daughter passed away. He is a brother-in-law of JAMES WATSON and PETER CRANE, and another brother-in-law, J.H. ROWSON of Sausalito, is also very ill. It is a sorrowful story. Miss NELLIE had two brothers and two sisters, all younger, to whom she was a mother, and one of the sisters aspires to a medical course in the University of California, in which Miss NELLIE determined to assist her. To this end she doubtless overworked herself in teaching, and hastened the sad outcome. Verily, she was a true hero. Brave, hopeful, self-denying, loving, and true. Her memory is blessed. Since the above was in type, the death of JOHN H. ROWSON has occurred.

J.P. DAVENPORT is now alone in his business of papering, painting, etc., and his shop is opposite the Water Co.'s office. The co-partnership of SWIFT & DAVENPORT has been dissolved.

Letter List

BROWN, TOREY C.	MAHONEY, Miss E.T.
CHRISTOPHER, TILLIE	MONTENAS, BERTIE
DOMINGO, MARY	MORRIS, W.C.
DRISCOLL, M.J.	MORAN, KATIE
DAVISON, D.H.P.	MANY, A.L.
FINCH, B.F.	McCOFFEY, BURT
GLASS, Mrs. H.	McDOUGAL, D.
GROSS, GEORGE C.	ORMUNA, F.M.
GRAHAM, SARAH	O'MALLEY, AUSTIN J.
GALLOWAY, AND	PEREZ, Mrs.
HEATH, Mrs.	PIERCE, E.T.
HOWE, A.D.	REARDON, M.
DACHLAM, Mr.	SHEPPARD, Mrs. A.D.
LUX, F.A.	SORE, Mrs. L.
LUNDBARK, JOHN	SCOTT, W.H. & Son
MERCER, EDWIN	SMITH, JEFF

MASON, GEORGE
THOMPSON, HARVEY M.
VOEHMANN, WILLIAM
VEILLER, LEYMOUR
TOLAND, Mrs. Dr.
VOGEL, MATHEW FIFE
ULENTE, CHARLES

Superior Court
AMELIA MANNER vs. BARCLAY MANNER
Decree of Divorce, $5 per week alimony, $25 to attorney

ELISHA DuBOIS vs. ELIJAH DuBOIS
Judgment for plaintiff

Estate of GEORGE LARSEN, deceased
Continued one week

Estate of JAMES WINANS, deceased
Continued one week

R. BULLIS vs. JAMES GALLAGHER
Dropped from calendar

Estate of EMILY GAMBERT, deceased
Decree that notice to creditors has been given

M.E. O'NEIL vs. W. SALE
Demurrer withdrawn, 10 days to answer

People vs. C.D. MASON
Information for resisting officer, set for arraignment December 18th

Estate of MARTIN SALM, deceased
Decree that notice to creditors has been given

M.A. COCHRANE, Admr. vs. A. BODIN
Judgment for defendant

Real Estate Transfers
Home & Farm Co. to LORENZO S. MUNCEY
Lots 2 & 4, Sunnyside Place, Novato - $10

E. WORMOUTH to WILLIAM N. SHELLEY
Lot in Mill Valley - $10

A.P. HOTALING to B.J. McKINNON
Lot 24, block 21, Golden Meadow - $500

J.B. HAGGIN to Sausalito Land & Ferry Co.
1.49 acres, Sausalito Rancho - $10

Home & Farm Co. to MANUEL S. DUTRA
Lots 32, 33, 34, 35, 36, & 37, block J, Novato - $10

JOHN R. SWIFT to JOHN P. DAVENPORT
Undivided half of lot on Reservoir Road - $10

Marin County Tocsin
Saturday, December 8, 1894

Born
BARR – In San Rafael, November 29, 1894, to the wife of WILLIAM BARR, a daughter.

MERRY – In San Rafael, December 6th, to the wife of RICHARD MERRY, a son.

TAYLOR – In San Rafael, December 5th, to the wife of F.S. TAYLOR, a daughter.

Died
MILLER – In San Rafael, December 2, 1894, NELLIE MILLER, aged 23 years and 6 months.

Notice for proving Will
    Estate of MARIA JESUS LAUFF, deceased
    Application of CHARLES A. & OSCAR LAUFF for letters testamentary
    E.B. MARTINELLI, Attorney for petitioners
    Filed December 6, 1894
                        THOMAS S. BONNEAU, Clerk
                        By D.T. TAYLOR, Deputy Clerk

Notice for proving Will
    Estate of URIAH WALLACE, deceased
    Application of LUCIE ADALINE WALLACE for letters of administration
    SUMNER V. MORES, attorney for petitioner
    Filed December 6, 1894
                        THOMAS S. BONNEAU, Clerk
                        By D.T. TAYLOR, Deputy Clerk

Local News
City Clerk DOUGHERTY has accepted a position as chief deputy under Assessor PARKS. The new incumbent of the office is to be congratulated on his selection of an assistant.

Superior Court
    People vs. CHARLES MITCHELL
    Charged with embezzlement, arraignment set for December 10th

    A.H. WHEELER vs. CHARLES LINARTY
    Tried and submitted

    J.D. ALLEN vs. M. ANTHONY etal
    Continued until Friday, January 11th, 1895

Real Estate Transfers
    EMIL A. RETY to JOSEPH V. SILVA
    Lots 3, 4, & 5, block 10 - $4,000

    Home & Farm Co. to NICHOLAS J.T. ANDERSEN
    14.7 acres of land on Black Point

Marin Journal
Thursday, December 13, 1894

Died
RYAN – On Monday, December 10, 1894, GERTRUDE THEODORE RYAN, daughter of ---- RYAN and wife of Sausalito, aged 4 years, 6 months, and 16 days.

PAGLIERO – On Sunday, December 9, 1894, Fairfax, in her 46th year, ANETTA PAGLIERO, a native of Italy.

Born
HEALY – In San Rafael, December 8, 1894, to the wife of JOHN HEALY, a daughter.

Local Intelligence
The firm of HAM & MINOTT has dissolved. Mr. HAM will continue the business alone.

Miss JENNIE POWERS, teacher of the San Quentin School, is spending her vacation with relatives in San Francisco.

The remains of JOHN HENRY ROWSON, temporarily interred in Mt. Tamalpais Cemetery, were yesterday removed to Sausalito Cemetery by Undertaker EDEN.

Miss ARMSTRONG has resigned from the telephone office, and will retire in a few days, and Miss BIRDIE McDONALD and Miss McKEON are prominent applicants for the place.

Mr. MILLER, father of the unfortunate young lady, Miss NELLIE MILLER, whose death we announced, still continues to improve. His chances for recovery are fair, although grave fears are entertained of the effect of a knowledge of his daughter's death, which, at last accounts, had been withheld from him.

A goodly number of his fellow countrymen and friends attended the funeral of CHARLES LEZZINI, at St. Raphael's Church, on last Saturday morning. His coffin was strewn with flowers and every evidence existed of sorrow for his loss and sympathy for his surviving relatives. Absolution of the body was given by Rev. Father CULLEN and interment followed in the Catholic Cemetery.

The wedding of Mr. WALTER CORBALLY and Miss ROSE ARMSTRONG will take place early in January.

Body Identified
On November 25th, GUISEPPE MOLFINO, an Italian aged 43 years, left his wife and home at No. 5 Vallejo Street, San Francisco, and did not return. It now transpires that the body found at Lime Point on December 8th, by lighthouse keeper JOHN MORGAN, was none other than that of the missing MOLFINO. The deceased was a crab fisherman by occupation, and his death was doubtless accidental.

Town Talk
H.M. CHAUNCY, for several years a resident of San Rafael, and well known here, died Saturday, alone in his room, in San Francisco. He was but 54 years old, but seemed much older.

Superior Court
    A.H. WHEELER etal vs. CHARLES LIMARUTY
    Submitted on briefs

    JOHN DeWITT ALLEN vs. CHARLES MITCHELL
    Continued one week

    People vs. C.D. MASON
    Continued one week

    GEORGE W. MONTEITH vs. his Creditors
    Continued one week

    Estate of GEORGE LARSEN, deceased
    Final account settled and estate distributed

    Estate of JAMES WINANS, deceased
    Executor allowed to withdraw petition for distribution

    Estate of JAMES BLOOM, deceased
    Order allowing creamery to be erected by executors
    First annual account submitted

    Estate of B. GALLAGHER, deceased
    Sale of personal property confirmed

    E. SCHWIESAU vs. ANNA GEIGER
    Demurrer overruled, 10 days to answer

Marin County Tocsin
Saturday, December 15, 1894

    Assignee's Auction Sale
        Creditors of F.C. DeLONG, an insolvent

All personal property
Sale at Novato Ranch Friday, December 21, 1894
S.C. DENSON, attorney for Assignee
HENRY PIERCE, Assignee

Local News
CHARLES LEZZINI, an old resident of this township, died at his home near Fairfax last Saturday.

Miss AMELIA HAYDEN has charge of the post office at Tiburon and will probably be appointed regularly later on.

Supervisor J.A. HARDING has sold his blacksmith business to Mr. SMITH, late of San Francisco, who is now in charge.

WILLIAM HAHN has purchased the business of Briggs Gardens, on Fourth Street, San Rafael. The new proprietor and his lady are first-class caterers and will doubtless maintain the high reputation that this resort secured under the former management.

D.W. MILLER, father of the late Miss NELLIE MILLER, whose untimely end was noted last week, passed away last Thursday. Deceased was a carpenter on the North Pacific Coast Railroad, and his fatal illness grew out of a trifling injury to a finger which developed a case of lockjaw. The funeral will take place today. The Order of Chosen Friends, of which he was a member, will attend in a body.

Telegraphic news of the week from the State of Washington makes mention of the suicide there of one J.T. WELCH, a railroad man. It is believed here that the victim is the J.T. WELCH who was formerly the master mechanic of the North Pacific Coast Railroad and well known in San Rafael and Sausalito. He was known to have gone to Washington after leaving the employ of the local road.

Superior Court
People vs. CHARLES MITCHELL
On motion of District Attorney, continued for one week

GEORGE W. MONTEITH vs. his Creditors
Meeting of creditors continued one week

FRANK C. DeLONG vs. HENRY PIERCE etal
Exempt personal property set apart to plaintiff

Real Estate Transfers
S.H. CHEDA to JEREMIAH COLLINS etal
Lot 28, map C, Short's addition, San Rafael - $10

G.L. RICHARDSON to HASBROUGH
Tideland lot 24 ½ and 26, sec 9, 28.1 acres - $10

H.C. CAMPBELL & T.B. KENT, trustees, to Novato Land Co.
10,200 acres more or less, comprising Rancho de Novato, exclusive of Blackpoint tract
$275,000

Estate of C.E. WHITNEY, deceased
Lot on corner of Laurel Street and Petaluma Ave.
Distributed to heirs at law by order of the Court

MARY C. FELT to PETER WILLIAMS
Part of lot 14, Short's addition to San Rafael - $10

J.P. ELLIOTT to A.G. ELLIOTT
Lot 16, Short's addition, San Rafael, also lot adjoining - $1,000

F. GARCIA to F.R. GARCIA
Lot on Third Street, near Tamalpais Ave – love and affection

JANE MOLSEED to W.J. MOLSEED etal
Tract of land in Tomales township – love and affection

BRIDGET LYNCH to MARY McNAMARA
3.124 acres in Laurel Grove Valley, near San Rafael - $10

E. McNAMARA to MARY W. McNAMARA
Part of lot 8, block 8, Ross Valley villa lots – love and affection

HENRIETTA McCUE to CHARLES R. WILSON
11 acres at Corte Madera - $10

Bank of California to CHARLES R. WILSON
11 acres at Corte Madera - $10

Marin Journal
Thursday, December 20, 1894

Real Estate Transfers
N.F. BARNUM to CHARLES PETERSON
3.78 acres in Novato - $10

LAURA M. PETERSON to GEORGE A. HUNNEWELL
Lot on Petaluma Ave. near Fourth St., San Rafael - $10

F.L. WILDERS to J.W. ECKLEY
Lot 39 Culloden Park tract, San Rafael - $10

JAMES TUNSTEAD to H. WILKINS
Lot on Fifth Ave, San Rafael - $10

H. WILKINS to JAMES TUNSTEAD
Lot on Irwin and Fourth Streets, San Rafael - $10

CHARLES McCARTHY to CH. LIPPMAN
Part of lot D, Sausalito Rancho – $10

Death of D.W. MILLER
The funeral of our late fellow townsman, D.W. MILLER, took place on Saturday afternoon, and was attended by many of the Order of Chosen Friends, of which the deceased was a member. The exercises were held at his late residence, Rev. E.A. HARTMAN officiating. Interment was in Mt. Tamalpais Cemetery. Mr. MILLER was an old time resident of this State, having crossed the plains in a covered wagon in 1854, settling in Contra Costa County. A native of Pennsylvania, he had early followed that great stream of population that turned its face towards the setting sun. In 1855 Mr. MILLER located in Marin County, and engaged in dairying, an occupation he followed until some 4 or 5 years ago, when financial reverses compelled him to abandon it. Since then he has been engaged in railroad bridge construction. Mr. MILLER is survived by 4 children, two boys and two girls. He also leaves two sisters still living, Mrs. JOSEPH ALMY of San Rafael and Mrs. PARROTT, the latter being of Humboldt County. All knowledge of the sad death of his eldest daughter was mercifully withheld from Mr. MILLER and they will meet only in the land of eternity.

Superior Court
F.C. DeLONG vs. HENRY PIERCE etal
Suit for possession of personal property, judgment for plaintiff

GEORGE W. MONTEITH vs. his Creditors
Hearing of motion of petitioner to set apart homestead
H.H. DEVOE elected assignee, bond $500

People vs. C.D. MASON
Plea of not guilty

M. PETRONI vs. his Creditors
Receiver's final account approved and settled

M.J. GREEN etal vs. B.F. LYFORD etal
Set for trial January 13th

GEORGE F. GRAY etal vs. H.B. WOOD etal
Demurrer argued and submitted

Married
VANDERBILT-McGUIRE – In San Francisco, December 11, 1894, by Rev. R.C. FONTE, FRANK H. VANDERBILT and LENA L. McGUIRE, both of San Rafael.

Letter List

ALLEN, WILLIAM B.	LINDSLEY, CARLETON
BARRATT, WILLIAM	MOLLER, AUGUST
BURNETT, CHARLES	MARTIN, HENRY G.
BOLLOTTI, L.B.	MURPHY, PAUL
BARRETT, W.	MILLS, CHARLES D.
BURKE, W.	McELNAY, JOHN
BUCKEN, G.F.	POWELL, SAMUEL G.
BROWN, EDWARD	POWERS, THOMAS
BROWN, ANDREW	ROMER, CHARLES
CRANE, WILLIAM T.S.	RUSSELL, ROBERT C.
COUICK, JOHN	RYAN, RICHARD
DOUGLAS, JAMES	RIX, EDWARD A.
EVANS, HENRY	RUEF, JOHANN
EUBANKS, COLONI	ROLLINS, CHARLES A.
FITZSIMMONS, JOHN	SHAW, THOMAS
FOX, EDWARD	SCHMIDT, RICHARD
GERAGHTY, EDWARD	SHINE, JEREMIAH
HOUCK, RICHARD A.	TAYLOR, FRED W.
HARRINGTON, ED	TERRY, BENJAMIN F.
HALLIGAN, FRANK	WRIGHT, CHARLES
KRUGER, JOHANN F.	WATTS, JAMES
KENNEDY, JOSEPH P.	WETMORE, CHARLES
KING, MANUEL	WELCH, EDWARD M.
LANDER, NELSON A.	WEST, JAMES A.
LYDIATT, AMOS	WILLIAMS, JOHN S.

Local Intelligence
Undertaker EDEN has removed all bodies interred in Sunny Hill Cemetery, Sausalito, and this old burying ground, as such, has become a thing of the past. Most of the remains have been buried in the new cemetery near Coyote Creek.

Mr. W.S. POND came down from Seattle last week. He visited friends in San Rafael, went to Auburn to see his mother, and returns north this week, where he is at the head of a large insurance business.

Mr. C.J. GOOCH of Red Bluff, an extensive cattle-raiser of Northern California, is now visiting his daughter, Mrs. A.H. McINNES of Mill Valley. We understand that Mr. GOOCH talks of disposing of his northern interests and investing in Marin County. The addition of so valuable a citizen would be a gain to the county.

Mrs. S.E. LEAN and her two little daughters, who have been residing at the Cypress Villa for the past year, left last Monday for Tucson, AZ, where they go to spend the holidays with Mrs. LEAN's father, Capt. JOHNSON, who has been Chief of Police there for the past 10 years. She will be greatly missed by her many friends hereabouts.

The San Rafael Fire Department held its annual meeting and election Tuesday evening, the 18th. The officers elected are:
President – L. HUGHES
Vice President – RICHARD KINSELLA

Secretary – T. HOCK
Treasurer – H.C. GIESKE
Steward – GEORGE FITZROY
Trustee – E. EDEN
Chief – T.B. ALMY
1st asst. – PETER KOPP
2nd asst. – L. JOHANSEN

Sausalito News
The funeral of MANUEL CORREIRA was held on Friday, December 13, 1894, and was attended by his friends and fellow-countrymen. Father VALENTINI officiated.

W.H. BAUSMAN, representing an Eastern Company, was in Sausalito this week looking about with a view of putting in a plant, to supply our town with electric light.

WALTER M. ADAMS, so long known as the genial host of the Ocean House in Bolinas, dropped in upon the News office last Wednesday.

Court Estrella
Court Estrella, No. 7906, A.O.F., at their regular meeting last Thursday night, elected the following officers to serve the ensuing term:
Chief Ranger – P. FORTIN
Sub chief Ranger – J.P. LACERDA
Financial Secretary – H.W. OTTEN
Recording Secretary – J.F. SCHETTLER
Treasurer – E. EDEN
Senior Woodward – L. ANDERSON
Junior Woodward – J.J. LAKIN
Senior Beadle – E. BURBANK
Junior Beadle – A.L. CONKLIN
Trustees – M.M. SALES, C. PEACOCK, and M. SHIELDS
Auditors – ROBERT SCOTT, M.J. CONWAY, and A. HINIKER

Death of E. DENMAN
Sonoma County lost one of her noblest men last Monday night when EZEKIEL DENMAN died. An old resident of Petaluma, he was one of the foremost of that body of strong men who have done so much to advance the material interests of that city. He was a good citizen, a genial man, unselfish, public spirited, intelligent, and honorable. He was president of the Bank of Sonoma County and largely identified in business with his son-in-law, Mr. GEORGE A. McNEAR. He was 67 years of age and a native of New York State.

JAMES MURRAY, brother of our popular fellow townsman, Lt. MURRAY of Company D, has shipped as quartermaster of the steamer Australia, plying between San Francisco and Honolulu.

Town Talk
Miss BIRDIE McDONALD has been appointed manager of the general telephone office in San Rafael.

Our esteemed fellow-townsman, M.C. DUFFICY, Esq., has been re-commissioned a Notary-Public by Governor MARKHAM.

Marin Lodge, No. 191, F.& A.M., elected the following officers last Wednesday evening:
JAMES SAUNDERS – W.M.
W.F. JONES – S.W.
W.G. CORBALEY – J.W.
B.W. STUDLEY – Treasurer
F.J. JACOBS – Secretary

Marin County Tocsin
Saturday, December 22, 1894

Dissolution of Co-Partnership
HAM & MINOTT

A.L. HAM will continue business
Dated San Rafael, December 11, 1894

                        ABNER L. HAM
                        J.P. MINOTT

Local News

GEORGE MILLER has returned for the holidays to San Rafael. He occupies a prominent and responsible position with a big lumber firm in Shasta County.

NATHAN HERZOG and NATHAN STRAUSS left for the Hawaiian Islands yesterday in charge of a herd of picked dairy cows, consigned by M. HERZOG of San Rafael.

Estrella Circle, C.O.F. elected the following officers at their regular meeting last week:
- Chief Companion – Mrs. E. SCHWIESAU
- Sub Chief – Mrs. A. JOHNSON
- Treasurer – Mrs. STUDLEY
- Financial Secretary – R. SCOTT
- Recording Secretary – Mrs. SHIPPLER
- Right Guide – Mrs. RICHARDSON
- Left Guide – Miss T. JOHNSON
- Inside Guard – Miss ANNIE SNEE
- Outside Guard – Mrs. FLAHERTY
- Surgeon – Dr. W.J. WICKMAN

Real Estate Transfers

M.F. COCHRANE to AUGUST BODIN
Lot 12, Block A, Short's addition to San Rafael - $10

SIDNEY B. CUSHING & GRACE CUSHING to JACOB GARDNER
General right of way over tract of land at Mill Valley - $10

Marin Journal
Thursday, December 27, 1894

Born

ALBUGAZIO – In San Rafael, December 25, 1894, to the wife of DAMIAN ALBUGAZIO, a daughter.

Died

THORNTON – In Larkspur, December 28, 1894, MARY J. THORNTON, beloved wife of HARRY N. THORNTON, and daughter of JAMES F. HOUGH, a native of San Francisco, aged 30 years and 6 months.

Letter List

ALLEN, WILLIAM B.	LANDER, NELSON A.
BROWN, ANDREW	MURPHY, PAUL
BROWN, EDWARD	MARTIN, HENRY G.
BUCKEN, G.F.	MOLLER, AUGUST
BURKE, W.	NIELLES, CHARLES D.
BURNETT, CHARLES	McELNAY, JOHN
BARRATT, WILLIAM	RUEF, JOHANN
CONICK, JOHN	RIX, EDWARD A.
CRANE, WILLIAM T.S.	RYAN, RICHARD
DOUGLAS, JAMES	RUSSELL, ROBERT C.
EUBANKS, CALVIN	ROLLINS, CHARLES A.
EVANS, HENRY	ROMER, CHARLES
FITZSIMMONS, JOHN	SHINE, JEREMIAH
FOX, EDWARD	SCHMIDT, RICHARD
GERAGHTY, EDWARD	SHAW, THOMAS
HALLIGAN, FRANK	WELCH, EDWARD M.
HARRINGTON, ED	WETMORE, CHESTER
HOUCK, RICHARD A.	WATTS, JAMES
KRUGER, JOHANN F.	WRIGHT, CHARLES
KING, MANUEL	WEST, JOSEPH A.

KENNEDY, JOSEPH P.	WILLIAMS, JOHN S.
LINDSLEY, CARLETON	TERRY, BENJAMIN F.
LYDIATT, AMOS	TAYLOR, FRED W.
ANDERSON, Mrs. J.K.	BOULWARE, GRACE
ALLEN, Mrs. H.H.	BERGMAN, H.
ANDERSON, W.A.	CHRISTOPHERSON, I.
ALDERMAN, OSCAR	CRANE, Mrs. BYRON G.
BEMENDERFER, M.	COLTON, Miss MINNIE
BRANDER, GEORGE L.	CARLTON, THEO.

Local News
Supervisor HARDING has sold his wagon and blacksmithing business to Mr. SMITH.

Mrs. MARY DAVIES will return to Nordhoff soon. She has passed two years in San Rafael, where she has many friends.

Funeral services over the remains of the late Mrs. THORNTON of Larkspur, were held in St. Raphael's Church on Wednesday morning.

FRED WOODWORTH, Esq., has moved his law office from Chronicle building to the Fifth floor in the elegant Mills building, San Francisco. Less than 2 years ago, Mr. WOODWORTH commenced practicing law in the metropolis, and already his business demands larger rooms.

An Old Resident Suffers a Stroke of Paralysis
Many Journal readers will remember JAMES A. GRANT, a prominent caterer who was here about 1880. He had a great fund of humor, was a fluent talker of the Fult. Berry School of oratory, and an all around good fellow. He served awhile as a Captain at San Quentin, and then drifted East, and is now living in Concord, NH. Last Admission Day he accepted an invitation to read a paper before the Boston Club of California Pioneers. Reaching Boston earlier than the hour for meeting, he called at the Revere House to see a friend and while there suffered a stroke of apoplexy. Mr. GEORGE MASON received a paper giving an account of it, the hope being expressed that the attack would not prove fatal.

Miss MAMIE EDEN has developed exceptional artistic gifts and has reason for no little satisfaction in some pieces from her easel, both in landscape and animate art. Her picture of a family of kittens was awarded first prize at the reception given last week by the Sisters of the Dominican Convent in San Rafael.

POWER-GROVER
A pretty wedding of Colusa people, well known in Petaluma and this county, took place at St. Stephen's Church, Colusa, on Tuesday morning December 18, 1894. The groom was RICHARD POWER, junior partner of the Colusa House and the bride Miss CAROLINE GROVER, second daughter of Mr. and Mrs. JOHNSON GROVER. Miss EVA JOSEPH presided at the organ. The ushers were GEORGE BROOKS Jr., and CHARLES DE ST. MAURICE. The bridesmaids were Misses GERTRUDE DE ST. MAURICE, CORA GROVER, and GRETTA ARNOLD; the maid of honor being Miss MABEL GROVER. Little MARIE BREDEFELD acted as page. The groom was accompanied by Mr. W.M. HARRINGTON in the capacity of best man. The ceremony was performed by Rev. JAMES GOPE.

Novato Notes
All the cows belonging to the various dairies of the DeLONG Ranch were sold at public auction on Friday last. The Syndicate owning the ranch property was the largest purchaser. The cows on the BEN HAYDEN Dairy brought the highest price, $29. The lowest price was $14, average $22 per head. There will be no particular change in the management of the dairies. MAX THEILIG will remain in charge of the DeLong orchard.

Miss FLORENCE DeLONG will shortly enter the Petaluma High School.

FRANCIS SUTTON has removed to San Francisco with all his belongings, including his famous hunting dogs. He and his family celebrated Christmas at 19th Street, with a 15 pound turkey from the GALLAGHER Ranch on the Summit of Monte Negro, Novato.

Dr. BURDELL and wife have recently returned home from an extended sojourn in Europe. Mrs. BURDELL, Sr. is laid up with rheumatism.

Mrs. JOSIE SWEETSER is confined to her home with measles.

Ex-Governor MACKIN, agent of the Novato Home and Farm Co., has made numerous sales of land of late, and new residences are springing up everywhere.

Mr. N.D. HOSKINS, the Colorado rancher, has sold his Novato residence to a German physician who will open a drugstore in connection with his practice.

JOHN MURPHY, formerly of Novato, has returned from Pescadero to accept a position as manager of a creamery for JAMES BURDELL in Petaluma.

Among the applicants for teacher's certificates at the recent examination held in San Joaquin County was Miss MAGGIE KEATING, late of Marin County.

LOUIS DEVOTO will rewarded for his labor with a fine crop of hay on his marshland during the coming season.

Superior Court
>	GEORGE W. MONTEITH vs. his Creditors
>	Continued one week
>
>	People vs. CHARLES MITCHELL
>	Bench warrant issued
>
>	Estate of C.G. MONDON, deceased
>	Partial distribution ordered
>
>	Estate of MARIA J. LAUFF, deceased
>	Will admitted to probate
>	Letters of administration issued to L.A. WALLACE, bond $3800
>
>	Estate of F.B. McKENNAN, deceased
>	Final account settled

Real Estate Transfers
>	I.G. INK etal to HARRIET J. INK
>	38.50 acres in Rancho Laguna de San Antonio - $10
>
>	E. FAUCRAULT to Bank of Tomales
>	58 acres in Tract No. 40 of Blucher Ranch
>	48.27 acres in Tract No. 41 of Blucher Ranch, Tomales - $4,052
>
>	M. DE SLAEF to CHARLES GARDELLE
>	Lot on A Street, San Rafael - $10
>
>	LEWIS STINSON to JOHN J. STUBBE
>	Undivided half of lot, division C, Novato Rancho - $10
>
>	NINA R. SPENCER to CHARLES F. ACKLEY
>	Lot 14, block 24, Golden Meadow, San Rafael - $10

Mr. A.C. DIGGINS, the street contractor, well known in San Rafael, died at his home in San Francisco last week. He was a good man and universally esteemed.

Sausalito Notes
J.B. MAHAR has secured the paper route for Tiburon.

W.D. CLAUSSEN has been elected a vestryman of Christ Church in place of GEORGE W. REED, on account of his removal.

The TILLINGHAST property between El Monte Hotel and Mr. W.G. BARRETT's property has been divided into Villa lots which will be placed on the Sausalito market this spring.

The well known RETY property has been sold to SILVA & Co. for $8000, but it will still be continued as a French Restaurant.

EWING BOWERS, son of the late Judge BOWERS of this county, was in Sausalito last Tuesday. Mr. BOWERS holds a clever position in the Mint, and is said to be very popular with the officials as well as with the operatives.

NAME INDEX

Abbink, G., 84
Abbott, Mrs. Alvin B., 239
Abbott, Mrs. W.H., 50
Abbott, W.H., 194
Abeille, Marie, 62
Abel, C., 92
Abel, Fred, 222
Ables, Horace, 90, 105
Ables, J.B., 244
Ables, James B., 174, 185, 197, 238
Ables, James, 175
Ables, Mrs. James, 175
Ables, Mrs., 78
Ables, T.G., 145, 152
Ables, T.J., 76
Ables, Thomas B., 174
Ables, Thomas G., 143
Abrams, Melville S., 171
Abrams, Mr., 59
Ackerson, C.H., 66
Ackerson, George E., 231
Ackerson, William W., 66, 231
Ackley, Alice, 249
Ackley, C.F., 68
Ackley, Charles F., 269
Ackley, Forrest, 199
Ackley, H.C., 32, 132, 137
Ackley, Henry C., 133
Ackley, Henry, 252
Ackley, Leroy, 62, 200
Ackley, M.D., 184
Ackney, H.C., 137
Adair, Hannah, 194
Adams, 59
Adams, D., 85
Adams, E.C., 159, 178
Adams, E.E., 20, 23, 33
Adams, Frank E., 36
Adams, G., 99
Adams, Grove, 23, 33, 178
Adams, H.O., 185
Adams, Holly, 42
Adams, J.B., 194
Adams, Jerry, 9, 128, 227, 228, 243
Adams, L., 85
Adams, Miss D., 11
Adams, Mrs. E.E., 227
Adams, Mrs. W.L., 178
Adams, R., 144
Adams, Ruby, 2
Adams, W.L., 152
Adams, W.S., 75, 173
Adams, Walter M., 266
Adams, Walter, 9
Adams, William J., 171
Adams, William, 123
Agestinho, Manholl, 253
Agnew, Edith, 200

Agnew, George, 103, 156
Agostino, F., 137
Ahen, C., 75
Aherd, A., 97
Ahern, James B., 183, 222
Ahern, Mrs., 161
Ahlberg, Carl F., 71
Aiken, Dr., 206
Aitken, A.N., 91
Aitken, J., 239
Aitken, May, 12
Alberti, J., 53, 111
Alberti, Joseph, 162, 164, 209
Albini, Guiseppi, 220
Albino, J., 2
Albugazio, Claudina, 62
Albugazio, Damian, 106, 267
Alcarazi, Daniel, 215
Alcarazi, Joe, 215
Alden, Mrs. C.E., 233
Alderman, Bertie, 62
Alderman, David, 61
Alderman, Eva, 62
Alderman, John, 25
Alderman, L., 137
Alderman, Mrs., 155
Alderman, O., 31, 68
Alderman, Oscar, 173, 220, 268
Alexander, Charles O., 208, 233
Alexander, Charles, 2
Alexander, F., 159
Alexander, G., 54
Alexander, Mr., 234
Alexander, N.P., 78
Alexander, T.N., 239
Alexander, W.A., 2, 5, 9
Alexander, William, 16
Alicarn, Michael, 178
Allen, Arthur, 241
Allen, General, 60
Allen, H.H., 32
Allen, H.P., 220
Allen, Harry Edwin, 155
Allen, J. DeWitt, 217, 218, 223
Allen, J.D., 261
Allen, John DeWitt, 249, 262
Allen, L.H., 2, 39
Allen, Laura, 102
Allen, M.H., 177
Allen, Mrs. E.M., 220
Allen, Mrs. H., 183
Allen, Mrs. H.H., 161, 268
Allen, W., 82
Allen, William B., 265, 267
Allison, J., 31
Almy, Charles, 206, 211
Almy, Joseph, 156
Almy, Mrs. Joseph, 264
Almy, T.B., 266
Alomada, A.P., 46

Alphonse, Adolph, 241
Alphonse, Louis, 241
Alvarado, J., 23
Alvarado, J.B.C., 159
Alvarez, J., 119, 121
Alverson, Edward, 176
Amaral, A.S., 206
Amaral, J.M., 159
Amaral, J.S., 11
Amaral, Joseph B., 66
Ames, A.M., 153
Ames, Augusta W., 151, 152
Ames, General, 60
Ames, H.A., 155
Ames, Mr., 143
Ames, Mrs. Pelham, 253
Ames, P.W., 153
Ames, Pelham W., 152
Ames, Worthington, 152
Amiot, Frank, 46
Amos, John, 66, 151
Andersen, Nicholas J.T., 261
Anderson, Alice, 155
Anderson, Andrew, 181
Anderson, Arthur, 62, 200
Anderson, Charles, 258
Anderson, George, 225
Anderson, I., 93, 111
Anderson, J.P., 244
Anderson, J.T., 95
Anderson, John, 159
Anderson, L., 266
Anderson, Leo, 178, 233
Anderson, Maren, 244
Anderson, Mary, 164, 166
Anderson, Mr., 206
Anderson, Mrs. J.K., 268
Anderson, Mrs. M.M., 155
Anderson, Mrs., 197
Anderson, Peter, 21
Anderson, Stephen, 206
Anderson, Theodore, 234
Anderson, W.A., 268
Anderson, W.M., 146
Anderson, W.W., 210, 222
Anderson, William N., 142
Andrew, B., 99
Andrews, Mrs. J.H., 253
Andrews, W.A., 9
Angelinetta, Pablo, 208
Angellotti, F.M., 8, 34, 50, 57, 70, 72, 73, 83, 89, 100, 129, 131, 164, 167, 191, 209, 213, 250, 259
Angellotti, Judge, 110, 132, 149, 166, 197
Angellotti, Mrs. F.A., 153
Ansenio, Bernardino, 128
Anthony, H.M., 217, 218, 223, 249

Anthony, M., 261
Appleton, George, 256
Aquinn, M., 46
Arbini, 30
Arbini, A., 9
Arbini, Antonio, 121
Arbini, Domenico, 220
Arbini, Joseph, 111, 144
Archer, Mr., 202
Archer, Mrs., 162, 166
Archer, Thomas S., 157
Archibald, James, 224
Ardner, E., 13
Argall, Mrs., 229, 233, 251
Ark, Henry, 161
Armand, E., 75
Armstrong, Agent, 4
Armstrong, Annie M., 256
Armstrong, J.L., 252
Armstrong, J.L.G., 25, 31, 166
Armstrong, John L.G., 244
Armstrong, John, 239
Armstrong, Miss R., 4
Armstrong, Miss, 11, 262
Armstrong, Mr., 202
Armstrong, Mrs., 11
Armstrong, Rose, 262
Armstrong, William, 54
Arnold, Gretta, 268
Arnold, Mrs. W.L., 233
Ashbridge, A.S., 32
Atchley, G.W., 4
Atchley, George, 60
Atherton, 168
Atherton, Clarence, 61, 168
Atherton, J.W., 30
Atkins, Mrs., 164
Atkinson, J.R., 119
Atkinson, Mrs. George, 69
Attenger, F., 37
Atwater, 120
Atwater, Edwin L., 106, 131
Atwater, H.H., 120
Atwater, Mr., 157
Atwater, Mrs., 78
Atwell, John, 171
Aucalbiter, A., 210
Augustine, Greta, 62
Augustine, Mattie, 115
Augustine, S.M., 22, 143, 185, 240, 243
Augustine, Samuel M., 174, 197
Augustine, Winifrede, 60
Austin, E., 75
Austin, Frank, 7
Austin, H.S., 15
Austin, Hiram Spellman, 53
Austin, Hiram, 47, 53
Austin, Mrs., 53
Avens, 23
Avery, Gus D., 245
Avery, Josephine, 27

Avery, Mrs. R.J., 190
Avilla, Joas Silveira, 103
Avilla, Jose S., 107
Avilla, M.V., 21
Avilla, Sherry, 204
Axen, Ida, 93
Ayadoux, Marie, 242
Ayers, Birdie, 97
Ayers, Mrs. A.D., 234
Azavedo, F., 25
Azavedo, Joas, 222
Azevedo, A.S., 206
Azevedo, F.S., 2, 12, 24, 46, 68, 117, 206
Azevedo, M.S., 68
Azevedo, Manuel, 8
Baar, S., 132
Babcock, Helena, 234
Babcock, William F., 234
Babcock, William, 45, 225, 234
Babcock, Willie, 234
Bacci, G., 46
Bach, Charles, 69, 191
Bachr, William Jr., 18
Backer, Rosa, 251
Bacollio, A., 206
Bacon, F.E., 96
Bacon, Mrs. F.C., 188
Baechtael, Gordon, 135
Baggi, J.W., 111
Bailey, F.T., 111, 173, 209
Bailey, H.F., 201
Bailey, Juanita, 62, 200
Bailey, P., 202
Bailey, Pauline, 62, 200
Bailey, Sadie, 203
Bain, Kittie, 74
Bain, Nellie, 168
Baker, C.C., 85
Baker, C.T., 58
Baker, D.E., 111
Baker, F., 93
Baker, Walter, 241
Baldes, Rafael, 188
Bales, George E., 66
Ball, Clara A., 82
Ball, F.F., 239
Ball, Franklin P., 95
Ball, Horace W., 82
Bamber, 102
Bancroft, W.B., 118
Banflemo, M., 132
Bangs, Benjamin, 255
Bannon, Cathrine, 192
Bannon, Jane, 192
Baptiste, A., 25
Baptiste, Anna, 159
Baptiste, F., 92
Baptiste, Mr., 202
Barazili, Antonio, 58
Barbara, Joaquin, 171
Barber, Carrie E., 86

Barber, Hattie, 86
Barber, Hyland E., 86
Barber, Mrs. H.E., 192
Barbie, Annie, 242
Barclay, A.J., 220
Barclay, Mrs., 147
Barclay, Sam, 203
Barclay, Samuel, 61
Bareuchi, Charles, 206
Bargate, George, 55, 158, 162, 158
Baright, Mary E., 189
Barkan, A., 154
Barkan, Adolph, 101
Barker, Annie E.H., 178
Barker, Miss R., 220
Barker, Mrs. D., 233
Barker, Mrs. W., 249
Barker, Mrs., 26
Barlow, Thomas E., 204
Barnard, E., 248
Barnard, Grace, 62
Barnard, Gracie, 200
Barnes, A.M., 171
Barnes, H.H., 194
Barnett, A., 96
Barnett, Jessie E., 73, 105, 126
Barnett, Josiah, 73, 105, 126
Barnett, William J., 73
Barney, C. Roy, 103
Barney, C.S., 26, 39, 117, 156
Barney, Charles S., 8, 78, 103, 104, 141
Barney, Charles, 64
Barney, John W., 26, 78
Barney, Roy, 3, 20, 75
Barnum, N.F., 90, 264
Barnum, Peter, 242
Barofoldi, A., 161
Barone, Belle, 102
Barr, F.H., 173
Barr, Mr., 168
Barr, William, 108, 167, 245, 259, 260
Barr, Willie, 62, 200
Barratt, William, 265, 267
Barrelo, Robert, 249
Barrets, Robert, 222
Barrett, A., 42
Barrett, W., 265
Barrett, W.G., 270
Barros, Barry, 14
Barrows, Joseph, 137
Barrows, Mr., 202
Barry, W.M., 155
Barstow, 30, 105, 246
Barstow, Annie Park, 61
Barstow, Garf, 62, 200
Barstow, Mr., 154
Barstow, Mrs., 154
Barstow, S.F., 169
Bartlett, Edward C., 95

Bartlett, G.H., 51
Bartlett, George, 165
Bartlett, Miss, 234
Bascom, D.I., 60
Basebe, C.E., 98
Basebe, Rosa, 98
Basker, Annie H., 192
Bass, H.B., 146
Bassett, David, 27, 28
Bassett, L.A., 244
Bassett, Laura A., 252
Bassett, Miss C.B., 165
Bassett, Mrs. William, 232
Bassett, William F., 160
Bassett, William, 244, 252
Bassford, J.M. Jr., 29
Bassi, M., 137
Batchelder, Elmer E., 42
Batchelder, K.C., 57
Batchelder, Kate C., 200
Batchelder, Kate, 74
Batchelder, Miss K.C., 27, 35
Batchelder, Miss, 62
Bates, Harry S., 220
Bates, Miss, 112
Bathurst, Angus, 224
Bathurst, Lizzie E., 169
Batista, B., 23
Batten, G.C., 173, 183
Battista, Z.G., 46
Bauer, Frederick H., 20
Baumstark, Ben, 178
Baur, C., 35
Bausman, W.H., 266
Baxter, H.B., 194
Baxter, Joseph A., 43, 45
Bayer, G.E., 183
Bayles, Ida May, 110
Bayley, Nora F., 208
Beach, Alva, 200
Beach, Alva, 62
Beach, Willie, 107
Beale, L.L., 204, 210
Beals, C.W., 170
Bean, A., 115, 117
Bean, Alex, 117
Bean, Ed, 105
Bean, Emma Jane, 117
Bean, James, 181
Bean, Lilla, 7
Bearn, Edwin, 102
Beasley, E.C., 199
Beaton, John J., 22
Beccio, A., 220
Beckendorf, B., 137
Becker, A., 185
Becker, A.R., 192, 196
Becker, Alex R., 40
Becker, Arnold, 40, 43, 196, 258
Becker, C., 237
Becker, Christopher, 88
Becker, G.J., 150, 153, 154

Becker, Louis, 68
Beckhort, Peter N., 58
Beckhuson, Miss M., 227
Becktel, H.W., 242
Bedell, Nellie, 225
Beedle, W.H., 210
Beedy, J., 78
Beeman, E.K., 228
Beeman, William, 134
Beer, Mary M., 27
Beermaker, G.W., 83, 94
Beggs, F., 210
Beggs, Tom J., 188
Beggs, William P., 103
Begley, D., 44, 167
Begley, J., 202
Begley, James, 61
Begley, Peter, 62
Behm, E., 143
Behm, Emanuel, 136
Beirao, Manuel T., 65
Beirao, Manuel, 74
Beisler, George W., 253
Beisler, John H., 198
Beisler, John Henry, 196, 197
Beisler, John, 147, 187, 189, 196, 197, 198, 253
Belgeri, G., 12, 14, 97, 102, 199
Belknap, D.P., 63, 250
Belknap, Marion, 251
Bell, A.F.L., 14
Bell, Arthur F.L., 16
Bell, Catherine, 245
Bell, Emma H., 139
Bell, Frank R., 233
Bell, Julia E., 94
Bell, Philip, 245
Bell, T.B., 145
Bellamy, Sam, 126, 239
Bellingham, Mrs., 97
Bellman, Vincent, 235
Bello, C.S., 206
Bellonde, J.S., 230
Bellow, J.M., 99
Bellrude, 144
Bellrude, J.S., 8, 150, 182, 188
Bemenderfer, C., 111, 123
Bemenderfer, M., 268
Bengston, O.V., 188
Bengton, B.W., 195
Benjamin, E.J., 24
Bennard, Charles, 195
Bennets, John, 192
Bennett, Frank P., 115
Bennett, Mrs. C.M., 115
Benson, C.H., 151, 213, 227, 245
Benson, Charles E., 167
Benson, Charles H., 7, 8
Benson, J., 111
Benson, M., 147
Benzen, L.P., 210

Berdugo, G., 97
Bergman, H., 268
Beri, W., 96
Berkham, Peter N., 214
Berkhart, P.N., 24, 55, 182, 236
Bernardo, M., 206
Bernstein, J., 183
Bernstein, Julius, 68, 188, 189
Berri, E., 214
Berri, Victrix, 214
Berry, Mindora F., 254
Berry, Mindora L., 98
Berry, Mrs. T., 119
Bertram, 157
Bertram, F.W., 129, 155, 164
Bertrand, J.F., 50
Bertrand, Joseph, 23
Bertrand, L., 51
Best, D., 108
Bethune, Ella, 195
Bettacker, James, 233
Betten, H., 9
Betten, Henry, 83, 125, 147
Betten, William, 70
Bettencourt, A., 25
Bettencourt, A.S., 81
Bettencourt, Antonio S., 45
Bettencourt, Frances, 1
Bettencourt, J., 143
Bettencourt, J.E., 1, 103
Bettencourt, John, 15, 199
Bettencourt, Jose M.T., 65
Bettencourt, M.A., 206
Bevier, H.N., 15
Beyries, Victor, 206
Bibby, Augusta, 159
Bibby, Mary, 159
Biber, Annie, 166
Bichard, N., 248
Bichard, Nicholas, 257
Bickerstaff, 229
Bierce, 113
Bierce, A., 85, 88, 91, 93, 95
Bierce, Ambrose, 72
Bierce, R.A., 77
Bigby, J., 82
Bigelow, 171
Bigelow, E.P., 201
Bigelow, Frank, 62, 200
Bigelow, J.F., 130, 186
Bigelow, John F., 154
Bigelow, Mr., 126
Bigelow, Mrs. F.W., 159
Bigelow, S.C., 14, 249, 251
Biggins, 173
Biggins, Honora, 94
Biggins, J.M., 244, 255
Biggins, James M., 185, 190
Biggins, James Michael, 197
Biggins, James, 66, 184
Biggins, Mr., 166
Biggins, T.J., 56

Biggins, Thomas J., 66, 101, 192
Biggins, Thomas Jefferson, 33
Biggins, Thomas, 54, 58, 172
Billings, George E., 36
Billo, George, 78
Birch, Reginald B., 6
Birch, Reginald W., 6
Birch, William A., 6, 65
Birchard, Nicholas, 253
Bird, Mabel, 194, 210
Birmingham, John, 236
Birrillier, L., 239
Bishop, Lillian, 220
Bishop, Mrs. L.A., 248
Bismark, Harry, 157
Bissell, A., 63
Bitter, J.S., 121
Bixby, Lelia E., 115
Black, James, 162
Blackledge, James, 244
Blaeirini, L., 7
Blain, Jane, 120
Blake, Mary E., 166
Blanchard, Rev., 190
Blanding, Mrs. Gordon, 195
Blanding, William, 195
Blaney, A.J., 163
Blankenhorn, George, 200
Blankenhorn, Louis, 105
Blasingame, J.A., 96
Bliel, George, 79
Blink, H., 60
Block, Thomas R., 259
Bloom, A.J., 181, 243
Bloom, Adolph J., 125, 146
Bloom, Adolph, 133
Bloom, James, 78, 84, 108, 109, 117, 119, 125, 133, 146, 228, 243, 262
Bloom, Joe, 119
Bloom, Joseph, 78, 169
Bloom, Josephine, 224
Bloom, Lucia M., 125, 133, 146
Bloom, Poldina, 74
Bloom, Ulysses, 224, 243
Blower, E.J., 192
Blum, Jacob, 72
Blumenthal, Al, 62
Blumenthal, Alfred, 200
Blumenthal, Florence, 62, 199
Blumenthal, H., 221
Blumenthal, M., 9, 106, 128, 142, 163, 178, 190
Blumenthal, Morris, 166
Blumenthal, Rita, 164
Boas, Judah, 67
Boden, Mr., 12
Boden, Mrs., 12
Bodin, A., 260
Bodin, August, 14, 16, 267
Bodin, Gertrude, 252, 254

Body, 19, 112, 115, 127, 128, 135, 155, 216, 223
Boetzear, C., 220
Boggenbare, A., 102
Bogginhan, A., 82
Bogiano, D., 206
Bohm, Al, 32
Boilnan, Miss L., 159
Boland, C.A., 5, 7, 19
Boland, Capt., 60
Boland, Thomas H., 62
Boland, Thomas, 111, 217
Bolini, Manuel, 250
Bolla, Peter, 76
Bollotti, L.B., 265
Bonam, J.B., 194
Bond, Mary A., 159
Bonestell, Louis H., 60
Bonetti, Barbolina M., 121
Bonetti, L., 146
Bonetti, Luca, 4, 121, 150
Bonneau, Clerk, 20, 181
Bonneau, Mrs. Thomas S., 41
Bonneau, T.S., 8, 167
Bonneau, Thomas S., 20, 28, 29, 32, 33, 43, 57, 70, 73, 100, 106, 125, 136, 143, 151, 158, 161, 174, 197, 198, 205, 224, 232, 245, 251, 252, 261
Bonnel, Mrs., 164
Bonney, Belle, 91
Boole, Anna E., 45
Boole, Fred W., 163
Boole, M., 253
Boole, Maude M., 163
Boomer, Mary J., 67, 178
Borau, Mrs., 78
Borba, Mariana, 204
Borbeck, E., 220, 251
Borbeck, H.E., 99
Borel, Antone, 71, 77, 165
Borella, A., 145
Borella, G.A., 258
Borella, Louisa, 92
Boreman, Thomas, 11, 15
Boren, P., 42
Borges, Manuel, 206
Borle, Mr., 233
Bornecke, L., 119
Bosqui, Benjamin, 197
Bossani, J., 15
Bosserman, C.H., 97
Bossi, A., 112
Bossi, Antonio, 28, 100
Bossoni, Joseph, 126
Bost, Eugene, 147
Bostwick, H.P., 105
Bothin, J.C., 67, 207
Botta, Mary De Silva, 5, 11
Bottarini, Charles, 152
Bottini, Batista, 206
Boulware, Grace, 268

Bouquet, Joseph, 159, 161
Bowden, M., 93
Bowen, Fred, 246
Bowen, George, 130
Bowen, M., 96
Bowen, Michael, 220
Bowen, Nellie, 62
Bowers, Annie, 251
Bowers, Ewing, 270
Bowers, Judge, 191, 270
Bowers, S.C., 164, 250, 251
Bowers, Stephen Calhoun, 149
Bowers, T.J., 94
Bowers, W.W., 85, 91, 94
Bowland, J.C., 205
Bowland, J.D., 22
Bowley, Kate, 156
Bowman, Ella, 178
Bowman, Henrietta, 143
Bown, M., 178
Boyce, H.A., 136
Boyd, 148
Boyd, G.D., 155
Boyd, H.C., 28
Boyd, J.D., 32
Boyd, J.F., 257
Boyd, Jane Frances, 106, 107
Boyd, Jessie, 75
Boyd, John F., 4
Boyd, Laura J., 192
Boyd, Mazy, 34
Boyd, Nellie, 195
Boyd, T.P., 227
Boyd, Thomas P., 122, 125, 145, 151
Boyd, Thomas, 213
Boyd, W.J., 50, 137, 151, 213
Boyd, William J., 111, 213
Boyen, A., 44, 56
Boyen, A.N., 202
Boyen, Albert N., 167, 238, 240
Boyen, Albert, 213
Boyen, Dora, 204
Boyen, Edward H., 167, 229, 232
Boyen, Emma, 62, 203
Boyen, Henry, 62, 200
Boyer, 129
Boyle, Carmelita N., 81, 91, 100
Boyle, H., 201
Boyle, Henry, 41
Boyle, Hugh A. Jr., 81
Boyle, Jane, 41, 139
Boyle, Miss Hugh, 194
Boyle, Sidney F., 91
Boyne, A., 11
Boysen, Mary, 35
Brackette, Wallace S., 40
Bradbury, 119
Bradbury, J.L., 98
Bradley, G.F., 123
Bradley, George F., 119

Bradley, James, 33, 35, 37
Bradley, Mrs., 211
Bradley, Thomas, 29
Brady, Annie, 113, 172
Brady, Edward, 100
Brady, J.E., 113, 205
Brady, James B., 240
Brady, James Bernard, 198
Brady, James, 100
Brady, John E., 100, 198
Brady, Maggie Agnes, 198
Brady, Maggie, 100
Brady, Mary, 198
Brady, Mrs., 100
Brady, Peter, 215
Bragg, Mrs., 97
Bralley, Maggie, 175, 177
Bramner, Miss, 164
Branco, A.F., 103
Brander, George L., 268
Brandon, Alfred, 26
Brandt, C., 134
Brandt, H., 51
Brandt, M., 108
Brannan, James, 241
Brauning, John, 242
Bravo, J.D., 64, 69, 112, 145, 162, 164
Bravo, John D., 165, 237
Bravo, Maddalena, 165
Bray, Adella L., 110
Bray, Reginald D., 193
Brazil, 240
Brazil, A., 195, 246
Brazil, A.M., 102
Brazil, Antone, 15
Brazil, Benjamin, 190
Brazil, J.J., 46
Brazil, Katherine, 15
Brazil, Mr., 230
Brazil, P., 188
Bredefeld, Marie, 268
Breen, William, 99
Bremer, William F., 147
Brenna, Mr., 193
Brennan, John H., 67, 186
Brennan, Mr., 10, 187
Brennan, O.M., 191
Brennfleck, M., 150
Brennfleck, Mr., 76
Brennfleck, Mrs. B., 10
Bresack, Portia, 159, 178
Bressnan, Mrs. P., 172
Bresson, 119
Bresson, Alphonse, 211, 212
Bresson, Dominga, 45, 123, 160
Bresson, Joseph, 123
Bresson, Josie, 200
Bresson, Mary Josephine, 42
Bresson, Mrs. J., 248
Bretton, Harry, 77
Bretzel, 32

Breyfogle, Dr., 125
Briare, R.M., 180
Brickwiedel, J.H., 73
Brickwiedel, Mr., 202
Bridge, H., 206
Bridge, H.S., 171
Bridgeman, Laura E., 156
Briel, Mrs. A., 239
Briggs, A., 131, 210
Briggs, A.C., 147, 162
Briggs, Amelia, 230
Briggs, Arthur C., 71, 215
Briggs, August, 164, 171, 195
Briggs, Cassie, 215
Briggs, Emelia, 257
Briggs, Emma, 62, 257
Briggs, Gustav, 257
Briggs, Hattie, 257
Briggs, John R, 255
Briggs, John, 230, 257, 259
Briggs, Lizzie Irene, 209
Briggs, Mr., 151
Briggs, Mrs. Arthur C., 159
Briggs, Mrs. E.E., 246
Briggs, Mrs. L., 208
Briggs, Mrs. M., 253
Briggs, Mrs., 162, 230, 248
Briggs, R.W., 242
Briggs, Ralph, 193
Briggs, William, 230
Brims, Alma, 222, 227
Briones, J., 66
Bristowe, Lizzie, 195
Britton, Joseph, 199
Brizard, Henry F., 208
Broderick, John, 174
Bronce, Manuel D., 82
Bronson, Aimee A., 7
Bronson, Andrew, 239
Brooks, 93
Brooks, B.S., 13, 14, 16
Brooks, Benjamin S., 156
Brooks, George Jr., 268
Brooks, J.F., 108
Brooks, J.T., 102
Brooks, James, 220, 227, 233, 234
Brooks, John Doe, 221
Brooks, John, 140
Brooks, Kate L., 13, 16
Brooks, W., 14
Brooks, Will, 13, 14, 16, 124
Brophy, Joseph, 1776
Brophy, Nicholas, 176
Brosin, Charles, 70, 72, 81, 86, 136, 143, 144, 223
Brown, 42, 119
Brown, A.H., 58
Brown, Amelia, 192
Brown, Andrew, 265, 267
Brown, Arthur M., 193

Brown, Belle C., 34, 38, 89, 180, 200, 244
Brown, C.B., 25
Brown, Charles, 67
Brown, Clyde N., 106, 107, 148
Brown, Dr., 159
Brown, E., 51
Brown, Edmund, 102
Brown, Edward, 265, 267
Brown, Ella M., 246
Brown, Emma, 80
Brown, Flora, 210
Brown, Fred, 7
Brown, G., 164
Brown, G.A., 164
Brown, George, 181, 194
Brown, Grace, 242
Brown, H., 75
Brown, H.B., 37
Brown, J. Dalziel, 242
Brown, J., 204
Brown, J.A., 192
Brown, James, 60, 258
Brown, John A., 132
Brown, Joseph, 75
Brown, M.A., 28, 259
Brown, Mary A., 89, 244
Brown, Miss B.C., 74
Brown, Miss M.J., 182
Brown, Miss, 61
Brown, Mr., 233
Brown, Mrs. C.G., 155
Brown, Mrs. Capt., 183
Brown, Mrs. Clyde N., 148
Brown, Mrs. Dr., 155
Brown, Mrs. J., 194
Brown, Mrs. W.W., 210
Brown, Mrs. William, 178
Brown, Mrs., 164
Brown, Ralph, 81
Brown, S.H., 67, 178
Brown, S.R., 81, 89
Brown, Samuel R., 89
Brown, Tony, 61
Brown, Torey C., 259
Brown, W.O., 43, 217
Brown, Will W., 22
Brown, Will, 147
Brown, William, 184
Browne, D., 78
Browne, Miss A.E., 182
Browning, I., 161
Broz, Frank, 6
Broz, Louisa, 6
Bruce, John, 53
Bruce, Joseph, 176
Bruce, Mr., 85
Bruce, William, 204
Brumer, Robert, 227
Brun, Maria, 232
Brune, Mr., 61
Bruner, Mr., 126

Brunn, C.D., 231
Brunn, Mrs. P., 216
Brunn, P., 213
Brunn, Peter C., 166, 240
Brunn, Peter, 140
Brunner, R., 220
Bruns, H.F., 248
Bruns, Henry F., 115
Bruns, Mr., 234
Bruson, A., 194
Bruton, J., 106
Bryant, Arthur W., 15
Bryen, Mrs. T., 164
Bubac, A.H., 92
Buchanan, A., 99
Buchanan, E.Y., 152
Buchanan, Henrietta J., 152
Buchanan, J.J., 113
Buchanan, John, 114
Buchanan, Mrs. J., 102
Buchanan, Mrs. O., 90
Buchanan, O., 90
Buckelew, Martha, 79
Bucken, G.F., 265, 267
Bucker, Carrie, 194
Buckley, Catherine, 240
Buckley, Katie, 240
Buckley, Mary, 108
Bueler, Cecilia, 239
Buelna, Octavia, 215
Buhne, Mrs. A.H., 194
Buker, Charles, 89, 199
Bulin, Miss Sal, 220
Bullard, Millie, 26
Bullard, Mrs., 248
Bullis, Catherine, 36, 52
Bullis, R., 4, 98, 253, 260
Bullis, Richard, 175, 244
Bullotti, Vergillo, 195
Bulotti, 178
Bulotti, V., 75
Buloz, Marianne, 233
Bulter, Miss J., 195
Buncy, 105
Bundy, 26
Bundy, J., 78
Bundy, Jessie E., 159
Bundy, Jessie, 161
Bunker, Charles D., 67
Bunker, Edward A., 67
Bunker, H.C., 67, 195
Bunker, Susie, 166
Bunn, Frances E., 216
Bunn, George, 69, 163, 165, 210
Bunn, Mrs. George, 230
Bunn, Nellie, 4, 64, 69
Bunnell, J.S., 134
Burbank, D.B., 146
Burbank, E., 266
Burbank, George W., 2, 8, 167
Burdell, Dr., 59, 253, 268
Burdell, Galen, 24

Burdell, J.B., 147, 171
Burdell, James B., 132, 143, 204, 244
Burdell, James, 269
Burdell, Mabel, 59, 244
Burdell, Mrs. S., 48
Burdell, Mrs. Sr., 268
Burgeson, 114
Burgess, William, 178, 192
Burgin, J.F., 38
Burgle, E., 137
Burgle, Eugene, 134, 140
Burke, 93
Burke, B.K., 176
Burke, Dr., 170
Burke, H., 17
Burke, J.T., 7
Burke, Mr., 8
Burke, Mrs. John, 251
Burke, T., 66
Burke, W., 265, 267
Burley, 202
Burmeister, O., 37, 144
Burnett, Charles, 265, 267
Burnett, H.D., 12
Burns, Elizabeth, 76
Burns, Ellen, 159
Burns, Emma, 76
Burns, Frank J., 76
Burns, J.F., 76
Burns, M., 32
Burns, Mrs. John, 237
Burns, Mrs. P., 87
Burns, Mrs., 145
Burreias, M., 147
Burrell, Mrs. P.F., 192
Burrell, Mrs. P.T., 243
Burress, Mrs. John E., 143
Burrey, Charles E., 182
Burrey, Charles, 80
Burris, Frank, 57
Burris, H., 134
Burrows, Frank D., 164
Burry, Mamie, 85
Burry, Valentine, 85
Burtchaell, 152
Burtchaell, Annie, 120
Burtchaell, Bert, 61, 62, 200
Burtchaell, Mr., 26
Burtchaell, Mrs. John, 120, 122
Burtchaell, P.T., 31, 38, 79, 120, 167
Burtchaell, William, 122
Burten, B., 206
Burton, Mrs. C.F., 63
Bury, Mamie, 116
Bury, Mary E., 139
Busini, Mr., 234
Bustin, F., 54
Bustin, F.J., 202
Bustin, J., 103
Bustin, J.F., 202

Bustin, John T., 167
Bustin, Mary A., 1
Bustude, Miss, 220
Buthman, J., 213
Buthman, Julius, 53
Butler, Adeline, 192
Butler, E., 26
Butler, George E., 67, 187
Butler, George, 50
Butler, J., 134
Butler, John W., 47
Butler, M., 4, 206
Butler, Michael, 246
Butler, Mrs. George, 157
Butler, Thomas F., 15
Butterfield, L.H., 42
Butterworth, Emma, 161, 222, 248
Butterworth, Mr., 202
Butterworth, William T., 100
Buttner, Lillie, 76
Buyers, 99
Byers, Annie E., 146
Byers, Ellen, 146
Byers, John, 146
Byers, Miss A., 240, 244
Byers, R.E., 246
Byers, Robert J., 146
Byers, Robert, 192
Byrne, C.H., 49
Byrne, Charles, 7
Byrne, J.D., 7
Byrne, J.E., 190
Byrne, M., 2
Byrne, Mary, 204
Byrnes, Bridget, 239
Byrnes, John, 239
Byrnes, Mary, 157
Cabral, Joao De Azevedo, 7
Cabral, John, 68, 186
Cabrall, Rosie, 2
Cadra, Rosi, 28
Caesar, Annie, 201
Caesar, J.S., 77
Caesar, Joseph Silvester, 23
Caesar, Joseph, 26
Caesar, W., 250
Caesar, William, 4, 223, 255
Cahill, James, 215
Cahoon, C.O., 164
Cain, Sarah, 58, 78
Cain, Thomas, 58, 78
Calahan, Hannah L., 20
Caldwell, Dr., 129
Caldwell, Jessie, 245
Calin, Aaron, 118
Callaghan, Mrs. Francis, 195
Callan, Michael, 160
Callan, Mrs. E.J., 113
Callender, Charles H., 201
Callestro, Miss M., 93
Callopy, Mr., 210

Callou, Mrs. E.J., 93
Camehl, S. Louise, 150
Cameron, Carroll G., 249
Camlin, T.J., 96
Camm, J.L., 247
Camm, L.J., 177
Camm, S., 166
Campbell, Donald Y., 21, 48, 186
Campbell, H.C., 172, 186, 193, 263, 251
Campbell, Henry C., 249
Candida, M., 121
Candido, N., 137
Candido, Umbelina, 258
Candolfi, P., 239
Caneereao, Cath, 25
Cannara, Frank, 155
Cannon, John F., 155
Cannon, Mamie, 220
Cantel, L., 172
Cantelen, Marie, 220
Cantell, Henrietta, 51
Cantwell, Mrs. J.C., 208
Caplain, Hannah, 220
Caplice, Edmund, 67
Cappelmann, Anna A., 169
Carater, General, 191
Carazean, 75
Carberry, Patrick, 73
Carder, Kate, 204
Cardoza, Clara Peirera, 7
Carechellow, Kate, 51
Carew, John, 63
Carey, James A., 3
Carey, James, 132, 134
Carey, K., 18
Carey, Miss K., 123
Carey, Mrs. K., 123
Carleton, J.M., 131
Carlson, T., 66
Carlton, Mary, 123
Carlton, Theo., 268
Carmichael, F.A., 236
Carmichael, Mrs. F.A., 236
Carmody, Annie, 48
Carmon, William, 69
Carnahan, W.M., 192
Carpenter, E.S., 206
Carpenter, G., 134
Carpenter, Grace, 159, 199
Carpenter, L.G., 144
Carpenter, Mr., 214
Carr, Carmichael, 126
Carr, H.P., 121
Carr, Mark, 16
Carr, Richard, 122
Carrigan, Andrew, 97
Carrigan, Clarence, 97
Carrigan, John, 97
Carrigan, Joseph, 97
Carrigan, L., 173

Carrigan, Louis R., 95, 97, 212
Carrigan, Louis, 119
Carrigan, Miss, 97
Carrigan, Mrs. Louis, 119
Carrigan, William, 97
Carroll, 109, 114
Carroll, C., 18
Carroll, Dennis, 195
Carroll, Fred H., 246
Carroll, Henry, 215
Carroll, Mike, 230
Carroll, Mrs. E.H., 178
Carroll, Nellie Paull, 161
Carroll, P., 87
Carroll, Thomas, 17
Carson, H., 93
Carter, Mary, 178
Carter, Miss U., 183
Cary, Katie, 119
Carzalleras, 240
Casarotte, Charles, 16
Case, A.B., 43, 45, 146, 151
Case, Arlo V., 143
Case, F., 242
Cassaday, Sarah, 116
Cassans, H., 131
Cassans, Henry, 104
Cassen, Andrew, 247
Cassidy, John, 148
Cassou, H., 37, 141, 195, 237
Castigan, A.B., 10
Castro, Dave, 93
Castro, Louisa, 157
Cattymenos, 2
Cauzza, 58
Cauzza, J.B., 2, 56, 63, 87, 226
Caveral, Jose, 183
Cayestri, A., 54
Cerini, Angelina, 80
Chabot, Mrs. Reni, 251
Chaddick, Miss R., 201
Chadwick, F.R., 77
Chadwick, G., 18
Chais, P., 51
Chaix, Adrien, 158
Chalewees, Miss A., 201
Chambers, Emma, 164, 173
Chambers, J.P., 85, 134, 201
Chambers, John P., 201
Chambers, S., 75
Chancy, Peter, 60
Chandler, Kate A., 213
Chandler, Miss K.A., 16, 34
Chapman, Cole, 248
Chapman, Harvey W., 210, 240
Chapman, Henry W., 234
Chapman, R., 177
Chapman, Russell, 202, 246
Chappalear, Alice, 200
Chappari, G., 67
Charlebois, David, 209
Charlebois, Mrs. David, 209

Charles, Mabel, 157
Charras, J., 54
Chase, Bertha C., 192
Chase, Charles M., 156
Chase, Miss, 226
Chassels, William, 162
Chauncy, H.M., 262
Check, Donald A., 201
Cheda, 73, 146
Cheda, A., 35
Cheda, E.S., 65
Cheda, Elvezio S., 152
Cheda, Iride, 62, 200
Cheda, Livio H., 162
Cheda, S.H., 232, 249, 254, 263
Cheney, Miss, 140
Cheney, Sadie C., 34
Cherry, Addie C., 246
Cheval, Jos., 206
Chevers, Florens, 39, 40
Chevers, Helen F., 67
Chick, A.G., 227
Chick, A.J., 151
Chick, Donald A., 67
Chick, Donald E., 222
Childrens, Hon., 63
Chisholm, C., 147
Chisholm, Christopher, 197
Chittenden, Charles R., 65
Chittenden, G.E., 40
Choynski, Maurice A., 12, 13
Christensen, C., 18, 255
Christensen, Martin, 159
Christianson, James, 49
Christieson, 110, 140
Christieson, J.P., 4, 9, 77, 140
Christieson, James P., 165
Christieson, Marks, 171
Christieson, Wood, 40
Christoffer, Niels, 178
Christopher, Telfer, 223
Christopher, Tillie, 259
Christopherson, I., 268
Christopherson, Neil, 213
Church, Adeline, 22
Church, Herman, 238
Civianno, Jose, 195
Clancy, Julia, 82
Clancy, Peter, 252, 253
Clapp, Charles, 78
Clark, A.C., 33
Clark, Catherine, 75
Clark, Estella, 67
Clark, Ethel L., 248
Clark, F.L., 25, 28
Clark, Frank, 16
Clark, Gordon, 67
Clark, Harry, 148
Clark, Helena, 201, 220
Clark, J.B., 99
Clark, J.H., 82
Clark, James, 148

Clark, John, 67, 148
Clark, M., 119, 123
Clark, Mary, 119
Clark, Miss A.M., 192
Clark, Miss H., 11
Clark, Miss M., 11
Clark, Mr., 11, 202
Clark, Mrs. B., 220
Clarke, Charles, 200
Clarke, Edw. G., 201
Clarke, Mrs. Edward G., 210
Clary, Father, 206
Claudianos, Mrs., 186
Claussen, H., 183, 245
Claussen, H.P., 16
Claussen, Henry, 184
Claussen, Mrs., 183
Claussen, P.H., 84
Claussen, P.H.C., 146
Claussen, W.D., 269
Clayton, Mrs., 26
Clearwater, D.D., 247
Clearwater, Daniel, 244
Cleary, Mr., 130
Cleir, Mrs. William, 48
Clementina, Mes. V., 183
Clemmer, C., 232, 235
Clemmer, Charles, 236
Clifford, Harold, 62, 200
Clifford, May, 61
Clifford, R., 203
Clifford, Reginald, 62
Close, Bessie, 234
Close, Mrs. D., 220
Close, Mrs., 233
Clough, J.A., 191
Cluver, Lena, 34, 80
Cluver, Louise, 27, 34, 80
Clyne, Mrs., 192
Coan-Hambly, Mrs., 161
Coarch, John, 220
Cobb, A. Jr., 238
Cobb, H.A. Jr., 238, 240
Cobb, H.A., 12, 107, 146, 180, 244
Cobb, Henry Alfred, 57, 73
Cobb, M., 95
Cobb, M.C., 12
Cobb, Melvina C., 13, 57, 73
Cobball, A., 4
Cobden, Mr., 3
Cochrane, 175
Cochrane, D.A., 103
Cochrane, J.W., 26, 44, 145
Cochrane, James W., 8, 11, 13, 29, 31, 83, 109, 125, 129, 134, 137, 146, 158, 165, 167, 171, 197, 209, 237, 244
Cochrane, John T., 6, 108
Cochrane, M.A., 260
Cochrane, M.F., 12, 66, 71, 110, 114, 168, 243, 254, 267

Cochrane, Mr., 41, 55, 101, 252
Cochrane, Mrs. P.H., 234
Cochrane, Mrs., 101, 175
Cochrane, P., 96
Cochrane, P.H., 50, 126, 234
Codoni, G., 146
Codoni, G.A., 16, 242
Codoni, J.J., 151
Codoni, Quinto, 167, 182
Codoni, Silvia, 151
Coffin, H.J., 48
Coffin, James A., 201
Coffin, James, 16, 189, 201
Coffin, Joe, 93
Coffin, Miss, 173
Cohen, B., 247
Cohen, Miss B., 247
Cohen, Miss C., 233
Cohen, Mr. 26
Cohen, Mrs., 26
Coit, Mr., 49
Coit, Mrs. M., 143
Coit, Mrs., 99, 145
Colann, M., 106
Cole, Charles M., 40
Cole, Kitty W., 180
Coleman, Carleton, 132
Coleman, Carrie M.P., 132, 163
Coleman, J.W., 90
Coleman, James V., 63
Coleman, John, 244
Coleman, L.B., 25
Coleman, Luther B., 29
Coleman, Mrs. C.M.P., 67
Coleman, Robert L., 53, 54, 58, 132, 155, 163
Coleman, W.P., 247
Coleman, W.T., 192, 228
Coleman, William T., 114, 120, 127, 128, 132, 191
Coll, Frank, 73
Collapy, G.M., 161
Collin, H.J., 42
Collins, C., 64, 72
Collins, C.D., 18
Collins, C.S., 75
Collins, Carrie E., 34
Collins, Carrie, 39, 174, 213
Collins, Catherine, 22, 23, 49, 55, 65, 77, 81, 89
Collins, E.M., 15
Collins, Fritz, 205
Collins, Hugh, 204, 205
Collins, Jeremiah, 263
Collins, John, 176, 215
Collins, Mary Alice, 198
Collins, Mary, 237
Collins, Miss P., 11
Collins, Mrs. H., 100
Collister, Thomas, 147
Collum, M., 160
Collurs, Ellen, 65

Collut, Elvina, 171
Colton, 132
Colton, Minnie, 268
Colwell, Jessie, 201, 230
Commonn, Annie V., 153
Conant, Russell, 241
Concusing, Mrs., 234
Condoni, G., 4
Conendt, A.L., 173
Conick, John, 267
Conklin, A.L., 266
Conklin, E., 97
Conley, Ada, 220
Conley, G.H., 93
Conley, George A., 182
Conley, William P., 247
Conly, M., 82
Connell, Eugene, 61, 181
Connell, J.O., 84
Connell, Morris, 67
Connell, N., 82
Connell, R.R., 125, 220
Connell, Richard R., 74
Connell, Richard, 176
Connell, Thomas, 176
Connelly, James, 215
Connelly, M.D., 237
Connelly, Mary, 247
Connelly, Mrs. M., 258
Connelly, Mrs. T., 201
Connelly, P.D., 144, 146
Conner, Albert S., 164
Connolly, A., 145
Connolly, Andrew, 205
Connolly, Annie, 243
Connolly, James, 215
Connolly, M., 27, 212
Connolly, P.D., 126, 145, 212
Connolly, Patrick D., 117
Connolly, William, 239
Conrad, Francis, 148
Conrad, J.H., 171
Conradson, Oscar, 58, 63
Conroy, Mrs., 204
Constant, Manuel, 81, 107, 116, 243
Constantini, R., 144
Contehuen, Marie, 220
Conterno, Miss N.E., 144
Contreas, Mrs. J., 188
Convery, 196
Conway, M.J., 61, 151, 266
Conway, Maggie, 171
Conway, Malana, 192, 234
Conway, Miles J., 149
Coogan, T.C., 31
Cook, Catherine W., 251
Cook, Edith, 179
Cook, H.N., 179
Cook, May, 156
Cook, Miss H.W., 144
Cook, Mrs. J., 204

Cookson, H., 206
Cooley, M., 137
Coop, Jane, 50
Cooper, Mary, 173
Copa, M., 102, 137
Cope, F.J., 224
Corbaley, Bert, 204
Corbaley, C., 203
Corbaley, Charles, 62
Corbaley, Lois, 200
Corbaley, Mrs., 27, 28
Corbaley, W.G., 143, 266
Corbally, Walter, 262
Corbin, Mayne, 62
Corbin, Mrs. William, 171, 178, 240
Corda, John, 68
Corda, Silvio, 76
Cordes, Clara, 62, 199
Cordes, Harry, 62, 200
Cordes, Lillie, 62, 200
Cornell, Richard, 118, 119
Cornell, S., 16
Cornwell, Joella G., 212
Cornwell, Mary S., 40
Cornwell, Mr., 69
Correa, John Enos, 206
Correia, A.V., 60
Correira, Manuel, 266
Corti, Christine, 62, 199
Corwall, 247
Cossa, 144, 206
Costa, A., 137
Costa, E.H., 134
Costello, Elifia, 129
Costello, G., 121
Costello, John, 17
Costigan, A.B., 15
Cotter, R.G., 34
Cottingham, R.T., 8, 80, 85
Cottle, Elmer E., 7
Couick, John, 265
Coulter, C.L., 126
Coulter, George, 67
Coulter, John, 69, 70, 71
Coulter, Olivia, 71
Couran, J., 137
Coursen-Roeckel, Mme., 209
Courtney, P., 60
Cowell, Harry, 85
Cox, E.M., 35, 119, 123
Cox, E.R., 16
Cox, Mr., 75, 80
Crafts, C.W., 78
Cragen, Mrs. R.W., 192
Craig, Annie C., 67
Craig, James, 3
Craig, Mrs. A.G., 204
Crall, George A., 205
Cramer, John D., 174
Crandall, Andy, 48
Crandall, Dollie Maria, 103

Crandall, Maria O., 109
Crandall, Mrs. William O.L., 101
Crandall, W.O.L., 9, 48, 245
Crandall, William O.L., 109
Crane, C.M., 144
Crane, Eliza A.R., 124
Crane, Henry, 198
Crane, James, 148
Crane, Mrs. Byron G., 268
Crane, P., 33
Crane, Peter, 189, 259
Crane, V.T., 121
Crane, William T.S., 265, 267
Crane, William, 198
Crawford, A., 228
Credon, H., 2
Creed, Constable, 57, 59
Creed, J.E., 167, 248
Creed, John E., 174, 245
Cremmings, Harry, 131
Cresalia, M., 54
Crider, J.W., 123
Crimmings, Mr., 196
Crimmings, P.J., 67
Crimmins, Anthony, 44
Crimmins, Henry, 106
Crimmons, 120
Crimmons, H., 120
Crisanti, G., 159
Crisanti, Geralamo, 187, 205
Crisp, 2
Crisp, Frances, 204
Crittenden, C.N., 54
Crittenden, Libbie, 217
Crittenden, Miss M.A., 34, 80
Crockard, Hugh, 67, 151
Crockett, Henry, 210
Crockett, J.B., 208
Crofts, F.E., 187
Crofts, Francis E., 56, 63
Crofts, Francis, 61
Crofts, Mr., 61
Crofts, Mrs. M.L., 178
Croker, A., 108
Cron, C.L., 254
Cron, Charles L., 217
Cronan, John, 74
Crone, Mr., 163
Crook, H.N., 135
Crosbie, W., 7
Crosby, Arthur, 1, 20, 33
Crosby, Mr., 223
Crosby, Mrs. A., 8
Crove, Marin, 200
Crover, Mrs. E., 233
Crowell, Harold W., 201
Crowell, Miss K.M., 165, 171, 204
Crowley, 80
Crowley, Annie, 7
Crowley, Father, 224

Crowley, John, 215
Crowley, Mazie, 204
Crowley, Mr., 26, 51
Crowley, T.J., 20, 31, 40, 52, 73
Crowley, William, 215
Crowne, Maria, 190
Crumpton, Clara, 203
Crumpton, H.J., 173
Cruz, Alexander, 241
Cruz, Alfred, 215
Cudworth, Johanna, 43
Cuiter, Charles E., 159
Culatto, Vincent, 148
Culbertson, S., 92
Cullen, Father, 262
Cullen, Mary, 24, 55, 58, 182, 214, 236
Cullenan, Dennis, 54
Cullie, William, 215
Culver, Charles, 215
Cummings, Ed, 150
Cummings, James, 71
Cumpton, SC., 165
Cunliffe, John, 148
Cunning, I., 92
Cunningham, Aloysius, 215
Cunningham, D.C., 182
Cunningham, Miss, 102
Cunningham, R., 159
Cupid, Samuel, 219
Curlett, Aleck, 200
Curlett, Celia, 229
Curlett, William A. Jr., 229
Curlett, William, 67, 229
Curley, John, 93, 241
Curran, Maggie, 213, 235, 236
Currey, Margaret, 169
Currey, Robert, 62, 200
Currey, T., 60
Currey, Thomas, 140
Curry, John, 67, 187
Curry, Thomas, 201
Curtis, A.R., 63
Curtis, C.W., 102
Curtis, Carlton, 62, 200
Curtis, Elizabeth, 239
Curtis, Ella E., 239
Curtis, Ella Eliza, 239
Curtis, J.F., 22
Curtis, Loomis, 239
Curtis, Miss A., 11
Curtis, Miss M., 11
Curtis, Mr., 126
Curtis, Ralston, 203
Cushing, Grace, 267
Cushing, Harriet R., 169, 193
Cushing, S.B., 147
Cushing, Sidney B., 169, 267
Cusick, James, 56
Cusp, M., 75
Cutter, Mrs. S.C., 178
Cutter, Mrs., 233

Cyphers, C., 96
Cyphus, C., 42
D'Arey, E., 66
D'Hierry, Paul, 10
Da Costa, A., 15
Da Rosa, A., 178
Da Silva, M. DeS., 46
Da Silveira, Marianna J. 148
Dacey, James, 195
Dachlam, Mr., 259
Dado, P., 147
Daggett, John, 55
Dailey, H.T., 239
Dailey, James, 60
Dailey, Michael, 195
Daily, Horace, 37
Dalessi, H., 13, 37, 145
Dalessi, Henry, 107, 161
Dalessi, Mrs. H., 182
Dalton, H., 134
Daly, H., 17
Daly, Helene R., 216
Daly, Thomas, 254
Daniels, J., 40
Daniels, James, 176
Daniels, William, 176
Danner, M.T., 172, 175, 179
Dans, William, 247
Danverkosen, R., 220
Darce, Feliciana, 218
Darcy, P.M., 121
Darden, Mrs. W.H., 85
Darner, Jos. S., 193
Darr, William, 116
Darui, Edvardo, 259
Daus, I., 151
Daus, Isidor, 149, 157, 159, 164, 172, 184, 190, 219, 221, 255, 257, 259
Daus, Susan, 151, 190, 259
Davenport, 56
Davenport, Eddie, 61
Davenport, Edward, 203
Davenport, Grace, 200
Davenport, J.P., 25, 31, 103, 141, 259
Davenport, John P., 48, 260
Davenport, Mr., 202
Daver, Kosen Edward, 67
Daves, Mrs. W.W., 195
Davidson, Charles, 63
Davidson, H.B., 248
Davidson, H.S., 244
Davidson, Helen R., 114
Davidson, J.B., 38
Davidson, James B., 16, 34
Davidson, Mrs. M., 234
Davidson, S.J., 245
Davies, Mary, 3, 268
Davies, Mr., 112
Davies, W.H., 95
Davis, Alice, 226

Davis, B.L., 213, 227
Davis, Dr., 125
Davis, G.W., 210
Davis, H.E., 234
Davis, H.H., 93
Davis, H.M., 243
Davis, Harriet B., 154
Davis, Hattie B., 153
Davis, Henry M., 256
Davis, Hirrel, 200
Davis, J., 178
Davis, J.B.F., 154, 226
Davis, Jennie T., 98
Davis, John, 72, 222, 250
Davis, M., 132
Davis, Miss H.B., 150
Davis, Mr., 145
Davis, Mrs. Andrew M., 222
Davis, Mrs. T.J., 240
Davis, Mrs. W.G., 75
Davis, Mrs. W.W., 159, 222
Davis, Mrs. William W., 165
Davis, Rev., 132
Davis, S.P., 121
Davis, W., 210
Davis, W.H., 30
Davis, W.K., 165
Davis, Winfield S., 187
Davison, D.H.P., 259
Davison, D.V., 240
Davison, H.B., 140, 258
Dawfery, Grace, 159
Dawley, Mr., 202
Dawson, George, 156
Dawson, J., 202
Dawson, Lena B., 228
Dawson, Margaret, 156
Day, George, 62, 200
Day, Ned, 62, 200
Dayton, E., 15, 28, 121
De Azevedo, Constantine T., 18
De Azevedo, F.S., 51, 65
De Azevedo, Francisco S., 179
De Borba, Antone, 39, 59, 156, 168
De Borba, Jose, 168
De Botta, M. DeS., 3
De Fiennes, H.J., 225
De Fiennes, Mary F., 28, 237
De Fiennes, Mary J., 225
De Fiennes, Mr., 146
De Fiennes, Mrs. R., 235
De Fiennes, Rudolph H., 220
De Frieze, P.A., 12, 32, 98
De Ghetaldi, Emil, 36
De La Montanya, H., 68
De Lacy, John, 199
De Metz, Ed, 62
De Metz, Edward, 200
De Ramos, A.E., 145
De Ramos, Anna E., 165
De Romero, Juan, 21

De Rosa, A, 188
De Rosa, Roque, 227
De Rosas, Domingo G., 14, 16
De Roza, Francisca Maria, 124
De Silva, 111
De Slaef, M., 269
De Souza, 111
De Souza, Manoel S., 116
De Souza, Maria E., 208
De Souza, Marie, 175
De Souza, Mrs. George, 230
De Souza, S.F., 127
De St. Germain, 93
De St. Maurice, Charles, 268
De St. Maurice, Gertrude, 268
De Veechi, P., 78
De Zapata, Maria Vila, 195
Deakin, Frederick H., 212
Dealy, E.V., 23
Dean, Isabella, 52
Dean, Peter, 146
Dearborn, Isabelle, 178
Deas, W.B., 15, 123
Deasy, Maggie, 204
Decker, Alice, 170
Decker, Miss, 180
Decker, Von De George, 178
Deering, 43
Deffebach, 236
Deffebach, J.O., 233
Deffebach, Jessie O., 108, 247, 249
Deffebach, M., 249
Deffebach, M.M., 81, 226
Deffebach, Mary M., 247, 258
Deffebach, Matilda, 182
Del Grosse, A., 60
Del Grosso, L., 46
Delaney, Mrs., 159, 183
Delcroix, Mrs. J., 206
Dellaven, Josie D., 220
Delmas, 197
DeLong, 99, 167, 247, 268
DeLong, Charles, 235, 237
DeLong, F.C., 59, 71, 72, 110, 112, 154, 174, 183, 190, 217, 262, 264
DeLong, Florence, 61, 268
DeLong, Frank C., 110, 219, 263
DeLong, Frank, 60
DeLong, George, 61, 181, 236
DeLong, Mr., 27, 101, 254
DeLong, Mrs., 29
Delpointi, A., 121
Delze, A.C., 161
DeManuel, E.T., 46
Demery, L., 106
Demetriatas, Vrasius, 176
Dempsey, E., 149
Dempsey, Joseph, 241
Dempsey, Minnie L., 82
Deniston, Maggie, 201

Denman, Ezekiel, 266
Denn, Nellie, 234
Dennery, Mrs. W., 139
Dennery, Winifred, 136
Dennis, M.E., 99
Dennison, Andrew, 3
Denson, S.C., 263
Des Nevos, M.F., 137
Deschler, Barbara, 130
DeSousa, J.A., 60
DeValin, George H., 227
DeValin, Mrs. E.E., 48
DeValin, W.H., 48
Devoe, H.H., 264
DeVoto, L.A., 245
DeVoto, Louis A., 74
DeVoto, Louis, 167, 269
Dexter, C.H., 106, 180
Dexter, Charles, H., 173
Deyony, Mrs., 251
Dias, 240
Dias, John S., 246
Dias, John, 76
Dias, Mr., 230
Diazen, A.F., 46
Dick, Nellie M., 194
Dickenson, Mr., 76
Dickenson, Mrs., 76
Dickinson, J.H., 51, 87, 173
Dickinson, John H., 245
Dickinson, Miss M., 227
Dickman, T., 51
Dickmann, 15
Dickow, 140
Dickow, Robert, 137
Dickson, Edwin, 78
Dickson, George E., 160
Dickson, George, 78, 109
Dickson, J.C., 175, 179, 240
Dickson, Mariah H., 220
Dickson, Robert, 189
Dickson, Taylor, 45
Dickson, W.J., 146
Dieckman, P., 249
Dietz, F., 141
Diggins, A.C., 3, 128, 135, 269
Dilk, Dr., 72
Dille, E. ER., 256
Dillon, Annie, 182
Dillon, George, 4
Dillon, Mary, 99
Dimock, F.H., 81, 83, 89
Dimock, Frank H., 33
Dimock, Jennie, 33, 81, 83, 89
Dinsmore, Paul, 161
Dioney, L.H., 258
Divier, Charles, 195
Dixheimer, John, 203
Dixon, Bessie, 143
Dixon, Frank, 230
Dixon, Marian, 143
Dixon, Mrs. Frank, 195

Doble, R. McF., 194, 218
Dodge, 59
Dodge, A.H., 144, 210
Dodge, Airmet H., 147
Dodge, G.M., 8
Dodge, George M., 4, 142
Doe, James, 162
Doe, Jane, 29
Doe, John, 29, 30, 86, 162, 214
Doherty, Emma, 42
Doherty, Mrs. P.E., 244
Dola, Miss J.M., 195
Dolan, Mary, 40
Dolcini, M., 127
Dole, Charles, 241
Dole, Raymond, 241
Dollar, Grace, 62, 199
Dollar, Janet, 200
Dollar, Mary, 200
Dollar, May, 62, 200
Dollar, Melville, 62, 200
Dollar, Stanley, 62
Dollores, Mr., 248
Dolly, H., 119
Domergue, G., 245
Domergue, Gaston, 173, 238
Domett, Ellen M., 156
Domett, Emma E., 156
Domingo, Joe, 230
Domingo, Jos., 192, 206
Domingo, Jose, 242
Domingo, M., 111
Domingo, Mamie, 247
Domingo, Mary, 259
Donahoe, Rebecca, 60
Donahue, Belle W., 121
Donahue, Belle, 236
Donahue, Isabel, 65
Donahue, James M., 5, 19, 20, 22, 23, 24, 28, 32, 38, 39, 42, 49, 51, 55, 64, 65, 70, 72, 77, 81, 102, 119, 121, 124, 127, 130, 133
Donahue, Mr., 87
Donahue, Mrs. J.M., 221
Donahue, Mrs., 11, 59
Donahue, R., 51, 244
Donahue, Richard, 233, 235, 238, 248, 255
Donahue, Thomas, 39
Donaldson, James, 111, 116
Dondero, G.B., 104, 121
Donnell, Henry C., 251
Donnelly, Alice, 201
Donnelly, Andrew, 196, 232
Donnelly, D., 132
Donnolly, Andrew, 209
Donohoe, Eliza R., 248
Donohoe, Marie Paule, 180
Donohue, Dennis Jr., 172, 226, 232
Donohue, Dennis, 186, 248

Donohue, Mr., 202
Donovan, Catherine, 208
Donovan, James, 208
Donovan, M., 230
Donzel, A.J., 159
Doody, Georgie, 200
Doolittle, J.E., 160
Doon, Lee, 79, 139
Dore, M., 129, 145
Dore, Mrs. Charles, 187
Dorr, William, 19, 79, 115
Dorsey, J.W., 207
Dotters, Emma E., 193
Doub, Val, 60, 191
Dougherty, Annie Baptist, 190
Dougherty, Hugh, 148
Dougherty, Marchie, 203
Dougherty, Marcia, 61
Dougherty, Millie, 61
Dougherty, Mr., 261
Dougherty, Mrs. T.E., 190
Dougherty, Mrs. W.F., 49
Dougherty, Sherman, 62, 200
Dougherty, W.F., 31, 38, 49, 50, 55, 126, 142, 167
Doughty, John, 95
Douglas, James, 15, 265, 267
Douglass, David, 147
Dow, George A., 220
Dowd, C.J., 147
Dowd, Charles J., 95
Dowd, Charles, 207
Dowden, John, 222, 248
Dowling, Jane T., 31
Dowling, Miss, 16
Downey, James, 180, 197, 222
Downing, Henry, 231
Downing, W.H., 214
Doyle, F.E., 144
Doyle, James, 247
Doyle, Thomas, 234
Doyle, William, 148
Drahm, Carl, 61, 203
Drake, Charles S., 7
Drake, Hester A., 57, 59
Drake, Olive, 81
Dreypolcher, Frederick, 178
Dreypolcher, W., 146
Driscoll, M.J., 259
Driscoll, May, 62
Du Jardin, L., 41
Du Reis, S., 15
Duarte, A., 12, 46
Duarte, Frank S., 102, 126
DuBois, 244
DuBois, 75, 103
DuBois, Charles, 209
DuBois, Dr., 162
DuBois, E., 25, 116, 146, 233
DuBois, Elijah, 226, 250, 255, 257, 260

DuBois, Elisha, 29, 193, 205, 217, 226, 245, 250, 255, 257, 260
DuBois, Eliza, 217
DuBois, Mrs. Charles, 26
DuBois, Rosena L., 3
Dudley, M.C., 24
Duff, Mrs., 178
Duffey, Thomas J., 67
Dufficy, Edwina J., 199
Dufficy, George W., 127
Dufficy, Josephine, 151
Dufficy, Judge, 1, 127
Dufficy, Justice, 26
Dufficy, M.C., 8, 30, 145, 166, 209, 266
Dufficy, Miss A., 201
Dufficy, Miss E., 74
Dufficy, Miss E.J., 35
Dufficy, Miss, 62
Dufficy, Mrs., 1
Dufficy, Rafael, 1
Dufficy, Veronica A., 196
Duffield, V.C., 94
Duffy, Julia, 158
Duffy, P.E., 119, 125, 131, 142, 146, 158
Duffy, Ray, 62, 199
Duffy, T.J., 188
Duffy, W., 159
Duggan, M., 129
Duggan, Sarah, 127
Dulip, J.M., 228
Dumond, Annie, 178
Dunand, Edward, 200
Dunand, George, 200
Dunand, Maurice, 200
Dunard, Lena M., 237
Dunaud, L.F., 88
Dunbar, Jennie M., 78
Dunbar, John, 165
Dunbar, L., 173
Dunbar, L.L., 207
Dunbar, Louis L., 78
Duncan, John, 216
Duncan, Robert L., 121, 122
Dunn, John, 67, 183
Dunn, Mr., 181
Dunne, Frank, 76
Dunon, John, 165
Duperyraux, B., 145
Duptry, J., 178
Duran, Mamie, 156
Duree, Charles, 178
Duree, Robert, 87
Dutra, 217
Dutra, E., 196
Dutra, M., 196
Dutra, M.D., 21
Dutra, Manuel S., 260
Dutran, M., 18
Dutton, Ermina, 159

Dutton, W., 186, 226
Dutton, Warren, 53, 95, 158, 248, 251
Dwinelle, C.H., 96
Dwinelle, Charles H., 89
Dwinelle, Charles, 92
Dwyer, John, 176
Dwyer, William, 44, 178
Earhart, P.L., 251
Earl, 5
Earl, W.E., 132, 222
Earl, William E., 219
Earl, William, 77
Easkoot, A.D., 4
Easting, J.M., 210
Eastland, Alice L., 120, 158
Eastland, J.G., 44
Eastland, Van Leer, 115, 120
Eastman, Harriet A., 249
Eastman, Mary, 161
Eastman, William H., 249
Eastman, William, 201
Eastman, Willie, 62
Easton, W., 172
Easton, Wendell, 6, 65, 78, 88, 92, 160, 171
Eaton, Darwin G., 180
Ebele, H., 121
Ebele, Henry, 242
Eckelman, Paul H., 171
Eckels, S., 254
Eckley, J.W., 264
Eddy, Mabel, 77
Eden, B., 96
Eden, Coroner, 13, 17, 19, 21, 30, 54, 70, 87, 90, 102, 104, 112, 127, 128, 135, 155, 161, 175, 188, 196, 206, 216, 217, 223, 247, 256, 257
Eden, E., 8, 35, 68, 72, 124, 144, 167, 213, 245, 253, 266
Eden, Edward, 3, 22, 30, 39, 52, 60, 63, 127, 134, 147, 200, 252, 253
Eden, Mamie, 268
Eden, S., 54, 56, 202
Eden, Stephen, 151, 227
Eden, Undertaker, 262, 265
Eden, William, 137
Edgar, J.C., 84
Edmeads, Elizabeth, 204
Edminster, Jessie, 84
Edward, William, 43, 143
Edwards, 41, 143
Edwards, Emanuel, 166
Edwards, Mrs. Legnia, 173
Eged, F., 49
Egera, M., 25
Ehlers, H., 144
Ehlers, Henry, 84
Ehman, Elizabeth, 76
Eickhoff, 194

Eickhoff, Edward, 83
Eickhoff, George, 83
Eickhoff, Henry, 83, 88
Eickhoff, M., 83, 89, 113, 150
Eickhoff, M.M., 150
Eickhoff, M.W., 89, 93, 113, 150, 178
Eickhoff, Magdalena, 93, 178, 220, 221
Eickhoff, Melocene W., 220, 221
Eickhoff, Mrs. Henry, 234
Eistner, Charles E., 242
Eklund, Mrs. J.P., 54
Eldridge, J.O., 199
Elliott, 49
Elliott, A.G., 263
Elliott, Adam G., 204
Elliott, Capt., 56
Elliott, E.M., 75
Elliott, Fred, 17
Elliott, J.P., 263
Elliott, Mrs. Thomas, 227
Elliott, N., 56, 202
Elliott, Pierce J., 24, 72, 73
Elliott, Ralph, 200
Elliott, Thomas, 234
Elliott, Tom, 83
Elliott, Vivan Pearl, 65
Elliott, W., 202
Elliott, W.W., 30, 35
Elliott, Walter, 62
Elliott, William, 93, 143, 201
Elliott, Zalie J., 43, 45
Ellis, C.L., 51
Ellis, J.V., 25
Ellis, Jennie, 197
Ellison, C.H., 236
Ellison, Surveyor, 4
Ellsworth, Ella A., 172
Ellsworth, L.R., 170
Ellsworth, Maggie, 235
Ellsworth, T., 170
Ellsworth, Timothy, 162
Elmerich, Anton, 42, 45
Elmerich, Harry, 199
Elmerich, Josephine, 45
Elmquist, G.E., 93
Eloesser, Leo, 6
Emerson, C.H., 46
Emerson, D.W., 196
Emerson, Frank, 187
Emerson, L., 213
Emerson, Luther, 46
Emerson, Percy W., 195
Emerson, Percy, 196
Emery, Cordella, 220
Emhoff, N., 137
Emhoff, Nic, 181, 222
Emmett, R., 28
Ench, Frank, 222
Enge, 37

Engel, Emil A., 179
Engel, J.G., 7, 159
Engel, John G., 68
Engelberg, E.A., 175
Engermann, Mrs. Capt., 227
Englefield, 99
English, William D., 125
Engstrom, Miss A.S., 195
Enlow, E.E., 174
Enos, 21, 180
Enos, Aleck, 48, 57
Enos, Catherine, 139
Enos, T., 25
Enright, Thomas, 207
Erease, A., 5
Erickson, Emil, 234
Erutia, Christiana, 39
Erving, A.M., 207
Erving, J.C., 119
Escalle, Ellen, 226
Escalle, J., 145
Escalle, Jean, 181
Escalle, Mrs. J., 84
Escallier, Maurice, 234
Escallier, V., 68
Escobar, J.M., 242
Essner, 168
Essner, Johanna, 55
Essner, M.E., 95
Essner, Mrs., 174
Estelita, Michael, 215
Estey, C.L., 84
Estey, T.H., 84, 146
Estey, Thomas G., 8
Estudillo, Lou, 253
Ettobart, Mary, 258
Eubanks, Calvin, 267
Eubanks, Coloni, 265
Euslu, F., 75
Eustace, D.F., 210
Eustace, Dan, 172
Evans, A.F., 230
Evans, Alexander, 256
Evans, H., 60
Evans, Harry, 86, 87
Evans, Henry, 98, 99, 149, 150, 153, 155, 170, 265, 267
Evans, Mary, 256
Evans, W.D., 84
Evans, W.H., 87
Ewald, Lizzie, 159
Fagan, James, 85, 95, 173, 175
Fagan, Mr., 69
Faggiano, Bob, 168
Faggiano, J.B., 7, 74, 159
Faggiano, Joseph, 61, 181
Faggiano, Rosa, 7
Fagundes, Clara, 86
Fair, J.G., 59
Fairbanks, Frank, 66
Fairbanks, Mary M., 106
Fairbanks, Mrs. W.R., 256

Fairbanks, W.R., 43, 146, 182
Fairbanks, William R., 131
Fais, A.B., 68
Falch, Otto E., 82, 154
Falconar, J.S., 11
Fallon, J.L., 93
Fallon, James L., 113
Fallon, Mrs. J.L., 93
Fallon, T.J., 29, 41, 86, 89, 129, 160, 161, 162, 202, 258
Fallon, Thomas J., 167
Fallon, Tom, 244
Fanning, Emma, 19, 66, 71, 81
Fanning, George F., 1, 27, 155
Farley, Benjamin Thomas, 82
Farley, Miss, 233
Farnum, J., 230
Farquhasson, R., 46
Farrell, Annie, 16, 34
Farrell, Jane, 184
Farrell, Jennie, 16, 34
Farrell, John, 184
Farrell, Martin, 124, 125
Farrell, Mary, 35, 62, 200, 235
Farrell, Miss M., 74
Farrell, Miss, 184
Farrell, Mr., 126
Farrell, Mrs., 85, 147
Farrell, One, 180
Faucrault, E., 269
Faucrault, Josie, 204, 206
Faucrault, Louis, 204
Faure, F., 77
Faust, E., 46, 93
Fay, Charles W., 40
Fay, Dennis, 108
Fechteler, Augustus F., 254
Fechteler, Frank, 112
Fechteler, Lt., 111, 112, 114
Feeney, Ann, 16, 52, 127, 164, 181
Feeney, John B., 67
Feeney, Matthew, 52
Feeney, William, 14
Feintuck, Morris, 29, 67
Fell, Thomas, 251
Fellmann, L., 85
Felt, Cornelia, 220, 233
Felt, Mary C., 263
Felton, Mrs., 187
Ferdinand, H. Carmati, 222
Ferdinando, C., 137
Fereira, Mary, 256
Ferguson, G.A., 2, 12, 17, 18, 24, 71, 122
Ferguson, P.T., 225
Ferguson, Phineas F., 214
Fernandez, M.S., 8
Fernandez, Manuel, 223
Ferran, Alfred, 200
Ferran, Eugene, 200
Ferrea, Stephen, 176

Ferris, John W., 46, 48
Ferry, Louise, 62
Fetheroff, Mrs. Ala L., 32
Fetherston, Mrs. George, 143
Fiedler, Carrie L., 218
Fiedler, Carrie, 34
Fiedler, F., 111, 115, 116, 219, 221
Fiedler, Miss C.L., 16
Fiedler, S.S., 87, 115, 116
Field, Fred, 147
Fife, George S., 178
Figel, Jos., 119, 123
Figora, L., 137
Figuera, N., 5
Filippini, Charles, 128, 245
Filippini, L., 147
Filippo, Pingitore, 173
Finch, B.F., 259
Finch, Sabra A., 34
Fineer, H.M., 119
Finger, H.M., 123
Finlayson, Tom, 200
Finnerty, 10
Finnerty, Ellen, 14
Fiori, Antonio, 1
Fischer, Charles, 175
Fischer, E.A., 82
Fischer, Mrs. Emil, 240
Fish, Alice, 181
Fish, C.H., 181, 243
Fish, Charles H., 167
Fish, Charles, 225
Fish, Hester, 61, 204
Fish, Mrs. Azel, 234
Fish, Mrs. C.H., 181
Fish, Mrs. Charles H., 170
Fish, S., 99
Fisher, 197
Fisher, A., 242
Fisher, A.L., 9
Fisher, A.M. 240
Fisher, Andrew L., 131
Fisher, J.S., 157, 166, 187, 190, 194, 213, 218, 227, 228, 243
Fisher, John, 67
Fisher, M., 42
Fisher, M.C., 171
Fitch, 51, 109, 114
Fitch, Oscar, 113
Fitzgerald, Minnie, 114
Fitzgerald, T.C., 76
Fitzgerald, William, 148
Fitzpatrick, William, 28
Fitzroy, G., 73
Fitzroy, George, 44, 266
Fitzroy, Maud, 3
Fitzroy, Sophia, 73
Fitzsimmons, J., 12, 15
Fitzsimmons, John, 265, 267
Flaherty, Dan, 198
Flaherty, E., 185, 190

Flaherty, Edward, 166
Flaherty, Miss M., 201
Flaherty, Mrs., 267
Flanagan, Daniel, 62
Flanagan, James, 199
Flanagan, Jennie, 110, 112
Flanagan, Lillie, 166
Flanagan, Maggie, 165
Flanagan, Mrs. Thomas, 112
Flanagan, Thomas, 112
Flanagan, William, 24
Flanagan, Willie, 62, 199
Fleisher, Herman, 215
Fleisher, Oscar, 215
Fletcher, Harry, 200
Fletcher, Mrs. C.H., 252
Fleury, Jules, 72
Fliat, J.M., 59
Flick, Lena, 161
Flick, William K., 143
Flint, N., 99
Flint, Ruby, 27, 29
Flood, 171
Flood, A., 66
Flood, J.L., 130, 154, 212
Flops, A., 131
Flores, C., 21
Flouan, W., 97
Floyd, H., 235
Floyd, Henry, 247, 249, 253
Flynn, John, 176
Flynn, Kate, 11
Flynn, Stephen T., 148
Foley, Mary E., 181
Foley, Richard, 210
Folker, George N., 256
Follett, L.A., 132
Fonte, R.C., 265
Foomberg, Mrs. J.M., 227
Forbes, A., 113, 117
Forbes, Charles, 219, 221
Forbes, Edith, 232
Forbes, Madame, 240
Forbes, Mary A., 82
Forbes, Miss E., 171
Forbes, Mrs. Alexander, 232
Ford, Ellen, 98
Ford, Mrs. Edwin, 165
Ford, Mrs., 27
Forrest, Charles, 147
Forrest, Jennie, 124
Forsati, James, 73
Forse, Bessie, 62, 200
Forsell, Carl Albert, 53
Fortin, P., 213, 266
Fortin, Pierre, 92
Fortio, Mr., 11
Fortrell, Thomas, 245
Fortune, Mrs. William, 192
Fortune, W.R., 68
Fortune, William, 252
Foss, J.W., 171, 172, 188
Foss, James W., 45, 175, 186
Foster, A.W., 3, 105
Foster, Charles L., 180
Foster, Constable, 4
Foster, F., 123
Foster, Frank, 30, 225, 248
Foster, J.D., 22
Foster, May A., 3
Foster, Mr., 11, 19, 126
Foster, Mrs., 11, 225
Foster, S., 43, 258
Fostino, Antonio, 207
Fottrell, Thomas, 167
Fowler, Elizabeth Ellen, 79
Fox, 110
Fox, Bern E., 220
Fox, Bernard E., 173
Fox, C.J., 108
Fox, Ed, 252
Fox, Edward, 265, 267
Fox, G.W., 12, 24, 49, 130
Fox, George W., 17, 20, 42, 81
Fox, Irene, 62, 200
Fox, Minnie, 62, 200
Fox, Nathan, 62
Fox, Nathaniel, 200
Fox, Patrick, 230
Fox, S., 151, 170, 202, 232
Fox, Susan, 12, 17, 20, 24, 42, 49, 81, 130
Fox, Thomas H., 171, 252
Frager, S.J., 28
Frajsrtadt, Chaja F., 193
France, W.M., 17
Frances, H., 193
Frances, Harry, 96
Francisco, A.M., 148
Franetta, George, 22, 242
Franetta, J., 30, 48, 146, 257
Franetta, J.F., 35
Franetta, John, 127
Franetta, Mamie, 201
Frank, Capt., 61
Franklin, M., 119
Franks, 40
Franzi, A., 207
Franzioli, D., 27
Frasier, Daniel, 4
Frazer, Manuel C., 249
Frazer, S.J., 25
Frazier, D.S., 84
Frazier, Davie, 87
Frazier, Mae, 182
Frease, A., 51
Frederickson, 28
Fredson, Esther C., 66
Fredson, George, 66
Freeman, W.D., 147
Freese, M., 18
Freis, Ellen, 247
Freitas, J.T., 46
Freitas, M.S., 68
Fremont, M., 99
French, Alice, 181, 201
Freshwaters, Milton, 166
Freud, Emily, 178
Frey, Franz, 3
Freyschlag, Miss, 230
Fricke, C., 40
Fries, Mr., 59
Fritch, George, 30, 64, 66, 67, 71, 77, 207
Fritz, George L., 165
Fritz, H., 202
Frohman, L., 161
Fronk, Edw. B., 173
Fronk, George G., 123, 173
Fronk, George, 48
Frost, J., 51
Frost, Mrs. L., 11
Fuchs, Hugo, 171
Fugazi, J.F., 30
Fugita, Y., 188
Fujito, T., 247
Fuller, Henry, 8
Fuller, M., 51
Fulton, Mrs. J., 181, 192, 195, 210
Furgeson, G.A., 68
Furlong, Amy, 203
Furlong, Arthur, 62
Furlong, Clarence, 200
Furlong, Irving, 199
Furlong, Marjorie, 157
Furlong, Perry, 62
Furlong, R., 8, 81, 106
Furlong, Robert, 54, 56, 57, 160, 167, 229, 233, 245, 252
Furlong, William, 241
Furnance, Nora, 190
Futch, George W., 94
Gabriel, Jose, 21
Gaffney, D., 168
Gaffney, J.J., 185
Gaffney, Miller, 240
Gage, W.S., 254
Galentine, P.W., 235
Galindo, Benedicto, 189
Gallagher, 75, 268
Gallagher, B., 205, 223, 231, 248, 254, 262
Gallagher, Bernard, 195, 196, 209, 232, 238
Gallagher, Catherine, 113, 117, 124
Gallagher, E., 146
Gallagher, Frank, 167
Gallagher, Harry, 210
Gallagher, Hugh, 61, 167
Gallagher, James, 260
Gallagher, John J., 132
Gallagher, M.J., 253
Gallagher, Mrs. P., 87
Gallagher, Nellie R., 218

Gallagher, Nellie, 74
Gallagher, P., 92, 98, 103, 105, 110, 117, 152, 185
Gallagher, Patrick, 174
Galloway, And, 259
Galloway, Florence C., 218
Galloway, Florence, 34
Galrachaer, B., 18
Gambert, Emily, 260
Gambetti, J., 186
Gambetti, Joseph, 22
Gamble, Prof., 220
Gamboni, G., 67
Gamboni, S., 191
Gamet, P., 86
Gannon, 9
Gannon, Col., 189
Gannon, Constable, 94
Gannon, Dennis, 227
Gannon, J., 245
Gannon, Jack, 10, 109
Garaghty, Fred, 176
Garaghty, Joseph, 176
Garcia, 2, 117, 118
Garcia, A.G., 266
Garcia, B., 92
Garcia, D., 54
Garcia, F., 119, 123, 263
Garcia, F.R., 263
Garcia, I., 86
Garcia, Joe, 132, 178
Gardelle, C., 60
Gardelle, Charles, 269
Gardelle, Justa, 55
Gardner, 2
Gardner, Delmore, 62, 201
Gardner, E., 23, 31, 167, 211, 245
Gardner, Edward, 201
Gardner, Edwin, 38, 62
Gardner, J., 12, 108, 110, 164, 188
Gardner, J.H., 105
Gardner, Jacob, 43, 45, 124, 167, 174, 193, 247, 267
Gardner, Justice, 206, 210, 227
Gardner, Mr., 26
Gardner, P., 12
Gardner, Peter, 113, 182, 207
Gardner, S.R., 84
Gardner, Sam, 78
Garrison, John, 62
Garrity, Richard, 87
Garvey, J.F., 212
Garzoli, Arnoldo, 163
Garzoli, Belardo, 163
Garzoli, Correno, 163
Garzoli, Placido, 64
Garzoli, Rosa, 17, 18, 27, 163
Garzoli, William, 17, 18, 163, 188
Gaspar, Jose Cardoza, 195

Gates, Alice A., 35
Gates, Miss A.A., 74, 241
Gates, Miss, 62
Gaudard, A., 258
Gaudaro, Alexis, 117
Gaver, Andrew P., 163
Gaver, John W., 126
Gaver, Mrs. A.P., 102
Gay, C.A., 207
Gay, Charles A., 68
Geary, Emma, 121
Geary, Sarah, 121
Geary, Thomas J., 255
Geary, W.W., 91, 98
Geary, William W., 89, 109
Gedding, Engineer, 17, 19
Gedersen, H.N., 111
Gedge, J., 51
Gehret, A., 37
Geiger, Anna, 168, 262
Geiger, F., 146
Geiger, Fred, 228
Gengenbach, 111
Gensen, H., 46
Genswindt, Mrs. M., 227
Geoghaben, T., 157
Geohogan, L., 230
Geraghty, Edward, 265, 267
Gergerding, Albert, 18
Gericke, A., 85
Gericke, Agnes, 74
Gericke, Anna, 213
Gericke, Miss N., 182
Gerlach, George, 24
Gerlach, William P., 24
Germaine, J.R., 49
Ghidossa, Misunio, 76
Giacomini, A., 87, 177, 181, 188, 211, 233
Giacomini, Angelo, 164, 224
Giacomini, G., 207
Giacomini, J., 149
Giacomini, J.B., 88
Giacomini, John, 108, 109, 129, 150, 153, 170, 248
Giacomini, Mr., 101
Giacomini, T., 97
Gibbons, A.S., 243, 246
Gibbons, Dr., 259
Gibney, Hallie, 62
Gibson, A., 2
Gibson, J.C., 75, 79, 81, 85, 247, 250, 252
Gibson, John C., 100
Gibson, R.E., 85
Gieske, 44, 45
Gieske, H.C., 31, 244, 266
Gieske, Henry C., 38
Gieske, Henry, 25, 232
Gieske, J.C., 104
Gieske, Johann C., 104
Gieske, Mrs. H.C., 244

Gilbert, Clifford A., 210
Giler, John, 241
Gilfilan, Walter A., 192
Gill, Eugene, 215
Gill, Walter, 215
Gill, William L., 228
Gilleran, Mrs., 11
Gilligan, M., 69, 108, 240
Gilligan, Mr., 239
Gilmore, Louis F., 110
Gilmore, Minnie, 110
Gilmour, Addie, 102, 104, 107
Gilroy, John, 245
Gilwert, N.N., 119
Ginn, George A., 58, 65
Gioli, L., 37
Giovianni, G., 121
Girth, F., 180
Girvin, Mrs. R., 220
Gitti, G., 2
Glass, Mrs. H., 259
Gleason, Miss A., 201
Gleeson, Edward, 176
Gleeson, Francis, 148
Gleeson, T.D., 129
Glidmacher, L., 23
Glinderman, William,, 37
Glover, Albert D., 126
Glover, Albert H., 238
Glover, Emily F., 18
Glover, Mrs. E., 252
Glynn, E., 18
Goad, W.F., 211, 235
Goddard, Alice, 62
Goddard, Frederick, 62, 200
Goerl, Conrad, 62
Goerl, Fritz, 31, 62, 201
Goerl, Jacob, 62, 200
Goggin, E.W., 207
Goirs, F., 75
Goldstone, Olenia, 249
Goltick, Mariano, 178
Gomes, Maranno Jose, 124
Gomez, Antone, 219
Gomez, Mary P., 43
Gomez, Peter, 166
Gonzales, J., 145
Gonzales, N., 96
Gooch, C.J., 265
Goodilll, J.M., 183
Goodman, 192
Goodrum, M., 42
Gope, James, 268
Gordi, F.L., 195
Gordon, A., 123, 132
Gordon, D.S., 63
Gordon, Olivia A., 6, 183, 245
Gordon, S.E., 245
Gordon, Susan E., 183
Gordon, U.M., 191
Gordon, Willie A., 242
Gorley, Belle, 239

Gorley, Capt., 239
Gorley, H.A., 10, 26, 59, 60, 105
Goss, Annie, 1
Goss, Louis A., 153
Goss, Mary, 192, 210, 219
Gossage, Winnie, 66
Goudy, William, 215
Gould, T.J., 190
Gould, Thomas, 147
Goulde, Julia, 183, 192
Gouzenen, J., 220
Grace, M.N., 240
Gracia, F.R., 60
Grady, M., 99
Graham, A.E., 162
Graham, A.H., 231
Graham, A.W., 236, 253
Graham, Adelaide E., 80
Graham, Bob, 30
Graham, C.A., 209
Graham, Charles K., 84
Graham, Clara Augusta, 234
Graham, George S., 191, 193, 234
Graham, Miss A.E.T., 258
Graham, Mrs. W.G., 234
Graham, Mrs., 96, 191
Graham, Nellie, 234
Graham, Robert, 27, 28
Graham, Sarah, 259
Graham, W.G., 234
Grandi, Salvatore, 4
Grandido, Eleanor, 62
Grandjean, Charles, 200
Grandjean, Edward, 199
Grandjean, W., 62
Grandjean, Walter, 200
Grange, C., 96
Grant, 7
Grant, H.C., 248
Grant, James A., 268
Grant, John F., 216
Grant, M.W., 75
Grant, Mary, 208
Grant, Miss, 97
Gras, Celestine, 241
Gras, Leon, 241
Grass, Charles, 217
Graves, Benjamin H., 151
Graves, Emma C., 220
Graves, Fred, 63
Graves, Hannah, 84
Graves, P.A., 75
Graves, William, 161, 242
Gray, F., 78
Gray, George F., 265
Gray, Giles H., 11, 16
Gray, Jesse, 213
Gray, Mr., 258
Grayham, W.R., 123
Greaver, Ed, 163
Greavor, Edward, 194

Green, 2
Green, A., 2
Green, Charles, 209, 220
Green, F.H., 59
Green, Floride, 27, 35, 197
Green, Frank, 162
Green, George, 214
Green, John, 246
Green, Lottie, 209
Green, M.J., 265
Green, Miss F., 74
Green, Miss, 62, 157
Green, Rosa C., 95
Green, W.A., 68
Greenberg, Leon, 186
Greenfield, S.E., 5
Greenwald, L., 77
Greenwood, M., 3
Greer, E.S., 125, 209
Greer, J.L., 167
Greer, John L., 28, 29, 142
Greffoz, Louise, 62, 203
Greffoz, Susanne Catherine, 250
Gregg, 131
Gregg, Eva N., 10, 19, 29, 40, 42, 54, 70, 72, 74, 75, 77, 133, 159, 160
Gregg, Eva, 32, 35, 65, 136, 240
Gregg, G.R., 75
Gregg, H., 35, 40, 133
Gregg, H.R., 42, 159, 240, 243
Gregg, Herbert R., 160
Gregg, Herbert, 54
Gregg, Miss, 44
Gregg, Mrs., 169
Gregory, Elise, 222
Gretchen, Alma, 240
Gretchen, Miss, 222
Grethel, 51
Grethel, P., 77
Grethel, Philip, 30, 64, 66, 71
Greuet, Eugene G., 103
Grey, Mr., 202
Grey, W., 42
Greyson, Emma E., 63
Griffin, John, 223, 226, 231, 233, 235, 240, 249
Griffin, Minnie, 225
Griffin, Mrs. E., 76, 99
Griffin, Mrs., 116
Griffin, S.R., 65
Griffin, Sarah O'Connor, 136
Griffith, 17
Griffith, E.L., 170
Griffith, Edwin L., 161, 176
Griffith, Jeannie, 45
Griffith, Mrs. E., 227
Griffith, Mrs., 235
Grin, 111
Grinter, G.W., 146
Groenwold, Mrs. L., 192
Groff, Andrew, 232

Grorbell, Mr., 190
Grosh, Mrs. E.T., 192
Grosiglia, G.B., 55
Grosjean, 142
Grosjean, C., 41, 179
Gross, Alfred, 111, 115
Gross, George C., 259
Gross, Louisa M., 115
Gross, Louisa, 111
Grossman, Clara, 62, 200
Grossman, Paul, 62, 200
Grove, Dr., 91, 99, 226
Grove, M.F., 13, 15
Grove, Milliard, 200
Grove, Mrs. O.W., 91
Grove, O.W., 99
Grover, Caroline, 268
Grover, Carrie, 259
Grover, Cora, 268
Grover, Johnson, 259, 268
Grover, Mabel, 268
Grover, Mrs. Johnson, 259, 268
Guay, John, 97
Guelmini, G., 207
Guerin, Felix, 183
Guglielmina, Mrs. Antone, 211
Guibbini, G., 202, 205
Guibbini, Gottardo, 191, 199, 231
Guintrand, Jean B., 82, 171, 220
Guldager, Albert, 204
Guldager, George M., 93
Guldager, George, 220
Guldager, H., 147
Guldager, Louis Jr., 84
Guldager, Mrs. L., 36
Guldager, Ruth E., 166
Guldager, William, 74
Gulde, Carl, 62
Gulde, Vesta, 62, 200
Gumpel, Clifford A., 178
Gumpel, Michael, 220
Gunn, Emily, 22
Gunn, George, 216
Gunn, Miss, 22
Guthel, P., 94
Haack, Helena, 123, 225, 232, 233
Haack, N., 122
Haack, Nicholas, 122, 123, 139
Haas, Emma, 62, 219
Haas, Frank, 62
Haas, Fred, 62
Haas, Mrs., 26
Haas, Nettie, 62
Hacker, L., 75
Haddeman, Jane A., 58
Hadden, J.R., 103
Hadler, J., 51
Hageisbeen, Leonard, 219
Hagerty, Michael, 171
Hagerty, N., 18

Hagger, H., 75
Haggin, J.B., 260
Hagon, Elizabeth S., 155
Hagon, Julius, 241
Hagon, Numa, 241
Hahn, Amanda, 160
Hahn, F.F., 227
Hahn, Mrs. F.J., 220
Hahn, Mrs. William, 258
Hahn, W., 46
Hahn, William, 37, 237, 256, 263
Hakes, D., 109
Hakes, Lee, 109
Halden, Edward B., 67
Hale, Sadie, 61, 203
Halenbash, Henry, 178
Haley, Harry, 200
Haley, Henry, 62
Haley, J., 67, 224
Haley, James, 201
Haley, John, 25
Hall, Bertha M., 236
Hall, Bertha, 213, 236
Hall, Emma E., 227
Hall, Frank J., 110, 112
Hall, H.H., 88
Hall, H.M., 84
Hall, James, 165
Hall, Mrs., 97
Halligan, Frank, 265, 267
Halloran, O., 42, 247
Ham, 142, 266
Ham, A.L., 68, 109, 127, 202
Ham, Abner L., 129, 267
Ham, Ellen, 202
Ham, Katie, 202
Ham, Mr., 261
Hamada, H.F., 204
Hamb, Margaret G., 32
Hamburg, Celia, 156, 157
Hamdt, John, 183
Hamerschlager, J.B., 219
Hamilton, Alice, 178
Hamilton, G.E., 219
Hamilton, George E., 37
Hamilton, Julia R., 117, 120
Hamilton, Julia S., 198, 255
Hamilton, Julia Shafter, 17
Hamilton, M., 134
Hamilton, Mrs. A.R., 90
Hamilton, T.E., 50
Hamm, Bessie, 200
Hamm, Lena, 203
Hamm, Stafford, 62, 200
Hamm, Woldemar, 62, 200
Hammel, Peter P., 173, 219
Hammel, R., 3
Hammond, 75
Hammond, J., 75
Hammond, Jane, 119
Hammond, L., 28

Hammond, L.G., 92
Hammond, P.S., 252
Hampton, Dr., 152
Handon, Maude, 192
Hankins, Mary P., 192
Hankman, Frank, 247
Hanlan, W., 169
Hanlon, C.F., 32, 55
Hanlon, Charles F., 20
Hanlon, Mrs. C.F., 32
Hanna, Frank, 60
Hanna, William, 82
Hannon, Catherine, 218
Hannon, J.A., 218
Hannon, Margaret M., 195
Hannon, W.H., 8, 218
Hansen, 140, 146
Hansen, Carl, 203
Hansen, Carson, 61
Hansen, Charles, 27
Hansen, Elizabeth, 254
Hansen, George, 61
Hansen, H., 203, 254
Hansen, Henry, 62
Hansen, J., 92
Hansen, Louis, 252
Hansen, M., 75
Hansen, Mr., 20, 26
Hansen, N.B., 227
Hansen, Sarah, 27
Hansen, Thomas, 4, 31, 38, 167
Hanson, B., 252
Hanson, C., 66
Hanson, Charles, 25, 30, 240
Hanson, H.T., 67
Hanson, John, 174
Hanson, S., 25
Hanson, Sarah E., 30, 36
Hanson, T., 168
Harcourt, George, 176
Hardenburg, Mrs., 11
Harding, C., 92
Harding, George, 28, 30, 32, 140, 145, 253, 255, 256
Harding, J.A., 8, 263
Harding, Mary, 253, 255, 256
Harding, Mr., 15, 135, 268
Harding, Mrs. George, 135
Hardman, S.H., 182
Hardy, 101
Harlan, Charles, 2, 12, 77, 79, 91, 95, 98, 102
Harlan, George, 197
Harlan, Marie, 12
Harlan, Olive M., 259
Harlow, Frank L., 32
Harmes, J.T., 147, 245
Harmes, John T, 173
Harmon, E.M., 183
Harmon, Edward N., 36
Harmon, M.H., 183
Harney, F., 63

Harning, D.B., 106
Harold, W.P., 36
Harridge, John, 242
Harries, Florence, 110
Harries, J.D., 70
Harrigan, Mary, 178
Harrington, Bartine, 227
Harrington, Ed, 265, 267
Harrington, H.B., 80
Harrington, W.M., 268
Harrington, W.V., 87
Harris, C.F., 208
Harris, Fannie, 61, 203
Harris, Isaac, 30
Harris, John, 215
Harris, Mr., 26
Harris, Mrs. Edwin, 97
Harrison, 115, 116, 143
Harrison, Agnes, 204
Harrison, Alice, 62, 203
Harrison, C.H., 55, 87, 150, 173
Harrison, Edward J.N., 179
Harrison, Edward, 22
Harrison, F., 78
Harrison, F.A., 177, 185
Harrison, H., 60, 103, 112, 113, 117, 124, 205, 216, 253, 257
Harrison, Harry, 66
Harrison, Henry, 29, 41, 49, 72, 86, 89, 129, 160, 161, 162, 164, 185, 191, 193, 197, 223, 244, 252, 258
Harrison, J.K., 21
Harrison, L.J., 110
Harrison, Laura, 169
Harrison, Mamie R., 169
Harrison, Mr., 152
Harrison, Robert, 173
Harrison, Sheriff, 224, 247
Harrison, W.P., 254
Harrison, Zoe M., 177
Harrison, Zoe, 185
Hart, Frank, 147
Hart, M., 27
Hart, Mary E., 71
Hart, Mathew, 139
Hart, R.C., 23, 182
Hart, W.F., 147
Hart, W.N., 190
Harte, Gregory, 214
Hartman, E.A., 80, 112, 236, 264
Hartman, Rev., 151
Harton, C.B., 108
Hartwell, George, 176
Hartwell, James, 176
Hartwell, John, 176
Hartzell, I.W., 134
Harukneh, 181
Harvey, Alice, 190
Harvey, LeRoy G., 45, 169, 256
Harvey, Miss A., 157
Harvey, Mrs., 192

Harwood, W.R., 17
Hasbram, K.J., 219
Hasbrough, 263
Haskell, 252
Haskell, G.S., 201
Haskell, L., 44
Haskell, L.F., 178, 209
Haskell, Llewellyn F., 61, 245
Haskell, N., 60
Hass, Charley, 219, 249
Hass, Mrs. William, 192
Hassett, E.L., 165
Hassett, Mrs. E., 59
Hassler, Margretha, 239
Hastings, Mrs. Robert P., 220
Hatch, Helen, 173
Hatch, Mr., 50, 167
Hatch, Mrs., 50
Hatton, Henry, 258
Hattroun, Miss, 219
Hauptmann, H.P., 60
Hauss, Matilda, 34
Haven, 57, 70, 83
Haven, Acton, 61, 151
Haven, J.Q.A., 112, 245
Haven, Lewis, 61
Havens, Howard, 143
Hawkins, 9
Hawkins, A.C., 223
Hawkins, Birdy, 187
Hawkins, Cory, 59
Hawkins, Fannie, 28
Hawkins, O.C., 25, 29, 67, 224
Haycock, M.A., 98
Hayden, Amelia, 263
Hayden, Ben, 268
Hayden, D.L., 4, 99, 112, 126, 136, 139, 144, 171
Hayden, Justice, 219
Hayden, Mrs. M., 219
Hayden, Mrs., 219, 220
Hayden, Wilbur, 167
Hayes, D.W., 90
Hayes, E.A., 90
Hayes, Fred, 119
Hayes, J., 66, 75, 219
Hayes, James, 120
Hayes, Mary, 6, 231
Hayes, Miss, 11
Hayes, Mrs. M., 82
Hayes, Pat, 2
Hayes, Patrick, 6
Hayne, R.T., 192
Hays, C.B., 195
Hays, Henry G., 7
Hays, Mrs. E.B., 171
Haze, 63
Hazzard, Frederick K., 76
Head, Rose, 204
Healey, Benjamin, 151, 259
Healey, Kate M., 149
Healey, Katie M., 151

Healey, William, 74
Healion, W.H., 182
Healy, Benjamin, 194
Healy, Frank, 8, 21, 87, 212
Healy, J., 252
Healy, James H., 145
Healy, James, 144
Healy, John E., 38, 167
Healy, John, 31, 41, 261
Healy, K., 82
Healy, M., 102
Healy, Marshall, 226
Healy, Minnie, 105
Heany, T.U., 178
Hearn, A., 220
Hearn, William, 203
Hearn, Willie, 61
Hearst, Mary, 219
Hearst, Phoebe A., 132
Hearst, W.R., 36
Hearst, William R., 54, 221
Heath, Mrs. Richard, 192
Heath, Mrs., 227, 259
Heathcote, B., 68
Heckel, Havier, 242
Hegan, Florence A., 164
Heidel, J., 189
Heidel, Thomas, 189
Heilfron, B., 147
Heilfron, Ben, 168, 209
Heilman, Mrs. I.W., 192
Helenschild, Mary, 85
Heller, M., 78, 97
Hellings, Desaree, 214
Helm, George, 37
Helm, Wilhelm, 219
Hemichson, Dorothy, 208
Heminway, Mrs., 84
Henderson, Mr., 140
Henderson, W.H., 34
Hendley, C., 219
Hendley, Charles B., 220
Hendley, Charles, 227
Hendley, Ineth, 195
Hendricks, Levi, 139
Hendry, Annie, 254
Hendry, George W., 170
Henermann, Margot, 117
Henigan, Hattie, 233
Henley, F., 108
Hennessey, 86
Hennessey, F.D., 60
Hennessey, M., 240
Hennessey, Thomas, 147, 178
Henre, J., 28
Henry, A.S., 129
Henshaw, Pat, 118
Henshaw, William, 119, 122
Hepburn, 107
Herbert, A., 227
Hernandez, Valentine, 170
Herrick, H.S., 89

Herzog, 189
Herzog, A., 92
Herzog, George, 61, 203
Herzog, Gusta,, 101
Herzog, Jennie K., 164, 165
Herzog, Jennie, 125, 159, 163
Herzog, Julia, 164
Herzog, Leonie, 62, 200
Herzog, M., 11, 25, 31, 67, 87, 95, 163, 192, 198, 244, 245, 256, 267
Herzog, Mr., 125, 189, 202
Herzog, Mrs., 125
Herzog, Nathan, 267
Herzog, S., 151, 227
Herzog, Sidney, 62, 200
Herzog, W., 46
Herzog, Z., 54, 164
Hesketh, Nellie, 182
Hess, E.L., 233
Hester, A.W., 134
Heuter, Edward L., 84
Hevens, Mattie, 61
Hewitt, Isabella, 106
Hewitt, William, 61
Heywood, Miss W.M., 19
Heywood, Mrs. Lou, 165
Heywood, Walter M., 156
Hibbard, Lee, 36
Hibbard, Olney, 31, 237
Hibben, Miss, 208
Hickey, W.C., 50
Hickey, William C., 230, 252
Hickey, William, 80, 231
Higgins, D., 63
Highton, H.H., 229
Hildebrand, B.J., 85
Hildreth, Alice L., 227
Hill, Charles S., 242
Hill, G.F., 33
Hill, George F., 183
Hill, Mary, 181, 201, 208
Hill, William H., 51
Hills, Frank E., 86, 216
Hills, J.F., 5
Hills, Joel F., 86
Hills, Sanford M., 86
Hilton, William, 124
Hilts, R.J., 54
Hinckley, Mrs. E.M., 119, 126
Hines, Mary, 219
Hines, Thomas, 157
Hiniker, 41, 163
Hiniker, A., 213, 215, 266
Hiniker, G.E., 215
Hiniker, J., 215
Hinz, August C., 183
Hoag, D.A., 131
Hoag, Emma, 200
Hoag, Miss, 20
Hoatmester, A.K., 99
Hobart, R.D., 51, 67

Hobart, W.S., 167
Hobbs, F.F., 239
Hobson, Arthur W., 162
Hock, Christina, 209
Hock, Diana, 178
Hock, T., 53, 111, 209, 266
Hock, Tobias, 245
Hoe, Frank, 162
Hoe, John, 162
Hoeft, George, 207
Hofer, F., 33
Hoff, Henry, 144
Hoffey, James, 215
Hogan, J.E., 99
Hogan, J.F., 137
Hogg, James, 48
Holbz, M., 51
Holite, Antonio, 222
Holland, 58
Holland, A., 75
Holland, F.W., 147
Holland, Mabel, 93
Holland, Mae, 204
Holland, Miss, 78, 104
Holland, Mr., 96
Holland, Mrs., 84, 96
Holland, N., 46
Hollenberg, Gus, 240, 252
Holloway, W.E., 139, 153, 155, 157, 160, 162, 164
Holloway, William E., 11
Holly, Dwight E., 177
Holm, Charles, 219
Holmberg, Augustus, 227, 233
Holmberg, Gus, 178
Holmes, C.S., 189
Holton, F.A., 110
Holton, Flora, 103
Holtz, G., 86
Homan, Jose M., 116
Homes, Joseph, 247
Hooper, C.A., 96
Hooper, J.G., 219
Hooper, K., 207
Hooper, Miss, 101
Hoover, J.C., 41
Hopkins, George W., 11, 16
Hopkins, Gertrude, 173
Hopkins, S.J., 120
Hopkins, Samuel J., 111, 115, 117
Hopkins, William E., 178
Hopkins, William Evelyn, 249
Hornsby, Annie L., 35
Hoskins, N.D., 269
Hoskins, Otto, 219
Hotaling, 115
Hotaling, A.P., 6, 108, 113, 238, 260
Hotaling, Anson P., 134, 197, 250
Hotchkiss, Miss M.S., 4

Houck, Richard A., 265, 267
Hough, James F., 267
Hourihan, Annie, 233
Houston, E.C., 213, 218, 245
Houston, Mrs. E.C., 213
Hoveland, J.L., 99
Hover, A., 7
Hovey, E., 37
Howard, Carrie, 219
Howard, F., 119
Howard, George, 123
Howard, Mary, 15
Howard, Mrs. S.D., 227
Howard, Mrs., 110
Howard, Teresa, 157
Howard, William C., 171
Howe, A., 154
Howe, A.D., 259
Howe, A.S., 120
Howe, Harvey, 119
Howe, Henry N., 193
Howe, Henry Nathaniel, 198
Howe, Juana B., 198
Howe, Juana D., 193
Howe, Mr., 119
Howe, Mrs. Albert, 118
Howe, Mrs. H.A., 176, 179, 182
Howe, Mrs., 178
Howell, Sadie, 252
Howitt, H.O., 84, 89, 141
Howitt, Isabella, 139
Hoxie, Hattie, 66
Hoxie, Joseph, 156
Hoxie, Vivian, 62, 201
Hoyer, S., 161
Hoyt, C.A., 208
Hoyt, Mr., 126
Hoyt, Mrs., 126
Hubark, J., 23
Hubbell, O., 4, 147
Hudson, Millard F., 6, 21
Hueter, Ernest L., 88
Huff, A., 242
Huff, Lulu, 102
Hug, Rosa K., 65
Hug, Wilhelm, 6
Hughes, Chief, 34
Hughes, D.T., 173
Hughes, J.F., 27
Hughes, Judge, 60
Hughes, L., 265
Hughes, Louis A., 213
Hulbe, C., 84
Hulbe, Martha, 60
Humboldt, W.B., 219
Hume, W.O., 258
Humphrey, Georgia Martina, 3
Hundly, Kate, 204
Hundly, Kittie, 78, 104
Hunnewell, Addie C., 225
Hunnewell, G.A., 175, 212, 225, 244, 258

Hunnewell, George A., 66, 88, 114, 144, 169, 243, 264
Hunnewell, George, 55, 83, 237
Hunnewell, J., 145
Hunnewell, Mr., 148
Hunnewell, W.G., 225
Hunt, 192
Hunt, George, 70
Hunt, Mrs., 97
Hunter, Christina E., 222
Hunter, E.F., 119
Hunter, E.T., 35
Hunter, Helen, 200
Hunter, J.H., 222
Hunter, Mrs. James, 115
Hurd, M., 23
Hurdle, Eddie, 215
Hurley, Annie J., 206
Hurley, Annie, 210
Hurley, K., 137
Hurst, H.C., 178
Hutchinson, Fernande, 67, 116
Hutchinson, Mrs. H.L., 195
Hutchinson, W.S., 23
Hyams, Ellen, 130
Hyams, Frank, 224
Hyatt, George, 24
Hyatt, Prof., 196
Hyde, A.S., 51
Hyde, Henry C., 37
Hyde, John, 73
Hyde, Mrs. George, 157
Hyde, Mrs. H.C., 178
Hydes, James L., 16
Hyiel, H.J., 28
Hyman, A.B., 78
Hymans, Mrs. F., 68
Hyne, Robin, 173
Hynes, Ferdinand, 176
Ibs, George, 67
Idal, Robert, 241
Ignacio, J., 25
Ignacio, M., 12
Ihle, Fritz, 111
Infant, 188
Ingelken, Miss M., 233
Ingermann, A., 146, 147
Ingram, P., 25
Ink, H.J., 212
Ink, Harriet J., 163, 269
Ink, Harriet Jane, 214
Ink, Harriet, 189
Ink, I.G., 269
Ink, T.H., 163, 189, 214
Inman, 105, 142
Inman, M.F., 134
Inman, Pratt C., 134
Irvin, Joseph, 204
Irvin, Mr., 99
Irvin, William, 204
Irving, Henry, 210
Irving, Thomas, 61

Irving, Tom, 245
Irwin, Estelle, 208
Iverson, A.G., 158
Iverson, George, 202
Iverson, H., 140, 202
Iverson, Hans, 240
Ivien, James, 148
Jackson, Annie, 246
Jackson, Arthur, 153, 155, 158
Jackson, C.R., 158
Jackson, E.W., 158
Jackson, Ernest, 204
Jackson, Frances, 132
Jackson, Martha, 57
Jackson, Mary Louisa, 158
Jacobs, 142
Jacobs, C.I., 19, 224
Jacobs, Charles I., 25, 29
Jacobs, E., 78
Jacobs, E.L., 77
Jacobs, Ella, 29
Jacobs, F.J., 143, 202, 266
Jacobs, Frank, 69, 127, 128
Jacobs, Olivia, 62, 200
Jacobs, S., 92
Jacobson, Charles A., 158
Jacobson, Fred, 187
Jacobus, Ida, 244
Jacoby, P., 37
Jacoby, S., 23
James, Hattie, 178
James, Ida, 227
James, John T., 231, 238
James, Mary H., 53, 54, 193
James, Wilber, 199
James, William E., 28
Jamieson, John, 200
Jamieson, Nellie, 61
Jamieson, Willie, 203
Jansen, J., 46
Janson, A., 97
Janson, O., 78
Jellet, S.J., 68
Jenkins, Joseph Lee, 131
Jenkins, Joseph, 58, 73
Jenkins, Mr., 59, 243
Jenkins, Mrs. J.H., 34
Jennings, C.B., 220
Jensen, Charles, 213
Jensen, M., 147
Jephson, T.P., 74
Jepson, Henry, 159
Jepson, Margareth Frances, 103
Jepson, Margareth, 139
Jerome, Chris, 208
Jessarich, T.M., 96
Jessup, Eddie, 200
Jessup, Isaac, 88, 111, 144, 212, 237
Jewell, B., 99
Jewell, Julia S., 67
Jewell, Miss H.L., 80

Jewell, Mrs. I.R., 27, 29
Jewell, S., 27, 28
Jewell, W.H., 22, 25, 31
Jewell, William H., 162, 177, 202
Jewell, William, 150
Jewett, Joseph M., 237
Joachim, Laurent, 242
Joaquin, J., 121
Joaquin, John, 183
Joaquin, Jose, 12
Jockers, Ludwig, 228
Johansen, L., 266
Johansen, M., 54
Johansen, Martin, 32, 259
Johansen, Mr., 202
Johanssom, Madame, 219
Johnson, 9, 48, 51, 75, 94, 96, 141
Johnson, A., 51, 99
Johnson, A.S., 208
Johnson, Alfred, 183
Johnson, B.B., 37
Johnson, C.F., 2
Johnson, C.S., 12
Johnson, Capt., 265
Johnson, E., 220
Johnson, Emma B., 210
Johnson, Emma P., 173
Johnson, F.H., 60
Johnson, Frank S., 187
Johnson, H., 108
Johnson, Happy Isabel, 14
Johnson, Hilda, 93
Johnson, Irving, 167
Johnson, J., 92, 233
Johnson, Kate, 132, 186, 255, 258
Johnson, L.J., 162
Johnson, Louis, 36, 238
Johnson, Lucy, 193
Johnson, Martin, 219
Johnson, May, 173
Johnson, Miss M.C., 34
Johnson, Miss, 80
Johnson, Mr., 25
Johnson, Mrs. A., 267
Johnson, Mrs. F.D., 173
Johnson, Mrs. S.S., 233
Johnson, Mrs. T., 267
Johnson, Mrs., 11
Johnson, R.W., 25, 31, 54, 56, 80, 81, 85, 167
Johnson, Robert W., 38
Johnson, Roger, 57, 71
Johnson, S., 46, 168
Johnson, T.B., 14, 134
Johnson, Thaddeus B., 16
Johnson, W.J., 31
Johnsson, 111
Johnston, 108
Johnston, Caroline V., 161, 176

Johnston, Mary, 178, 195
Johnston, Mrs. W.B., 233
Johnstone, C.V., 170
Jones, B., 82
Jones, Dr., 26, 27, 76, 162, 176, 245
Jones, E.D., 239
Jones, Edith A., 231
Jones, Edith, 62
Jones, Eleanor, 62, 200
Jones, Houston, 64, 66, 69, 251
Jones, Ivy, 66, 71
Jones, J.M., 26, 30, 31, 66, 69
Jones, John, 37
Jones, Lena, 74
Jones, Louis, 78
Jones, Mary, 8, 46, 168
Jones, Mettie M., 36, 254
Jones, Mr., 11, 126, 176
Jones, Mrs. J.M., 71
Jones, Mrs., 27
Jones, O.E., 137
Jones, P.W., 6
Jones, Paul, 59
Jones, Pembrose W., 78
Jones, W.F., 31, 38, 137, 143, 167, 235, 266
Jones, William, 144
Jonjor, A.L., 12
Jordan, Ciriano, 241
Jordan, Ed, 82
Jordan, Emma H., 169
Jordan, J.F., 226, 257
Jordan, John F., 28, 85
Jordan, Mrs. J.F., 31, 226
Jordan, Mrs., 11, 38, 69, 99, 187
Jordan, Pearl, 226
Jorgensen, A., 92
Jorgensen, Ada, 62, 203
Jorgensen, Diana, 62, 200
Jorgensen, Frederick, 70
Jorgensen, Katie, 62, 200
Jorgensen, P.M., 213
Joseph, Eva, 268
Joseph, Harry, 73
Joseph, M., 66
Joseph, U., 195
Josephine, E., 17
Jossa, 75
Josslyn, Alma, 64
Jost, M., 99
Joy, Minnie 34
Judson, Charles C., 165
Judson, Henry C., 165
Jukes, Mr., 184
Jukes, T.J., 56, 107, 150, 164, 207
Jukes, Thomas J., 153
Julian, John, 152
Kadel, Barbara, 92
Kadel, Mary M., 92, 110
Kahan, W., 23

Kahn, A., 8
Kahn, Lewis, 195
Kahn, Morse, 159
Kain, M.W., 18, 43, 49
Kaiser, Jacob, 204
Kalender, F.H.C., 195
Kamool, 97
Kaneen, C.S., 169
Kaneen, E., 203
Kaneen, Eddie, 62
Kaneen, Pattie, 62, 203
Kaneen, Sup., 180
Kanngeiser, Amelia, 247
Kanzie, George, 251, 252
Kappenman, 44, 203
Kappenman, A., 50, 54, 55, 83, 234, 245
Kappenman, Bertha, 62, 200
Kappenman, Charlie, 199
Kappenman, Hannah, 62, 200
Kappenman, Joe, 62, 200
Kappenman, Mr., 11
Kappenman, Mrs. A., 11
Kappenman, Mrs., 187
Kare, Thomas, 252
Kashaw, Israel, 198
Kaston, Wendell, 235
Katen, John, 207
Katon, W.H., 242
Kaufman, F., 132
Kaufman, Frank, 181
Kaufman, H.W., 217
Kaufman, H.W.E., 218
Kauger, E., 60
Kaupf, C., 234
Ke, Tong, 250
Keane, G.B., 227
Keane, J., 203
Keaner, Johannes, 6
Kearney, Mrs. R.M., 120
Kearney, R.M., 149
Kearney, William, 124
Kearny, John, 241
Keating, Maggie, 34, 168, 269
Keating, Miss, 213
Keating, Richard, 168, 184
Keck, F.C., 125, 171, 209
Keck, Fredrick C., 58
Keefe, J.H., 163
Keefe, Mary, 163
Keefer, Merrel, 62
Keek, F.C., 170
Keeler, J.B., 96, 119, 123
Keeler, Laura, 254
Keeler, Mrs. J.B., 195
Keen, George B. Jr., 213
Keene, Joe, 62
Keene, Mr., 63
Keigho, 166, 172
Keigho, John, 139
Keigho, Thomas, 170
Keil, Hugo D., 1

Keiner, Herman, 183
Kelf, Hugh D., 16
Kellegren, Henry, 176
Kelleher, Capt., 246
Kelleher, L., 42
Keller, J., 86
Keller, O., 66
Kelleran, Christina, 42
Kellerica, Thomas, 183
Kelley, A.C., 8
Kelley, Frank, 173
Kelley, J., 63
Kelley, K., 5
Kellner, H., 188
Kellogg, B.M., 158
Kellogg, Bertha M., 154, 156
Kellogg, D.O., 218
Kellogg, Karl, 16
Kellogg, Lansing, 208
Kellogg, Richard B., 193
Kellogg, W.J., 78
Kelly, Ellen, 198
Kelly, George, 178
Kelly, J.G., 108
Kelly, James V., 114
Kelly, Kate, 256
Kelly, Lewis, 195
Kelly, M., 227
Kelly, Mr., 99, 107, 230
Kelly, Mrs. J.S., 242
Kelly, Mrs. L., 51
Kelly, Mrs., 11
Kelly, P.H., 180
Kelly, R., 51
Kelly, Sally, 204
Kelly, W.D., 44, 177
Kendall, George, 60
Kendall, J., 40
Kendall, John, 183, 190
Kenman, I., 111
Kennedy, Bridget, 254
Kennedy, Delia, 246
Kennedy, John, 100
Kennedy, Joseph P. 265, 268
Kennedy, Mary Ellen, 97
Kennedy, Mary, 139
Kennedy, Michael, 148
Kennedy, Miss M., 90
Kennedy, Miss, 22
Kennedy, N., 93, 102
Kennelly, Mary, 239
Kenney, S., 75
Kenney, Sabina, 204
Kenny, Ella, 194
Kenny, J.P., 242
Kent, T.B., 186, 263
Keough, Michael W., 36, 162
Kerloor, J.G., 99
Kerr, Earl T., 91, 139
Kerr, J., 63
Kerr, William Watt, 211
Kerrigan, Mary E., 144, 145

Kerrigan, T., 202
Ketchum, William N., 214
Keyes, Edith, 102
Keyes, F., 77
Keyes, James W., 90, 237
Keyes, L.C., 175
Keyes, Mrs., 90
Ki, Tong, 248
Kiely, John, 148
Kiely, Patrick, 148
Kiely, Thomas, 148
Kifly, Hattie, 86
Killen, Eugene, 148
Killen, Thomas, 148
Kimball, W.E., 78
Kincaid, Dan, 202, 206
Kindsley, C.F., 181
King, Armia Ramos, 171
King, David, 86
King, Joe, 14, 15
King, Manuel, 265, 267
King, Nora, 230, 231
King, P., 228
King, W., 203
King, William, 53
King, Willie, 62
Kingsburg, Edith, 252
Kingwell, Frank I., 213
Kinnan, J., 134
Kinney, Bailey, 139
Kinney, Mrs. Marshall J., 80
Kinsella, 9, 141
Kinsella, Miss K., 201
Kinsella, R., 8, 213
Kinsella, Richard, 167, 265
Kircker, Johanna, 204
Kirk, M., 147
Kirk, Miss N., 135
Kirk, Nellie, 34, 76, 213
Kirkhoff, Clay, 252
Kirkhope, William, 173
Kirkoters, Mrs. W.C., 97
Kirkoters, W.C., 97
Kirkup, Dr., 60
Kirman, J., 99
Kirschner, Miss H., 258
Kirwan, David, 200
Kiser, Mr., 178
Kittle, Harriet De Witt, 51, 52, 151, 154
Kittle, J.G., 51, 53, 149, 199
Kittle, Jonathan G., 39, 43, 52, 151, 154
Kittle, Lucia Hamilton, 154
Kittle, Mrs. N., 233
Kittle, William, 233
Klein, 23, 141
Klein, C., 52
Klein, Christien, 187
Kleinclaus, G., 98
Klenhammer, Bertha, 133
Kletz, A., 106

Kline, J.E., 37
Klose, A.H., 207
Klose, Mr., 27
Knappenbach, Miss, 26
Knappenbach, Mr., 26
Knarston, J.H., 107
Knell, Barbara, 43, 45, 169, 232, 249
Knell, Frederick G., 56, 58, 232
Knell, John, 43, 45
Knight, E., 40
Knittel, Constance, 62, 200
Knittel, H., 254
Knittel, Henry, 7, 66, 212
Knittel, Mamie, 62, 200
Knox, George R., 195
Knox, George, 224
Koch, H., 77, 99
Koch, Louise A., 213
Koehler, Karl O., 31
Koehler, Vincent H.E., 31, 188
Koenig, A., 40
Koenig, Adolph, 58
Koenig, Mrs., 190
Koerner, C.H.W., 13
Koerner, Charles H.W., 169
Koerner, Charles, 181
Koerner, H.W., 16
Kogminsky, H., 54
Kohlberg, M.S., 123
Kohlberg, Mr., 59
Kohler, Minnie, 199
Kohlhoff, Gustav, 204
Kohlkoff, George, 37
Kohn, R., 255
Kohn, Rudolph, 92, 253
Kolling, C.E., 119
Kopp, P.F., 181
Kopp, Peter, 266
Koshland, Mrs. M.C., 248
Kouse, William, 215
Koutz, T., 92
Kowalsky, 14
Kowalsky, E.H., 102, 186
Kowalsky, Henry I., 8
Kraenbuhl, Miss J., 142
Kragen, Mrs., 208
Kramer, J.H., 99
Kramer, Miss S., 220
Kramer, Miss, 195
Kratzenstein, Emma, 95
Kratzer, G., 60, 77
Kreling, Ernestine, 224
Kreling, F.W., 224
Kremer, John, 230
Krenkel, Gustav W., 227
Kriegel, Edward, 195
Krouglair, P., 11
Kruger, Johann F., 265, 267
Krumpel, Fanny O'Connor, 136
Kruse, F., 101
Kruse, Fred, 89, 101, 106

Kruse, Frederick, 223
Krutz, Fred, 56
Kuhnle, F., 37
Kuler, Mrs. J.B., 178
Kunis, J., 145
Kunnemann, John, 160
Kuntry, Charles, 233
Kunz, Charles, 92, 126
Kunz, J., 106
Kuprion, C., 77
Kurtz, 140
Kurtz, Charles, 137
Kurtz, Eugene, 34, 35, 40, 139
Kusche, August, 214
Kusche, Earnest, 214
Kuttner, Mr., 220
Kynoch, Flora, 61
Kyser, Miss L.D., 210
L'Amoureaux, 257
L'Amoureaux, M., 89
La Page, Jane, 1, 5, 6, 14, 19, 25, 81
Laborde, Bertha, 104
Labourdette, Pierre, 235
Lacerda, 21, 100
Lacerda, J.P., 48, 57, 100, 213, 266
Lacey, Mrs. Robert, 257
Lacey, Robert, 257
Lack, Michael, 194
Lacy, H., 193
Lacy, Maud, 12, 13
Lacy, Miss N., 222
Ladato, Mary, 181
Lafranchi, A., 87
Lafranchi, G., 93
Lafranchi, P., 2
Lafranchi, Pio, 137
LaFranky, J., 23
Laftronn, Anna, 210
Lagan, 10
Lagan, Father, 136, 175, 176, 190, 194, 230, 231, 240
Lagan, Hugh, 23
Lagon, Dr., 76
Lake, H.W., 156
Lake, Nellie, 119
Lakeman, Helen M., 45
Lakin, Dr., 202
Lakin, J.J., 127, 213, 266
Lakin, Mrs., 11
Lamb, M., 60
Lambert, Hugh, 183
Lamerrow, J., 42
Lamplough, Cecil A., 239
Lampman, Henry, 79
Lamson, 78
Lancel, L.A., 246
Lancel, Leon A., 50
Land, C. Evans, 67
Land, John T., 107

Lander, Nelson A., 178, 265, 267
Landers, Mrs. John E., 246
Landgraf, Mr., 76
Landgraf, R., 184
Landgraf, Robert, 133, 149, 177
Lando, William, 168
Landon, Dr., 189
Lang, 164
Lang, Augustine, 62, 200
Lang, Otto, 66, 240
Languetin, M.E., 190
Lanham, Miss, 156
Lanini, Joseph, 227
Lanthum, E.P., 195
Lariche, Anna, 3
Larsen, A., 220
Larsen, C.F., 117, 247, 255
Larsen, George, 21, 160, 162, 194, 260, 262
Larsen, M.A., 99
Larson, Oscar S., 229, 230
Larssen, 17
Lassen, John, 222
Latham, Alice, 118
Latham, F.B., 118
Latham, Mrs. F.B., 195
Lathrop, Benjamin G., 242
Latronel, John P., 228
Laude, Mrs., 234
Lauff, Charles A., 261
Lauff, Charles, 20, 253
Lauff, M.J., 168
Lauff, Maria J., 269
Lauff, Maria Jesus, 261
Lauff, Mary J., 253
Lauff, O.B., 30
Lauff, Oscar, 261
Laughlin, Lester, 171
Laughlin, Mary, 256
Lauriano, J., 245
Lauriano, Joseph, 46
Lavada, Joseph, 67
Laviosa, Amelia, 62, 200
Laviosa, Emile, 62, 200
Laviosa, Louis, 62, 212
Laviosa, Mario, 200
Lawder, J., 109
Lawler, J.P., 157, 161
Lawler, James P., 150, 153, 155, 160
Lawler, M., 86
Lawler, Michael, 139
Lawrence, 21
Lawrence, A., 30, 45, 56, 147, 174
Lawrence, Antonio, 18, 50
Lawrence, William, 13
Lawrie, William, 73
Lawson, Charles W., 258
Lawson, Hannah, 258
Lawton, G.F., 96

Lawton, G.W., 102
Lawton, J.D., 211
Lawton, M.A., 23, 123, 135
Lawton, Mrs. D.B., 182
Lawton, Mrs. U.A., 178
Lawton, T.D., 137
Layng, J.E., 236
Le Cornec, Mr., 202, 229
Le Cornec, P., 61
Le Count, 97
League, Ida, 204
Lean, Mrs. S.E., 265
Leary, J.G., 108
Leary, William, 95, 178, 220
Leavenworth, Olivia, 87
Leavy, W., 23
LeCounty, 75
Ledgett, Mary E., 166
Lee, Allan, 4, 188, 199, 201
Lee, Allen, 205, 217
Lee, Benjamin B., 32
Lee, Mrs. S.A., 217
Lee, Sarah A., 201, 205
Leeds, Bertha E., 35
Leeds, Bertha, 182
Leeds, E.B., 84
Leege, Otto, 246
Leek, Christopher, 191, 238
Leek, Mr., 184
Lees, Fred, 69
Lees, Mrs. Capt., 69
LeFranky, 178
Legault, F., 33, 35
Leiale, Manuel, 256
Leis, Jennie, 190
Leitsch, Fannie, 191
Lelfehult, F., 134
LeMar, L., 171
Lenan, Ella, 183
Lenhart, Emily C., 63
Lennan, Meary, 234
Lennon, J.J., 63
Lent, C.H., 51
Lentz, Miss, 230
Leon, Capt., 61
Leon, F.G., 97
Leonard, George, 231
Leonard, M.S., 178
Leonarda, Julia, 2, 24, 25, 51, 65, 153
Leopold, C.M., 67
Leroy, C.C., 168
Leszynsky, Samuel L., 235
Leudgeon, Mr., 204
Levari, John Marle, 234
Leviston, W., 14
Leviston, William, 171
Levy, Louis, 205
Levy, Mrs. Eugene W., 165
Levy, Rebecca, 45
Lewis, A.C., 67
Lewis, Canby, 207

Lewis, E., 129
Lewis, Ed, 75
Lewis, Etta L., 112
Lewis, J., 74
Lewis, Joseph, 151
Lewis, L., 135
Lewis, M., 135, 210
Lewis, Mary E., 67
Lewis, Mrs. Benjamin, 194
Lewis, Mrs. G.H., 220
Lewis, P., 123
Lewis, Ruth, 15
Lewis, William C., 207
Lewis, William, 167
Lewis, Z., 37
Lewthwaite, Alex, 251
Lezzini, Charles, 13, 262, 263
Libbey, Edney S., 12
Libbey, Emily F., 35, 65
Libbey, Mr., 61
Liberty, Leland L., 165
Liberty, M.J., 165
Liberty, Mrs., 161
Lichtenberg, Charlotte, 188
Lichtenberg, W., 12, 14
Lichtenberg, William, 188
Lichtenstein, Bessie, 189
Lichtenstein, D., 78
Lichtenstein, Harry M., 125, 163, 164, 165
Lichtenstein, Harry, 159
Lichtenstein, M.H., 189
Lichtenstein, T., 189
Liebrecht, S.P., 164
Lilley, Michael, 235
Limaruty, Charles, 163, 199, 262
Limberg, J., 219
Linarty, Charles, 261
Lind, Fred, 150
Lind, Lizzie, 150
Lind, Mrs., 165
Lindaur, Max, 166
Lindquist, M., 123
Lindsley, Carleton, 265, 268
Lindsley, F.D., 174
Linforth, W.H., 229
Linscott, Ivan, 176
Lippitt, 20, 125, 146
Lippman, Ch., 264
Lisk, D.A., 128
Lisk, Marion, 128
Little, J.R, 225
Liveen, Mrs., 121
Liver, Otto, 222
Livingston, Grace, 62, 200
Livingston, Wallace, 62, 199
Livinston, A., 86
Lobenstein, S., 163
Lofsh, Herman, 56
Lofstrom, I., 96
Loftus, William, 84
Logan, James F., 175

Logan, T.O., 235
Lohse, Jesse C., 227
Lois, B., 33
London, Will, 56
Long, Clara I., 150, 158, 180
Long, John F., 158
Long, Lulu, 78
Long, Margaret, 36
Long, R.H., 68
Longley, C.J., 160
Longley, Charles, 167
Longley, G.W., 75
Loomis, Henry, 71
Lopes, Antonio S., 117
Lopez, H., 61
Lopez, J., 59, 118
Lopland, Frances M., 15
Lorch, Charles, 233
Lord, J., 2
Losee, Lydia T., 5
Losee, W., 5, 19
Losee, Welman, 3, 18
Loud, Lt., 112
Loudon, R.B., 20, 172
Loudon, Robert B., 242, 244
Loughad, H.W., 134
Loughborough, A.H., 136
Louheed, C., 99
Louini, Guiseppi, 231
Louis, J. Jr., 194
Lovejoy, W.H.L., 166
Lovie, F., 132
Low, J., 145
Low, Jennie, 195
Low, Lee Chung, 139
Lowden, Maggie J., 34
Lowden, Maggie, 38
Lowden, Miss M.J., 140
Lowder, J., 81
Lowe, J.A.S., 67
Lowe, Rev. 69
Lowe, Susan, 38
Lowenfield, B., 42
Lowenfield, Bernard, 178, 235
Lowney, Nellie, 239
Lowney, Thomas F., 108
Lubmenson, Annie F., 27
Lubrant, L., 60
Lucas, Cyrus L., 166
Lucas, H., 131, 168
Lucas, H.J., 37
Lucas, John, 25, 31
Lucas, Maria L., 98, 99
Lucas, William, 60
Ludolph, William, 67
Luiz, A., 259
Lull, Norman A., 139
Lunarnty, Charles, 156
Lund, 140, 146
Lund, Camilla, 87
Lund, E.C., 119, 146, 213
Lund, Elias C., 95, 96, 252

Lund, H.C., 96
Lund, Mrs. E.C., 216
Lundbark, J., 75
Lundbark, John, 242, 259
Lundquist, William, 210
Lundstrom, Annie W., 218
Luney, K.M., 131
Luney, Kate M., 230
Lunny, Sadie, 62, 200
Lunt, Lottie, 200
Lux, 165
Lux, A.L., 97
Lux, F. William, 97
Lux, F., 97
Lux, F.A., 259
Lux, George, 97
Luz, Ino, 161
Lydiatt, Amos, 265, 268
Lydon, James, 73
Lyford, B.F., 228, 255, 265
Lyford, Benjamin F., 165
Lyman, A.J., 67, 243
Lyman, Mrs., 258
Lynas, Minnie F., 40
Lynch, 86
Lynch, Bessie, 134
Lynch, Bridget, 54, 78, 264
Lynch, John, 60
Lynch, Margaret, 208
Lynch, Richard, 134
Lynn, W., 99
Lyon, J.L., 237
Lyon, Robert, 241
Lyons, Jennie, 96
Lyons, Mrs., 222
Maack, C.A., 4
MacDonough, Joseph, 67, 179
Machado, Antonio, 207
Machado, F., 8
Machado, L., 2
Machado, Lucas, 5
Machado, Manuel F., 67
Mack, B. Jr., 144
Mack, Mrs. A., 192
Mackay, 130, 171
Mackay, J.W., 78, 134, 154, 171, 192, 212, 216, 243
Mackay, John W., 1, 6, 21, 31, 45, 55, 66, 82, 109, 114, 133
Macken, John, 62
Mackenzie, E., 242
Mackenzie, Howard, 62
Mackenzie, Jane, 123
Mackenzie, Malcolm, 62
Mackenzie, Phebe, 62
Mackenzie, Rev., 177
Mackie, Emily Isabella, 50
Mackie, James B., 50
Mackin, Andrew, 175, 177
Mackin, J., 102
Mackin, Mr., 184, 269
Mackin, Mrs., 11

Mackinder, T.B., 258
Mackle, James B., 210
Maculy, W., 173, 178
Madden, James, 161, 210
Maddock, Nellie, 182
Madera, Raymond, 241
Madruga, Manuel F., 7
Madruga, Samuel P., 251
Madsen, Capt., 30
Madsen, M., 137
Magee, 92
Magee, Anna, 73
Magee, Florence, 62, 200
Magee, J., 123
Magee, James, 178
Magee, Mrs. James, 165
Magee, R.D., 4, 147
Magee, R.J., 52
Magee, Richard J., 51, 61
Magee, Richard, 4, 53
Magee, T., 88
Magee, Thomas, 84, 183, 186
Magee, W.F., 213, 227
Maggary, Mary A., 175
Maggetti, 69, 73
Maggetti, E., 64
Maggetti, J., 8
Maggetti, Louis, 207
Maggetti, Silvio J., 152
Magnes, Alberto S., 24
Magnes, Irving, 62, 200
Magnes, Moses, 193
Magnes, Mr., 190
Magnes, R., 4, 52, 76, 171, 212
Magnes, Robert, 193
Magnesen, Martin B., 6
Magneson, Bertha, 250
Maguire, Ellen, 38
Maguire, Laura, 39
Maguire, Mary Jane, 38
Maguire, Mrs., 56
Maguire, Olive, 38
Maguire, Susannah, 39
Maguire, Thomas Godfrey Jr., 39
Magus, M.S., 2
Mahar, 192, 193
Mahar, J., 111
Mahar, J.B., 196, 214, 269
Mahar, James, 194
Mahar, John B., 194
Mahar, Mrs. J., 178
Mahon, E.B., 3, 9, 22, 99, 134, 147, 232
Mahon, T.J., 4, 9, 24, 27, 128, 130, 135, 228
Mahon, Timothy, 3
Mahoney, 178
Mahoney, Ella, 62
Mahoney, L., 28
Mahoney, M., 178
Mahoney, M.J., 2

Mahoney, Michael, 210
Mahoney, Miss E.T., 34, 259
Mahoney, T.V., 188
Mahoney, W.H., 49
Mailliard, Annie A., 6
Mailliard, J., 37
Mailliard, John Ward, 161
Maison, Ludwig B., 27
Maker, Thomas, 241
Makin, James, 60, 233
Malatesta, Joseph, 175
Male, L., 210
Mallon, Charles E., 94, 96, 185
Mallon, Charles, 139
Mallon, H.M., 172
Mallon, Honora M., 67, 96, 101, 172, 190, 191
Mallon, Honora Margaret, 197
Mallon, Honora, 185
Mallon, Mr., 166
Mallon, Patrick, 67, 96, 165
Mallory, M., 33
Maloney, M.R., 165
Maloney, R., 51
Malore, J., 60
Malore, J.H., 60
Maltos, A., 207
Maltzen, C., 87
Maltzen, Charles, 16
Mamscheimer, U., 178
Mann, A., 60
Mann, Abner S., 151, 153
Mann, Arthur, 241
Mann, Emmet, 203
Mann, Maude, 145
Manner, Amelia, 260
Manner, Barclay, 260
Manner, C.V., 228
Manney, J.F., 30, 32
Mannheimer, M., 165
Manning, Charles, 177
Manning, Minnie, 188
Manny, James, 13
Mansebo, Manuel, 45
Mansfield, Dr., 89
Manuel, Joseph, 68
Many, A.L., 259
Marchant, 158
Marchant, Ethel, 62, 200
Marchant, William, 199
Marchant, Willie, 62
Marchats, D., 2
Marcus, Gustav, 6
Marcuse, Mr., 185, 187, 189
Marcuse, Mrs. B.M., 247
Marden, A.L., 183
Marden, Emma F., 67
Marder, Wilhemine L., 17
Marens, Gustav, 6
Mares, Maria C., 153
Maria, Jack, 248
Marilla, Michael, 187

Marinda, M., 75
Marini, V.A., 210
Marion, Washington, 67, 178
Markham, Governor, 266
Markham, J., 234
Marks, Frank B., 67
Marline, G., 75
Marquess, Alberto S., 230
Marriott, A.J., 246
Marshall, James, 114, 169
Marshall, Joe, 129, 132
Marshall, L., 123
Marshall, Louis, 68
Marshall, Mrs. Louis, 157
Marshall, S.A., 18, 196
Marshall, W.A., 196
Martelli, Martini, 50
Martens, D., 202, 213
Martens, Dick, 92
Martin, Arnold, 167
Martin, Arthur A., 21
Martin, Arthur, 64
Martin, Charles, 84, 135, 147, 191, 223, 224
Martin, Henry G., 265, 267
Martin, James, 68
Martin, Linda, 74
Martin, Mrs. Thomas, 30
Martinelli, A., 64, 69, 227, 228, 237
Martinelli, Attilio C., 65
Martinelli, E., 113
Martinelli, E.B., 28, 36, 38, 40, 44, 167, 188, 142, 202, 213, 215, 216, 245, 252, 257, 261
Martinelli, L., 36, 64, 147
Martinelli, Louis, 4, 38
Martinelli, Mrs. J.S., 213
Martinelli, O., 237
Martinelli, S., 207
Martinez, E. Francisco Sr., 194
Martinez, Ernest, 176
Martinez, Jose, 215
Martinez, L., 120
Martinez, Ladislao, 117, 124
Martinez, Manuel, 148
Martinez, S., 147
Marvin, I.F., 35
Marzoni, P., 60
Mason, C.D., 260, 262, 264
Mason, Clinton, 207
Mason, George, 81, 146, 245, 260, 268
Mason, John, 207
Mason, Laura P., 110
Mason, Mr., 184
Mason, Mrs. George, 250
Mason, S., 220
Massey, A., 165, 178
Mastings, Madame R., 220
Mastrup, Iver, 61
Mastrup, Maria C.S., 166

Mastrup, Miss, 11
Mastrup, Theodore, 62
Masuda, Mr., 220
Mather, E., 60
Matheson, A.C., 8, 144
Matheson, A.E., 222
Mathews, Manuel S., 204, 249
Mathin, Miss F.S., 230
Matsen, Carl, 91
Matsen, Charles, 77
Matsen, Charlotte, 117, 119
Matteson, E.P., 168, 174
Matteson, Mrs. E.P., 168
Matthews, E.S., 67
Mattlies, H., 5
Mattoni, Marion, 186
Mattos, 195
Mauricio, Maggie R., 30
Mauricio, Manuel, 30
Maurri, Mat, 178
Maxon, G.W., 46
Maxwell, A., 137
Maxwell, Ethel, 62
Maxwell, Harry, 222
Maxwell, Lawrence, 62
Maxwell, Mrs. H.J., 178
May, J., 132
Mayer, August, 223
Mayer, Clara Leontina, 82
Mayer, Louise, 194, 242
Mayer, Oscar, 35
Mayhew, Granville, 199
Mayle, J.W., 244
Mayne, Rev., 101
Mazeas, Frank M., 32
Mazeas, J.M., 51, 218
Mazeas, Jean M., 39, 43
Mazeas, Judith, 40
Mazza, Francisco, 70
Mazza, Frank, 44
Mazza, J.J., 70
Mazza, Louis, 71
Mazza, Luigi, 70
McAdams, Mr., 110
McAdams, S.A., 14, 16
McAlester, William, 223
McAllep, Lena, 87
McAllep, Miss L.C., 34, 218
McAllister, A.C., 95, 146, 213
McAllister, Alice, 204
McAllister, Archie C., 33, 35
McAllister, Archie, 27
McAllister, Bessie, 35
McAllister, Capt., 37
McAllister, Elliott, 170, 180
McAllister, Hall, 202, 210
McAllister, J.L., 2
McAllister, Kate, 36
McAllister, L., 121
McAllister, Miss, 62, 74
McAllister, Mrs. A.C., 143
McAllister, W.F., 170, 208

McAllmey, Mrs., 192
McArthy, J., 190
McArthy, Mary M., 258
McAulay, John E., 165
McBenna, A., 77
McBride, Laura, 200
McBride, M., 251
McBride, Thomas, 62
McBright, Joseph, 233
McBryde, Laura M., 249
McBryde, Laura, 62
McBryde, Violet, 62, 199
McCabe, N., 75
McCaffery, Burt, 222
McCaffoney, B., 234
McCallam, Christy Ann, 254
McCallister, A.C., 37
McCamish, Chester B., 120
McCamish, Chester, 139
McCamish, H.F., 19
McCamish, W.F., 120
McCamish, William F., 256
McCamish, Winnie, 120
McCarthy, Charles, 171, 264
McCarthy, Clarence, 200
McCarthy, E.W., 4, 25, 31, 167
McCarthy, Edward W., 38
McCarthy, Harry A., 233
McCarthy, J., 49
McCarthy, M., 123
McCarthy, Walter, 200
McChesney, E.J., 110
McChesney, Eliza J., 92
McChesney, H.M., 110
McChesney, Henry N., 92
McClashan, 5
McClellan, Bernice, 62, 200
McClellan, Blanche, 62, 200
McClellan, Lillie, 62, 200
McCloskey, Hugh, 241
McCloskey, Mrs. A., 179
McClosky, 179
McClosky, Michael, 90
McClure, D., 131
McCoffey, Burt, 259
McCollough, J., 42
McComb, J., 42
McComb, John, 48
McConnelogue, Catherine, 172
McCormack, J.P., 35
McCormick, Ellen E., 64
McCornick, Hugh, 18
McCoy, J.C., 222
McCrea, 231
McCue, Father, 149
McCue, Henrietta, 67, 207, 264
McCue, J., 165
McCue, Mrs. James S., 249
McCue. J.S., 65
McCullough, J., 51
McCune, L., 82
McCurdy, Samuel, 241

McCutcheon, E.J., 16
McDaniels, J.C., 80
McDermott, James, 62
McDermott, Lizzie, 163
McDermott, P., 109, 114, 245
McDermott, Patrick, 163
McDonald, 32, 48
McDonald, A., 97
McDonald, Angus, 20, 21, 35, 169, 246
McDonald, Birdie, 262, 266
McDonald, D., 230
McDonald, Dr., 180
McDonald, Effie, 56, 61, 63
McDonald, George M., 135
McDonald, Gilbert, 59
McDonald, Gracie, 61
McDonald, J.A., 227
McDonald, J.S., 61, 78, 79, 117, 119, 121
McDonald, James S., 61
McDonald, James, 28, 56
McDonald, John N., 22
McDonald, Lillie, 59
McDonald, Lizzie, 161
McDonald, Margaret, 62, 203
McDonald, Miss B., 11
McDonald, Mr., 69, 207
McDonald, Mrs., 11, 244
McDonald, R.H., 186
McDonald, Rebecca S., 180
McDonald, Rev., 63
McDonald, S.J., 233
McDonald, Thomas F., 85
McDonnell, Addie, 34
McDonnell, Miss, 16, 168
McDonough, J., 175
McDonough, J.H., 143, 144
McDonough, S., 178
McDonough, Samuel, 246
McDougal, D., 259
McElnay, John, 67, 265, 267
McElnay, Mary, 240
McElroy, Carolyn M., 157
McElwee, 229
McFarland, C., 33
McFarland, Harry, 226
McFarland, Mrs. J., 194
McFarrell, Annie S., 119
McGarin, Annie, 79
McGeary, John, 222
McGee, Charles, 5
McGee, Edward, 236
McGee, Thomas, 15, 18
McGillawey, Ann, 194
McGilliary, G.O., 179
McGillilwig, Annie, 179
McGinnis, Mrs., 87
McGinnis, Rev., 23
McGlerron, E., 66
McGlocken, Jack, 194
McGovern, Frank, 239

McGovern, P., 111
McGovern, Peter, 239
McGovern, Thomas A., 209
McGowan, Julia, 54
McGowan, Mr., 54
McGrass, Mrs. M., 253
McGrath, John, 251
McGreavy, Richard, 216
McGrew, W.H., 92
McGroth, Maggie, 201
McGuire, Frank, 242
McGuire, Lena L., 265
McGuire, Mr., 171
McGuire, Mrs., 179
McGurk, Francis, 176
McGurk, Frank, 73
McHugh, Thomas, 192
McInnes, J.H., 42, 89, 117, 134
McInnes, Mrs. A.H., 265
McIntosh, A., 75, 102
McIsaac, Miss E.K., 182
McIsaacs, Neil, 114, 120
McJohnstone, D., 60
McKay, 108
McKay, A., 121
McKay, Alex, 108
McKay, James A., 209
McKee, Charles, 84
McKee, J.C., 145
McKee, S., 28, 42
McKeel, Charles, 148
McKenna, B., 18
McKenna, Miss, 112
McKenna, P., 92, 106
McKennan, F.B., 214, 269
McKennan, Frederick Butler, 211, 216
McKennan, Hugh, 211
McKenzie, 108
McKenzie, Abbie, 62
McKenzie, E., 171
McKenzie, James, 62, 200
McKenzie, Mrs. Robert, 233
McKenzie, Mrs. William, 171
McKenzie, William, 171
McKeon, Miss E., 11
McKeon, Miss, 262
McKinney, J.C., 28
McKinney, William, 215
McKinnon, 35, 65, 81, 162
McKinnon, Alex, 60
McKinnon, B.J., 260
McKinnon, Father, 10
McKinnon, Frederick Butler, 206
McKinnon, Hugh, 206
McKnight, Mollie J., 238
McLattan, C., 119
McLaughlin, 207
McLaughlin, D.W., 37
McLean, David A., 238
McLean, J.N., 3

McLean, James T., 143
McLean, Miss L.M., 34, 74
McLean, Neil A., 238
McLeod, A.C., 147
McMahan, Mr., 107
McMahon, George, 75
McManus, Henry, 159, 179
McManus, Jessie, 103
McMillan, 92
McMillan, George, 37, 46, 86, 140
McMillan, R.J., 68
McMillan, William, 173
McMullen, Joseph, 258
McMullen, Mrs., 241
McMullin, James G., 47
McMurtry, L.B., 257
McMurtry, Leslie B., 251
McNabb, Mrs. James H., 236
McNamara, E., 264
McNamara, Edward, 13
McNamara, Ellen C., 206
McNamara, Ellen, 202
McNamara, Fred, 226
McNamara, J., 207
McNamara, J.H., 227
McNamara, Joe, 91
McNamara, John, 33, 111
McNamara, Joseph, 89
McNamara, M., 50, 126
McNamara, Mary W., 264
McNamara, Mary, 264
McNamara, Mrs., 201
McNear, George A., 266
McNear, George P., 190, 201
McNear, J.A., 116, 124, 154, 178
McNight, Mollie J., 191
McNutt, W.F., 211
McPhail, Ella, 34
McPherson, Katie, 173
McPhillips, Francis, 204
McQuaid, Father, 97
McQuaid, J., 149
McQuarrie, Etta, 62
McQuarrie, Father, 106
McQuarrie, Robert, 37
McRea, J.G., 9, 222
McShafter, James McM., 44
McSweeney, James, 73
McVanner, 35
Mead, Mamie, 236
Mead, Mrs., 236
Meagher, F.T., 242
Meagher, Frank T., 193, 202, 209
Meagher, Irene, 202
Meagher, Lizzie Irene, 193, 209
Meagher, Mrs. F.T., 191
Meeker, 41
Meeker, B.C., 165
Meeker, M., 192

Mehl, 23, 141
Mehl, F., 53, 145
Melano, A., 97
Melhus, Gugri, 192
Melville, Mrs. G.A., 210
Melville, W.R., 217
Melzer, J., 75
Menken, E., 230
Menken, U.E., 183
Menotti, Pasquinucci, 43
Menville, 75
Menzies, Thomas, 1
Mercer, Alice Jane, 131
Mercer, Edwin, 102, 234, 259
Meredith, G., 106
Merrill, John H., 55, 66
Merrill, Parker, 50, 217
Merrill, Ruth A., 75
Merry, Catherine, 252
Merry, Richard, 55, 246, 252, 260
Mersebach, Clara, 186
Mesa, 25, 92
Mesa, M.R., 5
Messer, W.T. Jr., 161
Metz, A., 96
Metzger, G.V., 245
Metzler, Anna, 165, 178, 188, 192
Metzler, N., 173
Meyer, 252
Meyer, Charles, 6, 185
Meyer, David, 67, 155
Meyer, Edward, 239
Meyer, Mary, 185, 205
Meyer, Miss E., 11
Meyer, Moritz, 70, 72, 86
Mias, Capt., 26
Michaelson, Mr., 53
Michels, Katie, 233
Micticker, Jos., 123
Middleton, J.W., 42, 48
Milano, H., 239
Milbury, W., 75
Miles, Henry, 64, 85
Mill, C.L., 154
Miller, 44, 45
Miller, A., 86, 108
Miller, Alphonso, 236
Miller, Annie, 54, 220
Miller, Anton, 130
Miller, B.T., 40
Miller, Bernard, 69
Miller, Bill, 92
Miller, Charles E., 67
Miller, Clara, 3
Miller, D.W., 263, 264
Miller, Daniel, 259
Miller, E.C., 99
Miller, Etta, 86
Miller, F., 146
Miller, Frank, 78

Miller, Fred, 218
Miller, George, 63, 154, 267
Miller, Grace, 204
Miller, J., 92
Miller, J.A., 205
Miller, James, 191
Miller, Lulu, 62, 200
Miller, M.B., 8
Miller, M.J., 153
Miller, M.R., 88
Miller, Magdalena R., 88
Miller, Max Henry, 51
Miller, Miss A., 247
Miller, Mr., 214, 262
Miller, Mrs. E.M., 222
Miller, Mrs. Fred, 218
Miller, Mrs. Isaac, 71
Miller, Nellie, 259, 261, 262, 263
Miller, O.C., 7, 45, 58, 173, 179, 228, 247, 249
Miller, W.A., 225, 243
Miller, W.H., 132
Miller, W.J., 31, 64, 154
Miller, W.P., 25
Miller, William Alfonso, 237
Miller, William H., 133
Miller, William J., 38, 135, 167
Milligan, 142
Milligan, R.T., 194
Millmeister, Agnes, 88
Mills, Charles D., 265
Mills, Charles, 194
Mills, J.W., 65
Mills, Juliet W., 57, 70, 83
Mills, Minnie B., 208
Mills, Mrs. W.G., 183
Mills, W.G., 4, 91
Mills, William G., 57, 65, 70, 83
Milton, 5
Milton, R., 195
Milton, Walter M., 232
Minami, F., 40
Minand, F., 210
Mineis, C., 25
Miner, Ella F., 22
Miner, Mary, 66
Minesinger, Estelle, 159, 161
Minielle, Denise, 178
Minor, D.K., 165, 247
Minor, E., 132
Minor, George, 73
Minott, 142, 261, 266
Minott, Capt., 127
Minott, J.P., 267
Minott, James P., 129
Mintie, A.E., 118, 224
Mintie, L.C., 224
Mintie, Lottie C., 118
Miraell, C., 137
Miranda, Mrs. S., 183
Miranda, S., 67, 195, 208

Mirander, Camille, 62
Missit, Annie, 233
Mitchell, Charles, 261, 262, 263, 269
Mitchell, J., 124
Mitchell, James, 65
Mitchell, John, 124, 125
Mitchell, Mr., 184
Mitchell, Theodore, 178
Mitton, R., 35
Mogollo, F.M., 108
Moims, M., 25
Molfino, Guiseppe, 262
Moline, A.J., 77
Moller, August, 265, 267
Moller, S.L., 33
Molseed, Jane, 264
Molseed, W.J., 264
Moltzen, Charles, 84
Monaghan, Kate, 234
Mondon, Antoinette, 62
Mondon, C.G., 269
Mondon, Caroline, 72
Mondon, Ed, 110
Mondon, Henry, 62
Mondon, Jeanette, 62
Mondon, Mary H., 151
Montague, H. De La, 208
Montalon, G.W., 91
Monteith, G.W., 253, 257
Monteith, George W., 208, 255, 262, 263, 264, 269
Montenas, Bertie, 259
Montgomery, A., 57, 67
Montgomery, Alex, 108
Montgomery, Alexander, 105, 119, 121
Montgomery, Mrs., 189
Montmayeur, Pierre, 258
Mooney, J., 180
Mooney, Richard James, 148
Moore, A.A., 258
Moore, Arthur, 60
Moore, Charles M., 40
Moore, Charlotte, 233, 251
Moore, Ellery B., 239
Moore, Ethel, 62
Moore, Florence C., 104
Moore, Fred L., 20
Moore, H.H., 92
Moore, J.C., 239
Moore, John, 241
Moore, Luther E., 115
Moore, Maud, 58
Moore, May, 34
Moore, Miss, 59
Moore, Mrs., 250
Moore, R.J., 247
Moore, S.E., 77
Moorhead, 44, 45
Moorhead, Grace, 62, 200
Moorhead, Harold, 20, 62

Moorhead, S.H., 234
Moorhead, S.P., 25, 31, 108, 245
Moorhead, Stanley P., 38, 252
Moorman, H.C., 162
Morais, M., 96
Moran, James, 176
Moran, Katie, 259
Moran, M., 119, 123
Moran, P., 168
Moras, J.M., 148
Moras, Maria Dos Angos, 148
Mordoff, Homer, 62, 200
More, Myreta W., 16
Morella, Anton, 226
Morello, G., 146
Mores, Sumner V., 261
Moretti, A.B., 13, 132, 140, 238
Moretti, G., 223
Morgan, Bertha, 200
Morgan, E.J., 2
Morgan, Ella, 165
Morgan, H., 66
Morgan, H.W., 27
Morgan, J.C., 178
Morgan, John, 155, 262
Morgan, Laura, 171
Morgan, Mary A., 125, 126, 141
Morgan, Maud, 199
Morgan, Miss, 101
Morgan, Mr., 219
Morgan, P. Brett, 15
Morgan, P.B., 13, 68, 125
Morgan, Ruth, 61
Morgan, Sam, 247
Morgan, Stella, 199
Morgan, W.H., 35
Morgan, W.I., 52
Morgansen, M., 137
Morinini, Joe, 178, 195, 222
Morinini, Joseph, 194
Morley, W.I., 178
Morns, M.J., 178
Morrill, Parker, 218
Morris, 85, 97
Morris, Anna, 222, 249
Morris, B.F., 92
Morris, E.B., 135
Morris, James, 134, 139
Morris, John, 6, 67
Morris, K.M., 8
Morris, M., 12
Morris, Mary, 18
Morris, May, 85
Morris, Mrs. E.B., 192
Morris, Mrs. Ignacio, 252
Morris, Mrs., 85, 187
Morris, Rebecca, 3
Morris, Roland S., 222
Morris, Rosa, 62, 199
Morris, Rowland, 230
Morris, Roy, 85
Morris, S.N., 170, 185, 192, 196

Morris, Sallie, 67
Morris, Sarah N., 258
Morris, W.C., 259
Morrissey, Peter, 3, 22, 32, 39, 56, 58, 72
Morrow, A.J., 121
Morrow, Andrew J., 165
Morrow, Anton, 190
Morrow, Eleanor, 112
Morrow, Judge, 37, 112
Morrow, Maud, 111, 112, 114
Morrow, W.W., 114
Morscheimer, A., 192
Morse, B.G., 146
Morse, Benjamin G., 216
Morse, Kate, 25
Morse, Mrs. B.G., 206, 211
Morse, Mrs., 121
Morse, W.H., 220
Mortimer, E.E., 165
Morton, David, 124
Morton, Ellen C., 131
Morton, Ellen Catherine, 125, 146
Morton, Eugene, 119, 125, 131, 146
Morton, J., 119
Morton, Mr., 74, 113
Morton, Nellie, 244
Morton, Owen, 125, 146, 219, 221
Mosson, William S., 42
Mossop, W.S., 102
Mouette, P., 3
Moulton, F.B., 202
Moulton, Florence, 21
Moyle, Mrs., 165
Moyle, N., 25
Muhlbeyer, Antone C., 133
Mulcahy, Mary, 243
Mulcahy, W., 202
Mulhern, E., 243
Mulhern, F., 56, 202
Mulhern, Frank, 151
Mulhern, J., 56
Mulhern, J.P., 202
Mulhern, M., 213
Mulhern, M.J., 50, 149, 167, 234
Mullen, A., 106
Mullen, F., 78
Mullen, Fred, 148
Mullen, J., 145
Mullen, Julia, 158, 179
Muller, 75, 108
Muller, B., 102
Muller, E., 92
Muller, Keteka, 258
Muller, L., 33
Muller, Mrs. Henry, 222
Muller, R., 51
Mulligan, Ella, 27
Mulligan, James, 176

Mulligan, R.T., 84
Mullins, John, 73
Mulvaney, P., 169, 226
Muncey, Lorenzo S., 260
Mundt, F.A., 89, 118
Mundt, Francis Augustus, 82
Mundt, T., 233
Mundt, Theodore, 89, 115
Muneo, James M., 153
Murbach, A., 97, 234
Murphy, A.B., 15
Murphy, Carrie, 222
Murphy, D.J., 83
Murphy, Edward W., 209
Murphy, Edward, 209
Murphy, G., 181
Murphy, George, 161, 170
Murphy, Hannah, 115
Murphy, I.J., 165
Murphy, J.A., 157, 158
Murphy, James, 157
Murphy, John, 115, 269
Murphy, Jos., 194
Murphy, L.J. 123
Murphy, Lawrence, 241
Murphy, M., 102
Murphy, M.L., 87, 204
Murphy, Maggie, 165
Murphy, Mary M., 115
Murphy, Mary, 139, 178
Murphy, Miss, 222
Murphy, Mrs. D.C., 233
Murphy, Mrs. J., 239
Murphy, Mrs. John W., 220
Murphy, Nina, 236
Murphy, P., 18
Murphy, Patrick J., 158
Murphy, Patrick, 157, 241
Murphy, Paul, 265, 267
Murphy, S.G., 39
Murphy, Will, 204
Murphy, William, 206
Murray, 127
Murray, A.B., 217
Murray, B., 233
Murray, Ben, 54
Murray, C., 98
Murray, Catherine, 82
Murray, Conductor, 4
Murray, Cornelius, 79, 82
Murray, F., 53
Murray, Frank J., 84
Murray, Frank, 62, 200
Murray, Fred, 61
Murray, George, 54
Murray, J.D., 183
Murray, J.J, 202
Murray, James L., 182
Murray, James, 266
Murray, Joseph J., 137
Murray, Lt., 266
Murray, M., 9, 49, 79, 146

Murray, Maggie, 204
Murray, May, 258
Murray, Michael, 7, 86, 151
Murray, Miss N., 201
Murray, Miss, 22
Murray, Mr., 187
Murray, Mrs., 187
Murray, T.J., 202
Murray, William, 62, 200
Murray, Willie, 62, 200
Muscio, Edna, 182
Myer, E., 92
Myers, Charles W., 219
Myers, D.U., 124
Myers, David, 4, 71
Myers, H.A., 256
Myers, John H., 28
Myers, Mary, 74, 108
Myers, S.L., 37
Myrick, 43
Nagel, G.A., 120
Nagel, Jacob, 13, 16
Nappenback, Henry, 220
Nash, Mrs. J.S., 76
Nason, F.T., 224
Nason, Mary P., 136, 149
Nathan, A., 93
Navarro, Jesus, 222, 226, 240, 255
Neal, 144
Neal, J., 2
Neal, R.W., 75
Neale, V., 14, 19, 44, 139
Neale, Vincent, 12, 128, 167, 192
Nearmann, J.S.S., 184
Nearne, Edgar A., 232
Needham, 25
Neel, J.F., 242
Neil, Mrs. Robert E., 167
Neil, Robert E., 167
Neimeyer, Josephine, 122
Neito, Rabbi, 165
Nelan, Mrs. M., 37
Nelson, A., 51
Nelson, Alfred, 115, 178
Nelson, Charles, 78, 233
Nelson, E., 108
Nelson, Ed, 254
Nelson, Edna M., 16, 34
Nelson, George, 254
Nelson, Johannes, 131
Nelson, M., 54
Nelson, Miss, 161
Nelson, Walter, 74, 204
Nelson, William, 62, 203
Neppard, Louis, 179
Nesbit, J., 77
Neumann, Adam, 133
Neumann, Julius, 157, 178
Nevez, Manoel F., 195
Nevin, Peter, 148

Newberry, William, 215
Newcomber, Mr., 225
Newcomer, J., 16
Newell, David, 82
Newlands, M., 145
Newman, Harry C., 166
Newman, Katrina, 56
Neyce, Mae, 34
Neyce, Miss, 140
Nichols, Andrew, 100
Nichols, Asa C., 36
Nichols, Charles C., 227
Nichols, E.H., 199
Nichols, Ella W., 31
Nichols, Ellen W., 36
Nichols, Lena, 62
Nichols, Martha, 62
Nichols, Miss E.H., 35, 74
Nichols, Miss, 62
Nichols, Thomas H., 37, 245
Nicholson, W.A.S., 23
Nickles, Andrew, 238
Nicolassen, J., 188
Nicolaysen, 183
Nielles, Charles D., 267
Nielsen, Heinrich, 178
Nielson, H., 60, 75, 111
Nielson, Hans, 146, 243, 245
Nielson, Mr., 78
Niles, Edward, 241
Nilson, Alfred, 111
Nilson, C., 66
Nilson, John, 244
Nilson, Krystie, 128
Nilson, O., 42, 46
Nippert, L., 97
Nisson, E.P., 84, 144
Nisson, Lena, 74
Nizzoli, Mr., 207
Noble, Dr., 61, 97, 104, 223, 233
Noble, H.H., 99
Noble, Mrs. C.J., 69
Noble, Rev., 63
Noble, W.B., 242
Noble, Willis, 231
Noe, Victor, 178
Nolan, Maggie, 65
Nolan, Michael, 237
Nolthing, William, 192
Noonan, Nellie, 29
Norden, L., 97
Nordling, E.E., 153, 155
Nordman, Joseph, 149
Noriel, Aneta, 93
Noriel, William, 199
Norman, John, 253
Norman, Mrs. Travis, 76
Northup, J.W., 231
Norton, C., 66, 88
Norton, Charles, 74, 83
Norton, John, 215
Nott, Charles, 167

Nott, Hiram J., 119
Nott, Hiram, 20, 117, 119
Nowell, George, 7
Nowell, J.A., 75, 180, 218
Nowell, Mr., 80
Nugent, James, 59, 168
Nugent, Robinson, 1
Nunes, Antonio, 129, 254
Nunes, Rita, 173
Nutting, L.B., 75
Nye, Caroline E., 191
Nye, D.F., 217
Nye, David, 142, 184
Nye, Mrs. David, 162
O'Brien, D.F., 66
O'Brien, Eleanor, 122
O'Brien, Eva, 3
O'Brien, J.J., 105
O'Brien, M., 109, 111
O'Brien, Michael, 104, 118
O'Brien, Miss M., 201
O'Brien, Mollie, 181
O'Brien, Mrs., 222
O'Brien, P.E., 137
O'Brien, Thomas V., 158
O'Brien, William, 54
O'Bryen, 33, 35
O'Bryen, Mrs. T.J., 114
O'Connell, Daniel, 58, 63
O'Connell, J., 207
O'Connell, John, 192
O'Connell, Nora, 74
O'Connor, 93
O'Connor, Agnes K., 136
O'Connor, Angela, 136
O'Connor, Ann W., 136
O'Connor, Catalina, 69
O'Connor, Charles F., 136
O'Connor, Fanny C., 136
O'Connor, Fanny Stone, 136
O'Connor, J.J., 168
O'Connor, James C., 136
O'Connor, Jennie, 204
O'Connor, John A., 136
O'Connor, John F.K., 136
O'Connor, M., 146, 234
O'Connor, M.J., 135, 162
O'Connor, Maggie K., 136
O'Connor, Mary Stone, 136
O'Connor, Michael J., 136
O'Connor, Mrs. M.C., 230
O'Connor, Mrs. M.J., 162
O'Connor, Mrs. T.C., 137
O'Connor, Mrs. W., 207
O'Connor, Sarah A., 136
O'Connor, Thomas D., 136
O'Connor, William, 136, 174
O'Donale, C., 230
O'Donnell, Myles, 101
O'Gorman, Mary, 136
O'Halloran, Mr., 252
O'Hara, 217

O'Keefe, Ellen, 231
O'Keefe, Robert, 215
O'Leary, Cornelius, 110, 116
O'Leary, Margaret, 116
O'Leary, William, 241
O'Malley, A., 111, 119
O'Malley, Austin J., 259
O'Malley, Dick, 240
O'Mara, M., 54
O'Neil, Lena, 222
O'Neil, M.E., 260
O'Neil, Miss K., 26
O'Neill, Charles, 149
O'Niel, Father, 59
O'Pope, George, 28
O'Reilly, J.J., 145
O'Reilly, T., 75
O'Rourke, Nellie, 35
O'Shaughnessy, M.E., 191
O'Shea, Henry, 233
O'Sullivan, Mrs. Catherine, 176
O'Toole, F., 201
Oakes, Frances, 66
Obitz, Harry, 200
Obitz, J., 166
Obitz, Jacob, 9, 19, 159, 160, 170, 226
Ochs, G.F., 23
Ochs, Gustav F., 56
Offutt, Isabel H., 258
Offutt, Isabel, 182
Oge, Gertrude, 61, 204
Oge, Mary, 61, 204
Oge, Willie, 62, 200
Ohae, D.C., 5
Ohlmann, E., 75
Ohm, 7, 18, 117
Ohm, E., 25
Ohm, L., 25
Oki, 181
Olbers, Mr., 59
Oldam, A., 123
Oldis, Josephine, 132
Olds, Daniel, 250
Olin, 27, 28
Olin, Miss M., 201
Oliveira, J.V., 5
Oliveira, S.M., 46
Oliver, 19
Oliver, George, 61, 236
Oliver, Margie A., 123
Oliver, O.L., 24, 32
Oliver, W.M., 24, 32
Olivia, Attilo, 215
Olivia, Charles, 176
Olsen, C.H., 66
Olsen, E., 203
Olsen, Hans Jacob, 70, 83
Olsen, J., 77
Olson, Charles, 192, 222
Olson, Edward, 62
Oman, August, 176

Onstott, John, 251
Ordway, W.F., 92, 93
Orlovere, L., 8
Orloza, L., 60
Ormuna, F.M., 259
Osborne, Cordelia, 95
Osborne, Melzer, 96
Osborne, O.E., 181
Osborne, W.H., 145
Osgood, Caroline L., 166, 175, 232
Osgood, Carrie L., 155
Osgood, James, 222
Osgood, Mrs., 23
Osgood, R.W., 228
Osgood, W.J., 166
Osment, Delia, 219
Oss, I., 132
Ostaera, Toney, 222
Osterman, Mrs. M., 227
Osterman, Mrs. S., 69
Ostini, F., 168
Oswall, L., 5
Otis, George E., 171
Otis, George, 68
Ott, Charles, 78
Otten, H.W., 266
Otton, Hedley, 127
Ottual, J., 42
Overman, E.C., 252
Owen, Anna, 200
Owen, J.W., 234
Owen, William, 234
Owens, W.W., 51
Owien, P., 207
Owler, Peter, 245
Oxnard, Louise A., 34
Oxnard, Mrs. R., 181
Oxnard, Mrs. Robert, 230
Oxnard, Thomas, 34
Ozann, A., 207
Ozann, Arthur Charles, 158
Ozann, C.A., 164, 177
Ozann, Charles Arthur, 158
Ozann, Charles, 21
Ozann, Louise N., 158, 164
Ozann, Natalie, 180
Pacdaneda, Joseph, 139
Pacheco, A.F., 82, 158
Pacheco, B.L., 157, 158, 223
Pacheco, G., 16, 158
Pacheco, Gumesindo, 158, 243
Pacheco, I., 203
Pacheco, John, 55, 92, 209
Pacheco, Juan, 158
Pacheco, Mercedes, 61
Pacheco, Ramon, 182
Pacheco, S., 202
Pacheco, S.A., 45, 53
Pacheco, Salvador A., 50
Pacheco, Salvador, 35, 147
Pacheco, V., 106

Pacheco, Vicenta, 1
Padret, N., 129, 145
Paff, 52
Paff, Charles, 65, 157, 160, 170, 172, 211
Paff, J., 174
Paganini, Charles, 148
Page, Arthur, 4, 186
Page, G.T., 212
Page, George T., 146, 237
Page, George, 248
Page, Gustav, 133
Page, Hamilton, 6
Page, Mrs., 195
Pagliero, Anetta, 261
Painter, R., 123
Palachi, G., 99
Palidini, Assunto, 179
Palm, Charles W., 194
Palmer, J., 137
Paloggi, A., 97, 102
Panchard, Ralph, 215
Pancoast, G.F., 66
Pareto, G., 256
Pareto, John, 21
Park, Ella F., 1, 152
Parker, George W., 70
Parker, Harry, 208
Parker, Henry, 188
Parker, Lillian A., 153
Parker, Miss Marion G., 34
Parkin, Hannah M., 254
Parks, Arvilla, 199
Parks, B.F., 195
Parks, I.H., 146, 252
Parks, Ira H., 167
Parks, Ira, 245
Parks, Mr., 167, 261
Parks, Mrs. L.F., 195
Parks, Sylvester, 110
Parlor, Taliaferro, 252
Parmarlee, Chauncey A., 42
Parrish, D., 108, 113
Parrish, Dillwyn, 197
Parrott, Mrs., 264
Parson, F.W., 212
Pascoe, 32, 48
Pascoe, W.F., 20
Pascoe, William F., 21
Pastori, 135, 139, 149
Pastori, C.S., 77
Pastori, Charles, 79, 130
Pastoria, Mr., 188
Patezan, James, 179
Pattarina, Mr., 131
Pattarina, Mrs., 131
Patten, W.H., 85
Patten, William, 146, 183, 230, 233
Patterson, Martha, 104
Patterson, W.J., 123
Pattison, J.H., 119

Pattridge, R.K., 2, 129
Paulino, Joe, 17
Paulsen, Karmen, 86
Peacock, C., 266
Peacock, Mr., 103
Pearce, George, 68
Pearl, Sophie W., 12
Pearson, Fannie M., 47
Pearson, Lewis, 188
Peckham, Lois A., 46
Pederson, H., 195
Pedranti, Antonio, 231
Pedrotti, A., 154
Pegetti, S.R., 253
Peireira, Frank, 207
Pellow, J.E., 213
Pelton, John C. Jr., 88
Pelton, John C., 90
Pendergast, James A., 99
Pendleton, Henry, 57
Penman, Edith, 21
Penman, George, 14, 21, 205, 221
Pennie, Judge, 134
Pennypacker, J.J., 225
Penrose, T., 75
Pepe, Joseph, 215
Pepper, G.B., 45, 221
Pepper, W.R, 221
Pepper, William R., 59
Peralta, Manuel, 241
Perara, F., 129, 143
Perara, Frank, 114, 121, 129, 126, 127, 130, 136, 221
Perata, J., 146
Percival, W.W., 218
Percy, Mrs., 252
Pereira, Antonio, 143
Pereira, J., 12
Pereira, Manuel S., 117
Perez, Mrs., 259
Perillat, A., 68, 130, 134
Perillat, Alexis, 11
Perillat, Marie, 100, 134
Perkins, A.T., 15
Perkins, S.H., 208
Perley, Emily L., 192
Perrari, John, 69
Perry, 181
Perry, Adela Downing, 230
Perry, Charles O., 205
Perry, Frank, 179, 195
Perry, Grattan, 26, 31, 201, 217, 230, 231
Perry, J., 82
Perry, J.E., 75
Perry, Kate, 68, 190, 207
Perry, Margaret L., 230
Perry, Mr., 234
Perry, P., 66
Perry, Risteome, 230
Person, Ola, 161

Persson, L.O., 145
Pertelchick, Jos., 181
Pesch, Mamie, 57
Peter, Antone, 207
Peter, Carlo, 231
Peter, Harry, 62, 201
Peter, Louis, 4
Peter, Mary, 197
Peter, Mr., 212
Peters, Frances A., 34
Peters, Henry, 207
Peters, Herrmann, 240
Peters, J.A.W., 96
Peters, Mrs. Charles, 113
Petersen, C., 137
Petersen, Grace, 62
Petersen, H., 213
Petersen, J., 25, 31, 99, 146, 167, 213, 257
Petersen, Lewis, 62
Petersen, Louis, 228
Petersen, Marie, 181
Petersen, Martin, 136, 180
Petersen, Mathilda, 227
Petersen, Minnie, 62, 200
Petersen, Olivia, 62, 203
Petersen, P.H., 212
Petersen, Tommy, 199
Peterson, 45
Peterson, A., 111, 121
Peterson, A.F., 69, 147
Peterson, A.S.F., 54
Peterson, Charles F., 197
Peterson, Charles, 156, 264
Peterson, Contractor, 13
Peterson, H.T.W., 139
Peterson, Henry, 26, 111, 148
Peterson, Johannes, 4, 9, 38, 148
Peterson, L., 66, 131, 203
Peterson, Laura M., 264
Peterson, Michael, 230
Peterson, P. Henry, 13
Peto, J., 121
Petrelli, Michele, 240
Petri, Narcisse, 72, 77
Petroni, L., 247
Petroni, Louis, 250
Petroni, M., 207, 247, 253, 257, 265
Petroni, Maurizio, 250
Petsch, M., 92
Pfeiffer, John L., 248
Phelps, Charles, 127
Phillips, J., 76, 80
Phillips, M., 93, 108
Phillips, Mrs. J., 80
Phillips, Mrs., 99
Phillips, Robert B., 24
Philpott, Hattie, 195
Phinney, Judge, 76
Piantanida, Francesca, 35
Pickering, Eveline, 93

Pickering, Mrs. Everline E., 179
Picket, Mr., 63
Pie, Pigozzi, 222
Pierce, E.T., 259
Pierce, Henry, 71, 110, 112, 154, 217, 219, 263, 263, 264
Pierce, M., 96
Pierce, Sarah C., 6
Pierce, W., 23, 131, 195
Pierce, William S., 6
Piezzi, Mary A., 182
Pimentel, Maria F., 7
Pinchello, Steve, 225
Pinkard, Belle E., 208
Pinot, C., 11
Pipin, E., 75
Pixley, A., 3
Pixley, Amelia v.R., 177
Pixley, Emma C., 243, 244
Pixley, Frank Jr., 92
Pixley, Frank M., 64, 132
Pixley, M.F., 243
Plank, F.F., 109
Plaritz, F.V., 99
Plaster, George, 179
Platt, Mr., 199
Plette, Alexander, 62
Plette, L., 202
Plette, Leza Catherine, 51
Plette, Louis C., 93
Plette, Louis, 187
Plow, Carl, 182
Polsen, Charles A., 190
Pomeroy, C.P., 44, 167, 222
Pomeroy, W., 17
Pond, Ella C., 43, 89, 185, 258
Pond, George, 216
Pond, M.S., 28
Pond, Mrs. W.C., 196
Pond, W.C., 196
Pond, W.S., 265
Ponjcan, A.M., 5
Porcella, Stephen, 248
Porcella, Steve, 168
Port, Mr., 234
Portatta, Mrs., 183
Porteous, Mrs. J.S., 61
Porter, Robert, 208
Portley, May, 78
Porto, Dal, 97
Potter, H.W., 15, 17
Poulet, Abel, 176
Poulet, Ali, 176
Powell, B.G., 106
Powell, M., 8
Powell, Mrs. R.C., 222
Powell, S.G., 66
Powell, Samuel G., 265
Powell, Walter, 36, 40
Power, Richard, 259, 268
Powers, Dr., 112
Powers, Harry, 195, 248

Powers, Jennie, 261
Powers, M., 23
Powers, Mrs. George H., 246
Powers, T., 66
Powers, Thomas, 145, 233, 265
Powers, W., 222
Powyle, H., 93
Praetzel, Mrs. C., 234
Pratt, Aleck, 189
Pratt, E.W., 123
Pratt, Elinor D., 258
Pratt, Fred, 189
Pratt, Leon E., 12
Prendergast, J.J., 198, 255
Prenty, 57
Prenty, Mrs., 173
Prescott, 229
Prescott, Effie G., 135
Prescott, Mabel, 62, 200
Prescott, Ralph, 61, 229
Prescott, Raymond, 204
Prescott, Roy, 62, 200
Preston, 35, 65, 81, 162
Pretzels, Mrs., 179
Prezzi, H., 48
Prida, Jos., 253
Pringle, J., 192
Pringle, James, 198
Pringle, Mamey, 258
Pritchard, Alonzo, 106
Protesti, G., 145
Proudfoot, Jessie, 62, 199
Prulley, Mrs. A., 188
Prunty, Catherine, 33, 54, 56, 58, 191, 192, 258
Prunty, Peter, 166
Pryor, J.H., 191, 212
Pryor, Mrs. P., 191
Puckhaben, H.C., 253
Puereri, Adele, 77, 79
Purvis, J.P., 92
Quackenbush, Thomas M., 212
Quarres, George, 58
Querke, 135
Quick, Mrs., 181
Quinn, I., 93
Quinn, John T., 237
Quinn, Mary J., 237
Quint, E., 32
Quint, L., 12
Quint, Leander, 98
Quist, John, 104, 106
Raab, Charles, 215
Raedanida, Gangicha, 103
Raedvida, 111
Raisch, Mrs. A.J., 248
Raleigh, Harry, 200
Raleigh, Mrs., 27, 28
Ralston, Joseph, 132
Ramos, 181
Ramos, A.E., 157
Ramos, Anna D., 14, 15

Ramos, Anna, 12
Ramos, J.B., 121
Ramos, Victor, 62
Ramsey, Lt., 112
Ramus, John, 241
Randeson, J.D., 93
Randit, Vincent, 82
Ranlin, H., 252
Ranzoni, L., 173
Rasmussen, James, 63, 200
Rasmussen, Jean, 62
Rasmussen, K., 234
Rasmussen, P.H., 213
Rasmussen, Peter, 17
Ratigan, Lizzie, 82
Rato, F., 132
Raulino, C.B., 178, 193, 198, 199, 219, 221
Raulino, Carolina B., 100, 109
Raulino, Carolina, 103, 236
Raulino, Joseph, 100, 103, 109, 113, 131, 235
Raulino, M., 106
Raulino, R., 106
Rawkins, O.C., 19
Rawlings, Joe, 192
Rawlings, Joseph, 91, 176
Ray, H.H., 123
Ray, Milan, 242
Rea, John, 91, 92
Reakle, J., 97
Reardon, M., 259
Reardon, Mrs. Dr., 90
Reatz, L., 75
Receker, Paul F., 150
Redding, Charles A., 61
Redding, Mrs. W.C., 91
Redding, W.C., 91
Redding, William, 91
Redfield, O.F., 123
Redington, Mrs. L.C., 189
Redmond, 168
Redmond, Bertha C., 112
Redmond, Johanna, 96
Redmond, Mary E., 96
Redmond, Miss K., 201
Redmond, Miss, 131
Redmond, Timothy, 214
Redmond, Walter, 200
Reed, C.H., 35
Reed, Dr., 38
Reed, George W., 269
Reed, J., 60, 222
Reed, J.J., 84, 147
Reed, J.P., 84
Reed, Mrs. G.B., 42
Reed, Mrs. G.W., 157
Reed, Mrs. J., 190
Reed, Mrs. J.J., 190
Reed, Mrs., 216
Reese, C., 18
Reeves, J.R., 16, 84

Regan, Henry, 203
Regan, J.C., 75, 195, 222
Regan, Mrs. J.C., 192, 195
Regendes, A.T., 12
Reglay, George, 241
Reichert, Mollie, 242
Reichert, Theodore, 158, 242
Reichert, Thomas, 242
Reilly, Agnes, 200
Reilly, Barney, 174
Reilly, Bernard W., 174
Reilly, Charles J., 64
Reilly, G., 75
Reilly, Joe, 62, 199
Reilly, M., 202
Reilly, William, 215
Reinfelt, M., 15
Reinholdt, Peter, 245
Remillard, Ed, 145
Remillard, P.N., 158
Remington, A.D., 174, 188, 190
Reoubeois, Mr., 179
Resch, M., 121
Resch, M.R., 97
Resendes, A.T., 42
Resendes, Manuel, 17
Resiga, Ellen, 234
Resiga, Frank, 234
Resiga, John, 234
Resiga, Josephine, 234
Respini, Jeremiah, 223
Rety, 270
Rety, Emil A., 261
Reusche, August Jr., 193
Rey, C., 66
Rey, J.J., 68, 191
Rey, Jane Ann, 248
Rey, Jane, 191
Rey, V.A., 44
Rey, V.J.A., 179
Reyes, M.M., 33
Reynolds, Annie M., 252
Reynolds, Bertha, 69
Reynolds, E.W., 2
Reynolds, James, 102
Reynolds, John, 60, 191
Reynolds, Lottie, 62, 200
Reynolds, Maude, 62, 200
Reynolds, Miss C.E., 234
Reynolds, Miss, 64
Reynolds, Mrs. L.E., 16, 27
Reynolds, Mrs. L.E.S., 35
Reynolds, Mrs., 136
Reynolds, T., 75, 82
Rhodes, Jessie, 215
Rhone, L., 60
Rice, Clara, 78
Rice, J.B., 83, 147, 170, 181, 207
Rice, J.R., 161
Rice, John, 147
Rice, Joseph, 83

Rice, P., 254
Rice, Pat, 150
Rice, Patrick, 130, 133, 135, 136, 177, 190
Rice, W.H., 60
Richard, A., 75
Richard, H., 75
Richard, Mrs. F.E., 210
Richards, C.O., 179, 192
Richards, Emma, 68, 235
Richards, J., 87
Richards, John, 173, 209
Richards, Miss, 234
Richards, Mrs., 249
Richards, William A., 78
Richardson, D., 92
Richardson, E.T., 72, 75
Richardson, Frank, 226
Richardson, G.L., 93, 167, 263
Richardson, George L., 44, 142, 167, 224, 236, 245, 252
Richardson, Josie, 204
Richardson, M., 227
Richardson, Martha, 204
Richardson, Mr., 105
Richardson, Mrs., 11, 267
Richardson, R., 99
Richardson, S., 44
Richardson, Stephen, 41
Richardson, Thomas, 132
Rideout, Alvira Jane, 7
Ridge, Thomas, 215
Riditer, Mrs. Fritz, 233
Rieger, William, 88
Riehard, N., 249
Righetti, A., 162
Righetti, Aquiline, 136
Righetti, C., 98
Righetti, Candido, 117, 118, 136
Riley, Charles, 234
Riley, J., 131
Riley, John, 123
Riley, K.A., 93
Riley, Mary, 208, 242
Riley, Thomas, 221
Ring, Byron, 192
Ring, David, 79, 149, 151
Ring, George E., 52, 146
Ring, Herbert E., 165
Ring, Herbert, 37
Riordan, Mrs. Dr., 96
Riordan, P.W., 5, 46, 48, 56, 207
Riordan, T.D., 152
Rippert, Firmin, 161
Riscioni, Mrs. S., 182
Ritchie, Agnes, 197
Ritchie, William, 68, 207
Rivas, J., 119, 123
Rix, Edward A., 265, 267
Rixford, G.P., 18
Rixford, Loring P., 40
Rixon, Harry, 179
Rizzini, 130, 135, 139, 149
Rizzoli, R., 207
Roach, David, 215
Robbins, Mr., 179
Robbins, Mrs. Thomas G., 179
Roberts, George F., 68, 69, 179
Roberts, Harry, 63, 200
Roberts, J., 60
Roberts, J.F., 242
Roberts, J.H., 35
Roberts, J.M., 46
Roberts, J.P., 141, 224
Roberts, Joe, 252
Roberts, M., 149
Roberts, Mary E., 186
Roberts, Mr., 170
Roberts, Walter, 200
Robertson, Fanny J., 122
Robertson, Fanny, 121
Robertson, John, 216, 253
Robertson, L., 75
Robertson, Miss D., 182
Robertson, Mr., 63
Robertson, Mrs. J.H., 115
Robertson, Rose L., 213
Robertson, Roxie, 153
Robertson, William, 126
Robinson, A.T., 96
Robinson, Aaron, 218
Robinson, C.J., 99
Robinson, Charles F., 22
Robinson, Ethel, 62, 199
Robinson, Franklin, 173
Robinson, J.F., 37, 202
Robinson, Kate, 208
Robinson, Leone, 62, 200
Robinson, Merrit, 37
Robinson, Mrs. J., 78
Robinson, Sarah F., 248
Robison, S.S., 111, 115
Roccatagliata, Lillie A., 175
Roccatagliata, Mary, 175
Roche, Rena, 200
Roche, Susie A., 104
Rochefort, Paul, 207
Rockford, Amelia C., 124
Rodd, M.E., 135
Rodden, Ada Maud, 95, 97
Rodden, Edna, 97, 197
Rodden, G., 245
Rodden, G.F., 227
Rodden, G.W., 97
Rodden, George F., 39, 142, 151, 213
Rodden, George, 17, 97
Rodden, Judge, 230
Rodden, Judge, 56, 79
Rodden, Justice, 10, 194, 228, 235
Rodden, Mrs. George, 97
Rodden, Mrs., 234
Roddy, Kate, 195
Rodey, M.A., 60
Rodgers, Clara, 34
Rodgers, Francis, 194
Rodgers, Frank, 21
Rodgers, J.P., 198
Rodgers, James, 235
Rodgers, M., 92
Rodgers, Manuel, 113, 131, 178, 188, 199
Rodman, Miss N.A., 11
Rodrigues, J.M., 102
Rodrigues, Joan M., 195
Rody, M., 92
Roe, John, 162
Roe, Richard, 29, 162, 214
Roe, Thomas, 162
Roeder, J.A., 5, 7
Roeder, J.A.C., 3
Rogalle, A., 106
Rogers, Dr., 37
Rogers, J., 204, 206
Rogers, Manuel, 193, 198, 219, 221
Rogers, William Reuben, 135
Rogerson, F., 77
Roggenlan, Adolf, 157
Rokie, Attilo, 215
Rolen, Carl A.A., 28
Rolineo, John, 128
Rollins, Charles A., 265, 267
Rolls, Mrs., 257
Roma, J. Mariano, 71
Roma, J.M., 189, 205
Romer, Charles, 173, 265, 267
Ronberg, E.A., 259
Ronberg, Emile, 62
Rooney, James, 241
Roos, B.C., 43
Roos, Laura, 62, 173
Root, E.M., 207
Root, J.F., 160
Roscelli, Attilo, 73
Rose, 27, 28
Rose, A., 102, 121
Rose, Henry, 232
Rose, J.P., 25
Rose, Mrs. Adena, 228
Rosecrans, W.S., 108
Roselli, Andres, 121
Rosenberg, Jacob, 7
Rosenthal, J., 175
Rosenthal, Joseph, 68, 114
Rosenthal, M., 191
Rosenthal, Marcus, 68, 114, 117
Rosfarini, V., 15
Roslett, J., 60
Rosme, E., 97
Rosme, W.E., 121
Rosner, E.M., 92
Ross, Ann S., 111, 116
Ross, Frank E., 234
Ross, John J., 71

Ross, M.L., 68
Ross, Marie, 207
Ross, Mary, 203
Rossefalle, Magnesen, 195
Rosseter, John H., 11
Rossi, L., 2
Rossini, Pietro, 217
Roucheto, Baptiste, 148
Rouke, Mr., 87
Roullier, A., 10, 15
Roullier, Albert, 84, 88
Rourke, Barnard, 171
Routstein, I., 156, 157
Rowland, Grace, 50
Rowson, Henry, 51
Rowson, John H., 259
Rowson, John Henry, 262
Roy, Alexander, 120, 187
Roy, J.A., 5, 20, 22, 47, 49
Roy, James A., 119, 172
Roy, James, 101, 103, 104, 113, 124, 127, 133, 134, 139, 183, 242, 250
Roy, John A., 7, 32
Roy, T.B., 37, 120, 172
Roy, Thomas B., 4, 6, 120, 187
Roza, J.S., 243
Ruddick, P.H., 24
Ruef, Johann, 173, 265, 267
Ruger, Miss, 112
Rumbold, Dr., 257
Rumbold, Mrs. Thomas F., 257
Runfeldt, M.A., 46
Runkel, George, 84, 253
Runyon, Fred F., 213
Runyon, Frederick F., 64
Rush, Mrs. Peter, 30
Russell, A., 145
Russell, Ernest, 151
Russell, F.W., 5, 86
Russell, Florimel E., 19, 86
Russell, J., 137
Russell, K., 137
Russell, M., 82, 106, 121
Russell, Mr., 11
Russell, Mrs. A.D., 195
Russell, Robert C., 265, 267
Rust, E.C., 36
Rutherford, Thomas W., 173
Rwiefel, Potter, 195
Ryall, P., 145
Ryan, A., 131
Ryan, Anna, 42
Ryan, Charles, 215
Ryan, Daniel J., 112
Ryan, Daniel, 235
Ryan, Father, 151
Ryan, Gertrude Theodore, 261
Ryan, Katie, 62, 200
Ryan, Lena F., 161
Ryan, Leonora, 204
Ryan, Lizzie, 60

Ryan, M., 97
Ryan, M.J., 222
Ryan, Maggie, 74
Ryan, Mamie, 62, 200
Ryan, Nora, 74
Ryan, Richard, 265, 267
Ryan, T.R., 246
Ryan, Thomas R., 55, 255
Ryan, Thomas, 41, 71, 256
Ryland, Mary A., 253
Sabine, 154
Sabine, R.H., 147
Sadler, Minnie C., 195
Sage, E., 75
Sais, Albert, 199
Sais, Alfred, 62
Sais, Ed, 200
Sais, Edward, 62
Sais, Jesus M., 1, 136
Sais, M.W., 169
Sais, Manuella M., 56
Sais, Pedro, 129, 131, 135
Sais, Willie, 199
Salazar, J.U., 195
Sale, Eva, 62, 203
Sale, Kittie, 62, 203
Sale, Martha, 62, 199
Sale, W., 260
Sale, W.T., 33
Sale, Willa, 62, 199
Sale, William T., 4
Sale, William, 140
Sales, M.M., 266
Salina, Modesta, 194
Salling, Miss E., 233
Salm, Martin, 122, 125, 146, 260
Salm, Mary, 189
Salme, Lena, 62
Salme, Martin, 125, 127, 131, 139, 146, 248
Salmon, 137
Salsberg, Clara M., 28
Sammy, George, 205
Samuels, Mr., 168
Sanchez, F., 137
Sanchez, N., 129
Sanchez, Nellie, 247
Sanciven, M., 12
Sander, Maria Rey, 248
Sanders, William, 148
Sanderson, Charlotte H., 24, 207
Sanderson, George R., 24
Sandoval, Mrs. Pablo, 73
Sanford, Arthur, 176
Sanford, James, 176
Santana, John M., 7
Sapin, Cline Elizabeth, 79
Saratte, Jon, 102
Sargent, Atiglia, 195
Sargent, C.R., 208
Sargent, Cyrus R., 40
Sargent, Elizabeth R.C., 208

Sargent, George C., 33
Sarmento, M.T., 82
Sarry, Mrs. M.E., 210
Sartori, Charles H., 133
Sartori, Charles, 48, 56
Sartori, Ersilia, 62, 203
Sartori, I., 137
Sartori, Ignazio, 7, 81, 82
Sartori, Kate, 62, 200
Sartori, Laura, 62, 200
Sartori, Olive, 51, 60
Sastkowske, F., 25
Saudman, Jannie, 222
Saudman, Kate, 222
Saul, Otto, 156
Saultry, Mr., 26
Saunders, 142
Saunders, Emily, 200
Saunders, Gertie, 62
Saunders, J.D., 98
Saunders, James D., 165
Saunders, James, 143, 266
Saunders, Jennie, 61, 204
Saunders, Mrs. James, 127
Saunders, W.H., 244
Saunders, William H., 165, 230
Savage, Amelia C., 160
Savage, J., 92
Savage, Mrs. C., 165
Savell, William B., 171, 183
Sawlet, G., 60
Sawyer, Ed, 78
Scanlan, David, 162
Scanlin, Mary E., 191
Scannell, Chief, 34
Schaer, Emma, 185
Schafer, Beckie, 96
Scharrer, Louis Herbert, 53
Scheeline, Simon C., 70, 72
Schengle, A.G., 111
Scherbe, Miss B., 183
Schereer, Paul, 195
Schettler, J.F., 266
Schetzel, Kate F., 209
Schilling, Pauline, 20
Schippers, John, 69, 70, 77, 83121, 124, 125, 196, 219
Schladitz, Charles, 88
Schlingman, J.F., 101
Schloper, Dr., 96
Schlosser, H., 32, 146, 257
Schlosser, Henry, 79, 160, 167
Schlosser, Hy, 31
Schlosser, Jacob, 230
Schlosser, Mr., 176, 202, 222
Schmeirer, Fred, 148
Schmerdt, Babetti, 254
Schmidt, A., 12
Schmidt, Bernhardt, 200
Schmidt, Henry, 11
Schmidt, John, 227
Schmidt, Mrs. R., 220, 233

Schmidt, R., 97, 248
Schmidt, Richard, 183, 265, 267
Schmiedell, Henry, 232
Schmitt, Annie, 71
Schmitt, Louise, 66
Schmitt, Rudolph, 66
Schmitt, William W., 71
Schneider, 141
Schneider, Annie, 23, 227
Schneider, D.M., 54
Schneider, Dora L., 48, 53
Schneider, J.J., 31, 130, 188, 201
Schneider, John F., 151
Schneider, Mrs., 201
Schneider, O., 207
Schneider, Oscar H., 48, 212
Schneier, William, 232
Schnell, J., 42, 65, 146
Schnell, Jacob, 49
Schnell, John, 4, 68, 87, 173
Schoellomer, A.M., 240
Schoeneman, 56
Schoeneman, Clara, 145
Schoeneman, Fred, 54
Schoeneman, Mr., 202
Schoobert, John E., 230
Schoonmaker, Cyrus, 183
Schoonmaker, James B., 171
Schreeves, Mrs. F., 252
Schrock, W.A., 237
Schroder, Gustav F., 123, 124
Schroder, Gustav, 101, 123
Schroder, H., 37
Schroder, Louise, 123
Schueler, John, 183
Schuemann, Fritz, 223
Schuetzen, Mrs. P., 84
Schufeldt, F.C., 85, 91
Schultz, D.H., 87
Schultz, Harry, 241
Schultz, Sarah J., 40
Schultz, Susan A., 228
Schutz, Matilda, 235
Schwerin, Mrs. R.P., 247
Schwettler, J.F., 269
Schwiesau, E., 14, 16, 24, 27, 41, 51, 128, 135, 148, 168, 185, 186, 223, 243, 250, 255, 262
Schwiesau, Mrs. E., 41, 51, 57, 267
Schwiesau, Mrs., 11
Schwiesau, S., 190
Scilacci, P.F., 84, 245
Scott, 54
Scott, A.E., 202, 213, 227
Scott, Annie Maria, 210
Scott, Arthur, 39, 217
Scott, C., 203
Scott, Carrie, 217
Scott, Charles, 62
Scott, George, 53, 61, 69, 204, 256

Scott, Georgiana, 35
Scott, H.T., 123
Scott, Hazel, 199
Scott, Helen, 200
Scott, J.E., 123
Scott, Miss Georgie, 16
Scott, Mr., 126
Scott, Mrs. A.D., 59
Scott, Mrs. H., 11
Scott, Mrs., 4
Scott, R., 213, 267
Scott, Robert, 180, 213, 266
Scott, Sadie, 62, 203
Scott, W.A., 53
Scott, W.H., 259
Scott, W.P., 123
Scott, William A., 29
Scott, William, 200
Scott, Willie, 62
Scown, 26, 125
Scown, A.G., 32, 39, 146, 167
Scown, Adolph G., 43
Scown, Mary, 125
Scown, Mr., 168
Scown, Mrs. A.G., 236
Scown, Mrs., 40, 168
Scudder, Judge, 236
Scudder, Pearl, 48
Seabel, Philip, 199
Searles, H.L., 245
Sears, A.S., 25
Sears, Ben, 222
Sears, Laura, 244
Sease, Nicholas J., 229
Sebastian, Anton J., 238
Sebrean, Mrs. John, 70
Secombe, Ada, 62, 200
Secombe, Sadie, 62, 200
Secondino, P., 41
Sedgwick, A.V., 179
Seehind, Dora, 26
Seet, William, 28, 35, 185
Seibel, Christine, 62
Seibel, F., 146
Seibel, Fred, 60
Seibel, Herbert, 200
Seibel, Mrs., 145, 219, 257
Seibert, Don, 62
Seibert, Mrs. 183
Seibert, Roy, 63
Seligman, Caroline, 169
Selkirk, W.A., 257
Selkirk, W.N., 53
Semler, Arthur, 82, 88
Senomec, Mont Luigi, 240
Sepes, Emma, 17
Settaro, Fernando, 215
Seven Oaks, Mrs. J., 69
Seven Oaks, Mrs., 75
Sewell, C., 33
Shaffer, R.E., 97
Shafter, 115

Shafter, Helen, 74
Shafter, J. McM., 21, 98, 102, 132, 235, 255
Shafter, James C., 118
Shafter, James McM., 90, 186
Shafter, Jayne J., 82
Shafter, P.J., 4, 98, 115, 120, 169
Shafter, Payne J., 111, 117
Shafter, R.B., 96
Shain, Joseph, 41, 89
Shand, David O., 249
Shand, Maggie C., 149
Shane, Carrie, 26
Shane, Mrs. M.E., 174
Shank, Fanny, 62
Shank, Frank, 62
Shank, William, 62
Sharker, Grover, 241
Sharkey, John H., 195
Sharon, F., 119
Shattuck, D.D., 68, 171
Shaunessy, M.M., 68
Shaver, Aaron, 149, 206, 209, 210
Shaver, Charles B., 58
Shaver, Harriet B., 83, 104
Shaver, Isaac, 79, 83, 88, 91, 191
Shaver, Ivy, 22
Shaver, J., 230
Shaver, Mrs. Aaron, 209
Shaver, R.F.B., 227
Shaver, Raymond, 62, 200
Shaver, Roy B., 213
Shaver, Roy, 151
Shaw, Mr., 183
Shaw, Thomas, 111, 195, 265, 267
Shay, T., 175
Shay, Timothy, 179
Shea, Francis, 215
Shea, John, 215
Shearer, George D., 114, 182, 216
Shearer, L.W., 93
Shearman, J.S., 166, 174, 247
Shears, Mrs., 183
Sheehan, 145
Sheehan, Jeremiah, 201
Sheehy, John, 8, 25, 31, 62, 106, 194, 200
Sheehy, Veronica Darling, 106
Sheehy, Veronica, 106, 139
Sheehy, Winifred, 194
Sheek, Matilda, 29
Sheek, William, 29
Sheeline, Simon C., 86
Sheels, H., 129
Sheerin, David, 68
Shelley, Frances, 146
Shelley, Mrs. W.N., 183
Shelley, Samuel Gilman, 146
Shelley, W.N., 130, 146

Shelley, William N., 43, 45, 104, 108, 118, 260
Shelton, J., 68, 207
Shelton, Mrs., 69
Shenton, Mrs., 184
Sheppard, E., 131
Sheppard, Mrs. A.D., 259
Sheridan, P.J., 150
Sherman, 177
Sherwood, H.M., 222
Sherwood, John, 27
Sherwood, Lily, 237
Sherwood, Miss H.M., 237
Shield, John, 17
Shields, M., 266
Shields, Marcia, 5
Shields, Mrs. J., 195
Shields, Mrs., 1, 187
Shields, Oleta, 62, 200
Shilling, Amir, 161
Shilling, Annie, 183
Shine, George, 252
Shine, J., 42, 76, 150
Shine, Jeremiah, 40, 48, 49, 265, 267
Shine, Jerry, 10, 133
Shine, John, 7, 22
Shine, Mrs. Jerry, 10
Shippler, Mrs., 11, 267
Shoberg, Albert S., 46
Shoberg, Miss S., 11
Shoberg, Mrs., 211
Shoberg, Sophia, 46, 216
Shoemaker, E.H., 111
Shoemaker, Mr., 112
Shoobert, Elizabeth J., 2
Shoobert, J.E., 24, 146
Shoobert, John E., 2, 4
Shorb, S., 97
Short, J., 147
Short, J.O.B., 11, 15, 63, 120, 146, 186, 222, 225, 238, 254, 258
Short, John O.B., 28, 46, 50, 92, 249
Short, O.B., 107
Short, Orey, 61
Short, Walter E., 15, 108
Short, Walter, 11, 107
Shortridge, 197
Shotwell, E.E., 42
Shotwell, J.M., 186
Shotwell, Joseph M., 205, 250
Shotwell, Marianne Tourgee, 205
Shotwell, Mr., 187
Shreve, E.D., 110
Shreve, Esther, 62, 200
Shuck, Mary L., 210
Shuck, Mrs. McL., 207
Shueman, Fritz, 205
Shufelt, F.C., 81

Shute, Mrs., 220
Shutz, Matilda, 237
Sibley, James, 45, 208
Sibrean, M.M., 95
Siemsen, H., 182
Silacci, P., 93
Silberstein, J., 58, 61, 114, 185
Silva, 237, 270
Silva, A., 60
Silva, A.M., 42
Silva, Antonio Machado, 40
Silva, J.A., 118
Silva, J.E., 188, 193
Silva, J.M., 109
Silva, J.P., 109
Silva, John Enos, 113, 131
Silva, John Foster, 116
Silva, John, 119, 121, 127, 129
Silva, Joseph V., 261
Silva, M. DeM., 211
Silva, M., 207
Silva, M.A., 118
Silva, M.G., 238
Silva, Manuel D., 24
Silva, Manuel DeM., 184
Silva, Manuel, 65
Silva, Mary, 56, 139
Silva, R.E., 42
Silva, Rosa Emily, 40
Silveira, 21
Silveira, F., 13
Silveira, F.A., 211
Silveira, Feliz A., 184
Silveira, J., 25
Silveira, Jose H., 238
Silveira, Mary, 105
Silverman, J., 97
Silvius, Herman T., 68
Simand, E.T., 157
Simand, Maude, 157
Simard, S.T., 174
Simard, Sam, 145
Simard, Samuel T., 158
Simes, Mrs. C.H., 182
Simmons, Joseph, 241
Simoni, P., 46, 121
Simontacchi, Antonio, 35
Simpson, Loretta, 195
Simpson, Mr., 20
Simpson, Richard S., 183
Simpson, Silas S., 34
Simpton, A.M., 153
Simpton, G.W., 8, 245
Simpton, George W., 182
Sims, Alice, 175, 177
Sims, Charles, 177
Sims, Mrs. Charles, 177
Sinclair, A.M., 2
Sinclair, A.U., 183
Sinclair, Edward A., 27
Sing, Hop, 156
Sing, Lee, 154

Singley, G.W., 177
Sjogren, Louisa J., 81
Skiffington, Matthew, 241
Skinner, W.D., 84
Skybarker, Mr., 61
Slack, Eliza, 179
Slancer, Mrs., 183
Slater, George, 241
Slayton, Miss E., 183
Slevin, Bessy, 235
Slinkey, 115, 116
Slinkey, Brother, 198
Slinkey, Colonel, 13
Slinkey, Daniel, 55, 150
Slinkey, J.E., 73, 168
Slinkey, Lillian, 198
Sloss, 7, 12
Slosser, H., 25
Small, Mamie, 246
Small, Reuben, 154
Smart, G.T., 247
Smith, A., 12, 75, 92, 129
Smith, A.A., 202
Smith, A.C., 51
Smith, Alonzo C., 201
Smith, Amanda, 249
Smith, Annie Pardee, 78
Smith, Annie, 93
Smith, Artie W., 173
Smith, Bella, 62
Smith, Blanche, 179
Smith, Charles, 63
Smith, Clara A., 249
Smith, Cora B., 204
Smith, Dr., 233
Smith, E., 202
Smith, E.H., 123
Smith, Emily A.P., 169
Smith, Ethel S., 247
Smith, Eugene W., 245
Smith, F., 5
Smith, F.D., 59
Smith, Fanny, 242
Smith, Francis L., 242
Smith, George F., 208
Smith, George W., 68
Smith, H., 23
Smith, Harry, 62, 63, 200
Smith, Hattie, 62, 200
Smith, Henry, 5, 237
Smith, J. Glover, 78
Smith, J., 2, 23, 111
Smith, J.C., 233
Smith, J.G., 222
Smith, J.H., 77, 99, 111
Smith, J.M., 42
Smith, J.N., 129
Smith, J.R., 183
Smith, Jean, 18
Smith, Jeff, 259
Smith, Julia, 61
Smith, K., 15

Smith, Lucy Virginia, 23
Smith, Lucy, 148
Smith, Manuel, 179
Smith, Margaret K., 228
Smith, Margaret, 204
Smith, Marston, 148
Smith, Mary, 195, 204, 228
Smith, May, 222
Smith, Mr., 19, 263, 268
Smith, Mrs. A.H., 213
Smith, Mrs. G.B., 201
Smith, Mrs. G.F., 258
Smith, Mrs. S., 183
Smith, O., 203
Smith, Ora, 131
Smith, P., 147
Smith, R., 2
Smith, Russell, 176
Smith, S., 227
Smith, S.H., 123
Smith, S.L., 179
Smith, Sidney V., 71
Smith, Susie, 62, 179, 240
Smith, Temple, 153
Smith, Thomas, 51
Smith, Tom, 180
Smith, W., 129
Smith, W.H., 93, 96, 99
Smith, William, 51
Smith, Willie, 63
Smith, Z., 203
Smith, Zekie, 62
Smyth, Bertha, 62, 203
Smyth, C.S., 34, 38, 61
Smyth, Clara B., 35
Smyth, Hudson, 20
Smythe, C.B., 229
Smythe, C.S., 92, 135, 179
Smythe, Margaret, 213
Snee, Annie, 267
Snee, Mary, 28
Snell, Mrs. E.L., 71
Snook, George A., 1
Snook, George Clement, 1
Snook, S., 92
Snyder, 119
Soares, A.J., 8
Soares, F., 8
Soares, Joaquin De Souza, 116
Soares, S.J., 144, 149, 164, 166
Soares, Severino J., 129
Sodre, M.V., 97
Sohncke, H.G., 156
Soldate, M.A., 69
Soldati, James, 99
Soldati, Joe, 99
Soldavini, A., 9
Soldavini, Angelo, 258
Sonlae, J., 248
Sore, Mrs. L., 259
Sorenson, Lottie, 62, 200
Southwick, D.S., 44

Southworth, Mary J., 238
Southworth, S.S., 238
Souza, Antonio F., 153
Souza, Antonio, 69
Souza, J.J., 207
Souza, Mariana S.R., 194
Spalding, J.D., 208
Spaletto, E., 97
Sparrow, E.D., 173
Sparrow, Edward D., 6
Spaulding, Sarah, 92, 96
Spear, Joseph Jr., 190
Spear, Joseph S., Jr., 190
Specula, John, 241
Spedding, Dr., 105, 110
Spellman, Erastus, 47
Spellman, Festus, 53
Spence, A.S., 18, 166, 174, 177, 184, 247
Spence, F., 82
Spencer, 144, 177
Spencer, Clara A., 227
Spencer, F.W., 12, 14, 19, 128, 139
Spencer, John C., 104
Spencer, Mr., 23
Spencer, Mrs. A., 190
Spencer, Mrs., 23
Spencer, Nina R., 192, 269
Spencer, Sydney, 129
Spenney, Charles, 42
Sperry, J.W., 71, 97, 173, 258
Sperry, James W., 88, 94, 111, 115
Sperry, Mrs. E., 179
Spinney, C., 66
Sponey, J.B., 42
Spony, John B., 195
Spony, Mr. J.W., 183
Spoor, Mrs. H.C., 183
Sprague, R.H., 236
Spreckels, Adolph B., 36
Spreckels, J.D., 40
Srivers, H., 5
Stack, Joseph, 233
Stack, Thomas, 28
Stadfeld, Jacob, 45, 56
Stafford, J., 145
Stagg, Cornelius, 132
Stahl, E., 173
Stalford, 103
Stalford, John P., 15
Stalow, J., 51
Stamfelde, A., 77
Standley, Annie E., 189
Stanley, John P., 136
Stark, Ferdinand, 246
Starkey, E., 54
Starr, R.S., 161
Starrett, J.F., 69
Statter, 5
Stearnes, Eliza A., 208

Stearns, Mary, 204
Stedman, Robert, 204
Steel, Fred, 190
Steel, William, 238
Steele, 59
Steele, James, 233
Steele, Jane C., 182
Steele, T.J., 147
Steen, Annie, 95
Steen, John A., 95
Steenshorn, J., 247
Stefert, Louise, 219
Steffins, Capt., 183, 219
Steffins, E.J., 46, 119
Steffins, Mrs. N., 248
Steffins, Mrs., 219
Steinecke, Sophia, 28, 85
Steinmetz, 35
Steinwood, E.A., 46
Steitz, H., 129
Steiz, Henry, 153
Stemple, 125
Stemple, Charles, 126
Stemple, E.A., 115, 116
Stemple, Eliza A., 126
Stemple, Eliza Ann, 117
Stemple, Leonard S., 117
Stemple, Poole, 17
Stencil, Miss A., 254
Stephen, Dr., 105
Stephen, J.J., 110
Sterling, Henry, 252
Stern, Charles K., 180
Stetson, J.B., 128
Stetson, Maria, 128
Stetson, Mr., 101
Stevens, Ella, 195
Stevens, M., 137
Stevens, Mrs. T.J., 68
Stevens, William, 80
Stevenson, C.C. Jr., 30, 222
Stevenson, Jane Haight, 222
Stevenson, Mrs. C.C. Jr., 223
Stewart, Adam, 94
Stewart, Frances D., 155
Stewart, H.M., 220
Stewart, John, 183
Stewart, Miss, 247
Stewart, Mrs., 87
Stewart, R.F., 145
Stewart, W.K., 233
Stimpson, J.S., 208
Stimpson, Jane, 1
Stine, Mrs., 254
Stinell, A., 66
Stinson, A.H., 26, 103, 208
Stinson, Lewis, 269
Stinson, Nathan H., 105
Stocker, M., 42
Stocker, Maud, 204
Stockmeyer, Mrs. D., 219
Stolp, O., 66

Stolph, Mr., 202
Stone, C.B., 205
Stone, DeLancey, 241
Stone, J., 46
Stone, Miss H., 230
Stone, O.C., 183
Stone, Peter V., 68, 165, 183, 208
Storlim, William, 148
Story, 23
Stout, M., 123
Stow, S.H., 18
Stowell, Aggie, 73
Stowell, E.H., 183, 195, 210
Stoy, Sam, 182
Stoy, Samuel, 173
Stozynske, Teiphil, 48
Strain, Henry, 5
Strand, G.B., 46
Strand, Maggie C., 136
Strasser, Leopold, 3
Stratton, Charles C., 6
Stratton, Charles, 19, 33, 35
Stratton, Edith, 62, 63
Stratton, J.S., 31, 167
Stratton, John S., 38
Stratton, Mr., 26, 63
Strauss, Levi, 208
Strauss, Nathan, 245, 247, 250, 267
Strecker, A., 37
Streeten, James M., 36, 40, 45, 77, 256
Strittmatter, Jacob, 68
Strittmatter, Mrs., 11
Strobel, James, 215
Strong, E.B., 116, 235, 247, 253
Strong, Edward B., 249
Stuart, John Percy, 23
Stubbe, John J., 269
Studley, Arthur, 62, 201
Studley, B.W., 143, 266
Studley, Mrs., 267
Stump, Irwin C., 132
Stumpf, John, 14, 16
Stutt, James, 60
Sullivan, 60, 185, 188
Sullivan, Con., 195
Sullivan, M., 78, 108
Sullivan, Mary A., 156
Sullivan, Mary J., 259, 251
Sullivan, Mary, 40
Sullivan, Mrs. J., 219
Sullivan, P., 195
Sullivan, P.J., 184, 250
Sullivan, Peter J., 36, 40, 237
Sullivan, Peter, 251
Sully, Minnie, 179
Sumard, E.I., 155
Summerfield, 48
Surrienburg, George, 62
Susavilla, J.S., 174
Sussman, S., 191
Sutcliffe, D.D., 207
Sutcliffe, F.E., 2
Sutcliffe, Julia Ann, 68, 207
Sutcliffe, Thomas E., 129, 207
Sutherland, D., 146, 213
Sutherland, Helen, 200
Sutherland, William, 212
Sutter, Allen M., 186
Sutton, 96
Sutton, Aiden, 168
Sutton, Francis, 174, 268
Sutton, Frank, 101, 180, 229
Sutton, Minnie, 74, 174
Sutton, Thomas, 236
Svenson, A., 46
Svenson, Augusta, 230
Swain, Ellis M., 205, 208
Swain, Hattie E., 205
Swan, Jabez, 246
Swanson, A., 28, 60
Swanson, John A., 81, 156
Swanwell, Ivy, 17
Sweeney, 75
Sweeney, L., 51
Sweetser, Fred W., 182
Sweetser, J.R., 146
Sweetser, John R., 4
Sweetser, John, 181
Sweetser, Josie, 269
Swiefel, Peter, 39, 40
Swift, 259
Swift, J.R., 48, 123
Swift, John R., 260
Swift, K., 33
Swift, Patrick, 116
Swift, R., 141
Swisher, B.F., 124, 214, 244
Swisher, Bella F., 58, 109, 125, 170, 182, 185, 190, 192, 196, 207, 209, 219, 221
Sylva, F., 214
Sylva, Florence, 210
Sylva, John, 50
Sylvester, A., 102, 121
Taboas, Franco, 63
Taboas, Manuel, 62, 199
Tabor, Adeline, 62
Tabor, Mary E., 243, 256
Tabor, W.J., 243
Tachiria, 102
Tackney, John, 218
Tackney, M., 218
Taft, Frank W., 61
Taft, H.F., 64
Taft, L.R., 167
Talbot, Mary, 54, 78
Talbot, Mrs. A.P., 179
Talbot, Mrs., 208
Talbot, William, 78
Taliaferro, Dr., 60
Tanforan, F., 42
Tanjle, Homer, 201
Tann, Amanda, 20, 24, 30, 42, 91, 101, 126, 128, 139, 144, 155
Tannebaum, B., 242
Tanner, R., 201
Tanner, Ralph, 62
Tarr, C.B., 12
Tay, Charles Fox, 176
Taylor, 93, 144
Taylor, Andy, 249
Taylor, D.T., 43, 73, 198, 151, 205, 251, 261
Taylor, Dan, 109
Taylor, F.S., 261
Taylor, Fred W., 265, 268
Taylor, Frederick S., 45
Taylor, Frederick W., 195
Taylor, G., 93
Taylor, George, 62
Taylor, H.W., 150, 188
Taylor, Henry W., 182
Taylor, J.W., 7
Taylor, James D., 116
Taylor, James I., 11, 49, 50, 64, 66, 72, 74, 79, 113, 119, 123, 207
Taylor, James, 126, 149, 179
Taylor, Kate R.E., 45, 186
Taylor, Mr., 85
Taylor, Mrs. D., 173
Taylor, Mrs. S.W.I., 193
Taylor, S.T., 211
Taylor, Sarah I., 208
Taylor, Sarah W., 179
Taylor, Sarah W.I., 93, 124, 127, 235
Taylor, T., 46
Taylor, T.W., 12
Taylor, W.P., 16, 124, 146, 168, 245
Taylor, William, 121
Taylor. D.T., 263
Tebi, Fred, 230
Teixeira, Macheda, 254
Teixeira, Rosa, 196, 199, 255
Teixera, J.A., 25
Tellerson, Henry, 166
Ten Broeck, A.H., 214
Ten Broeck, Ellen M., 214
Tenir, Martin, 254
Terra, M.M., 161
Terris, Mary, 103
Terry, 107, 195
Terry, B.F., 46
Terry, Benjamin F., 265, 268
Terry, J.M., 95
Terry, Mrs. M., 222
Terry, William, 108, 133, 210
Tetcovitch, Blas, 215
Tetiques, Mr., 230
Tetterberg, A.H., 153
Tevis, William S., 208

Tharpe, Julia, 62, 200
Thatcher, Mrs. E.S., 220
Thaxter, William S., 3
Thayer, Clifford, 63, 200
Thayer, Lucy H., 172
Thayer, Wilbur, 200
Thederman, 111
Theilig, Max A., 66, 75
Theilig, Max Arno, 36
Theilig, Max, 268
Theyer, A., 157
Thomas, D., 247
Thomas, G.W., 108
Thomas, George A., 59
Thomas, H., 51
Thomas, H.B., 173, 230
Thomas, J.J., 46
Thomas, J.S., 230
Thomas, Jacques, 90
Thomas, John, 212
Thomas, L., 75
Thomas, Lizzie J., 146
Thomas, W.J., 209
Thomay, A., 8
Thompson, C.T., 136, 155
Thompson, Charles T., 21, 110, 160, 161
Thompson, Charles W., 186
Thompson, Guy, 62, 199
Thompson, Harvey M., 260
Thompson, J.A., 77, 135
Thompson, Jefferson, 59
Thompson, John A., 70, 83
Thompson, Mabelle S., 77
Thompson, Mary E., 158, 160, 186
Thompson, Mr., 243
Thompson, Mrs. J.E., 247
Thomson, A.B., 9, 23, 86, 141
Thomson, George, 106
Thomson, Mrs. R. MacGregor, 173
Thomson, R. MacGregor, 173
Thon, C.H., 92
Thon, Margaret, 92
Thorne, Walter, 211
Thornton, Harry N., 267
Thornton, Mary J., 267
Thornton, Mrs., 268
Thors, Louis, 228
Thosoph, M., 75
Thrasher, David, 43
Throckmorton, I.W., 93
Thurn, 25
Tibbey, E.F., 231, 236
Tibbey, Edney S., 162
Tibbey, Emily F., 68, 81, 162, 253
Tibbey, Millie Byers, 108
Tierney, Mrs. William, 76
Tierney, Mrs., 26
Tierney, W.F., 112

Tierney, William, 157
Tilden, Charles, 106
Tilghman, George, 32
Tilghman, W.P., 179
Tillinghast, 270
Tilton, S.S., 124
Tilton, W.M., 229
Tilton, Walter M., 124
Timony, A., 37, 168
Timony, Anthony, 117, 229
Timony, F., 2
Timony, Mrs. A., 225
Tobin, John, 175, 177
Tobin, Roy J., 161
Todd, Hugh G., 146, 151
Todd, Hugh, 162, 194
Todhunter, T.E., 163
Todtmann, Theo E., 23, 172
Tognazzi, Mr., 100
Tognazzi, Peter, 103
Tojetti, Edward, 75
Toland, D., 42
Toland, Mrs. Dr., 260
Tomasini, G., 162
Tomasini, L., 14, 150
Tomasini, Louis, 13, 18, 177
Tomasini, M., 183
Tomasini, Matthew, 1
Tonini, Antoinette, 88
Toofry, J., 46
Toohey, B., 251
Toohey, Cornelius, 231, 251
Toplitz, F., 102
Torra, M., 207
Torre, John, 194
Tourgee, Mrs., 187
Towle, George W. Jr., 161
Towle, Kate, 196
Towne, A.N., 3
Towne, A.P., 10, 13, 146
Towne, Hiram, 3, 10, 139
Townsend, Alice C., 208
Trachney, Mr., 130
Trainor, Peter, 154
Traversi, Joseph, 183
Traxler, Earlington, 114
Treanor, Mary A.C., 251
Treanor, Mary, 74, 251
Treanor, W., 74
Treanton, Mr., 202
Treanton, P., 56
Tree, T., 135
Tree, Treeda, 121
Trefile, Simeon D., 235
Treweek, Fred J.R.M., 106
Trouette, A., 2
Troy, R.P., 8, 69, 86, 226
Tubaini, L., 60
Tuchler, A.S., 239
Tucker, Henrietta, 39
Tucker, Mrs. J.D., 39, 155
Tuckey, A.R., 110, 214

Tuckey, Matilda R., 208
Tuginan, A., 75
Tuher, John, 216
Tully, M., 137
Tumelty, Ellen, 45
Tunstead, Dora, 122
Tunstead, James A., 88
Tunstead, James, 33, 44, 45, 50, 63, 71, 83, 95, 98, 104, 107, 115, 120, 144, 154, 171, 179, 180, 183, 191, 205, 222, 224, 233, 237, 243, 244, 258, 264
Tunstead, Mary A., 154
Tunstead, Mary, 180
Tunstead, Mr., 173
Tunstead, Mrs., 102
Tunstead, Thomas, 120, 122, 152
Tunzi, I.L., 235, 240
Tunzi, M., 235, 240
Tunzi, P., 87
Turner, Charles F., 122
Turner, Dell, 204
Turner, Emma, 90
Turner, Fannie, 62, 173, 203
Turner, Frank, 249
Turner, Mrs. A.E., 173
Turner, Mrs. O., 113
Turner, Thad, 123
Turrell, Ada, 114
Twilia, M., 46
Tyrrell, Eliza A., 63
Uheldi, Lulf, 121
Ulente, Charles, 260
Unch, Frank, 204
Ungarth, Mr., 232
Unger, Cress, 46
Unknown, 243, 257
Upshain, Benjamin P., 179
Upton, A.H., 105
Upton, Archie A., 105
Upton, James W., 105
Upton, Mr., 60
Urban, Dr., 85
Urban, K., 116, 141
Urschman, Mr., 11
Utschig, John, 37
Valencia, A., 51
Valencia, Catalina C., 158
Valencia, Catalina, 158
Valencia, Mrs. C.C., 69, 80, 207
Valencia, Ramon, 44
Valencia, T., 42
Valencia, V., 42
Valentine, 7
Valentine, T.B., 12, 81, 108, 177, 178, 218, 226
Valentine, Thomas B., 233
Valentini, Father, 15, 100, 256, 266
Valesquez, I.M., 96
Vallette, Ellie O'Connor, 136

Van Arsdale, Nellie, 211
Van Arsdale, W.W., 211
Van Balveron, W.E.J., 227
Van Dyke, H.J., 20, 177
Van Dyke, Henrietta, 180
Van Dyke, Henry J., 33, 180
Van Dyke, J.H., 208
Van Ness, T.C., 20
Van Palveren, W.E.J., 181
Van Sickle, C., 93
Van Slyke, E.W., 217
Van Slyke, E.W.S., 201
Van Tassell, Thomas, 162
Van Wic, Miss A., 195
Van Wie, Miss N., 252
Vance, W.K., 84, 86, 103, 105, 141
Vanderbilt, 56
Vanderbilt, F., 202
Vanderbilt, Frank H., 265
Vanderbilt, Mr., 202
Vanderbilt, William, 8, 155, 160, 161
Vandercook, Edward P., 65
Vanderlip, G.G., 246
Vanderlip, J.F., 246
Varney, 181
Vater, Mrs., 38
Vater, Rosalie A., 208
Vater, Rosalie V.R., 179
Vater, Rosalie, 31
Vaughan, D.E., 97
Vaughan, W.H., 87
Vaughn, George, 66
Vaughn, Mrs. W.H., 122
Vaughn, Mrs., 76
Vaughn, Thomas, 226
Veiller, Leymour, 260
Veiller, S., 51
Velan, Heloise R.C., 3
Velasco, M.L., 153, 157, 158, 222
Velasco, Maria L., 149
Verruder, Mrs. R., 210
Vesaria, Harriette L., 88
Vesaria, Louis, 18, 88
Vestry, B., 25
Viale, 192, 193
Viale, J., 214
Viale, Jos., 196
Victorino, J., 25, 96
Victorino, V.J., 60, 193
Vidal, Justo, 84
Viel, Mr., 188
Vierra, 100
Vigreanie, Miss C., 210
Vining, Everett A., 181
Vinwink, Garret, 165
Voehmann, William, 260
Vogel, Agatha, 209
Vogel, Charles, 232
Vogel, Frieda, 62

Vogel, H.B., 106
Vogel, Hans B., 88
Vogel, Mary A., 209
Vogel, Mathew Fife, 260
Vogel, Miss A., 233
Vogel, Mrs., 232
Vogel, Philip, 237
Von Gunten, Miss B., 208
Von Manderscheid, 126
Von Metzer, Mrs. E., 181
Von Retzer, Carl, 210
Von Schroeder, Jeannette, 39
Von Schroeder, John Henry, 39
Von Seibourj, Otto Jos., 195
Vonsen, J., 84
Vonsen, John, 144, 147
Vonsen, Katie, 74
Vrang, George, 62
Vrang, Morton, 63
Vrang, Mr., 103
Vrang, Mrs., 216
Vrnwink, G., 69
Wagner, Dr., 214
Wagner, E., 93
Wagner, George W., 254
Wagner, Henry L., 210
Wagner, Henry S., 202
Wainright, H.H., 65
Wainwright, Charles A., 225
Walker, Agnes, 133, 250
Walker, Albert, 62
Walker, Celestine, 63
Walker, Ella, 61, 204
Walker, H., 95, 108
Walker, Helen, 176
Walker, Hugh, 62, 68, 95, 100, 109, 110, 126, 232
Walker, J.P., 60
Walker, Jessie, 176
Walker, Lizzie, 204
Walker, Lydia J., 258
Walker, M., 86
Walker, Mrs. Oscar V., 176
Walker, Oscar V., 176
Walker, W.J., 25, 102
Walker, William, 208
Walker, Zelma, 62, 200
Wall, Alice M.M., 155
Wall, Delia, 46, 238
Wall, J., 145
Wall, J.H., 106
Wall, James, 48
Wall, Mrs. Willie, 234
Wallace, 197
Wallace, A.D., 242
Wallace, H.M., 208
Wallace, Harry, 148
Wallace, L.A., 269
Wallace, Lucie Adaline, 263
Wallace, Marguerite, 221
Wallace, Michael, 148
Wallace, Uriah, 261

Wallace, W.T., 221
Wallace, William, 60
Wallis, 181
Wallis, H.B., 97
Wallis, Jerusha M., 205
Walliser, T., 99
Walls, A.W., 5
Walls, Bert, 151, 173
Walls, Eleanor Louise, 173
Walls, Mrs. Bert, 173
Walls, Mrs., 242
Walsh, E.G., 258
Walsh, Emmet, 201
Walsh, F.S., 5
Walsh, George, 63, 200
Walsh, J.H., 99
Walsh, J.R., 209
Walsh, James E., 98, 109, 133, 134
Walsh, Jeff, 192
Walsh, Kate, 242
Walsh, M., 75
Walsh, Maggie, 208
Walsh, Mary A., 217
Walsh, Mr., 130, 171
Walsh, Mrs., 235
Walsh, Richard I., 213
Walsh, Sarah, 249
Walsh, Walter A., 217
Walsh, Walter, 31, 112, 116, 211, 216
Walters, Fred, 26
Walters, Julia H., 68
Walters, Mrs. L., 11
Walters, Mrs., 252
Wambold, May L., 182
Wambold, May, 213
Ward, C.W., 66
Ward, E., 60
Warden, A.L., 123
Warden, D., 146
Warden, David, 5, 36, 43, 63, 180
Warden, R., 203
Warden, Robert, 62
Ware, Mrs. S., 252
Warfield, Mr., 191
Warmouth, E., 110
Warner, 2
Warren, Rita, 220
Warrington, Nellie V., 63
Warron, Robert, 183
Washington, F.B., 24, 88
Wasser, Miss J., 11
Waterhouse, F.G., 127
Waterhouse, Frank G., 95
Waters, Michael, 73
Waters, Patrick, 155
Watkins, E., 96, 97
Watson, 180
Watson, Agnes, 62, 203
Watson, Eddie, 62

Watson, Henry, 227
Watson, J., 203
Watson, J.H., 2
Watson, J.W., 8
Watson, James, 62, 198, 212, 218, 259
Watson, John, 248
Watson, M., 15
Watson, Marvin, 252
Watts, J., 51
Watts, James, 265, 267
Watts, John, 7
Weber, Anne, 41
Weber, Annie, 96
Weber, Ignaz, 249
Weber, John Peter Henry, 232
Weber, Mack, 228
Weber, P.H., 217, 219, 221, 222, 226
Weber, Peter H., 232
Weber, Peter, 10, 12, 41, 94, 96
Weberbeck, E., 75, 77, 82
Webster, Samuel, 136
Weeks, F.L., 129
Weeks, Miss, 236
Weeks, S.P., 253
Weigand, Frank, 73
Weightman, J.C., 107, 150
Weilly, O.F., 78
Weiner, Axel, 215
Weingarth, Miss, 232
Weislli, E., 106
Weistenstein, 17
Welch, E.M., 42, 183
Welch, Edith, 66
Welch, Edward M., 265, 267
Welch, J.T., 263
Welch, John F., 5
Welch, Myrtle, 249
Welch, R.F., 53
Welker, Hugh, 114
Wellington, Arthur E., 45
Wellmore, I.R., 18
Wells, Clarence, 241
Wells, M.M., 3
Wells, Miss, 230
Wells, O.T., 5
Welsh, A., 60
Welsh, Cate, 233
Welsh, E.M., 195
Welsh, Ed, 25
Welsh, J., 42
Welsh, M., 102
Welsh, Maggie, 240
Werleff, F., 23
Werlen, F., 78
Wertz, Louis, 26
Wesson, R.S., 25
West, E.F., 104
West, Emma J., 254
West, G., 82
West, Grace, 200

West, J., 213
West, J.A., 233, 249
West, James A., 265
West, John C., 129
West, Joseph A., 267
West, Mr., 202
Westerberg, H., 66
Westfall, Annie D., 40
Wetmore, Charles, 265
Wetmore, Chester, 34, 183, 267
Weyl, Anna, 135
Whaley, Miss N., 11
Wheatley, W.F., 30
Wheeler, A.H., 70, 209, 245, 261, 262
Wheeler, Albert H., 256
Wheeler, Arthur, 82
Wheeler, F.A., 195
Wheeler, Frederick A., 40
Wheeler, George H., 40
Wheeler, Harold, 68, 208
Wheeler, Robert S., 24
Whelan, Francis, 241
Whitaker, Alfred E., 195
Whitaker, Laura E., 7
White, A., 96
White, Alec, 200
White, Alice, 62
White, Annie, 62, 200
White, Cy, 36
White, Dr., 44, 86, 87, 122
White, Eddie, 200
White, Esther J., 31
White, F.J., 80, 82, 103, 139, 195, 201
White, Franklin J., 91, 100, 205
White, Fred, 204
White, George L., 248
White, J.H., 38
White, J.T., 25
White, Jean, 199
White, Jennie, 62
White, John, 141, 162
White, Laura J., 6
White, Laura L., 84, 154
White, Laura M., 88
White, Laura S., 6, 65
White, Lovell, 84, 88, 186
White, M.V., 99
White, Martha, 62, 199
White, Mary Jane, 38
White, Mary V., 91, 100, 169
White, Mrs. Dr., 181
White, Mrs. F.J., 105, 122
White, R.T., 75
White, Rose M., 130
White, Thomas, 162
White, W.J., 108
Whitelaw, Henry W., 112
Whitmore, W., 240
Whitney, C.E., 263
Whitney, J.S., 202, 218

Whitney, Mr., 20
Whitney, William J., 6
Whittel, George W., 68
Whittenburg, Mrs. W., 242
Whyte, Mrs., 230
Wiard, G.E., 77, 78
Wickersham, I.G., 238
Wickman, Dr., 30, 76, 87, 102, 159, 175, 211, 214, 218, 226, 229, 245
Wickman, Hettie B., 40
Wickman, Mrs. W.J., 20
Wickman, W.J., 27, 31, 38, 100, 167, 211, 246, 267
Wieland, Albert G., 71
Wieland, Charles S., 71
Wiggin, Charles, 77
Wilders, F.L., 264
Wile, R.E., 240
Wiler, Joe, 233
Wiley, G.E., 51
Wilke, R.A., 162
Wilkins, Alice, 203
Wilkins, B.L., 93
Wilkins, H., 61, 65, 145, 180, 183, 189, 194, 199, 205, 238, 255, 264
Wilkins, Hepburn, 6, 8, 11, 33, 41, 43, 45, 50, 55, 59, 86, 98, 100, 109, 154, 171, 174, 179, 192, 197, 216, 251
Wilkins, James H., 8, 167, 244, 252
Wilkins, Louise N., 31
Wilkins, Mrs. Lucy A., 177
Wilkins, W.W., 84
Willard, C.E., 191
Williams, Anna, 235
Williams, Annie, 233, 240
Williams, Charles L., 3
Williams, Charles, 156
Williams, Clara P., 192
Williams, Eck, 252
Williams, Fred, 62
Williams, George B., 257
Williams, George R., 198
Williams, Hannah Neil, 167
Williams, Hannah, 196
Williams, J.E., 181
Williams, J.L., 218
Williams, Joe J., 119
Williams, John S., 265, 268
Williams, Juliette, 167, 196
Williams, Laura M., 61
Williams, Lucy N., 192
Williams, Mary, 240, 242
Williams, May, 227
Williams, Miss A.N., 183
Williams, Miss M.J., 258
Williams, Mr., 22
Williams, Mrs. George B., 198, 257

Williams, Mrs. L.N., 183
Williams, Neil, 19
Williams, P., 145
Williams, Peter, 7, 81, 144, 163, 242, 263
Williamson, J.P., 249
Williamson, John A., 240
Williamson, Nettie, 237
Williamson, P., 77
Willis, Harry R., 41
Willis, J.A., 240
Willye, Mr., 84
Wilson, A.C., 195, 210
Wilson, Carrie E. Ladd, 68
Wilson, Carrie E., 246
Wilson, Carrie E.L., 183
Wilson, Charles R., 264
Wilson, Charlotte S., 50
Wilson, Edgar M., 125, 191, 238
Wilson, Ettie S., 249
Wilson, George E., 146, 150
Wilson, Gertrude, 91
Wilson, J.H., 25, 220
Wilson, J.N., 220
Wilson, J.N.E., 166
Wilson, J.W., 75
Wilson, John Ward, 50
Wilson, Mr., 50, 112
Wilson, Mrs. A.E., 183
Wilson, Mrs. John A., 248
Wilson, Mrs. John, 249
Wilson, Mrs., 50, 235
Wilson, P.S., 173
Wilson, Peter S., 208
Wilson, R., 75
Wilson, Robert, 3
Wilson, S., 137
Wilson, S.M., 183
Wiltspiel, J., 49
Winans, David, 250
Winans, E., 257
Winans, E.F., 255
Winans, Emeline F., 250, 251, 252
Winans, James, 260, 262
Winder, E.C., 227
Winder, Ed, 119
Windmiller, Maurice, 46
Winn, 108, 113
Winn, A.H., 156
Winn, Mr., 169, 172
Winn, W.B., 14, 91, 93, 95, 101, 141, 151
Winnigar, G.H., 33
Winse, Mrs. M., 183
Winslow, Margaret, 101, 103
Winslow, Mrs. E.J., 208
Winstedt, H., 102, 119, 123
Winter, Ed, 253
Winterburn, George H., 58, 71, 160
Winteringham, Mr., 126

Wirkan, Anna, 133
Wise, E.B., 77
Wise, H.E., 208
Wise, H.W., 237
Wise, Marion, 202, 210, 214
Wise, Mr., 101
Witke, Albert, 242, 249
Wolf, A., 106
Wolf, Lester, 103
Wolfe, 4
Wolfe, J., 137
Wolfert, Josephine, 2
Wood, 110, 140
Wood, B., 42
Wood, David, 179
Wood, Frank E., 230
Wood, H.B., 228, 265
Wood, Henry B., 15, 212, 246
Wood, John C., 246
Wood, W.P., 127
Wood, Wintler, 110
Woodard, A., 120
Wood-Hall, Mary C., 179
Woods, E., 68
Woodward, J., 2
Woodward, Mr., 157
Woodword, Silas S., 31
Woodworth, A., 5, 79
Woodworth, F., 126
Woodworth, Fred, 87, 198, 268
Woodworth, Miss M., 204
Woodworth, Mr., 56
Woodworth, Mrs. A., 97
Woodworth, Ralph, 79, 202
Wormcastle, Anna R., 164
Wormouth, E., 2, 12, 108, 113, 124, 130, 164, 166, 174, 188, 208, 247, 260
Wormouth, J.A., 154, 208
Worn, George A., 229, 239
Worn, George R., 229
Wosser, Bertha, 204
Wosser, Edward F., 17
Wrench, William, 58
Wright, Afred, 199
Wright, Charles, 37, 51, 265, 267
Wright, F.G., 11
Wright, Frederick G., 15
Wright, Georgiana A.M., 242
Wright, J.L., 131, 137
Wright, Jennie C., 106
Wright, Lottie, 63, 200
Wright, M.M., 96
Wright, Mattie, 106
Wright, Mrs. James L., 179
Wright, W., 28
Wright, Whitaker, 201
Wurtenberg, Flora, 240
Wuth, Gertrude, 233
Wyatt, H., 2, 129
Wyman, L.S., 123

Wynans, Mrs., 3
Xavier, P., 137
Xavier, Paulino, 179
Yates, W.H., 252
Yates, William Henry, 64
Yelmorini, A., 69
Yelmorini, Maria, 68
Young, Emily, 179
Young, F.O., 37
Young, George M., 60, 68, 208
Young, Harry, 234
Young, Mr., 32
Young, N.R.K., 179
Young, W.G., 80, 235
Young, William E., 51
Zabiana, M.S., 46
Zander, W.E., 98
Zanike, William, 179
Zaniol, M. Natale, 240
Zellar, Joseph, 192
Zellar, Sophia S., 139
Zellar, Sophia Steinecke, 31
Zellar, Sophia, 28, 38, 39, 47, 85, 221, 228, 231, 233, 235
Zellerbach, M., 219, 221
Zenglar, Ed, 252
Zetterberg, August H., 155
Zicovich, Mary, 168
Zierenberg, Ida, 62
Zimmerman, George, 74
Zimmerman, Louisa, 74
Zincke, 235
Zincke, E., 46
Zincke, William, 119, 192
Zindelar, Mr., 181
Zingler, Mrs. Ed, 234
Zinkand, C.A., 25, 31, 145
Zinkand, Charles A., 1, 6, 58, 60
Zinkand, Mr., 26
Zinkand, Sophia, 58, 139
Zinkand, William, 62
Zolezi, P., 68
Zook, F.K., 48
Zopf, H., 253
Zulotti, 75
Zumini, G., 81, 100, 237
Zumini, Joseph G., 96
Zumini, Mr., 207
Zwiebel, Peter, 244